Praise for *Wealth Preservation and Protection for Closely-Held Business Owners (And Others)*:

"I have found Jonathan Blattmachr to be an exceptionally talented and creative strategist. His advice and counsel are always of the highest caliber, and this book is an illustration of his brilliance."

> RICHARD T. FARMER
> Chairman
> Cintas Corp.
> Cincinnati, Ohio

"If you are really serious about protecting and preserving what you have built, you had better read this book. . . . Perhaps, even more important, have your lawyer and accountant read it!"

> GEORGE F. RUSSELL, JR.
> Chairman
> The Frank Russell Company
> Tacoma, Washington

"If you believe, as I do, that planning is important, that the most effective planning depends upon marshalling the best resources, and that the proper implementation of plans depends on obtaining a balanced structure of possible options, you will be immensely intrigued and assisted by Jonathan Blattmachr's latest book, *Wealth Preservation and Protection for Closely-Held Business Owners (And Others)*."

> EDWARD C. RAYMUND
> Founder and Chairman Emeritus
> Tech Data Corp.
> Clearwater, Florida

"A comprehensive treatise on a broad spectrum of financial issues of critical importance to business owners. It is clearly written and presented so that even the most complex concepts can be understood by those individuals with no previous familiarity with this subject matter."

> GAIL SCHNEIDER, ESQ.
> Senior Vice President
> The Chase Manhattan Bank,
>   N. A.
> New York, New York

"Here are all the answers—easy to find and in plain English—for all the estate planning questions of an owner of a business or a person of means."

> HERBERT G. WELLINGTON
> President
> H. G. Wellington & Co., Inc.
> New York, New York

"An excellent, all encompassing, treatise for owners of the closely-held business. An invaluable guide for those involved in planning or operating a closely-held business."

> SIDNEY KESS
> CPA & Lawyer
> Noted Lecturer & Author
> New York, New York

"Jonathan's advice and wisdom are invaluable to those who work in the estate or business succession environment. This book is a collection of his personal experiences and observations set forth in an easy to read format that will help business owners and their advisors more effectively identify and address personal wealth management issues."

> ANDREW D. PAINTER
> Partner
> Ernst & Young
> Atlanta, Georgia

"The most comprehensive wealth preservation and estate planning book I have read. Not only are tax and estate issues covered in depth but most essential topics such as 'How to select the proper lawyer' are covered at length. The step-by-step outlines provide an organized and comprehensive review of all aspects of wealth preservation, estate planning and transfer of ownership so essential to so many private businesses going through generation transfer. The format and organization would make it a perfect textbook for any course on protecting the future in a closely-held business."

JAY KESTENBAUM, CPA
President
Refrigeration Sales, Inc.
New York, New York

"The book provides valuable insights into sophisticated estate planning techniques in a very readable format."

PAUL N. FRIMMER, ESQ.
Irell & Manella
Los Angeles, California

"One of those rare books written in a concise manner in which business owners and families have *real* answers to questions that are asked daily.

Jonathan has produced a book that should become the main text for every serious business owner. *A MUST* read for every financial advisor."

THOMAS J. DOUMANI
Chairman of the Board
Advanced Planning Concepts,
    Inc.
Orange, California

"This is a very comprehensive book with many ideas on how to build, preserve, and transfer wealth. These ideas are presented very clearly and straightforwardly and will lead the reader to take action."

TERRANCE J. DOBSON
Executive Vice President
WestOne Bancorp
Boise, Idaho

"This is important reading for anyone who has accumulated, or who has the ambition to build, an estate. I am not aware of another book like it."

WILLIAM G. STROECKER
Former Chairman
First National Bank of Fairbanks
(Alaska)
Director, Key Bank of Alaska

"[This] book is to the point, easy to read and understand, and answers all the questions that closely-held business owners will ask themselves. I recommend it and will use it as part of my resource library."

LARRY B. SCHWEIGER
President
Unisyn, Inc.
Fort Lauderdale, Florida

"Jonathan Blattmachr's 'Wealth Preservation' volume is extremely useful for both property owners and professional estate planners. It is comprehensive, thorough, and refreshingly readable for a technically sound reference. It contains a wealth of material essential for business owners and other property owners alike."

P. THOMAS AUSTIN, CPA
Retired Partner
Ernst & Young
Cleveland, Ohio

"The book was great—once I started it I couldn't put it down. This book is a must for every life underwriter who works in the business and estate planning market."

DALE E. YODER
TransAmerica Life
Fairbanks, Alaska

"This book is a jewel. It should be in the office of every advanced life underwriter. It is clear, to the point, and easy to understand."

MUN CHARN WONG, CLU
Honolulu, Hawaii

"Wealth Preservation and Protection for Closely-Held Business Owners (And Others) . . . is extremely comprehensive and readable. It is a valuable reference, and should be required reading for all successful business owners who are trying to preserve what their efforts have produced. It is also quite timely, since the remainder of the 1990's should produce a flurry of growth in closely-held businesses."

> BARRY S. BERG
> Vice President,
> Finance & Administration
> Lappin Communications, Inc.
> Palm Beach, Florida

"An unusually candid, comprehensive and readable book designed for businessmen, trusts and estates attorneys, and other interested parties. It's the first time I can recall reading and understanding a book of this nature."

> HERB ORNSTEIN
> Hascoe Family Investments
> Greenwich, Connecticut

"If this book had been available several years ago, it would have saved me millions of dollars.

The person who really needs to read this book is the person, who thinks he has nothing to worry about and will never need to protect himself. The time to protect yourself is when you don't need to."

> RALPH E. WHITMORE, JR.
> President
> International Drilling Co.
> Beverly Hills, California

"What a book! Anyone who reads it will have to say, at least once, 'I wish I had known that.'"

> MIKE HARTMAN
> Independent Businessman
> Fairbanks, Alaska

"Jonathan's new book and his insights on the subjects are invaluable. He makes a very complex subject of the tax law very comprehensible and therefore very usable. It is not a book that will just stay on the shelf."

GEORGE E. GOERIG, ESQ.
Davis & Goerig
Anchorage, Alaska

"I have known Jonathan Blattmachr for many years. Without question, he has the most innovative and creative mind in tax and wealth transfer issues.

This new book is a must for the business owner or his advisor."

CLUNE J. WALSH, JR., CLU
President—1981 Million Dollar
Round Table
Detroit, Michigan

"This book comprises one of the most comprehensive analysis in layman's language of the tax and non-tax aspects of the accumulation, preservation and disposition of assets by and between family members and others that I have ever read."

THOMAS P. SWEENEY, ESQ.
Past-President
American College of Trust &
Estate Counsel
Wilmington, Delaware

"A thorough, informative and eminently readable book by one of the most knowledgeable and innovative people in the estates and tax planning field. Must reading for closely-held business owners and their advisors."

W. TIMOTHY BAETZ, ESQ.
McDermott, Will & Emery
Chicago, Illinois

"[The book] is fantastic. It will be of great benefit to those fortunate enough to obtain it and read it."

LEONARD A. KESTENBAUM
Chairman of Refrigeration Sales
    Co, Inc.
Long Island City, NY

"The title is totally accurate and descriptive. Jonathan has presented his readers with a wealth of invaluable information on an extensive range of important concerns. His writing style is compelling, yet provides for easy and enjoyable reading."

HOWARD P. SEARS, JR.
President
Sears Oil Co., Inc.
Rome, New York

"Jonathan's book equips the layman to be on parity with the professionals. As you make your financial plans, this book presents the entire field of options with the advantages and disadvantages of each one; better decisions will result."

JOHN A. THOMPSON
Former Chairman and Controlling
    Shareholder
Thompson-Hudson, Inc.
Montgomery, Alabama

"Jonathan's book is the first relevant text for our clients whose net worth averages in excess of $100 million. I feel comfortable in recommending Jonathan's book to the wealthiest and most sophisticated business owners in America and their advisors."

GARY M. KORNMAN
Chairman
The Heritage Organization, Inc.
Dallas, Texas

WEALTH PRESERVATION AND PROTECTION FOR CLOSELY-HELD BUSINESS OWNERS

(AND OTHERS)

WEALTH PRESERVATION AND PROTECTION FOR CLOSELY-HELD BUSINESS OWNERS (AND OTHERS)

Jonathan G. Blattmachr

The Libey Business Library

LIBEY PUBLISHING INCORPORATED
An Eagle Publishing Company

Washington, D.C.

Library of Congress Cataloging-in-Publication Data

Blattmachr, Jonathan G.
    Wealth preservation and protection for closely-held business owners (and others) / Jonathan G. Blattmachr.
        p.   cm. — (The Libey business library)
    Includes index.
    ISBN 1-882222-03-2 (acid-free paper)
    1. Estate planning—United States. 2. Close corporations—United States. I. Title. II. Series.
  KF750.B53 1993
  346.7305'2—dc20
  [347.30652]   93-8803
                                                CIP

Published in the United States by
Libey Publishing Incorporated
An Eagle Publishing Company
422 First St., SE, Suite 300
Washington, DC 20003

Distributed to the trade by
National Book Network
4720-A Boston Way
Lanham, MD 20706

Printed on acid-free paper.

Manufactured in the United States of America.

10 9 8 7 6 5 4 3 2

For Betsy

ACKNOWLEDGMENTS

I have been exceptionally fortunate to have so many talented individuals review parts of the manuscript and make important suggestions for its improvement. These include Jeffrey Brinck, Howard Buschman, Bill Crandall, Tom Doumani, Jessica Feder, Mike Hartman, Ed Inouye, Joe Hanna, Barry Kaye, Gary Kornman, Larry Lederman, Frank Logan, Herb Ornstein, Sam Polk, Barry Radick, Madeline Rivlin, Mark Ross, Paula Ryan, Georgiana Slade, Jay Swanson, my brother Douglas and my wife Betsy. I extend my deep thanks to each of them and to my tireless friend and secretary, Irene Landeros, who volunteered to type the manuscript in her free time.

TABLE OF CONTENTS

Chapter 12   WHAT SHOULD I DO IF MY SPOUSE IS NOT THE PARENT OF ALL MY CHILDREN?

Chapter 13   WHOM SHOULD I CHOOSE AS MY EXECUTORS AND TRUSTEES?

PREFACE

Over the next two decades, approximately 10 trillion dollars will be transmitted from the most senior generation of Americans to their children and grandchildren. That enormous wealth hangs as ripening fruit in front of desperately hungry government officials and other potential claimants. The time when the government and litigants will begin to bite ever more deeply into that property soon will begin. Those who do not plan to protect themselves will lose the most. Those who take action will face the smallest erosion of their and their family's property.

The political climate for the government to justify demanding a greater majority of that portion of the nation's wealth also is ripening. During the twelve years of the Reagan-Bush administrations, there was greater spending than ever before by the government but also a greater shift in the burden of taxation. Reflecting the economic policies of those administrations, the percentage of nation's taxes imposed on the wealthiest sector of the country was reduced in an attempt to spur greater economic growth for the entire country. History has demonstrated that reduction in taxation, especially capital gains tax, often does result in economic growth. However, the change in administrations has resulted in a change of economic philosophy. It is almost certain that a greater part of our country's tax burden will be shifted onto the shoulders of the wealthiest of our nation.

A significant portion of the wealth that will be transmitted over the next 20 years now is represented by interests in closely-held businesses. Those businesses represent the economic backbone of virtually every community in America, providing the majority of new jobs. A large part of the ownership of those businesses will be shifted from one generation to the next, and without proper planning, taxes will prevent the shift from effectively occurring.

In fact, even before the last session of Congress ended, in the fall of 1992, our senators and congressmen introduced bills foreshadowing the government's awakening to the possible imposition of additional tax on its citizen's wealth. For example, several representatives proposed reducing each American's estate tax exemption from $600,000 to $200,000 or less. Although some have claimed that the government would not dare do that, the government has already done it to all well-to-do Americans. Without much question, a further erosion of that exemption for all, and its entire elimination for many, is certain to occur. In addition, although the federal estate tax rates were reduced to 50% on January 1, 1993, because of legislation passed in 1981, it is certain that the rates soon will rise again, perhaps to 70% or higher. Because of a second tax, on the books since 1986, on transfers to grandchildren, wealth left to them will be eroded by over 90%. If you live in a state with an extra death tax, the erosion will approach 100%. But that is only the beginning. Even before he took office, President Clinton proposed a capital gains tax at death. That change would eliminate the major tax savings mechanism in preserving wealth in America.

Compounding the erosion of property held by the private sector on account of the government's constant quest to own and control more of the nation's wealth and income is the fact that each year the number of claimants and the size of their claims grows. In fact, over half of Americans will face a serious creditor's claim during their lifetime. One of the reasons is a simple one: More than half of American marriages end in divorce, and the spouse with less property will claim an entitlement to the assets of the other under relatively new laws passed in most states. Moreover, an increasing number of Americans face an increasing number of other claims each year. The reasons for that are many, but a primary one is the government's constant passage of new laws and regulations which provide itself and other claimants with new grounds to sue for someone else's money and property.

Unfortunately, owners of closely-held businesses are prime targets of taxes and claims. In addition, owners of private companies face other hurdles in attempting to preserve and protect their wealth. Those include the failure to hold a diversified base of wealth, difficulties in finding appropriate successor managers of their businesses, lack of liquidity to pay estate taxes and other claims, and complexities in choosing appropriate fiduciaries to manage their affairs.

The picture, however, is not that dark for those who undertake a thoughtful and professional approach to managing, preserving and protecting their wealth. In fact, many of the apparent detriments of owning closely-held business interests can be converted into advantages, but only with early and significant planning.

Ours is truly a government of laws rather than of men. Those laws, such as the ones which impose taxes, can be used as a weapon against you, but some laws can be used as a great shield for you. One of the most important endeavors you can take during your lifetime is to inform yourself about legal and related matters and how they will affect your base of wealth. Regardless of how successful you have been in building your wealth, your property can be dissipated almost instantly if certain conditions occur. By informing yourself, you will be able to reduce the probability of your wealth being eroded.

Wealth Preservation and Protection for Closely-Held Business Owners (And Others) is not a handbook on operating your business. It does not tell you what to manufacture for customers, what lines of businesses to drop and what services to provide. It does not even go into detail in sound business practices, such as having an independent board of directors. However, it will provide you with general guidance as to the preservation and protection of your wealth during your lifetime and after your death. It is not a "do it yourself" kit, however. No one, not even the most informed professional, knows all of the economic, tax and legal matters which can effect the erosion of wealth or its preservation and protection. This book, rather, provides you with important information so that you can work best with your professional advisors in protecting and preserving your base of wealth.

This book presents hard questions, such as whether you should diversify your wealth, whether you should have your children and grandchildren become members of your business, what should you do if you are in a second marriage situation and whether you can provide in a confidential way for individuals outside of your family. However, this book also provides guidance in how you can best answer them for yourself, your company and your family.

One technical matter should be mentioned. At the time that I wrote most of this book, the federal estate and gift tax rates were at 55%. Although they have dropped to 50%, as noted above, many of the examples in the book use a 55% rate of taxation. Whether the rate is 50%, 55%, 60% or more, the examples illustrate the same profound story: The government wants to be a major beneficiary of your wealth.

JONATHAN G. BLATTMACHR
New York, New York

WEALTH PRESERVATION AND PROTECTION FOR CLOSELY-HELD BUSINESS OWNERS

(AND OTHERS)

CHAPTER 1

WHY SHOULD I BOTHER WITH PROTECTION AND PRESERVATION PLANNING?

INTRODUCTION AND OVERVIEW OF CHAPTER

All of us tend to focus our attention on immediate matters, the day-to-day concerns of our family and work. Often we avoid looking ahead to anticipate and formulate plans to overcome difficult situations which may lie ahead. "Planning" by its nature connotes taking action in anticipation of later events, and planning is necessary for the preservation and protection of your business interests and other assets both during your lifetime and after your death. This Chapter will discuss some basic reasons why planning often is critical and almost always beneficial to preserve and maintain wealth and to assist your family in maintaining a lifestyle you believe is appropriate.

A FEW INTRODUCTORY MATTERS

A Few Thoughts As You Get Started

This book is addressed to owners of closely-held businesses to provide them with practical advice about estate and financial planning. It is not a guide on operating a business, although many parts of it deal with matters directly affecting your company.

Some of the Chapters deal with methods by which you can enhance your retirement, help protect yourself and your family from claims of creditors, provide greater insulation of part of your business from creditors during adversity and how to protect yourself and other members of your family from the inevitable and adverse economic pressures which occur at death and in divorce. As you read this book, you should keep in mind that over half of American marriages end in divorce. Do not believe that it cannot happen to you or members of your family. Also, you may wish to keep in mind that more personal bankruptcies are attributed to the breakdown of a marriage than any other single cause.

Premises

I start with several premises. One is that you have an interest in at least exploring estate and financial planning for yourself, your business and your family in order to preserve and protect your wealth. I also assume that you are willing to devote adequate personal time to the steps necessary to implement any plan you adopt. You should accept, however, that estate and financial planning is not a "one time" activity but is, finally, a lifelong process. I also anticipate that you are willing to incur the costs of planning, which can be considerable, if you are confident that the returns to yourself, your business and your family are adequately high. I assume that you have been successful in your business, in part, because of careful planning—indeed, I assume that you have learned that planning is an essential key in building a successful enterprise.

You Plan for Your Business, Don't You?

Very few people who have built a successful company allow their businesses to be run "at random." In fact, you probably have observed repeatedly in watching your employees and your competitors that those who undertake the most careful planning generally are the ones who achieve the most significant and profitable results. In many ways, the planning you do for your business should be inexorably intertwined with planning you do for the protection and preservation of your wealth. Why should you bother to plan for your business if you don't simultaneously plan for the other financial aspects of your and your family's life? In fact, a failure to plan for these other aspects can cause significant problems for your company.

An Overview of
Estate and Financial
Planning

Estate planning, as a category, usually means the orderly transmission of property from one person to another. However, effective estate planning encompasses much more. It includes, among other things, taking action to protect your assets from claims of creditors including an estranged spouse either of yours or a child of yours. Estate planning also means taking action to prevent having more than one-half (and, in some cases, much more than one-half) of your wealth eroded by tax when you die. Financial planning is much more than picking stocks. It involves virtually all matters which affect your economic base, and in particular, means the development of significant wealth outside of and independent of your business and, in most cases, using the value of your business to develop that independent base of wealth.

This book is designed to provide you with adequately detailed information to allow you, with the help of professionals, to achieve two broad goals: (1) to develop, preserve and protect your base of wealth, (2) to develop and implement, in a cost effective way, lifetime and testamentary estate planning, which is necessary to preserve and protect your wealth for others.

REASONS FOR
PLANNING FOR
WEALTH
PRESERVATION
AND
PROTECTION

For Yourself and Your
Family

No matter how successful your business is, it is subject to the vicissitudes of the marketplace. Every enterprise and industry goes through cycles. Although you may be the exception, many individuals and their businesses fail because of inadequate attention to independent wealth planning. Undertaking estate and financial planning enhances the probability of you and your business having the greater ability to survive through difficult financial times.

That ability to survive will provide you with many additional benefits. First, it will help maintain family and personal relationships. In the experience of many advisors, a major reason for divorce is adverse financial pressure. Your relationship with your wife or husband definitely will change if your business falls on hard times. Perhaps, your relationship will grow stronger because of the greater challenge the two of you will face and have to accept together. However, experienced lawyers often note a significant increase in the number of marital dissolutions when business conditions become bleak.

Second, no matter how strong your relationships are to your employees or how great their loyalty to you, adverse financial times of your business will adversely affect their relationship with you. Your initial response may be that you don't care, but you will in the long run: You will lose some of your most valued employees and, more important, perhaps, the experience base which they represent to your business. You may also lose their commitment to the organization whose success they have contributed to.

Third, independent wealth can help you maintain your health. Your health, and the health of other family members, may be adversely affected when your industry and business face hard times. Think back over your own lifetime and you may recall several instances where men and women who were very successful became physically, if not mentally, ill during adverse times for their businesses.

You and those closest to you will benefit by your undertaking and completing estate and financial planning for yourself. In addition, careful planning also will determine how you are perceived by others when you are gone. Even if we care more about ourselves than anyone else in the world, including the immediate members of our families, each of us probably wants to be "fondly" remembered and for our reputation to continue to be respected even after we die. If you leave your family and your business in a position where neither can survive financially, you will be remembered as a person who had neither the ability nor the good sense to plan for his or her business, family and the causes he or she cared about.

For Your Business

Closely-held businesses are the financial backbone of almost every community, large and small. Planning will help perpetuate your name in a positive way and allow you to leave an important legacy to your community. Failure to plan properly means that during difficult financial times your business and your community will suffer.

Planning will enhance the probability that your business will be maintained for your employees, your business associates, your family and others. Among other things, the development of an independent base of wealth can be used to help your business. When times become tough for your company, that independent wealth can be used to recapitalize the company or take other action to salvage some or all of its operations. If your company is experiencing difficulty with creditors, as it almost certainly will during hard times, your ability to bargain effectively with them will be enhanced if you have independent means which can be available for the business if you decide to use them for that purpose.

PLANNING WILL SAVE YOU AND YOUR FAMILY MONEY AND HEARTACHE

To summarize what has been said so far: Planning can significantly reduce the risks of your assets becoming subject to the claims of creditors during your lifetime and after your death. It can help immunize your business from adverse times. It can provide an independent financial base even if virtually all of your assets are tied up in the operation of your business. Planning can significantly reduce estate and related taxes thereby making more money available to your family and less to the tax authorities.

Your family almost certainly will save by your lifetime estate and financial planning. The savings not only will come from a reduction in estate and similar wealth transfer taxes, but also a reduction in income taxes, as well as more efficient administration of your estate and the more effective operation of your business after your death. Perhaps, more important, planning may significantly reduce fights over the financial spoils at your death and promote family harmony and respect. Probably, more fortunes have been lost in family feuds than in taxes. But make no mistake about it: Without proper planning, more than half of your wealth will be eroded by taxes. If your business represents a significant portion of your wealth, the burden of those taxes will fall on your company. There are very few businesses which could comfortably survive, or survive at all, when more than half of their wealth is dissipated by governmental claims.

EARLY PLANNING AND ACTION ARE THE KEYS

Many individuals pay for advice from professionals about estate and financial planning and then ignore it, somehow convincing themselves that they have unlimited time to take action. Others go through the planning process a single time never to be repeated, even though circumstances change. The results of either course of action are uniform and inevitable: the significant erosion of the base of wealth which had been built over years of struggle and risk—and all lost because the individual was unwilling to undertake early planning and action even for his or her own personal benefit.

HOW TO GET STARTED WITH YOUR PLANNING

Don't Wait for the Perfect Moment or Conditions

The time to begin your planning is now. Oh, I know, you are much too busy to get started with it right now. The inventory has to be counted, the plans for the business for next year have to be made, the bank loan has to be secured, and the golf game (for business reasons, of course) has to be played. Engaging in estate and financial planning is not easy and for most of us is not very enjoyable. Unfortunately, it also can be expensive. But there will never be a more perfect moment to start than now. Some people seem to believe the perfect moment is immediately before death. Although some planning can be taken shortly before death with some good results, nothing replaces getting started as early as possible.

If conditions for you and your business are especially good, now is a good time to start planning. If conditions for you and your company are bad, it is even more important to start planning now because, if conditions get worse, the beneficial effects of good planning may be foreclosed.

Information You Should Gather

The most important information you can gather to do your planning is to sort out your goals. Later in this Chapter, specific goals which are common are discussed. Later Chapters set forth how they can be implemented. Generally, you should decide right now if you want to immunize, to the extent legally and economically practical, aspects of your business from the business cycle and the claims of creditors, if you wish to develop a financial base of wealth independent of your company and how large that base should be and if you want to preserve your wealth for your family after your death. You should make some estimate of where you are right now with respect to those goals: what percentage of your wealth base is represented by your business; what independent base of wealth do you have; what independent base of wealth will be available (after the inevitable taxes) for your family when you die; who are the individuals (other than yourself, of course), causes and institutions you care about most; and who will be the most capable people to manage your business when you cannot do so. It shouldn't take you five minutes to write those things down. However, try to be as accurate as you possibly can, neither inflating or reducing the value of your property, and take an extra minute to make sure everything is listed.

| Ascertaining Your Goals | ### WHY YOU SHOULD HAVE SPECIFIC GOALS |

Counsellors have long observed that individuals and businesses which develop specific goals are much more likely to achieve the results desired. One of America's largest companies, which was to some degree "at sea", hired a new young CEO. He made it his first job to adopt specific goals for the company. The enterprise, after nearly a century in operation, was experiencing erratic earnings and its stock, which was publicly traded, was selling at a very small multiple of earnings, even in the best of its recent years. The CEO adopted as the company's primary specific goal that it would be either first or second in any industry in which it competed. He decided that if they could not achieve that within five years, they would sell out of that industry and expand in another in which they had achieved that goal or go into another industry where they felt they could achieve it. Was it a perfect solution? Probably not, but the company again is regarded as one of America's premier ones and its stock is back selling at a much greater multiple than it was before the new CEO took over. How did the company's recent success happen? No doubt, it is attributable to many factors. Certainly, however, the adoption of specific goals was a primary one.

Your goals for your business, yourself and your family should be similarly specific. Perhaps, your estate and financial planning goals may have to be even more refined.

COMMON FINANCIAL AND ESTATE PLANNING GOALS

In any case, many owners of closely-held businesses have similar financial and estate planning goals. Among typical ones are:

- Maximize Benefits—maximizing potential benefits for the family.
- Control—preserving control of assets, especially the family business, for the senior family members.
- Preserve the Business—preserving the family business or its worth for its current owner's lifetime and as it passes to other family members.
- Facilitating Sales—providing the mechanism for a sale of assets, including the family business if that becomes appropriate.
- Management—providing for effective management of a family business and other assets.
- Tax Savings—saving (and/or deferring) taxes, including income, gift, estate and generation skipping transfer tax at all government levels.
- Flexibility—maintaining maximum flexibility to react to changing family needs, economic circumstances and tax and other law changes.
- Creditor Protection—protecting family wealth from unnecessary evaporation as a result of divorces and other creditor claims;

- Opportunities for Others—providing family members with the greatest opportunity to achieve their potential, whether that is in business, teaching, philanthropy or another positive pursuit.
- Harmony—generating harmony and respect among family members and with employees and management of the family business.
- Perpetuate Ideals—perpetuating high standards for the family and the family business.
- Independent Wealth—developing a wealth base independent of the family business.
- Benefit the Community—benefitting selected charitable and other institutions within the community.

Your goals may be more or less extensive or may be different from the foregoing list. The important point is that you make a list of your goals.

SEEKING PROFESSIONAL ASSISTANCE

Regardless of your level of current financial success, and regardless of the business you may be in, you almost certainly need professional assistance to effect significant and long-lasting wealth preservation and protection for your family and yourself. Tax, property and financial matters which affect the preservation and protection of wealth are so complex that few if any owners of closely-held businesses can hope to master them all. In addition, without professional assistance, you will tend to neglect several aspects of your own planning and the implementation of goals. A strong indicator of your commitment to undertake significant planning will be seeking professional advice. Part of that advice may include the services of a personal counsellor (such as a psychologist) who, in appropriate circumstances, can work with you in reasoning out why you may have difficulty either in adopting a timetable, or in following the advice of other professionals you have hired and in implementing plans.

SUMMARY AND CONCLUSIONS

Just as you undertake methodical planning for your business during the course of its life, so too should you undertake careful planning for your estate and financial planning and that of your family. You, your business, your employees, your community and, perhaps most important, your family all can benefit through your undertaking planning in a significant and responsible way. Early planning is the key. Rarely will planning be adequate if it is undertaken just before the occurrence of events such as your death or the bankruptcy of your business, which almost certainly will cause a shifting in personal relationships and the imposition of significant claims. Your estate and financial planning should be an integral part of your overall planning for your business as well. An accurate analogy can be made to insurance. No reasonably intelligent person does without adequate fire, theft and liability insurance. But too many people do without adequate estate and financial planning. Do not let yourself be one of them.

CHAPTER 2

SHOULD I DIVERSIFY MY WEALTH DURING MY LIFETIME?

INTRODUCTION AND OVERVIEW OF CHAPTER

This Chapter will provide you with guidance in determining whether and the extent to which you should diversify your wealth during the time that you own your business. No matter how successful your company has been and is expected to be in the future, part, and perhaps a growing part, of your wealth base probably should be represented by assets and interests other than your core business. This Chapter also discusses matters for you to consider in determining how much of your wealth you want represented by your business.

THE STATE OF THINGS

The Life Cycle of Your Business and Industry

Every person, every community, every business and every industry go through cycles. The forces of competition, technological change, government regulation and shifting markets necessarily mean that things will be different tomorrow than they are today. Even if your business always has been profitable, its level of profitability has varied from time to time. Perhaps, you made 25% last year. Was that more or less than the year before? It has not always been 25% and it will not always be 25%. You probably are in a position to best know the life cycle of your business and when it is "up" and when it is "down." To a large degree, the life cycle of your business may reflect the life cycle of your industry and the economy in general. Perhaps, however, to an even greater

13

degree, it will reflect your life cycle. You will be a different person at age 75 than you were at 35. Your interests and attitudes will change and that will be reflected in the operation of your business even if all other things are equal (but of course they will not be anyway). You may not like the fact that things will change, but there are some matters, such as aging, that you cannot effectively control. If you accept the inevitability of the cycle of your company, you will be in a better position to protect it and yourself from adversity.

Determining Your Level of Wealth Concentration In General

You probably do not need to hire a Big Six accounting firm to determine what percentage of your wealth is concentrated in your business. You should know what assets you own, and their value outside of your business. Nonetheless, the value of your company may be difficult to estimate. Your industry may have certain standards (such as ten times earnings) which are used as a general guide to value enterprises in that business. Specifically, some reference to value can be obtained by looking at somewhat comparable public companies. However, the public companies will not be identical to yours and, in any event, interest in privately-held businesses usually sell at a significant discount compared to their counterparts which are publicly traded. If you do not have a reasonable estimate of the value of your business, it will be appropriate for you, in the planning process, to obtain a value from a professional valuation company. In fact, some lifetime planning (such as transferring interests in your business by gift) will necessitate hiring a professional and independent appraiser. (That will be discussed in Chapter 14, dealing with estate and related taxes.)

Risks And Rewards Of Investing In Your Own Business

The rewards of investing in your business are many. There are few accomplishments in life as enjoyable as creating a successful business. You become an important figure not just to your family because of the financial means you provide but also to your employees, suppliers, customers and all those who "feed" off your business, such as accountants, lawyers and others. For many, those rewards are more important than the financial base which is built. Many clients take salaries significantly below what the business reasonably could afford to pay and far below what comparable CEOs are paid in the industry. In fact, one of my clients does not, at this stage, take anything out of the business at all, not even a salary. Other than reinvestment of capital in the business, his profit sharing plan distributes all profits each year to his employees. He regards it as a privilege to work and build a business. He is also smart: He has learned that his people work much harder when they realize that they are the sole apparent beneficiaries of their action. Most of them do not even take coffee breaks. However, he also realizes that higher profitability means higher reinvestment in the capital of the business which has expanded significantly since he adopted the program of "I won't even take a salary."

The financial rewards of investing in your own business can be extraordinarily great, far surpassing the rate of return of a more diversified portfolio. Ask Ross Perot, Bill Gates, Marvin Davis or any of the other individuals who have made fortunes and they obviously will say that their best investment was in their own business. In fact, other than being very lucky (or, perhaps, insightful) in making investments with others, virtually the only way to build up a significant base of wealth is to invest in your company.

In addition to the obvious and subtle rewards of investing in your own business and being your own boss, there are several risks. The risks include losing the entire investment if things are structured poorly, as they often are with owners of closely-held businesses. Perhaps, even worse, is the "psychological" trauma of having a business you operate fail. There may be a thousand excuses you will find for the failure of your business but you may have to blame yourself as well.

Perhaps the Best Question You Can Ask Yourself

In determining the extent to which you should diversify your wealth, ask yourself the following question: If I had cash representing the net value of my business today, would I invest all of it in my current business? In other words, if your business is worth $10 million, and you had $10 million in cash, would you buy your business? My strong guess, based upon real life experience with clients, is that you never invest more than one-half of your capital base in your current company. If that is true for you, it means that you should start on a program of wealth diversification.

Diversification provides one of the greatest forms of protection from having your wealth eroded by claims of creditors and other factors. However, you may have to separate and insulate the independent wealth base from your business in order to protect it from being lost if your company becomes unprofitable.

There is another question you should ask, even if you would put all of your money into your business today. That question is: If you had the cash, would you direct for all that money to be used to buy your business to be operated by your family after your death? In other words, even if you think your wealth is best invested exclusively in your company during your lifetime, you may feel otherwise about that after your death. Again, experience indicates that many would answer that they would direct for little of their wealth to be used to buy interests in the family business if it were to be operated by other members of the family.

Perhaps, you will regard those questions as unfair ones because they do not reflect the current state of affairs, which is that you do have a significant investment in your closely-held business and changing that state of affairs is not easy to accomplish for a variety of reasons. As a consequence, it also is appropriate to consider some of the traditional reasons for continuing to hold or to sell a business.

REASONS FOR CONTINUING TO HOLD THE BUSINESS

Greater Control Over Your Investment

Few shareholders in publicly-traded companies have much impact on how the company is operated. In addition, although such investors generally are free to sell their investments, you probably can never obtain as much information about public companies as you can about your own. Accordingly, you are in a position to make more informed decisions about your investment and have more control over it if it is in your company rather than that of someone else.

Psychological
Security

Many individuals find significant psychological security in owning their closely-held businesses. Starting or operating a successful privately-held company is often one of the most important and fulfilling accomplishments in life. If you own a controlling interest in your business, you cannot, as a practical matter, be fired from any position you hold in it. You are much more a master of your destiny and it is difficult, if not impossible, to be able to value that.

Avoiding Taxation

Privately-held businesses are favored under the tax laws in more ways than are public ones. (More about that will be discussed in Chapter 14.) Special tax opportunities, many of which can result in legally avoiding or lowering taxes, are available only to owners of closely-held businesses and such businesses themselves. In fact, on average, interests in a closely-held business may be valued for tax purposes at 50% or less of comparable interests in publicly traded companies. That lower valuation can result in the significant reduction in death taxation, and, as a consequence, the passage of greater wealth to your family. On the other hand, the tax situation for a privately-held company or its owner can be a disaster if not correctly handled. In addition, the sale of your company, particularly if it has been successful, may result in significant taxes. Much of those taxes are "forgiven" at the death of the owner, if the affairs of the business and its owner have been properly structured.

Greater Impact in
Your Community

The respect you get, and deserve, often has more to do with your position of providing jobs and financial security for your community than from the fact that your business may make you a wealthy person. In both large and small communities, closely-held businesses are the major providers of new jobs. In fact, they are the financial backbone of virtually every community in the nation. Important other players in the economic community, such as bankers, lawyers, accountants and other small and large business owners, understand that. They will cater to you to get your business. In fact, you can have a much greater impact on their lives and their businesses than you probably could if your wealth were just represented by a broad based portfolio of publicly traded stocks and bonds.

That greater power to affect your community can be used by you to determine many factors in your community. If you are just another wealthy person in town, your views on matters may receive little more attention than the opinions expressed by someone else. However, because of the control you have over so many people, your opinion will carry greater weight. In addition, you will be in a position to explain how certain decisions will help your company, thereby increasing the base of economic security for your community than if decisions are made other ways. It is doubtful that you could make such persuasive arguments if you did not own an important company.

Greater Continuity for Employees and Customers

If you want to strike terror in the hearts of employees of most companies, start a rumor that the company is going to be sold to a competitor. In many circumstances, the new owners will come in and discharge a significant number of employees. Often, it is the management team which is discharged but, in many cases, it is lower level employees who are discharged as well. The reasons for that can be many but two are prime ones. First, an acquirer regards itself as the winner in the competitive struggle for business. Your company is regarded as the loser because you have sold out, and, accordingly, your managers should be discharged—they are losers rather than winners regardless of what is said during the "courting" practice to buy your business. Second, there is often a duplication of personnel. Most companies do not need two comptrollers, a double set of receptionists or whatever workers the acquiring company already has. In addition, an acquirer will tend to close down those divisions of the acquired company which are least profitable, thereby discharging people. Hence, your employees may perceive that they have greater prospects of continued employment if you remain the owner of the business. Obviously, there can be exceptions to that. If your company has fallen onto hard times and needs an influx of capital (or needs more capital to expand) being acquired can provide that additional base of capital and thereby enhance the prospect of continued employment.

Because of the possibility of termination of certain divisions or operations of your company, regardless of the reason it is acquired, your customers may also be affected by your selling your business. Certainly, they will be substantially affected if you liquidate your business but it is also likely that they will be affected if you sell it to someone else.

Provide Jobs for Family and Friends

Often, a significant portion of the value of a closely-held business is harvested, on an annual basis, through salaries, bonuses and benefits provided to employees. In any case, as the owner of the company, you can choose members of your family and your friends to be employees. Where the profits of the business are distributed as salaries, bonuses and benefits, it may be appropriate to grant jobs to family members and friends. In addition, family and friends are likely to be more loyal employees to you than others will be, all other things being equal. However, your company will operate in a different way if family and friends are part of it. In some cases that will be beneficial, but in other cases it may be detrimental, as is discussed in more detail below.

Lower Income Tax

To some degree, you have greater control about the timing of taxation of income if you own your own company than if you invest in other businesses, whether they are private companies or publicly held. Often, you can delay a sale or otherwise defer the receipt of proceeds, or income, until a later time. Generally, it is best to defer income. On the other hand, where it is anticipated that tax rates will be higher in a later year, you sometimes are able to accelerate income into an earlier one, thereby reducing overall taxation. That is much more difficult to accomplish if you are not in control of the company and its decisions.

REASONS TO SELL

Greater Liquidity

From time to time during your life, and certainly after your death, there will be a need for cash. If your wealth is represented almost exclusively by interests in your business, it may be difficult to raise cash. If you own a portfolio of marketable securities, for example, raising cash is as simple as calling a broker and directing a sale.

After your death, there will almost certainly be a need for cash to pay the expenses associated with your death including estate and inheritance taxes which may be due. As is discussed in more detail in Chapter 14, in some cases, and to a limited degree, the payment of death taxes can be postponed. However, eventually, they must be paid and they must be paid in cash. If cash assets have already been accumulated, or can be made readily available, the costs of liquidating assets to raise cash are eliminated or reduced.

Greater Diversification

Most great family fortunes have been made in one industry, and often one company. However, over time, the family usually diversifies its holdings. In fact, many families which made their wealth in one industry, such as railroads, would be in the poorhouse today if they had not effected diversification.

As explained above, the probability of your building a large base of wealth by holding a broad diversified portfolio is not as great as choosing one outstanding investment, such as your own company. On the other hand, the risk of failure and complete loss is greater if all of your wealth is represented in one business rather than a broad and diversified portfolio of assets. Usually, it becomes appropriate to consider diversification when you have built a significant base of wealth and want to ensure that it will exist, as a practical matter, for the rest of your life and for surviving family members. That often only can be done if you hold assets in addition to those related to your business.

Greater Personal Freedom

Many owners of closely-held businesses devote virtually all of their energies to the company's successful operation. They have little opportunity to engage in other activities because they have little time. Most owners of restaurants, for example, will tell you that personal involvement in the business makes the difference between success and failure. That is true for many other companies as well. Needless to say, if your base of wealth is more broadly diversified, you will have the opportunity, even if you choose not to take it, to devote less time to your company because it will represent less of a financial stake for you. Obviously, that may adversely affect the operation of your business. Nonetheless, as explained above, your business is likely to go through financial cycles in any event and you need to be less concerned about them, and therefore need to spend less time trying to overcome them, if your wealth is diversified.

Obviously, if you sell your business, you need to devote no time to it, except to the extent that you have an obligation to continue to work there or your payment for the company is dependent upon continued profitable operation of it. Selling your business, however, will provide you with the greatest personal freedom of all. It provides you with an opportunity to devote more time to your family, other investments, charity and recreational pursuits.

Force Family Members to Choose Alternative Careers

As will be discussed in more detail in Chapter 7, it may not be appropriate to have other family members work in your business. However, in many circumstances, family members, as well as friends, will work in the company. Sometimes, that is not in their best interests. By selling your business, you may be able to force family members to choose alternative careers. In fact, adopting a plan even during the development stages of your company that you will sell it at an appropriate time means that family members will understand that they eventually will have to choose alternative careers.

Funding Estate Taxes

As explained in more detail in Chapter 14, death taxes can erode between 50% and 80% of a property owner's base of wealth at death. Although, in some cases, a portion of the estate tax may be postponed for a while, eventually it must be paid and it always must be paid in cash. Selling your business may provide that cash to pay the taxes. Especially when you have arranged for the sale during your lifetime, the best price, under the best terms, may be obtained. If your survivors are forced to sell the business because the taxes must be paid, they may not obtain the best price or even a good one.

In addition, if your business is sold prior to your death, there will be no disagreements with the Internal Revenue Service (IRS) as to the value of the company at your death. The IRS, in estate tax audits, makes more money from changes in values than all other legal issues combined. Increasing the value of a closely-held business is one of the most lucrative ways for the IRS to collect additional taxes. The cost of administering your estate probably will be significantly greater if you own your business at the time you die. If it is sold prior to your death, those problems and disagreements probably will not arise.

On the other hand, a sale prior to death almost necessarily means the payment of significant capital gains taxes, unless special arrangements are made. If it is possible to arrange for the sale of your business shortly after your death, the sales price almost certainly will be accepted as the company's value for estate tax purposes, thereby avoiding disputes with the IRS, and providing the cash necessary to pay taxes and other expenses associated with your death. Also, in almost all cases, the income tax basis of your business in the hands of your estate will be equal to its estate tax value. That means a sale of your company after your death will result in no gains tax at all.

Greater Opportunities to Reduce Tax

Although interests in closely-held businesses, as explained earlier in this Chapter, usually are valued at significantly less than interests in public companies, opportunities to engage in certain estate planning may be foreclosed if virtually all of your wealth is represented by interests in a closely-held business. First, you may be hesitant to dispose of interests which are not in your business because that adversely affects your own base of diversification. Moreover, you may not be able to engage in certain estate planning strategies, some of which are discussed in Chapter 14, unless you have cash or at least assets which produce a different level of income or growth than that represented in your business. Furthermore, on account of a restrictive agreement among co-owners or because of tax or other rules, you may be unable to make gifts of interests in your business to family members or otherwise effect important estate planning. Nonetheless, such statements must be tempered by the fact that often interests in closely-held businesses are ideal subjects of transfers both during lifetime as well as at death.

Greater Opportunities to Protect Your Wealth from Claims of Creditors

Chapter 16 discusses in some detail steps you can take to protect yourself and your family from claims of creditors. It also discusses how you can take steps to reduce the impact of claims which are made against your business. However, as a practical matter, you probably will be able to effect greater protection for your wealth if it is represented other than by interests in your business.

For example, in some states, investments in policies of life insurance are not subject to claims of the owner's creditors. Only cash may be invested in a policy of insurance and thereby effect that protection. Similarly, in some states, your home, regardless of how valuable it is, is free of claims of your creditors. Your ability to own a valuable home, free of indebtedness, may not be as great if your wealth is tied up in your business. Overall, your ownership of interests in your businesses is more likely to be widely known, including being known by potential claimants against you, than other wealth you hold. As a consequence, interests in your business may appear to be more an inviting target than other assets held by you.

On the other hand, there are things you can do which can reduce the chances of interests in your business being subjected to claims of creditors.

Diversification Within the Company

To some degree, you may be able to retain your company and effect a type of wealth diversification plan by diversifying the assets held by your business and having those assets held in a separate subsidiary company. For example, as your company has cash available, it might purchase a portfolio of broad-based marketable securities, other independent closely-held businesses, real estate or other appropriate investments which effect a good diversification from your core operations. In fact, sometimes it may be less expensive from a tax perspective to do that than distribute cash from the company to its owners. Nonetheless, that type of diversification plan really only is effective if these newly acquired assets are immunized from claims which could arise with respect to your core operations. In some cases, that can be achieved by "dropping" operations into separate subsidiary corporations or limited partnerships. You cannot have wholly owned corporate subsidiaries if your business is an S corporation (sometimes called a Subchapter S corporation) but, as a general rule, it can have limited partnership subsidiaries. (An S corporation is one where the company's earnings are taxed directly to its shareholders and not to the corporation itself.) If your core business is in partnership form, it can hold partnership or corporate subsidiaries although these corporate subsidiaries cannot qualify as S corporations. More on how to structure the affairs of your company to prevent a liability in one of its parts from infecting the others is contained in Chapter 16.

If you diversify sufficiently within your company, it can become a type of holding enterprise. In some cases, parts can be split-off free of income tax. Nonetheless, you will continue to own and operate your core business with all of the advantages and disadvantages which that involves.

SUMMARY AND CONCLUSIONS

The profitability and the worth of your business will change over time. If almost all of your wealth is concentrated in your company, your personal ability to survive times of business adversity will be reduced. On the other hand, if your company, while you own it, goes through a period of significant success, your base of wealth may be more secure. There are many reasons to continue to hold your business, including greater control over your investment and being able to have a greater impact on your community and your family. In some cases, your family also will benefit because your wealth is concentrated in a successful business. For example, taxes at your death may be lower because interests in privately-held businesses tend to be valued significantly lower than comparable interests in public companies. On the other hand, you may find that there are several reasons you should consider selling at least a portion if not all of your business. Selling it will provide you with a greater base of diversification, thereby reducing the risk of complete financial failure if your company or industry falls on extremely hard times. In addition, selling your business provides you with greater personal freedom, may provide greater opportunities to protect your wealth from claims of creditors and may allow you to engage in more diversified estate planning arrangements.

CHAPTER 3

HOW DO I PLAN FOR THE SUCCESSOR MANAGERS OF MY BUSINESS?

INTRODUCTION AND OVERVIEW OF CHAPTER

Regardless of how long you have been the key manager of your company, some day the reins of control will pass to others. That may be when you retire, are adjudged incompetent, die or choose to take on a different role in your business. Whatever the reason, your financial future then will rest, in large measure, in the hands of the successor managers of your company. Hence, it is critically important for you to choose, well before your retirement or death, successor managers of your business or the mechanism by which they will be chosen. In fact, it may be appropriate for you to have successor managers in place even if you plan to sell your company. This Chapter will discuss approaches to determining the necessary qualifications for those managers, what to do when you decide to choose a successor manager from outside the company and how to determine the appropriate compensation for the successors.

WHY YOU SHOULD PLAN FOR YOUR SUCCESSOR MANAGERS

An essential ingredient to almost any successful business is superb management. Although it may be difficult for you, as the current owner of your business, to assess objectively your own abilities as a manager, you may be in the very best position to determine the qualifications of anyone who succeeds you. Experience often is a key ingredient in being a good manager. That experience, of course, can come from operating other businesses including those of your competitors, but every company, at least to some degree, is unique. The experience, therefore, gained at your particular business may constitute an important element of its successful management.

Your failure to plan for successors means you delegate that responsibility to someone else. Members of your family, if they become the successor owners of your company, may not be in a position to make an appropriate choice on account of their own lack of experience or business acumen or on account of a desire to promote themselves rather than the best interests of the company. Often, family members have no choice but to turn to the surviving workers in the business for their advice as to successors. Almost certainly, recommendations will be made to choose someone within the business. That may not be the best choice for your company but it may be almost impossible for your family to ascertain that.

Even if your family seeks the advice of outside advisors as to the selection of successor managers, the outsiders probably will not have your base of experience and knowledge as to the necessary qualifications of the manager.

Perhaps, most important, your failure to choose successor managers during your reign in operating the business means that you will fail to observe the chosen successor in operation. Watching that person perform the requisite and growing tasks and responsibilities of the job to replace you probably is the most important opportunity to assess whether or not that person will do a good job. No matter how carefully you try, you will not get 100% "accurate" information about anyone you hire outside of your company. Any employment service will be in the business of getting you to choose someone who is available to be hired whether or not that person is the best one or even an appropriate one for the job. Although you may be aware of an apparent good manager in a comparable business (perhaps, someone working for your competition), the information you receive will be somewhat filtered by other people's views and those views may not coincide with yours. In addition, successful experience as a manager in one business may not be transferable to yours for a multitude of reasons.

No doubt, you have observed that regardless of the quality of the industry, a poor manager can ruin an otherwise successful enterprise. Failure to plan for your successors greatly increases the probability of that happening to your business. Even if there are several "senior managers" in addition to you already in your company, you still should plan for successors. It may turn out that all of them leave or die at about the same time or that your surviving business owners, who are also co-managers with you, fail to plan for successive management. Obviously, if your business is owned and operated by persons in addition to you, you should make a joint decision as to the mechanism for the selection of successor managers. In any event, an agreement should be reached that the co-owners will implement a plan over a reasonable period of time to select successor managers.

ASCERTAINING THE NEEDS OF THE BUSINESS FOR SUCCESSOR MANAGERS

Every company needs managers but the appropriate number and levels of managers varies from business to business and industry to industry. In your industry, it may mean selecting successor directors to oversee the long-term planning and the strategic decisions for your business. Almost certainly, it will involve choosing the day-to-day executive and operating officers of your company. Certainly, you should approach the determination about the various levels and needs for successor managers objectively. Relying on what you have done alone probably is not an appropriate measure.

Your commitment to your business probably will be greater than that of any successor manager. In addition, you may be able to provide appropriate checks and balances for the continued profitable and successful operation of your business by choosing different tiers of the successor managers than you have used while you operated the company. Once you leave, the successor senior manager, even if you have seen him or her in operation for a long period of time, will operate the company in a different manner than you did. You may discover that, for example, a person who has had the best interest of co-workers at heart suddenly becomes more concerned about his or her own interests. Anyone you choose as a manager of your company is certainly going to be an intelligent person. He or she may know how to "play" you but once you are out of the picture that person will operate in a somewhat different way. Allowing one person entirely to control the show after you have gone may result in an inappropriate balance of power over the company.

You may find it appropriate to study the management structure of public companies in your industry, or larger companies, even if privately-held, which have been operated by other than the founder for some period of time to determine the management structures which have been successful. To some degree, you may wish to model the successor management structure of your company on some of those companies that you believe are most comparable to your business and your circumstances and have been successful.

It also may be appropriate for you to consider hiring an expert who has assisted in finding successor managers for other concerns. A number of "boutique" investment banking firms, particularly those which specialize in acquiring and "turning around" bankrupt or financially-distressed companies, often have significant experience in finding successful replacement managers. Such a company may be able to assist you in determining the appropriate characteristics and necessary skills of successor managers. Some employment or executive placement companies also have adequate experience in such matters and can be very helpful in recommending and finding senior managers for your company.

TIMING OF IMPLEMENTING THE PLAN FOR SUCCESSOR MANAGERS

Introduction

It Could Happen Sooner Than You Think

Regardless of your age or the current life cycle of your business, it is appropriate for you to consider successor management now. Perhaps nothing will be more important for the continued financial success of your enterprise than having that plan in place.

The need to find successor managers can happen for positive as well as negative reasons. Although individuals typically consider the need for successor management only in connection with their death, successor management may be necessary in the event of retirement or incompetency. In addition, opportunities may arise which divert your attentions from the day-to-day operation of your business. Such events can include "positive" ones, such as an opportunity to head a commission for the government, run for public office, or oversee an important charitable or community activity or similar event. Although you may view your departure from the day-to-day operations of your business as a temporary one, your service in another capacity may be prolonged and, in any event, failure to have successor management in place even during relatively brief periods of time may adversely affect your business. I represent a man who, for two years, left his construction company to operate a fuel service business. Other members of his family, who worked in the construction company with him, advised him that they felt they could operate the business and during the two-year period they kept assuring him that things were "just fine." When the client returned to the construction company, he found out that although the quality of the work done had continued to be high and the volume of business had been maintained, the financial position of the company was horrible. Uncollected accounts receivable had tripled and the costs of operation had increased to such a degree that the company, which had been profitable from its first year of operation, actually was operating at a loss. In the client's own words, "My mistake was not really taking the time to assess what management needs were necessary while I was away. To the extent I considered it at all, I assumed that my field operators could run the 'business' side of my company as well as they had done other work. That mistake cost me dearly." In fact, the client stated that if he had not returned to the construction company when he did it probably would have been lost resulting in the client facing significant personal liabilities.

You May or May Not Be the Best Judge of the Abilities of Successor Managers

There is a strong likelihood that you know your business better than anyone else in the world. As a consequence, you probably are in the best position to assess the needs of managers of your business. However, that is not always the case. Often, the style of management of a company's founder will be difficult for others to emulate. Not all founders who operate their own businesses take the time to become professionally trained as managers. It seems that as often as not the force of their personality, their commitment to the business and their native capacity offset their lack of "classic" management style. It is unlikely, however, that any successor will have those same qualities of the founder. As a consequence, it may be difficult for you to assess the needs of management in your business enterprise. Again, it may be appropriate for you, with the assistance of an expert, to assess the needs of your business in part by comparing it to the management structure of successful public companies or even private companies in your industry which have non-owner managers in place.

HOW TO HANDLE THE "POLITICS" OF HAVING OUTSIDERS BECOME THE SUCCESSOR MANAGERS

People join and leave businesses every day. That probably happens in your business as well. New people become accepted members of the team and join the "old boy" network after some period of time. In many professional organizations, such as law firms and accounting firms, that period may be years. In other businesses, such as banks, where movement at the management level occurs with much greater frequency, the time period generally is much shorter. In any case, once a person becomes a part of the framework of the company, his or her promotion to important management positions is more likely to be accepted by others who also work in the business. However, those who have been around longer, and are at the same, or even a higher, level of management, probably will resent the promotion of people who arrive at a later time and have not proven their worth. The transition of placing that newer person into an important successor management slot will be much smoother if that person has been with the company during your tenure in operating it.

Nonetheless, there may come a time (for example, by reason of your retirement) when you must hire someone who is a complete outsider to your business and make that person an important successor manager of your company. Regardless of the reason, if you decide to hire one or more outsiders to fill top positions in your company, a common circumstance where you will decide to recruit an outsider as the top or, at least, one of the top executives of your company is where your business has grown to such a level that no one on your present staff has the capacity, aptitude or experience to move the business further along. In other words, you may decide you need "new blood" as the life cycle of your business reaches a new level. There may be resentment among other top employees in your business. It becomes your responsibility to approach the problem head on and talk to all of the other key persons in your business about your decision. Although, obviously, you will have to gear the message about the new manager to fit the particular circumstances of your business and its needs, there are some messages which appear to have been more effective than others.

First, you should approach the insiders yourself for introducing the outsider. You may wish to compliment the current key workers for their performance and dedication and advise them that it is not a lack of competence, ability or commitment which led you to the decision to hire an outside person.

Second, it probably will be best if you can demonstrate that in making your decision you sought the advice of an expert who, after a careful analysis, concluded that the company would prosper better under new or additional managers. This message may include, for example, an explanation of the highly-competitive nature of your business and the need to gain the experience of others in the industry. In fact, if you have an outside board of directors (something almost all experts recommend), you can "blame" them (as well as any consultant you have hired) for the decision.

Generally, it may be best not to overemphasize the importance of the outsider but explain that he or she is just one member of the team, even if a very important one. You might analogize here to hiring a new starting pitcher for your favorite baseball team. It does not necessarily denigrate the rest of the team to go and hire an outsider even if the pitching staff is already strong. In no event should you apologize for your decision.

Third, you may wish to explain that you are taking the greatest risk of hiring the outsider. In the event of failure, you bear the brunt of the economic loss. However, you also may want to explain that based upon that person's experience and prior "track record" you anticipate enhanced profitability for the company which you believe ultimately aids the rest of the work force.

Perhaps, the most important message, however, you can relay is one of "minimal shakeup." There appears to be a propensity of new managers to discharge virtually every person directly underneath them and to hire replacements. The reason, actually, does not relate to the quality of the new manager's staff; rather, it relates to building loyalty. The new manager, in order to secure his or her own new position, may attempt to hire others who appreciate that their positions are attributable directly to him or her. Such action is, unfortunately, extremely common in American businesses and it often results in adverse consequences: Continuity of performance and knowledge is lost; it becomes a pattern and workers who remain know from prior experience that the owners of the business will not stop it from happening in the future; it probably will be costly as some of the successor staff managers chosen by the new manager will receive higher compensation than those who are discharged.

One of the most effective ways to prevent that purging of other current key employees from occurring is for you to hire the successor manager while you are still completely active in the business. Not only will you be able to observe the propensity of the successor manager to discharge people under him or her, it will also provide an opportunity to build a strong level of loyalty among all members of your staff while you are still active. In addition, it will, over time, tend to sever the loyalties which the successor manager had to persons with whom he or she formerly worked. The person chosen as the successor manager will begin to rely on the existing staff. If the successor manager feels changes should be made, he or she can discuss that matter with you and you will be in a position, and also hold the direct day-to-day authority, to implement or reject those suggestions. That all goes back to the fact that the time for you to consider the placement of successor management is now—not the year before you retire (when your attention may be diverted to other matters) or leaving the decision to your family after you die.

DETERMINING THE COMPENSATION PACKAGE OF SUCCESSOR MANAGERS

Make no mistake about it: The reason people work is primarily attributable to their perception as to the adequacy of their compensation. Putting all the explanations aside, when a person leaves one job for another, nine out of ten times it will be as a result of an enhanced compensation package. One of the worse things you can do is to hire someone, which results in a promotion of that person's position from another enterprise, and then inadequately compensate him (or her) so that he leaves as soon as a better financial package is offered. It is much easier to go from the presidency from one company to another than from a vice president in one enterprise to the presidency of another. Once you promote someone from the lower ranks to the higher ranks, their desirability as a more senior manager necessarily increases because they now have a better and more thorough experience base at that higher level. Here, again, the advice of an outsider, such as an executive placement agency or consulting firm, may be helpful. An agency which specializes in the placement of high-level managers in a certain industry may be aware of the types of compensation packages which not only attract top executives, but also the types which hold them to a position as well.

Executive compensation is often a complex matter. Cash compensation may be relatively easy to determine. You may be aware of what comparable positions in your industry are commanding. Even if you are not, that information generally is available from executive search firms and similar organizations. In some cases, you may have to offer more than the "going" rate to attract a particular executive. As mentioned, most people move because they believe they will receive higher compensation. In fact, very often, senior executives seek an equity position in the business for which they work or are asked to move to. In some cases, equity rights can be used to attract and hold superior managers where they cannot obtain equity in their current position or believe that the equity you offer them is more likely to become valuable in the future. Sometimes, for example, a person who probably would not move to your company under ordinary circumstances even as its chief operating officer, may accept your offer of employment if it is coupled with the promise of equity. The person may believe he or she can make that equity increase in value to such a point that he or she becomes a very wealthy person. Hence, coupling authority to make decisions which will affect the success of the business with equity in it can be a very effective way to acquire and hold senior executives.

Furthermore, equity packages often provide tax benefits for both the employer and the employee. For example, the issuance of certain stock options does not result in immediate taxable income to the employee and, upon exercise, may result in a deduction to the employer, although, at that time, the employee may have taxable compensation equal to the benefit derived from the exercise of the option. From the employee's perspective, value of the equity builds without current taxation. From the employer's perspective, compensation has been paid without any out-of-pocket cash cost so the deferral of any deduction for compensation is not adverse.

Moreover, there are limitations, as a general rule, on cash compensation which is "reasonable." Depending upon the industry, and the location in the country, salaries in excess of several hundred thousand dollars may be viewed as excessive and cause animosity within the company and outside of it as well. In fact, most of the extremely high compensation payments made from public companies to senior executives are not cash compensation but result from the exercise of stock options or other participation in equity. As you are no doubt aware, the tax law denies a deduction for compensation paid to the extent it is unreasonable. Moreover, if it is paid to an owner of the business, the excessive compensation may be taxable to the owner as a distribution from the company, such as taxable and nondeductible dividends.

Employees often are willing to gamble by taking equity in lieu of cash compensation and realize that if they can make the company perform well, they can build a significant base of wealth and often on a tax-favored basis. In fact, perhaps, a good equity program is one where executives do not receive "free" equity but have to pay for it at its current value or at a bargain price. That allows them to really make a choice as to whether or not they want to invest in the company they work for or whether they want to invest in other companies, including those which are publicly traded.

There are problems, however, with almost all "real" equity programs. You now have a co-owner to whom you are responsible to answer for your actions at least to a limited degree. As a practical matter, it is more difficult to remove an executive who holds a significant stake in equity than one who does not. To protect his or her equity in your company investment, litigation is much more likely. Furthermore, once the "genie is out of the bottle" it is almost impossible to put it back in without paying a large price which may include the potential, or perceived, tax benefits which the executive would derive by appreciation in the equity.

On the other hand, equity plans which provide for gradual vesting of ownership sometimes can be used as "golden handcuffs" to hold an employee in a position: The employee, wishing to capitalize on the actual or anticipated increase in the value of equity, can only do so by remaining on the job until vesting occurs. Such vesting can be done with cash compensation as well although, obviously, it is more expensive, from a cash flow perspective, for a company to pay compensation than issue additional stock to an employee.

Participation in equity also may cause a senior executive to work harder and to be more creative and courageous in operating a business because he or she will participate in the financial goals which are reached. Nonetheless, there is almost a universal consequence of granting real equity: You will be pressured to take the company public or to sell it out to someone else because that may be the only real way in which the executives can ever "cash in" on their investment during lifetime or early enough in lifetime to really enjoy it. Perhaps, your arrangement will not give the other executives adequate voting power to be able control the decision as to whether to go public or otherwise to sell out. Nonetheless, the executives always will hold the power of persuasion and also the threat of quitting. In some companies, senior executives who have been awarded equity threaten to quit unless the company is taken public or sold out. They claim that they don't care what happens to the company since they cannot cash in on their investment anyway. Hence, any predilection to award equity, even on a deferred basis, should be approached with caution. Also, awarding equity to your employees may inhibit your company's ability to sell the same percentage of equity to outsiders for cash.

Phantom Stock Plans

One alternative is to use "phantom" stock plans. A comparable program can be used even if the business is in the form of a partnership, a proprietorship or even an S corporation which usually can have only one class of equity. Rather than issuing real equity, selected employees receive phantom equity. You pretend (and everybody knows you are pretending) as though the employees received stock at the beginning of the year. That stock is revalued at the beginning of the next year and the employees receive an amount equal to the increased value of the stock. Often, a fixed formula, usually recommended to the business by a valuation service, investment banker or another, will be used as the formula to determine the amount of the value in the phantom stock. It is appropriate for both you and the employees to acknowledge that the formula may produce results which do not reflect real changes in value but that there will be no recourse even if someone feels the results are unfair. Often, the payment to the executives of the annual increase in their phantom stock is postponed until after the close of the year or an even longer time and that can cause a serious problem for the company. For example, the value of phantom stock increases so much in one year that the executives become entitled to significant payment. However, by the time the payment must be made, the company has fallen on very hard times. That means the executives become major creditors for the company, which can make things somewhat uncomfortable for everyone. Hence, certain other limitations (e.g., no one year's phantom stock payment can exceed 75% of the profits for the year in which payment is due) should be considered. Moreover, if the payment of the phantom stock compensation must be paid in cash, as it almost always is, a serious cash flow problem can be generated for the company.

Basically, you can design a phantom stock plan in as imaginative a way as you wish, including using vesting schedules and forfeitures in the event of discharge for cause or any other conditions. However, the tax and economic ramifications must be carefully considered. For example, the formula used to determine the value of the phantom stock may produce an unreasonable value. If the value is too low, you are always in a position to grant additional compensation, such as through bonuses, provided the total compensation is not unreasonable. On the other hand, if the result is that the value of the phantom stock is much too high, your company may become unreasonably indebted to its executives. As stated above, probably the worst case is where you have had a very high valuation, payment of the compensation is deferred, and then the company falls on hard times. Also, the IRS may contend that the phantom stock formula price determines the value of your stock for gift and estate tax purposes. The IRS may not be successful in that contention but is likely to make it if it would increase taxes. In any event, you should consider a phantom stock plan only after consultation with an advisor experienced with such plans.

Make the Executives Buy Equity: An Equity Program Which May Be Appropriate for Your Company

One potential equity program is to restructure the ownership of your company so that you and your family, in effect, have an entitlement to the current value of your company and to allow your executives to share, with real equity, future increases in the value of your company. For example, it could be restructured tax-free so that you and your family receive preferred interest, such as preferred stock if your company is a regular corporation. (That cannot be done with an S corporation as it can have only one kind of equity—common stock.) In addition, your family would receive that proportion of the common stock which you determine is appropriate allowing your executives, up to certain limits, to subscribe for additional stock from the company. Although only experienced advisors can tell you how much the common stock would be worth, often in a recapitalization the value of the common stock can be depressed to about 10% of the current value of the company by having the preferred stock absorb 90% of current value. You would permit your executives to purchase part of the common stock currently representing 10% of the worth of the business. The executives would be required to pay current value for the stock. Each executive, therefore, would have to face the decision as to whether he or she believed that an investment in the equity of your company was the best way to invest a portion of his or her cash. In effect, the executive would only participate in future growth of the company because most of the current value has been absorbed by the preferred stock held by you and your family.

From your company's perspective, the cost of such a plan is very low. If the stock is fairly valued, your company will receive real equity which can expand its base of operations. Second, executives who buy the stock are likely to stay with the company because they have more direct control over the fate of their investment compared, for example, to investment in a public company where they can have virtually no impact.

It is possible, as well, to impose rights to purchase the stock back if an executive leaves prior to a certain time (such as a number of years with the company) or is discharged for cause. Perhaps, it will be fair to provide for the stock of such a departing executive to be purchased back at the original purchase price plus an interest factor or, alternatively, pursuant to the use of a formula. A further alternative is to have the value determined by an appraiser. In any case, if you want a buy-back option, a mechanism to determine price over which there could be little disagreement should be used. You do not want to wind up in court over a disagreement over what the stock is worth if you have an option to buy or the executive has a right to put it back to the company, which can be part of the arrangement.

Especially where executives are paid large cash compensation, including generous bonuses, giving them an opportunity to buy real equity in your company, whether it is voting or non-voting equity, for its current value but with a real opportunity to participate in future growth of your business may be appropriate both for you and for them. For those executives, including new senior managers, who harp for equity, it will give them an opportunity to put their money where their mouths are and to demonstrate that they are willing to make whatever commitment to the business is necessary to make "their" company and "their" equity grow in value.

WHAT YOU SHOULD DO IF YOU HAVE NOT CHOSEN YOUR SUCCESSOR MANAGERS

Perhaps, you will not find the time or make the effort to choose successor managers. In that case, at a minimum, you should set into motion a mechanism by which an appropriate successor to you can be chosen. One of the most effective ways is to consider carefully who will own the equity in your business after your death. Leaving the equity to members of your family will put them in control. Often, there are many benefits to transferring your assets, including equity in your business, to trusts for members of your family or other loves ones. Chapter 9 discusses that matter in detail. A strong case can be made for use of trusts. The trustees become owners of the assets in the trusts even though they are held for the benefit of others, such as members of your family. In fact, in most cases, members of your family can be trustees. However, if members of your family are not the best ones to choose the successor managers of your business, use of some outside trustees who are better able to make those decisions should be considered. In fact, those outsiders can be special trustees whose duties are limited to certain tasks, such as voting the stock in your business or otherwise controlling the decision as to the selection of successor managers.

Many owners of closely-held businesses find that an independent board of directors, or at least having some outsiders on the board of directors, is one of the most important and helpful steps they can take in the successful operation of their business. Naming similar people as trustees of trusts, or otherwise arranging them to choose the successor managers of your business, may be an appropriate step for you to consider.

SUMMARY AND CONCLUSIONS

Because the management of most businesses is an essential ingredient to their success, planning for successor managers to you is important. Because you will hold special insights about the appropriate qualities of the senior managers, you should plan for the mechanism to choose your successors, or actually choose them and start them in your company long before you step down as the senior executive of your business. A thorough study, undertaken by you or experts on your behalf, of non-owner managers of businesses similar to yours may be an appropriate step for you to consider. You run a great risk of harming the continued success of your company if you do not have a successive management plan in place at the time that you stop the day-to-day management of your business. In some circumstances, it will be appropriate for you to consider hiring an outsider rather than someone currently working in the business with you. Having that person come in during your tenure will smooth the transition of having him or her accepted as your successor as well as providing you with a better opportunity to observe whether that individual is the appropriate successor to you. A critical factor in attracting and holding top executives is their compensation package. Generally, that is the reason they work. Designing the appropriate package again may require the advise of an expert. In some circumstances, an offer of equity is appropriate but awarding equity has potentially far-reaching effects. For many businesses, even where equity participation should be considered, phantom equity participation or equity which is purchased at current value may be a better route.

CHAPTER 4

HOW DO I GET OUT OF THIS BUSINESS ALIVE?

INTRODUCTION AND OVERVIEW OF CHAPTER

For several reasons, the better choice for you may be to dispose of your business prior to death. This Chapter will discuss several opportunities to do that and some of the difficulties in disposing of your business during your lifetime.

DIFFICULTIES IN SEPARATING YOURSELF FROM YOUR BUSINESS

Introduction

Arranging for the disposition of your business long before your death and even before your retirement may be appropriate for you to consider for a variety of reasons. Those reasons may be personal as well as business-oriented. You may have a better idea of the real worth of your business than most of your advisors. Your ability to negotiate the most financially lucrative disposition of the company may occur while you are still fully in control of the business as well as your faculties. The successor owners of your business may not be able to operate the business as well and, in any event, may not be able to arrange for a sale as well as you can. You probably know the likely buyers of your business and may be able to make the best deal. Nonetheless, in almost every case, you probably will face difficulties in disposing of your company.

Successor Management

As explained in Chapter 3, finding successor managers for your company probably will not be easy. If you intend to keep your business, however, during your retirement and pass it along to your family when you die, it probably is best if you take on the task of finding appropriate successor managers. Also, you will have to face the sometimes unsettling prospect of sharing responsibilities with them prior to the time that you leave the business. You may be unable to find completely satisfactory successor managers and as long as you own the company that is your problem. However, if you sell your business, successor management falls on the shoulders of the successor owners. Nonetheless, some potential buyers of your business may insist upon your continuing to operate the company. In fact, the sale of your company may be structured so that you are bought out over time and for the ultimate purchase price to depend upon the continued success of the business. That may mean that you must continue to operate it or to find managers whom you are confident will do a sufficient job to make sure that you are paid in full. To some degree, you place yourself at their mercy: As you remove yourself from the business you lose knowledge and experience relating to its successful operation and that knowledge and experience is gained by the others, thereby exposing you to financial risk over which you constantly lose more and more control.

Taxes

The most significant tax savings in estate planning occurs by the income tax-free, step-up basis in property owned at death: For most assets owned at death, all of the inherent gain in them is entirely forgiven upon their owner's death. The change in income tax basis applies, as a general rule, even if the property is subject to no or only a partial estate tax. As a consequence, there is a tremendous incentive to hold an appreciated business until death. Selling the business prior to death, generally even on the installment basis so that gain is postponed, will result in taxation of the inherent gain. As a result of the imposition of taxes upon the lifetime disposition of the business, in most cases, you face a significant erosion of your wealth base.

Moreover, and as will be discussed in Chapter 14 in more

detail, interests in closely-held businesses generally are valued significantly lower than their public company counterparts for estate tax purposes. Lower valuation means lower death taxes reserving more eventually for the family.

There may be other tax impediments to the disposition of a business during your lifetime as well. Although there are some mechanisms to reduce, and in some cases even avoid, those taxes, generally the potential erosion of the worth of your company by taxes represents a significant impediment to the disposition of your business during lifetime.

"Psychological" Factors

Nonetheless, experience indicates that the greatest stumbling blocks to the disposition of a business during lifetime are "psychological" factors. Building and operating a successful business is one of the most fulfilling experiences of life. Most businessmen and businesswomen find that their position in the family and in the community is enhanced by reason of having an important direct impact on the lives of many people (including employees, suppliers, customers and even competitors). It is a more profound impact than that of just another rich person down at the golf club. Most owners of successful companies can take personal pride in the successes they have brought to the business and to other people's lives. That is often an extremely difficult thing to give up. Hard work often is its own reward and producing beneficial results for many people, and your community, by that hard work, therefore, can be doubly satisfying.

The critical point is that when you sit down to consider whether you should sell your business you will face those psychological or emotional barriers. They are real and important factors to consider. Your life will be very different if you sell out. In some cases, clients seek personal professional counselling to "talk through" those issues and to determine what they really want for themselves, their employees, their business associates and their families during the balance of their lifetimes.

MECHANICS OF SEPARATION

Making A Plan

GOALS

Determining whether and if so how you should separate yourself from your business, it is first appropriate to determine your goals. Why do you want to get rid of the business? As explained earlier, at least tax and psychological factors probably will tend to inhibit you from disposing of your company. Nonetheless, maintaining the business may be incompatible with other goals you have. Those goals may include a desire to spend more time with your family, to take up another profession, to enjoy more recreation time, to devote yourself to a charitable or community cause or to diversify your wealth. It also may be that your business has "plateaued" and that you can build a greater base of wealth by selling your current business and going into other ventures.

In any event, you should have your goals clearly in mind as they will affect not only the timing of the disposition of your business but implementing the plan as well. For example, if your concern is the liquidity of your assets at the time of your death, and the inability to have cash to pay taxes or to allow your family to have wealth independent of the business, other steps, including the acquisition of life insurance, may be appropriate alternatives. Those other options may eliminate the need for disposition of the business.

Wanting to have more time to engage in other activities sometimes also can be adequately achieved by finding a solid successor management team. On the other hand, whether those other alternatives are as attractive as disposing of the business during lifetime is often a difficult determination to make. But ascertaining what alternatives are available depends upon the goals that you have and the degree to which maintaining ownership of the business inhibits obtaining those goals and the degree to which disposing of the company helps achieve them.

TIMING

The time to implement a sale of your company is important. Waiting until the law changes which, for example, may reduce the tax on the sale, may be an appropriate reason to wait, if you are certain that reduction in taxation will occur. Also, certain changes in the operation of the company may make the sale of the business more propitious at a somewhat later time than now. The outside perception of your ability to continue to operate your company successfully also may affect the price for which it will be sold. If you have suffered a disability, such as a heart attack or stroke, the potential buyer may conclude that it is better to wait and let you fail to achieve your business goals believing that you will be more prone to sell the company and at a lower price.

Personal factors also may affect timing. Your spouse may be retiring and you may want the sale of your business to be geared with your spouse's retirement. Reaching your retirement age also may be an appropriate time to consider the disposition of the business. However, as indicated earlier, you may get a better price if it is perceived that you have the capacity and the willingness to continue to work hard at your company and personally assure its success.

PROFESSIONAL ASSISTANCE

Many businessmen and businesswomen dispose of their businesses without first seeking the advice of an expert. Sometimes they are successful. Most times, however, they will do better with the advice of counsellors. Tax and related laws are so complicated that even a modest change in the structure of a disposition can save significant amounts of money. Professionals also may be able to provide mechanisms to build up significantly the price which will be paid or to reduce the liabilities to which you may be exposed in the transaction. In addition, an advisor may find you a much better deal.

One client of ours almost doubled the price that he received for his business because he sought the advice of competent outside advisors who found a group willing to pay a much higher price (almost twice as much) for his business than the original prospective purchaser was willing to pay. That made the difference between him being an exceedingly wealthy man and just a wealthy man. (He enjoys being exceedingly wealthy.)

Implementing the Plan

SELLING OUT PART OR ALL OF THE BUSINESS

ESOPs: GENERAL DESCRIPTION

An Employee Stock Ownership Plan (ESOP) is a special type of retirement plan for your employees that has many special advantages under the tax law. Under certain circumstances, selling your stock to an ESOP can allow you to cash out without paying income tax, and provide your business with tax incentives that make the purchase more economically feasible than it otherwise might be. As a result, ESOPs can be extremely attractive vehicles for disposing of some or all of a closely-held corporation, with or without an outside buyer's involvement. ESOPs can be used only by regular corporations. They cannot be used by S corporations or partnerships.

Description of a Typical ESOP Stock Purchase

An ESOP is the only type of retirement plan specifically designed to borrow money in order to purchase assets for the benefit of the employees covered by the plan. First, a trust is established to do the borrowing and hold the stock for participants. A loan is then arranged, usually from a bank. The bank, of course, will want to ensure repayment and normally will require a guarantee of the loan by the company or, if the company is not sufficiently creditworthy, by the selling shareholders. The trustee of the trust uses the proceeds of the borrowing to buy the stock from the company's stockholders; to qualify for the tax-free "rollover" tax benefit the trustee must borrow enough to purchase at least 30% of the total stock. The price must be a fair one, determined by an independent appraiser.

When the stock is first purchased it is placed in a "suspense account", a kind of holding pen. The ESOP trustee repays the loan with normal company retirement plan contributions, which are made to the ESOP just like contributions to any other qualified retirement plan. As the loan is repaid, proportionate amounts of stock are released from the suspense account into individual employee accounts.

Employees typically become vested in the stock in their accounts over a three to five year period; if they leave prior to vesting, the stock in their account is allocated to other active participants in the plan. Although there are many special rules about when the stock is distributed to employees, it will usually be held in the plan until the employee retires. During the time that the stock is in the plan, it can usually be voted by the trustee. This gives both management of the corporation and any lenders comfort that the company will continue to be operated in an orderly and predictable way. Nonetheless, the most successful ESOP companies are those that treat the employees as the owners that they have become.

There is good and bad news about stock which is distributed to employees from an ESOP. Because the stock will often constitute a substantial portion of an employee's retirement base, the law requires the company to offer to buy the stock back if there is no public market for the stock at the time of distribution; special rules can allow this payout to be deferred over a period of time, however. The good news is that the company can place a "right of first refusal" on the stock, ensuring that it will have the right to buy it before any third party. Obviously, that permits the company to control who its shareholders are.

Tax Advantages to the Seller

Probably the most important reason to consider an ESOP transaction is the possibility of obtaining the tax-free rollover noted above from privately-held shares into a broad base portfolio of marketable securities. Again, if the ESOP owns more than 30% of the company's stock after the sale, the seller is not a regular corporation (for example, you are the seller), and the stock is not traded on an exchange, a rollover will usually be possible. The seller is required to reinvest the proceeds in securities of a United States operating company within one year to obtain the benefit. This means that you can reinvest in your own new business (assuming it not related to the old one) or, more usually, in a portfolio of stocks and/or bonds of active companies. Remember that this is only a deferral of the tax, and that you will take a "carryover" basis in the new investments; thus, the inherent gain in the transaction is subject to tax on disposition of the replacement securities (at least up until the time you die when the inherent gain will be forgiven for income tax purposes).

One interesting possibility exists that virtually assures the deferral is effectively permanent, however. Several high credit-quality institutions will issue very long term floating rate bonds to individuals who use the ESOP rollover. The bonds have a maturity date certain to be after the death of the seller, whose estate will take a stepped-up basis in the bond at that time as explained earlier; because the floating rate should mean that the fair market value of the bond will be near par, the step up should be to the full value of the stock sold to the ESOP. Thus, no income tax is ever paid on the gain realized on the sale to the ESOP. Some individuals have borrowed against the bond (which is usually very good collateral) and used the funds to invest in assets that, if purchased directly with the proceeds of the stock sale, would have disallowed the rollover (like yachts!).

Tax Advantages to the Company

Aside from the tax-free "rollover" for a selling shareholder, an ESOP offers important advantages to the company sponsoring the plan. Sometimes, these benefits will significantly enhance the "doability" of a proposed transaction. First, it is important to realize that the way ESOP loans are repaid— through tax-deductible contributions to a retirement plan— the principal, as well as the interest, of an ESOP loan is effectively made deductible for income tax purposes. For a highly profitable company, this additional tax break can be quite meaningful. Second, where more than half of the company's stock is purchased by the ESOP, the ESOP lender (such as a bank) is permitted to pay tax on only half of its interest income, so that the interest rate on the loan should be lower than would otherwise be the case. Finally, dividends on the stock held by the ESOP, which would not usually be deductible, do effectively become deductible if they are used to repay the loan (or are passed through directly to the plan participants). Together, these benefits can add up to substantial savings for the corporation compared to a non-ESOP stock repurchase program.

Leveraged Buyout: Two Types

MANAGEMENT BACKED BY OUTSIDERS

Sometimes, other senior executives of a company may constitute an appropriate group to whom to sell the business. Rarely, however, will such a management team have the resources to buy you out for cash. In such a case, you may choose to sell your business to management for debt. However, that means that you continue to run the risks of ownership of the company without the power to operate it.

As a result, sales to management are often completed only where management is "backed" by an outsider. The outsider may be a group of passive investors, an investment bank, a large pension fund or any other entity which will provide the cash to buy you out. Many public as well as many private companies have been sold in such ways. Sophisticated outsiders, however, often will want to bargain with you asking that you take less favorable terms and a lower price. Your moral obligation to consider such offers and to be accommodating will be greater if you have raised with your management team their buying you out with the assistance of an outsider. You will be in a much better bargaining position if they raise it with you.

COMPANY BORROWING

At least a partial alternative to a sale to someone may be for your company itself to redeem your stock. Such a redemption as a general rule will be taxable to you, as a dividend, if your company is a regular ("C") corporation and your percentage interest in the company is not reduced by at least 20%, rather than as capital gain. For example, if you own 100% of the stock in your business, any redemption still leaves you with 100%. Similarly, if you are only a partial owner, but all owners are redeemed pro-rata, your percentage of ownership of the stock will remain the same.

If you are not the sole owner of stock, you will be able to arrange to be redeemed to a lesser or greater degree than others. In some cases, those types of non-pro-rata redemptions can result in the payments to you being treated as a purchase of your stock and, therefore, treated as capital gain rather than as ordinary income. However, as indicated, that will result in some shift in the percentage of ownership of the corporation and can result in a change in control.

The company usually can redeem your interests using its own cash or other assets. Generally, if the company is a C corporation, and sometimes even if it is an S corporation, it will recognize gain on any assets it uses to redeem shareholders. Usually, but subject to some important exceptions, it will not have to reorganize gain if the company is a partnership. Alternatively, the company may be able to raise cash to make the redemption by borrowing against its own assets and credit worthiness rather than making the redemption with its own assets.

In any case, your company will become saddled with debt if it borrows. Almost always, you will have to disclose the purpose for the borrowing. Where the lender, whether it is a bank or buyers of debt obligations of your company, knows that the funds will be used to buy part of your equity and not kept in the business, the lender is likely to insist on greater rights and control and higher interest. Hence, the risk of the lender taking over the company is greater.

DIFFERENT EFFECTS

The two types of leveraged buyouts can have different effects not only under the tax law but in the degree to which you continue to be dependent upon the success of the business as the basis of your wealth. Moreover, you may find that employee reaction to the two different types of buyouts is very different. Employees who participate in the buyout may become more committed to the entity. However, some employees who become owners, no doubt, will wish to take the company public as soon as possible or to be bought out themselves. Moreover, employees who do not participate in the change in control may leave the company. Often, the debt service payments necessary to finance the buyout by management cause a reduction in compensation and benefits not only to the management buyers but to the other employees as well.

Borrowing Against Equity

NEED TO AVOID PERSONAL LIABILITY

A de facto disposition may occur by borrowing against the equity in your company. In many cases, the lender will require that you be personally liable on any borrowing. Such recourse borrowing means that if the value of your equity is not adequate to pay off the loan including interest, the lender can move against your other assets. In that case, as a practical matter, you really have not effected a disposition of your business or a diversification of your wealth. Arrangements sometimes can be made, even with respect to privately-held companies whose stock is not marketable, to borrow on your equity without having personally to guarantee the loan. The terms, as a general rule, will be less favorable than if you do personally guarantee the loan. Again, whether you should risk personal recourse depends upon the goals you are trying to achieve. If you are concerned about real diversification, personally guaranteeing any loan based upon your equity does not effect true diversification. Moreover, as is discussed in more detail in Chapter 16, becoming personally indebted is one of the most common ways to wind up in personal bankruptcy, causing you to lose your business, and most of your other assets.

PRACTICAL LIMITS

Whether or not you are willing to guarantee a loan made on equity in your company, there will be limits. It is doubtful if you will be able to borrow more than 25 or 30% of the real estimated value of the equity in your business from any lender. The more you borrow, the higher the interest rate you will pay and the more restrictive the terms of repayment will be. Your lender, as a practical matter, will view itself as a co-owner of your business during the time that the loan is outstanding. You may even discover more concern about the operation of the business than if a loan were made directly to the business itself. The lender appreciates that you, and not your business, are holding the money lent and the business has not had the benefit of it. Often, lenders will have rights, pursuant to the lending contract, to acquire voting equity in your company if you default on payment or the value of the company goes down, thereby shifting control of the business to the lender.

OTHER FACTORS LENDERS CONSIDER

Whether you borrow on your equity or the company borrows to redeem part of your equity, any sophisticated lender will consider your personal situation in determining whether it will lend and under what terms. For example, it may ask what steps you have taken to fund your estate taxes. It will realize that upon your death the IRS may become the major creditor of your estate with a lien on the entire equity of the company and that can cause the operation of your business to be impaired. Hence, it is usually best if your estate planning is in order before you or the company seeks such financing. In fact, many lenders will insist that insurance on your life be carried and be made payable to the lender so it is sure to be paid off when you die. It may also limit salaries, bonuses, sales of substantial assets and affect other operations of the company.

Sales

DIRECT

The simplest and often the most effective way to separate yourself from your business is to sell it lock, stock and barrel for cash. The consequences usually are quite predictable. Nonetheless, your business may be in such a form (such as a proprietorship or partnership) that its sale can result in unexpected and adverse tax and other consequences. You should consider a sale, or any other disposition of your company, only after careful consultation with your advisors. For example, a sale, or even the pledge, of your equity may allow lenders to call loans made to you or to your company.

In almost all sales, certain representations and warranties will have to be made to the buyer by you and your business. You may be asked personally to guarantee certain items, such as that there are no pending lawsuits or even of the outcome of certain lawsuits currently pending against the company. Representations and warranties with respect to debt obligations, accounts receivable, accounts payable, level of inventory, actual and contingent liabilities, funding of retirement plans and many other matters are typically requested by the purchaser of a business even if the purchaser is buying stock and not the business assets themselves. If the company founders after the purchase, you should be prepared to accept the fact that the new purchaser will use almost any excuse to go back against you. As a consequence, the integrity, business reputation and character of the purchaser of your business may be important. Also, in many cases, bargaining away certain representations or warranties may be worth a lower price in the long run.

INSTALLMENT SALES

Sometimes, as explained earlier, you may have an opportunity, or will be requested, to sell your business in part for debt. In such a case, you will be paid for your business in installments. Such installment sales occur for tax and non-tax reasons. Whenever you receive debt as part of the payment, you are, in effect, making an installment sale. Depending upon whether the debt is guaranteed by a purchaser who has other assets, as opposed to only by your business itself, you may or may not continue to be dependent upon the success of your company to be paid off in full. You should carefully check as to where your debt on an installment sale "stands" compared to other indebtedness of the company. In some instances, installment noteholders have even been placed behind people who are really equity owners.

In any event, as a general rule, an installment sale can result in the postponement of the recognition of gain on the sale. For example, if you receive only 25% of the purchase price in cash and the other 75% is paid with a debt obligation, 75% of the gain usually may be postponed for income tax purposes until the debt is paid off. That can be beneficial. First, it provides you with an opportunity, in some instances, to gear the payment of that indebtedness to a time when your tax position is better. For instance, you may be a resident of a high-tax state. At the time that the installment obligation is paid (and the gain must be recognized) you may have become a resident of a state which has no effective capital gains tax. By moving, you may avoid state and local taxes; however, there are exceptions and you should check whether a change in residency will reduce taxes. Second, because the debt has not been eroded by capital gains tax, any interest you are paid on that indebtedness will be greater than if the amount had already been eroded by taxes. That interest will be taxable. Also, in some cases, you must pay interest to the IRS on the deferred tax liability and, in others, installment sales treatment is denied. In any case, you can elect out of installment sales treatment, which sometimes can be beneficial. Whether an installment sale is best for you depends upon many factors and that should be determined only in consultation with your advisors.

Tax-Free
Reinvestments

LIKE-KIND EXCHANGES

For a limited group of assets, the federal tax law permits you to exchange one property for another on a tax-free basis. As a general rule, real estate may be exchanged for another piece of real estate, even though it is of a somewhat different kind and quality. For example, you own a single-purpose building (such as one which is used to operate your manufacturing business). As a general rule, that building could be exchanged for a triple-net leased building with a class-A tenant which produces a yield somewhat comparable to a bond.

Such an exchange not only can be accomplished tax free but it can extricate you from some of the risks of an operating business. Even if you keep a building at the time you sell your company and you rent it to the business, what and whether you are paid rent will depend, in the real world, on the continued successful operation of your business by its new owners. Many persons who have made such arrangements find, out of necessity, that they must continue to give advice and, as a practical matter, work for the business in order to ensure its success and thereby continue to be paid rent.

It should be noted that like-kind exchanges are not difficult to arrange. The tax law permits any person who would have acquired your building for cash, in effect, to buy the replacement property you want and trade it to you. As a consequence, the real trick is finding a purchaser who will pay an adequate price for your business. You then can reinvest the proceeds, in effect, into the type of property you wish to operate which may include one which has an independent manager and minimal risk. For example, a building which is triple-net-leased to a governmental unit may involve no more management commitment on your part than owning a bond.

Certain other assets, such as certain investment assets, but not including stocks and bonds, also may be exchanged on a tax-free basis for other assets although the law more severely limits the classes of assets as to which the exchange may be effected.

Whether or the extent to which you can or should attempt to effect a like-kind exchange is a complex matter. Obviously, if you believe such an exchange may be appropriate, you should seek the advise of a competent tax counsellor.

Tax-Free Mergers

The tax law also, as a general rule, provides that if your company is "taken over" by another and you receive stock in the company buying yours, the receipt of the stock may be tax-free. Where your company is taken over by a strong, well-run and diversified public company, you will have effected significant diversification and hold an asset which, as a general rule, can be further diversified, although often only with a recognition of gain. All other things being equal, a tax-free merger or takeover will result in a larger wealth base for you than a taxable disposition of your company. Again, as a general rule, all of the inherent gain, including that carried over from your original stock will be forgiven at your death even if, for example, you leave it all to your spouse and no estate tax is paid by reason of the estate tax marital deduction.

Charitable Remainder Trusts

A potentially very powerful estate planning tool can also be used in some cases to help achieve tax-favored diversification. It is called a charitable remainder trust. The trust provides for annual or more frequent payments to beneficiaries for a fixed number of years (not in excess of 20 years), or until the named beneficiaries die. What remains in the trust then passes to charity. Although distributions from the trust generally are includable in the taxable income of the individual beneficiaries, the charitable remainder trust itself, as a general rule, is entirely income tax exempt. It may experience gain and collect otherwise taxable income without paying any gains or income tax. To the extent that the trust does not distribute such gain or income to the beneficiaries, it accumulates and builds on a tax-free basis. You can create such a trust for yourself, your spouse or both of you for life (even though that is longer than 20 years) entirely free of gift and estate tax. In addition, you may be entitled to a partial charitable deduction and the assets can be made to pass after your death and that of your spouse also if he or she is a beneficiary, to a charity your family controls. Also, properly structured, interests in certain closely-held business can be contributed to a charitable remainder trust and sold by the trustee tax free. However, there are dangers in doing that and promoters of such trusts almost never give such warnings.

It is the position of the IRS that if there is an understanding between the trustee and the person who creates the trust, usually called the "grantor", that the property contributed will be sold by the trustee, then the gain will be taxed to the grantor even though the understanding is not legally enforceable. Although the IRS's position has not been fully tested in the courts, it is appropriate to attempt to avoid it. As a consequence, there should be no understanding between the grantor and the trustee that the contributed property will be sold. Often, it will be best to use an entirely independent entity, such as a bank, as the initial trustee. If you serve as trustee and sell the appreciated assets you add to the trust, you may find it difficult to convince the IRS or a court that there was no understanding with yourself that the property would be sold upon its receipt, if that in fact occurs. Hence, it is best to avoid being the initial trustee of a charitable remainder trust to which you will contribute appreciated assets. It may also be difficult to convince the IRS or a court that there was no understanding that the appreciated assets contributed to the trust would be sold by the trustee where the trustee is a close relative of yours. Many find that using an independent bank as trustee is the safest course to take.

Even if there is no understanding between the grantor and the trustee that the appreciated assets will be sold, the gain nonetheless may be taxed to the grantor if the grantor has entered into a contract to sell such property. That almost certainly will be the case if the contract is legally enforceable and it may well be the case even if it is not legally enforceable but there is an understanding between you and the purchaser that the asset will be sold once it is put in trust.

There also is some indication in the tax law that if the trustee of a charitable remainder trust would be economically compelled to accept an outstanding offer to buy that the gain will be taxed back to the grantor of the trust. For example, where an offer has been made to purchase the shares of stock in a company and the person making the offer has the right to buy any shares not offered if the purchaser winds up owning, for example, 90% of the other outstanding shares. In that case, the trustee, as a practical matter, will be economically compelled to accept the offer where it is virtually certain the 90% threshold will be reached by others agreeing to sell. In such a case, it is likely that the IRS will contend that the gain experienced by the trust should be taxed back to the grantor. However, it should be emphasized that the law is not well developed in this area. If you seek to avoid gain by contributing appreciated property to a charitable remainder trust you should see your tax counsel long before any sale is anticipated. Unfortunately, in the "real world", individuals often consider charitable remainder trusts only in the latter stages of disposition of an interest in property whether it is a closely-held business, publicly-traded stock or raw land.

In any event, properly structured, it is usually possible to arrange the transaction so that the gain is not automatically attributed back to the grantor of the trust. That means that the entire base of the property is available to generate payments to the grantor of the trust, and, perhaps, other members of his or her family, for life. Economically, the property owner and members of the family may be better off that way than selling the property for cash and having a smaller wealth base. More about the "economics" of charitable remainder trusts is discussed in Chapter 8 dealing with retirement planning.

It also should be kept in mind that charitable remainder trusts are subject to a number of restrictions imposed by the tax law. Among these are that the grantor of the trust and members of his or her family, and entities in which they have significant interests, can have virtually no economic dealings with the charitable remainder trust. That means, for example, that you and your children cannot purchase assets held by the charitable remainder trust. The tax law imposes several other important rules which may make it inappropriate to use a charitable remainder trust. However, your company can redeem the shares held by a charitable remainder trust, as a general rule, if an offer is made to all shareholders to redeem their shares on the same basis. That means, for example, that you can contribute shares of closely-held stock to the charitable remainder trust and if the company then makes a redemption offer to all shareholders, the trustee of the charitable remainder trust probably would be able to accept that offer without running afoul of the tax law provided the offer is at least at the full fair market value of the stock. It appears that a similar procedure can be used to redeem partnership interests if your company is in the form of a partnership.

Charitable remainder trusts are very complex arrangements. Generally, only very experienced attorneys understand them well and, therefore, only they are competent to advise you as to the effect of creating and funding one. By the way, charitable remainder trusts are not eligible shareholders of an S corporation.

Sale of New Equity by the Business

One way to reduce the risks associated with operating a business at a loss is to obtain new equity for it. In addition, obtaining new equity provides a larger base of funds to upgrade operations and maintain cash reserves for economically adverse times. However, obtaining new equity does not result in separating yourself from your business. In fact, you may find that your new investors, as one would expect, may become anxious about the operation of the business and expect you to devote more time to the company and for you also to put in more equity if the business plan under which they invested is not met.

Going Public

Offering equity to the public may or may not result in separating yourself, in whole or in part, from the business. If the only shares offered to the public are new shares issued by your company, you will wind up owning the same shares and your wealth base will not be diversified. On the other hand, after the company sells its stock to the public, often the shares which you hold can be offered to the public and that may effect a diversification. Sometimes subject to rather strict security law rules, you will be able to sell shares on the public market.

Going public may seem attractive but there can be adverse effects as well. First, your company will be pressured to maintain or increase earnings and dividends quarter after quarter after quarter. You almost certainly will find it more difficult to engage in long-range strategies for your business which may adversely affect current earnings even though earnings would increase substantially over the long term by reason of those strategies.

Depending upon the percentage of shares held by the public, you may find that a reduction in the price of your shares may result in those who deal with your business in other capacities (such as bank lenders, jobbers and purchasers) expressing concern over the health of your business and to be less prone to do business with your company. If a significant portion of your shares are held by the public, you may find that an offer is made to buy out the public shares and to take over all or a portion of the company. Although the movie and play *Other People's Money* is fictitious, it represents the real world takeover scene. You should see it before going public.

Going public also imposes additional reporting responsibilities under federal (and often state) law. The penalties for violating those laws can be severe, including civil damages, massive fines and incarceration. Generally, if your stock is publicly traded, you, as an "insider," will not be able to sell a significant portion of your stock under the law on the public market and if you "dribble" your stock out, as is permitted, you may find that the price of your company's stock is adversely affected: Not only will you be increasing the supply of shares available for purchase (which generally depresses value) but also disclosure of your sales will have to be made and that may make other investors less prone to buy your company's stock, as they will wonder why you, as an insider, wish to reduce your own holdings in it.

Overall, going public may not be an appropriate way to separate yourself quietly and completely from your business. It should be considered primarily to raise equity where that is the most effective way to achieve a particular business goal.

Determining the Price

As indicated above, in a number of circumstances, you will have to determine the price at which interests in your business will be offered for sale. That may include, for example, an offer of redemption made by your company to a charitable remainder trust (and all other shareholders) to purchase the shares it owns. Similarly, if you decide to sell out your business in whole or in part you will have to determine an appropriate price. If you decide to take your company public, the price at which the company's shares will be initially offered to the public will have to be determined. In the latter case, however, the underwriter (i.e., the investment bank or similar entity which will actually arrange for the sale of the stock) probably will play a major role in determining the price at which the shares are offered. In fact, in most circumstances, it may be appropriate for you to seek the advice of a professional to determine the range of prices at which the interest in your business could be sold. Keep in mind, however, that a minority interest in a privately-held business is worth considerably less (often 50% less) than a comparable interest in a publicly-held company. In other words, in the real world, you may not be able to command much of a price for minority interests in your privately-held business. If your stock is publicly traded, minority interests are usually very easy to sell, and as a result, usually at a much higher price. Hence, taking your company public may allow you a more simple and lucrative way to diversify a part of your wealth.

Need for Independent, Professional Advice

The decision whether and how you should separate yourself from a business probably should be undertaken only with the advice of a professional. You may be disappointed to learn that your business is not worth as much as you thought it was or that you will face an enormous erosion of the value of your business through expenses, such as broker or underwriter fees, and taxes. In many jurisdictions, capital gains taxes can exceed 40%. Keep in mind, however, that almost all professionals you approach for assistance will have a predilection as to how they wish you to come out. For example, if you approach an investment banker, the banker probably will wish you to sell your interests rather than holding them. There is a strong likelihood that you will hire that banker to assist you in the sale and the banker will receive fees for arranging for the sale of your business and, in some cases, those selling fees to the banker may be dozens of times greater than the fees which you will be charged for general advice. You may find it appropriate to speak initially to an attorney and, perhaps, someone else who is at least no longer in the field of representing sellers of businesses but has an adequate background to provide you with sound advice as to appropriate approaches and the appropriate people from whom to seek assistance.

A Special Word of Caution in Selling Out

As indicated throughout this and other Chapters, your business may fail after you have disposed of it, whether you do so by sale, redemption or otherwise. Whenever the disposition involves borrowing (whether it is a leveraged buyout by management or some other way), there is some chance that you will be sued. One of the common grounds alleged in such a case is a claim of "fraudulent conveyance." The charge may be that you rendered your company insolvent by the payment you received. The contention is the amount which you are paid, whether it is by an actual redemption of your stock by the company or otherwise was the equivalent of a dividend which rendered the company insolvent. The burden of proving that, of course, will be on the person who makes the claim. However, you may become deeply and expensively involved in protracted litigation even if the claim is one you eventually could defeat. Hence, you probably will want to reduce the possibility of such a claim being made and to increase the probability of successfully defending against one. In that connection, you should consider three additional matters when selling out, regardless of the identity of the purchaser. First, you should have some concept about whether the new owners and managers will be able to manage your company reasonably well. Second, you should obtain the opinion of a valuation expert, as well as, perhaps, a bank, that your company will be solvent after the transaction is completed. In fact, it also may be best to have any lender involved in the transaction (whether it is a bank, a qualified retirement plan, a group of private investors or any other) certify to you that it has done a thorough investigation and concluded that your company is solvent and will remain so, after the transaction, despite the imposition of any debt. Third, it shows the extreme importance of hiring experienced advisors before you become deeply involved in negotiations to sell your business. Failure to appreciate the somewhat subtle, but extremely far reaching, effects of various methods of disposing of your business can result in financial disaster.

SUMMARY AND CONCLUSIONS

For several reasons, you may wish to sell all or a portion of your business or at least to separate yourself from the day-to-day operation of the business. Continuing ownership but not being involved with day-to-day management responsibilities can be difficult and dangerous. A key is carefully selecting successor managers of your company. If a decision is made to sell out the business in its entirety, many approaches may be used, including creating an ESOP and selling shares to it, making an installment sale to postpone taxes, having your company redeem shares, contributing them to a charitable remainder trust, selling out to insiders (such as other managers) or outsiders or taking your company public. The tax and other effects of different methods of disposition vary widely. In all cases, it will be appropriate for you to discuss diversification plans with tax and other advisors. However, you should keep in mind that some advisors may personally benefit by your decision to sell or not to sell.

CHAPTER 5

HOW CAN I PREVENT MY BUSINESS FROM BEING SOLD?

INTRODUCTION AND OVERVIEW OF CHAPTER

For a variety of reasons, you may wish to prevent your business from being sold during your lifetime or after your death. Although the law generally does not permit prohibitions on sales, arrangements can be used to eliminate most incentives for the owners to sell. However, the consequences of using such mechanisms can be far-reaching and may make it extremely difficult or costly for a sale to occur, even where you later decide that one should be made. In this Chapter, practical ways to inhibit your business from being sold during your lifetime and after your death and their consequences are discussed.

DURING YOUR LIFETIME

Remaining the Sole Controlling Owner

IN GENERAL

A most effective way to prevent your company from being sold is to become and remain its sole owner. Sales of businesses generally occur by selling equity interest (such as shares of stock representing the ownership) in the companies or selling the operating assets of the enterprises. Most individuals who do not want their companies sold wish to prevent a sale of both the equity and the key operating portions of the business. As a general rule, by remaining the sole controlling owner, you can prevent such sales from occurring. If you have co-owners, they, in certain circumstances, can sell their interests and if they become day-to-day operators may be able

69

to make inroads in the disposition of portions of your company. Such attempts at sale, however, are much easier for you to control during your lifetime. Nonetheless, without further action, your business may be sold out from under you during your lifetime even if you currently are the sole owner.

CREDITOR PROBLEMS

Creditors of Your Business

All businesses have creditors. Creditors include not only institutions which have loaned your business money, but also owners of traditional debt (such as bondholders) as well as your customers, your suppliers and others.

Creditors of a company are given rights under the law to foreclose, as a practical matter, against the assets of the business. In some cases, the rights of the creditor, such as a bank to whom your company is indebted, will be specified and limited pursuant to a contract. Other creditors, however, such as customers who claim your company has failed to perform as they allege you were required to, may have rights against your business which arise under the law. Generally, the amount of claims of debt holders of your business can be determined with reasonable precision. However, claims of other creditors may not be readily ascertainable and may be almost unlimited. For example, if a customer is injured by your product or the activities of your employees, the claim may be enormous. Unfortunately, juries not infrequently award damages for an individual's pain and suffering in the millions of dollars.

Your company also can be made liable for crushing "punitive" damages. Recently, the United States Supreme Court held that a jury could award punitive damages of 100 times the actual damage suffered by a plaintiff. Punitive damages are those which are imposed to punish the defendant because of conduct which, in effect, is regarded as outrageous. In the famous *Pennzoil* v. *Texaco* lawsuit, billions of dollars of punitive damage were awarded to Pennzoil against Texaco relating to the purchase by Texaco of Getty Oil stock. The government may become a creditor of your business as well. If your business owns an interest in real estate which contains toxic waste, governmental agencies can proceed against your business and force you to pay the costs of "clean up" even if it exceeds the value of the property involved and even if your business was not responsible for the pollution. Similarly, your company could become liable to pay the government enormous damages if it can prove your company violated RICO ("racketeering" activities, which encompass much more than organized crime) or anti-trust (including certain action regarded as unfair to your competitors) laws.

Although you can buy insurance to protect your business from claims of creditors, there will be limits on what you can purchase. First, insurance can become extremely expensive, thereby eroding the profits of your business. Second, insurance companies will limit the amount of insurance you can buy. Moreover, carrying large amounts of insurance can make your company a more inviting target of a claim.

In any event, if claims enforceable against your business are great enough, your company may be forced to go into either a full liquidating bankruptcy or a reorganization bankruptcy if it meets the criteria for such a reorganization. However, even in a bankruptcy reorganization your ability to continue to operate the business and maintain control over its operations may be significantly inhibited. Even if your company does not qualify for bankruptcy, creditor-imposed problems can be such that you will be forced to sell off your company's best assets to try to preserve the enterprise. Hence, creditors of your business, as a general matter, may be able to force at least part of your business to be sold. (Chapter 16 discusses some ways in which you may be able to reduce the probability of that happening).

Creditors of Yours: Introduction

Creditors of your business cannot take the equity interests which you hold in the business. However, as demonstrated above, they may be able to ruin the value of the business and force its operating assets to be sold, thereby destroying its value. Your own creditors, in effect, can take your equity interest in your business and operate the company without your participating in either its management or its ownership.

Debt Holders

The most likely circumstance in which you will have the equity interest in your business attached is by your borrowing money. Probably, the primary reason that some of the fortunes made in the early 1980s were lost in the late 80s or early 90s was the burden of debt taken on by a business or its owner. Debt can be either recourse or non-recourse. Non-recourse debt generally means that the individual or company which arranged for the indebtedness is not personally liable to pay it. The lender only has an interest in the asset with respect to which the loan was made and may only look to the value of that asset to be paid. Not infrequently, real estate is purchased with non-recourse indebtedness. The lender can be paid from the operation of the property or by the person who owns it, but, in the event that payments cease, the lender, as a general rule, has recourse only against the property itself.

Recourse indebtedness usually means that the individual or company who arranged for the indebtedness, in effect, has personally guaranteed it. If, for any reason, the debt is not paid as due, the lender usually can sue the individual personally regardless of whether the asset for which the loan was obtained still has adequate worth to secure the debt. Sometimes, however, special arrangements are made as to when, and under what circumstances, the lender can proceed against the individual or company personally.

In many cases, it will not matter whether you are personally liable on the indebtedness or not. The lender may foreclose upon the business asset for which the loan was made and you will lose it. The result may be the same if you are sued individually.

However, a lawsuit against you individually means that you can lose much more than the business asset itself. Usually, it will be best if you can arrange to borrow money on a non-recourse basis and have only the asset with respect to which you incurred the borrowing liable for it. Some lenders, however, even on a non-recourse basis, will seek additional security. For example, if you borrow money to acquire one tract of land, the lender may agree to non-recourse financing only if you pledge your equity interest in another asset as well.

The bottom line is that you significantly reduce the probability of losing the equity in your business if you do not incur personal indebtedness and do not pledge that equity for a loan.

Other Judgment Creditors

However, just as your business may face creditors other than those who hold debt against it, you may face creditors other than debt holders. A stock transaction you arrange, an accident involving your automobile, a claim of sexual harassment or the thousands of other grounds upon which you individually can become a defendant in a lawsuit may result in a significant judgment against you and an attachment, in effect, of the equity interest in your business, as well as your other assets.

Your Spouse as Your Almost Certain Creditor

Over half of American marriages end in divorce rather than in death. In the vast majority of those cases, your spouse will become a creditor of yours. If you live in a community property jurisdiction, such as California, it may be found that the interest in your business represents a community asset and, accordingly, your spouse owns one-half of it. Even if initially your business interests did not represent a community asset, some courts have found that your continuing to work at the company effects a "transmutation" of part of the business into a community asset. If you live in a non-community property jurisdiction, such as New York, your business interest may be found to be a "marital" asset. The court having jurisdiction over your divorce action will be able to award an "equitable" portion of your assets, including your business assets, to your spouse. In long-term marriages, the courts almost always give each spouse one-half of the value of each marital asset.

Courts, generally, have the power to award the interest in a business to one spouse who operates it and to make an "offsetting" award to the other spouse with other assets. In some cases, that other asset may include indebtedness which you owe to your former spouse. However, that means your spouse will be a debt holder of yours and potentially cause the problems with respect to the continued ownership of your business which any other debt holder could.

Even if you and your spouse do not become divorced, your spouse may become a creditor of your estate because of rights granted to your spouse under state law. In most cases, the best protection against claims of your spouse is a enforceable prenuptial or postnuptial agreement. However, you may find your fiancé or spouse unwilling to sign one.

What Can You Do About Your Creditors?

Chapter 16 discusses ways in which you can try to protect yourself and your family from claims of creditors. That Chapter also includes a discussion of protecting your business from claims of its potential creditors.

You Cannot Prohibit Sales by Others

If you are the sole owner of your business, no one can force you to sell out or force your business to sell its assets. (One exception is where the government takes assets under its eminent domain powers, but you will be reasonably compensated if that happens.) However, creditors of yours or your business, in effect, can attach your equity in your business or its assets.

If there are co-owners of your business, they may be able to sell their interests or, in certain circumstances, arrange for a sale of the business assets. For example, if your business is operated as a general partnership (a dangerous practice, by the way, as discussed in Chapter 16), any partner, usually, can sell any and all of the assets of the business. In addition, individuals are free to sell their equity interests in any business enterprise, in most cases. You cannot prohibit such sales. The law generally will not recognize any prohibition on sale and certain other significant restrictions on the transfer of property. Regardless of what you have heard, the circumstances of when you can actually prohibit a sale are greatly limited and those exceptions almost never apply to interests in a business. Hence, for example, if you and the other co-holders agree that none you will sell interests in the business and one of you does so, you may hold no power to stop the sale.

Obtaining and Implementing Rights of First Refusal

However, you can provide, as a general rule, for you or your company to have the right to purchase any equity interest in your business in the event that any co-owner wishes to or attempts to sell, exchange, give or otherwise transfer his or her interest in the business. Usually, the price can be set to be so low and the terms of the purchase so favorable that, as a practicable matter, no sale is likely to occur. Such rights of first refusal can be a powerful mechanism to prevent outsiders from acquiring interests in the company. Unfortunately, however, many such agreements are unenforceable or leave the door open to avoiding their intended impact by indirect means. You should not attempt to negotiate or implement such an agreement yourself. Rather, you should seek the services of an attorney (or other advisor) who has had significant experience in implementing and successfully defending such agreements.

Typically, when one owner feels compelled to sell his or her equity interest, that owner will attempt to evade the terms of the agreement. Unless the agreement is "airtight", you may find that the agreement does not provide you with the protection against sales of other owner's interests to outsiders and on terms favorable to the seller.

The cases are legion of individuals attempting to avoid rights of first refusal. Common grounds for such attacks include that the owner is selling under an exception. For example, often the agreement will permit distributions of business interests to descendants of a property owner. The owner will distribute the business interests to a child who, at the direction of the parent, will sell the asset, claiming that he or she is exempt from the right of first refusal agreement. Other common grounds for attack include that the agreement is not enforceable because the parties were acting under a mistake of fact, one party unlawfully induced into signing it, the terms violate public policy, or that the agreement is unenforceable because each party did not have independent legal representation. The latter is a common ground for attacking pre-marriage property settlement agreements. In some cases, minority owners of businesses also have used it to attack restrictions on limitations imposed by contracts that they have entered into contending that they were forced to use the majority owner's counsel (or counsel to the company) and did not understand the importance of what they were signing. Although there are not many cases where such attacks have been totally successful, many are settled out of court with the minority owners receiving considerably more than that provided under the terms of the agreement.

Despite the foregoing, obtaining rights of first refusal can be a most effective way in preventing sales to outsiders by other co-owners during your lifetime and after your death. However, as indicated earlier, in obtaining such right, you should seek the assistance of counsel who has experience in drafting such agreements and successfully having them implemented.

Other Clauses

Sometimes, the owners will not believe it is reasonable to allow the one of them who is more financially secure to be able to buy out at a low price the others who may be forced to offer up their interests for sale. Several mechanisms can be used to overcome such concerns. A common one is to provide for the purchase of an interest to be determined pursuant to a formula which is designed to reflect its current worth. A typical method is to multiply a "weight forward" average of yearly earnings times a capitalization factor which often is used to value companies in industry. Earnings in later years count more in determining the value at which the interest is sold than the earnings in earlier years. An average of yearly earnings is accordingly determined and that is multiplied times an appropriate capitalization factor. The capitalization factor, of course, reflects what is a fair return on investment. For example, if the fair return is 12%, the capitalization factor is 8.3 (i.e., 100% divided by 12%). An alternative, and better used for some businesses which have investment, as opposed to the production of services or goods, as their primary purpose, is to use an adjusted book value. Assets are revalued at market, liabilities are subtracted, and that difference is multiplied by the percentage of the business being sold. Not infrequently, discounts will be applied to reflect the fact that a minority interest is being sold. For example, the fair market value of the holdings of a real estate company is $5 million. Liabilities are $1 million. The four equal owners agree that when the first of them dies, his or her interest can be purchased with a 30% discount by the company. When the first dies, his or her estate will receive $700,000 (25% times $4,000,000 net value times 70%, to reflect the 30% discount). Not infrequently, the business agreement provides that at the death of an owner his or her interest must be purchased by the company or the surviving co-owners, rather than just being subject to an option to buy.

In still other cases, the right of first refusal will be one which merely provides the co-owners (or the business itself) with a right to match any offer made to purchase one of the co-owner's interest. Hence, if a minority co-owner finds someone willing to pay $2 million for his or her interest, the other co-owners or the business itself, in exercising the right of first refusal, must pay $2 million. If they do not, the co-owner wishing to sell is free to dispose of the interest at that price. Usually, fair market value is substituted for purchase price when the transfer will be by gift or any other way, such as a transfer to a spouse in a divorce, where there is no readily ascertainable purchase price. In any event, rights of first refusal do commonly prevent the sale of interests as they have a "chilling" effect on outsiders even making offers to buy.

Another mechanism which the co-owners may find appropriate, and which also can have the effect of preventing the interests from being sold to outsiders, is to add a "bullet" clause. A bullet clause is one under which any of the co-owners can specify the price either at which the others can buy him or her out or at which he or she can buy the others out. Hence, if the co-owner exercising the bullet provision sets a price which is unreasonably high, the others will choose to sell to him or her. On the other hand, if the price is unreasonably low, presumably the others will exercise the right to buy out the owner exercising the bullet provision. In some ways, bullet clauses are fair, but when the business becomes very valuable and some co-owners have little in the way of independent resources they have little choice but to sell because they have inadequate resources to buy. In any event, the bullet clause can sometimes be used as an effective method to get the owners to agree on a mechanism designed to prevent or inhibit sales to outsiders.

AFTER YOUR DEATH

You Cannot Prohibit the Sale of the Business by the Successor Owners or the Sale of Assets by the Business

The same rule which, in effect, prevents you from prohibiting the sale of your interests in the business or the sale of assets by the business itself prevents you, in effect, from prohibiting the sale of the business by those who succeed to the property upon your death or to prohibit the sale of the assets by the business after your death. However, practical restrictions can be imposed which makes it so difficult and/ or uneconomical to sell the interests that there is a high probability that your wishes will be respected for a long time after your death.

One Key: Selecting The Best Successor Owners

INDIVIDUALS

Carefully choosing the successor owners, such as the member of your family whom you trust most, can as a practical matter result in the continued ownership of the company and the assets by the business itself. However, any individual owning the interest can sell it. You cannot prohibit the sale. In addition, the creditors of the successor owner may attach the interest, thereby forcing a sale. Mechanisms providing for forfeiture of the interest if the successor owner sells the interest may or may not be enforceable. However, such forfeiture provisions are rarely the most effective and efficient methods of preventing the sale.

TRUSTEES

Probably the most effective mechanism to prevent the sale of your company is to place it in trust for your beneficiaries. You can prohibit the sale of trust interests themselves and that is what the individual beneficiaries will own. No one will purchase their interests in the trust because such sales, if the trust has been properly constructed, are void under the law. Although the beneficiaries may be paid for their interests in the trust, they keep the trust interests, or those interests will be effectively shifted to other beneficiaries, thereby preventing the purchaser from acquiring the interests in the trust or the underlying trust assets.

On the other hand, the trustee generally will be permitted to sell the trust assets. Provisions in trusts prohibiting the trustee from selling the assets generally are not enforceable. However, the probability that your business will be sold can be reduced to its practical minimum if you select the most trustworthy individuals or institutions as trustee, and if appropriate provisions are contained in the trust.

However, absolutely prohibiting the sale of assets by the trustee probably is not wise even if it can be made enforceable. Regardless of the success of your business and its prospects, the actual future for your company will be different from that which is forecast. Economic conditions for the economy as a whole, your industry, and your business may be significantly different than those you anticipate. Moreover, a decision by the government to enforce certain laws more rigorously, such as the anti-trust laws, environmental rules, labor practices and similar regulations can adversely affect your business to the point where it makes no sense to attempt to hold on to it.

Joseph Pulitzer, who built a tremendous newspaper

empire, forbid in his Will the disposition of the World Herald stock which he owned at the time of his death. The stock was placed in trust and the trustees were prohibited from selling it. They continued to hold the stock even though the World Herald Company fell on extremely hard times. The trustees were successfully sued for not disposing of the stock before the company completely fell apart. The Pulitzer story teaches us two morals: First, prohibitions on the disposition of assets, even as to trustees, probably are not enforceable under the law; second, and perhaps more important, it may make no sense to prevent a company, or its assets, from being sold under all circumstances.

Accordingly, if you want your business held, you should use a mechanism which prevents precipitous action to dispose of it. A system of checks and balances preventing the sale of the business or its assets on a whim probably should be your goal. Over time, such circumstances are almost certain to arise. If a child of yours is going through a divorce and needs funds to pay off his or her spouse, the sale of all or a portion of the business (or its assets) may be the "quick fix" that looks like the right one at the time. Such emotionally driven, and perhaps, short-term financially pressing circumstances, should not control what should be a decision made with a long view. Generally, trustees will not be driven by such personal, short-term, emotional decisions. Hence, you should consider having the business owned by a trust if you wish to reduce the probability of the sale of the company. On the other hand, be sure to discuss with your attorney the desirability of the trust including provisions (1) exonerating the trustees from any duty to diversify the trust holdings, (2) exonerating the trustees from liability for continuing to hold the interests in the business even if it loses money, (3) requiring unanimous consent of all trustees to sell interests in the business (including the issuance of significant new equity in the company or the issuance by the company of significant debt) or a sale by the business of a significant part of its assets or operations, and (4) requiring the trustees to obtain the consent of some or all of the competent and adult beneficiaries of the trust to any sale of the company or similar action.

In addition, if your company is owned by a trust, the creditors of your beneficiaries cannot attach the interests of the beneficiaries in the trust or the company. The trust, properly structured, represents one of the most efficient shields against claims of creditors of individuals. (See Chapter 16 for more information about how trusts can be used to protect property from claims of creditors.)

Another Key: Diversifying The Number of Holders

Hence, the real key to prevent a precipitous sale of your company after your death is to require that a number of individuals and, perhaps, institutions have to consent to the disposition of the business or a significant portion of its assets. For example, even if you leave the interests in your business for all of your children, you may make all of your children the trustees of the trust for each of them. Moreover, you might consider unanimity, or at least a super-majority, of the trustees to agree to the sale of the business or the adoption of a plan resulting in the significant disposition of its assets. Be sure you broadly define disposition. Taking on significant debt, granting options to sell and issuing new stock all can lead to the disposition of the business (or its assets). Again, you should seek the advice of professionals in determining what is the appropriate mechanism to use for your family and for the particular circumstances of your business. You also should be prepared to spend not an inconsiderable amount on legal fees and other advice if you want a first-class job.

You also should consider requiring the consent of at least one "outsider" to effect the sale of the business or a significant portion of its assets. That person should have no personal stake in how a decision comes out. Often, owners of businesses are prone to choose the successor CEO of the company as a person whose consent is necessary to sell the business or its assets. Almost certainly, the new CEO's immediate reaction will be to protect himself or herself or to attempt to buy the company himself or herself. Perhaps, the "input" of the CEO would be appropriate, but you probably should consider requiring the consent of a real outsider. That outsider could include, for example, a colleague in a different line of business who has demonstrated common sense and good business judgment over the years. He or she should act in the role as a trustee or a special trustee and should receive reasonable compensation for services. (Chapter 13 discusses other matters relating to trustees including how to set their compensation.)

Some of the duties and responsibilities of the outside trustee may be limited. For example, an outsider may not wish to be involved with day-to-day decisions of investing other assets. In addition, the outsider may not wish to be involved with decisions as to whether the trust should make distributions of property to a beneficiary unless the decision directly involves the business.

Not infrequently, different classes of trustees will be used. Your outside trustee's duty can be limited or expanded as much as you believe appropriate for the circumstances. Of course, the outside trustee may turn out to be recalcitrant or uncooperative. You should have a mechanism to remove each trustee and for the appointment of successors. (Those matters, also, are discussed in more detail in Chapter 13.)

You may find it appropriate to have at least three outside special trustees, a majority of whom must vote in favor of the sale of the business or a significant portion of its assets.

Because the trustees legally own the interests in the company and, therefore, can control the decisions of the business, they can prevent the enterprise or its assets from being sold, unless you have left a "gap" where someone else can trump their authority—that is a question of properly structuring the arrangement. It also will be appropriate for you to add some sort of "indemnification" language so that if the outside trustees refuse to accept an offer to purchase the business or its assets they cannot be held individually liable if their judgment to hold turns out not to be the most correct one. Within certain limits, the law allows you to grant rather broad indemnification to the trustees. It is a matter you should discuss in detail with your attorney. You should approach the matter of describing the authority of and providing the indemnification to the special trustee as you would if a colleague of yours asked you to serve as an outside trustee for his or her family.

A Further Key: Granting Cross Rights Of First Refusal

THE MECHANISM

Earlier in this Chapter, it was explained how obtaining and granting rights of first refusals among co-owners, if properly structured, can prevent a sell out of the business or its assets. Obviously, you do not need that if you hold all of the stock. However, through the years, the ownership of your business is likely to be split either among family members or trusts for their benefit. In fact, even if you only want one trust, it will be appropriate to authorize, if not direct, the division of the trust into separate parts in certain cases.

Because the ownership of the business or its assets or operating parts may be divided during your lifetime or after your death, it may be appropriate for you to arrange for the grant of cross rights of first refusal among the owners, even if the owners are trustees. As discussed earlier, you may structure the right of first refusal in many ways but even granting a right to match any offer to purchase may have a sufficiently chilling effect that it will be difficult for one family line, or group of trustees, to act precipitously in selling out. An appropriate mechanism may be to provide for the right of first refusal to be exercised at a discount price and to allow the purchase to be made by the other family members or trusts for their benefits with notes. You do not want the other family members who are the trustees to have to turn down an offer to purchase because of problems with cash flow—being able to pay with notes makes it more likely that the others will be able to make the purchase.

THE PRICE

As indicated, a key element is the price and terms under which the right of first refusal may be exercised. At a minimum, you may wish to grant every other family member or trust for each family line the right to match any offer to purchase. Perhaps, the purchase price should involve a premium. What is appropriate depends upon the goals you wish to achieve. Keep in mind that if an outsider winds up owning a majority of the interest in the business, there is a strong likelihood that the new majority owner can squeeze out the other family members or trusts for their benefit. That may or may not be an appropriate thing to happen. Sales generally result in the imposition of capital gains tax and there may be a significant erosion of wealth of the minority holders in such freeze out.

The other extreme would be a right to buy out at a very low price any family member, or a trust, which attempted to sell or transfer the business interest. There can be dangers in such a procedure, however. For example, the IRS has taken the position that if someone holds a right of first refusal (or option) to buy property inherited by the property owner's surviving spouse, the marital deduction may be denied and estate tax will be due. The marital deduction probably will not be disallowed if the option is to buy at fair market value with fair market value being determined without regard to the option to buy. However, this is a developing area of the law and one with which you should seek the advice of a competent tax practitioner very early in the planning process especially if you are concerned that your spouse, or a trustee for your spouse's benefit, may be prone to sell the business interest. (See Chapter 12 for a discussion of some other matters you may wish to consider if your spouse is not the parent of all your children.)

In any event, regardless of the right of first refusal provisions which you put into effect, someone in the family may lose and someone may win. Those who are wealthier may have the privilege of waiting out the others. Not infrequently, one line of the family will wind up running the business and will receive salaries, bonuses and other payments which will keep them "in the chips". The other family members may receive little in the way of dividends or distributions from the company and they will feel pressured to sell out to the others. That, fortunately or unfortunately, usually is the natural progression of a business as it moves from one generation to another. Having independent and professional trustees often can prevent such a situation from developing into one which results in unfairness or forces the branches of the family which do not operate the business, or are not as well off as the others, from having to sell out to the others for a price which is unfair.

Another Way: Change in Equity or Control Rights

As indicated above, the issuance of new equity in your business can result in a change of control and, therefore, the ownership of the company or its assets. Rather than have that occur against your wishes, you may be able to set up a mechanism to help achieve goals you wish to see accomplished. For example, you might provide that if any equity in your business is transferred by the issuance of new equity (or by sale, gift, transfer and divorce or otherwise), any voting rights which the equity has will be expunged. That means, in effect, that even if part of the ownership in the business is transferred to another, all voting powers or management rights which it represents are eliminated. You should be aware, however, that in certain jurisdictions stock may have to have at least some voting rights. You should discuss with your attorney the extent to which you can use the elimination of vote or management as a mechanism to prevent changes in the operation of your business. Where that is the rule, you may be able to arrange to have your equity converted into super voting control.

A further way to minimize the possibility of a change in management is to use a voting trust or an irrevocable proxy. A voting trust is an arrangement under which some or all of the shareholders of a corporation transfer their voting rights, in effect, to one or more persons who are the voting trustees. In some cases, the equity which the shareholders continue to own can be transferred, but, in any event, for as long as the voting trust lasts the vote with respect to the equity will be held by the voting trustee alone.

Generally, in most states, a voting trust cannot last for more than ten years. However, shareholders sometimes can agree ahead of time to renew the voting trust arrangement after the term expires. You should discuss with your attorney whether or not such an automatic renewal provision would be enforceable in your state. In some cases, you may be able to reincorporate your business in another jurisdiction which provides better rules for voting trusts, but you should consider the tax and other consequences of such reincorporation.

Irrevocable proxies generally can last for much longer time than a voting trust. As a consequence, the equity owners can grant someone a very long term irrevocable proxy to vote the stock and that can be used to prevent outsiders from participating in the operation of the business.

In any case, voting trusts and the irrevocable proxies may prevent the exercise of voting and management rights in a way which you would regard as inappropriate. Nonetheless, those mechanisms alone will not prevent the transfer of the underlying equity interest in the business. Other mechanisms have to be used in order to prevent that from occurring, as a practical matter. You should be aware that even non-voting co-owners of your business will have certain rights under the law, including the right to information about the company's operations. They also will hold the right to object to certain practices which they claim are not in the company's best interests, such as the failure to pay dividends in some cases and the payment of unreasonably high salaries, bonuses and benefits.

Another way which may prevent a change in control of the business is to have you, or other persons, hold the rights to subscribe for additional voting stock. For example, if a shareholder transfers an equity interest without the consent of the company, you would have the right to acquire additional voting stock which will provide you with whatever majority or super majority is necessary completely to control the operation of a company. Even with a so-called S corporation, that voting stock can represent virtually very little equity. In other words, you can be granted the right to acquire super-voting equity even though it represents very little additional equity interest in the enterprise. In fact, if you arrange to hold super-voting stock, it may allow you to transfer significant equity in your business but for you to continue to control the company.

Regardless of which mechanism you use to retain control of the business, or allow another trusted person to do so, it is important for you to discuss with your counsel the potential gift and other tax consequences of such action. For example, in certain circumstances, the elimination of certain rights that can cause the liquidation of a business can result in a deemed gift being made under the tax law. Similarly, the exercise of the right to buy equity at a price less than the current fair market value of the business can cause adverse effects. Your counsellor may be able to advise you how you can reach the goals you want to see achieved without causing adverse tax consequences. In fact, in some cases, you will be able to achieve beneficial tax effects at the same time that you set into effect mechanisms to prevent a shift in control of your business to inappropriate persons.

After Death Creditors

THE PROBLEM

As explained in more detail in Chapter 16 and earlier in this Chapter, even if you are the sole owner of your business, your creditors, in effect, can force you to sell your business or to foreclose upon it. That also can happen after your death with respect to creditors of your family members. Keep in mind that, on an average, more than half of your children will wind up "being divorced" and, in such a case, your child's spouse will become a creditor of your child.

Similar to your own circumstances, your child also may wind up owing money for a variety of different reasons and such creditors will be able to foreclose on interests in the business owned by your children. Also, both before and after your death, your company's creditors may be able to attach the assets of the business and, in some cases, effectively shut down its operations.

POTENTIAL SOLUTIONS

Several Business Entities, Where Appropriate

One of the most effective mechanisms to prevent creditors from ruining the entire business is to have businesses operated through several entities. Properly structured, each entity can be treated as a separate debtor for creditor-rights purposes. Nonetheless, in some circumstances, the separate businesses can be treated as one business for tax purposes, and that may be beneficial.

A common "mistake" is to have the operating business and its facilities owned by the same entity such as one corporation. Perhaps, you run a manufacturing business in which the business owns the plant and facilities as well as the operating business. One significant error in the operating business means that creditors can foreclose on everything, including the plant and equipment. It may be better for the plant to be owned by one entity, for the manufacturing equipment to be owned by another and for the operating business to be owned by a third one. Arrangements for the use of such facilities, such as through leases, usually can be arranged so as not to interfere with the day-to-day operations of the fundamental business. Moreover, if your company has several lines of business, each can be owned by a separate legal entity which probably will provide significant protection from the claims of creditors against one of them.

Similarly, where your business involves several operations you should consider holding each in a separate legal entity. For example, you may own several pieces of real estate which are either rented or used in the operation of your core business. A creditor problem in one building can make all of them liable. For example, suit is brought by a tenant of an apartment building your company owns. A judgment against the company which owns the building can make all of that entity's assets liable for any judgment. If you own the building directly, or you are a general partner of a partnership which owns it, all of your assets, including other businesses you own and, in turn, their assets, may be liable for any judgment awarded to the tenant. Considering that juries often award judgment in the tens of millions of dollars, it is appropriate for you to consider ways in which to insulate assets from each other. (See Chapter 16 for more detail on how you can protect yourself, your family and your business from claims of creditors.)

Cross Rights of First Refusal

Just as cross rights of first refusal can effectively prevent a business from being sold, it can also be used, at least to a limited degree, to thwart claims of creditors. If a creditor attempts to foreclose upon an asset, that action could result in a sale of that asset by a court or otherwise. The sale, however, can trigger the right of first refusal, effectively preventing the business from becoming controlled by outsiders. The time to set such a mechanism in place, however, is long before creditor problems arise. Part of your estate plan to be effected at your death should include the use of cross rights of first refusal among family members, or entities on their behalf, as you and your counsellors determine is appropriate.

Use of Trusts

As is discussed in more detail in Chapter 16, the trust, under American law, probably provides the greatest protection from claims of creditors. However, a trust alone may not adequately prevent creditors from attaching your business or its assets.

First, and not all attorneys are aware of it, a trustee of a trust may be **personally** liable for the obligations of the trust. For example, you transfer title to real estate to a trust with your most trusted child as trustee. Someone on the property is injured and brings suit. The injured party will sue the trust and in all likelihood will sue the trustee, not only in the capacity of the trustee, but individually as well. Under the law of many American jurisdictions, the judgment will be rendered against the trustee personally. The trustee may, or may not, be permitted by the court having jurisdiction of the trust to use the trust assets to pay any judgment. However, if the assets of the trust are insufficient to pay the judgment, the trustee will be personally liable at a minimum for any excess. You should keep that in mind when thinking about whom you would like to name as trustee for your family and whether you would take on trustee responsibility, and potential liability, for one of your friends, colleagues or family members. Because any judgment in excess of the trust assets will be the personal responsibility of the trustee in many states, the cross rights of first refusal may wind up protecting your family (because the rights of first refusal are exercised at a relatively low price) but leaves the trustee of the trust to greater exposure. For example, if the building has a real fair market value of $5 million but the option price is $2 million, the trustee faces potential personal liability on at least the $3 million difference. Chapter 16 explains some ways in which you can significantly reduce the probability of a trustee being personally liable. However, the time to consider that is at the formation of the business or a reorganization during your lifetime or after your death.

The trust can, however, insulate assets from claims brought against beneficiaries personally. For example, a judgment held by one spouse in the event of a divorce, usually cannot be collected from the interests held by the other spouse as a beneficiary of a trust. Hence, using trusts greatly reduces the probability of the assets being involuntarily transferred. It also significantly reduces the probability of the beneficiaries acting precipitously; the beneficiaries do not individually own the property and, therefore, cannot individually sell the assets.

On account of the personal liability in some states of trustees for claims against the trust, you may wish to discuss with your attorney having any trust you create being formed upon the laws of a state where trustees usually cannot personally be made liable for judgments against the trust. Also, you may wish to consider forming a special purpose corporate trustee, such as your family's own trust company, to reduce personal liability. Such special purpose trust companies are discussed in Chapter 13.

SUMMARY AND CONCLUSIONS

Usually, individuals are permitted to sell or otherwise transfer their interest in businesses. Often, however, the owner of a closely-held business will not want that to occur either during lifetime or after death. Although prohibitions on the transfer of property generally are not enforceable, other mechanisms, such as a right of first refusal, can act as effective inhibitors of sales. Even in the circumstance where you own 100% of the interest in your business, it may be appropriate for you to allow other family members to own parts of the business so that by entering into a co-owners agreement with them they will be able to purchase your interest if someone, such as the creditor, attempts to attach your interests in the business. With respect to interest owned by other persons, generally the most effective way to prevent a precipitous disposition of the business or its assets is to have equity transferred to a trustee. Interests you create for other persons in the trust can be made to be not attachable by anyone, including creditors. Nonetheless, the trustee will be permitted to sell interest in the business although, again, mechanisms can be set in place to inhibit that from occurring. In any event, creditors of your business can attach to the assets of the company. Separating certain business activities from each other, and following other steps set forth in Chapter 16, often can be used to reduce the probability of creditors effectively being able to attach business assets and interfering with operations of the company.

CHAPTER 6 · HOW CAN I KEEP MY EMPLOYEES WITH MY BUSINESS AFTER MY DEATH?

INTRODUCTION AND OVERVIEW OF CHAPTER

Employees are often the key to profits. Although some employees may be fungible and can be replaced easily, others are more critical to the continued successful operation of your enterprise. Often, the more senior managers of your company will make the differences between the successful performance of your business and its failure. As you age and certainly once you die, the importance of the other key employees of your company will grow.

In this Chapter, the importance of employees to the profitability of your company will be discussed. The Chapter will explain that the only reason your employees stay with you is because they perceive it to be in their best interests to do so. Finally, it will discuss how that perception can be used by you and your successors to keep your most valuable employees with your business and avoid pitfalls in attempting to do so.

93

WHY IT IS IMPORTANT TO DETERMINE THE IMPORTANCE OF YOUR EMPLOYEES TO THE FINANCIAL HEALTH OF YOUR BUSINESS

Your Employees May Be Your Company's Greatest Key to Profitability

For businesses and many industries, employees are less important than they have been in prior decades. Computers do the work of tens of thousands of individuals, including clerks, bookkeepers, record keepers, and others. For any service business, however, employees will remain, in all likelihood, a significant component in determining the success or failure of the business. Even industries, such as those involved with oil and gas production, where employees are not a significant part of the overall operation and expense, certain managers are key to profitable business. Your company's dependence upon specific key employees may be as great whether your business has many workers or only a few. That might be especially true if your industry is highly-competitive. As a result, it is likely that you, or the employees who succeed you, may be the key to continuing the profitability of your business and allowing it to maintain its competitive position.

You Need to Determine Which Employees or Positions Are Most Important

Perhaps you will conclude that you are the only employee who is important to the success of your business. All others are either expendable or easily replaceable. Even if that is true, you also are going to have to be replaced sometime and, by your own premise, you will be difficult to replace. In fact, you may find that you need to hire several people to replace you. That is not as unusual as it sounds; many owners are so dedicated and spend so much time in their businesses that it is impossible to find one individual, especially one who is not an owner, who will perform all the functions you have and put in the hours which you have.

It may be appropriate for you to seek the advice of a professional to study which aspects of your company's key areas of profitability are dependent upon certain persons or positions. That knowledge is important to you, and your family, as it will establish your greatest points of vulnerability. Once those positions (or individuals) are determined, you can take appropriate action to attempt to increase the probability of getting those people to stay with your business after your death or to find appropriate replacements.

Distinguishing
Between Employees
and Owners

INTRODUCTION

In many industries and businesses the roles of owners and workers become blurred. In many service businesses, such as law, accounting, medicine, architecture and engineering firms, the owners also are the workers in large measure. Although those professions are adequately profitable to continue to draw individuals into them, they are more inefficient because of the inability to clearly distinguish the roles of the owners and the workers. To some degree, that can occur, and does occur, in every industry.

ROLE OF OWNERS

Reasons to Become and Remain an Owner

The owner of a business, by definition, ultimately receives the benefits of success and bears the burden of a failure of the enterprise even if the failure is limited to an initial investment in business. In addition to receiving the financial rewards of owning your own business, there are other reasons to become an owner. A common one is a desire to be your own boss. Also, building a successful business can be one of the most fulfilling experiences of life. A successful businessman or businesswoman will find that he or she becomes an increasingly important person in the community and family as the business prospers and grows. People are dependent upon you for their livelihood, and you are likely to receive extra respect and accommodations because of that. Ultimately, however, the reason to become an owner is to derive the profits from the successful operation of the business. Few become owners for any other primary reason.

The Power of Owners

The owners also ultimately make all major decisions with respect to the business. In some cases, they may choose to delegate, or abdicate, those decisions to others. However, the fact remains that they have the power to affect virtually every aspect of the company, including the lines of business which will be operated, the number of people who work for them, the salaries which key executives will receive, the making of new owners, policies to borrow and to repay debt, and decisions to expand or contract the company. It does not necessarily follow, except in very few professions such as law and accountancy, that the owners must also work in the enterprise. If that does occur, it happens because of a belief that will help the success of the business or because the owner enjoys being involved in that particular business or industry.

The Proper Exercise of the Owner's Powers

The best exercise of an owner's power is one which results in the greatest profitability of the business. Over time, almost all of those associated with the business, including employees, will benefit more if the company is more profitable. If you track the history of virtually all industries, you will discover that greatest pay increases for its workers occurred during the times of the greatest economic growth and profitability for such industries. In fact, in almost every industry the story is the same, those who are most profitable generally pay their workers more. That is one way to maintain your competitive edge. In some cases, much of the rewards go to those who are perceived to make the greatest contribution, such as members of senior management. In any event, the fact remains that a primary exercise of your powers as an owner is to make sure that your business operates at its most profitable.

ROLE OF EMPLOYEES

Employees Should Be an Implement by Which Profits Are Produced

The only reason you should have employees is to assist you in making your business profitable. If you have hired anyone for any other reason you have made a decision that you do not wish to peak your profitability. Of course, you probably have many employees who are not "on line" in producing profits. Such jobs include compliance people—that is, those who prepare reports and/or provide advice to make sure the company is operating in accordance with certain government or industry regulations or rules. Similarly, bookkeepers, and even those involved in high-level matters, such as design of operation of pension and other plans for your employees, are not involved in direct profitability. Nonetheless, those positions are critical to the successful operation of your business. If they are not, you need to rethink why your company has those positions.

In any event, you should view your employees in the first instance as an implement by which profits are produced.

Employees Often Are the Major Cause of the Inability for the Business to Reach Maximum Profitability

There may be several reasons your business is prevented from reaching its maximum profitability. You may be making decisions which are counterproductive to the best interests of the company and its highest level of profitability. If you fail to achieve the greatest profitability and your competitors do, it is almost certain your business eventually will fail; a common reason that a company fails to achieve its maximum profit potential is because the decisions of its owner or operator are no longer designed to maximize profitability but to achieve some other goal.

It is difficult to avoid being arbitrary and capricious when you are in a position to do so. Arbitrary and capricious, of course, mean that the decisions are not made pursuant to a reasonable and publicized procedure or toward a fixed goal. Your workers, who realize that they owe their jobs to you, will tend to agree with virtually any decision you make if they realize that what you really want is for them to agree with you. Even if you profess that you want them to do only what is in the best interests of the company, your real underlying desires, which may be to control people's lives or to make yourself look important, probably come through. That, by the way, is one of the reasons for the failure of so many businesses which pass from one generation to the next. Fewer than 35% of businesses which were highly-successful in the first generation survive the second. Under 10% survive the third. Studies show that it is not the industry which fails but the owners. Many advisors believe that the failures occur not just on account of lack of aptitude but lack of proper attitude; rather than objectively doing what is in the best interest of the company the owners begin to make decisions of emotion or based on other factors which over time are almost certain to retard the company's profitability.

In any case, regardless of your ultimate responsibility for failing to adopt, implement and carry out policies designed to maximize your company's profitability potential, your employees are likely to be a major reason for the failure of your company to reach its maximum profit.

MEASURING YOUR EMPLOYEES' AND YOUR COMPANY'S SUCCESS

Your company's and your employees' success is not that difficult to measure reasonably. That measurement is by a "peer" review. As will be discussed in more detail in Chapter 18, if you want to find the best lawyer, ask other lawyers to exclude themselves and to rank their colleagues. Professional jealousy will affect some decisions but the cream usually will rise to the top with a peer review. The same is true with your business. Whether you have made money or lost money in your business last year, the measure of success usually is a comparison to your competitors. If your business dropped 10% during a recession and your competitors' dropped 30%, you and your employees ran your business like geniuses. On the other hand, if your business increased 20% and everyone else in your industry increased 40%, you may have a problem. Of course, creative accounting sometimes can cause bad results to look good and good results to look great. Therefore, a review which fairly measures comparative performance should be used. Also, a real key is to measure your company's performance not just on a short-term basis (how did we do last year compared to the other people in our industry) but over a longer period of time. In fact, one of the great potential benefits of owning your own business is that you can give up short-term results and aim for longer-term ones which ultimately make your company stronger and more competitive. Public companies often cannot do that because of pressure of current shareholders to maximize current profits.

CONCLUSIONS

The job of the owner is to set the way in which the company will operate. Owners do not have to be on-line workers. Workers, on the other hand, should be an implement by which the profits are produced. You need to determine who are the most critical employees toward fulfilling the mission of high profitability for your business.

THE ONLY REASON WHY YOUR EMPLOYEES STAY WITH YOU

They Perceive It Is in Their Best Interests

LOYALTY MAY NOT BE A MYTH BUT IT IS A MISNOMER

The primary reason people work and work for a particular company is because they perceive it to be in their best interests. Usually, that best interest is perceived to be maximum compensation. Lawyers leave the active practice of law, which historically has been an enjoyable way for many to earn a living, because they can make more money by going into other businesses. Physicians operate medical supply companies because that produces more in the way of profits than being an active practicing doctor. Certainly, several other factors determine why employees work in or leave certain positions. For example, a desire to live in a certain area of the United States may be more important than higher pay available elsewhere. However, within that particular location where the employee desires to live, the employee usually will choose the job which provides the greatest pay. Of course, admitting that is a little crass. When you ask someone why he or she changed jobs, you will hear a variety of reasons such as "opportunity" or "challenge". But the real reason almost always is the perception that more money will be made in the new position.

Of course, employees often turn down opportunities to

move for what they regard as somewhat marginal increases in pay. Workers understand that they have built up a critical "good will" in their current companies and that can be used to protect them in some cases. If you have been a highly-productive and well-regarded worker for ten years, you may decide not to leave; you realize that if you make a mistake things will be less hard on you than if you go to a new job and the mistake is made shortly after you take the new position. Also, employees tend to build up friends and familiarity with their surroundings. Lack of inertia is, in many ways, the employer's best friend in keeping workers on the job.

However, at the higher levels of management, factors such as loyalty and aversion to risk change. Higher ranking individuals tend to be hard working, and to some degree greater risk takers, and that, in part, is a measure of or a reason for their success.

CREATING AN ATMOSPHERE TO PROMOTE THE BELIEF THAT IT IS IN YOUR EMPLOYEES' BEST INTERESTS TO STAY WITH YOUR COMPANY

The most important thing you can do to keep workers with your business is to create a belief in them that they are better off with you than with anyone else. Avoiding decisions which are arbitrary and capricious and making sure that what you pay your employees is competitive are critical factors in creating that atmosphere. Profit sharing alone will not do that particularly if your business is not as profitable as others or if your top managers have an opportunity to switch to other industries where profits are greater.

Although it is true that employees often leave because of a perception that they will be paid more by changing jobs, there are certain things you can offer your employees which others perhaps will not. One of those is an attitude of acceptance, respect, importance and appreciation. Perhaps, your company cannot or should not afford to provide pay raises more than once a year. Certainly, it will not do so every time an employee does an outstanding job. You can, however, continuously let your employees know that you appreciate their importance.

Few employers provide such psychological compensation for the employees as a regular matter. You as an owner of a closely-held business can provide that form of compensation and it generally will inure to your benefit to do so. In fact, each day you should consciously consider how you would want to be treated to stay with someone else's company; you should treat your workers that way.

Why Your Employees May Leave When You Die

A CHANGE IN PERCEPTION OF WHAT IS IN THEIR BEST INTERESTS

Not infrequently, employees critical to the operation of a business leave after the principal owner dies. The reason is that they perceive that it is no longer in their best interest to stay. Sometimes, competitors will be able to hire your best people away on account of a perception that your business is in a weakened position because of taxes, lack of management and direction. Where that perception accurately reflects the position of your company, hiring away your best people can put the final nail in your company's coffin. (Putting competitors out of business can be the most effective way to operate although it is sometimes illegal.)

Often, key employees leave because they believe the successor owners will change the method of operating the company. They may believe that their efforts will no longer be rewarded or respected in the same way they were during your lifetime. Employees know that a new owner, especially one who may not have been involved in the company, may have a greater propensity to be arbitrary or capricious. If it is perceived that your surviving spouse or child will take over the day-to-day operation of the business and your spouse or child does not have good relations with the key employees, it is probable that many of them will leave.

THE SUCCESSOR OWNER COMPLEX (AND, UNFORTUNATELY, IT IS SOMETIMES REAL)

Again, very few businesses survive the death of their founder. The reason is attributable, in large measure, to failure to plan to obtain the appropriate successor managers of the company. Employees know when there is lack of appropriate management and realize that it is in their best interests to leave your company at the first opportunity; they will seek to obtain a position with a business which is perceived to be more stable and, ultimately, will be more profitable.

WHAT YOU CAN DO TO KEEP YOUR EMPLOYEES WITH YOUR COMPANY

Seek Their Advice

THE BENEFITS OF SEEKING IT

Your death will have an impact not just on your family but on your business as well. Your top employees probably are in a good position to help you assess the impact of your death at least with respect to the day-to-day operation of the business. Sometimes, owners will have an advisor survey their top executives to discover their views of what will happen when the owner dies. Although employees will usually answer direct questions as to the impact, they usually also express their own concerns about the company and their future with it. An employer who gathers that information can use it to address concerns of employees and to increase the probability of the employees staying rather than leaving when the owner dies.

Employees may, however, give guarded advice. They appreciate the advice will go back to the owner and are likely to say as little as possible which is regarded as critical of the owner. They often will even avoid what is truly constructive criticism. However, they usually will express their own concerns about the death of the owner and that will provide you with an opportunity to address them.

THE DISADVANTAGES OF SEEKING IT

Unfortunately, your employees are unlikely to give the entire truth. They may believe that you will react very adversely if you receive any criticism about yourself or your operations and may sacrifice telling the truth even if it would aid the company—they will regard keeping their jobs as paramount. In addition, if your employees express certain concerns which you cannot or will not address, the employees may regard you as being arbitrary or capricious. For example, suppose your employees believe that your oldest child will become the president of the company when you die, and they believe that is not in the company's best interest. What will they do with that information? Your failure to address the problem or the *perception* of the problem will be read as demonstrating that you do not put the interests of the company above all else. That means key employees will be more likely to leave than if you do acknowledge and address the problem. (By the way, it usually does not matter whether the problem is real or not; what matters is that the key employees believe it to be real.)

Overall, it probably is best to seek the advice of certain employees but you may have difficulty in discerning what is true from what is false. You may also have difficulty knowing how to use that information to get employees to stay with your company when you retire or die.

Sharing Their Concerns

If you conclude that your employees have stated logical and legitimate concerns about the operation of the business after your death, you should determine whether you can or will address them. You may find it appropriate to acknowledge openly their concerns and to advise them that you will undertake a formal program, including using the advice of outsiders, to address them. Employees may express concern over a heavy debt burden being placed on the company on account of death taxes associated with your death, a failure of you to designate clearly the successor chief operating officer of the company and your failure to take action to prevent arbitrary and capricious actions by successor owners. Ultimately, however, the more senior and, therefore, more key workers in your company are likely to express concerns over the possible loss of profitability of your company because they know that means they will earn less.

The Key: Creating Economic and Atmospheric Incentives to Stay

MAKING OTHER EMPLOYEES OF THE BUSINESS PART OF EACH EMPLOYEE'S EXTENDED FAMILY

Building loyalty at your business is one of the least expensive and most effective ways to keep employees together. Sponsoring truly enjoyable social functions is one of the best ways to develop a feeling of solidarity. However, mandatory "you will show up and you will have fun" events may not work well. You will know that, in part, by the number of the employees who attend. Regular social opportunities among your employees, such as a monthly meeting where you supply a first-rate meal and which allows all the employees to participate and express their views may be helpful.

SHORT-TERM INCENTIVES WITH LONG-TERM REWARDS

Deferred Compensation

Providing your employees with additional compensation is one of the most effective ways to keep them on the job. That compensation may be deferred and may be made subject to forfeiture. For example, you can provide employees with a growing base of wealth to fund retirement or to be paid at a later time but provide for it to be forfeited, in whole or in part, if the employee leaves before certain events, such as retirement, or requisite working periods, such as ten years, are reached.

Equity Participation

Deferred compensation, as a general rule, really is a sharing in the equity of the business. The reason, of course, is that profits retained in the company build equity. If you share that profit, you are in a real sense sharing equity. In a way, deferred compensation may be better to your employees than regular equity because it usually is paid regardless of whether the value of the business goes up or goes down.

Most employees, however, if given any opportunity, want to participate in real equity (that is ownership) of the business. That, of course, can be provided to employees as well and is often an excellent way to keep them on the job if granting equity is properly structured. Such equity participation also can be made subject to forfeiture.

Maximizing Efficient Tax Incentives

Just like you, your employees hate paying more tax than they have to. Deferred compensation and certain equity participation can be structured so as to provide the employees with tax-deferral and in some cases, legitimate avoidance of taxes. In some cases, however, you will have to sacrifice the best tax efficiency to achieve goals. For example, if your company is in a higher tax bracket than your key employees are, which is often the case, using deferred compensation under which both your deduction and the taxation to the employee are deferred does not maximize tax efficiency. However, the importance to your employees of receiving benefits of tax deferral may more than off-set the tax inefficiency which is generated by the arrangement.

Avoiding Arbitrary and Capricious Action After You Are Gone (A Question to Ask Yourself)

Probably more labor problems are attributable to arbitrary and capricious behavior than any other single factor. Nothing infuriates individuals more than an inability to predict what they are supposed to do. Many men and women have started their own businesses because they were so angered by such action of the people they worked for. It is difficult, however, not to fall into the pattern yourself. Every day, you should ask yourself whether you would want to work as a subordinate to yourself. If you will not ask yourself that question, you are demonstrating an attitude of non-caring and that may mean that you are not trying to maximizing your company's profit. Ultimately, you pay for your arbitrary and capricious behavior by your failure to look at the operation of your business, including the performance of your employees, in the most objective way. In addition, your employees may not advise you as to what is in the best interest of your company.

Testing the Waters Before You Leave

One of the best things you can do is to see, at least in a microcosm, how things might happen when you die. If you think that your surviving spouse or your children can operate the business successfully, have them take it over for a while without your assistance. If they are not ready, then you had better ask yourself when will they be ready. If you will not do that, then you do not care enough about keeping the employees with your business after your death and maximizing its profitability after you die. Testing can be implemented gradually but you should try it for some considerable period of time and long before you die or retire so you have time to implement any appropriate change.

If you are not willing to so test the waters, you should seriously consider arranging for the sale of your business during your lifetime or to take effect shortly after your death. You run a very substantial risk of your business being among the two-thirds which do not survive the next level of successor owners.

SUMMARY AND CONCLUSIONS

Employees are a critical factor in the profitable operation of your business. Even if you are the only key employee and all others are expendable or easily replaced, you ultimately will have to be replaced. Determining which individuals, or at least which positions, are critically important to the operation of your business will help you plan for the success of your business after your death. You need to identify the key employees or positions long before your death occurs in order to provide the smoothest transition in the operation of your entity. Seeking the advice of your employees may help you determine the importance of your role and how they view the roles of others. The key in holding the most important employees is to create economic incentives and the proper atmosphere to promote that. Perhaps, the most important thing you can do is to "test" your conclusions before you die or retire. It will provide you with an opportunity to make corrections if your plan does not appear to work the way you hoped it would. If you will not do that, you ought to consider arranging for the sale of your business before you die.

CHAPTER 7

WHAT ABOUT KIDS IN THE BUSINESS?

The statistics are not pretty: Fewer than 35% of successful privately-held businesses survive the passage of ownership from the first generation to the second and fewer than 10% survive the passage of ownership to the third. One reason for this phenomena is the failure to plan adequately for the payment of estate taxes on the death of the senior generation. However, a more significant and common reason is the adoption of poor or inappropriate business practices by the successor owners. This Chapter discusses whether or not you should involve your children in the ownership and the management of your business. Not only will it be one of the most important decisions for you to make, it also will be one of the most difficult. There is a strong predilection for owners of businesses to want their children to follow in their footsteps. This Chapter explores the reasons why that may or may not be appropriate and, if it is appropriate, how you can arrange the passage of ownership and control to your children in a way which is designed to prevent your business from becoming one of the casualties of the statistics.

BEFORE DECIDING WHETHER OR NOT TO HAVE YOUR CHILDREN WORK OR OWN INTERESTS IN YOUR BUSINESS, DETERMINE WHETHER AND WHY YOU WISH THE BUSINESS TO CONTINUE AFTER YOU RETIRE OR DIE

Introduction

People like to share good experiences. Most individuals who have built and operated successful ventures find that it is one of the most rewarding experiences of their lives. It is natural for them to want to share that experience with those who are closest to them, such as their children and grandchildren. However, arranging for your children or other family members to own and operate your business may be one of the biggest mistakes you can make. In order to decide if it is appropriate to consider transferring ownership and control of your business to your descendants, it is appropriate to explore why you may have a desire to do that.

Why Your Business Is Important to You

If you have operated your business for a considerable period of time, you are probably in it for more than the money, especially if it has been successful for a long time. If, however, the only reason you have built and operated your business is to maximize your base of wealth, you should consider arranging for the disposition of your business during your lifetime or after your death. In fact, if you are in it only for the money, you probably should arrange for the sale of your company, whenever you conclude that your wealth would be greater if invested elsewhere. Chapter 4 explores ways in which you might dispose of your business during your lifetime. You alternatively may wish to arrange for the disposition of your business after your death. One tax benefit of death is that the inherent capital gain liability in most assets you own is then forgiven. That substantially eases the ability of your successors to dispose of the business after your death.

Most individuals, however, derive additional satisfaction from operating their own businesses. As stated earlier in this book, the owner of a closely-held business, unlike other well-to-do individuals, often has a more direct and important impact on his or her community and family than other individuals of comparable wealth whose asset base is more diversified. Your success deservedly has given you respect and that respect will continue to grow as your company becomes more successful.

Moreover, people like to share good experiences. If you enjoy golf, fishing, or any other hobby, it will be natural for you to want to share that with your children and grandchildren. The same may be true for your business. Sometimes, children and grandchildren fall right along in the steps of their ancestors and will have the same interests and abilities. However, that is not always the case. For example, your daughter may have a greater interest in tennis than in golf. Your son may be more interested in journalism than manufacturing. The point is that the reasons the business has been important to you may not apply to your children.

Why You Wish to Have Your Business Continue After You Retire or Die

One of the most important questions for you to deal with is whether you want your business to continue after you retire or die, as opposed to selling or liquidating it and, if so, why.

Let's take a look at some of the commonly offered reasons and see how they relate to your situation.

PERPETUATE FAMILY AND BUSINESS IDEALS?

Each business has a personality. To a large degree, your values, ideals and other individual characteristics will be reflected in that personality. To some extent, your values will reflect those of the family. Also, the values of the business will be brought home to your family and the values of your family will be transported to the business. In fact, they will tend to reinforce each other. Perpetuating the business is likely to perpetuate those ideals if your children or other family members work in the business. Indeed, there are probably few ways in which you can ensure such significant reinforcement of the values of your family other than by having your family work in the business with you.

For many of us, that is an enviable goal to attempt to achieve. On the other hand, allowing your children to break away from the family and its ideals will allow them to learn new ones. Sometimes, those new ideals will come back and provide new perspectives to the family which can help it achieve more of its goals. In other words, it can prevent what might be viewed as unhealthy "inbreeding" of ideas and even ideals.

PERPETUATE RELATIONSHIPS AMONG YOUR CHILDREN, GRANDCHILDREN AND YOU?

Most Americans lose their children, as a practical matter, when they become adults. They often move away to other parts of the country and even if they do not, they develop their own families, lives, careers and interests, all of which reduce the time they may spend with each other and with you. Our relationships with our blood relatives are extremely important and many of us have significant aspects of our lives, including where we live, controlled by our relationship with members of our family. Many retired individuals, for example, move to a location near where their children or grandchildren live.

Having your children and other descendants work in a business with you ensures that you will have a continuous and long-term relationship with them. You may grow even closer to them and to their families than if they were not in business with you. Similarly, your children who work at your business probably will maintain a more constant and, therefore, closer relationship with each other than if they did not work together.

PROVIDE EMPLOYMENT FOR YOUR DESCENDANTS?

Obviously, if you control the company you can provide jobs to whomever you wish, including your descendants. That provides an opportunity, as explained earlier, for your descendants to share in the base of wealth and its fruits which you have created. You may be able, for example, to provide your children who are in an appropriate position with stock options, bonuses and other benefits which, in effect, shifts wealth from you to them in a tax efficient way.

On the other hand, if you pay your descendants only what they are worth, it may be that they can earn just as much, if not more, if they had employment elsewhere. Also, if they work for someone else, at least for a time, they will compete in a different arena than the one which is controlled by the family. The family-controlled arena is not necessarily an easier one for them to succeed in. In fact, in many families, each descendant must demonstrate superior skills to receive the same treatment that outsiders receive with more ordinary skills. The point simply is that the circumstances under which they will work will be different because it is controlled by the family.

ALLOW YOUR DESCENDANTS TO SHARE THE CONTROL YOU HAVE ENJOYED?

Many owners of closely-held businesses find that the control they have over their destiny, and, to a limited degree, their community, their employees and others, is very fulfilling. Being the controlling officer of a successful enterprise often is an enjoyable experience. If it is your company, you can share that control, and its benefits and enjoyment, with your descendants to the degree you determine appropriate. Sometimes, however, it may be difficult for a parent or grandparent to make an objective assessment of the ability of descendants to operate and control an enterprise. Moreover, jealousies often will arise among siblings or other family members who want to hold the control. Although, to some degree, control of an operation may be shared, it is usually best if there is one ultimate master of the enterprise. You may discover that not all of your descendants will happily accept, or in some cases, willingly accept your decision as to which family member shares the control with you and eventually succeeds to it entirely.

TRANSFER OF WEALTH AT LITTLE COST?

Without question, you can legitimately transfer wealth to family members who work in the business with little additional cost. For example, you may pay family members, or other employees, salaries and bonuses, and other benefits, without adverse estate and gift tax consequences, as a general rule, unless the level of total compensation becomes unreasonable. The determination of a reasonable level of salaries often is complex, but usually if a family member is paid the same amount as other people in the industry, or comparable positions in other industries, the compensation will be regarded as reasonable provided the family member has the requisite skills for the position and carries them out with reasonable diligence.

In fact, it is not uncommon to grant employees, including those who are family members, opportunities to gain an equity interest in the enterprise. In some circumstances, beneficial tax effects can occur as a result of such arrangements. However, on account of recent changes made to the Internal Revenue Code, it is possible that granting equity to family members, even in the course of their employment and even at levels comparable to those granted to non-family members, can cause adverse gift and estate tax consequences. As a result, a plan which results in a transfer in equity in your business to family members (including stepchildren and children-in-law) should occur only upon the advice of your tax counselor.

In any event, opportunities to transfer wealth to other family members may be increased where they work in the business with you.

THE BEST QUESTION TO ASK?

In determining whether or not you want your children in your business, the most important question you should ask is whether you would want them to be in the business if you were not part of it. As a practical matter, it is likely that you will cease working in the business, on account of your retirement or death, before other family members do. As a consequence, their commitment to your business may extend well beyond your lifetime and you need to determine whether you will want them in the business if you are not there.

Determining Which
Descendants Should
Be in the Business

INTRODUCTION

It may not be appropriate for all of your descendants to work in the family business. Jealousies may arise because the descendants will be competing with each other either for the material gain which the business offers or for approval of their contribution to the company as compared to the contribution being made by other family members. Only one of your descendants at any one time can succeed to the position of the senior officer in the business, such as its chief operating officer. It may be difficult for you to make decisions as to which descendant should be chosen even if one demonstrates greater skills and propensity to fulfill that position than the others do since other personal and family matters will necessarily have to be taken into account. An older child, for example, may feel it is a matter of birth right to be the senior family officer.

DEMONSTRATION OF INTEREST AT AN EARLY AGE

Often, some of your children will demonstrate an interest in working in the family business at an early age. That interest can be encouraged, if you find that appropriate. Others may develop an interest in working for the business later in life. Sometimes, however, that later developed interest may be attributable to other factors, such as an inability to advance at other jobs or a perception that it is the only way to ensure receiving a fair share of the worth of the business. You may wish to set forth certain ground rules as to when family members will or will not be permitted to become part of the business. It may be uncomfortable for you, and other family members, if another member of the family who has not succeeded in other positions wishes to join the family business and expects to begin at the level that others who have worked there for a longer time are at. Because of the personal relationships involved, it is often difficult to refuse to hire such a person or to give that person an undeserved position and level of compensation. In some cases, that can cause personal relationships to become worse rather than better.

DEMONSTRATION OF APPROPRIATE SKILLS AND ATTITUDE

You may find it appropriate to allow descendants into the family business only if they have demonstrated the requisite skills and aptitude compatible to become part of the team who works at the company. If your company requires people with a certain aptitude, it may be unfair and inappropriate to allow a descendant, or other family member, to work in the business who does not have that aptitude. Sometimes, other positions can be found for such a person but that may mean that he or she cannot progress to the same level of control or compensation which other family members do. If you create an artificial position for that person, in order to give them the apparent control and to provide them with a real compensation comparable to what other family members receive, you may find that the other family members become resentful. That, in turn, can worsen family relationships. Accordingly, you may find it appropriate only to allow in the business those who demonstrate the requisite skills for the business.

DEMONSTRATION OF AN OVERWHELMING DESIRE TO WORK FOR THE FAMILY BUSINESS

Many owners of closely-held businesses allow descendants to become part of the enterprise only if they show an overwhelming desire to be part of that company as opposed to others. They believe that a descendant should show a special commitment to the company because it is a family enterprise. If it is "just another job" to a family member, he or she is not hired. Often, and as will be discussed in more detail later, the atmosphere created with other employees, who are not family members, can be regarded as adverse if it appears that the family members are being given jobs because they simply want to work there and have no real commitment to the enterprise. If members of the family do not have a significant commitment to the enterprise, why should non-family members?

HOW TO PREPARE YOUR DESCENDANTS TO TAKE OVER THE BUSINESS

Introduction

In some families, it is understood from the earliest of ages that certain descendants will become part of the business enterprise. In some cases, that understanding will be generated by the satisfaction and enjoyment of working which older members of the family manifest. If your descendants perceive that you, and other leading members of the family, find great fulfillment and importance in what you do at the company, it is likely that attitude and feeling will develop in at least some of your descendants. That may not be enough, however, to make you want to have a certain descendant in your business. That descendant may have to demonstrate other characteristics in order to be allowed to become part of the business. In any event, you may find it appropriate to foster the notion that only those who are the most deserving will have the privilege of working at your company.

Early Experience May Be an Important Key

IT MAY DEMONSTRATE CAPACITY AND INTEREST

Allowing your descendants to work at your business at an early age may prove whether they have the necessary capacity and interest to work in the business. Some children, for example, may be especially gifted for your particular business. Others may not. Observing them in the earliest stages of their lives actually working in the business may show whether or not the family member has the propensity and interest to work in the family business. It may also demonstrate whether or not the family member will conform to the practices of the business or whether he or she will seek such special treatment because of the family relationship and, thus, may be a destructive or disruptive force in the business rather than a beneficial one.

IT MAY PROVIDE GREAT OVERALL UNDERSTANDING FROM THE ''GROUND UP''

If a family member has worked in each aspect of the business, he or she will know it better and will probably make a better leader and manager of that business. One of the most effective lawyers I have ever known and who had essentially one company as his sole client clearly was effective, in part, because he not only studied each aspect of the business, from the loading docks to the senior corporate officers, but he would often work in various aspects of the business during his "vacations." Eventually, the board of directors of that large public company asked him to leave private practice and become the chairman and president of the company. He did an excellent job in those capacities, as he had done for the entity while he was their outside general counsel, and he often told me that part of the reason was his knowledge of virtually every aspect of the business from first-hand working experience.

The same may be true for your company. If a family member works in the business during summers during high school and college, for example, he or she will have a better understanding of how things really operate. Through the years, the child can be "promoted" or moved laterally from one operation to another. It will provide that person with a much greater understanding about why things in the business work well and why, in some cases, they do not.

Choosing an Appropriate School Curriculum

Obviously, if your business requires employees or managers to have special skills, such as in financing, economics, medicine, engineering or certain sciences, it will be best if your child chooses a school curriculum which is compatible with the needs of the business. On the other hand, almost every business requires people with different skills. Regardless of how technically oriented your business may be, you will probably need a chief financial officer, and, if your business is a relatively large one, a personnel manager, a manager of benefits and certain other people who have more general business oriented skills. Even if a family member does not have the interest or aptitude for the technical aspects of your business, it may be possible for that family member nonetheless to become an important member of the business team by developing skills which the business also needs in order to operate efficiently. In some cases, that may reduce rivalry among siblings. For example, one child, who has the technical skills needed for the business, can be a manager or chief operator of the business. Another child, whose skills are geared to more general matters, such as personnel management, could be in charge of that operation. Competition between the two with respect to the day-to-day operations may be reduced because each child has a confined area of control. Nonetheless, it is likely that at least one of your family members will succeed to a higher position as well as a higher level of compensation than the others will. That alone may cause family rivalries to develop and interfere with the operation of the business as well as to cause a breakdown of personal relationships between the individuals and their families.

In many cases, even if your business requires individuals with certain skills, it may be that the high school or even college curriculum of a family member is not critically important because post-graduate education will provide the family member with the requisite skills to become an important part of your business. Almost all individuals find that unrelated studies and experiences help them develop into a more rounded person and eventually become a better manager of people. As a consequence, you may find it appropriate not to push your family members to adopt a certain curriculum designed expressly for your business where the education can be provided by specialized education later in life.

Make Your Child Have At Least One Work Experience in a Totally Unrelated Field

Most individuals find that having a significant work experience in a totally unrelated field, such as in the military, helps develop their total overall capacity. Regardless of how well developed the technical skills of a person are, that person probably will be a better manager if he or she has had broader experiences during lifetime. Too much "inbreeding" within the same industry may not produce the capacity to be able to use business methods that have worked in other industries. Bringing in a fresh point of view, even from a totally unrelated industry, may greatly help your business, particularly in the long run.

Make Your Child Work for a Competitor

Similarly, making your child or other family member work for a competitor of yours, even if it is not a direct competitor, such as someone in the same industry but another market area, probably will prove beneficial for both the family member and your business. An ability to see what works and what does not work in another company will provide your family members with a broad base to produce greater results for your own company. A family member may never be able to understand why your competitors do well, or fail, unless he or she has worked for one or more of them. In fact, some owners of family businesses adopt a rule that no family member can work in the business unless he or she has had a significant work experience outside of the company. It is somewhat similar to a rule some of the best graduate schools have adopted: You may not apply until you have had some outside real world experience which will make you a more important contributor to the school, your fellow students and yourself.

Do Not Supervise Your Child Directly

It is doubtful whether you can treat any member of your family objectively. The emotional and family relationships you have will cause you to be somewhat too hard or somewhat too easy on that person or to treat that person in a different manner from how you treat someone who is not related to you. At least in the early stages of a family member's employment in the business, you should avoid supervising the child directly. Your child's capacity to develop and to be critiqued more independently will occur only in that way. On the other hand, you may find it impossible to get your child's supervisor to give you an objective analysis of your child's progress and abilities. As an alternative, to determine how well your child is doing, you might have a confidential peer review. A peer review often is the best indicator of someone's capacity. Nonetheless, your child, in one sense, will have no peers at your organization. Everyone will know that he or she stands in a different position than everyone else does.

If you have demonstrated a strong desire for your child to

be part of the business and to succeed, it is likely that those who supervise your child will tell you what they believe you want to hear. Nonetheless, in many circumstances, you will be able to use objective criteria, such as the level of sales your child has made, or the productivity which he or she otherwise demonstrates, to compare your child to others. On the other hand, you should be aware that it is always possible for data to be skewed or tests to be set up so that your child will appear to have done better or worse than an objective testing standard would demonstrate.

Compensation and Promotion of Your Children

As indicated earlier in this Chapter, it is possible for you to spread family wealth and income by having children or other family members in the business with you. However, you may find it best, at least in the early stages of your child's employment with your business, to ensure that the child is paid and promoted on as an objective basis as possible. Not only may you generate resentment and anger among other employees of the business if you do otherwise, but you may provide your child with a false sense of importance and accomplishment. You may find that making your child compete with others produces a more healthy overall atmosphere and work environment than giving your child more than he or she deserves based on production at work alone.

THE CASE FOR NOT HAVING DESCENDANTS IN THE BUSINESS

The "Numbers" Are Not Encouraging

As indicated earlier, most family businesses do not survive the transfer of ownership and management from the first generation to the second and very few survive by the time it is transferred down to the third generation. Clearly, some children and grandchildren have made a family enterprise a success. In those cases, the measure should be from that person's generation downward. Again, in those cases, the statistics for continued success are not encouraging. There are many reasons for this phenomena. Certainly, one is that children or others are forced into the family business when they really do not want to participate in it. Second, often the incentive to build a large base of wealth is dissipated because the child or grandchild already understands that the wealth is there and has grown to believe that his or her goal in life is to spend that wealth rather than continue to build it. Regardless of the reasons, you probably should approach having members of your family, including children and grandchildren, in your business on a very cautious basis.

Finally, having family members in your business may adversely impact the business. For example, rivalries may develop among family members and you may not be able to attract high-quality outside persons because they believe that they will not have a fair opportunity to succeed because they are blocked by family members who will receive special treatment.

Face It: Neither You Nor Your Descendants Can Be Objective

In fact, before you invite or arrange for your descendants to become part of the business you must accept the fact neither you nor they can be objective with respect to dealing with each other. The reason that many amateur sports organizations, such as certain Little Leagues, prohibit a parent from being the coach on any team where the child is a member is because it has observed on a constant basis that the parent cannot treat his or her child objectively. The parent will either be too hard or too easy on the child. Either way, the relationship between the parent and child does not develop in the most positive way it can and the child's ability to reach his or her maximum potential almost certainly will be stifled.

There Can Only Be One President

If you are the president or CEO of your company, your child no doubt will strive to succeed to that position as well. If you have more than one child, or other family members in the company, rivalry among them to reach that top position almost certainly will occur. Just as you cannot be objective about your children nor they objective about you, similarly your children cannot be objective with respect to each other. More often than not, it is the older child who succeeds to the more senior position. That may be the natural order of things in the family, and probably has been from the time your first child was born, but it is not necessarily the way things develop in business. Certainly, to some degree, seniority, even with respect to succeeding to top management positions, is a factor which is used in businesses. However, most businesses strive to make promotions on the basis of demonstrated skills and commitment rather than seniority alone. Yet the way in which your family has treated its members will necessarily be transferred, at least in part, to your business.

A more serious problem, however, for your business in the long run is your inability to attract the most competent persons for other senior management positions. The most skilled people may refuse to come to your company because they perceive that they will be blocked by or will have to compete on an uneven playing field with family members. Your business may do just fine with the individuals whom it does attract for certain senior management positions but it is likely that you will not be able to get the very best if you have members of the family in your company. The most skilled people have reached their levels of success in part because of their ability to understand human nature. They will understand very well that (regardless of what you state) your children and grandchildren will be competing in a different arena than they will be. Even if you hire someone directly as the president or CEO of your company, that person will know that his or her ability to deal with family members will be stifled and cannot be totally objective. It may be that you can still hire such a person but the very best probably will turn you down.

In fact, many companies adopt "anti-nepotism" rules. Those rules prohibit family members, at least within a certain degree of relationship, from working in the business. Many family businesses which have successfully survived many generations have done so because, over time, family members were not allowed to work in the business, except in the most extraordinary circumstances, and the family hired outsiders to manage and operate the business. In fact, if you study the wealthiest families in the United States you will find that almost certainly is the case, with few successful exceptions.

Stifling Your Child's Initiative

Most parents want their children to reach their maximum potential. In many circumstances, having your child work in the family business will not encourage that happening but will stifle it. Part of the reason is that your child's initiative may be discouraged. If you are too easy on your child, your child may learn that he or she does not have to work as hard to obtain the same incidents of success as someone else. On the other hand, if you are overly hard with the child, you are likely to stifle your child's initiative. You will accept your child's ideas more quickly or less quickly than you would with another employee. That will have an effect on your child which, in the judgment of many professionals, is not always a positive one. As a consequence, you should try to discern, perhaps with the advice of another advisor, what the likely impact on your child or grandchild will be if you have him or her become a member of the family business.

Resentment of Other Managers and Employees

No matter what you are told by your fellow managers and employees in your family business, it is likely that they will resent having members of your family become part of the company. They will realize that their treatment will change once family members become involved in the enterprise. As a consequence, they will treat your family members in a different way than they would independent co-workers. Unfortunately, over time, that may have an adverse impact on your business.

HAVE AN EXIT STRATEGY

Overall, having members of your family become part of the business may be beneficial. On the other hand, it may turn out to be adverse for you, the family and the company. As a consequence, before you invite family members to become part of your business, you should have appropriate exit strategies. These strategies should include ways in which you can eliminate rivalries among family members from occurring, can remove family members from inappropriate positions without causing personal strife and embarrassment and can adopt anti-nepotism rules without unfair treatment of certain family members who have not yet joined the business. For example, if you have more than one child or grandchild working at the business, you might have each one become in charge of a separate division. If horrible rivalry which adversely impacts the business occurs, it may be possible to split the business so that one child owns and operates (perhaps with you) one division with the other child owning and operating a different division. Obviously, there can be many consequences, some of which may be adverse, to such action. Nonetheless, you should consider these exit strategies at the time you invite family members to join the business. Otherwise, you may find it virtually impossible, without ruining personal relationships and severely damaging the business, to cope with problems which arise among family members on account of their presence in the business.

Your children and grandchildren will be different people after they have worked in your company for a long time. They will have challenges, disappointments and joys in their own life and in the business which will affect them. Some of them will grow stronger and better as a result of those experiences and some will grow worse. Your 25-year-old child, fresh out of business school, will be a different person when he or she is 55 years old and operating your business. It may not be appropriate for him or her to succeed to that top position or to maintain it. If you want your business to survive what could be adverse times, you had best be in a position to be able to change the situation in a way which is likely to cause the least damage. Planning ahead is the key for that circumstance.

IN-LAWS IN THE BUSINESS

Not infrequently, you will be encouraged or expected to hire in-laws in the business. Because more than half of American marriages end in divorce, there is a superb chance that your child-in-law (or grandchild-in-law) will be divorced from your child (or grandchild). That can cause severe problems in the operation of a family business. Few divorces are totally amicable. You probably will side, out of love and affection, with your own blood relative and against your in-law. Yet, if your in-law is an important member of your management team, it is likely that your business will be injured as a result of the breakdown of the marriage. In addition, it is possible that your child will be very resentful of your continuing to have a close working relationship, especially on a day-to-day basis, with someone whom your child now regards as an enemy and someone to be despised.

What will make the situation worse is if you provide your in-law with equity in your company. Although there are few "you should never do it" rules in planning, one that comes very close is the one which says *never* give equity in your company to an in-law. If you want to transfer an interest in the business, transfer it to your child, even if he or she does not work in the business and his or her spouse does. As long as the marriage remains a healthy one, your in-law can enjoy the fruits of that equity through the ownership in the hands of his or her spouse, who is your blood relative.

However, even if you do not put equity in the hands of an in-law, you should be aware of the high probability of divorce, regardless of the current length or stability of the marriage and again have an appropriate exit strategy to remove that in-law from the operation of your business if a breakdown of the marriage with your child or grandchild occurs and that breakdown is disruptive to the business.

THE INEVITABLE RESULTS

Introduction

Family businesses tend to go through a life cycle just as many other entities do. Some business will fail over time. In fact, as indicated at the beginning of this Chapter, most family businesses fail after ownership and management is transferred to the children's generation and almost all fail after the enterprise is transferred to grandchildren. Yours may fare better, but there still will be a likely order of events which occur even with the most successful family enterprise.

Going Public

Not infrequently, the company will be taken public. As is discussed in more detail in Chapter 4, there are advantages and disadvantages of your company becoming a publicly-owned one. Family businesses which are successful rarely stay in private hands for generations although there are exceptions. Often, those exceptions occur where family members are not involved in the day-to-day operation but remain owners and comprise a part of the board of directors. In fact, you may wish to ask your advisors to conduct a study of successful family enterprises and, to the degree you believe appropriate, try to pattern some of your activities after those which you feel provide good models for your company to follow. Again, you will discover that several of those companies eventually are sold off to the public.

Private Sale

TO OUTSIDERS

In addition, private businesses are often sold to outsiders. The outsider may be a public or private company and your business may be merged into or become a subsidiary or division of the purchaser. That frequently is an effective strategy especially where members of the family are not involved in the day-to-day operation of the business either because of anti-nepotism rules or lack of interest or aptitude to operate the business. Often, family members will decide that diversification is important and that selling off the business is an important way to effect diversification and obtain its benefits, some of which are discussed in Chapter 2.

SALE TO ONE GROUP OF DESCENDANTS

Once people marry and form their own families, their loyalty toward other family members, even brothers and sisters, often begins to dissipate. Almost always, there is less love, affection and loyalty paid to cousins (and even less to second cousins and more remote relatives) than to one's immediate family. Although, in a few cases, family businesses continue to be owned down to the fourth and fifth generations of the founder with control and profits being shared on a basis which all regard as fair and equitable, more frequently disagreements about the future of the business, its operation and its disposition arise.

Not infrequently, one particular family line will demonstrate a capacity and interest greater than the others to operate the business in a successful manner. Those who do a more successful job may be resentful of others who live off the profitability which they are producing. On the other hand, owners who are not involved in the operation of the business may become resentful of salaries and other benefits which the operators receive or believe that the operators are not doing as good a job as they should. As a consequence, disagreements over the future of the business typically arise. Not infrequently, as a consequence, one family line will sell out to another.

In any event, as you go forward with plans for the disposition of your business, you need to accept that eventually not all of your descendants will participate equally in the business either as to its operation or its ownership. You may wish to discuss with your advisors ways in which you can minimize results which some of the family members will regard as inequitable in order to reduce the inevitable problems which can result from that.

SUMMARY AND CONCLUSIONS

The decision as to whether or not to allow your descendants to become managers or employees of your business is one of the most important ones you make. Eventually, you will have to pass the reins of management and operations to another. Perhaps, that will be best if it is a member of your family. That family member may have greater loyalty to you and the other owners in the enterprise than an outsider would. However, having descendants work in a business can cause problems as well, including stifling a descendant's initiative and creating resentment among other managers and employees. Some companies, in fact, eventually adopt anti-nepotism rules so that, except in the most extraordinary circumstances, family members can only be on the board of directors and cannot be operators of the business. Obviously, what is best depends upon the circumstances and the particular aptitude and attitude of your descendants. Eventually, however, not all of your descendants will participate in the operation of the management of the business to an equal degree. That in turn almost certainly means that the ownership will not remain equal. Usually, even a successful family company eventually is sold to the public or to others. In some cases, the sale will be made to that one group of descendants which shows a greater propensity to participate in the business and a desire to own it.

CHAPTER 8

HOW CAN I PLAN FOR MY RETIREMENT?

INTRODUCTION AND OVERVIEW OF CHAPTER

Much of estate planning, as well as a considerable portion of financial planning, revolves around transferring assets to other persons. Giving assets away is the antithesis of what most of us have been taught is a primary mission in life, which is to aggregate as much wealth as possible. In other words, we have been taught "he who has the most toys wins." Giving assets away runs counter to that logic. One aspect of estate planning, however, is compatible with accumulating as much wealth as possible. That is to plan for our own retirement. Planning for retirement can be a complicated matter. It is one aspect of planning, as much as any other, which requires action as early as possible. In this Chapter, retirement goals, particularly retirement vehicles, their tax effect, and the impact of retirement planning on your family will be discussed.

RETIREMENT GOALS

Introduction

Planning for retirement is complex. It includes determining how you will spend your time after you stop working, where you will live during your golden years, whether you have sufficient health insurance and so on. Financial decisions necessarily become a critical ingredient of that planning for most people. Many benefits provided in the workplace, such as health and life insurance, may no longer be provided once you are separated from your job. Even if those benefits continue, there may be income tax to pay on them. Resources to

131

pay those taxes must be found. The primary financial goal, however, of retirement usually involves securing an adequate income to allow you and your family to enjoy an appropriate lifestyle during what may be a significant number of years.

Legacy for Descendants

In planning for your retirement, an important, although often a secondary goal, is to increase the inheritance which your descendants will receive. To some degree, the goals of maximizing your financial base during your lifetime and increasing (or at least maintaining) the amount your family inherits from you conflict. However, through proper planning, those goals, in large measure, can be appropriately balanced.

Protection from Claims of Creditors

Regardless of how well you have saved for your retirement, claims of your creditors (or creditors of your employer if your employer is paying your retirement) can erode or eliminate the base of wealth which produces that income for you. As a consequence, protecting your assets against claims of your creditors should be part of the overall planning strategy of placing yourself in the financial position you want to be in (and maintain) during your retirement. Don't forget that your spouse will be a creditor if you get divorced.

THE KEYS TO RETIREMENT PLANNING

The Magic of Compounding

One of the most important aspects of building wealth is to allow "money" to compound. Compounding simply means that interest is paid on interest which previously has been earned. At one time, compounding was largely unknown in the financial world. In recent times, more and more opportunities have been offered to provide compounding on an accelerated rate. Money will grow faster if it is compounded daily rather than weekly, weekly rather than monthly, monthly rather than quarterly and quarterly rather than annually. The effects of compounding, particularly over a long term, can be extraordinary. See Chart 8.1 for a comparison of compounding.

CHART 8.1
Comparison of Compounding—$1,000,000
8% (After Tax) Rates of Annual Earnings

Time in Years	No Compounding	Compounding Every Day	Compounding Every Year
0 (start)	$1,000,000	$1,000,000	$1,000,000
1	1,080,000	1,173,489	1,080,000
2	1,160,000	1,271,214	1,166,400
..	..	..	..
..	..	..	..
..	..	..	..
..	..	..	..
10	1,800,000	2,225,338	2,158,925
..	..	..	..
..	..	..	..
..	..	..	..
20	2,600,000	4,952,128	4,660,957
..	..	..	..
..	..	..	..
..	..	..	..
30	3,400,000	11,020,158	10,062,657
..	..	..	..
..	..	..	..
..	..	..	..
40	4,200,000	24,523,574	21,724,521
..	..	..	..
..	..	..	..
..	..	..	..
50	5,000,000	54,573,234	46,901,613

Risks and Rewards of Investment Returns

Different actuaries (the people who forecast earnings and future values on earnings) use a different range of projected annual earnings and other factors to forecast the future value of money. However, most actuaries agree on certain fundamental guidelines. First, the greater the return, the greater the risk. Over time, those who take a greater risk may not receive an enhanced return over those who take a more conservative approach. Consider, for example, those who bought junk bonds paying rates between 15% and 20% when a risk-free investment (such as a U.S. Government bond) paid under 10%. The default on (and reduction in value of) junk bonds has been high, bringing the average actual return on investment of junk bonds to something approaching the risk-free return. For many investors, of course, the return on junk bonds and other speculative investments has been far less than the return on risk-free investments; in fact, the returns have been negative. Second, the yield on non-taxable investments (such as municipal bonds) tends to approach the after-tax return of taxable investments of comparable risk. For example, a grade-A taxable bond producing a 10% per year return, when the effective income tax rate is 40%, will mean that comparable risk bonds producing tax-free interest will tend to produce only slightly more than 6% (that is, the same as a 10% taxable yield after a 40% income tax). Third, diversification reduces the risk of total loss for any particular investor and, therefore, may enhance the over-all return (by reducing the risk of failure of a particular investment).

Starting as Early as Possible

One maxim is to start saving for your retirement as early as possible, in order to build the maximum during your lifetime from the magic of compounding. When I returned from the Army I asked the law firm I worked for to adopt a retirement program. The managing partner laughed and said it was ridiculous for me at age 27 to be concerned about retirement; that was for folks in their 50s and 60s. The head of the firm's pension group backed me on that matter. I worked there just a little over four years. The firm set aside only $7,000 in a retirement account for me. But when I am 65, the fund (assuming it earns 8% a year) should provide me with over $15,000 a year for life. Why? Because I started early and got the magic of compounding working for me.

If you want to retire at age 65, and you would start to save for it at age 62, you will be required to put aside massive amounts each year in order to have the base of wealth necessary to provide you with the return necessary to enjoy an appropriate lifestyle during your retirement. If you had started at age 30, the amount you would set aside in total (and not just each year) is much smaller. An illustration is contained in Chart 8.2. **Look it over**. It should inspire you to consider maximizing your retirement savings as early in life as is compatible with a reasonable lifestyle and other personal and business goals which you want to accomplish during your working years.

Rates of Return

Many people, when they consider what will be available for their retirement, make an estimate of the rate of return they believe they can earn on the base of wealth they will have saved and assume that will be their annual retirement income. For example, if $1 million is invested and the annual rate of return is assumed to be 5.5% a year, the fund will earn $55,000 annually. Many persons in estimating their retirement income, consider such an estimated rate of return as what they will have to live on.

However, as the owner of property, you not only have the right to spend the income (or profit) which your investment generates, but the underlying assets as well. In other words, you can enhance the annual amount you can spend by amortizing or annuitizing the principal. Perhaps, a better way to look at it is as the "cannibalization" of your corpus. However, spending your capital will provide you with considerably more to spend. For instance, with $1 million, and if you live for 20 years, and earn 5.5%, the amount you could spend each year (without considering the impact of any income tax on the earnings) is $83,679.

The problem, of course, is that you may live longer than 20 years. That means, of course, that your entire base of wealth will be eroded. Because of the possibility of the complete erosion of the base of wealth, and the desire to consume the principal over a lifetime (and thereby have more to spend each year), some property owners purchase **life annuities** from insurance companies. The insurance company knows (on average) exactly how long you will live. It, therefore, knows how much of your capital you can spend each year in

CHART 8.2
**The Amount Needed to Set Aside to
Accumulate a $500,000 (at 8% assumed earnings)
Retirement Fund at Age 65 Years**

Starting Age	Annual Amount Set Aside	Total Put Aside	Total Fund at 65
25	1,930	77,200	500,000
30	2,902	101,570	500,000
35	4,414	132,420	500,000
40	6,839	170,975	500,000
45	10,936	218,520	500,000
50	18,415	276,225	500,000
55	34,515	345,150	500,000
60	85,228	426,140	500,000
63	240,385	480,770	500,000

addition to income. Of course, you will not live for exactly the time the insurance company forecasts. In the judgment of many advisors, however, the amount of earnings paid by the insurance company on your investment is relatively small compared to prevailing market rates of return. However, it is, as a practical matter, the only way to be sure that you can consume your capital during lifetime but make sure it is not entirely depleted prior to your death. Nonetheless, you do take the risk that the insurance company will suffer financial problems and be unable to pay the annuity for your full life.

Tax-Deferred Compounding

The power of compounding is magnified when the compounding occurs on a tax-free or tax-deferred basis. Take a look at Chart 8.3. It compares the amount which will be accumulated over various periods of time with and without immediate taxation. The chart uses an assumed 10% annual rate of return and a 40% rate of taxation. After 40 years, the amount of wealth available to generate income for you is more than four times greater if the tax is deferred. (Take a look at that bottom of column two and compare it to the bottom of column three.) By the way, the assumed rate of return also is important in comparing the *relative* impact of tax deferral. In other words, as the annual earnings rate increases (for example, 10% a year rather than 5% a year), the benefits of tax-deferred compounding also increases. Compare the results in Chart 8.3 with those in Chart 8.4.

Therefore, coupling early savings with tax-deferred regular compounding can produce a significant base of wealth. Unfortunately, opportunities to obtain tax-deferred yields are limited by law. Although tax-free yields (such as interest produced by municipal bonds) are available, their yield approaches the after-tax yield of comparable risk taxable returns.

CHART 8.3
$100 Invested at 10% a Year Taxable
Interest Rate and 40% Tax Rate

(1) End of Year	*(2)* Gross Amount by Deferral (Before Taxation)	*(3)* Net Amount with Current Taxation	*(4)* Net Amount (After Tax on Deferred Income)	*(5)* Percentage Increase in After Tax Wealth Base
1	110.00	106.00	106.00	-0-
2	121.00	112.36	112.60	.002%
3	133.10	119.10	119.86	.65%
4	146.41	126.25	127.85	1.27%
5	161.05	133.83	136.63	2.09%
*	*	*	*	*
*	*	*	*	*
*	*	*	*	*
*	*	*	*	*
10	259.37	179.09	195.62	9.23%
20	672.75	320.71	443.65	38.33%
30	1,744.94	574.35	1,086.96	89.25%
40	4,525.93	1,028.57	2,755.56	167.90%

CHART 8.4
$100 Invested at 5% a Year Taxable
Interest Rate and 40% Tax Rate

(1) End of Year	(2) Gross Amount by Deferral (Before Taxation)	(3) Net Amount with Current Taxation	(4) Net Amount (After Tax on Deferred Income)	(5) Percentage Increase in After Tax Wealth Base
1	105.00	103.00	103.00	
2	110.25	106.09	106.15	0.06%
3	115.76	109.27	109.46	0.17%
4	121.55	112.55	112.93	0.34%
5	127.63	115.93	116.58	0.56%
*	*	*	*	*
*	*	*	*	*
*	*	*	*	*
*	*	*	*	*
10	162.89	134.39	137.73	2.49%
20	265.33	180.61	199.20	10.29%
30	432.19	242.73	299.31	23.31%
40	704.00	326.20	462.40	41.75%

Selling Off Assets to Create the Pool

The investment you have made in your business has effected, if your business has been successful, a compounded buildup of wealth. Many forms of businesses allow for that to occur, in effect, on a tax-deferred basis. For example, if you started your business 30 years ago and invested $100,000 in the stock of the company, your compounded annual return has been about 12% if your business is now worth $3,000,000. If your business is worth $5 million, your compounded rate of return is almost 14%. Although the earnings of the business may have been taxed as earned, the income tax basis in your stock (that is, the amount at which you measure gain or loss upon sale) probably has remained at $100,000.

Your business can serve as an important base of wealth for your retirement although you may have to sell it in order to provide a base of wealth from which income can be regularly derived. Selling off your company to create a base of wealth may not be compatible with the long-term goals you have for the business. Also, the sale of your business may result in a significant tax to pay. In any event, the balance of this Chapter will turn to somewhat less extreme methods by which a base of wealth may be created to carry you through your golden years.

RETIREMENT VEHICLES

Self-Savings: The Old Fashioned Way

INTRODUCTION

A program reasonably designed to save money for retirement is the oldest form of retirement planning. Unfortunately, doing that takes tremendous discipline. There is no penalty for not making the contribution or spending what you have saved. There are, however, specific advantages and disadvantages of a self-savings program.

ADVANTAGES

No Tax Law Limits or Penalties

The tax law, as will be discussed below, provides certain benefits but imposes certain limits and restrictions in using certain tax-favored retirement or savings vehicles. A self-savings program, however, contains no limitation on the amount which can be saved or how it can be invested and there are no extra penalties associated with such savings.

Complete Flexibility in Timing, Amount or Method

In fact, there is complete flexibility in the timing of what you save, the amount you save and the method of investing. If you believe that speculative investments will produce the greatest overall return by the time you retire, you can make them. However, most advisors will tell you that speculative investments are not appropriate for retirement funds. Usually, and recent history supports the wisdom of such advice, investment of retirement funds should be among the most conservative undertaken by a property owner. Conservative is not synonymous with fixed income but rather means a well-balanced portfolio of stocks, bonds, real estate and cash equivalents. In other words, speculative investments should not be considered. Speculative investments are regarded as such because the individual investment has a high probability either of returning many times in excess of the return of a risk-free investment or returning zero (or close to it). In fact, many more speculative ventures fail than are successful. Perhaps, you will be lucky enough to choose some speculative investments which pay off with high multiples. In fact, you may convince yourself that your investment prowess is such that you don't need luck. For most of us, however, a conservative approach for investing our retirement funds, even though it may be a self-investment program, is a more appropriate way to proceed. Additional amounts, if compatible with our investment philosophies, are the ones which can go into more speculative investments.

It is, perhaps, appropriate to note that your investment in your business (whether you bought it, invested the money or inherited it) probably would be regarded, by most counsellors, as a speculative investment. Nonetheless, you have made that investment, and presumably done well. Consequently, you probably have taken adequate risks in speculative investments during your lifetime and your retirement "nest egg" should be invested on the other end of the investment risk spectrum.

Avoiding Professional Fees to Set Up the Plan Or to Administer It

Many forms of retirement planning and investing involve hiring professionals. Even "tax approved" retirement plans are created pursuant to written agreements. You will be charged, one way or the other, to have yours written to meet your particular needs or goals or, at least, to have a professional review even a standardized form. Because of the potential adverse tax effects which can occur if certain tax-favored plans are not properly administered, professionals may have to be hired to ensure compliance with the law. You avoid these fees, which reduce effective yield, with a self-savings retirement program.

Step-Up in Basis at Death

As will be discussed in more detail in Chapter 14, most assets which you own when you die have all the inherent gain in them forgiven. For example, an investment you made for $10,000, which is worth $150,000 when you die, will have its gain or loss (after your death) measured from $150,000. If you had sold the investment prior to your death, gain or loss would be measured from your original cost of $10,000. **That income tax-free step-up in basis is the most significant tax-savings device in estate planning.** However, as will be discussed below, the basis in assets in certain retirement vehicles does not change when their owners die. That means that the assets will be subject to both estate tax and income tax. The rate of taxation often will be 80% and in some high-tax jurisdictions can approach (and in some cases exceed) 100%!

As a general matter, your estate (or beneficiaries) will secure the tax-free step-up in basis at your death on any asset held in any self-savings program.

DISADVANTAGES

Complete, Current Income Taxation

One disadvantage of a self-saving program is immediate taxation of income and gain, in most cases. Although you could acquire investments which produce tax-free income (such as municipal bonds), their yield will tend to approach the after-tax yield of comparable-risk investments. As demonstrated in Chart 8.3, the difference between current taxation and postponing (or eliminating) tax can be enormous.

A second "tax" disadvantage that self-saving retirement programs suffer from is a failure to get a deduction for the contribution made to the plan. Suppose, for example, that after income tax on your salary you have $100,000 to save for retirement in a particular year. If you could have deducted the amount you save, you would have had $166,666 to invest in the retirement program if you had been in a 40% tax bracket, and $200,000 to invest if you were in a 50% income tax bracket. All other things being equal, the base of wealth you create in your retirement will be that much greater if you are able to deduct the investment. Some retirement options, but subject to severe limits and conditions, allow a deduction for amounts saved.

Creditors' Claims

As a general rule, all funds you own may be attached by your creditors. In some cases, exemptions from claims of creditors may be available for certain retirement vehicles. The extent to which you need to be concerned about claims of creditors depends, in part, on other aspects of your life. If you engage in activities where the risk of significant liability against you is high, other action can sometime reduce the probability of your personal assets becoming subject to claims of creditors. For more detail, see Chapter 16. In most cases, the amount you have in a self-savings program can be attached by your creditors.

Qualified Retirement Plans

INTRODUCTION

The law relating to tax-favored plans is complex. Such plans enjoy certain benefits under the tax law. A plan is said to be "qualified" when it meets the requirements of the law to enjoy those benefits.

ADVANTAGES

Deduction for Contributions

Contributions to qualified retirement plans are deductible. Hence, you get to derive the earnings from the funds that otherwise would go to the government as taxes. The law, however, imposes limitations (as well as conditions) on the amount which is deductible. The types of plans vary, and the law relating to them is complicated.

Basically, two types of plans are permitted. One is called a defined **contribution** plan. The amount contributed for each employee is determined usually pursuant to a formula (such as a percentage of salary). There is an annual maximum, however, of not more than $30,000 for each employee (including yourself). Each employee's fund at retirement will depend upon the total contributed and its investment experience. It may be large or small, relative to the employee's needs. The other type of plan is called a defined **benefit** plan. The benefit the employee is to receive during retirement years is determined usually pursuant to a formula (and as a percentage of pre-retirement salary). There is a 1993 maximum targeted annual benefit of about $115,000. Actuaries advise the employer how much must be contributed each year to build the fund to the size necessary to produce the targeted level of retirement income for each particular employee. Obviously, much more must be contributed each year for an older employee than for a young one when starting the plan.

If you need a fund of $500,000 to pay an employee's retirement beginning at age 65, you are going to have to set aside $455,000 for an employee who is 64 years old assuming the fund earns about 10% for the year. For an employee who is only 50 years old, you may have to set aside only $15,737 a year from the time the employee is 50 until the employee reaches age 65. Which is better? It depends on your perception, but the total you set aside for the younger employee is much smaller. The reason is that you get the benefit of tax-deferred compounding for the younger employee for a much longer time. That means, again, that starting as early as possible probably is much better.

The overall point is that regardless of the type of qualified retirement plan you choose, the law imposes severe limits on the amount which can be contributed to the plan and deducted. However, the effect on the amount available to invest on account of receiving the deduction, as explained above, can be enormous. In a 50% income tax bracket, it can double the amount of wealth base which is available.

Tax-Deferred Compounding

The second benefit is that earnings, if properly invested, can compound (that is, grow) on a tax-deferred basis. As indicated by Chart 8.3, your wealth base can easily triple or quadruple over your lifetime on account of tax-deferred compounding compared to current tax compounding.

The combined effect of receiving a deduction for contributions in tax-deferred compounding can be enormous. In a 50% tax bracket amounts contributed will grow, over 40 years, to more than five times than what they would have had no deduction been given for the contribution and if the earnings had been currently taxed. See Chart 8.6.

However, the benefits of the tax deduction for the contribution to the plan and of tax-deferred compounding is not as great for contributions made close to retirement when the

CHART 8.5
**Effect of Deduction for Contribution
and Tax-Deferred Compounding Related to
Time Between Making of Contribution and
Retirement at Age 65 Years**

$30,000 Invested at 10%, Compounded Annually

(1) Age at Time of Contribution	(2) Amount Contribution Growth at Age 65	(3) Multiple
25	1,357,778	45.26
35	523,482	17.45
45	201,825	6.73
55	77,812	2.59
60	48,315	1.61
64	33,000	1.10

CHART 8.6
Combined Effect of Receiving Tax Deduction and Tax-Deferred Compounding of Contributions
$100; 50% Tax-Bracket; 8% Assumed Earnings

Year	Tax-Deductible and Tax-Deferred Contributions		Non-Tax-Deductible and Currently Taxed Contributions	
1	$100	$100.00	$50	$ 50.00
2	100	208.00	50	102.00
3	100	324.63	50	156.08
4	100	450.61	50	212.32
5	100	586.66	50	270.82
*	*	*	*	*
*	*	*	*	*
*	*	*	*	*
10	100	1,488.66	50	600.31
*	*	*	*	*
*	*	*	*	*
*	*	*	*	*
20	100	4,576.20	50	1,488.90
*	*	*	*	*
*	*	*	*	*
*	*	*	*	*
30	100	11,328.32	50	2,804.25
*	*	*	*	*
*	*	*	*	*
*	*	*	*	*
40	100	25,905.65	50	4,751.28

earnings in the plan begin to be withdrawn and taxed. That suggests that the benefits from a qualified retirement plan are maximized by saving the most you can as early as possible.

Some Protection from the Claims of Your Creditors

The law is not entirely developed but it appears that interests in qualified retirement plans (but, perhaps, not individual retirement accounts) are not subject to the claims of your creditors. That protection, however, does not generally apply to claims of your spouse in divorce. In addition, in many states, your spouse may have other rights to claim ownership of interests in your qualified retirement plan. Also, some states have special rules about immunizing individual retirement accounts and certain other tax-deferred retirement arrangements from claims of creditors.

DISADVANTAGES

Set Up and Maintenance Costs

Depending upon the type used and the particular circumstances involved, qualified retirement plans can be expensive to set up, on account of legal and consulting work. More important, however, is the fact that plans usually have to be modified to reflect changes in the law. Virtually, every year, since the modern tax pension provisions were enacted in 1974, Congress has enacted significant changes to the rules which require amendments to plans. Those amendments are often extremely difficult to make. How plans have to be amended is often unclear, and the costs of consulting a lawyer (or other pension specialist) can be high.

For some plans, the advice of others must be obtained. Certain plans have their tax effects determined, in part, by actuaries. Their fees, like the fees of accountants and attorneys who are involved in the maintenance and administration of a plan, can be considerable. Those expenses must be considered in determining what the enhanced yield will be by the tax benefits of a qualified retirement plan. The net yield will be reduced by those expenses thereby reducing the benefits of a qualified retirement plan.

Need to Cover Other Workers

One of the major costs of setting up and maintaining a qualified retirement plan is that most other workers in your business must be covered by the plan. That means that contributions must be made on their behalf as well as your own. The tax law provides rules as to how much (or how little) you must provide for your workers in order to provide benefits for yourself (and other so-called "highly compensated" managers). The costs, for many businesses, are considerable. **In fact, often the amounts which you must set aside for other workers (even though those amounts, also are tax deductible) more than off-set the benefit of receiving a deduction for the amounts you set aside for yourself.**

Of course, you may wish to provide your workers with retirement benefits in any case and doing that on a tax-favored basis may be best for you as well as them. However, from a purely "what's best for me" perspective, it is doubtful that the tax benefits of a qualified plan will offset the costs of having to make contributions for your other workers, if you have many of them.

Need to Begin Taxable Withdrawals by Age 70½ (*And Not to Take Withdrawals Before 59½*)

At least after a while, you will "own" your interest in a defined contribution qualified retirement plan (and certain other tax-favored arrangements, such as IRAs), as your workers will own theirs. Generally, you can demand your interests in such a plan at any time once it is regarded as yours under the terms of the plan (which will reflect certain requirements and options provided under the tax law). However, receiving distributions from your qualified plan before age 59½ (or your disability) can result in the imposition of non-deductible penalties in addition to the income tax you almost always pay on what you receive from the plan.

Because of the government's constant hunger to collect more taxes, you are required to begin withdrawals from qualified retirement plans (and certain other tax-favored arrangements, such as IRAs) by about age 70½ and pay income tax on these or pay severe penalties for failure to do so. Although you can, within certain limits, slowly "dribble" amounts out of the plan (almost all of which will be subject to current income taxation), there are minimum amounts you will be required to take out each year, even if you continue to work.

Other Penalties

The tax law imposes additional penalties as well. Contributions which are made too early, too late, too large in amount, or too small in amount will result in imposition of penalties. Similarly, taking distributions out of the plan too early, too late, too small in amount, or too large in amount also will result in penalties.

The tax law, in effect, also restricts the kind of investments which can be made. Investments must be made under a "prudent person" standard. That standard, a familiar one under the law, requires that the funds be invested with care, skill, prudence and diligence under the circumstances then existing that a prudent person acting in a like capacity and familiar with such matters would use in the conduct of an enterprise of a like character and with like aims. It also generally requires diversification to avoid large losses unless under the circumstances it is clearly prudent not to diversify. Obviously, reasonable people can disagree as to what is prudent and what is not. However, if you (or the person administering the plan) step over at the wrong side of the line, penalties can be imposed.

In large measure, you will be restricted to traditional portfolio-type investments—those producing interest and dividends although, to a limited degree, a qualified retirement plan may receive rents and royalties too. However, investment in proprietorships or partnerships which operate businesses will result in an immediate income taxation, in most cases, on such income. For example, if your qualified retirement plan invests in a partnership which operates a spaghetti factory, the income allocated to your qualified retirement plan as a partner will be subject to immediate income taxation and the exemption from taxation which the plan enjoys will be ignored for purposes of that income.

Another penalty, and one of the most unfair ones, is the successful investment penalty. If your plan experiences more than mediocre investment performance, the excess, as it is distributed to you (under certain complicated formulas) or at your death can be subject to a non-deductible 15%

penalty. Although the political backers of the tax made a sufficient "theoretical" justification for the tax, it is nothing but a tax on excellent investment performance. The penalty should be repealed but, unfortunately, it generates a sufficiently large amount of revenue that it probably will not be.

For certain types of defined benefit plans, your company's own assets are "on the line" even though you have paid over to the plan all the amounts the law requires. The rules make your company guarantee up to 50% of its net worth if, for virtually any reason, your workers do not get paid their full retirement benefits from the plan. That should concern you greatly. Check with your pension advisor to determine if that is the type of plan you have or the type you are considering adopting. As a general rule, your company should avoid such plans as your business itself receives no significant extra benefits by adopting plans it must guarantee.

Tax-Deferred (Deferred Payment) Annuities

INTRODUCTION

An annuity is an annual payment, usually of a fixed sum. The insurance and other investment industries have been creative in designing and promoting annuities. Although the tax law does not provide as many benefits for annuities as it once did, some advantages still are available. In addition, as explained earlier in this Chapter, certain annuities are the one way in which you can be sure (subject to the insurance company suffering financial difficulties) that you will be paid for your entire lifetime, constantly consuming corpus, but never running out of payments. A tax-deferred (deferred payment) annuity contract is different from certain "qualified" tax-deferred annuity arrangements used by tax-exempt employers (such as churches and schools) as the retirement plans for their employees.

ADVANTAGES

No One Else Needs to Be Covered

Unlike a qualified retirement plan, a tax-deferred (deferred payment) annuity need not provide any comparable benefits for any other workers in your business. Moreover, although benefits in qualified retirement plans are limited to people who "work" for a living (as opposed to persons who receive passive income, such as interest and dividends), a tax-deferred (deferred payment) annuity can be used by any individual taxpayer.

Tax-Deferred Compounding

Most individuals can acquire tax-deferred (deferred payment) annuities from insurance carriers. Funds invested are retained by the insurance company (or, in some cases, invested at the direction of the annuity contract's owner into certain funds maintained by the insurance company) and the earnings are tax-deferred. Neither the insurance company nor the annuity contract owner pays an immediate income tax on profits. As illustrated by Chart 8.3, the effect of that tax-deferred compounding can be significant.

Income Tax Exclusion

The investment in a tax-deferred annuity usually is made with income which already has been taxed. Insurance companies, as a general rule, will accept only cash. Because the investment is made in cash, any portion of a payment which is considered a return of that cash is not taxed (as it already had been taxed). That provides for an exclusion from taxation of the payment. However, under most annuity contracts acquired since 1982, payments are deemed first to consist of taxable income and only of investment once only the value in the policy is no more than what has been paid for the annuity contract.

Payment for Life

Certain annuity products guarantee that you will be paid for life, regardless of how long you live. Those are known as "life annuities." You may acquire the annuity for your own life and for that of your spouse (or you and another person). Provided the insurance company remains financially sound (something, contrary to popular opinion, not guaranteed by the federal government), you will be paid regardless of how long you live. The insurance company will consider your health and certain other information (such as your sex) in determining how long it believes you will live and propose an annuity payment for life accordingly.

Some annuities have refund features if you die prematurely. However, any such guarantee will reduce the annual payments you receive.

Also, with certain products (such as where investments are made "inside" the annuity contract) the annual payment you receive each year for life will vary with your contract's own investment experience. Those are known as "variable" annuity contracts. One particular advantage of a variable product is that, as a general matter, the cash or investment value of an annuity contract is not subject to the claims of creditors of the insurance company which has issued it. That provides you with some protection from any financial woes the insurance company may suffer.

DISADVANTAGES

Penalties on Distributions Before Age 59½ Years

As with qualified retirement plans, the tax law imposes certain penalties if you make withdrawals from the annuity contract before age 59½ (subject to certain exceptions for disability and for certain payments "spread" over a certain period of time). Hence, you need to be relatively certain that you will not want payments before age 59½ years if you decide to acquire a tax-deferred annuity.

Loss of Tax Deferral If Held Other Than by an Individual

As a general matter, if the annuity contract is acquired by other than a human being (such as a trust) the deferral of taxation is lost. Trusts are often used to prevent property from being attached by creditors (see Chapter 16), and the deferral of taxation may be lost if certain types of trusts are used to hold an annuity contract. Although many lawyers believe that a transfer to (or acquisition by) a fully *revocable* trust will not disqualify the annuity from tax deferral, there is inadequately developed law on that point to say for certain that the deferral from taxation is not lost by a transfer of the annuity contract to a revocable trust. Indeed, generally, the mere transfer to another of the tax-deferred annuity will cause all of the inherent untaxed income to be taxed to its former owner. Although strong arguments can be made that no such acceleration of taxation should occur on the transfer to a revocable trust, there does not appear to be direct definite authority on point.

Lack of Investment Flexibility

Some annuity contracts (known as *variable* annuity contracts) allow the annuity contract owner to select among a series of mutual funds (and often money market accounts) as to how the funds will be invested. Some of these funds may have outside managers (such as an independent investment bank) or the insurance company may manage some or all of the funds itself. Although you have broader selection, you will be limited to the funds (and accounts) offered by that particular insurance company.

Lack of Estate Planning Flexibility

A significant part of effective estate planning involves the transfer of assets to others during lifetime. Once an annuity contract is acquired, however, any transfer of it usually results in immediate income taxation.

Moreover, an annuity payable for the life of one person may not be an appropriate asset to transfer to another. If the annuitant dies early, the amount which the new owner will receive will be small compared to the gift tax value of the transfer.

Double Taxation at Death

As explained earlier in this Chapter, the income tax-free, change in basis to current market value at death is the most important tax saving mechanism in estate planning. Certain assets, however, owned at death are not entitled to that automatic change in basis. Rather, their inherent income tax liability never goes away. Annuities do not receive the automatic change in basis. Typically, those assets also are subject to estate taxation (unless an exemption, such as the marital deduction for transfers to the surviving spouse, is allowed). Although there are some offsetting factors, an annuity contract which survives the death of its owner will be subject to both estate tax and income tax. The effective rate of taxation may be 80% or more (except as to any portion of the contract representing the owner's investment in the contract which he or she has not been paid during lifetime).

Claims of the Insurance Carrier's Creditors

The serious financial problems which some insurance companies have faced has resulted in certain annuity contract owners not receiving their payments. Most insurance contracts are not guaranteed by the government although some states do make certain guarantees. If the insurance company fails, the annuity contract owners may not be paid or not paid in full. An important exception is for certain *variable* contracts (where the owner selects the investments). The cash (or investment) value represented by the annuity probably is not subject to the claims of insurance company's creditors (unless the investment is in what is called the company's "general account"). However, as was explained earlier, you cannot obtain an annuity for life where you control the investments through a variable product.

Commissions and Other "Loads"

People are paid to sell things and annuity contracts usually are not an exception. Often 6% (and in some cases more) of what you invest in the annuity contract will go to the sales representative. Some companies are beginning to offer "no load" (i.e., no sales commission) insurance contracts. However, almost all companies charge annual management fees on investments in annuity contracts.

Life Insurance

Introduction

In Chapter 15, we will explore in some detail some uses of life insurance. Typically, life insurance is considered a mechanism by which the financial cost associated with death (such as the loss of the salary) is shifted to an insurance company. Life insurance is a unique type of property and is specially (and generally favorably) treated under the tax law. Subject to the limits provided by law, it can be an excellent mechanism to build a retirement fund. If you have an independent reason to carry insurance on your life or that of a family member or key employee, you should explore with your advisors using the income tax favored aspects of the policy to build a retirement fund (or other savings program) for yourself or for your employees.

Advantages

No One Else Needs to Be Covered

Unlike a qualified retirement plan, a life insurance policy need not provide any comparable benefits for any other workers in your organization. (There is an exception for a special form of group-term insurance, but we are exploring a totally different type of program.) Indeed, although benefits in qualified retirement plans are limited to people who work for a living (as opposed to those who receive passive income, such as interest and dividends), a cash value life insurance policy can be used by any taxpayer.

Tax-Deferred Compounding

Except for so-called "pure term" policies, most policies provide for a "cash" build-up. In fact, the funds are not held in cash but are invested. Depending upon the type of policy, the insurance carrier (or its advisors) or the owner of the policy will determine how the cash is invested. Provided the policy constitutes a life insurance contract under the tax law, the profit (whether ordinary income or capital gain) which the policy earns is not currently taxed. That means that compounding "inside" the policy occurs on a pre-tax basis. Again, your attention is invited to Chart 8.3 which demonstrates the dramatic effect of accumulating earnings on a tax-free or tax-deferred basis.

Income Tax-Free Withdrawals of Basis

If you acquire a tax-deferred annuity or place funds in a qualified retirement plan, any withdrawal you make, as a general rule, will be deemed to consist (in whole or in part) first of any income which has been earned under the annuity contract or in the qualified retirement plan. Life insurance, unless it is a single premium or other "modified endowment contract" policy, permits its owner to withdraw basis first. The effect can be very beneficial.

For example, suppose you "invest" (i.e., pay total premiums of) $100,000 in your life insurance policy. Provided there is adequate cash (or investment) value, you will be permitted to withdraw $100,000 at any time completely free of income tax unless the policy is a modified endowment contract.

Under the tax law, basically, modified endowment contracts are those where you pay a single premium (or very few premiums in the early years) and which insure you for life. However, properly designed, a policy can avoid modified endowment contract status but nonetheless allow a very quick buildup of cash (or investment) value.

That means that if your policy is not a modified endowment contract you can withdraw your investment in the policy and allow the earnings to continue to build on a tax-deferred basis. For instance, at the time you retire, you have paid total premiums (that is, made an investment in the policy) of $500,000. The policy has a cash or investment value of $1 million. During your retirement, you would like to receive $50,000 after tax (or tax free) each year. With a tax-deferred annuity contract or qualified retirement plan, funds distributed to you will be subject to income tax. If the effective income tax bracket is 50%, you would have to receive $100,000 from the annuity contract or the qualified retirement plan in order to net the $50,000 you wish each year for your retirement.

However, you could withdraw $50,000 tax-free from a life insurance policy (provided it is not a modified endowment contract) for ten years. That means you have avoided paying tax on $500,000 ($50,000 a year for ten years). The taxes you have avoided paying continue to work for you, further compounding your base of wealth. Chart 8.7 provides an illustration of the effect of making tax-free withdrawals as opposed to taxable ones.

The key point is that if you have need for life insurance in any case (such as to replace a lost salary or to fund estate taxes), you should consider acquiring a policy which permits the tax-free build up of wealth which can be used for retirement (or any other purpose which will be achieved by the tax-deferred buildup of a portfolio-type investment). Chapter 15 provides additional details and specific examples of how you, members of your family and people who work in your business can use special tax strategies in acquiring, paying for and carrying life insurance. If you are virtually certain that there never will be withdrawals or borrowings from the contract, you may conclude that it does not matter if the policy is a modified endowment contract.

Income Tax-Free Receipt of Proceeds at Death

As a general rule, regardless of the level of premiums paid and the rate of return, proceeds paid upon the death of the insured usually are received free of all income tax. For example, if only $30,000 in premiums are paid, the insured dies prematurely and $1 million in proceeds is paid, the entire $1 million will be received free of income tax, as a general rule. The tax law contains certain exceptions to the income tax-free receipt of proceeds at death. The most important of those exceptions is known as the "transfer for value" rule. Basically, the difference between the proceeds paid and the amount invested in the policy is subject to income tax if the owner of the policy bought it from someone other than the insurance company. There are a number of important excep-

CHART 8.7
Effect of $50,000 Annual Withdrawal Tax-Free As Opposed to $100,000 Taxable (Resulting in Net of $50,000)

Initial Contribution is $500,000; Fund Grows to $1,000,000 at 10% in 7 Years

Year	Tax Free Withdrawal	Amount Left	Taxable Withdrawal	Amount Left
1	50,000	950,000	100,000	900,000
2	50,000	995,000	100,000	890,000
3	50,000	1,044,500	100,000	879,000
4	50,000	1,098,950	100,000	866,900
5	50,000	1,158,845	100,000	853,590
6	50,000	1,224,730	50,000	888,949
7	50,000	1,297,202	50,000	927,844
8	50,000	1,376,923	50,000	970,628
9	50,000	1,464,615	50,000	1,017,691
10	50,000	1,561,076	50,000	1,069,460

tions to the transfer for value rule. The bottom line is that you should consult with your professional insurance advisor and your tax advisor before acquiring or transferring any life insurance policies.

Protection from Claims of Your Creditors in Some States

Several states (such as New York) appear to provide an unlimited exemption in bankruptcy from claims of creditors for interests you hold in policies of life insurance on your life. That means, for example, that if the cash (or investment) value of your policy is $2 million, that amount is not subject to the claims of creditors in bankruptcy, even though you could withdraw it at any time. Other states (such as California) provide no or little special protection from claims of creditors for interests in life insurance policies. Although the law varies from state to state, as a general matter, whether your interest in a policy is protected from the claims of creditors is determined by the state of your principal residence (which lawyers call "domicile").

Even if you reside in a state which does not provide protection for interests in life insurance policies from the claims of creditors, Chapter 16 provides further guidance on how you may be able to protect your life insurance from creditors.

Some Investment Flexibility for Some Policies

As stated above, in most policies, the cash (or investment) component of a policy is invested as directed by the insurance company. One type of policy, known as a *variable* policy, allows its owner to direct investments among a portfolio of mutual funds (and, perhaps, money market accounts). In well-designed variable policies, the owner can "asset allocate" among the funds and make changes from one fund (or account) to another without adverse tax consequences. Although the owner of a policy cannot choose which individual bonds and stocks to buy, the owner typically can choose among a blue-chip stock fund, an aggressive stock fund, an international fund, a treasury bond fund, a corporate bond fund and similar types of co-mingled funds.

Freedom from the Claims of the Insurance Company's Creditors for Some Policies

An insurance company's creditors usually can attach all of its assets if the company falls into financial trouble. If the insured dies, those financial troubles may prevent the company from paying the death claim because, as a general rule, the insurance company's other creditors will have claims with a higher "priority" than those of insurance policyholders and their beneficiaries. In addition, the cash (or investment) component of the policy also may be subject to the claims of the insurance company's creditors. However, in modern times, no insurance company has failed to pay any death claim which has arisen although not all payments required under annuity contracts have been made. In any case, the insurance company is not treated as owning the cash (or investment) component of a variable policy unless it is invested in what is typically called the "general account" of the carrier. Hence, the cash (or investment) component of a variable policy is not usually subject to the claims of creditors of the insurance company. Even though the insurance company is not treated as owning the cash (or investment) component, the tax-free buildup in value inside the policy nonetheless occurs. However, because the protection from claims of the insurance carrier's creditors does not apply to certain accounts even in a variable policy, you should make sure, if protection from claims of the insurance company's carriers is important to you (as it should be), that you do not invest any significant portion of the cash (or investment) component of the policy in such accounts which can be attached by the insurer's creditors. More important, you should consider acquiring only a variable policy so as to protect the cash (or investment) component from the claims of all of the insurance company's carriers.

If you are interested in acquiring a variable contract, you should keep some factors in mind. First, to sell a variable policy, the life insurance sales representative must hold a certain type of securities license. That license requires additional training and testing and not all life insurance sales representatives hold such licenses. Second, the insurance company whom the sales representative represents may not carry a variable product. Third, generally, an insurance sales representative can sell only a variable product of one company. If you want to see illustrations of variable products from other companies, you may have to contact representatives of several companies. Fourth, you must be willing to undertake to exercise the responsibility of having investment options. Unlike other insurance policies, the owner of a variable policy directs how the funds are to be invested (among a complex of mutual funds and money market accounts). The owner should be willing to undertake that responsibility or obtain something other than a variable policy.

DISADVANTAGES

Cost of Term Insurance, Commissions and Other "Loads"

In order to secure the tax benefits attributable to the cash (or investment) component of the policy, such as the ability to withdraw money from the policy income tax free, it must be a life insurance policy. To be one, there must be a "term" (or "pure" insurance) component. In fact, the amount which you can invest in the policy (and the maximum value it can reach) is dependent upon the level of term insurance (or its cost). (In Chapter 16 there is a further discussion of what the term component policy is.) In order to "access" those benefits, you have to pay for the term insurance. If you have an independent need for life insurance (such as funding estate taxes), and the policy is well designed, over time there may be no extra cost by acquiring a cash value contract in order to access the income tax benefits of the policy. However, if you have no need for the death benefit, it probably is not economically sound to acquire a life insurance policy just to access the income tax benefits of a life policy. As indicated above, in some states, there may be considerable protection from claims of creditors for cash in a policy. Perhaps, that feature, coupled with the tax-free buildup on the cash (or investment) component, would justify the cost of acquiring the term insurance even if you have no need for the death benefit, but that is doubtful as well.

Tax Law Limits on Investments Through the Policy

In order to constitute a life insurance policy and receive the benefit of the tax-free buildup, the policy's cash (or investment) value cannot exceed certain limits. There are complex tests set forth in the tax law to determine these. In large measure, those limits are tied into the level of *term* insurance which is acquired or the cost of that insurance. Those, in turn, are dependent upon the age of the insured.

Those limits are different from the "modified endowment contract" rules which limit how quickly you can pay premiums in the early years of the policy.

Surrender Charges on Withdrawal on Some Products

Some products are designed so that sales and other charges are deferred rather than all imposed when the premium is paid. Generally, that means that is more cash value "working" in the policy for you. However, if you withdraw cash from the policy or cancel it, surrender charges will be imposed so that the deferred charges can be recovered by the insurance company. When you review illustrations or consider making a withdrawal from the policy, you should consider whether there will be surrender charges.

Lack of Investment Flexibility

As indicated above, unless you acquire a variable product, the insurance company will determine how your cash (or investment) component is invested. Even with a variable product, you will be limited in your choices. You will not be able to direct, for example, that you want to be invested for the next six months only in IBM common stock. However, with a variable product, there will be some choice as to how the funds are invested and, often the funds will be managed by professionals other than the insurance company and its affiliates. You may well determine that such professional managers can do as good a job in picking stocks and bonds as you can.

Limitations on Contributions and Growth

As indicated, the tax law imposes limitations on the contributions you can make (i.e., total premiums you can pay) and the amount to which the policy can grow. How much the return will have to be depends on various factors. In any event, the insurance company will advise you as to what point your investment will exceed the limits provided by the tax law. You will be given the right to buy more insurance (without proof of your insurability) in order not to have to withdraw cash from the policy. The alternative, as indicated, is to withdraw the cash from the policy so it meets the limits of the tax law.

Losses Attributable to the Insurance Company, Creditor Problems and Poor Performance

The return on the cash (or investment) component in your life insurance policy may depend upon certain aspects of the operation of the insurance company. The performance of cash value policies (sometimes called "whole life" policies) typically depends, in part, upon how well the insurance company is operated. If the insurance company's costs of doing business increase, the investment performance of your cash value may decrease. Also, if the insurance company has creditor problems and you hold other than a variable product, the cash value (or investment) component, and the death element component for all policies, will be subject to the claims of the insurance company's creditors. In addition, regardless of the type of policy you acquire, including a variable policy, poor investment performance probably will mean a lower cash value for your policy. The performance among insurance companies on investments (and the funds they provide through variable policies) varies considerably over various periods of time. One potential way to protect yourself against such changes is to acquire several comparable policies to "spread" your risk and effect a type of diversification. If you acquire other than a variable cash value product, acquiring insurance from several carriers also will spread the risk of insurance company creditor problems. In some cases, you will be charged more per $1,000 of insurance coverage if you buy policies with smaller face amounts.

The Private Retirement Trust[sm1]

INTRODUCTION AND DESCRIPTION

As indicated, one of the major advantages of investing in a qualified retirement plan is that the earnings, until distributed to the worker for whom the contributions were made, are exempt from income tax. That occurs because the qualified retirement plan itself is exempt from income tax, just as

---

[1] Private Retirement Trust and PRT are all service marks of Jonathan G. Blattmachr.

a charity is, as a general rule. Charities, usually, can receive unlimited quantities of taxable income and yet avoid paying any income tax on those earnings because charities are granted an exemption from taxation under the law. There is a special type of trust, known as a charitable remainder trust, which is exempt from taxation even though benefits in the trust are split between individuals and charity. Usually, payments are made to one or more individuals for life and then what remains in the trust passes to charity.

Payments from the trust must be made each year to individuals until the property passes to charity. The payments may be one of three types: (1) a fixed dollar amount each year (known as an annuity), (2) a fixed percentage (such as 8%) of the annual value of the fund (known as a unitrust payment), or (3) the lesser of *accounting income* or the unitrust percentage specified in the trust instrument. They are known, respectively, as charitable remainder *annuity* trusts, charitable remainder *unitrusts*, and *income-only* charitable remainder *unitrusts* and are sometimes called "type 1", "type 2" and "type 3" charitable remainder trusts.

Within certain limits, the determination of what constitutes *accounting income* is made by the state law which governs the trust and by the terms of the instrument. Accounting income is different from tax income. Accounting income usually includes interest, dividends, rents and royalties. It typically excludes capital gain. The third type of trust, as indicated, is different than the other two because it provides that no more than accounting income for the year is to be paid to the beneficiary. Generally, distributions to the beneficiary will be includable in the beneficiary's income in a way somewhat similar to the way distributions from a qualified retirement trust are taxed to a worker. Because the charitable remainder trust is tax exempt, keeping earnings in the trust, rather than currently distributing them, provides for the tax-deferred compounding. Again, your attention is invited to Chart 8.3 which illustrates what the effect of tax-deferred compounding can be. The third type of trust (the income-only charitable remainder unitrust) may be structured and its investments made so that no distributions are currently made and taxed to the individual beneficiaries. It is called the Private Retirement Trust^{sm} because it simulates some of the effects of a qualified retirement plan but does so on a separate, or private basis for you, and not for your employees.

ADVANTAGES

No Limit on Amount Contributed

Unlike qualified retirement plans and premiums paid (that is, amounts deposited) on a life insurance contract, the tax law imposes no limit on the amount which may be contributed to a charitable remainder trust.

Contribution of Appreciated Assets

Except for certain employee stock ownership and similar plans (discussed in detail in Chapter 4), contributions to a qualified retirement plan, tax-deferred (deferred payment) annuity or life insurance policy must be made in cash. However, contributions to a charitable remainder trust (or contributions directly to charity) may be made with non-cash assets, subject to very few exceptions. These non-cash assets can include those which are appreciated. For example, you purchased stock for $10,000 and it is now worth $75,000. You can contribute that stock to a charitable remainder trust and, if the contribution is properly structured, you will not be taxed on the gain even if the trustee sells the stock after it is received from you. Except in unusual circumstances, the trustee will pay no tax on the profit of $65,000 because the trust itself is exempt from taxation.

The effects to you (and your family) of contributing appreciated property to a charitable remainder trust as opposed to selling it, recognizing the profit and having to pay a tax on it, can be significant. As is illustrated by Chart 8.8, the economic value to you of making a contribution of an appreciated asset to a charitable remainder trust, rather than selling it, can provide you with much greater economic wealth. It is appropriate, however, to add several words of caution.

CHART 8.8

The Effect of Contribution of Appreciated Property
to a Charitable Remainder Trust as Opposed to Selling it

A. *Sale*

Fair Market Value	$ 100,000
Tax (Cap. gains at 28%)	<28,000>
Net	$ 72,000

B. *Contribution to Charitable*
   Remainder Unitrust

Contribution to CRUT	100,000
Tax	-0-
Net	100,000

1. Tax deduction for remainder interest of 17,429 at 31%. Tax Savings   5,403
2. Life interest: Annual payout   8%

First, it is the position of the IRS that if you have an understanding with the trustee that the appreciated assets contributed to the trust will be sold by the trustee once you have contributed them, the profit will be taxed directly to you. If you act as trustee of the charitable remainder trust, and the appreciated assets you contribute to the trust are sold by you shortly after they are contributed to it, you probably will have a difficult time convincing the IRS or a court that there was no "understanding" between yourself as the contributor and yourself as the trustee that the appreciated assets contributed to the trust would be sold. You may have a similar problem of credibility if a close member of your family or your "best friend" acts as trustee. Probably, it is best to use an independent individual or corporate fiduciary (such as a bank or trust company) as the initial trustee of a charitable remainder trust. In any case, you should *not* discuss with any prospective trustee any expectation you may have that the appreciated assets contributed to the trust will be sold. Corporate fiduciaries, as a general rule, do confer with beneficiaries as to their personal financial goals after the trust has been set up, and in appropriate circumstances, the corporate trustee will conclude that the contributed assets should be sold. In fact, most corporate fiduciaries like to diversify holdings. Hence, if you contribute one "brand" of asset, there is a high probability that the contributed assets (whether or not they are appreciated) will be sold. However, by using an independent corporate fiduciary, you significantly reduce the possibility of a successful IRS contention that the gain should be taxed to you.

The rules relating to charitable remainder trusts are extremely complex. You should undertake creating, funding or administering one only with the advice of an accountant or lawyer who is experienced with them. There are many "promoters" (some of whom are former tax shelter promoters) of charitable remainder trusts. Sometimes, their motivation is to get you to create such trusts because they sometimes are paid, often by the charity and without disclosure to you, a portion of the amount which you contribute to the trust. You should seek the advice of an independent lawyer or tax accountant *before* becoming significantly involved in a plan to create a charitable remainder trust.

Tax-Deferred Compounding

The effect of avoiding the tax on the inherent gain in assets contributed to the charitable remainder trust produces a form of tax-deferred compounding. In addition, to the extent that the trust earns taxable income in excess of the amounts which are paid out currently to the individual beneficiaries, tax-deferred compounding also occurs. However, the law requires that the annuity or unitrust payout amount be at least 5% per year. Hence, for the usual charitable remainder trust, tax-deferred compounding can occur only to the extent that taxable income exceeds the payout rate (which must be at least 5%). Unfortunately, if the payout rate is as low as permitted (5%), it cannot be increased when a larger payout is desired.

The Private Retirement Trust[sm], at least to a significant degree, may eliminate those disadvantages. It permits the trust, through investment in special types of investment, including investment partnerships and special bank common trust funds, to earn taxable income without the receipt of accounting income. Because the Private Retirement Trust^{sm} pays the *lesser* of the unitrust amount or accounting income, and because accounting income can be kept very small (in fact, in some cases zero), nothing need be paid out from the trust on a current basis. As a result, the earnings can compound on a tax-deferred basis and a much larger fund is built to provide payments during retirement years.

Income-only charitable remainder trusts, such as the Private Retirement Trust^{sm}, can contain what is known as a "make-up" provision. Under the make-up provision, the beneficiary receives the difference between what the unitrust percentage payment was calculated to be for the year and the amount of accounting income actually earned when, in a later year, accounting income exceeds the unitrust amount for that later year. For example, in the first year the unitrust amount is $80,000 but because *accounting* income is zero the beneficiary receives nothing and the *taxable* income earned by the trust will accumulate on a tax-deferred basis. In the tenth year, the unitrust amount is $100,000 and accounting income $180,000. If the trust contains a make-up provision, the entire $180,000 will be paid to the beneficiary: $100,000 is paid as the unitrust amount for the current (tenth) year and $80,000 is paid for the first year when no payment was made.

The Private Retirement Trust^{sm} has been specially designed to allow a trustee to produce large quantities of accounting income in later years to effect the make-up payments. Because of the structure of the Private Retirement Trust^{sm}, the beneficiary can retain relatively high unitrust percentage (such as 8% or 10%) without having income currently taxed during the early years of the trust.

As indicated earlier, charitable remainder trusts are complex. The Private Retirement Trust^{sm} may add additional benefits but it also adds an additional layer of complexity.

Charitable Deduction

Contributions to charity generally are deductible for income (as well as gift) tax purposes. However, because the benefits in a charitable remainder trust are split between individuals (for which a charitable deduction is not allowed) and charity, the tax law permits an income deduction only for the tax value of charity's interest in the trust. Usually, the deduction is relatively small. A number of factors will affect the size of the deduction. Those factors include the IRS published interest rates (which are used to determine estimated earnings each year in the trust), the length of time which the trust is expected to last (and usually they last until the individual beneficiary or beneficiaries die) and the percentage used to determine the annuity or unitrust payment. Chart 8.9 provides an illustration of what deduction can be produced. Although the deduction is relatively small, it is permitted at the time that the trust is created even though the charity has to wait to receive anything.

By using appreciated assets, and especially if the Private Retirement Trust℠ is used, it is possible to conclude that you will derive more benefits by creating a charitable remainder trust than not creating one. However, it probably would be inappropriate for you to consider creating a charitable remainder trust unless you had a sincere interest in benefitting charity. You (and any other individual beneficiary of the trust) may die prematurely. If that happens, the potential economic benefits for the individuals will not be reached and the charitable interest will be accelerated prematurely. There are ways to hedge against that, including having a minimum fixed term (of up to 20 years) and/or buying life insurance on the life of the beneficiaries to replace the remainder if it passes prematurely to charity.

Nonetheless, charitable remainder trusts are irrevocable, are largely inflexible and were designed primarily to benefit charity as well as individuals. You should, as a result, consider creating one only if you have a sincere interest in benefitting charity. Still, charitable remainder trusts can be powerful arrangements and can provide an excellent method

CHART 8.9
Factors

Annuity/Unitrust for a Stated Term
Term: 5 years
Payments per year: 1   Unitrust Computation: IRS Method
Months between Valuation Date and First Payment Date: 12
IRS Interest Rate: 6.80%

Payout Percentage to Individual Beneficiary	Charitable Deduction as a Percentage of Amount Contributed (*Annuity Trust*)	Charitable Deduction as a Percentage of Amount Contributed (*Unitrust*)
5%	79.3888%	78.6841%
6%	75.2665%	74.8942%
7%	71.1443%	71.2525%
8%	67.0220%	67.7538%

Annuity/Unitrust for a Stated Term
Term: 10 years
Payments per Year: 1   Unitrust Computation: IRS Method
Monthly between Valuation Date and First Payment Date: 12
IRS Interest Rate: 6.80%

Payout Percentage	Charitable Deduction as a Percentage of Amount Contributed (*Annuity Trust*)	Charitable Deduction as a Percentage of Amount Contributed (*Unitrust*)
5%	64.5552%	61.9136%
6%	57.4662%	56.0919%
7%	50.3772%	50.7702%
8%	43.2882%	45.9071%

Life Annuity/Unitrust
Age: 40
Payments per Year: 1   Unitrust Computation: IRS Method
Months between Valuation Date and First Payment Date: 12
IRS Interest Rate: 6.80%

Payout Percentage	Charitable Deduction as a Percentage of Amount Contributed (Annuity Trust)	Charitable Deduction as a Percentage of Amount Contributed (Unitrust)
5%	36.248%	21.152%
6%	23.497%	16.232%
7%	10.747%	12.676%
8%	00.000%	10.068%

Life Annuity/Unitrust
Age: 50
Payments per Year: 1   Unitrust Computation: IRS Method
Months between Valuation Date and First Payment Date: 12
IRS Interest Rate: 6.80%

Payout Percentage	Charitable Deduction as a Percentage of Amount Contributed (Annuity Trust)	Charitable Deduction as a Percentage of Amount Contributed (Unitrust)
5%	42.365%	30.824%
6%	30.839%	25.191%
7%	19.312%	20.834%
8%	07.785%	17.430%

Life Annuity/Unitrust
Age: 60
Payments per Year: 1   Unitrust Computation: IRS Method
Months between Valuation Date and First Payment Date: 12
IRS Interest Rate: 6.80%

Payout Percentage	Charitable Deduction as a Percentage of Amount Contributed (Annuity Trust)	Charitable Deduction as a Percentage of Amount Contributed (Unitrust)
5%	50.708%	42.809%
6%	40.850%	36.916%
7%	30.992%	32.070%
8%	21.133%	28.056%

of supplementing retirement income. That may be especially true for the Private Retirement Trust[sm]. Chart 8.10 provides a detailed illustration of a comparison of a self-investing retirement program and using the Private Retirement Trust[sm]. The charts are difficult to decipher. You will probably need the assistance of an experienced advisor to take you through them. The illustration uses a 10% per year rate of earnings and a 40% income tax bracket. The *relative* benefits of a Private Retirement Trust[sm] compared to a regular savings program will be the same regardless of the rate of earnings (assuming they are identical). As the tax bracket increases, the Private Retirement Trust[sm] on a relative basis will look better; at a lower tax bracket it will not be as good as the results illustrated.

Potential Creditor Protection

As a general rule, in the United States, creditors can attach any interest you have in any trust you create. In most states, that will include the unitrust or annuity interest you retain in a charitable remainder trust. Your creditors probably cannot break the trust because the remainder is vested in charity but your retained annuity or unitrust interest probably can be attached. Nonetheless, the Private Retirement Trust^{sm}, in a practical way, can discourage creditors from attempting to attach your interest in the trust. Because the trustee can invest in such a way to produce no accounting income, and because you are only entitled to receive accounting income, your interest in the trust may not be worth much and your creditors may be willing to settle for a relatively nominal amount and permit you to keep your interest in the trust. However, a charitable remainder trust is not the most practicable or foolproof method of protecting yourself from claims of creditors. It is a potential benefit only, and it probably would be inappropriate for you to consider creating a charitable remainder trust, regardless of the kind, for creditor protection alone.

DISADVANTAGES

Investment Limitations

As with most trusts, a charitable remainder trust generally must be invested under the "prudent person" standard. Few trustees will undertake speculative or extremely risky investments regardless of projections of return except, possibly, for a small portion of the trust. In addition, as a practical matter, a trust cannot invest in proprietorships or partnerships which operate businesses, because that will cause the trust to lose its exemption from taxation for the year. As a result, the overall return may be less than investing on your own. However, as stated earlier, investments for your retirement probably should be among the most conservative you undertake in any case.

Penalties on Certain Activities

Charitable remainder trusts, like private (family) foundations, are subject to a number of penalties as are certain people associated with them, in some cases. For example, there is, as a practical matter, an absolute prohibition in your (or anyone in your family) selling assets to or buying assets from a charitable remainder trust. This rule prohibits, in fact, almost all economic activities between you, members of your family, entities in which you have a significant interest (such as your business), on the one side, and the charitable remainder trust, on the other. The rule prohibiting such economic transactions is a broad one. Recently, the IRS took the position that the rule would be violated if an undivided interest in a piece of real estate were transferred to a charitable remainder trust and the creator of the trust maintained an interest in the same property. The moral is a certain one: Consult with a legal expert on charitable remainder trusts prior to creating or dealing with one.

Loss of Principal to Charity on Death

The ultimate price you pay for using a charitable remainder trust is that the property in the trust will pass to charity upon the death of all the non-charitable beneficiaries. Life insurance can be acquired on the beneficiaries' lives in order to replace that loss. That, in part, is an economic decision. If you are motivated primarily to benefit charity, acquiring life insurance may not be necessary or even appropriate. However, if a motivating factor is to provide for a base of wealth for the beneficiaries and their families, acquiring life insurance almost certainly should be considered.

Non-Qualified Employer Plans

INTRODUCTION

The rules relating to qualified retirement plans are so complex and onerous that many companies no longer use them or do not maximize potential benefits under them. Even if such plans are offered, the level of retirement income they produce for several categories of employees (particularly those who are highly compensated) will be inadequate. As a consequence, in addition to saving for themselves, employees often seek to have employers provide supplemental retirement benefits in a non-qualified form.

COMMON TYPES

Unfunded Promises to Pay

Probably, the most common type of non-qualified retirement program which employers provide are those where the employer does not transfer assets outside of the company to fund the retirement ahead of time. If the company is able to do so when the employee retires, the payments will be made, provided that the promise to pay is legally enforceable (as it usually will be by retirement). However, if the company goes out of business, there may be no assets available to pay the benefits.

ADVANTAGES

No Current Taxation

The good news for the employee is that he or she is not currently taxed on the promise to pay. The employee will be taxed, however, as payments are received. In addition, should the obligation be funded at a later time, the employee may be taxed at the time of funding.

Plan Flexibility and Lack of Regulation

As a general rule, employers can pick and choose which employees will receive such promises to pay and can negotiate individualized terms. As a practical matter, neither federal nor state law will regulate the design of the unfunded plan. However, as indicated earlier, the employee may (or may not) have a right to enforce the promise to pay if it is not met. The employee typically will stand behind other creditors of the company.

DISADVANTAGES

No Current Deduction

Although the employee does not include anything in income before the right to receive the payments occurs, the employer receives no current deduction. That result should be contrasted to qualified retirement plans. For those plans, the employer receives a current deduction, and yet the employee has no current income. The effect is to make taxable income disappear and that is one of the primary reasons why companies put up with the hassle, risk and expense of qualified retirement plans.

Claims of the Company's Creditors

From the employees' perspective, one of the greatest disadvantages of an unfunded promise of the employer to pay retirement amounts is that the employer's assets which are used to pay the benefits are subject to the claims of its creditors. From the employer's perspective, that may be viewed as an advantage or a disadvantage. It is advantageous to expose such assets to claims of creditors because they build the base of the company's net wealth. On the other hand, the employer may be providing less to the employees and, accordingly, it provides less of a hold on them.

Forfeiture Provisions

Often, promises to pay non-qualified retirement benefits are subject to forfeiture by the employee. No benefits (or less in the way of benefits) may be paid if the employee leaves service, at least by quitting the job, prior to normal retirement age. In some cases, it will be expressly provided that the payments are discretionary by the employer, meaning they can be stopped or terminated at any time.

Double Taxation at Death

All forms of deferred compensation, as a general rule, will be subject to both estate tax and income tax at death. Although there is a deduction for income tax purposes for the federal (but not the state) death tax paid, the effective rate of taxation on deferred compensation which the employee "owns" at death often exceeds 80% even in states with no income tax and can approach (and sometimes exceed) 100% in high-tax jurisdictions. As a consequence, deferred compensation usually should not be viewed as the method by which the employee will build significant wealth to pass on to his or her family.

Lack of Compounding

Although different plans provide different features, it is common for such unfunded promises to pay to have no compounding feature in them. The employee will receive a stated amount (such as an extra $50,000) a year. There will be no opportunity for the amount to be increased unless the contract between the employer and the employee so provides.

Rabbi Trusts

INTRODUCTION

Several years ago, a synagogue wished to provide a retirement program for its rabbi. The synagogue sought the advice of the IRS as to the effect of setting money aside for the rabbi in a fund but under which the fund would be subject to the claims of the synagogue's creditors. The IRS made clear its position with respect to the taxation of such a trust. Because the first of these trusts was for a rabbi, they are called "Rabbi Trusts" by pension consultants. Under a Rabbi Trust, funds are transferred, usually each year, to a trustee who holds them for eventual distribution during the retirement years of the employee. The trust is designed so that its assets are subject to the claims of the employer's creditors. The IRS has ruled that that prevents the employee from being currently taxed as contributions are made to the trust. As long as the assets in the trust remain subject to the claims of the employer's creditors, the assets are not treated as transferred as compensation to the employee. The employee is taxed only as payments are made from the trust to him or her. It is possible that the IRS will change its views on the taxation of such trusts.

The employee need not be a rabbi, or a clergy person at all, and the employer need not be a synagogue or a church. In fact, they are widely used by taxable companies.

ADVANTAGES

A Funded Promise

From the employee's perspective, seeing his or her retirement funded provides a type of psychological comfort. Under the law, it is the same, as a practical matter, as if the assets had remained in the employer's hands. Many employees, however, believe that the probability of being paid is greater if the employer does undertake annual funding of the plan.

In addition, many Rabbi Trusts provide for the trustee to loan the funds back to the employer and for the employer to pay (or credit) to the trust each year a fixed (or floating) interest rate. Where that occurs, the funding is, to some degree, a mirage.

No Current Taxation

Like other forms of other non-qualified plans, the employee is not currently taxed as funds are set aside. However, the contributions to the Rabbi Trust are not deductible. Where the employer is in a higher income tax bracket than the employee, a type of mismatch occurs. The amount of tax paid could be reduced by, in fact, paying that extra compensation to (or vesting it in) the employee.

Compounding

Typically, a funded Rabbi Trust does provide for earnings to be accumulated. Under the tax law, the earnings will be taxed to the employer even if the earnings are accumulated by the trustee of the Rabbi Trust. Hence, the employee gets the benefit of a tax-deferred compounding because the earnings are currently taxed to the employer. Again, where the employer's effective income tax bracket is higher than the employee's, waste is occurring under the tax law. Under current law, in most circumstances, a successful company (the employer) will be in a higher effective tax bracket than the employee. However, other factors may outweigh this waste under the tax law. (Note that a church, synagogue or other tax-exempt entity which is the employer is in a zero tax bracket so it is best that the employee is not currently taxed.)

Lack of Regulation

There is virtually no state or federal regulation of Rabbi Trusts. The employer may discriminate as to which employees it wishes to cover by Rabbi Trusts and which it does not. The trust may be individually designed for different employees and their needs (although, as a general rule, employers may wish to avoid an appearance of being arbitrary and discriminatory among employees of the same rank).

DISADVANTAGES

Claims of the Company's Creditors

As stated above, a major disadvantage of a Rabbi Trust is that the assets in the trust are subject to the claims of the employer's creditors. It might be anticipated that the employer will transfer the assets outside of the company when financial conditions suggest that the company's creditors might attach that property. In certain cases, even if the employer does make such transfer, it will not be effective in preventing creditors from attaching the assets in the trust. In addition, in the real world, during troubled times, the employer will be less prone to reduce the company's base of wealth, including the base which creditors know is available to satisfy their claims. Hence, because creditors of the company can attach the property in the Rabbi Trust even after the employee retires, such trusts may be viewed as not providing significant retirement income security.

No Current Deduction and Current Taxation

Until compensation, in fact, is paid to the employee from the trust, there is no deduction to the employer. In addition, taxable income earned by the Rabbi Trust will be taxed currently. As explained above, it will be taxed to the employer and not the employee. Often, the employer will be in a higher tax bracket than the employee, meaning that waste under the tax law is occurring. Where the trustee of the Rabbi Trust loans the funds back to the employer who merely "credits" on its books interest to the Rabbi Trust the trust usually will not have any taxable income. However, if the employing company is profitable, it will have additional earnings from the operation of its business and those earnings will be taxed to it. The company will not be entitled to a current deduction for the interest merely credited to the Rabbi Trust.

Because of the current taxation of the Rabbi Trusts, they are occasionally funded with tax-favored or tax-free investments, such as municipal bonds or life insurance.

Methods have been developed by which interests in a policy insuring the life of an employee can be shared (or split) between the employee (or an entity on the employee's behalf), on the one side, and either the Rabbi Trust or the employer on the other. By doing that, the Rabbi Trust and the employer can enjoy the benefits, to the extent permitted by the tax law for life insurance products, of tax-deferred compounding. There can be an additional benefit as well. As long as neither the Rabbi Trust nor the employer pulls out from the policy more than the premiums the company has paid, the amount pulled out will be tax free. Even if it uses those funds to pay the retirement benefits to the employee, the employer will be entitled to a deduction for such payments. That is extremely efficient under the tax law especially where the employer is in a higher effective income tax bracket than the employee is. The employer is funding a deduction with, in effect, tax exempt income and even though the employee must include such payment in income, the value of the deduction to the employer saves more tax dollars than the receipt of such a taxable payment in the hands of the employee produces in taxes.

Secular Trusts

INTRODUCTION

In contrast to so-called Rabbi Trusts, Secular Trusts were developed. (The name is merely to contrast them to the Rabbi Trusts.) Under a typical Secular Trust, regular payments are made by the employer to a trust. However, the assets in the trust are not subject to the claims of the company's creditors. As a result, it is believed that the employee must include such payments to the trust as income, and the employer is entitled to a deduction for them.

ADVANTAGES

Freedom of Claims of the Company's Creditors

A major advantage of a Secular Trust over a Rabbi Trust is that the payments to an employee are funded and are free from the claims of the employer's creditors. However, it is possible that creditors nonetheless may attempt to attach such property if the Secular Trust is in fact discharging an obligation of the employer. Before constructing Secular Trusts, you should seek the advice of a specialist.

Compounding

Because the funds, in fact, are held by the trustee of the Secular Trust, the earnings will compound (at least prior to the time that they are paid to the employee). Unlike a Rabbi Trust, the earnings will be taxed to the employee (or to the trust). In many cases, however, that will be more tax efficient than the Rabbi Trust where the earnings are taxed to the employer which often will be in a higher tax bracket than the employee.

Current Deduction

The employee must include the payments to the Secular Trust as income. The employer, however, is entitled to a current deduction. Again, where the employee is in a lower tax bracket than the employer, an efficiency occurs under the tax law.

Lack of Forfeiture

In almost no Secular Trust will the interests of the employee be subject to forfeiture. If they were subject to forfeiture, the interests in the trust probably would be subject to the claims of the employer's creditors and the trust would not, in effect, be a Secular Trust or achieve the results which a Secular Trust generally is designed to accomplish.

Lack of Regulation

As with most forms of non-qualified employer plans, Secular Trusts are not, as a practical matter, regulated by state or federal law.

DISADVANTAGES

Current Taxation

Earnings in the Secular Trust, like those in the Rabbi Trust, are currently taxed. Again, sometimes the trust will be funded with tax-favored or tax-free investments. It is possible to split the ownership of a policy on the employee's life. That allows the Secular Trust to invest in the cash value component of the policy which can cause a tax-free buildup on earnings and the eventual receipt of tax-free death benefits.

Claims of Your Creditors

Although interests in a Secular Trust are designed so as not to be subject to the claims of the employer's creditors, your interest in the trust may be subject to the claims of your creditors, including your spouse in the event of a divorce.

SUMMARY AND CONCLUSIONS

The real key to effective retirement planning is to start saving as early as possible. Compounding is a major factor in financial planning. Starting shortly before retirement is inefficient. Better yet is tax-free or tax-deferred compounding, such as that provided by a qualified retirement plan. Qualified retirement plans also provide an opportunity to make taxable income disappear because the employer receives a current deduction for contributions for such plans and the employees do not currently have to include such payments

CHART 8-10A

Effects of Taxation on Income Accumulated in *Taxable* Side Fund
(No Private Retirement Trust[sm])

Yr	Age M	Age F	Annual Investment	Investment Income	Gross Income	Income Taxes @40%	After Tax Income	Account Values	Net To Heirs
1.	35	35	$50,000	$5,000	0	$2,000	0	$53,000	$23,850
2.	36	36	50,000	10,300	0	4,120	0	109,180	49,131
3.	37	37	50,000	15,918	0	6,367	0	168,731	75,929
4.	38	38	50,000	21,873	0	8,749	0	231,855	104,335
5.	39	39	50,000	28,186	0	11,274	0	298,766	134,445
6.	40	40	50,000	34,877	0	13,950	0	369,692	166,361
7.	41	41	50,000	41,969	0	16,787	0	444,874	200,193
8.	42	42	50,000	49,487	0	19,794	0	524,566	236,055
9.	43	43	50,000	57,457	0	22,982	0	609,040	274,068
10.	44	44	50,000	65,904	0	26,037	0	698,582	314,362
11.	45	45	50,000	74,858	0	29,943	0	793,497	357,074
12.	46	46	50,000	84,350	0	33,740	0	894,107	402,348
13.	47	47	50,000	94,411	0	13,764	0	1,000,753	450,339
14.	48	48	50,000	105,075	0	42,030	0	1,113,798	501,209
15.	49	49	50,000	116,380	0	46,552	0	1,233,626	555,132
16.	50	50	0	123,363	0	49,345	0	1,307,644	588,440
17.	51	51	0	130,764	0	52,305	0	1,386,103	623,746
18.	52	52	0	138,610	0	55,444	0	1,469,269	661,171
19.	53	53	0	146,927	0	58,778	0	1,557,425	700,841
20.	54	54	0	155,743	0	62,297	0	1,650,871	742,892
21.	55	55	0	165,087	0	66,034	0	1,749,923	787,465
22.	56	56	0	174,992	0	69,996	0	1,854,918	834,713
23.	57	57	0	185,492	0	74,196	0	1,966,213	884,796
24.	58	58	0	196,621	0	78,648	0	2,084,186	937,884
25.	59	59	0	208,419	0	83,367	0	2,209,237	994,157
26.	60	60	0	220,924	0	88,369	0	2,341,791	1,053,806
27.	61	61	0	234,179	0	93,671	0	2,482,298	1,117,034
28.	62	62	0	248,230	0	99,292	0	2,631,236	1,184,056
29.	63	63	0	263,124	0	105,249	0	2,789,110	1,255,100
30.	64	64	0	278,911	0	111,564	0	2,956,457	1,330,406

INCOME DISTRIBUTION BEGINNING IN AT AGE 65

31.	65	65	0	295,646	118,258	177,387	2,956,457	1,330,406
32.	66	66	0	295,646	118,258	177,387	2,956,457	1,330,406
33.	67	67	0	295,646	118,258	177,387	2,956,457	1,330,406
34.	68	68	0	295,646	118,258	177,387	2,956,457	1,330,406
35.	69	69	0	295,646	118,258	177,387	2,956,457	1,330,406
36.	70	70	0	295,646	118,258	177,387	2,956,457	1,330,406
37.	71	71	0	295,646	118,258	177,387	2,956,457	1,330,406
38.	72	72	0	295,646	118,258	177,387	2,956,457	1,330,406
39.	73	73	0	295,646	118,258	177,387	2,956,457	1,330,406
40.	74	74	0	295,646	118,258	177,387	2,956,457	1,330,406
41.	75	75	0	295,646	118,258	177,387	2,956,457	1,330,406
42.	76	76	0	295,646	118,258	177,387	2,956,457	1,330,406
43.	77	77	0	295,646	118,258	177,387	2,956,457	1,330,406
44.	**	78	0	295,646	118,258	177,387	2,956,457	1,330,406
45.	**	79	0	295,646	118,258	177,387	2,956,457	1,330,406
46.	**	80	0	295,646	118,258	177,387	2,956,457	1,330,406
47.	**	81	0	295,646	118,258	177,387	2,956,457	1,330,406
48.	**	82	0	295,646	118,258	177,387	2,956,457	1,330,406
49.	**	83	0	295,646	118,258	177,387	2,956,457	1,330,406
50.	**	**	0	295,646	118,258	177,387	2,956,457	1,330,406
TOTAL				5,912,920	3,811,804	3,547,740		⇨ 1,330,406

Net to Heirs *after* Federal Estate Taxes $ 1,330,406

10.00%	Payout Rate
10.00%	Investment Interest Rate
6.00%	Side Fund Interest Rate—Net After Tax
55.00%	Estate Tax Rate

CHART 8-10B

Private Retirement Trust℠—with Deferred Income and Replacement Trust

	Joint Age	Annual Gifts	End of Year PRT℠ Values	Insurance Premium	Gross Income	Income Taxes @40%	After Tax Income	Net to Heirs PRT℠	Makeup Amounts	Net Available
1	35	$50,000	45,615	8,532	0	0	0	2,956,457	4,147	2,488
2	36	50,000	96,137	8,308	0	0	0	2,956,457	12,878	7,727
3	37	50,000	151,502	8,308	0	0	0	2,956,457	26,651	15,991
4	38	50,000	212,514	8,308	0	0	0	2,956,457	45,970	27,582
5	39	50,000	279,626	8,308	0	0	0	2,956,457	71,391	42,835
6	40	50,000	353,450	8,308	0	0	0	2,956,457	103,523	62,114
7	41	50,000	434,657	8,308	0	0	0	2,956,457	143,037	85,822
8	42	50,000	523,983	8,308	0	0	0	2,956,457	190,672	114,403
9	43	50,000	622,243	8,308	0	0	0	2,956,457	247,240	148,636
10	44	50,000	730,328	8,308	0	0	0	2,956,457	313,633	188,180
11	45	50,000	849,222	8,308	0	0	0	2,956,457	390,835	234,501
12	46	50,000	980,006	8,308	0	0	0	2,956,457	479,926	287,956
13	47	50,000	1,123,868	8,308	0	0	0	2,956,457	582,096	349,258
14	48	50,000	1,282,116	8,308	0	0	0	2,956,457	698,652	419,191
15	49	50,000	1,456,188	8,308	0	0	0	2,956,457	831,033	498,620
16	50	0	1,601,807	0	0	0	0	2,956,457	976,652	585,991
17	51	0	1,761,988	0	0	0	0	2,956,457	1,136,833	682,100
18	52	0	1,938,187	0	0	0	0	2,956,457	1,313,032	787,820
19	53	0	2,132,005	0	0	0	0	2,956,457	1,506,851	904,111
20	54	0	2,345,206	0	0	0	0	2,956,457	1,720,052	1,032,031
21	55	0	2,579,727	0	0	0	0	2,956,457	1,954,573	1,172,744
22	56	0	2,837,699	0	0	0	0	2,956,457	2,212,546	1,327,528
23	57	0	3,121,469	0	0	0	0	2,956,457	2,496,316	1,497,790
24	58	0	3,433,616	0	0	0	0	2,956,457	2,808,463	1,685,061
25	59	0	3,776,978	0	0	0	0	2,956,457	3,151,825	1,891,095
26	60	0	4,154,676	0	0	0	0	2,956,457	3,529,523	2,117,714
27	61	0	4,570,143	0	0	0	0	2,956,457	3,944,991	2,366,995
28	62	0	5,027,157	0	0	0	0	2,956,457	4,402,005	2,641,203
29	63	0	5,529,873	0	0	0	0	2,956,457	4,904,721	2,944,633
30	64	0	6,082,860	0	0	0	0	2,956,457	5,457,708	3,274,625

Income Distribution beginning in at Age 65

31	65	0	6,082,860	608,286	243,314	364,972	2,956,457	5,457,708	3,274,625
32	66	0	6,082,860	608,286	243,314	364,972	2,956,457	5,457,708	3,274,625
33	67	0	6,082,860	608,286	243,314	364,972	2,956,457	5,457,708	3,274,625
34	68	0	6,082,860	608,286	243,314	364,972	2,956,457	5,457,708	3,274,625
35	69	0	6,082,860	608,286	243,314	364,972	2,956,457	5,457,708	3,274,625
36	70	0	6,082,860	608,286	243,314	364,972	2,956,457	5,457,708	3,274,625
37	71	0	6,082,860	608,286	243,314	364,972	2,956,457	5,457,708	3,274,625
38	72	0	6,082,860	608,286	243,314	364,972	2,956,457	5,457,708	3,274,625
39	73	0	6,082,860	608,286	243,314	364,972	2,956,457	5,457,708	3,274,625
40	74	0	6,082,860	608,286	243,314	364,972	2,956,457	5,457,708	3,274,625
41	75	0	6,082,860	608,286	243,314	364,972	2,956,457	5,457,708	3,274,625
42	76	0	6,082,860	608,286	243,314	364,972	2,956,457	5,457,708	3,274,625
43	77	0	6,082,860	608,286	243,314	364,972	2,956,457	5,457,708	3,274,625
44	78	0	6,082,860	608,286	243,314	364,972	2,956,457	5,457,708	3,274,625
45	79	0	6,082,860	608,286	243,314	364,972	2,956,457	5,457,708	3,274,625
46	80	0	6,082,860	608,286	243,314	364,972	2,956,457	5,457,708	3,274,625
47	81	0	6,082,860	608,286	243,314	364,972	2,956,457	5,457,708	3,274,625
48	82	0	6,082,860	608,286	243,314	364,972	2,956,457	5,457,708	3,274,625
49	83	0	6,082,860	608,286	243,314	364,972	2,956,457	5,457,708	3,274,625
50	84	0	6,082,860	608,286	243,314	364,972	2,956,457	5,457,708	3,274,625
TOTALS				12,165,720	4,866,280	7,299,440			

Net to Heirs *after* Federal Estate Taxes $2,956,457

10.00%	Payout Rate
10.00%	Investment Interest Rate
6.00%	Side Fund Interest Rate - Net After Tax
55.00%	Estate Tax Rate

CHART 8-10C

Private Retirement Trust℠—with Deferred Income and *No* Replacement Trust

Yr	Age M	Age F	Annual Gifts	End of Year PRT℠ Values	Gross Income	Income Taxes @40%	After Tax Income	Net to Heirs PRT℠	Makeup Amounts	Net Available
1	35	35	$50,000	55,000	0	0	0	0	5,000	3,000
2	36	36	50,000	115,500	0	0	0	0	15,500	9,300
3	37	37	50,000	182,050	0	0	0	0	32,050	19,230
4	38	38	50,000	255,255	0	0	0	0	55,255	33,153
5	39	39	50,000	335,781	0	0	0	0	85,781	51,468
6	40	40	50,000	424,359	0	0	0	0	124,359	74,615
7	41	41	50,000	521,794	0	0	0	0	171,795	103,077
8	42	42	50,000	628,974	0	0	0	0	228,974	137,384
9	43	43	50,000	746,871	0	0	0	0	296,871	178,122
10	44	44	50,000	876,558	0	0	0	0	376,558	225,934
11	45	45	50,000	1,019,214	0	0	0	0	469,214	218,528
12	46	46	50,000	1,176,136	0	0	0	0	576,135	345,681
13	47	47	50,000	1,348,749	0	0	0	0	698,749	419,249
14	48	48	50,000	1,538,624	0	0	0	0	838,624	503,174
15	49	49	50,000	1,747,486	0	0	0	0	997,486	598,491
16	50	50	0	1,922,235	0	0	0	0	1,172,235	703,341
17	51	51	0	2,114,459	0	0	0	0	1,364,459	818,675
18	52	52	0	2,325,905	0	0	0	0	1,575,905	945,543
19	53	53	0	2,558,495	0	0	0	0	1,808,495	1,085,097
20	54	54	0	2,814,344	0	0	0	0	2,064,344	1,238,606
21	55	55	0	3,095,779	0	0	0	0	2,345,778	1,407,472
22	56	56	0	3,405,357	0	0	0	0	2,655,356	1,593,213
23	57	57	0	3,745,892	0	0	0	0	2,995,892	1,797,535
24	58	58	0	4,120,482	0	0	0	0	3,370,481	2,022,288
25	59	59	0	4,532,530	0	0	0	0	3,782,529	2,269,517
26	60	60	0	4,985,783	0	0	0	0	4,235,782	2,541,469
27	61	61	0	5,484,361	0	0	0	0	4,734,360	2,840,616
28	62	62	0	6,032,797	0	0	0	0	5,282,796	3,169,677
29	63	63	0	6,636,077	0	0	0	0	5,886,076	3,531,645
30	64	64	0	7,299,685	0	0	0	0	6,549,684	3,929,810

Income Distribution beginning in at Age 65

31	65	0	7,299,685	729,968	291,987	437,981	0	6,549,684	3,929,810
32	66	0	7,299,685	729,968	291,987	437,981	0	6,549,684	3,929,810
33	67	0	7,299,685	729,968	291,987	437,981	0	6,549,684	3,929,810
34	68	0	7,299,685	729,968	291,987	437,981	0	6,549,684	3,929,810
35	69	0	7,299,685	729,968	291,987	437,981	0	6,549,684	3,929,810
36	70	0	7,299,685	729,968	291,987	437,981	0	6,549,684	3,929,810
37	71	0	7,299,685	729,968	291,987	437,981	0	6,549,684	3,929,810
38	72	0	7,299,685	729,968	291,987	437,981	0	6,549,684	3,929,810
39	73	0	7,299,685	729,968	291,987	437,981	0	6,549,684	3,929,810
40	74	0	7,299,685	729,968	291,987	437,981	0	6,549,684	3,929,810
41	75	0	7,299,685	729,968	291,987	437,981	0	6,549,684	3,929,810
42	76	0	7,299,685	729,968	291,987	437,981	0	6,549,684	3,929,810
43	77	0	7,299,685	729,968	291,987	437,981	0	6,549,684	3,929,810
44	**	0	7,299,685	729,968	291,987	437,981	0	6,549,684	3,929,810
45	**	0	7,299,685	729,968	291,987	437,981	0	6,549,684	3,929,810
46	**	0	7,299,685	729,968	291,987	437,981	0	6,549,684	3,929,810
47	**	0	7,299,685	729,968	291,987	437,981	0	6,549,684	3,929,810
48	**	0	7,299,685	729,968	291,987	437,981	0	6,549,684	3,929,810
49	**	0	7,299,685	729,968	291,987	437,981	0	6,549,684	3,929,810
50	**	0	7,299,685	729,968	291,987	437,981	0	6,549,684	3,929,810
TOTAL				14,599,360	5,839,740	8,759,620			

Net to Heirs *after* Federal Estate Taxes $ 00

Payout Rate	10.00%	Side Fund Interest Rate	6.50%
Investment Interest Rate	10.00%	Estate Tax Rate	55.00%

CHART 8-10D

The following is a financial comparison between the Private Retirement Trust[sm] with and without replacement Trust to a Taxable Side Fund.

Assumptions:

A 35-year-old individual is willing to contribute annually $50,000 for the next 15 years to an account that will be providing the highest income for he and his wife for the rest of their lives. He wishes to begin receiving income at age 65. He also wishes to provide an inheritance to his heirs.

Investment of $50,000 /yr for 15 Years
Interest Rate on Investment 10%
Federal Income Tax Rate 40%, Federal Estate Tax Rate 55%
Age at Retirement 65
Percentage withdrawal per year at Retirement 10%
The life insurance premiums are included in the total annual contribution of $50,000.

	Taxable Side Fund	PRT[sm] Without Replacement	PRT[sm] With Replacement
Contribution	$ 750,000	$ 750,000	$ 750,000[1]
Fund Value at			
Yr 10	$ 698,582	$ 876,558	$ 730,328
Yr 20	1,650,871	2,814,344	2,345,206
Yr 25	2,209,237	4,532,530	3,776,978
Yr 30	2,956,457	7,299,685	6,082,860
Gross Income At Retirement (*Annual*)	295,646	729,968	608,286
Total Income at Retirement (over 20 years)	$5,912,920	$14,599,360	$12,165,720
Total Net (after tax) Income Received (over 20 years)	3,547,740	8,759,620	7,299,440
Amount to Heirs	1,330,406[2]	0	2,956,457[3]
Amount to Charity	0	7,299,685	6,082,860

[1] Includes Life Insurance Premiums paid
[2] Reflects a 55% Federal Estate Tax
[3] Value of the Replacement Trust

in income. However, the law imposes many burdens with respect to qualified retirement plans and the amounts which can be contributed are limited. Other retirement vehicles, such as self-savings, Rabbi Trusts and Secular Trusts do not provide similar advantages to qualified retirement plans. However, discrimination among employees is permitted and through the use of other investment vehicles (such as life insurance policies in an appropriate case) some of the benefits available to a qualified retirement plan can be achieved. The Private Retirement Trust℠ can be an ideal supplemental retirement vehicle. Contributions can be made with appreciated assets, and if properly structured, the appreciation is never taxed. Moreover, earnings in the Private Retirement Trust℠ can build on a tax-deferred basis.

CHAPTER 9

ARE TRUSTS FOR ME AND MY FAMILY?

INTRODUCTION AND OVERVIEW OF CHAPTER

The concept of the trust is one of the most important developments of English common law, the type of law which governs throughout almost all of the United States. Trusts can be used as a powerful financial, estate and business planning tool. One of America's great Supreme Court justices, Oliver Wendell Holmes, once wrote, "Put not your trust in money but rather put your money in trust." Justice Holmes knew what he was talking about. This Chapter explains the different types of trusts, and how trusts can benefit you and your family by providing a mechanism to better manage your wealth, to protect your assets from claims of creditors, and to reduce your taxes.

SOME BACKGROUND ABOUT TRUSTS

What Is a Trust?

IT IS SIMPLY A LEGAL RELATIONSHIP

You are involved with many legal relations. Your relationship to your spouse is a legal relationship as is your relationship to your children. Similarly, you also have a legal relationship with your company as its owner. If you are employed by your company, you have another legal relationship with it. A trust is simply another form of legal relationship. It is one which can arise by expressed agreement or, in some cases, can be implied either by the circumstances or by the law. The consequences of the legal relationship of a trust usually are very well defined.

191

The "Players" and What They Do

Almost always, a trust involves three positions: (1) a property owner who transfers legal ownership of assets to (2) a trustee who, in turn, holds those assets for the exclusive benefit of the (3) beneficiary (or beneficiaries) of the trust. The transferor of the assets to the trust does not necessarily have to be a natural person and, in fact, many corporations create trusts primarily for business and tax reasons. The person who creates the trust may be known by many names: creator, grantor, settlor, trustor, or donor. Because the trust relationship is a contractual one between the grantor and the trustee, the property owner must have the ability to enter into a contract in order to create a trust. It may be possible, in some circumstances, for someone acting on behalf of a minor or an incompetent person (such as a guardian of the property of the minor) to be authorized by a court to create a trust with the minor's or incompetent's property.

Under the law of most states, the trustee either must be a competent adult or an entity authorized, under state law, to act as a trustee. Usually, the only corporations which are permitted to act as trustee are banks and trust companies. In many states, however, other entities (such as charitable organizations) are permitted to act as trustee of trusts for their own benefit, and it is common for a charity to act as trustee of trusts created for its own benefit by others.

As indicated, the grantor generally transfers legal title to property to the trustee. The trustee usually is required to register ownership in a way which publicly discloses the fact that the ownership is in a trust. The title might read, for example, "Honest Trust Company, as trustee for Mary Little under agreement of trust created by John Little."

As indicated, the trustee holds only *legal* title to the property. Under the law, the *beneficial* title is held by the beneficiaries.

General Types of Trusts

PENSION TRUSTS

Most retirement or pension plans are in the form of a trust. Usually, the grantor is the company which makes the contributions. The company may also be the trustee although often an independent institution, such as a bank or trust company, is the trustee. The beneficiaries are the employees for whom contributions have been made. Pension trusts are specially treated under the tax and other laws which apply to them. Those matters are discussed in more detail in Chapter 8.

BUSINESS TRUSTS

In some states, it is common for certain businesses to be operated in the form of a trust. For most tax purposes, however, business trusts are taxed as if they are corporations and they are not taxed under the normal rules which apply to most trusts.

PERSONAL TRUSTS

Most trusts fall under a category which can be regarded as personal trusts. These are gratuitously created trusts formed primarily to manage assets for beneficiaries, and are subject to the jurisdiction of the courts which deal with decedents' estates and related matters.

Why Trusts are Formed

Generally, trusts are such flexible legal relationships that they can be formed to accomplish a tremendous variety of different tasks. A trust will sometimes be formed to hold property to be transferred in connection with a business arrangement. The trustee is charged with certain duties which will be rigorously enforced by the law, so that transferring the property to the trust enhances the probability that the transaction will be completed as agreed to among the parties involved. Similar arrangements, such as escrow agreements, are, in effect, a form of trust where the escrow agent functions as a trustee, although the title used to describe the fiduciary position may be different than "trustee."

Most personal trusts are created to provide benefits and protection for beneficiaries. As a general matter, interests in trusts which are created for you by someone else are not subject to attachment by your creditors or the creditors of the person who created the trust. In many ways, the trust provides the ultimate protection against claims against property.

Because legal ownership of the property is held by a trustee and the interests of the beneficiaries can be structured so that their interests are not assignable or attachable, it becomes impossible, as a practical matter, for someone to "con" the beneficiary into transferring his or her interest in the property. Usually, the interest cannot be sold or assigned as a gift, and if someone attempts to buy a beneficiary's interest in a trust, in almost all cases, that buyer will not be able to obtain the interest but may be able to retrieve the money paid to the beneficiary. That provides significant protection against the beneficiary's own imprudence.

Trusts also can be used to ensure that funds are received by the beneficiary at a specific time. For example, you can structure a trust so that, with virtual absolute assurance, certain levels of money will be made available to your children or grandchildren as each reaches a certain age, such as 35 years or when a certain event occurs, such as marriage.

Trusts can be used to ensure that the purpose for which the trust was designed is fulfilled. For example, you want to be assured that funds you have made available to pay for your child's college education are used only for that purpose. If you give the money to the child, the child may well decide that purchasing a car, investing in a friend's business, contributing the funds to a religious organization or some other worthy purpose is more important than using the funds to pay for a college education. If the funds are held by a trustee for the benefit of that child, you can be certain that the funds will only be expended for that child's education. An alternative disposition will be provided for the property, if your child has not attended college by a certain age, such as a direction that it be paid to your favorite charity. That can provide an incentive for the child to go to college; otherwise, the child will receive no benefit from the money.

A trust can be used as an incentive to cause actions in other ways. The trust can provide, or authorize the trustee to take action so that the child receives matching distributions from the trust based upon earnings which the child achieves. For example, the trust for your grandchild could provide that the trustee is to distribute one dollar to him or her for each dollar he or she earns at a job. It is likely there will come a time in her life when doubling income will be important and knowing he or she can access the property from the trust only by achieving certain levels of income production could inspire the grandchild to do so.

Obviously, people achieve goals in different ways. Usually, we wish our property to be used to protect family members and to provide them with the opportunity to achieve their potential. That potential may be success in business but it may also be certain successes in humanities, medicine, philanthropic work, teaching or other activities which the family regards as productive. The trust is probably the most powerful and flexible arrangement to help use your property both to protect your family from the vicissitudes of life and to provide an opportunity for members of your family to strive to achieve their potential. Unfortunately, money can be as destructive for people as it can be constructive. Trusts can be used, perhaps, more than any other arrangement to increase the probability of your goals being achieved with your wealth.

As indicated, you can provide for the trust property to be used or restricted in just about any way you wish. For example, if you want to encourage the entrepreneurial spirit in your child, you might place language in the trust encouraging the trustee to make funds available to allow the child to start his or her own business. You might wish also to express that the trustee should provide funds for that purpose only if the child can raise matching capital contributions from others. You might further provide that no more than one year's income of the trust should be dedicated to such a venture by the child. Generally, however, it may be best not to make such matters mandatory requirements or restrictions but make them recommendations only so that the trustee can deviate from them if circumstances warrant.

Duties of a Trustee

The primary duties of a trustee are to safeguard, manage and distribute or apply the assets of the trust in accordance with the instructions contained in the trust agreement. As indicated earlier, trusts may be created for any lawful purpose and, accordingly, the terms may vary widely. The most common personal trust created in the United States provides for the income of the trust to be distributed currently to a named beneficiary (such as the spouse or child of the person who created the trust). Usually, when that named beneficiary dies, the property is distributed outright to others, usually descendants of the person who created the trust.

As a general rule, the terms of the trust can be made much more flexible. Usually, the trustee can be given the power to accumulate income and pay the income and principal among a class of beneficiaries as the trustee chooses, or in accordance with specific instructions provided in the instrument, such as to provide for the health, support and education of a group of beneficiaries.

The hallmark of the trustee's duties, however, usually is to invest the assets in accordance with instructions of the trust and the restrictions imposed by law. For example, the trustee usually will be required to invest in the manner as would a prudent person interested in the preservation of capital and the production of a reasonable level of income. Normally, that means that the trustee will not be permitted to make speculative investments, such as trading in "naked" options and similar investment activities. In some cases, the restrictions imposed by law can be expressly waived in the trust agreement. That may be appropriate, for example, where you wish trust assets to be made available to members of the family who wish to start new business ventures. Usually, new ventures are regarded as speculative and unless expressly authorized to do so by the instrument most trustees will not invest in them.

The law usually also prohibits a trustee from engaging in any economic activity with himself or herself. For example, the trustee cannot sell or buy his or her own assets to or from the trust. Again, that prohibition sometimes can be waived by express provision in the instrument.

How Trustees Are Paid

States have different rules regarding the manner in which trustees are paid. For example, state law may provide for trustees to be paid a fixed percentage of the value of the trust each year and a certain percentage of the value of assets at the time the trust terminates. In other states, fiduciaries are entitled to "reasonable compensation." In some cases, the trustees must share one fee; in other cases, up to three trustees may receive separate fees. Although people may disagree as to what is "reasonable", a corporate trustee generally publishes a schedule of its fees and charges those fees to the trust unless a beneficiary objects. In fact, most states use a reasonable compensation determination of fees for all trustees, whether they are individuals or corporate fiduciaries. For small trusts, the fees may be 1% of the annual value of the fund. For larger trusts, the fees may be significantly lower.

The critical point is that in almost all circumstances, you can specify the compensation the trustee will receive. The trustee can either accept the position at the specified compensation or refuse to accept that compensation, and a substitute trustee may be appointed either using that same fee schedule you have specified or, if no one will serve under that schedule, with some other arrangement. Usually, where the trust is created during your lifetime and the trustee begins to act immediately, an agreement can be reached and specified in the trust agreement. If the trust is created at your death, the trustee will have the right to refuse to accept the trusteeship for any reason, including the fact that the trustee will not serve for the compensation you have specified. Where you wish to specify the amount of compensation (which sometimes is a wise thing to do), it will be appropriate to discuss it with the individual or institution whom you propose to appoint to make sure that the compensation level is acceptable. In any case, your instrument also should provide a mechanism for the appointment of successor trustees and how they will be compensated.

FORMS OF PERSONAL TRUSTS

Revocable and Irrevocable

Trusts may be revocable or irrevocable. Revocable trusts are ones which can be revoked and the assets held by the trust reclaimed by the grantor. Usually, a trust is revocable only if the instrument expressly so provides or the circumstances clearly support such a conclusion. Usually, so-called "living" or "lifetime" trusts which are used primarily as a substitute for a Will for the passage of property at death are fully revocable. A more complete description of revocable trusts and use of revocable trusts as Will substitutes is contained in Chapter 11.

Most trusts, however, are irrevocable and cannot be revoked by the person who created them. For example, a revocable trust which is used as substitute for a Will for the passage of property at death becomes irrevocable upon the death of the property owner who created it.

Usually, the trusts you create for your family members will be irrevocable. If they are revocable by you, the transfer of property to the trust will be regarded as incomplete for estate and gift tax purposes and, as a result, the property will be includable in your estate. (Even if the trust is irrevocable, the property may nevertheless wind up in your estate.) Usually, if you have transferred property in trust for a member of the family, you will not want the property to be includable in your estate. Similarly, if the trust can be revoked by you, all of the income (including capital gain) experienced by the trust will be taxed directly to you.

Of course, you can allow a beneficiary to terminate the trust and withdraw all the assets. Typically that type of trust is not regarded as revocable because the beneficiary, rather than the person who created the trust, has the power to terminate the trust and obtain direct legal ownership of the assets.

For Yourself or for Someone Else

Usually, you can create a trust for yourself and/or someone else. Most trusts you create for yourself are designed to be revocable by you during your lifetime. However, in some cases, it will be appropriate to consider creating an irrevocable trust for your own benefit. In possibly one state in the United States (Missouri), and in many jurisdictions outside of the United States, your creditors will not be able to attach property which you have placed into an irrevocable trust for yourself. Also, in some states, your spouse will be entitled to take a minimum share of any property you have placed in trust for your own benefit if the trust is revocable by you. If the trust is irrevocable, however, it may not be subject to your spouse's claims to property at your death.

You also can create certain types of irrevocable trusts for your own benefit which will only last for a limited period of time. Such trusts can sometimes reduce the estate and gift tax cost of transferring property to other persons but usually only if they are completely irrevocable. Those matters are discussed in Chapter 14.

Similarly, some trusts are required by the tax law to be irrevocable. These include charitable remainder trusts. Such trusts provide for payments to be made to one or more individuals for a term of years or for the individuals' lives and then for what remains in the trust to pass to charity. Tax benefits are sometimes available in creating those trusts even if you are the sole individual beneficiary. However, to derive those benefits the tax law requires that the trust be irrevocable.

Typical Interests in Trusts

INTRODUCTION

As stated earlier, trusts can be exceptionally flexible arrangements and may be designed, subject to very few limitations, exactly the way the grantor wishes. Over time, certain patterns of rights or interests granted to beneficiaries in trust have developed. These are discussed below.

RIGHT OR ELIGIBILITY TO INCOME

Most trusts provide for the beneficiary to receive the income from the trust as it is earned, although, for administrative convenience, that income may be distributed only every month, quarter or at the end of the year.

The definition of "income" for purposes of trust administration is different from the concept of income for other purposes, including that under the tax law. Tax income includes regularly recurring income, such as interest and dividends, as well as profit derived from the sale or other disposition of the property, such as capital gain. As a general rule, some receipts, such as interest on municipal bonds and life insurance proceeds, are not considered income for most tax purposes.

Trust accounting income, however, generally consists of regular periodic receipts, such as interest, dividends, rents and royalties. Capital gain almost always is not considered trust accounting income even though it is income for tax purposes. The capital gain usually is retained in the trust as part of its corpus.

The concept of paying income from a trust is so well ingrained in property law that the tax law uses that concept in many circumstances. For example, most trusts which qualify for the estate tax marital deduction (as transfers to a spouse) require that the trust accounting income be paid annually to the spouse for whom the trust was created. Because the concept of accounting income varies from state to state (and, within certain limits, under different governing instruments even under the same state law), different spouses will receive different amounts of income from different trusts even though the trusts are comprised identically, have the same receipts and are required to distribute income currently. Similarly, one type of a trust which is an eligible shareholder in an S corporation is required to distribute its accounting income (not its tax income) currently.

Sometimes, the trust instrument will provide that trust accounting income does not have to be distributed currently but may be accumulated and possibly distributed at a later time. Usually, such trusts authorize, but do not direct, the trustee to distribute income on a current or delayed basis, in whole or in part, as the trustee determines. The trustee may be given broad discretion regarding when to distribute income (such as what the trustee determines to be in the best interests of the beneficiary) or under more clear guidelines (such as to support the beneficiary).

Similarly, the trust may permit the trustee to pay income among a class of beneficiaries. Such authorization typically is granted so that the trustee can pay the income as the trustee believes is best. For example, if one beneficiary has fallen on hard times, the trustee may be prone to distribute more to that beneficiary than to others. Again, the trustee may be given either detailed guidance or broad discretion in exercising such a power to "sprinkle" income among a class of beneficiaries.

RIGHT OR ELIGIBILITY TO PRINCIPAL

In many trusts, the beneficiary is entitled or eligible only to receive only trust accounting income. The trust principal (or corpus as it is sometime called) is preserved for the persons who receive the property when the income beneficiary's interest in the trust ends (usually when that beneficiary dies). Those successor beneficiaries are typically called remaindermen.

In a number of instances, the trustee is authorized, in the exercise of discretion, to pay principal as well as income to the beneficiary or beneficiaries. Sometimes, the trustee will be given broad discretion as to whether and how much principal to distribute from time to time. In other cases, the discretion will be narrow, such as distributions only for a beneficiary's health or education. In a few circumstances, a beneficiary will be given a right to demand principal at a certain time, such as upon obtaining a certain age.

Occasionally, trusts will provide for an annuity (a fixed amount) or a unitrust amount (a fixed percentage of the annual value of the fund) to be paid to the beneficiary even if that amount is in excess of the trust's accounting income. In those cases, the beneficiary will be entitled to receive adequate corpus to make up any shortfall between the amount required to be distributed and accounting income earned.

CONTROL OVER THE DISPOSITION OF TRUST PROPERTY

In most trusts, the grantor directs how the property will be disposed of when the income beneficiary dies. Sometimes, the grantor will allow the beneficiary to specify how the property will be disposed of at the beneficiary's death. Such a power of disposition is known as a "power of appointment." If the beneficiary has the right to appoint the trust property to himself or herself, directly or indirectly, the beneficiary usually is treated as owning the property for tax purposes. Hence, the tax estate of a beneficiary holding such a broad power must include the property subject to the power. On the other hand, the grantor may provide that the property may be appointed among a very narrow class of people, such as the beneficiary's own descendants.

Sometimes, the beneficiary will be given the right to direct the trustee to give the property to other persons during the beneficiary's lifetime. In some cases, the exercise of that power can cause tax problems for the beneficiary. You should discuss such matters with your attorney if you wish to give a trust beneficiary such a power.

Common Uses of Personal Trusts

PROFESSIONAL MANAGEMENT OF ASSETS

Not all individuals have the training or inclination to invest their own assets in an appropriate manner, and trusts provide a ready-made vehicle for the professional investment of assets if an appropriate trustee is selected. A trustee such as a bank or trust company, for example, may provide professional management of assets.

Generally, the law restricts the entities which may act as a trustee. For instance, most asset management firms cannot serve as trustee. Nonetheless, an individual eligible to serve as a trustee can be authorized to hire and fire such managers and pay for their services.

Usually, it is important to ensure that the assets will be professionally managed while they are in trust. Assets in a closely-held business are sometimes placed in trust. The management skills in such a case are different from those where a broad-based portfolio of marketable securities is managed. The selection of the appropriate trustee for such circumstances is discussed in detail in Chapter 13.

PROTECT ASSETS FROM CLAIMS OF CREDITORS

Except perhaps in Missouri and some jurisdictions outside of the United States, you usually cannot create a trust for your own benefit and immunize the assets from the claims of your creditors (including your spouse in the event of a divorce). Generally, to the extent you retain the right or eligibility to receive assets from the trust, your creditors can force the trustee to give those assets to your creditors (on your behalf). On the other hand, assets which are placed in trust for a beneficiary by someone else can be immunized from the claims of the creditors of both the beneficiary and the person who created the trust. For example, any trust you create for your spouse or a child usually can be structured to be absolutely immune from the claims of their creditors, including a spouse in the event of a divorce or at death. In fact, in the United States, the trust probably represents the greatest shield against claims of creditors if it is properly structured and administered. More on how trusts can be used in such ways is discussed in Chapter 16.

Once assets are distributed from the trust they usually lose their immunization from the claims of creditors. Sometimes, a property owner will decide that his or her children should receive property when they reach certain ages. Once the property is distributed to the children, however, the property becomes subject to the claims of creditors and, occasionally, the timing could hardly be worse.

For example, you provide for assets in trust for your daughter to be distributed to her when she is 35. At that time, your daughter is embroiled in a bitter divorce and is seeking a large settlement from her husband. Her receipt of significant assets from the trust is likely to "turn the tables" in the negotiations against her. Similarly, you provide for your son to receive property when he is 50. At that time, your son is suffering from a terminal illness. He will receive the assets just in time to have them form part of his taxable estate and have half of them (or more) eroded by taxes.

CENTRALIZED CONTROL OF WEALTH

Centralization of management occasionally produces better results than if management is dispersed. A similar benefit can occur with respect to the centralization of wealth. For example, if you leave your business in separate shares to your children, there is no central control mechanism with respect to the ultimate operation of the business or its disposition. By placing your business interests into trust for your children, centralization of control and wealth can be maintained. Even if you create a separate trust for each child (which often is better than one trust for all of them), centralization of control and wealth can occur by naming the same person or at least one common person as trustee.

PREVENT DISSIPATION OF WEALTH

The propensity to spend money is reduced if property is held in trust. Many individuals are spendthrifts and assets pour through their hands like water. A critical factor is that dissipation of wealth (whether it is complete or partial) can be prevented or at least slowed by having the assets held in trust. Usually, it is the job of the trustee to prevent dissipation and preserve the assets for the long term.

LONG-TERM CONTROL OF A BUSINESS OR OTHER ASSET

DIVIDE MANAGEMENT RESPONSIBILITIES FROM THE BENEFITS OF ENJOYING WEALTH

The individuals or institutions whom you wish to benefit from your wealth may not be the best people to manage your property. For instance, your children may have no interest in operating your business but want to enjoy the wealth it represents. In many ways, the only practicable solution, or the only one which will almost assuredly achieve the result you want, is to provide for the legal ownership of your business to be held by a trustee, whom you believe is the best manager of your business (or who is in a position to select the best manager) and for the trust to be dedicated to the benefit of your children.

As explained in more detail in Chapter 5, a trust is one of the most effective ways to assure that your business is not sold after your death, or if it is, that it is not sold precipitously.

SAVE TAXES

In several circumstances, trusts can save significant taxes. At one time, it was possible to use trusts to prevent any estate taxes (or similar duties) from being imposed when the benefit of property passed from one generation to another. Now the federal tax law limits those benefits. Nonetheless, trusts can save gift, estate and similar taxes, and in some circumstances income taxes as well, compared to the outright ownership of property. More about such savings is discussed in Chapter 14.

PROTECT ASSETS FROM BEING THE SUBJECT OF GIFTS

Sometimes, an individual is easily persuaded to part with his or her property, or a significant portion of it. Children sometimes find that threats of withholding love and affection from a widowed parent is an exceptionally effective method of convincing that parent to make the transfers the child wishes.

Some individuals are more prone to make unwise investments than others and, when such people own assets directly, they can lose them as a result.

However, if the assets are held in trust, it becomes much more difficult (if not impossible) for assets to be foolishly lost.

For example, a widowed mother of adult children is the beneficiary of a trust, under which corpus can be distributed to her only in the discretion of the trustee. Her son goes to her and requests that she give him several hundred thousand dollars so he can start a business, which he is confident will capture the fishing lure business in the United States. The son has no experience in that or any related business but he loves to fish. Because she loves him, believes in him, or just cannot say "no" to him, she would give him all the money he requests. However, she does not own it—it is owned by the trustee. It is unlikely that the trustee would agree to her request to invade the trust so she could give the funds to her son for that purpose. Perhaps, a modest investment would be made or, alternatively, the trustee might loan funds to the son. It is more likely that the trustee will simply refuse to advance the funds to the son or will impose conditions such as investing in the company only if the son can raise equal capital from others.

In any case, trusts really do prevent the dissipation of wealth and, accordingly, provide a more long-term base to protect your family from the vicissitudes of life and help them achieve their potential.

COMMON TYPES OF TRUSTS IN ESTATE PLANNING

Introduction

Subject to very few restrictions in the law, a property owner can draft a trust in almost any desired way. However, in some cases, the law requires that a trust be in a certain specified form in order to produce certain effects. That is common, for example, with respect to certain tax provisions. Even if you are familiar with the requirements of the law, you nonetheless should confer with an expert in the field: Often, provisions in one part of the trust (such as the powers granted to the trustee to manage assets) will cause the IRS to argue that another provision, required by the tax law, has been so restricted or limited that the trust no longer produces the desired tax effect. The following are common types of trusts, the form of which is prescribed by the tax law or is customary to achieve certain results.

QTIPs and Other Marital Deduction Trusts

As is discussed in more detail in Chapter 14, under federal law and the law of many states, you can give or bequeath all or as much of your property as you wish to your spouse free of estate tax by reason of what is commonly known as the "marital deduction." (In a few rare circumstances, the nature of the asset will prevent the transfer of the asset to your spouse from qualifying for the marital deduction; your attorney should be able to advise you as to whether or not you hold any such assets. Also, if your spouse is not a U.S. citizen, special rules apply.) Subject to extremely rare exceptions, the outright transfer of the asset to your spouse (unless he or she is not a U.S. citizen) will qualify it for the marital deduction. However, you may well decide that it would be preferable, for a variety of reasons (not the least of which is that you want to be certain that the property eventually passes to your children rather than your spouse's subsequent husband or wife), for a trust to hold the assets for your spouse for the balance of his or her lifetime. Fortunately, federal law (and the law of most states) allows a marital deduction for assets placed in trust for a spouse if the trust is in a certain form. These trusts usually take one of three forms: (1) a "qualified terminable interest property" or "QTIP" trust, (2) a trust virtually identical to a QTIP except that you also give your spouse the power to appoint the property during lifetime or at death to whomever your spouse wishes (including a subsequent husband or wife), or (3) an arrangement known as an "estate trust", in which your spouse has no entitlement to income, as a general rule, but which will terminate in favor of your spouse's own probate estate and allow your spouse to control the ultimate destiny of the entire property in the trust. Today, almost all marital trusts are in the form of a QTIP although in a very few states there may be tax advantages of using one of the other two types of trusts. However, if your spouse is not a U.S. citizen, a fourth form of trust must be used to obtain the marital deduction.

QTIP trusts were made to qualify for the marital deduction, beginning in 1982, as a consequence of the fact that many married property owners had children from prior unions. Other forms of transfers which qualified for the marital deduction (whether an outright transfer to the spouse or another type of marital trust) allowed the surviving spouse to control the ultimate destiny of the property. That put the property owner on the horns of a dilemma: To use the marital deduction to postpone the tax until the spouse died provided a larger base of wealth for the surviving spouse, but allowed the surviving spouse to deflect the property away from the property owner's own family.

With a QTIP trust basically only two conditions have to be met: Your spouse must be entitled to all of the accounting income generated by the trust each year (and your spouse must be given the right to force the trustee to make it reasonably productive of that income), and no one other than your spouse can receive distributions from the trust during your spouse's lifetime. (There are a few other "technical" and important requirements but they are more mechanical and your tax advisor should know about them.) When your spouse dies, you can be sure that the assets in the trust will be paid as you have directed after the payment of any estate tax attributable to the assets then in the QTIP trust.

As indicated, you cannot prescribe that your spouse's income interest or other rights to property in the trust terminate other than by your spouse's death. For example, you cannot provide that your spouse's right to property will be diminished if your spouse remarries. If you do that, the trust will not qualify for the marital deduction. As indicated, your spouse must be given the right to force the trustee to make the property reasonably productive of accounting income and that can be a problem in some closely-held businesses. Your business may not regularly distribute dividends (if it is in corporate form) or regular distributions (if it is in partnership or proprietorship form). You can provide that the trustee is not required in all events to make the property reasonably productive of accounting income but your spouse must hold the right (either under the terms of the governing instrument or state law) to force the trustee to make the property reasonably productive of income. Where your business cannot (or wishes not) to make regular distributions, your spouse will hold the power, in effect, to force the trustee to dispose of a significant portion (if not all) of the business interest held in the trust unless the trust holds other assets which produce such a level of accounting income such that, on balance, the trust is regarded as reasonably productive of income. Chapter 12 provides additional guidance as to how that dilemma can be resolved. The important matter is that you discuss it in detail with your attorney in constructing your estate plan.

In any case, the QTIP trust is widely used by many married persons with extremely beneficial results in preserving property, providing for the spouse and preventing the dissipation of wealth outside of your family line.

S Corporation Trusts

For many years, trusts could not be shareholders of S corporations (sometimes called Subchapter S corporations). Such corporations, as a general rule, are not taxed on the income which they earn. Rather, the income is taxed directly to the shareholders whether or not it is distributed, in a way similar to the manner in which partners of a partnership are taxed on partnership income. S corporations can save considerable taxes over regular (often called C) corporations. First, regular corporations pay a tax on their earnings and then the shareholders pay a tax on any dividends distributed. If both the corporation and the shareholders are on a 50% effective income tax bracket, for example, earnings which are distributed to shareholders will be subject to an effective rate of tax of 75%. In an S corporation, only the shareholders pay the tax so that the effective rate of taxation, under similar assumptions, is only 50%. Second, regular (C) corporations are often in a higher effective income tax bracket than their individual shareholders. By electing S corporation status where allowable, the income is taxed at the lower brackets of the shareholders. Third, the IRS, as a general rule, will not challenge the level of salary and bonuses paid to corporate officers who are shareholders of an S corporation. With respect to a C corporation, the IRS frequently attacks such salaries and bonuses as unreasonably high. If the IRS is successful, the salaries and bonuses usually are converted from deductible compensation to non-deductible dividends (which are subject to the double taxation regime of earnings of regular corporations).

For many years, a trust could not qualify as an eligible shareholder of an S corporation. If the trust held the S shares for even a moment, the corporation lost its S corporation status. Now, however, basically two types of trusts can qualify as eligible shareholders: so-called "grantor trusts" and "Qualified Subchapter S Trusts" (QSSTs).

Under the Internal Revenue Code, the existence of certain trusts is, in effect, ignored for income tax purposes. Although trusts usually are regarded as taxpayers separate and independent of their beneficiaries and grantors, a grantor trust has its income taxed directly to its grantor (or in a few cases directly to its beneficiary) as though the trust did not exist. A grantor trust is, therefore, a mere transparency under the income tax rules. This type of trust will automatically qualify as an S shareholder as long as its income is taxed directly to the person who created it and that person could be an S shareholder. One simple way to do that is merely to authorize the trustee to distribute the trust income and corpus to your spouse. Even if your spouse never receives a dime from the trust it will be an eligible S shareholder if you could be one. A trust may be a grantor trust (with its income attributed to you) in several other ways.

A few additional words about such trusts are appropriate. First, the rules relating to grantor trusts are some of the most complex under the tax law. Even the IRS, charged with enforcing those rules, has made errors in interpreting them. For example, the IRS has issued a number of rulings to the effect that a trust was a grantor trust, and therefore an eligible S shareholder, based on an incorrect interpretation of the law. Although the taxpayer who received the ruling may rely on it, other taxpayers may not. In addition, a trust may clearly be a grantor trust in the year it is created but may lose that status at a later time. For example, it is not entirely clear what the status of the trust will be if the trustee is authorized to distribute income and principal of the trust to your spouse (which almost certainly will make it a grantor trust when created) and if your spouse predeceases you or you become divorced. The bottom line is that you should carefully discuss with your tax advisor the necessity of the continuing status of the trust as a grantor trust to hold shares in your S corporation.

Second, the income of the trust will be attributed to you even though it is accumulated or distributed to others, such as your children. For example, you may create a trust to hold stock in your S corporation for the benefit of your children with a trustee making distributions to your children as the trustee determines is best. Unlike a QSST which can have only one eligible beneficiary and must distribute all of its accounting income each year to that beneficiary, a grantor trust will be an eligible S shareholder even if the trust has multiple beneficiaries (and even if some or all of those beneficiaries are not eligible S shareholders). You get the "privilege" of paying tax on income which is not going to be distributed to you. Although at first glance this may seem detrimental, it is possible that it can be beneficial. If you, the trust and its beneficiaries are in approximately the same income tax bracket, having the income taxed to you will not result in an overall increase in taxation. Furthermore, many knowledgeable tax practitioners believe that you are not making a taxable gift by paying income taxes under the grantor trust rules (as required by the law) on income which is distributable to another. As a result, the income for your children is not eroded by income taxes, thereby building their base of wealth free of gift tax, and your base of wealth (and later estate taxes on it) is reduced by the income tax.

As set forth above, the other type of trust which is an eligible shareholder of an S corporation is the QSST. Basically, a QSST can have only one beneficiary (who must otherwise be an eligible S shareholder, such as an individual American taxpayer) and the accounting income earned in the trust must be distributed currently to that beneficiary. Two important matters about these trusts should be noted. First, contrary to popular belief, the trust instrument itself does not have to require that its accounting income be distributed, as in the case of a QTIP trust for your spouse. (A QTIP trust constitutes a QSST if your spouse is an American taxpayer.) However, the trust must, in fact, distribute all of its accounting income. However, by merely authorizing the trustee to distribute all of the accounting income (rather than require it), the trustee can stop making those distributions once the S shares are no longer held in the trust (or the corporation otherwise loses its status as an S corporation).

Second, for the QSST to be an eligible shareholder of the S corporation, its sole beneficiary must agree to be taxed on the earnings of the S corporation as though the beneficiary directly held the shares in the QSST. For example, if the QSST holds 10% of the S corporation stock, the beneficiary (such as your child) of that trust must agree to be taxed on 10% of the earnings of the S corporation, whether or not those earnings are distributed. Although the QSST must distribute all of its accounting income, the corporation is not required to distribute its earnings to the QSST. That means that the proportionate share of income earned in the S corporation will be taxed directly to the beneficiary of the QSST whether or not the corporation makes any distribution. In other words, the earnings in the S corporation are not considered accounting income of the QSST unless the earnings, in fact, are distributed by the corporation to the trust. Obviously, that can be a problem. (In fact, being an S shareholder who has to report income of the corporation can be a problem even if the shares are directly held because the income of the corporation will be taxed to the shareholder even if no distribution is made.) For that reason, shareholders of a S corporation often enter into an agreement which provides that the corporation must distribute an amount sufficient to allow the shareholders (or others to whom the income is taxed) to be able to pay the income taxes. You probably should consider such an agreement if your corporation is a Subchapter S status, whether or not shares are held in any QSSTs.

In any case, stock in an S corporation can be held in trust thereby preventing the shares from being subjected to claims of creditors of the beneficiary, as well as obtaining the other attributes of trust ownership.

Upon your death, you will have no choice, as a practical matter, but to use a QSST if you want the shares of the S corporation to be held in trust. During your lifetime, however, you probably have a choice of using a QSST or a grantor trust. Which you should use depends upon the circumstances. Properly structured, however, it may be possible to go from one form of trust to another providing for more flexibility in planning.

Family Trusts

Often, property will be placed in trust granting the trustee discretion to pay income and corpus among all members of the family. For instance, you might place property in trust to pay the income among a group consisting of your spouse and all your descendants living from time to time until the trust ends. That way, the trustee will have the authority to use the trust property where the trustee perceives it can do the most good. Such trusts will not qualify for the marital deduction. Hence, gift or estate tax will have to be paid on the transfer of property to such a trust unless the transfer falls under an exclusion or an exemption. Whether you should use such a family trust depends upon whether you believe the purposes for making the transfer can be best achieved by transferring it to a discretionary trust.

Generation-Skipping Trusts

As a general matter, property held in trust for your own benefit will not be considered owned by you for estate or gift tax purposes if someone else created it for you. Hence, when your interest in the trust terminates at your death, the trust assets will not be includable in your estate unless you hold or have held the power to pay the property to yourself or to your estate (or your creditors or the creditors of your estate). An exception is where the trust was created by your spouse and it qualified for the marital deduction as a QTIP trust. Similarly, if you place property in trust for your daughter providing her with the right to the income and certain access to the corpus (such as in a discretion of a trustee other than herself), the property will not be includable in her estate when she dies and is transferred down to your grandchildren. That provides an opportunity to avoid an estate or gift tax at your daughter's generation. In fact, subject to certain limitations contained in the law, the benefits of the property could be transferred from one generation to another, over and over again, without any erosion of the property by estate or gift taxes. Eventually, that will mean an enormously enhanced base of wealth for your family compared to exposing it to taxes as the property moves from one generation to another.

As a general rule, however, the law imposes a tax, in addition to the estate and gift tax, as the benefits in property move from one generation to another. This duty, known as the generation-skipping transfer tax, is a very effective one and property you place in trust for your child will be subjected to the generation-skipping transfer tax when your child's interest in the trust ends and the property is distributed to or held in further trust for your grandchildren. However, as is discussed in more detail in Chapter 16 as well as below in relationship to the Megatrust[sm2], some exceptions and special rules are available which may reduce, and in some cases eliminate, the impact of the tax.

Whether or not the tax can be reduced or eliminated, generation-skipping trusts (under which the benefits of property pass through trusts from one generation to another) may be beneficial when compared to leaving the property outright. As mentioned, at a minimum, the trust probably can be structured so as to avoid being attached by creditors of the beneficiaries, including a spouse in a divorce or at death.

Educational Trusts

Sometimes, individuals will create trusts designed specifically to provide for the education of their children or grandchildren. In some cases, special benefits of creating a trusts for such purposes are available. Usually, it is not appropriate to limit the trust assets to only that use. Rather, it usually is

---

[2] Megatrust is a service mark of Jonathan G. Blattmachr and Richard Oshins.

better to authorize the trustee to be able to pay or apply the property for other purposes for the beneficiary but provide guidance to the trustee that the primary purpose of the trust is to provide for the education of the beneficiaries.

Trusts for Minors

PROBLEMS OF MINORS RECEIVING PROPERTY

The term "minor" has different meanings under the law. Generally, however, individuals who are minors (in most states, those under the age of 18 years are considered minors) cannot enter into contracts. Because of that, they cannot effectively take title to and manage property. As a result, the law provides special ways for the property to be held on behalf of minors. One of those ways is to have a guardian of the property appointed for the child. Usually, it is a terrible arrangement, involving constant court supervision and the generation of significant legal fees. Other methods are available and you should be certain that your estate plan provides for the use of these methods rather than forcing the court appointment of a guardian of the property for your child. (Chapter 13 contains more detailed information about the various types of guardians.) Usually, these alternative arrangements are in the form of trusts or function like trusts.

SPECIAL TRUSTS FOR MINORS

2503(c) Trusts

Description

Transfers in trusts usually do not qualify for the $10,000 gift tax annual exclusion. To facilitate transfers to minors and allow the $10,000 annual exclusion, the tax law provides for a special type of trust. It is set forth in section 2503(c) of the Internal Revenue Code and is typically called a "2503(c) trust."

Advantages

Because the details of a 2503(c) trust are set forth in the Internal Revenue Code and Treasury Department Regulations, a standard type of form, used widely by attorneys, has developed. Because it is standardized, it generally is relatively inexpensive to have a 2503(c) trust drafted. In addition, transfers to the trust qualify for the $10,000 annual exclusion. In its most basic form, such a trust is relatively easy to administer, and many individuals have trusted lay persons to act as trustees of such trusts.

Disadvantages

The law allows for little flexibility in drafting the terms of the 2503(c) trust. As a consequence, "customizing" such a trust to take into account the special circumstances of a child may not be permitted. Generally, the trustee must be authorized to spend all of the income and principal for the benefit of the child. Placing limitations on the trustee's ability to so use the property will prevent it from qualifying as a 2503(c) trust. Furthermore, only the child for whom the trust was originally created can benefit from the trust during the child's lifetime. For example, you could not provide that the funds in a 2503(c) trust for your oldest child be used for the benefit of your younger child, no matter how great the need.

As with almost any other trust you create for someone, you should not serve as the trustee—if you do, the IRS will contend (and probably successfully) that the assets in the trust for the minor are includable in your estate as a result of the controls you hold as trustee over the beneficial enjoyment of the property (one of the general grounds for inclusion of property in the estate of the person who gave it away during lifetime). Less obvious, however, is the potential problem which can arise if you serve as trustee of a 2503(c) trust for your child even if the trust was created by someone else. For example, your mother creates a 2503(c) trust for the benefit of your son naming you as trustee. The probability is extremely high that the IRS will contend that the property in that trust is includable in your estate because you can discharge your obligation to support your child by using the trust assets. Although it may be possible to structure a 2503(c) with you acting as trustee, you should consider doing that only if you receive assurance from your tax counselor that your serving as a trustee will not cause adverse problems for you.

One of the major disadvantages of the 2503(c) trust is that your child must receive the property (or have the right to demand the property) no later than when the child reaches age 21. When individuals make gifts to young children, little thought is given to the consequences of the child receiving the property (together with its income and growth) when the child becomes 21 years old. Most individuals discover that no matter how responsible a person is, age 21 is too young to receive significant amounts of property. Fortunately, the law has developed so that the child can be given the right to withdraw the property for a limited period of time after she or he reaches age 21 (such as 30 days). If the child does not demand the property within that time, the property can remain in trust for the child. Unfortunately, many parents do not tell their children about their rights and the time for the child to withdraw the property expires. There is little question that the child would be successful in court in demanding the property where his or her right of withdrawal was hidden and later discovered. Moreover, by giving the child the right to demand the property, all of the income of the trust will be taxed directly to the child and the ability to "split" income between the child and the trust (which sometimes can reduce overall taxation) will be lost. Furthermore, because the child once held the right to demand all the property, the child's creditors (including, in some states, the child's spouse) might be able to attach the assets in the trust.

The Extra-Crummey Trust[sm][3] described later and in Chapter 14 solves some of those disadvantages for transfer to minors.

UGMA Or UTMA Gifts

Every state has a special mechanism for transferring certain assets to children. Some states use what is known as the Uniform Gifts to Minors Act; others use the Uniform

---

[3] Extra-Crummey Trust is a service mark of Jonathan G. Blattmachr.

Transfers to Minors Act. Although not called trust arrangements, they operate in an almost identical fashion. For instance, under the Uniform Gifts to Minors Act (used in most states), a fiduciary called the "custodian" holds the asset for the child until the child reaches majority. Some states limit the type of property which can be added to the trust to cash, securities and life insurance. Other states allow other types of property interests to be added to the trust.

The child must be entitled to receive the property at age 18 or 21, as prescribed by state law (or in some cases, as specified by the person who makes the transfer). Virtually all of the disadvantages, including potential problems for a parent who acts as the custodian under a UGMA or UTMA transfer, that arise under 2503(c) trust also occur with UGMA or UTMA gifts. Again, the Extra-Crummey[sm] trust may be a better vehicle to use.

The Extra-Crummey[sm] Trust

Many years ago, the IRS agreed with a federal court which ruled that where minor beneficiaries of a trust are given the right for a limited time to withdraw property from a trust, transfers to that trust qualified for the gift tax annual exclusion. The case is known as *Crummey* v. *Commissioner*. Such powers of withdrawal which allow the transfer to the trust to qualify for the annual exclusion are known as "Crummey" powers.

Because of the complications of the tax law, using Crummey powers to qualify transfer for the annual exclusion is complex. By altering the method of using powers of withdrawal, having the transfers to the trust qualify for the annual exclusion is simplified. Moreover, using this "Extra-Crummey[sm]" power makes it possible to have transfers qualify for the annual exclusion and yet hold them in trust, as a practical matter, as long as the transferor wishes, including the child's entire lifetime. Although the beneficiary will have a brief period of time to withdraw all or a portion of each contribution to the trust (which, probably can be as short as 15 days), experience indicates that such short-term powers are rarely exercised. Moreover, it seems likely that the creditors of the beneficiary will not be able to attach the property which remains in the trust. More detail about the Extra-Crummey Trust^sm is set forth in Chapter 14.

Special Trusts for Special Needs

Attorneys and other counsellors have found additional ways to creatively use trusts to solve problems for special needs. For example, trusts are now often used to allow an individual to qualify for special state medical care which would not be provided because of the wealth base of available to the beneficiary. By placing property into special trusts, it is sometimes possible to allow the grantor of the trust to avoid disqualification from such government provided medical benefits while still, through the trust, having access to the trust property in the discretion of a trustee.

Similarly, trusts have been created for family members with special needs. Often, again, it is appropriate to use such a trust to avoid disqualification from government-sponsored programs.

Trusts may also be used to camouflage transfers for special friends and others as discussed in Chapter 17. In fact, the trust is such a flexible arrangement and is so useful in achieving tax, business as well as personal goals, that you may find it one of the most powerful tools in all of your planning.

THE MEGATRUST^sm: AN IDEAL WEALTH PRESERVATION VEHICLE

Introduction

Many people know that the purpose of life is to be happy. Some of them also believe that having more things will make them happier and their purpose of living will be more completely fulfilled (see Chart 9.1). Some people also believe that trusts were created by lawyers to keep them from owning their rightful inheritances. As a matter of fact, a trust can provide more benefits for a beneficiary, particularly over a long term, than direct ownership of assets. Therefore, trusts can provide greater happiness than outright ownership of property.

In the course of their practices, lawyers often note that certain trusts do not grow but, in fact, begin to be dissipated.

CHART 9.1
Why People Want Assets

- Receive income.
- Use assets (buy them).
- Direct investments.
- Control where property goes at death.
- Consume property.

Generally, that is not attributable to poor investment decisions by the trustee, but the constant demands of beneficiaries for more and more property. The beneficiaries always have "excellent" reasons for their requests: a desire for another home, the need to complete a collection of objects of art, a wish to start a business, or a requirement to fulfill a charitable pledge. Distributing property out of a trust to beneficiaries, however, can cause adverse effects. First, once an asset is owned by an individual it will be included in his or her estate unless the asset is dissipated prior to death. Moreover, once it has left the trust it will be subject to the claims of the creditors of the beneficiary (including, in many cases, the claims of a spouse in a divorce or a death). Property directly owned can be lost in other ways, such as by unwise investments or gratuitous transfers to others. Almost all of those can be avoided through the use of trusts.

But the dilemma seemed unsolvable: Why be a beneficiary of a trust if you do not receive property (or at least the income) from it? The Megatrust^{sm} was especially developed to resolve that dilemma.

The Megatrust^{sm} Concept in General

The Megatrust^{sm} has been designed to maximize the level of wealth which passes through multiple generations while maximizing the use of tax exemptions and the protection from claims of creditors.

Assets in Trust

Generally, the law limits the amount of time that property remains in trust. That is known as the "rule against perpetuities." Generally, property can remain in trust only for 21 years after a group of a limited number of identified individuals die. Sometimes the person who creates a trust specifies that the trust may last for 21 years after all of his or her descendants who are living when the trust was created die. Not all lawyers are aware that there are alternative methods of measuring a length of a trust. First, you may choose to direct that the trust's length will be measured by the lives of people who are not beneficiaries. For example, you could direct that a trust is to last until 21 years after a group of individuals die, including all of your descendants and the ten youngest descendants of Joseph P. Kennedy or some other people who were living at the time the trust was created. There is a strong probability that someone in that group will live for almost 100 years. By tacking on the additional 21 years allowed under the rule against perpetuities, the assets may remain in trust for upwards of 120 years.

Second, some states in the United States (such as Idaho and South Dakota) permit personal trusts to last perpetually. Hence, if you wish, you can have assets remain in the trust for as long as you wish. You should note that as a general rule you may not prohibit the trustee from selling assets in the trust, and only the wealth which the assets represent can be forced to remain in trust. Because of the inability to foresee all the circumstances which would make extending the trust for a long period of time unwise, it almost certainly is appropriate to allow the trustee to terminate the trust (even if under a rather strict standard) or to allow selected beneficiaries to terminate their trusts by appointing the property outright to members of their family upon the beneficiary's death. In any case, you are able to create a very long-term (or if you go to the proper jurisdiction, a perpetual) private trust and to obtain the benefits of trusts for that period of time.

The typical Megatrust^{sm} provides for such long-term trusts although it also usually permits the trustee to terminate the arrangement, in whole or in part, if appropriate to do so and permits certain beneficiaries to appoint the property outright to members of the family upon death.

Most trusts provide for payments of property to beneficiaries. In some cases, the trusts also permit the *application* of assets for the beneficiaries as well. For example, a trustee may be permitted to pay medical expenses, including long-term nursing home care, for a beneficiary. The Megatrust[sm] allows that but it goes further: It permits the trustee to buy assets for the beneficiary's personal use. For example, the beneficiary asks the trustee to distribute property to the beneficiary to purchase a home. If the trustee does so, the beneficiary will own the home but the wealth it represents will no longer receive the benefits of being in trust. The Megatrust[sm] authorizes the trustee, in lieu of distributing property to the beneficiary, to buy one (or more) homes for the beneficiary's personal use and the use of others whom the beneficiary wishes.

For example, you create a Megatrust[sm] for your daughter. Your daughter marries and wants her own home. If the Megatrust[sm] buys a home for your daughter several potentially beneficial results occur. First, mere ownership of the home by the trust should not be treated as generating taxable income. If the trustee made regular distributions to the daughter so she could make mortgage and other payments to maintain the home, it is likely that the trust would generate taxable income which would be taxed to the daughter. Second, use of the home by the daughter at the discretion of the trustee probably will not result in any imputed income to the daughter. By holding the asset for her use, both the trust and the daughter can avoid income tax. Third, in almost no case will the home be subject to claims of creditors of the daughter, even if she should be forced into bankruptcy. Her interest in the home is through a trust (and the use is discretionary) so it cannot be attached by creditors. Fourth, if the daughter's marriage breaks down, her husband will be unable to demand that the home (or any other assets held in the trust which is provided for the use of the daughter) be transferred to him. In fact, many individuals who create a Megatrust[sm] provide for their children-in-law to be potential beneficiaries of the trust but only as long as they are married to and living with one of their children as husband and wife.

Consider how potentially beneficial it would be if your daughter could say to her husband when he has run off with a neighbor and comes back and demands the home in the marital settlement, "I'd love to transfer the home to you. But, you see, I don't own it. My use is only discretionary. And the real shame is that until you left me you were a potential beneficiary of the trust as well."

Because assets are generally not distributed from the trust but only made available for the beneficiary's use they do not form part of the beneficiary's own wealth base for estate and gift tax purposes. As a consequence, when a beneficiary dies, or the assets are made available for the use of another beneficiary, the beneficiary is not, as a general rule, subject to estate and gift tax on the transfer. If property had been distributed to the beneficiary so the beneficiary could acquire the assets, an estate or gift tax probably would be imposed (unless falling under exception or exemption) when it is transferred to someone else. As mentioned above, if the assets in the trust eventually are held exclusively for the benefit of persons in a generation younger than that of the current beneficiary, a generation-skipping transfer tax (somewhat akin to a gift or estate tax) may be imposed. However, and as is discussed in more detail later, the Megatrust^sm is probably the ideal vehicle to use the $1 million generation-skipping tax (GST) exemption.

In summary, then, the Megatrust^sm provides an ideal method to protect assets and preserve family wealth. Although the trustee is authorized to distribute property from the trust to beneficiaries the trustee is generally encouraged, instead, to buy assets for the beneficiaries' use. As a general rule, the beneficiaries are expected to pay for their own consumable and wasting assets, such as vacations, food and transportation. The trust may provide homes, works of art and ownership of businesses for the beneficiaries. The potential benefits to you and your family of such a trust are summarized on Chart 9.2. Beneficiary interests in such a trust are summarized on Chart 9.3.

Common Megatrust^sm Special Features

Giving the beneficiary the right to demand property from the trust (whether it is income or principal) generally means that the beneficiary is treated as owning the property for estate,

CHART 9.2
Potential Benefits of Creating Trusts

- Preserving control over the disposition of assets.
- Maximizing effective tax planning, including income, gift, estate and generation-skipping transfer taxes.
- Maintaining maximum flexibility to react to changing family needs and tax law and other changes.
- Protecting family wealth from the claims of creditors, including the claims of spouses incident to a divorce.
- Making optimum use of gift and/or generation-skipping transfer tax exemptions.

gift and income tax purposes. But the law allows beneficiaries to hold certain rights with respect to the trust property without being considered its owner. Generally, the beneficiary can be given the unilateral right to demand property for the beneficiary's support, maintenance, health and education as the beneficiary chooses. Although a demand by a beneficiary could be resisted by other persons interested in the trust (such as the beneficiary's own children who are also current beneficiaries or future beneficiaries of the trust), practical methods of preventing their complaining too loudly are available. For example, if you arm your child with

CHART 9.3
Beneficiary Interests in Trusts

- Entitlement to all income or use of assets (or eligibility to receive income or use of assets).
- Entitlement to demand 5% or $5,000 of corpus each year.
- Entitlement to demand corpus for support, maintenance, health or education of the beneficiary.
- Eligibility to receive corpus for any reason.
- Ability to direct payment of all assets to others (lifetime or by Will).
- Entitlement to direct all investments of the trust.
- Entitlement to name successor trustees.

a power to appoint the property among a broad class of individuals at the child's death, the ability to appoint the property away from his or her own descendants probably will act as a shield from complaints by those beneficiaries. In other words, as Ed Halbach, one of the nation's foremost law professors, stated, "A power of appointment also can also be a power of disappointment."

You may well decide that giving your child such a power may not be wise. Moreover, if your child has withdrawn property clearly outside of the scope of what is permitted under the instrument, the IRS may try to include the assets in the trust into the beneficiary's estate under the theory that the right to withdraw property held by the child was really broader than provided in the trust instrument. The IRS may not be successful in its contention (except in rare cases) but because of the possibility of such an attack, and for other reasons, you may not wish to arm any beneficiary with a unilateral right to withdraw property under any circumstance. In any case, your attention is invited to Chart 9.3 for a summary of powers which could be held by a beneficiary, as a general rule, without causing significant estate and gift tax or creditor problems for the beneficiary. The more fixed rights to interests you grant a beneficiary, the more probable that creditors and others will attempt to attach those interests even while they remain in trust.

The Megatrust℠ Provides the Most Effective Use of Exemptions

Although our nation imposes its highest taxes on the gratuitous transfer of wealth, limited exemptions are provided. As a general rule, for example, each individual can transfer up to $600,000 free of estate or gift tax and up to $1 million free of generation-skipping transfer tax. The scarcity of these exemptions make them valuable. One of the most effective ways to use them is to use the exemptions as early as you have the resources to do so. Conversely, failure to use the exemptions as early as is practical means that they will be eroded by inflation. In addition, many proposals have been made to reduce significantly the amount of the exemptions. If they are used early, a practical type of "grandfathering" of their use almost always is provided under the law. For instance, if you use your $600,000 exemption when you are 55 years old rather than using it at your death at age 85, the effect is to have the exemption grow from $600,000 to over $6 million at the time of your death if the property grows at 8% a year. Conversely, if inflation averages 4% per year over the 30-year period, the value of your exemption in terms of current dollars will be reduced from $600,000 to only about $175,000. The effects with respect to the GST exemption are even more dramatic because the exemption is larger. Once property is placed in trust under the protection of that exemption, it remains exempt from gift, estate and generation-skipping transfer tax until the trust terminates. The ability to avoid that tax by using your GST exemption early and having the trust last for a long term (such as 120 years) can mean a tremendous difference in wealth. Your attention is invited to Chart 9.4. Note that with just 8% compounded growth a year, the $1 million grows to over $10.25 billion at the end of 120 years. Because the Megatrust^sm more than other trusts is more probable not to make distributions out of the trust (while nonetheless providing benefits to the beneficiaries by providing assets for the use of the beneficiaries), the chances of such sustained growth is greatly enhanced.

CHART 9.4

Annual After-Tax Growth	Value of Megatrust^sm After 120 Years	Value of Property If No Trust
3.00%	34,710,987	2,169,437
4.00%	110,662,561	6,910,410
5.00%	348,911,561	21,806,999
6.00%	1,088,187,748	68,011,734
7.00%	3,357,788,383	209,861,774
8.00%	10,252,992,943	640,812,059
9.00%	30,987,015,749	1,938,688,484
10.00%	92,709,068,818	5,794,316,801

How the Megatrust^{sm} Can Be Used to Operate a Business

Assisting a child or other beneficiary in starting a business is a typical reason property owners set forth for requiring the payment of assets to beneficiaries of the trust out of its corpus, rather than leaving the matter to the entire discretion of the trustee. Perhaps, one of your descendants will become the next great business person amassing a tremendous fortune. Of course, during your descendant's lifetime, those business assets will be subject to the claims of his or her creditors and will be eroded by government taxes when the descendant dies. If the child divorces during marriage, there is a high probability that his or her spouse will make claims (some of which may be successful) against a portion of the value of the business.

The Megatrust^{sm} allows the trustee to make payments to a beneficiary for such purposes or for any other purposes you specify in the governing instrument. But the Megatrust^{sm} provides an alternative: Split off a portion of the trust, make the child the sole investment trustee of the trust and allow the child to run the business through his or her powers as the investment trustee. The child, with those powers, can select the board of directors (or managing partners if the business is operated in partnership form) and, in turn, select the president and other key officers of the business. The child, serving on the board of directors (or a comparable position in a partnership) and as the CEO can receive a salary, which, of course, must be reasonable under the circumstances.

In that way, if your child is America's next great self-made billionaire, the value of the business will remain in trust, providing the protection and tax benefits which only trusts can provide. In addition, the trust created for such a child can be merged back into the "main" trust. In fact, the Megatrust^{sm} can be designed to split, split again and reform in any ways which the controlling trustee deems appropriate. See Chart 9.5.

As explained earlier, trustees are very hesitant to make speculative investments, even if authorized in the governing instrument. However, by naming one of your descendants as

CHART 9.5
The Many Benefits of the Megatrust℠

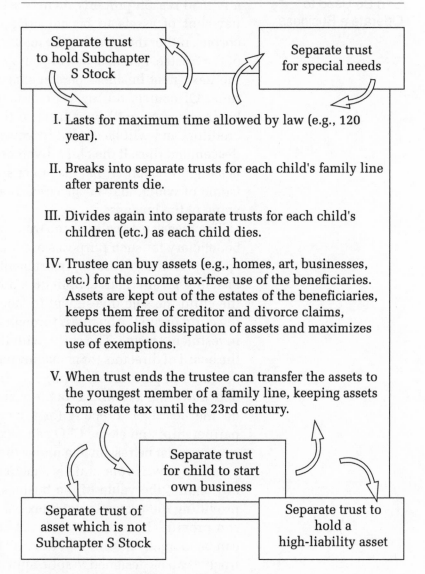

Separate trust to hold Subchapter S Stock

Separate trust for special needs

I. Lasts for maximum time allowed by law (e.g., 120 year).

II. Breaks into separate trusts for each child's family line after parents die.

III. Divides again into separate trusts for each child's children (etc.) as each child dies.

IV. Trustee can buy assets (e.g., homes, art, businesses, etc.) for the income tax-free use of the beneficiaries. Assets are kept out of the estates of the beneficiaries, keeps them free of creditor and divorce claims, reduces foolish dissipation of assets and maximizes use of exemptions.

V. When trust ends the trustee can transfer the assets to the youngest member of a family line, keeping assets from estate tax until the 23rd century.

Separate trust for child to start own business

Separate trust of asset which is not Subchapter S Stock

Separate trust to hold a high-liability asset

the investment trustee, as expressly permitted in the governing instrument and as encouraged in lieu of making direct distributions to that beneficiary, the original trustee can alleviate himself or herself, in larger measure, from criticism if the venture does not turn out to be a profitable one.

Management in a Megatrust^{sm}

At least one non-beneficiary individual or institution must be named as a trustee of the trust. That trustee will have the exclusive authority to make discretionary (non-required) distributions to the beneficiary or beneficiaries, although beneficiaries can be given the right to demand property for support, maintenance, health and education. The non-beneficiary trustee also will determine which beneficiary, if any, obtains the use of assets owned by the trust. Nonetheless, any person, if adult and competent, can be a trustee for investment and other management purposes, even though he or she may be a beneficiary of the trust, without causing, as a general rule, adverse income or wealth transfer tax or creditor-type problems.

Because a Megatrust^{sm} may last an exceedingly long time and may grow to a very large size, special consideration on the choice of trustees must be made. Chapter 13 provides more guidance for choosing trustees and the use of a Trust Protector, an individual or institution which can monitor the actions of the trustee and remove a trustee in appropriate cases without the necessity of going to court.

Spousal Megatrust^{sm}

Often, individuals will conclude that they cannot afford to permanently part with assets prior to death. Generally, if you provide that assets from the trust may be returned to you they will be includable in your estate and subject to the claims of your creditors. Nonetheless, practical methods of being able to continue to enjoy the benefits of property transferred in trust during your lifetime are available. One of the most effective methods, if you have a secure marriage, is to make your spouse a discretionary beneficiary of the trust. By authorizing the trustee to pay income or corpus to your spouse, or providing assets of the trust for your spouse's use, you may be able to enjoy the fruits of the property in the discretion of your spouse (after he or she has received such benefits or use at the discretion of the trustee). It appears relatively certain that you can define your spouse as the person to whom you are married from time to time. Hence, if you and your current spouse are divorced or your current spouse predeceases you, any new spouse of yours will become a discretionary beneficiary of the trust.

However, transfers to such a trust, where your spouse's rights to property are discretionary and/or your spouse is defined as the person to whom you are married from time to time, will not qualify for the marital deduction. As a result you will be required to use certain exclusions or exemptions to place property in the trust or you will be required to pay gift tax in connection with transfers to the trust.

Nonetheless, you must be careful that the assets transferred to a trust in which your spouse has interests are not treated as owned, in whole or in part, by your spouse. For example, if you reside in a community property jurisdiction (or the assets are treated as community property even though you might live in a non-community property state), your spouse will be treated as co-contributor of the trust, and the assets will potentially be subject to claims of your spouse's creditors and be includable in your spouse's estate. Usually, you can avoid such characterization if proper planning steps are taken prior to the contribution of the assets to the trust. You should make certain that you receive the advice of your legal counsellor before attempting to create any trust, especially where you want your spouse to be a beneficiary but do not want the assets subject to the claims of your spouse's creditors or included in your spouse's estate.

SUMMARY AND CONCLUSION

Ascertaining the goals you want to achieve with respect to your financial estate planning is the proper beginning point to determine whether trusts are appropriate vehicles for you. Discussions with your legal and tax advisors will help to "focus" those goals and how trusts can be used to achieve them. Trusts, by their nature, prevent the dissipation of property and tend to preserve ownership of assets. They tend to prevent compulsive decisions, and can greatly reduce taxes and eliminate the claims of creditors, including that of a spouse in a divorce. No estate or financial plan is complete unless the use of trusts to help achieve important goals is considered.

CHAPTER 10

WHY DO I NEED A WILL?

INTRODUCTION AND OVERVIEW OF CHAPTER

The privilege of specifying how you wish to dispose of your assets at your death does not exist under all legal systems. Subject to certain restrictions, a property owner in the United States may specify how assets directly owned at death will be disposed of by executing a valid Will. A Will may perform several other functions as well, such as designating who will administer your estate and who will be the guardian for your minor children. Regardless of other estate planning steps you have taken for the disposition of your property (such as the execution of a living revocable trust), you should execute a Will. In this Chapter, matters relating to Wills, including Will contests, are discussed. Living Wills and health care proxies are also discussed in this Chapter.

PROPERTY WHICH PASSES AT DEATH

Assets Which Pass at Death

Significantly more than what you own in your own name will pass to others when you die. It is important for you to be aware of these kinds of property and to take steps to make sure they are disposed of, to the extent you can, in a way which best fulfills your estate planning goals.

JOINTLY OWNED PROPERTY

Not infrequently, an individual will own an asset with one or more other individuals; in fact, almost all assets can be owned by more than one person. Basically, the law provides for three types of common ownership. The first is known as a "tenancy in common." A tenancy in common is a typical form of common ownership with persons other than your spouse. For example, if you and your brother have inherited a piece of land from your parents, and the property stands in both your names, you probably own it as tenants in common. Under a tenancy in common, each of you owns your respective share (usually one half, but it can be any other percentage). You can sell your half without the other owner's consent (unless there is an agreement to the contrary) although that sometimes is difficult to arrange; for example, the new owner will become a co-owner with your brother, which may not be regarded as desirable. In addition, you can give your interest away without the consent of the other person and you can dispose of your interest in the property at your death by your Will.

If you want to sell the entire property but the other owner or owners do not, as a rule you can commence an action in court to effect what is known as a "partition" of the property. From a theoretical perspective, this means that the court will award you your share of the property and you will own it separately and alone and the balance will be held by the other owner or owners. This can happen, for example, where you and your sister own one half each, as tenants in common, of 100 shares of stock. If your sister will not agree to split the ownership, you can probably get a court to order that the shares be reissued in two certificates: one 50-share certificate for you and one 50-share certificate for your sister. With respect to real estate and certain other unique assets (such as furniture or works of art), the court usually cannot effect a partition or division of the property. The "south 40" of the 80-acre parcel you own with your brother may have less worth than the "north 40." Perhaps the south 44 would be equal in value to the north 40 but the court is not going to take that chance. Rather, the court will order what is known as a "partition sale" in most cases, meaning that the court will hold an auction (at which you and the other owners may bid) and divide the proceeds among the owners.

An important point to remember is that you can, at your death and by your Will, dispose of your interest in property held with others as tenants in common. That is not the case with certain other forms of property owned in common with others.

The second type of property owned in common is known as a "joint tenancy with rights of survivorship." Sometimes this form of ownership is simply referred to as a joint tenancy. Almost any type of property can be owned by persons as joint tenants with rights of survivorship. During lifetime, the owners' rights are very similar to those of tenants in common. The primary difference is what happens when one of the co-owners dies. The right of survivorship means that the surviving co-owner or co-owners will automatically receive the property. As a general matter, even if you direct in your Will or another document that your interest in the property will pass to someone other than the surviving co-owner or co-owners at your death, the provision usually will be ineffective and the co-owner or co-owners will succeed to ownership of the entire property.

In some cases, the title to the property will indicate that it is one that contains survivorship rights. Bank accounts, for example, that contain the letters "JTWS" connote rights of survivorship, as the letters mean "joint tenancy with rights of survivorship." Similarly, "EOS" on a bank account connotes a survivorship feature—the initials mean "either or survivor."

Sometimes it will not be clear whether rights of survivorship is intended. The law of some states, for example, creates a presumption that a bank account in the name of two persons connotes that the bank account is intended to confer survivorship rights. In some states, in fact, it is possible to designate that the account is maintained in joint name only "for convenience", meaning that there is no ownership interest created in the new co-owner and that survivorship rights are not intended. Such an account might be opened when a parent wants a child to be able to sign checks on the parent's checking account in order to help the parent pay bills, etc. The parent does not intend to make a gift to the child of one-half of amounts deposited in the account or for the child to receive (to the exclusion of other children) the full amount in the account at the time the parent dies. If an account "for convenience only" has not been created, the child who has been named as the co-owner of the account will succeed to the entire amount in the account by virtue of survivorship rights which are implied by the joint nature of the account.

The third type of common ownership is known as "tenancy by the entirety." A tenancy by the entirety is a form of joint ownership with rights of survivorship which can exist only between a husband and wife. In many states, any property held by a husband and wife is presumed to be held a tenancy by the entirety. In some jurisdictions, a tenancy by the entirety can be created only in real estate and cannot be created, for example, in bank accounts, stocks or automobiles. A major difference between a regular joint tenancy with rights of survivorship and a tenancy by the entirety is that one co-owner in a tenancy by the entirety cannot alone terminate the co-ownership arrangement and the rights of survivorship which go with it. Any co-tenant of property held as joint tenants with right of survivorship can sever the joint tenancy and rights of survivorship at any time (up until death). However, if you and your spouse own property, such as your home, as tenants by the entirety, neither of you alone (without the consent of the other) can change the form of ownership. In any case, property held between you and your spouse as tenants by the entirety will automatically pass to the survivor of the two of you when the first of you dies. (In some states, if you die under circumstances such as a common accident, where the orders of your death cannot be clearly established, each of you may be able to dispose of one half. Of course, it is very rare for that to occur.)

Again, it is important to realize that in most states property which you hold with your spouse (at least if it is real estate) will be presumed to be held by you and your spouse as tenants by the entirety. That will significantly limit your ability to dispose of the property to others at the time of your death and, in some cases, will limit your ability to provide the most effective planning for that property, even if you want your spouse to benefit from it.

LIFE INSURANCE

In most cases, life insurance proceeds will be paid, upon the death of the insured, to a beneficiary who has been designated by the policy's owner. (In many cases, the insured will be the owner of the policy, although Chapter 16 will explain in detail why that may be inappropriate.) Even if you specifically provide for the disposition in your Will of the life insurance proceeds, that disposition will be ineffective if you have also completed a valid beneficiary designation form. As a general matter, you can name any person, institution or entity (such as a trust) as the recipient of life insurance proceeds. If an effective designation is not made (for example, you name your mother as the only beneficiary and she dies before you), the proceeds usually are paid to your estate. In addition, you can designate your estate as the recipient of the proceeds, although as will be explained in Chapter 16 that rarely is a wise thing to do. In any case, where you have named your estate as the beneficiary or the beneficiary designation you have made is ineffective (or you have failed to make one), the proceeds will be received by your estate and will be disposed of by your Will.

RETIREMENT BENEFITS

Usually retirement benefits are disposed of in the same way that life insurance proceeds are—that is, in accordance with a completed beneficiary designation form. In some cases, the retirement plan will require that the proceeds be paid to a member of your family and you will not be permitted to designate any beneficiary (or you will be permitted to designate a beneficiary only as to part). In some cases, as with life insurance proceeds, you will be able to name the recipient of the retirement benefits or, should you fail to name a recipient, the benefits will be paid to your estate for disposition by your Will.

CONTRACTS

In effect both retirement benefit designations and life insurance designations are designations made pursuant to contracts. For example, your insurance policy represents a contract between you (or other owner of the policy) and the insurance company, and the contract gives you the right to name the beneficiary by using a designation form. In addition to retirement benefits and life insurance, there are several other ways in which property will be disposed of by contract at your death. For example, if you have used a revocable living trust as a substitute in whole or in part for your Will, the assets owned by or payable to the trust at your death will be disposed of by contract, because the trust is nothing but a specialized type of contract.

Often co-owners of businesses enter into contracts with respect to the disposition of the business assets when one of them dies. You may be required, for example, to sell all or part of the ownership in your business back to the company or to the surviving owner when you die. Other types of options, which usually are a form of contract, will control the disposition of the property at your death.

Similarly, you may have entered into a property settlement agreement with your spouse or former spouse which will require that certain assets be transferred at your death. You may be required by the agreement to keep a Will in effect providing for the disposition.

POWERS OF APPOINTMENT

Not infrequently, one individual will grant to another the power to specify how property held in a trust or similar arrangement is to be disposed of when someone dies. For example, if your grandmother created a trust for your benefit, she might have granted you the power to say by your Will, or by an instrument executed during your lifetime, who is to receive the trust property when you die. Often a power to appoint property to others will be exercised in a specific way (such as by making specific reference to the document under which you hold the power). The persons to whom you can appoint the property may be limited (for instance, to your descendants or your spouse). As indicated, in some cases the power of appointment can be exercised by your Will only. (In some cases, your Will will be deemed to have exercised the power even if you do not make specific reference to it.) In other cases, however, you can execute the power only by a document executed during your lifetime. Usually if you fail to exercise a power of appointment, the property will pass to beneficiaries specified in the document which conferred the power of appointment to you.

ASSETS DIRECTLY OWNED

Assets which you own directly at the time of your death generally can be disposed of by your Will when you die. (As indicated above, if you have transferred assets to a revocable living trust, the terms of the trust will dispose of the assets, as the assets will not be directly owned by you at the time of your death.) If you do not die with a valid Will, or to the extent that your Will fails to dispose of certain of the assets which you own directly at the time of your death, usually those assets will pass pursuant to the "intestacy laws" of the state in which you reside at the time of your death. (Certain assets, such as real estate, usually will pass pursuant to the intestacy laws of the state where the assets are located.)

An Overview of Intestacy Laws

You do not want to die intestate with respect to any of your property. If you do, state law will decide how your assets are disposed of. If you do not die with close relatives, your assets will pass to the state. For example, except for a minimum amount (which varies from state to state), if you die with a spouse and children, your spouse will not be entitled to receive all of your assets. Usually, at least one third and in some cases two thirds of your property will pass pursuant to the intestacy laws to your descendants. It is probable that your estate will follow the poorest tax and administrative plan possible if you die without a Will. Among other matters, it is almost certain in most jurisdictions that the individual who ends up administering your estate will have to post a bond. The bonding company will charge for the bond, and either the administrator or your estate will have to pay for it. In almost all cases, the bond requirement can be waived by your Will. Also, if you have minor children, your failure to have a Will will probably mean that you have failed to designate a guardian. If your spouse does not survive, there is likely to be a lengthy and costly legal proceeding, if not a bitter one, involving members of your family and your spouse's family as to the selection of the guardian.

LIMITATIONS ON YOUR ABILITY TO DISPOSE OF ASSETS AT DEATH

Introduction

As a general matter in the United States (contrary to rules which exist in several other countries), you are free to dispose of assets by your Will in any manner which is regarded as lawful. (For example, you cannot leave your property in a way which is intended to promote crime.) However, in some cases the law imposes limitations on the amount of property which you are free to dispose of if certain other persons exercise their rights to it. In addition, there are limitations on the manner in which you can dispose of your property. Moreover, for anyone holding any significant amount of wealth, taxes may erode more than half of the property, meaning in effect that you can only dispose of the balance.

Spousal Rights

COMMUNITY PROPERTY

Under community property laws in certain states, each spouse owns basically one half of all community assets. Community property jurisdictions in the United States are Louisiana, Texas, New Mexico, Arizona, California, Nevada, Washington State, Idaho and Wisconsin. Generally, all assets acquired by either spouse during marriage (as opposed to those which are brought to the marriage) other than by gift or bequest constitute community assets. Because each spouse owns only half of each community asset, each spouse can dispose of no more than his or her half even if title to the asset is held in the name of one spouse. The rules relating to community property are extremely complex. They are discussed in greater detail in Chapter 12. In some community property states, assets which you acquire in a non-community property jurisdiction are, in effect, converted to community assets for purposes of disposition at death if you reside in the state when you die. Moreover, there is a presumption that any asset held by either spouse is a community asset unless, as a general rule, the spouse can prove otherwise by persuasive evidence. (As a practical matter, the courts are inclined to find community property.) Furthermore, if you have resided in a community property jurisdiction, the community property nature of the asset may carry over even if you die a resident of a non-community property state.

As a consequence, unless you have never resided in a community property jurisdiction or acquired an asset in such a jurisdiction, or unless your spouse has effectively waived any rights to community property in a valid agreement, you should discuss with your attorney what limitations your spouse's community property rights may place on your ability to dispose of property standing in your name. You should also discuss your right to dispose of a portion of assets, as community property, even if title to those assets is held by your spouse.

Minimum Share Rights

Virtually all of the non-community property states give a surviving spouse the right to receive a minimum share of the deceased spouse's estate. The minimum share typically varies between one third and one half of the estate of the first spouse to die, depending upon state law and certain other conditions (such as whether the spouse dying first has any descendants). What assets are included in the estate for purposes of a surviving spouse's minimum share varies from jurisdiction to jurisdiction as well. Usually, a spouse may waive his or her rights to the minimum share from the estate of the deceased spouse but the procedure for doing so is sometimes complex and, in many states, will be closely scrutinized by the court. The type of interest which will satisfy your spouse's rights to a minimum share of your estate also varies from jurisdiction to jurisdiction. In a few states, putting the share in trust for your spouse and providing your spouse with the income for life (and no other rights) will be satisfactory. In other states, interests in trusts do not count at all, and your spouse may demand to receive his or her share outright. As discussed in Chapter 12, you may be able to take actions to minimize or limit your spouse's right to a minimum share of your estate. The important point, however, is that you consult with your attorney to determine what your spouse's rights are and take appropriate action in light of those rights toward completing your estate planning goals.

DOWER AND CURTESY

In very few jurisdictions, a wife or husband is awarded certain rights in real estate owned, respectively, as "dower" and "curtesy." As indicated, usually these rights pertain to real estate only. If you hold real estate, you should have your attorney advise you as to whether your spouse has dower or curtesy rights in it.

WIDOW'S/WIDOWER'S SET OFF

In addition to an entitlement to a one-half share of community property and/or minimum percentage of the estate of the surviving spouse, virtually all states provide that a surviving spouse has a right to certain property. Typically, this property is of a personal nature, such as furniture and furnishings, an automobile, a family bible and, certain livestock. In some states, the entitlement may include relatively modest amounts of cash. The monetary value of the entitlement typically is very limited, so that as a general rule, that it will not have a significant impact on your estate planning. Nonetheless, it is possible that your spouse may be entitled to an asset which you would prefer to go to someone else (perhaps a family heirloom which does not have significant fair market value). Depending upon state law, there may be action you can take (such as giving the asset away during your life) which will effectively defeat your spouse's right to demand the asset. Typically, the right of your surviving spouse to the assets "set off" in your estate do not count against your spouse's minimum share and cannot be defeated by creditors of your estate.

CONTRACT RIGHTS

If you have entered into an agreement with your spouse relating to property rights, your spouse may have rights under the agreement which are enforceable against your estate. For example, even if your spouse has waived any right to receive property from your estate under the intestacy laws, community property laws or minimum share law, you may have agreed to leave your spouse a certain amount of money, specified assets or a percentage of your property. Usually, such rights are enforceable against your estate. Moreover, in at least some jurisdictions, to comply with such an agreement you may have to provide, in effect, for those assets to pass to your spouse free of any estate tax which may be due. (Although property passing to your spouse usually qualifies from exemption from estate tax by reason of the marital deduction, the deduction is not available in all circumstances and may not be available for purposes of state death tax.)

In addition, if your marriage has broken down prior to your death, your spouse may have rights against your estate under local "equitable distribution" or similar rules.

OTHER RIGHTS MAY APPLY TO OTHER PROPERTY

Your ability to dispose of property at your death may also be limited by other legal rights of your spouse or descendants. For example, as a general matter, your spouse will be entitled to certain payments from any qualified retirement plan which was maintained for your benefit or which you own at the time of your death.

Moreover, your spouse may contend that assets in your name are really held for his or her benefit under an implied agreement or trust arrangement. As discussed in more detail in Chapter 12, your spouse may also contend that a portion of the assets in your name belong to him or her by reason of an oral or implied business partnership between the two of you.

Obtaining advice from competent legal counsel is the only way you can be certain of the extent to which your spouse has rights to your property which will limit your ability to dispose of it.

Rights of Other Family Members

FORCED HEIRSHIP

In Louisiana, as in certain foreign jurisdictions, a decedent's descendants may be entitled to a certain share of property owned at death. Even if you do not live in Louisiana or one of those foreign jurisdictions, your descendants may be entitled to a share of your property located there. If you own property in Louisiana or a foreign country, it may be appropriate for you to discuss with your attorney (who, in turn, may have to contact an attorney in that jurisdiction) whether or not your descendants have a right to property by forced heirship.

CONTRACT RIGHTS

Although parents rarely contract with their children to leave them property at death, it does happens from time to time. What is more common is for a husband and wife in connection with a divorce to contract to leave to their children a certain percentage of their estates. The extent to which the children can enforce such rights (as opposed to enforcement by the surviving spouse on their behalf) is not always certain. You should discuss with your attorney the extent to which any such contract rights will limit your ability to dispose of your assets at your death and, if you wish, the extent to which you can restrict or eliminate their rights.

FAMILY PROPERTY

Just as a surviving spouse may be entitled to certain property (such as an automobile, furniture and furnishings), many states give such property rights to other family members, such as children. Usually, the value of such property is very limited and will not materially interfere with the disposition of your estate.

Under certain employer-provided benefit plans, children (or at least minor children) may be entitled to certain benefits, thereby limiting or eliminating your ability to dispose of those benefits.

Other Limitations

TIME LIMITS ON "TYING UP" PROPERTY

Most states restrict the time during which you can restrict the disposition of property. In fact, subject to very few exceptions, you cannot prohibit the sale of an asset. (Effective ways to simulate that result, however, are set forth in Chapter 5.) As a practical matter you can prevent the sale or other transfer of a property interest by placing the interest in trust. Every state permits you, subject to very few limits, to prohibit the sale or transfer of a beneficial interest you create for someone in a trust. Almost all states limit the time during which you can restrict the transfer of such an interest. Under the "rule against perpetuities", you cannot provide for a trust to last longer than 21 years after the death of the last to die of a group of identified persons who are living when the trust was created. For example, if you have two children and three grandchildren, you can provide, as a general matter, that the trust can last until 21 years after they all die. You cannot state that the trust will last until 21 years after all of your grandchildren die because you may have grandchildren who are born after you die, and the rule against perpetuities would be violated. Idaho and South Dakota (as well as certain foreign jurisdictions) do not, as a general rule, impose a rule against perpetuities. Among states that do impose a rule against perpetuities, the exact terms of the rule vary.

CHARITABLE BEQUESTS

Some states limit the percentage of your property that you can leave to charity or how close to your death you may make a Will creating charitable interests created under your Will. Through careful planning, you usually can avoid those restrictions. However, it will be appropriate for you to discuss with your attorney whether those restrictions will apply, and if so, what action you will need to take to achieve your planning goals.

CREDITORS' CLAIMS AND EXPENSES OF ESTATE ADMINISTRATION

The costs of your funeral and burial, the charges for administering your estate (including fiduciary commissions, court costs, appraisal expenses and attorney fees) as well as claims against your estate will almost always take precedence over debts and bequests under your Will. Debt obligations almost always take precedence over bequests. In some circumstances, those claims, expenses and charges can be made against property which passes outside of your will (such as assets held in a revocable living trust at your death). As mentioned above, your spouse, your ex-spouse or your descendants may have contractual rights and will be creditors of your estate on account of contractual rights under property settlement agreements entered into prior to your death.

Taxes

OVERVIEW OF THE AMERICAN DEATH TAX SYSTEM

The American death tax system is one of the most complex in the world. All audits of estate, gift and generation-skipping transfer tax returns are conducted by IRS attorneys. All other tax audits are conducted by highly trained lay persons.

Currently, the estate, gift and generation-skipping transfer taxes (collectively called "wealth transfer taxes") are the highest taxes imposed under American law. The rate of tax can reach 60% without considering any additional taxes which some states impose. Each individual, as a general matter, has a $600,000 "exemption" against lifetime gifts or testamentary transfers. Tax rates on amounts above that level usually commence at 32% and reach 55% when the base of wealth (including the $600,000 exemption amount) reaches $2.5 million. As a consequence, more than half of the estate of virtually anyone with significant wealth will be eroded by taxes. This presents a severe limitation on the disposition of your wealth and a major incentive for effective tax planning during your lifetime in order to eliminate the impact of those taxes.

MORE DETAIL IN CHAPTER 14

Chapter 14 presents more detail on the American wealth transfer tax system and contains approaches to reducing wealth transfer taxes. However, to achieve the reduction of those taxes you should promptly seek the advice of a competent tax practitioner.

CHOICE OF FIDUCIARIES

The People Who Will Handle Your Affairs After You Die

EXECUTORS, PERSONAL REPRESENTATIVES AND ADMINISTRATORS

Any person or institution you name to administer your estate is called an executor or, in some states, a personal representative. The executor literally "executes" the terms of your Will. If you have no Will, or the person you name as executor does not serve, the person who administers your estate is usually called an administrator. As a practical matter, the duties and obligations of an executor, personal representative or administrator are identical and will be referred to interchangeably in this Chapter.

Upon qualifying in court, your personal representative acts to take title to all of your property, pay your creditors and death taxes and ultimately distribute the property to those who are entitled to receive it.

Your personal representative generally becomes the legal owner of your assets and can decide unilaterally which assets to sell, trade or hold. In addition, a personal representative may be able to decide which assets are given to which beneficiaries. (For example, if you have left half of your assets to your son and the other half to your daughter, the executor may be able to decide which assets each receives.) Failure by your executor to carry out the duties of office carefully can result in significant penalties against your estate. For example, your executor will be charged with filing your estate tax return. Almost always, severe penalties will be imposed if the return is not filed on time. For example, if the return is filed one day late, your estate almost certainly will have to pay a fine equal to 5% of the tax due even if the taxes are paid on time.

Your personal representative may also be personally liable for your debts, pre-death income taxes and estate taxes if they are not paid in full when due. In addition, if your executor fails to administer and invest your assets prudently (something about which reasonable persons can disagree), your executor may be personally liable for any loss or damage which your estate suffers. Your personal representative also may be liable if assets belonging to you are not discovered and collected and your estate loses the ability to obtain them (as sometimes happens). Thus, your executor could be subject to a high degree of personal liability.

For owners of closely held businesses, the choice of an executor is an especially important one. The executor usually will become the legal owner of your business interests and, therefore, able to decide whether to continue the business, sell it, merge it, change lines of business, fire and hire personnel and take all of the other steps which you during your lifetime could take with respect to the disposition and operation of the business. The choice of an executor is often the most critical one in an estate plan; it is even more essential to choose the right personal representative for the estate of the owner of a closely held business.

In any event, in almost all circumstances you can choose whoever you wish to serve as your executor. That choice is one of the most important legal privileges you have. Generally, the only restriction is that you choose a competent adult (and, in some states, someone who is a U.S. citizen). You can usually choose more than one person or institution to serve. Chapter 13 contains more detail about executors and other fiduciaries.

TRUSTEES

Any trust which you create will be administered by one or more trustees. Usually, a trustee will receive assets directly at your death (as when you name the trust or trustee as the recipient of proceeds of insurance on your life) or will receive them upon distribution from the personal representative of your estate during or at the end of the administration of your estate. The trustee becomes the legal owner of the assets received, although they must be held for the exclusive benefit of the beneficiaries of the trust. As the owner, the trustee can decide which assets to sell, trade, buy or hold. If assets in your business are transferred to a trustee, as a general matter the trustee will be in the same position that you were in to control the disposition of the business and to operate it. In many ways, the powers of the trustee are more extensive than those of your personal representative. First, the administration of a decedent's estate is generally much more limited in time than the administration of a trust. Second, an executor usually has limited flexibility in deciding how much a particular beneficiary will receive or when the beneficiary will receive assets. It is common, and with good reason, for a trustee to hold significant power to decide which of a group of beneficiaries will receive property and when it will be received. Again, you can usually choose whomever you wish to serve as trustee, subject to very few restrictions. In some circumstances, the restrictions will be more severe if the trust is created under your Will than if it is created by a written agreement during your lifetime (such as a revocable living trust which acts as a substitute for your Will).

GUARDIANS

As is discussed in more detail in Chapter 13, as a general matter, you may select the guardian or guardians of the person and property of any minor child of yours if the child's other parent does not survive you. The selection of guardians for your children may be one of the most important functions served by your Will. In most states, by executing a Will you can specify who that person should be and your wishes will be respected.

If you fail to designate a guardian effectively, the court will have latitude in deciding who the guardian should be. Usually, a relative is chosen as the guardian of the person (with whom the child probably will reside). However, if extensive property is involved, the court may decide that someone other than a family member should be guardian of the property. If you want to enhance significantly the possibility that the best person will be guardian, you need to name that person in your Will.

ATTORNEYS AND OTHER PROFESSIONALS

As a general matter, you will not be able to require your executor, trustee or guardian to employ a particular attorney or other professional, such as an accountant, to assist in the administration of your estate. You may strongly suggest that a particular person be retained for such purpose although many attorneys regard it as "bad form" for an attorney to prepare a document in which the attorney (or the attorney's law firm) is recommended to be hired. As a practical matter, you can achieve that result by naming a corporate fiduciary (such as a bank or trust company) or naming the professional as the fiduciary. Almost all banks in the United States follow a policy of hiring the attorney who prepared the Will to represent that institution in its capacity as a fiduciary under the Will. If you name the professional as the fiduciary, the professional can generally choose himself or herself (or his or her firm) to perform professional services. For instance, if you name your accountant as the executor under your Will the accountant will generally be able to hire his or her own accounting firm to perform accounting services for the estate.

How Those Fiduciaries are Chosen

As indicated, you can specify in your Will whom you wish to serve as executor, trustee or guardian. You should be aware, however, that even if only a very small amount of property passes under your Will (because, for example, you have used a revocable living trust as a Will substitute), the powers and duties of your executor (or administrator if you have no Will) will probably be very extensive. For example, under the tax laws it is your executor or administrator who is personally liable to see that your estate tax return is filed and all estate taxes paid, even with respect to property not under the control of the executor or administrator. The executor or administrator also is singularly empowered to make certain far-reaching elections under the federal and state tax laws and other state laws. As a consequence, no matter what other planning you have done, you should execute a Will and name as personal representative the person or persons or institution you believe are best qualified to carry out the important duties of an executor. (More information about making this decision is set forth in Chapter 13.)

If you fail to make a Will, or if the person or institution named in your Will fails to serve, the court having jurisdiction of your probate estate (the part of your estate that you could have disposed of by Will) will choose the person to administer it. State law will provide a suggested order or priority for persons to be chosen, usually starting with the surviving spouse (if any). However, the courts will not be required to follow that suggested order in all cases. In fact, some courts, in effect, appoint individuals or institutions the court favors. The court's choice may not be the choice you would make or the choice that will turn out to be best for your family or business.

As indicated, you can specify the individuals or institutions to serve as trustees of trusts created under your Will, including any trusts that you create by exercising a power of appointment under your Will. If you fail to name a trustee, the court will appoint one for the trust. The courts usually have much greater latitude in selecting a trustee than in appointing an administrator. The person or institution which the court chooses may not be what your family wishes or what ultimately turns out to be in your family's best interests. You can assure that the best choice is made only by having an effective designation in your Will or other controlling instrument.

How Fiduciaries are Compensated

Usually, state law will provide specific rules, or at least guidance, as to how fiduciaries are to be compensated. In some states, fiduciaries may receive compensation computed as a percentage of the property which they administer. In other states, they receive "reasonable compensation." In those states the court will determine reasonable compensation if requested, although in most cases the fiduciary usually fixes the compensation unless a beneficiary objects to the amount of that compensation. Attorneys and other professionals are usually compensated in a similar way.

Subject to certain limitations, you can specify the method by which your fiduciaries will be compensated. If your estate is an extremely large one, and your property will be administered under the laws of a state providing fixed compensation, the level of compensation determined under state law may be unreasonably high. In New York, for example, generally speaking each executor (up to a maximum of three) of a large estate is entitled to 2% of the estate. Two percent of an extremely large estate (especially if there are multiple executors) probably is an unreasonably large amount. Generally, you can specify what the fiduciary's compensation will be under the Will or other instrument. More detail about that is contained in Chapter 13. However, if you fail to so specify, or you die without a Will, statutory rates probably will apply. If you have a large base of wealth, you may be able to save your survivors considerable amounts if you impose a reasonable limit on the amount which your fiduciaries are paid.

Bonds and Other Costs of Serving

In many jurisdictions, all fiduciaries must post a bond to secure their performance. Generally, the bond can be waived (and the cost of it therefore saved) only if the bond requirement is expressly waived in the Will or other governing instrument. In some cases, avoiding the cost of the bond will in itself pay for the preparation of the Will. In addition, some states require that fiduciaries render a written report of all transactions undertaken for the estate or trust (called an accounting) at certain fixed intervals, such as every year. Usually, the cost of preparing the account is borne by the estate or trust. Because an accounting involves a legal proceeding, the expense of attorneys fees is almost always necessary. Generally, your Will may waive the requirement of periodic accountings, and that will mean significant savings to the estate or trust. A valid Will containing such waiver provisions is usually required to effect those savings.

How Fiduciaries are Controlled

POWERS TO ACT

State law (and to some degree federal law) will arm your fiduciaries with certain powers. Usually, those powers include the right to safeguard and invest assets. A fiduciary's powers do not always include other common commercial powers such as the power to borrow or to operate a business. However, subject to very few restrictions, you can grant extensive commercial powers to fiduciaries who act under your Will. It usually is critically important, as an owner of a closely held business, that your Will (and other estate planning documents) expressly authorize the fiduciaries to have such additional extensive powers. For example, you may decide that the personal representative of your estate should also become the chairman of the board of your company. In some states, it will be questionable whether the executor can serve in that capacity unless expressly authorized in your Will.

COURT PERMISSION AND INTERFERENCE

In some jurisdictions, the fiduciary will need the permission of the court to take certain actions. In addition, the court can interfere with or block certain actions which the fiduciary proposes to take and which usually may be taken without express court authorization. To some degree, by provisions in your Will you can limit the necessity of receiving the court's permission and interference with the administration of your estate.

WHERE TO SAFEGUARD YOUR WILL

Lost Wills

Rules relating to the execution of a Will are much more strict than those relating to the disposition of other property, such as the execution of the form by which proceeds of insurance on your life are paid. Usually, in addition to being competent, you must sign your Will at its end, have it witnessed by two persons who are adult and competent (and not beneficiaries under the instrument), and declare the instrument to be your Will (although you do not have to disclose anything about its contents). Even if you have complied with all of the formalities for execution of the Will, there is a presumption that the Will was revoked if the original is lost. No matter how careful a person you believe yourself to be, there is some probability that the original Will (as opposed to a photocopy) will not be able to be found after your death. Moreover, if the Will is executed in more than one original counterpart, the failure to be able to produce *all* executed counterparts will result in a presumption that you revoked the Will and it may be denied admission to probate. In either case, legal fees probably will be extensive. A word to the wise is *never* to execute more than one original of your Will. If your attorney insists otherwise, you should check that advice with another attorney, experienced in estate matters, before you do so. In any case, if the original of your Will or all original counterparts cannot be produced when you die, your estate probably will face litigation and attendant expenses.

Major Choices

NOT AT HOME

Although you may be inclined to take the original of your Will with you after it has been executed, taking it to your home probably is not a good idea. If you were to die in a fire at home your Will could be destroyed at the same time. In addition, there is a chance that someone—spouse, child, maid or even you might inadvertently throw your original Will away. Keeping your Will at home is not a wise choice.

Recently, a client of mine became comatose. She had insisted on keeping the original Will with her, and her brother and I had a most difficult time finding the original instrument. I was very worried that she would remain comatose and not be able to execute another Will. Her brother finally found the Will stuffed in the back of a drawer together with newspaper clippings and other unimportant papers.

SAFE DEPOSIT BOXES

Documents are sometimes held in a safe deposit box for safekeeping. In some states, however, there are restrictions on access to the safe deposit box of a deceased owner. If you want to control, more or less directly, where your Will is located, your safe deposit box may be a viable choice. If, however, the law of your state restricts access to the box after your death, a special proceeding will have to be commenced in court. This will cost money and will delay the admission of your Will to probate and, therefore, delay the administration of your estate. In any case, make sure that someone (such as the person whom you have named as the Will's executor) knows that the Will is contained in a safe deposit box. Of course, make sure that the key to the box also can be found.

Another choice is to have your nominated executor or a trusted family member hold the Will in his or her own safe deposit box. In fact, many banks and trust companies will retain the original of your Will in their own vault without charge to you if you have named that institution as the executor.

You may feel uncomfortable allowing the bank or trust company to retain the original because, if you decide to remove the bank or trust company as the nominated fiduciary, you might be hesitant to ask for the Will back (as the institution is sure to ask why). Usually, you will not have to ask for the Will because you will be executing a new Will and the fact that the bank retains the old one will be of no consequence.

ATTORNEY SAFEKEEPING

Many attorneys will retain the original of your Will in the firm's safe deposit box (typically called its Will vault) without charge. As with a Will retained by a bank or trust company, you may not have to face the embarrassment of asking for the instrument back. If you want the instrument back, it is probably because you intend to execute a new Will. You can execute the new Will without having possession of the original of the current Will. Once the new Will is executed, possession of the old Will may not be significant.

In a few cases, however, retrieving the original Will can be important. First, you may change the disposition of your property in such a way that you would not want the contents of your prior Will ever to come to light. In other words, you may want the prior Will (and all copies) to be destroyed. You can instruct the person (such as a bank or your attorney) to destroy it for you. Usually, the institution or attorney will not do that but rather return the original to you so that you can destroy it yourself. Whether it is necessary or appropriate to destroy the original (and copies) of a prior Will depends upon the circumstances. In some jurisdictions, people in possession of a Will may be compelled to file it in court making it a matter of public record. You should discuss these matters with your attorney at the time you sign your Will. In most cases, however, your attorney will not be compelled to deliver the prior Will to anyone, although if there is a Will contest, the attorney may be required to deliver it upon demand in court proceedings.

In any case, you should retain a photocopy of the original Will. In fact, it is probably better to retain a photocopy than a "conformed" copy in which the names of the person who signed the Will and the witnesses are typed in. As stated earlier, in some circumstances, a Will can be admitted to probate even if the original document is lost. However, as a practical matter, that will be much easier to do if you have an exact photocopy including showing signatures. For one thing, the witnesses will be able to verify their signatures.

SUMMARY

The decision as to how best to safeguard your original Will is rather complex. If you have named a bank or trust company as the executor or personal representative, an appropriate choice will probably be to leave the original in the safekeeping of that institution and add a notation to that effect on copies retained by you and your attorney. Placing the original in your attorney's Will vault may also be an appropriate choice, if you are relatively confident that you will not want to retrieve the original from your attorney (as you might if you changed attorneys) or if you can retrieve the original from your attorney without feeling uncomfortable.(You may be able to do the latter simply by writing a letter instructing your attorney to send it to you.)

PROBLEMS TO AVOID IN MAKING A WILL

Do Not Use Family Witnesses

The rules relating to the formalities for execution of a Will (such as requiring, in virtually all circumstances, that the Will be witnessed, that all parts of the Will be in writing and that it be signed at the end) are among the strictest of all legal rules. Usually your designation of a beneficiary on a life insurance policy does not have to be witnessed (even though the policy may represent a significantly greater amount of wealth than the amount that you dispose of by Will).

One common error is to have family members or other beneficiaries of your Will act as witnesses. Although having a beneficiary witness a Will does not necessarily, in all states, invalidate the Will, it will make the admission of the instrument to probate much more complex and costly. It may also increase the probability of a Will contest and require that the beneficiaries who acted as witnesses forfeit their bequests.

Do Not Write It Yourself

No matter how tempted you may be to write out your own Will by hand, type it yourself or use a form provided by a commercial company, do not try to prepare your Will yourself. Ben Franklin reputedly said, "The lawyer's best client is the man who writes his own Will." What Ben meant, of course, is that a lay person is so likely to make egregious errors that lawyers will get rich in straightening things out afterward.

The amount which your attorney will charge you for preparing your Will depends upon many factors. The charge may vary from a few hundred to tens of thousands of dollars, depending upon the circumstances. Having a lawyer prepare your Will is probably one of the best investments in lawyer's time you can make. Of course, your Will will have no real effect upon you during your lifetime; it will only affect your family and other beneficiaries after you die. You may not want to spend *your* money to benefit others after your death. If that is your attitude, perhaps you do not want a Will at all. But if you do want to make a decision regarding the proper disposition of your own property, you must execute a Will and you should have it prepared by an experienced attorney.

Never Execute More Than One Copy

As stated above, your Will will not be invalid because you execute multiple originals, but you are asking for trouble if you do so. The big winners will be the attorneys who will have to convince the court that the instrument should be admitted to probate even though all of the originals cannot be found. There could even be a contest after your death (resulting in greater legal costs) as to whether the Will should be admitted under any circumstances. Keep in mind that those who would take under prior Wills and those who would take if there were no Will may argue that the instrument offered for probate as your Will is not valid.

If you have already executed a Will in more than one original copy, go back to your lawyer, have a new instrument prepared, sign only one original and have it kept safe in the manner suggested above.

Never Make Changes to the Original Signed Copy

If you keep the original of your Will (something you probably should not do), and you want to make changes to it, do not write on the original instrument. Even though Wills have been around for centuries, the law as to when a writing on a Will will invalidate it is not as clearly developed as one might assume. The handwritten changes almost never will be regarded as valid but they may result in the invalidity of the underlying instrument. The one thing you can be certain of, if you do make changes on the original instrument, is that your estate will incur significant legal costs after your death.

WILL CONTESTS AND HOW TO AVOID THEM

Why Will Contests Happen

Wills and certain other instruments which effect the transfer of property at death (such as designation forms for the proceeds of life insurance policies or pension plans) often have their validity challenged in court. If the instrument is a Will, the lawsuit is known as a "Will contest." Basically, the validity of a Will can be attacked on one or more of three grounds: the incapacity (incompetency) of the person who signed it; failure to conform strictly to the formalities of execution of the instrument (such as having the appropriate number of witnesses); and fraud or "undue influence" practiced on the person signing the Will.

The motive for mounting a Will contest is usually to obtain more property under a prior Will or the intestacy laws (which specify how your property is disposed of if you have no valid Will). For example, you have bequeathed to your spouse the minimum share of your estate to which he or she is entitled. However, under the intestacy laws (or a prior Will executed by you), your spouse would be entitled to more property. Your spouse will have an economic motivation to attack your last Will and seek to have the more advantageous disposition take effect.

One circumstance, perhaps more than any other, which is likely to cause a Will contest is that in which the decedent has treated one child differently from another under a Will or has significantly disinherited one or more children. For example, for reasons good and sufficient to you, you leave all of your estate to one of your children to the exclusion of the others. Obviously, your other children fare better under the intestacy laws. There may be a high probability of a Will contest under those circumstances.

Although Will contests are commonly believed to be motivated by simple greed, the motivation is quite often hurt feelings or frustrated expectations on the part of those who are disinherited or who would receive less than others.

I was once called in to assist in the settlement of a dispute in which a son had commenced a Will contest against his father's Will. The father had left about 75% of his estate to his daughter, who lived in dire poverty, whose husband was dying of cancer and whose children barely had enough to eat, and only about 25% to his son, who was a very wealthy bachelor physician. The son did not even need the additional 25% which he would receive if the Will contest were totally successful. But the son had convinced himself that his father could not have intended to discriminate against him because he viewed any discrimination as a lack of love and respect. This was the case even though the father recited in his Will that he was leaving more to his daughter than to his son because the son was in a stronger financial position than his daughter and he was confident that his son's abilities would allow his son to maintain and improve his financial position.

As Tough as It Is, Tell Your Family Your Plans

Individuals who decide to discriminate among their children or who significantly disinherit them, risk harming relationships among their children or between their children and the beneficiaries of the Will. For example, even though the case just mentioned was settled, the son has refused ever to contact his sister or her children again and has reputedly disinherited them (although under his prior Wills he had left his estate to them). The sister did not know of the father's plan, but the brother has vented his anger and hurt feelings against her and her family. Whatever your reasons for discriminating among your children or disinheriting them, you are almost certainly guaranteeing a similar fate for your surviving family members. For example, if you have children by a previous marriage and leave a significant portion of your estate to your spouse, it is almost certain that the relationship between your children and your surviving spouse will be impaired after your death.

Moreover, you are almost certain to ensure that additional legal costs will be incurred by your estate and the surviving family members as charges and counter charges are made after your death. Lawyers will be the big winners. In fact, in some cases involving post-death lawsuits among family members, lawyers have received a larger portion of the estate than any family member.

In almost all circumstances, if you plan to discriminate by your Will against your children or anyone else who would be a natural object of your bounty it is preferable to explain your testamentary plans to them during your lifetime. That will provide an opportunity during your lifetime for them to try to persuade you to do otherwise. If you are worried about hurting your relationship with those persons, think about how their relationships with other family members might be hurt when you die. In many circumstances, I recommend to parents who are disinheriting or discriminating against a child to send or have me send to the child a copy of the Will, giving the child plenty of opportunity to lobby for a change. In addition, the child usually comes to accept the fact that it is the parent's wish that the child receive less or be disinherited entirely. Because the underlying motivation for bringing the Will contest often is a belief that the parent could not have intended it, the fact that the parent has advised the child of the discrimination or disinheritance during lifetime forces the child more readily to accept it, thereby defusing the probability of a Will contest.

Where Legal, Use an In Terrorem Clause

EXPLANATION OF IN TERROREM CLAUSES

In many states, you may include an in terrorem clause in your Will. An in terrorem clause is one which is expected so to "terrify" a possible Will contestant that he or she will not contest. It is very simple in design: You make a modest bequest to the possible contestant and then provide that if the contestant (and sometimes others) contest the Will, or threaten to contest it, the bequest is revoked in its entirety. An in terrorem clause can be very effective in jurisdictions where it is legal. There are several states where it is not legal.

The exact design of an in terrorem clause depends upon the circumstances. It does not involve simply leaving the proverbial "one dollar" to a child to show that you did not forget the child, but involves providing a significant bequest to the possible contestant, so that the forfeiture would be expensive. For example, you have a son and a daughter and you want to leave virtually all of your estate to your daughter.

Because you have no spouse, each of your children would receive one half of your estate if you had no Will. Whether or not you advise your son that he will be receiving less than his sister, you anticipate that your son would contest your Will (and there is nothing you can do to prevent him from mounting the attack as he will have legal standing to do so). What you might do would be to provide for your son to receive a percentage of your estate (such as 15%) or a fixed amount of money (such as $100,000), taking into account the amount which will be disposed of under your Will. You would then provide that if your son threatens or commences a Will contest (or joins with others to do so, or if such a suit is commenced by his descendants), his bequest is forfeited and will pass as though he died, without any descendants, before you did.

How to Use them Anywhere

In terrorem clauses can be extremely effective in preventing Will contests. However, such clauses are not legal in all states. Some jurisdictions regard them as invalid as being against public policy. The theory is that it is best to allow adversaries to argue about matters in court so that the court can discern the truth and deny probate when there are valid grounds for denial of probate.

For example, you become ill and are living with your daughter who takes care of you. You become very dependent upon her. She hires a lawyer, has a new Will prepared for you in which you leave virtually all of your estate to her and almost none to your son. You do not really want to do this but your daughter influences you unduly (by threats not to take care of you, for example) to sign the instrument. Alternatively, you may have become incompetent (because of the administration of medicines) so that you do not even know what you are signing. (Yes, it is unfortunate, but true, that there are lawyers who get involved in such matters.) Your daughter's lawyer is smart enough to have an in terrorem provision placed into the instrument you sign as your Will. Because the son will forfeit the bequest provided for him under that instrument if he contests it, the son will be deterred from contesting it unless he is absolutely certain of success. Very few Will contests are successful and the son's attorney may advise him after your death that the prudent thing to do is to accept the modest bequest and not run the risk of forfeiting it by contesting the instrument.

If you reside in a state where in terrorem clauses are not valid, there are methods to use them effectively without moving to another state. One method may be to direct that your Will be admitted to original probate in a state where in terrorem clauses are valid. That probably will be effective to validate the in terrorem clause. Alternatively, you can create a revocable living trust which acts as a Will substitute and include an in terrorem clause, but create it under the laws of a state where in terrorem clauses are valid. If you transfer substantially all of your assets to the revocable living trust before your death, most of your wealth which would have passed under the Will will now pass under the revocable living trust. This may effectively remove the incentive to bring a contest against the Will because the Will does not control the bulk of your estate. If the bulk of your estate is in the revocable living trust, any challenge to the trust will trigger the in terrorem provision and result in a forfeiture of the modest benefits provided for the contestant under the trust instrument.

ALTERNATIVES TO WILLS

As discussed in detail earlier in this Chapter, assets may pass at your death pursuant to legal arrangements other than your Will. The advantages and disadvantages of those alternative forms of disposition are also discussed above. If you do not wish to have property pass under your Will, you have two primary alternatives: the transfer of assets into a joint tenancy of assets with rights of survivorship and the transfer of assets in trust prior to your death. As explained above, placing property in joint name with rights of survivorship may not be a wise choice in many circumstances. First, in many jurisdictions you are likely to be deemed to have made a gift at the time that you create the joint tenancy. Second, in most jurisdictions, you cannot revoke the transfer of the one-half interest, although you may be able to terminate the right of survivorship to your retained one-half interest unless the joint tenancy is a tenancy by the entirety created between you and your spouse.

Revocable trusts are probably the most effective alternative to Wills. In one form or another, revocable living trusts are a valid method of transferring your assets at death, provided you have effectively transferred ownership of the assets to the trust prior to your death. The trust may even provide that it is revocable only with the consent of an independent third party, such as an attorney, accountant or bank which acts as trustee or as co-trustee with you during your lifetime. It is not a good idea to provide that the trust can only be revoked with the consent of one or more of your children. If a child whose consent is required to revoke or change the trust is entitled to benefits under the instrument when you die, you probably will have been deemed to have made a taxable gift at the time you set up the trust, because the child's interest in allowing you to revoke or amend the trust is regarded as "adverse." Revocable living trusts are discussed in more detail in Chapter 11.

POWERS OF ATTORNEY

Explanation

As a general matter, you can delegate certain of your legal rights and powers to an agent. This delegation can be accomplished in many ways. The most common is execution of a document known as a "power of attorney." By a power of attorney you name another person as your "attorney-in-fact" to act as your agent. Typically, that person is authorized to engage in some, or all, transactions which you could engage in yourself. This includes, for example, the ability to use your money to buy assets, or to sell assets which you own. In many circumstances, the attorney-in-fact's power will be limited to certain discrete matters, such as selling or buying a specifically identified piece of property. (In California, for example, most house closings are done pursuant to powers of attorney which are granted to the broker who has represented you in the sale or acquisition of the home.)

Why You Should Have a Power of Attorney

ABSENCE

If you own significant property, there may come a time when action should be taken to safeguard it, but there will be no one with the legal authority to do so. For example, you are on a business trip, and a political or military uprising occurs which prevents you from leaving the country or communicating with the outside world. Events at home may arise which require certain action to be taken with respect to your property (such as the voting of shares of stock in your business). More realistically, perhaps, is the case where you are on an extended vacation and cannot be contacted, but circumstances arise which suggest it would be prudent for certain legal action with respect to your property to be taken. If no one has been authorized to take such legal action, it cannot occur.

If you have executed a power of attorney, the attorney-in-fact can take action on your behalf even in your absence.

DISABILITY

Virtually all of us become disabled at one time or another during our lifetime. While undergoing an operation, you are disabled. If you suffer from an illness, such as Alzheimer's disease, you may become legally incompetent, temporarily or permanently. You may suffer a disabling heart attack or stroke. For many reasons, it may be appropriate for action to be taken with respect to your property while you are legally disabled from doing so. There are procedures which can be implemented by the courts to effectuate legal actions when you are incompetent. However, those procedures are usually time-consuming and very expensive. In addition, to go forward, those procedures usually require proof that you are incompetent. Presenting that proof may be inappropriate or distasteful. Yet, if there is no other mechanism (such as a power of attorney) in effect, your family or colleagues may have little choice but to undertake those procedures.

At one time, a power of attorney was automatically revoked when the grantor of the power became disabled. Now, in all American jurisdictions, the power of attorney can be made "durable," so that it will survive incompetency.

Selecting Your Attorney-In-Fact

An attorney-in-fact does not have to be an attorney-at-law. Generally, any competent adult can be an attorney-in-fact. In addition, you can name more than one person as the attorney-in-fact. You can provide that your attorneys-in-fact must act together, by majority or severally (that is, separately). In addition, you can specify that certain of your attorneys-in-fact can take certain actions, while others cannot. For example, you should not give a family member the power to make gifts to family members, for tax and other reasons discussed later.

It often is best to appoint one trusted family member and one third party as attorneys-in-fact. You might, for example, name the person appointed as the executor of your Will (if that person is not a close family member) to be the "independent" attorney-in-fact. That person could make gifts to members of your family or expend funds on their behalf. You should also consider appointing a trusted family member and providing, as long as he or she is available, that only he or she can take action with respect to the commercial disposition of your property, such as its sale. Usually, however, most people provide for both the family and the independent attorney-in-fact to be able to make decisions with respect to the sale or purchase of property and for the independent attorney-in-fact alone to make gifts or other transfers to family members.

If you give a family member the power to pay money or property to himself or herself, the IRS almost certainly will take the position (although not necessarily successfully) that the person has the power to take all the property, and you have made a gift of all your assets to that person. Although the IRS might not be wholly successful with that argument, do not take the risk. Provide for an independent attorney-in-fact to make the gifts.

While a standard form of power of attorney will not include the power to make gifts, the ability to make gifts to family members may be exceptionally important in the event that you become disabled. First, it will permit funds to be expended to maintain your family (such as providing support and maintenance for your spouse) without the necessity of going to court for authorization of such expenditures. In addition, gifts made immediately prior to your death (a time when it is more probable that you will be legally disabled) can be exceptionally effective from an estate planning perspective. If you have not expressly authorized your attorney-in-fact to make such gifts (or provided an alternative methods for doing so), you may not be able to obtain the estate planning benefits of making such gifts. Again, it may be possible to go to court to obtain authorization for such gifts to be made, but the costs of doing so are likely to be high and the procedures in almost all states are complex, time-consuming and a matter of public record.

Safeguards Against Abuse of Powers of Attorney

In General

In the movie *Rocky V*, Rocky loses all of his money because while training for his fight in the Soviet Union, his accountant, pursuant to the power-of-attorney Rocky granted to him, used the power of attorney to transfer Rocky's assets to himself. Believe it or not, that can happen. In the real world, however, people are not prone to act immediately when presented with a power of attorney, especially when the transaction is significant. In New York, for example, it used to be so difficult to get banks and other financial institutions to accept the validity of a power of attorney that a law was passed making it unlawful for such institutions to refuse to honor a power of attorney. The law also provides for indemnification of an institution if it honors a power of attorney, even if it turns out to have been revoked. The law has no teeth, however, because there is no penalty if the institution fails to honor the power of attorney.

Despite such laws, people who are presented with a power of attorney typically ask for proof that the principal (that is, the person who signed the power) has not revoked the power and that the person is still alive. Unless the power is durable, expressly providing that it survives the legal incompetency of the individual, the third party will probably ask for further proof that the principal is not legally incompetent.

The hesitation of third parties to deal with an attorney-in-fact provides a practical safeguard against the abuse of the power. Nonetheless, abuses can occur. As a consequence, you should be exceptionally careful granting a power of attorney. For example, if you do not name your lawyer as attorney-in-fact, you might ask him or her to retain the power of attorney and not disclose its existence until a specific reason to use it occurs. For example, you might instruct your lawyer to hold the power of attorney until he or she learns that you have become legally disabled, and then to deliver the power to the persons named as attorneys-in-fact.

Another excellent safeguard is to require joint action and to name multiple attorneys-in-fact. For example, if you name your accountant (as Rocky did) and your child and require that they must act jointly, your accountant cannot act alone. Furthermore, naming a bank or trust company as attorney-in-fact can be an excellent safeguard in states where you are permitted to do so. Even if the bank officer improperly or unlawfully uses the power of attorney, it is highly likely that the bank will be required to "make good" on any losses which your property sustains and most banks carry insurance which further enhances the probability that you will be made whole for any abuse of the power.

"Springing" Powers of Attorney

In many states, you can execute what is called a "springing" power of attorney. The power has no effect until a certain event occurs, at which time the powers "springs" into life.

Typically, the event that causes the power to become effective is the principal's incompetency. One potential problem, however, is that you may have to go to court to prove incompetency. In some states, a judicial proceeding is not required and the power can then provide that it becomes effective upon certification by your physician (who probably should be expressly named) that your ability to manage your financial affairs has become substantially impaired.

Alternatives to Powers of Attorney

As mentioned above, one problem with a power of attorney is the fact that many third parties will refuse to accept them. The typical "poor person's" power of attorney is a joint bank account, which may be used, for example, to help a parent who becomes unable to manage his or her own financial affairs. As explained above, creating a joint account with your child has its own ramifications, some of which can be adverse unless you are in a state which provides for a "convenience only" account and you carefully designate it as such. This will permit you, for example, to sign checks and make deposits to the account for your parent. Other assets can also be placed in joint name and, as a practical matter, provide you with a method of dealing with such assets. However, as explained in more detail above, placing property in joint name may produce adverse results overall.

Another method is to transfer assets to a revocable living trust and to provide for a third party (that is, a person other than the one who signed the trust) to be the trustee. Virtually all commercial institutions will deal with a trustee more readily than an attorney-in-fact. Nonetheless, even if an attempt is made to transfer all of the person's assets to a revocable trust, a power of attorney is still a good idea.

LIVING WILLS AND HEALTH CARE PROXIES

Background

Under general principles of American law, each of us can direct what medical care we do or do not wish to receive. Unfortunately, however, individuals who need medical care are often incapacitated and cannot make their wishes known. If you are in an automobile accident and are unconscious, you cannot tell the physician whether you want your leg removed to enhance the probability of your surviving. Similarly, during a final illness, decisions as whether or not to take heroic measures to sustain your life briefly, even though the probability of your recovering or your regaining consciousness is remote, cannot be made by you because you are not able to express your wishes.

The law gives effect to documents by which you make your wishes known or name another person to make binding decisions for you if you are not able to do so. These documents are known, respectively, as "Living Wills" and "Health Care Proxies." Health Care Proxies are known by other names, such as Medical Powers of Attorney, in some states.

The publicity given to Karen Ann Quinlan and to *Cruzan* v. *Harmon* shows the importance of using a Living Will to express your wishes as to prolonging your life by means of medical technology. The moral question is whether you will determine the nature and extent of your medical treatment or leave that determination to be made by the courts. Even if you would wish to expend all of your financial resources to keep you alive artificially, you should make your wishes known to ensure that they will be carried out.

Contents of a Living Will

DESCRIPTION

Usually, by your Living Will you specify whether you wish life-sustaining procedures to be used when the probability of your recovering is remote—for example, when you are "brain dead." Perhaps nine out of ten individuals who sign a Living Will state that they wish to have the "plug pulled" at the point when they are brain dead. Others, however, wish their lives to be sustained. Whatever your wishes, you should make them known by executing a valid Living Will. The United States Supreme Court has upheld the validity of Living Wills but requires, in effect, that they be in writing. Your attorney should know the form which is best for you. Usually, a Living Will validly executed in one jurisdiction will be respected in another.

WITNESSES

Different states prescribe different formalities for executing a Living Will. In some states, you have a choice of having your Living Will witnessed or notarized.

Often Living Will forms will be provided by a health care provider, such as your doctor or hospital. In the event that the instrument must have witnesses, it is a good idea not to have family members act as witnesses.

COPIES, NOTICE AND STORAGE

Although you should never execute your Will in more than one original, it is perfectly fine to execute multiple copies of a Living Will. In fact, execution of multiple copies is a good idea because it permits you to deliver an original to several persons or institutions to make sure an original is on file. You probably should keep an original yourself, allow your spouse or child to safeguard one, and send one to each of your primary physicians. It may also be appropriate to have a copy filed with the hospital in your community. It is also a good idea to give an original to your attorney for safekeeping.

Contents of Health Care Proxy

DESCRIPTION

By a Health Care Proxy, you designate an individual to decide what medical procedures should or should not be undertaken for you when you are unable to make that decision. Typically the Health Care Proxy is used not to "pull the plug" but to give that individual the authority to make decisions on your behalf with regard to specific medical procedures, such as transfusions, amputation or other surgical procedures.

CHOICE OF HEALTH CARE AGENT

In most states, you can name only one individual (and not an institution) as your agent by a Health Care Proxy. However, you can name successors or alternates in the event that the first person named cannot act or cannot be found. Most individuals name their spouse or child as the primary health care agent. A close relative is usually in a better position to make medical decisions than your attorney or accountant. Generally, however, you can name anyone you wish, although in some states you cannot name your physician or a health care provider such as a hospital.

DURATION OF HEALTH CARE PROXIES

State law determines how long a Health Care Proxy remains in effect. You should ensure that your Health Care Proxy is re-executed if required under the law of the state where you reside or spend considerable time (such as a state where your summer home is located).

WITNESSES

If witnesses are required, the rules governing the witnessing of a Health Care Proxy are similar to those governing the witnessing of a Living Will. Your attorney will be able to advise you as to proper procedures.

COPIES, NOTICE AND STORAGE

As with a Living Will it is usually best for you to execute several copies of a Health Care Proxy. One copy should be delivered to the primary and secondary Health Care agents named, as well as to your physician. You should keep a copy, as should your spouse (even if your spouse is not named as the agent) and a copy should be kept by your lawyer.

HOW OFTEN SHOULD I REVIEW MY WILL?

At Least Every Two Years

As a general rule, you should review your Will in consultation with your attorney at least every two years. Changes in the law are often subtle, but important in cumulative effect. By reconsidering the disposition of your property every two years, you can ensure that your Will reflects your wishes and the interests of those who survive you. Periodic review with your attorney will help to ensure that your Will takes advantage of changes in the laws from time to time.

Whenever a Major Financial, Health or Family Event Occurs

In addition, you should review your Will, with your attorney, whenever a major financial, health or family event in your life occurs. The sale of your business or your retirement would be financial events which would warrant a call to your attorney. Similarly, the receipt of a significant inheritance by you or your spouse should prompt you to call your attorney about your own Will.

If your health, or the health of a major beneficiary of your estate plan should change significantly, you should also call your attorney about your Will. For example, if your spouse develops a terminal illness, you and your spouse should contact your attorney about your Wills to see if changes are appropriate.

You should also call your attorney whenever there is a major change in family relationships or events. This would certainly include your own divorce, but would also include the divorce of a child or grandchild, your child's or grandchild's marriage or the birth of a child or grandchild.

In other words, whenever something happens to you or your family which could have a financial impact, you should call your attorney and discuss whether it would be advisable to revise your Will.

SUMMARY AND CONCLUSIONS

Your Will is often the centerpiece of your estate plan. Although several types of assets will pass at your death other than by your Will, you should ensure that you have an up-to-date Will. Your Will should dispose of your assets in the manner that will best effect your desired estate plan, naming those individuals or institutions that you want to carry out the administration of your estate and any trusts which your Will creates and granting those fiduciaries appropriate powers to assist them in carrying out their responsibilities.

Generally, you have broad flexibility in disposing of your assets pursuant to your Will, although your spouse and others may have rights that will limit disposition. Although Will contests occur somewhat infrequently, and rarely are entirely successful, you may anticipate a contest whenever you discriminate among the natural objects of your bounty or disinherit them totally or substantially. To avoid the erosion of your wealth by attorneys' fees in such a case, and to avoid aggravating relationships among surviving family members, you should consider steps to remove any motivation to commence a Will contest. Discussing the disposition of your estate with your family members well before your death may be the most effective way of preventing a Will contest, even though you may regard the task as a very disagreeable one. In addition to signing a Will, you should consider executing a power of attorney with respect to your property, as well as a Living Will and Health Care Proxy.

CHAPTER 11

SHOULD I AVOID PROBATE?

INTRODUCTION AND OVERVIEW OF CHAPTER

Property is transferred at death in a variety of different ways. Probate is one of the methods by which others will receive property you own at your death. Although probate often is regarded as something to avoid, that is not always the case. This Chapter will explore whether you should attempt to avoid probate with respect to some or all of your assets.

WHAT IS PROBATE?

The "Technical" Meaning

The word "probate" is derived from the Latin phrase "to prove." Technically, it means the court process by which a certain instrument is **proved** to be your Last Will and Testament. The procedures by which that happens vary from state to state. Some procedures are rather complex; some are quite simple.

The "probate proceeding" is the legal action by which the instrument is proved (or not proved) as the property owner's last Will. In some states, it involves a lawsuit in which a formal legal action (a lawsuit) is brought against those who would inherit your property if you died without a Will. Those individuals are your closest relatives under the law and usually will consist of your spouse and descendants if you have any. If your closest relatives do not, in effect, agree that the instrument is your last Will, an action is typically started against them in which they are sued. In the lawsuit, the court will determine whether the instrument submitted, in fact, is your last Will. As a general matter, the probate proceeding itself has nothing to do with the administration of your estate. The probate proceeding can be a complex proceeding and expensive or it can be a simple one and relatively inexpensive.

In other jurisdictions, the instrument is submitted to a court or administrative officer (who may not be a judge) without notice to any other persons. Typically, notice is published in a local newspaper advising anyone who reads the paper that an instrument has been submitted purporting to be your Will. Usually, people have a limited time to come in and contend that the instrument is not your Will. Normally, only your close relatives (or those individuals who contain they inherit from you under another Will) can contend that the instrument submitted is not your Will.

Usually, the person named to administer your estate is the one who will submit the Will to the court or administrative officer with a request that it be found to be your Will. That person is called your "executor" or, in some states, your "personal representative." As a general matter, the terms can be used interchangeably.

Hence, the meaning of probate (and the probate proceeding) is quite limited: consisting only of proving or disproving that an instrument is your last Will.

The "Common" Meaning

To most people, probate means the entire administration of a property owner's estate. Although most probate proceedings (in the technical legal sense) are short lived, the administration of any sizeable estate is likely to last at least three years, and often, for the estate of an owner of a closely-held business, will last more than ten years. (In fact there are tax reasons why it can be beneficial to prolong the administration of the estate—that is discussed in Chapter 14.) Usually, but not always, when people react adversely to the word "probate" they are thinking about the entire process of administration and not just the proceeding of proving that an instrument is or is not the property owner's Will disposing of certain assets owned by that person at death.

WHY PROBATE IS VIEWED AS SOMETHING TO BE AVOIDED

It Is Associated with Death

A Will does not "operate" on assets until the person who wrote it dies. Hence, there can be no probate (or probate proceeding) unless there is a death. For most of us, our own death is regarded as a most unpleasant state of affairs and is to be avoided at almost any cost. Therefore, it is not surprising that even in the most narrow sense probate is something which people want to avoid.

The Entire Process of Dying Can Be Horrendously Expensive

In virtually every family, stories can be told about disastrous results which occurred when someone died. Dark secrets about a person sometimes come to light. If the breadwinner dies, the surviving family members may be destitute. In addition, almost always there will be significant expenses associated with a transmission of property at death. If your estate is a significant one, and unless you leave it to charity (leaving it to your spouse will only postpone the problem), very significant taxes may be paid to the government. If your affairs have not been carefully planned, the costs of administration may be very high. Lawsuits (including expensive Will contests which may arise in the probate process) can consume the entire value of the estate. Sometimes, lawyers and judges and other persons involved with the administration of estates are dishonest or, at least, overreach and assets are diverted to them rather than going to those who really should receive them. However, avoiding the use of a Will does not necessarily guarantee any reduction in the cost of dying or any other adverse consequences of dying. One of the most common misconceptions is that somehow avoiding using a Will (and using a revocable or living trust, discussed in more detail later) will eliminate taxes. Nothing is further from the truth. In fact, on balance, avoiding using a Will, on average, probably will increase the amount of overall taxes paid. In some cases, avoiding probate can reduce some expenses but it will not eliminate them altogether and, in many cases, will not reduce them significantly at all.

Poor Planning Produces Emotional Wounds Which Cannot Be Healed

As discussed in more detail in Chapter 1, one of the easiest things to do in life is to put off planning for things which will happen after your death. What do you care? You won't be around. Lack of planning, or poor planning, not only will almost certainly guarantee that your family pays the highest calculable taxes and expenses, but is likely to produce emotional stresses among surviving family members. One of the first estates I ever administered was that of a trust officer of a major bank in New York City. The officer was only 40 years old. He literally hounded his colleagues and customers to have up-to-date estate plans including an up-to-date Will. He died of a heart attack at his desk and, of course, without a Will. He had been married less than two years and had a six-month old baby from his second wife. His first wife had died and the two teenagers from that marriage still lived with him. Their relationship with their stepmother was very poor. Higher taxes than necessary were paid at his death. In addition, his failure to have a Will and designate whom he wished to be the guardian of his children from the prior marriage produced the almost certain fight among his parents, his deceased wife's parents and his widow. The matter was compromised but only after the expenditure of tens of thousands of dollars in legal fees. The battle was so bitter that relationships among the family groups never healed.

Again, every family can tell stories such as those. They are associated with someone's death but they seldom are attributable to the probate process but rather poor planning.

In Some Jurisdictions, Probate Can Be More Expensive Than Other Methods of Transferring Property

In some states, probate can be significantly more expensive than other methods of disposing of property. Some states, for example, have fees payable to the probate court and they increase sharply as the amount of property subject to the court's control increases. Some states have minimum attorneys' fees for property which is disposed of under a Will or assets which are disposed of under the intestate laws of the state (that is, the assets which could have been disposed of under your Will but where you die without a valid Will). Similarly, some states have fixed (and relatively high) fees paid to executors and personal representatives to administer the property disposed of under your Will (or in intestacy). Some courts can appoint "appraisers" to determine the value of your estate; in some jurisdictions, their fees are ridiculously high compared to the services they render. If some of the people who would take your property if you died without having a valid Will are minors or incompetent, many states will appoint a lawyer to represent those persons in the probate process or in the process which occurs with respect to assets which will be disposed of under the intestacy laws.

Not all states have such high costs and, in some jurisdictions, it is not practicable to attempt to avoid them. However, in some states, it is possible to reduce the expenses of administering your property significantly if you minimize the amount of property which passes under your Will or under the intestate laws.

Will Contests are Less Likely

Generally, anyone who would take property if you died without a valid Will can contend that the instrument offered to be proved is not your Will. Sometimes, people who inherit under alternate instruments (such as an earlier or later Will you have signed) also can object to having a particular instrument admitted to probate as your Will. Will contests (or at least threatened Will contests) occur in some jurisdictions with significant frequency. Although few of such attacks are successful (with a jury or judge making a finding that the instrument offered is not a valid Will), hundreds of cases are settled each year by payments to those who object to the admission of the instrument to probate as the Will.

Fewer attacks and settlements are made and fewer successful lawsuits are brought when property is disposed of by different means, such as the designation of a particular person as the beneficiary of life insurance proceeds. At first, that may seem contradictory. After all, the law imposes strict standards for executing Wills and the threshold of competency to make a Will is about the lowest under the law (even less than that to enter a contract, as a general rule). With all the formalities and safeguards, it might seem that it would be easier to attack a pension plan or a life insurance designation which merely has been signed by the property owner and mailed into the insurance company or the person who administers the retirement plan. The law usually requires that a Will must be witnessed (with some states requiring three witnesses), must make certain recitals, requires the person signing the Will to declare to those who are witnesses that he or she knows it is a Will, must be signed in a certain place in the document, effectively prohibited from acting as witnesses, in addition to other requirements The law even imposes special rules about the way in which a Will can be revoked or modified. Moreover, if more than one copy of the Will is signed and not all the copies can be found when the property owner dies, the instrument may be denied probate. In addition, many lawyers follow additional safeguards such as having the client sign every page of the instrument and not just at its end.

Unfortunately, all of the safeguards provide, in effect, additional grounds to attack the instrument as not a valid Will. For example, the requirement that the Will must be witnessed (as well as signed) raises the possibility of an attack where the witnesses are also persons who take benefits under the instrument. Generally, if beneficiaries under the Will act as the witnesses, it will not be admitted to probate unless those persons waive their rights to take under the instrument. Lawyers who take extraordinary precautions to ensure that there is a clear record of what occurred at the time the instrument was signed as the Will sometimes discover that an objectant contends that the attorney engaged in such extraordinary actions because the attorney was concerned about the validity of the instrument.

In any case, experience indicates that a contest over the validity of the disposition of property is more likely to occur with respect to a Will than virtually any other kind of disposition method. For instance, where a revocable or living trust (discussed in more detail later) is used as a substitute for a Will, contests are less frequently brought and generally have been less successful than Will contests.

It is appropriate to note, however, that the probability of a successful Will contest (or any other attack on the disposition of property which is to take effect upon your death) can be reduced significantly. For example, a Will (or other document) usually can be designed to provide a forfeiture-of-bequest provision if a beneficiary who takes under the instrument attacks or even threatens to attack the validity of the instrument. Those are known as "in terrorem" clauses because they are supposed to terrorize a potential objectant into not acting. (They are discussed in more detail in Chapter 10.) Of course, if you provide no bequest which would be forfeited there can be no effective forfeiture provision. Some states, as a matter of public policy, prohibit the use of such clauses but, through careful planning with your attorney, you should be able to simulate a similar effect.

WHY PROBATE MAY AFFECT LITTLE OF YOUR WEALTH EVEN WITHOUT PLANNING

Probate Generally Applies Only To Assets Directly Held

In the not-so-distant past, significant wealth was represented primarily by land. Ownership of land had to be carefully recorded. A Will was almost the exclusive method by which title to land could be transferred upon its owner's death. Now, however, most wealth is not represented by land but by other assets, such as securities, interests in partnerships, cash, life insurance, pension proceeds and similar assets which do not usually represent an interest in real estate.

Although it is discussed in more detail in Chapter 10, it is sufficient here to simply point out that your Will and probate process will apply only to assets, as a general rule, which you own directly at death and for which no alternative disposition method has been made. For most people, much more of their assets will pass outside of probate than under it. If the significant part of your wealth, however, is represented by direct ownership of interests in your business, probate will apply to most of your wealth unless you take other steps to avoid that.

What Happens to Your Other Assets?

Your other assets will be disposed of by alternative dispositions you make or which are made for you if you do not affirmatively make them. For example, life insurance proceeds probably will be paid upon your death pursuant to a beneficiary designation form you have filed with the insurance company prior to your death. Similarly, your interests in retirement plans will pass pursuant to a designation form you filed with your company before your death. Property owned jointly with others usually will be transferred automatically to the other co-owner when you die. Assets which you have placed in trust will pass as you have specified in the trust instrument even if you can revoke the trust up until the time you die.

Sometimes, although alternative methods of disposing of assets (such as life insurance proceeds) are available, you will fail effectively to do so. For instance, in many law firms, if a partner fails to designate who the successor interest to his or her partnership interests is, those interests will be paid to his or her estate. Probably, most lawyers throughout the country have failed to fill out such forms. Lawyers, however, are not the only ones neglecting their planning. Many individuals fail to fill out beneficiary forms for retirement plan proceeds that are held for the worker at the time of death. Usually, in such cases, property will be paid to the estate and will become subject to disposition under the Will (or the intestacy laws if there is no Will). As a consequence, there will be a disposition of the asset.

Usually, it will be better to use the alternative methods of disposing of property (such as life insurance proceeds) than having them paid to your estate. For example, as a general rule, life insurance proceeds paid to a beneficiary other than your estate will not be subject to the claims of your creditors. If you either name your estate as the beneficiary or fail to make a designation which is effective at your death (because, for example, the beneficiary you named predeceases you and you had named no alternate), the proceeds will be paid to your estate and may become subject to the claims of your creditors. Obviously, if the claims of your creditors otherwise will be satisfied by assets in your estate, making the proceeds payable to your estate may not be a disadvantage. In fact, in a few cases, it may be advantageous to have items such as retirement plan proceeds paid to your estate. In any case, it is appropriate for you to discuss the disposition of those types of assets with your attorney.

THE ADVANTAGES OF PROBATE

Sometimes, the Results Are More Certain

Wills have been around for centuries and are widely known throughout the world. Every state has specific rules about how Wills must be signed, etc. As indicated above, other methods of disposing of property are much more recent developments and, almost as a necessary consequence, less certain. For example, and as will be discussed in more detail later, it is not absolutely certain in a few states that a disposition of property by death through a living trust will be effective, at least in certain circumstances.

Also, in any case, you will not be able to be certain that you have disposed of all of your assets by alternative methods. You are likely to own something in your own name at the time you die, and that asset either will be disposed of by your Will or, if you have none, under the intestacy laws.

It Is Simpler During Lifetime

As a general matter, your Will will have no operative effect until you die. You do not have to re-register title (which typically is something you must do to use an alternative form of disposition to a Will) or pay someone to manage property because it is not in your name but in the name of a living trust, or an agent for you. You can buy and sell assets as you have in the past and your Will will have no practical effect, except in the most rare circumstances, to you while you are alive. Moreover, you may amend or revoke your Will at any time prior to your death.

Obviously, I am not attempting to underemphasize the importance of your Will which may be the most important document, from your family's perspective, which you ever sign. However, during your lifetime the Will will have little practical effect on how you operate and conduct your affairs. Many alternative methods will result in some interference (although it may be modest) in your life.

In Some Cases, The
Tax Effects Are Better
or At Least More
Certain

LIFETIME

Your Will will have no effect on you from a tax perspective
during your lifetime. Arranging for an alternative method of
the disposition of your property may. For example, you may
decide that you will have property held in joint name with
you and a member of your family (such as your spouse).
Perhaps, you may have read that having property held in
joint name with you and your spouse will avoid probate and
get the results you want. Joint ownership, however, is more
likely to cause adverse effects than beneficial ones. During
your lifetime, however, a number of questions will arise with
respect to that asset. For example, if you and the other joint
owner have a parting of the ways, who is entitled to the
property? You will contend that the joint ownership was
created only to provide a simplified method of disposing of
the property at your death and you never intended to transfer
any ownership during your lifetime. The other person will
contend to the contrary. The results almost always will be
uncertain. In addition, the IRS may charge that you have
made a gift at the time you placed the property in joint name.
Although there probably will be no tax if that other person is
your spouse (unless your spouse is not a U.S. citizen), the
IRS is likely to contend that there is gift tax consequences if
anyone other than your spouse is the other co-owner of the
property. Similarly, there may be questions as to who is taxed
on any income (or entitled to any deductions) generated by
the property—should it all be taxed to you or should a portion of it be taxed to the other co-owner? Again, if the other
co-owner is your spouse and you file a joint tax return for
federal, state and local purposes, there may be little in the
way of consequences. If the beneficiaries are other than your
spouse, there may be significant tax effects.

The federal tax law has developed to provide, in effect,
that where you place assets during your lifetime into a revocable or living trust, the income tax effects during your lifetime are the same as though you continued to own the
property in your own name. However, there are some poten-

tially important exceptions. For example, the tax-free build up of earnings in a tax-deferred annuity is not available if the annuity contract is owned other than by a human being. There is no definitive law which states that that tax benefit will be available if the annuity contract is held by a revocable trust. There are other potential adverse consequences as well.

If you use a revocable trust as the alternative methods of disposing of most of your assets which otherwise would be disposed of by your Will, a separate tax return for that trust will have to be filed unless you are the sole trustee or a co-trustee of that trust.

DEATHTIME

The differences between disposing of property by your Will and virtually any other mechanism often are more sharp when it comes to what happens after you die. Although it would be appropriate for you to discuss the matter with your attorney to get more detail, suffice it to say that, on balance, tax consequences of disposing of property by Will is preferable to almost any other disposition methods. For example, your company is an S corporation. Only United States individuals and certain other entities can qualify as S shareholders. Your estate can be an S shareholder even if your estate remains in administration for many years following your death. If you dispose of the S stock by a revocable trust, the revocable trust will be an eligible shareholder for only two years following your death, although, in turn, the shares might be distributed, pursuant to your plan, to another eligible shareholder within two years.

Your lawyer or tax accountant should be able to provide you with more detail about whether or not the effects of probate to you (or your family) will be more beneficial than disposing of your assets by alternative methods. Make sure you discuss that matter in some detail with your counsellors.

THE PRIMARY ALTERNATIVE TO PROBATE: THE REVOCABLE LIVING TRUST

Introduction

One of America's great law professors and estate planners, James Casner, who spent most of his career teaching at the Harvard Law School, suggested over 30 years ago using a revocable trust instead of a will. Although many lawyers initially were skeptical of using them, revocable trusts, sometimes called living trusts or lifetime trusts and many other names are now widely used in many areas of the United States. Many misconceptions have arisen with respect to revocable trusts but, in appropriate circumstances, they can be important and beneficial.

A revocable trust is one which simply means it can be revoked and the property taken back by the person who creates it. That person usually is called the "grantor." Usually, the right to revoke it and reclaim the assets is retained until death. In some cases, the right to revoke will be limited to certain circumstances such as the time during which the person who created the trust is unmarried or only with the consent of someone else, such as an independent trustee. By and large, the revocable trust will have virtually no tax effect during the lifetime of its grantor. The use of a revocable trust itself will provide no special estate tax savings over disposing of your property by Will. Almost every day in the United States, ads are run in newspapers which claim that a particular form of revocable trust will save taxes when you die. The implication is that it will save more than if you dispose of your assets in another way, such as by a Will. Those claims are false and, as explained earlier, a revocable trust may produce less in the way of potential tax benefits than disposing of your property by Will, at least in some cases.

Advantages

GREATER CONFIDENTIALITY ABOUT THE DISPOSITION OF YOUR WEALTH

In almost all states, your Will, once it has been admitted to probate, becomes a public document which may be inspected by anyone requesting to see it. One banker's and lawyer's journal used to run a "Will of the Month" column in which the Will of a famous person (such as Nelson Rockefeller) would be described in detail. Perhaps, you will not care (and perhaps no one else will care) that the disposition of your property is a matter of public record. Often, however, it will be appropriate to keep such matters confidential. For instance, if you decide that one of your children should not receive his or her inheritance outright because of the child's propensity to destructive behavior, legal disability, incarceration, creditor problems or other factors, you may not want that publicly disclosed. Moreover, if you made a bequest to someone who is not a natural object of your bounty (such as a gift to a "special friend"), you may not want that to be a matter of public record. Using a revocable trust, in most states, can provide confidentiality as to the disposition of your wealth.

However, the confidentiality may not be maintained in all cases. For example, if a creditor brings a claim against the revocable trust or a member of your family claims the instrument is not valid (or wants it interpreted in a certain way), the document is likely to have to be filed in court and, in most cases, will become available to public inspection. For many, however, the revocable trust will provide a greater probability for confidentiality about the way they left their assets.

AVOIDING CERTAIN COURT FILING FEES

Usually, a fee will be charged by the court or administrative office where your Will is filed for probate. Often, the level of fee will be directly related to the amount of property which is disposed of by your Will. The less disposed of by your Will, the lower the filing fee. In most states, the filing fees may not be regarded as significant. But much depends upon your individual perspective. In some states, for example, the probate filing fees are as low as $25 (for small probate estates) to over $1,000 (for large probate estates). New York also charges the same fees when the state estate taxes are fixed by the state. That system sounds a little unfair, doesn't it? Well, that filing fee to have the state determine your taxes applies whether you have a Will or not. The state will impose a fee again if your executors decide that they want to account to the court for how they have administered your estate and to receive the court's discharge. (Some executors choose to settle all questions about the propriety of their actions by an agreement with the beneficiaries outside of court. In that case, the filing fee can be ignored.) If your assets are disposed of by a revocable trust, some or all of the filing fees will be avoided.

Some states have other fees, such as for appraisers. Often, these are "political" appointments and the fees are unreasonably high in relationship to the responsibility or work which the appraiser performs. You should discuss with your attorney whether your estate could be subject to such fees and whether those fees can be avoided or reduced significantly by using a revocable trust.

In many states where your Will is offered for probate, the court may appoint an attorney to represent any minor beneficiaries of your estate or minors or incompetents who would take your property in the event that you had died without a Will. In most states, the fees for such attorneys are reasonable but, in almost all cases, they can be avoided by using a revocable trust. Again, you should discuss with your attorney whether your estate is likely to have such an attorney appointed and what the fees will be.

POSSIBLY REDUCING THE PROBABILITY OF "WILL CONTESTS"

As explained earlier, in the real world, Will contests are less probable if you dispose of little property under your Will. An attack on a revocable trust usually is much more difficult for many reasons. First, the revocable trust will have an impact during your lifetime. You probably will have registered title to property in the name of the trust during your lifetime demonstrating that you knew it existed. It is very probable that independent people will have had dealings with the trust during your lifetime establishing that it was regarded as a valid document well before your death. Sometimes, people will contend that the instrument you signed is not your valid

Will because you did not know that you signed it or that your signature is a forgery. That is almost impossible to successfully contend where you have had property titled in the name of the trust and you have taken actions on behalf of the trust during your lifetime. Similarly, objectants may contend that you were incompetent at the time you signed your Will. Again, you will probably have had many transactions involving the trust during your lifetime. It will be much more difficult for a credible case to be made that you were incompetent at the time you signed the trust but were competent thereafter when you dealt on its behalf.

In considering whether it is appropriate to use a revocable trust to avoid a Will contest, it is appropriate for you to consider whether a Will contest is likely to occur. That matter is discussed in more detail in Chapter 11. However, your lawyer probably can advise you whether the probability of a Will contest is high. If you are leaving your estate, in effect, equally among your children, the probability of a Will contest is vastly reduced compared to what might happen if you favor one child over another. Chapter 11 explains in more detail how you can reduce the probability of a Will contest even if you use a Will. However, you can probably further reduce the possibility of an attack (or a successful one) on the disposition of your assets by using a revocable trust. Nonetheless, it will be appropriate for you to discuss that with your attorney.

POSSIBLY REDUCING FIDUCIARY FEES

Generally, those who administer your estate will be entitled to be paid for their services. Many states provide fixed fees to be paid to an executor (or personal representative) based upon the size of the probate estate. Those fee schedules can be avoided, usually, by using a revocable trust. However, those same states typically provide for trustee's commissions to be paid to those who administer your revocable trust after your death (when it becomes irrevocable). Whether the trustee's fees for administering your trust after your death will be more or less than the fees which a personal representative would be paid for administering your estate if you dispose of it by Will can be calculated by your counsellor. You can then decide whether it is appropriate to attempt to avoid or reduce certain fees.

However, another option may be better whether you choose to use a Will or a revocable trust to dispose of your assets at your death. Generally, you can set the level of fiduciary fees in the governing instrument. In effect, you will condition the appointment of a certain person as the trustee of your revocable trust or as executor under your Will upon that person's agreement to a certain level of compensation and no more. If the person named wishes to serve as the fiduciary, the fee arrangement set forth in your governing instrument (whether it is a revocable trust or a Will) will control. Whether it is appropriate for you to use a certain fee schedule is discussed in more detail in Chapter 13.

In a Few States, Avoiding Minimum Attorney's Fees

In some states, such as California, there is a minimum attorney's fee that has to be paid with respect to property disposed of under a Will. In one case, for example, a man died with an estate of $3.6 billion. The attorneys for the estate received a fixed fee of $36 million. That fee could have been avoided if the individual's assets had been disposed of by a revocable trust. In fact, revocable trusts are widely used in California to avoid the minimum attorney's fee schedule. (Also, in California, attorneys are entitled to additional fees for almost everything else they do in addition to getting the Will admitted to probate, such as work relating to filing and auditing of the estate tax return.) In most states, however, the level of an attorney's fee is determined by a "reasonable" standard. Typically, the fee is set by agreement between the fiduciary (such as the executor or trustee) and the law firm or, alternatively, by the court or with the beneficiaries. In many cases, the amount paid to the attorney will be the same whether property is disposed of by Will or by revocable trust.

However, by avoiding a Will contest, which will necessarily result in significant attorneys' fees, the revocable trust, in fact, may result in a significant savings of lawyers' fees. Again, it will be appropriate for you to discuss that matter with your own counsellor and to receive an estimate about whether significant attorneys' fees will be saved by disposing of your assets by revocable trust rather than by Will.

IN A FEW STATES, AVOIDING "ARCANE" COURT PROCEDURES

In some states, the administration of an estate is much more complex if assets are disposed of by Will rather than revocable trust. In California, for example, having to obtain permission from the court to sell real estate and having to hold an in-court auction with respect to the sale of real estate is almost certain to occur if the property is disposed of by Will. Other states have other rules where permission of the probate court will be necessary in order for certain actions to be taken. In almost all states, those rather arcane and potentially expensive procedures can be avoided by using a revocable trust. Indeed, that is another reason why revocable trusts are so prevalent in California.

Again, you should discuss with your own attorney whether or not your estate is going to face significant procedural hurdles in court if your assets are disposed of by Will.

AVOIDING POTENTIAL DELAY IN THE ADMINISTRATION OF YOUR WEALTH

Usually, your executor or personal representative will have no power to take any action with respect to your assets until your Will is admitted to probate by the court. That means, in effect, that the administration of your probate estate will be delayed. In some states, the delay will be very short. In other states, however, particularly where a Will contest is threatened or brought, minors are involved, witnesses cannot be found or the attorney is "too busy" to turn to the probate proceeding promptly, the administration of your assets will be delayed. Delay often means expense and almost certainly means frustration. In certain cases, the named executors or personal representatives can get permission of the court to take certain action, such as to distribute an asset to a surviving family member for support. However, such proceedings almost certainly will involve hiring an attorney. The attorney will be paid for such work. It is possible for your family to save considerable expense (and emotional distress) if you use a revocable trust. However, whether the savings will occur depends upon the circumstances and the procedures in your state. You should discuss the matter with your attorney and weigh the importance and likelihood of achieving those savings in determining whether you should use a revocable trust to dispose of a significant part of your assets.

IN A FEW STATES, PROTECTING SOME ASSETS FROM CREDITOR CLAIMS OR CLAIMS OF A SPOUSE TO A MINIMUM SHARE OF YOUR ESTATE

Chapter 16 discusses protecting your assets from claims of creditors in detail. Here, however, it is merely appropriate to point out that in a few states, your assets may be protected from certain claims of creditors or a claim of your spouse to a minimum share of your estate if you use a revocable trust rather than allow the assets to be disposed of by your Will. In Connecticut, for example, assets which are placed into a valid revocable trust before you die generally will not be subject to the claims of your spouse to a minimum share of your estate. If you are concerned about claims of creditors or claims which your spouse may make against your property, you should discuss the matter with your attorney and determine whether a revocable trust can be used to safeguard your assets from those claims. Even if the revocable trust will not achieve those results under the law of the state where you reside, you may wish to discuss with your attorney whether creating a revocable trust under the laws of another state will achieve the result you want.

Providing Asset Management During Your Disability

Unfortunately, many of us become unable effectively and prudently to manage our financial affairs during our lives. The law provides mechanisms for the management of your affairs while you are so disabled. Your family, for example, can commence a proceeding to have a conservator of your property appointed who will be empowered by the law to take certain actions to safeguard your assets and to manage them on your behalf. In addition, it may be possible to have you declared fully incompetent and have a guardian (in some states called a committee) who will become, in effect, the legal owner of your assets while you are incompetent. Those proceedings, however, are expensive and, in some cases, may be embarrassing to you and your family. They are, in effect, actions of last resort.

An alternative, and one widely used in the United States today, is for you to execute a **durable** power of attorney. (Powers of attorney are also discussed in Chapter 10.) The person appointed under the power of attorney is called an attorney-in-fact, although that person does not have to be an attorney licensed to practice law. In effect, the attorney-in-fact becomes your agent for managing your assets. The power of attorney is said to be durable because it is effective even if you become incompetent. In the real world, however, people do not like dealing with attorneys-in-fact. Indeed, in New York State, a law has been passed which makes it unlawful for banks and other financial institutions to fail to honor a power of attorney. (It is a law without teeth, however, because there is no fine imposed for failing to respect a power of attorney.) Moreover, powers of attorney are narrowly construed under the law.

A revocable trust is a much more flexible and powerful method for your assets to be managed during your disability. Typically, the revocable trust will provide for a trustee to be appointed in your place, if you are acting as trustee, upon your incompetency. Often, incompetency does not have to be established in court, usually, the instrument merely provides that upon the certification of your attending physician (and sometimes your lawyer as well) that you are experiencing significant difficulty in managing your assets, the person named to take over becomes the trustee. The critical factor is that the trustee will then legally own the assets and will be able to manage them and use them on your behalf in a much more direct and certain way than an attorney-in-fact could.

PROPERLY STRUCTURED, ASSISTING IN LIFETIME ESTATE PLANNING

Because the trustee will be the legal owner of the assets in the revocable trust, the trustee if so authorized in the instrument can take action to effect lifetime estate planning for you, even if you are legally incompetent to transfer assets yourself. Although you may authorize an attorney-in-fact to make gifts and take other actions for you during your lifetime, the results are less certain than having the trustee of a revocable trust do so. An example will demonstrate why.

For many years, one of my partners represented a woman, whom I will call Sally. Sally had two things she cared about: her mother, who was in her 90s, and her alma mater. My partner recommended that Sally create a charitable remainder trust upon her death providing payments to her mother during her mother's remaining lifetime, if she survived Sally with the remainder over to the college. One day, Sally called my partner and said she was moving to another part of the United States where we did not have an office. She explained that it would be simpler for her to have her personal affairs handled by a lawyer there. My partner agreed and offered to be of any assistance. Soon thereafter, my partner received a letter from Sally's new lawyer in her new location. The lawyer asked my partner to review the new Will he had prepared for Sally to sign, which was almost identical to the one my partner had prepared for her. A few years later, Sally's secretary called my partner and explained that Sally was comatose and was expected to die soon. She added that Sally had never signed the new Will and would die with the Will which my partner had prepared for her many years ago. The secretary wanted confirmation that the Will was still "A-Ok." My partner advised that the IRS had retroactively changed the rules with respect to charitable remainder trusts and the one under Sally's Will would not be qualified. Accordingly, no charitable deduction would be allowed with respect to it and millions of dollars of unnecessary estate tax would have to be paid. My partner flew out to the town where Sally was in the hospital and waited there several days until the doctors revived her adequately so that she could instruct my partner to sign a codicil to her Will on her behalf. The codicil was found to be valid and admitted to probate securing the estate tax charitable deduction for Sally's estate.

Although the Internal Revenue Code has since been amended, in effect, to prevent the IRS from taking such retroactive action with respect to charitable remainder trusts, the important point is that the entire problem relating to Sally's incompetency could have been avoided had she used a special form of revocable trust, called the Master Living Trust©*. Among other powerful authorities granted to the trustee, it permits the trustee, prior to the death of the property owner, to amend any of the provisions so as to ensure their qualification for appropriate treatment under the tax laws. Recently, for example, the United States Tax Court entered a decision which would have disqualified thousands upon thousands of trusts under people's Wills from qualifying for the marital deduction. Although that decision was later reversed by an appellate court, attorneys throughout the nation scrambled to have their clients execute codicils to existing Wills or new Wills to cure the problem which the Tax Court contended was present in those instruments. Not only did that result in considerable expense for both lawyers and their clients, but it was a frightening circumstance where clients were incompetent and unable to amend their Wills. No one, not even an attorney-in-fact, could amend their Wills. However, if the

* Jonathan G. Blattmachr holds the common law copyright to Master Living Trust.

trust had been contained in the Master Living Trust©, the trustee acting under the instrument could have effected the cure even though the grantor of the trust was then incompetent.

The revocable trust is not, however, a cure all for all planning. In fact, a revocable trust will cause adverse effects if certain lifetime planning is effected. Recently, for example, the IRS and at least one court have held that any transfer out of a revocable trust within three years of the property owner's death will be brought back into the taxable estate. Generally, the transfer-within-three-years-of-death rule was repealed in 1982 but a technical defect in the Internal Revenue Code (which the IRS has attempted to exploit to its unfair advantage) may continue to apply the old law to revocable trusts. It is likely that legislation will be enacted by the Congress which will cure that problem for revocable trusts. However, differences under the law will continue to persist between having assets held in and transferred by a revocable trust and having the assets held directly by you and transferred by your Will. Only by discussing the matter in detail with your counsellor will you be able to determine in what circumstance the revocable trust will provide different consequences for you and your assets and whether those consequences will be advantageous or not.

PERHAPS, AVOIDING PROBATING YOUR WILL IN ANOTHER STATE

If you own real estate (and sometimes tangible personal property, such as works of art, furniture, boats or automobiles) in another state, your Will may have to be admitted to probate there as well as your home state. Some jurisdictions, however, provide simplified methods of proving your Will in their state. Nonetheless, almost all of those proceedings will involve additional expense in the administration of your property in the other state. Often, placing such property in a revocable trust prior to your death will be effective in avoiding probate in another jurisdiction and, thereby, reducing the costs of administering that property.

PREVENTING PILFERING OF YOUR ASSETS DURING YOUR LIFETIME

I had an uncle who was a disabled war veteran. Although he was legally competent, he was prone to almost every suggestion anyone made including suggestions for him to give his property to others. My father had almost all of my uncle's assets placed in a revocable trust with a local bank as trustee. Although the trust was revocable, my uncle was required to give the bank and to my father (and, after my father's death, to me) notice of an intent to revoke. Although he gave away almost all cash he ever had in his pockets to almost anyone who would ask for it, the revocable trust prevented the vast majority of his property from being given to others.

When my uncle finally decided he wanted to own his own home, I purchased it for him through a revocable trust. This time, I made it even more difficult for him to revoke the trust or transfer the interests in it. The trust was revocable only with the consent of an independent third party. From a tax perspective, no adverse consequences occurred by creating such a trust (although there might have been had a member of his family had to consent to the revocation). In any case, the revocable trust can prevent property from being taken from someone who would be prone to take the suggestion of others. All of us, at one time in our lives and, sometimes, for extended periods of our lives, may become subject to unreasonable and unfair demands of others. Properly structured, the revocable trust can provide some real protection from that in some cases. A Will cannot do that.

By the way, an adverse consequence of using the revocable trust to own my uncle's home arose, and I will discuss that next under "Disadvantages."

Disadvantages

EXTRA COST OF CREATING A REVOCABLE TRUST

Make no mistake about it, your attorney is going to charge you an extra fee for drafting a revocable trust for you. You should ask your attorney how much more it will be and then you can weigh that against the potential savings or other benefits which may be derived by executing one.

In addition, it may turn out that your attorney will need to research certain effects of the revocable trust. For example, you may ask the attorney whether the revocable trust will prevent your new spouse from being able to take a minimum share of those assets. Your attorney may have to research that to provide you with an answer. Similarly, your attorney may be asked to research what the effect of transferring your stock options are to a revocable trust. Moreover, your attorney may state that it would be better, because a significant part of your estate is being dedicated to charity, for you not to use a revocable trust. Your attorney probably will be right but it is likely that your attorney will have to research the arcane rules of section 642(c) and section 681 of the Code. Not all lawyers will know the answers to all questions about the potential consequences of using revocable trusts. You should not be disturbed if your attorney suggests that he or she be authorized to research certain matters. On the other hand, the cost of your attorney doing so should be weighed against the benefits which might be derived by creating the revocable trust.

YOU WILL NEED A WILL ANYWAY

Even the most avid promoters of revocable trusts will acknowledge that you still need a Will. It is doubtful that you will transfer everything you own to your revocable trust before you die. Even if you attempt to do so, you may die holding certain claims against other people (such as for pain and suffering you have experienced in the automobile accident which brought about your death) which will not have been and could not have been assigned to a revocable trust. Moreover, under the tax law, if you do not have an executor or personal representative named under a Will which is admitted to probate, there is no clear and certain person who is responsible for dealing with the IRS. In fact, in that case, everyone who holds property which is includable in your estate (and not just the trustee of your formerly revocable trust) will be responsible for filing your estate tax return and seeing that all your taxes are paid. You can imagine the pandemonium if your nephew who received a $10,000 life insurance proceeds payment, your girlfriend (or boyfriend) who succeeded to the jointly held bank account you maintained with her (or him), your infant daughter who succeeded to the proceeds in your pension plan, as well as the trustee of the revocable trust all want to decide how certain matters should be handled with IRS.

The bottom line is that you will have to have a Will prepared as well as a revocable trust. In most states, your Will can simply provide, as a practicable matter, for all assets which you still own directly at death to be "poured over" to the formerly revocable trust at your death and name an executor (who probably will be the same person who is trustee of your revocable trust) and certain other matters. In other states, however, such pour overs may not be permitted or if the revocable trust is for any reason not valid, your Will will have to recite again each and every disposition which is contained in the revocable trust.

In any case, it will cost you more, almost certainly, to have both a revocable trust and a Will. But in the scope of things that additional cost probably should not be a reason you fail to use a revocable trust if circumstances dictate that benefits can be derived from using one.

EXTRA TROUBLE OF CHANGING TITLE

To be most effective, the revocable trust will have to become the owner of almost all of your assets prior to your death. If you create the revocable trust and do not put assets in the name of the trust your Will will continue to be the major estate planning document. Even if your Will pours over all of the assets to the revocable trust, the possibility of a Will contest, delays in getting the Will admitted to probate, the appointment of an attorney to represent minor members of your family and all of the other potentially adverse effects of having your Will admitted to probate will occur.

Changing title to your assets is not simple. Although in

some states, such as in California, the use of revocable trusts is so commonplace that procedures have been simplified. In states where revocable trusts are not as commonly used, you should not be surprised to learn that there is resistance to changing title to that of a revocable trust.

Many law firms will provide assistance in changing title for you. That work is often done by paraprofessionals rather than lawyers. However, you can anticipate paying for such services and you should not be surprised if you run up several thousand dollars of fees in changing title to many assets. Certainly, you can attempt to do the work yourself but you may fall victim of the "cobbler's children" syndrome: The client promises the lawyer that he or she will change title to all of the significant assets, such as securities, homes, etc., right away but it does not happen. Often, when I check back with a client after a few months and then again after a few years, I get many excuses as to why the transfers have not occurred. Often, we are rehired, eventually, to make the changes in title.

If you are going to use a revocable trust, you should commit to have the transaction completed which includes changing ownership of the appropriate assets to the trust. If you are not willing to incur the bother or expense, you probably should not consider using a revocable trust even though significant benefits eventually may inure to your family by doing so.

Uncertain Effect in a Few States

In most circumstances, you initially will be the sole trustee of your own revocable trust. In a very few states, there may be some question as to whether such a trust is valid because you are the sole grantor, sole beneficiary and sole trustee during your lifetime. The argument has been made that nothing has really occurred and that the transfer is illusory.

Your lawyer will be able to advise you as to whether there is any such a danger in your state, and if so, recommend a way to ensure that the revocable trust will be regarded as valid in your state or, possibly, recommend that you create a revocable trust under the laws of another state.

A Few Potential Problems During Your Lifetime

Earlier, I told a story of my uncle, a disabled veteran, for whom we used revocable trusts to protect his assets from those who might convince him to give his property to them. A problem arose, however, when my uncle created a revocable trust with me as trustee to hold title to his home. As a disabled veteran, my uncle was entitled to the reduction in the real property taxes on his home. In fact, it would have cut the taxes by about 75% and on Long Island, New York, where my uncle lived, one of the highest real estate tax jurisdictions in the world, the savings was meaningful. I was unable, however, to convince the local tax assessor that the veteran's exemption should apply. It would not have been cost effective to take the matter to court and I was considering whether to terminate the trust (and use an alternative method to prevent my uncle from transferring the home to someone else) when my uncle died, and the question of the veteran's exemption became moot.

Another case where you may have a problem is with respect to local transfer taxes. New York City, for example, imposes a tax on the gross value (which you cannot even reduce by the value of a mortgage debt) on real estate which is transferred. The City is so aggressive in imposing the tax that almost correcting the spelling of your name on the title will result in its imposition. In any case, the City takes the position that almost any change in title, even if there is no change in the beneficial ownership of the property, entitles it to collect the tax. You should make sure, before creating a revocable trust and transferring assets to it, that such special local taxes will not apply.

As mentioned earlier, using revocable trusts as a substitute for Wills is a new one in the law (realistically, not more than 30 years old). As a consequence, all of the ramifications of using a revocable trust have not yet been determined. In addition, the lawmakers may not always take into account the fact that people may be transferring title of assets during their lifetimes to revocable trusts although, by and large, Congress has, of late, in making new tax laws, generally prescribed the same results whether title is held directly by an individual or a revocable trust (although significant differences may remain with respect to tax laws that have been on the books for quite some time).

If you want to transfer title to your home to a revocable trust you had best first check with the mortgagee (that is, the institution that holds the mortgage interest in your home). Often, mortgage agreements provide that you must pay off the entire mortgage if you transfer title to the property unless you get the mortgagee's consent. Some states have special laws which prevent those problems from happening when you change title to a revocable trust. Not all states have such rules. Where revocable trusts are not commonly used, you may well get resistance from your bank (or other mortgage lender) when you ask permission to transfer title. The important point, of course, is to make sure that you ask permission before you transfer title; otherwise, you face the threat of a claim that the mortgage balance is due immediately.

TAX RESULTS AFTER DEATH MAY NOT BE AS BENEFICIAL FOR SOME

In many ways, as stated earlier, the tax effects of having property pass under your Will may be better, in some cases, than having the property pass pursuant to a revocable trust. As mentioned, that may occur with respect to S corporation stock or if you leave a significant portion of your estate to charity. There are several other differences. Although proposals have been made to the Congress to attempt to harmonize the treatment for tax purposes for property whether passing under a revocable trust or a Will, not all of those proposals have been adopted and it seems likely that some differences will remain for quite some time. You should take the responsibility of asking your tax advisors as to whether there would be adverse consequences to your estate plan by using a revocable trust at least with respect to certain assets.

SUMMARY AND CONCLUSION

As a practical matter, you will not be able to avoid having a Will admitted to probate (or having assets pass under the intestate laws if you die without one). In some states, the probate proceeding can be complex and expensive, at least in certain circumstances. In other states, procedures dealing with the admission of Wills to probate and the administration of assets passing under the Will are simplified and costs significantly reduced. In any case, you can avoid, to a large degree, the probate process by using a revocable trust or another alternative form of disposing of property when you die. Whether that will be beneficial depends upon a variety of circumstances. In many states, using revocable trusts probably will save expense and is likely to thwart a successful Will contest. However, using a revocable trust, in some cases, can be less beneficial than having property be directly owned by you throughout your lifetime and having it pass to others on your death under your Will. Only by discussing the matter in detail with your lawyer will you be able to make an informed decision as to what degree you should attempt to avoid having property pass under your Will and, if so, the appropriate method of doing so. In any case, alternative methods of passing assets at your death, such as using a revocable trust, are not likely to reduce the estate taxes which are payable on your assets. Claims by promoters to the contrary simply are not true. Nonetheless, a revocable trust can be a powerful tool to manage assets for you during your lifetime, provide confidentiality of the disposition of your wealth and to effect lifetime estate planning for you if you become incompetent.

CHAPTER 12

WHAT SHOULD I DO IF MY SPOUSE IS NOT THE PARENT OF ALL MY CHILDREN?

INTRODUCTION AND OVERVIEW OF CHAPTER

Many times during our lives we have to resolve conflicts. Sometimes, two goals we are pursuing are worthy ones, but, at least to some degree, they conflict. Almost certainly, that will occur where you face estate planning decisions and you are married to a person who is not the parent of all your children. You will face emotional as well as financial questions in trying to do the "right" thing both for your children and your spouse. In addition, in most jurisdictions, your spouse will be entitled to certain payments or property whether your marriage terminates by death or divorce. Although there are no perfect solutions, this Chapter includes practical approaches to consider in resolving some dilemmas you will face in a subsequent marriage.

THE STATISTICS OF MARRIAGE

More Marriages End in Divorce than Death

Demographers appear to agree that more American marriages end today in divorce rather than death. That appears to be the case for virtually all lengths of marriages. The longer the marriage, the lower the likelihood of divorce; nonetheless, even if you have been married for quite a long time (such as 20 years), there still is a significant possibility of divorce. Growing percentages of long-term marriages (those which have lasted more than 10 years) are now ending in divorce.

Many Households Have Children from a Prior Marriage

Not surprisingly, especially in light of divorces in longer-term marriages, more and more married persons have descendants from prior marriages (or from another union). The problems of deciding how you should dispose of your wealth probably will be just as vexing whether or not your children are being reared by your new spouse. In fact, as will be discussed below, the financial decisions you make as to the disposition of your property may be more difficult in that circumstance.

THE "TYPICAL" ESTATE PLAN FOR A SINGLE-MARRIAGE FAMILY

First for the Spouse, then for the Children

The vast majority of estate plans for married persons who have children only of their common union is to provide for all (or almost all) of the assets to be dedicated to the surviving spouse and then for them to pass to the couple's descendants. Although there are tax and other reasons (discussed primarily in other parts of this book) for not leaving property outright to a spouse even where all of the children are of the common union, most estate plans provide for an outright disposition to the survivor. In any event, an outright disposition to the surviving spouse where either of them has children of a prior marriage is almost certain to produce hardships, cause ill-will between your spouse and the children of your prior marriage, and significantly increase the probability of litigation after your death.

The Children Run the Business for Spouse's Benefit

For many married owners of closely-held businesses who have children only of that one union, it is common for the children, or at least those of them who are involved in the business, to run the family company, at least in part, for the surviving parent's benefit. Although that will sometimes reduce conflicts between the children of the surviving parent (as is discussed in more detail in Chapter 9), conflict, and sometimes vicious and expensive litigation, may arise where your surviving spouse, who is not the parent of your children, has an interest in the business which is run by your children.

CONFLICTS IN THE SUBSEQUENT MARRIAGE

Inheritance by Your Spouse Will Defeat the Inheritance of Your Children of a Prior Marriage

Often, each spouse will make a pledge to the other that anything which is inherited from the other spouse will be left to the deceased spouse's children by the survivor spouse. Believe it or not, sometimes the spouses even intend to keep their promises at the time they are made. However, time almost definitely will erode the "memory" or "conditions" of the promise or will eradicate it in its entirety. Even if your spouse has no children of her or his own, you are almost certainly providing for the disinheritance of your children with respect to anything you leave to your spouse. Except in Louisana, children have no right under American law to any inheritance.

Even if your spouse refers to your children of another marriage as "her" or "his" own children, and even if the children have been raised in the household you have maintained with your spouse since the time of your children's infancy, your spouse probably will not view your children as her or his own, unless your spouse legally adopts them. Certainly, there are exceptions to that rule which arise from time to time. But the adage that blood is thicker than water often runs true, and you are taking a great risk if you rely on an understanding, or worse yet, your perception, that your spouse will leave all assets to all of your children when she or he later dies. In addition, you are placing a heavy psychological burden on your surviving spouse. She may want to do the right thing by your children but is pressured by his or her own children to favor them over yours.

A Trust May Help but It Will Not Eliminate the Conflict Altogether

HOW TRUSTS WORK

Chapter 10 discusses trusts in detail. All we need to state here is that with a trust one person (called the "trustee") holds legal title to property for the benefit of another (called the "beneficiary"). Usually, a trust provides for income (and sometimes additional amounts) to be paid to one beneficiary for life and then for the property to pass to others. By using a properly structured trust, you can provide for your surviving spouse for life (or until remarriage or any other event you specify) and then have the property which remains in the trust pass to your children (or anyone else you specify). Again, if the trust is *properly* structured, you will eliminate the disinheritance of your children when your spouse dies but still provide for your spouse for life.

As a general rule, a trust can be structured as creatively and flexibly as you want it to be. As indicated, you can provide for your spouse to receive the income from the trust until your spouse dies or later remarries. You may even provide for your spouse's rights to be terminated in the event your spouse co-habits with another person. You may permit a trustee to pay, in addition to income, other amounts to your spouse for any reason you specify (such as support, maintenance, health or education of your spouse) or, in effect, for no specific reason at all (so that additional amounts can be paid to your spouse for the luxuries of life). In fact, you can even provide the trustee with discretion to pay income among a class consisting of your spouse and all your descendants as the trustee chooses. Regardless of how you structure the trust, conflicts will arise. For example, if you give a trustee discretion to pay income (and other amounts) among your spouse and your children, each beneficiary is likely to complain if any payments are made to the others. You can be assured that even pro-rata payments (unless you have directed them) are likely to be criticized. Moreover, if you want to obtain certain perceived benefits under the tax law, such as postponing the tax until your spouse dies, you will have much less flexibility in structuring the trust.

The Marital Deduction

As explained in Chapter 14 in detail, subject to very limited exceptions, the marital deduction permits you to leave your entire estate outright to or in trust for your spouse free of estate tax. Even though, as is explained in Chapter 14 in detail, using the marital deduction for your entire estate may not ultimately reduce the overall tax burden on the property, most individuals like to postpone tax for as long as they can. The marital deduction accomplishes that, although the property you leave your spouse will be taxed on your spouse's death.

The law allows the federal marital deduction even if you do not leave the property outright to your spouse but place it in trust for your spouse. However, the form of trust is severely limited. You must, at a minimum, provide that your spouse receive all of the trust income for life, even if your spouse remarries. This special form of marital deduction trust ("qualified terminable interest property" and typically referred to by its initials QTIP) can ensure an eventual inheritance by your children while allowing you to provide for your spouse and postpone taxes until your spouse's death. Unfortunately, to obtain the state equivalent of the federal marital deduction in some jurisdictions, it is necessary to leave the property outright to your spouse or to give your spouse the power to control the disposition of the property when she or he dies. Failure to obtain the marital deduction at the state level, in turn, can cause such large state taxes as to cause federal taxes to be paid even though you have provided for your whole estate to pass in a form which appears as though it would qualify for the marital deduction for federal tax purposes.

THE PRODUCTIVE INCOME PROBLEM

The rules relating to the QTIP have further complexities. For example, your spouse must have the right (either under the terms of the instrument which creates the trust or state law) to force the trustee to make the property reasonably productive of income. Often, that causes a severe problem for the estate of an owner of a closely-held business. Your business may produce very little in the way of income. Salaries, consulting fees and bonuses may be paid, but the amount of distributions in the way of dividends or partnership distributions may be limited or nonexistent. The law does not require your spouse to make the property productive but, in effect, it must give him or her the right to force the trustee to make it productive within a reasonable time. In extreme cases, the spouse could force the trustee to sell interests in the business which are held in the trust in order to make the property productive. Giving your spouse the right to make the closely-held business interests productive is not usually a problem in a circumstance where all children are of the union with your spouse.

Even if the property is reasonably productive of income, your spouse, as the primary beneficiary of the trust for life, will be in a position, as a practical matter, to criticize business decisions which reduce income. Your spouse, for example, may have standing to question the level of salaries, bonuses and other benefits provided to your children (or others) who operate the business after your death. Careful planning can reduce the probability of such an attack being successful, but it cannot eliminate the possibility of the attack being made in all cases.

An alternative form of marital deduction trust, called an "estate trust", does not have to provide for your spouse to receive all of the trust income or to make the trust reasonably productive of income. However, the entire trust must be paid to your spouse's estate at his or her death, thereby giving him or her control (by Will) over the disposition of the entire trust property. Hence, the estate trust probably is not a wise choice for you if you are in a subsequent marriage and you or your spouse have descendants of a prior marriage.

THE TIME USE OF MONEY PROBLEM

In any event, from your children's perspective, providing for all (or a significant portion) of your wealth to be placed in trust for the benefit of your spouse will not be in their financial best interests even if their ultimate inheritance is assured and even if using the marital deduction reduces overall taxation (as it sometimes can). The reasons are relatively simple: Your children have to wait to receive the inheritance and during your surviving spouse's lifetime all of the income will be paid to the spouse and not accumulated for your children's benefit.

This problem was present in a recent Will contest case involving a great fortune. The husband had left the inheritance he had received from his first wife (who was the mother of all of his children) to his second wife. The second wife was approximately the same age as his children. Even though he left the property in a QTIP trust for his second wife, the children waged a bitter (although totally unsuccessful) Will contest. Assets of the estate, to some degree, were tied up for years. Fortunately, the assets consisted largely of publicly-traded stocks and bonds. If a closely-held business had been involved, however, the results could have been disastrous for the business. In such circumstances, courts often resort to court-appointed administrators who hold the legal power to administer all assets, including interests in a closely-held business.

Tensions in the Business

DEMANDS FOR MORE INCOME AND DIVERSIFICATION

Regardless of the type of trust you create for your spouse, and especially if you leave the interest in your business outright to your spouse, it is likely that your spouse will make increasing demands for more income from the business and for the interests of the business to be sold for reasons of diversification. Regardless of how good the relationship between your spouse and your children of a prior marriage is up to your death, that relationship will change after you die, and often for the worse. Your spouse can no longer rely on you for judgment so will turn to others. Even if he or she initially turns to your children, there is a strong likelihood that your spouse will turn to other advisors over time. Those advisors, whether or not they have your spouse's best interests at heart, are likely to recommend changes in the operation of the business, in order to diversify holdings and reduce the risk of adverse developments in the business, or to recommend that the business be sold.

DEMANDS TO PARTICIPATE IN MANAGEMENT

Often, the surviving spouse's demands (again, often fostered by "new" advisors) will include a right to participate in the management of the business. Your spouse is likely to demand a right to sit on the board of directors and, perhaps, participate in day-to-day decisions in the operation of the business. That rarely reduces conflicts; more likely, it will increase them as your spouse becomes more involved in the way the children are operating the business.

CONFLICT BREEDS LOSSES

The conflicts between your spouse and your children are likely to reduce the profitability of your business. Perhaps, accommodations will be made to your spouse so that more of the business assets are paid to her or him or because attention will be turned away from business to personal conflict which has developed. Your children may be inhibited in exercising their best business judgment or may make decisions which are intended to injure your spouse because she or he is beginning to interfere in the business.

Ways to reduce those potential conflicts are discussed later. In few cases, however, is it as simple as deciding that you will disinherit your spouse, to the extent the law allows you to do so.

Your Spouse's Rights to Your Property

IT'S AN ASYMMETRICAL WORLD

As a married person, you have certain rights from and obligations to your spouse. During your marriage, you are required, in effect, to support your spouse and your spouse is required to support you. In an amicable marriage, charges over rights and obligations are rarely made. They do arise, however, where the marriage ends, whether by divorce or death. Strangely, perhaps, the rights and obligations are different depending upon how the marriage terminates. In some cases, rights will be greater in divorce; in other cases, they will be greater at death.

RIGHTS IN DIVORCE

Alimony

Why Alimony Is Paid

Alimony (sometimes called "maintenance") is the payments which one spouse must make to another for support following divorce. Many theories may be advanced for the payment of alimony, such as a payment to reflect a "buyout" of the marital partnership which existed between the husband and wife. The real reason is the government's self-interest. If you do not support your spouse, the obligation will fall, at least to a limited degree, on the government. Needless to say, the government wants to shift that burden back to you. In any event, ex-husbands (and, yes, sometimes, ex-wives) very often have an obligation to pay alimony.

The Law's Arm Is Very Long and Hard

In a property settlement, the husband and wife will usually agree on the amount of alimony and the conditions under which it will be paid. It is not voluntary on the part of the payor, however. The husband, or in some cases, the wife, knows that the law has the power to impose on him or her the obligation to pay a significant portion of his or her income each year to the other. The agreement to pay the other something reflects nothing but a settlement of the obligation.

The law is quick to enforce rights to alimony. Usually, procedures to enforce the alimony payment are summary (that is, quick) in nature. Because the law is interested in shifting the burden of support to you, it has little patience with technical and even equitable arguments you may make why you should not pay alimony. For example, a charge that your spouse is not entitled to temporary alimony because she or he has committed adultery is not going to meet with warm reception from the judge. (Many spouses have tried and they all have failed.)

In addition, even if your spouse has agreed to a certain level of alimony, he or she can go to court and attempt to have it increased under "subsequent change of facts." Often, spouses are successful in increasing alimony because of change in circumstances. Sometimes a payor spouse can get alimony reduced if his or her income is reduced on account of illness or retirement or the payee spouse has succeeded to good fortunes of his or her own.

Child Support

As strongly as the courts enforce alimony obligations, the courts are even more rigorous in enforcing child support obligations. Although much publicity is given to the number of fathers and mothers who do not pay court-required child support, many fathers and mothers do pay it. As an owner of a closely-held business, you have nowhere to hide. Some parents move after the marriage has ended, and the enforcement of claims for alimony and child support obligations becomes more difficult (although recent federal legislation has increased the enforcement of support obligations). As an owner of a closely-held business, you are an easy target.

Levels of child support can be very high. In some states, a significant portion of your pre-tax income must be devoted to your children unless you are awarded custody. If you go through a divorce and you have children whom you are obligated to support (because they are not adults and emancipated), it is a matter you should discuss most carefully with your divorce lawyer. Child support payments, unlike alimony, are *never* deductible for income tax purposes. Recent changes in the tax law are designed to prevent you from camouflaging (even with your ex-spouse's consent) child support as tax-deductible alimony.

In any event, if your spouse is awarded custody of your children, he or she will have a right to enforce child support payments against you; and as your fortunes increase (or your children's needs do), your spouse may have the right to seek additional amounts of child support, and there is a likelihood that he or she, if adequately represented, will be successful.

Property

Community Property States

Louisiana, Texas, New Mexico, Arizona, California, Washington, Nevada, Idaho and Wisconsin are America's community property jurisdictions. Community property laws vary from state to state but some common principles apply. Generally, any asset acquired during the marriage, other than by gift or inheritance, is a community property asset and each spouse is immediately a 50% owner in that property. However, any property you bring to the marriage, regardless of how you acquired it, and any gift or inheritance acquired during the marriage is not a community property asset, but rather a "separate asset." Spouses are entitled only to interests in community property, unless an agreement or extraordinary circumstances arise.

If you started your business after you were married, there is a high probability that it will be regarded as a community property asset unless you can establish that you started it with assets you brought to the marriage or with assets you received by gift or inheritance during the marriage. Even if you can establish that, or if you brought the business to the marriage, your spouse may claim that, over time, the business has been "transmuted" at least in part into a community property asset. Typically, the claim is founded on the fact that your efforts expended during the marriage have made the business a success. (Is it likely that you will argue that your efforts have nothing to do with your business's success?) Such claims have met with varying success, but usually the spouses compromise the matter rather than submit it to a court.

Separate assets may lose their separate nature if they are "co-mingled" with community assets or title is held, for at least a time, with the other spouse. You should be careful not to allow that to happen with your business interests, but in an amicable marriage it sometimes does. By the way, some states convert your separate assets into community property in some cases if you and your spouse move, for example, to a community property state when you retire.

Other States

The non-community property jurisdictions in the United States have different rules for allocating property to each spouse in the event of a divorce. Those states use the concept of "marital property" which is similar to the concept of community property in the community property states. The major difference is that with a community property asset, each spouse owns from the time of its acquisition a 50% undivided interest in it. With a marital asset in a non-community property state, only the spouse who actually owns the property has any interest in it until the marriage breaks down. Once the marriage breaks down, the other spouse becomes entitled to an interest in the property. Theoretically, that spouse's interest is to be determined by a court who can award as little or as much of it to each spouse as the court wishes. Most courts have adopted a practice of a 50/50 division for marriages over 10 years.

In non-community property jurisdictions, if you brought your business to the marriage or acquired it by gift or inheritance during your marriage, it does not fall into the category of marital property. However, as in the case of community property jurisdictions, arguments have been made to show that at least a portion of the asset has been transmuted into marital property because of the efforts of the spouse who operates the business during the marriage, and those arguments have sometimes been successful.

Joint Property

Property which is held in the names of both spouses is presumed to be owned one-half by each. Sometimes, spouses will claim that the title does not reflect the "real facts." Rarely, are such claims successful. What is important for you to realize is that if you register property in joint name with your spouse there is virtual certainty that she or he will receive one-half of that property.

Even though all, or a portion, of your business may be a community (or marital) property asset, your spouse may not be awarded part of the interest. The courts are authorized to award your spouse other assets (including a note from you) so that the business does not have to be "broken up" merely because the marriage has "broken down."

Pension Plans

Federal and state laws generally provide a spouse with certain rights to your qualified retirement plans and similar tax-favored arrangements, such as individual retirement accounts (IRAs). If your interests in those plans have been acquired during your marriage, there is a strong possibility that your spouse will be awarded one-half of the interests in those plans when you divorce.

RIGHTS AT DEATH

Community Property States

In most community property jurisdictions, your spouse is entitled only to her or his one-half interest in community property assets. In no jurisdiction is your spouse entitled to an income interest equivalent to alimony when you die. Occasionally, however, property settlement agreements will provide for alimony to continue even after the spouse paying it dies.

Other States

The non-community property states use an entirely different system, as a general rule, with respect to determining a surviving spouse's interest in her or his deceased spouse's estate. Most states provide for a minimum share of the estate which must be left either outright or in a trust for the surviving spouse. The minimum share is called by different names in different states such as "elective share." The make-up of the estate varies from state to state as well. Some states include assets which cannot be disposed of by Will, such as life insurance proceeds, pension benefits, joint bank accounts and similar items. Other states do not include them. The minimum share varies in size, typically being a minimum of at least one-third to as much as one-half of the deceased spouse's estate. It also varies in nature. Some states provide for an outright payment, others for a trust. Typically, the minimum share is approximately equal to what the surviving spouse would receive if the deceased spouse died without a Will.

Joint Property

Jointly owned property can take several forms. Sometimes, it will include the "right of survivorship", which is the right to receive all of the property when the first of the two owners dies. Sometimes, but not always, the form of ownership will be noted in the title. For example, if you and your spouse own a bank account together and after your name appear the letters "EOS" or "JWRS", the survivor of you and your spouse will succeed to the entire ownership in the account, as a general rule. ("EOS" means "either or survivor"; "JWRS" means "joint with rights of survivorship.")

Many states provide a presumption that any assets held in both the husband's and wife's names are intended to include a right of survivorship.

You should know what the effect would be, upon your death, of owning assets in joint form with your spouse. You should discuss the matter with your attorney to make sure that the form of ownership reflects the way you want it to be considered at the time you die. You also should be aware, and discuss with your attorney, the considerations involved in changing the form of ownership of assets held by you and your spouse. For example, one form of common ownership between a husband and wife, known as a "tenancy by the entirety", cannot be changed by one spouse alone. You will need your spouse's consent to change a tenancy by the entirety asset to any other form of ownership. In many states, a tenancy by the entirety can be created only in real estate and not other assets, such as stocks and bank accounts. In addition, in many states, the creditors of the estate of a deceased spouse cannot attach that deceased spouse's interests in tenancy by the entirety property. If you anticipate significant claims of creditors with respect to your estate, it therefore might not be a good idea to terminate a tenancy by the entirety form of ownership for another form which would make your interest in the property subject to the claims of your creditors at your death. Finally, tax consequences also can occur by changing ownership; before you change the title to any asset, consult with your attorney.

Pension Plans

Under federal law, your spouse, as a general rule, will be entitled to succeed to certain interests in your retirement plans when you die (other than individual retirement accounts (IRAs). Subject to rather strict rules, your spouse may waive her or his rights in your qualified retirement plan.

PARTNERSHIPS WITH YOUR SPOUSE

It Doesn't Have to Be in Writing

Sometimes, a husband and wife will operate a business together pursuant to a written partnership agreement. More often, however, even if they work together in the business, they will not have a written partnership agreement. In fact, often one of the spouses will regard the business as his or her own proprietorship. In some cases where there has been no partnership agreement, courts have found that the husband and wife intended there to be a partnership between them. The partnership may be a 50/50 partnership or the law may find some other percentage ownership between the spouses. In addition, whether you live in a community property or a non-community property state, if your spouse works for your business there is a good chance that your spouse will claim that a portion, or all, of the business has been transmuted into a community property or marital asset.

If your business is in corporate form, there is a much smaller probability that the court will find that it represents a partnership between you and your spouse. Nonetheless, if your spouse works in your business, the courts may find that a portion of it has been transmuted into community property or a marital asset. In addition, your spouse may claim that all of your assets constitute a type of partnership and the stock in your corporation is merely one of the *partnership's* (and not your separate) asset.

Making the Record Clean

Having your spouse acknowledge, pursuant to the formalities of a marital property agreement, that your business is your sole and separate property probably provides the best protection against having your spouse successfully claim that your business interests are owned in part by your spouse as a partner. In any event, if you and your spouse do work in the business together, it would be best for you to have a written "partnership" agreement. Not only will that make the record more certain in the event of a divorce (or your death if you do not wish to leave your business to your spouse), but it is more likely to avoid surprises under the tax law. Usually, courts will respect a written partnership agreement if the partners have acted pursuant to that agreement. If you have no such agreement, the IRS has much more latitude in contending that the arrangement is other than the way you and your spouse have treated it.

HOW TO LIMIT YOUR SPOUSE'S RIGHTS IN YOUR PROPERTY (IT CAN WORK FOR OR AGAINST YOUR CHILDREN TOO)

Pre-Marital Agreements

Overview

As a general matter, the law permits two people, even prior to their marriage, to agree to how their property will be treated both during their marriage and in the event of divorce or death. Such agreements are commonly called "pre-nuptial agreements" or "pre-marital" or "ante-nuptial" agreements or contracts. Although courts will carefully scrutinize the circumstances under which the agreement was entered into, the agreement usually will be enforced if the requirements of local law are met. Among other requirements, the agreement usually cannot have been unreasonable at the time that it was entered into or unconscionable at the time that it takes effect. The meanings of "unreasonable" and "unconscionable" vary with the circumstances. However, if you have entered a marriage with the understanding that your spouse will abandon her or his job to provide a more comfortable home life for you, it probably would be regarded as unreasonable if your spouse abandoned in a pre-nuptial agreement all claims to alimony or property in the event of divorce. Even if what your spouse has agreed to is reasonable at the time that the agreement is made, a court may find it to be unconscionable, especially if circumstances have changed, at the time of divorce. For instance, suppose your spouse suffered a debilitating condition or disease during the marriage. Even if your spouse has waived any entitlement to alimony (because your spouse intended to continue work but later quit the job), there is at least some chance that a court would find that the "no alimony" provision is unconscionable at the time of the divorce. Keep in mind, again, that the government's purpose in making you pay alimony is to shift the burden of maintaining your spouse from the government back to you.

In any case, a pre-nuptial agreement probably provides more protection than any other arrangement in minimizing or limiting your spouse's right to your property.

Fair Disclosure Requirements

Virtually all states require that you disclose to your future spouse the nature and extent of your assets and income prior to having that person sign a pre-nuptial agreement. Many people balk at the idea of disclosing their financial circumstances to their betrothed. Disclosing it at the time you get married, however, will be much less harmful to you than having to disclose it at the time of divorce. Unless you and your spouse have signed a binding pre-nuptial or similar agreement, your spouse will have an absolute right to all financial information about you (and for the years during your marriage) at the time of a divorce action. Many husbands and wives have been brought to their knees because of demands for financial disclosure by the other spouse in divorce, especially where the husband or wife has engaged in questionable activities (such as failure to report all income on tax returns). The bottom line is that as uncomfortable as you feel it might be to disclose information about your financial resources at the time of marriage, it will be much more painful for you to do so at the time of divorce.

Fair, Independent Legal Representation

Most states also require, either explicitly or as a matter of practice, that your betrothed have independent legal representation at the time of execution of the pre-nuptial agreement. You are begging for problems if you attempt to have your lawyer represent both you and your future spouse. In addition, the lawyer who represents your future spouse should have no financial dealings with you and probably should have never represented you in any matter. In one case, the attorney's malpractice carrier paid nearly $5 million to a spouse who had been represented by a lawyer who, although he had not represented her husband, had represented his company. She contended that the attorney was in a position of conflict and had not adequately represented her interests. The only reason she did not go after her husband as well was because he was in bankruptcy. Her claim instead was aimed at her attorney and, as indicated, he paid "through the nose."

The Myth of Post-Marriage Agreements

In most states, the law also permits spouses, after marriage, to enter into property ownership and alimony arrangements. Whether or not your marriage is healthy, it is extremely unlikely that your spouse will agree to enter such an agreement. Why should your spouse abandon claims which your spouse holds against you and your property? Your spouse's lawyer probably will urge him or her not to sign the agreement. In the real world, one spouse approaches the other about signing such an agreement only if there is a problem with the marriage even if the other is not aware of it. In any case, you should not hold out any hope that your spouse will sign such an agreement after your marriage (unless it is in the context of a divorce). If you wish to limit your spouse's rights to your property and your spouse's rights to alimony, you should cover it in a pre-nuptial agreement.

Effects on Your Children

A pre-nuptial agreement is intended to limit each spouse's rights to property, alimony and certain other rights (such as the right to serve as the administrator of your estate if you die without a Will). Usually, you will be permitted to give your spouse, either in a divorce or at death, more than the minimum provided in the pre-marital agreement. Hence, if your spouse agrees that she or he is entitled to only 20% of your estate at death, you would be permitted to leave your entire estate to your spouse when you die. In some cases, however, the children of the spouse who dies first will contend that they are beneficiaries of the pre-marital agreement and that you are prohibited from leaving your spouse any more than the minimum your spouse has agreed to under the pre-nuptial contract. As bizarre as such claims may seem, it is a good idea to ensure that any pre-nuptial agreement or any other property contract you enter into with your spouse expressly provides that it does not limit any voluntary transfer of property and that it is not intended to provide anyone else, including your and your spouse's children, any rights under the agreement.

Special Trusts

In many jurisdictions, property which you place in trust may remove it from the scope of claims of your spouse in the event of divorce or death. The kind of trust which accomplishes this varies widely from jurisdiction to jurisdiction. In some states, for example, a fully *revocable* trust created after marriage will remove the assets in the trust from claims to part of your estate by your spouse. In other states, only an irrevocable trust will accomplish that, and in some states even more extreme action will have to be taken to remove assets from the basket against which your spouse can make claims. It will be best for you to discuss that matter with your attorney prior to getting married. Even if you do not discuss it with your attorney prior to marriage, you may wish to do so after marriage to see how you can limit your spouse's rights to your property through the use of special trusts. You should keep in mind that if you or your spouse change your principal residence from one state to another, you and your spouse's rights to each other's property may change.

Lifetime Transfers

In General

In some cases, if you make a gift to someone other than your spouse, it will be beyond your spouse's reach in the event of divorce or death. That is not the case, however, in all states. In some community property states, for example, your spouse has a right to void a transfer you have made by gift to another person, any time during the marriage, with respect to your spouse's one-half interest in a community asset. In most states, however, your spouse will not be able to make such claims to gifts already made if your spouse has con-sented to them. Consent usually is liberally found, such as where your spouse agrees to "gift split" on your gift tax return (that is, your spouse pretends, as the law permits your spouse to do, that your spouse has made one-half of all gifts made by you). Again, because the law varies so widely from jurisdiction to jurisdiction, you should discuss with your lawyer your spouse's right to attach property you have given away to other people during your marriage.

Special Limitations

Property you give away during lifetime is much more likely to be successfully attached by your spouse if you retain interests in it. In many states, for example, if you create an irrevocable trust but retain the right to receive the income from the trust for your life, your spouse will be able to claim rights to that property.

Contracts with Others

In General

Through contracts, you may have created rights in persons other than your spouse to your property. In many cases, the rights of those other persons will take precedence over the claims of your spouse to the property. That may even be the case where the asset is a community property asset, but you have been the manager of the asset for both you and your spouse during the marriage.

Rights of First Refusal and Related Business Agreements

You may have entered into an agreement with the co-owners of your business giving them the right to buy your interest in the business if you attempt to transfer it during your lifetime (commonly called a "right of first refusal"). Hence, if you should attempt to transfer (or the court orders you to transfer) an interest in your business in a divorce, the co-owners of the business may have a right to buy it from you. In many cases, those rights will take precedence over your spouse's rights to the interest. That can be particularly important where the price which the co-owners have to pay for the interest is less than its current fair market value.

A right-of-first refusal agreement must be bona fide and cannot be used as a way to defraud your spouse of property. For example, you cannot have your brother, who is the co-owner of the business with you, buy your interest at a low price with an understanding that he will sell it back to you as soon as your divorce is complete. On the other hand, such an agreement made prior to divorce and which is enforceable against you and your spouse, probably will be respected by the courts. By the way, sometimes when parents transfer property in the business to their children they expressly cover circumstances in the event the child may become divorced. Such agreements prevent the son-in-law or daughter-in-law from getting an interest in the business. (Using a trust may be a much better way to accomplish that, however—see Chapter 16.)

Structuring Your Own Inheritance

In General

Usually, only assets you hold or could have held in your own name are subject to attack by your spouse in the event of divorce or death. If you have never owned the asset, it probably is not attachable by your spouse even if you have an interest in it.

For example, if you have received the interest in your business by gift or bequest from your parents, your spouse will be entitled to a minimum share of the business (or its worth) in the event of your death in most non-community property states. As discussed above, if you live in a community property state, and your spouse has worked in the business, a court may find that your efforts have converted the property, in whole or in part, into a community property asset and your spouse will be entitled to one-half (or less) of the business or its worth in either the event of divorce or your death. You can avoid the foregoing results if you structure your own inheritance and gifts from others in a better way, as discussed below.

Working with Your Parents' Advisors

Whether it is your business interest or other assets which you will acquire from your parents or other family members, working with them and their advisors to help you structure your own affairs to limit your spouse's (and other creditors') rights to your assets is essential. As a general matter, any interest in a trust which your parents (or others) have created for you will not be attachable by your spouse. In some states, however, a court can award part of your fixed rights in a trust created by another to your spouse. Hence, to maximize protection from claims of all creditors (including your spouse in the event of divorce or death), it is best to limit your interest to a discretionary one. Chapters 10 and 16 discuss using trusts to protect property from claims of creditors (including claims of a spouse) in more detail.

Your Spouse's Rights to Information About You and Your Finances

As mentioned above, upon death or divorce, in most cases, your spouse will have almost an absolute right to obtain all financial information about you, including interests you have in trust or otherwise. Therefore, entering into a pre-marital agreement, taking other action prior to marriage as advised by your attorney, and structuring receipt of gifts or inheritance from others to you through trusts, or other arrangements, are some of the best ways to protect yourself from having to leave property to your spouse when you die or having to give assets to your spouse in the event of a divorce.

ESTABLISHING YOUR ESTATE PLANNING GOALS AND PRIORITIES IN A SUBSEQUENT MARRIAGE

In General

Almost everyone has some estate planning goals which are in conflict. For example, when you want to maximize the amount which is available for your spouse but also want to maximize what is available for your descendants, you have a conflict. Leaving assets outright to your spouse may maximize her (or his) economic interest but decreases the probabilities that those assets eventually will be received by your children.

Division of the Estate

NEVER USE TAX-DRIVEN FORMULA CLAUSES

As will be discussed in more detail in Chapter 14, the tax law provides certain exemptions which can be used to reduce taxes on your property at your death and as that property eventually is transferred down to your grandchildren. As a practical matter, it is impossible for your attorney to know exactly how big those exemptions will be or what will be the best way to use them until after your death. As a consequence, your estate planning documents probably will use those exemptions by describing them in terms of the tax result sought to be achieved. For example, your lawyer will probably tell you that the estate tax exemption is $600,000 and that your estate planning documents will be prepared to take maximum advantage of that exemption. In fact, the available exemption is rarely exactly $600,000. Your lawyer knows that and, in fact, your lawyer will not make a bequest under your Will of $600,000. Rather, your lawyer will use language which describes the results sought to be achieved. The language may be something similar to "the maximum amount by which my taxable estate, determined without regard to this bequest, can be increased without increasing the federal estate tax on my estate." Certainly, without a strong tax background, it is difficult to understand what the language is trying to accomplish. But lawyers know, because they are experienced, that the phrase is attempting to use exactly the maximum available estate tax exemption.

Although use of such tax-oriented formula clauses to divide an estate commonly are used, it often is a mistake to use them as the method of dividing an estate between your spouse and your children. Tax-oriented formula clauses are almost guaranteed to cause conflict. There are literally thousands of cases where that has occurred. Unfortunately, many lawyers continue to use them.

Certainly, reducing taxes is an important goal. As a consequence, attorneys place a premium on using exemptions exactly (and no more or no less). However, it is inappropriate to use such tax concepts as the basis for dividing your estate between your spouse and your children.

For example, you estimate your net worth at $1.2 million. Your lawyer has told you that your estate tax exemption is $600,000 and you understand that you can leave that amount to your children free of estate tax. You can leave the other $600,000 to or in trust for your spouse under the protection of the estate tax marital deduction. (Of course, using the marital deduction only postpones the tax until your spouse later dies.) You have decided that a 50/50 division of your estate between your spouse and your children makes sense any way, so you instruct your lawyer to leave the estate tax exemption amount to your children and balance to your spouse. Let's take a look at some of the obvious things that can go wrong with that plan. First, your estate may grow or shrink. For example, if your estate grows to $2 million at the time you die, your children would receive only the estate tax exemption amount and your spouse would receive the balance or $1.4 million. Second, you may use the exemption for lifetime gifts that exceed the annual exclusion (which, as discussed later, is $10,000 per donee if your spouse splits the gift). The use of that exemption for gifts will occur even if you did not know you made the gift and even if you do not want to use the exemption for such gifts: The law requires you to use it against gifts. Hence, the full $600,000 may not be available when you die. That means that more of your estate will be transferred to your spouse and less to your children. Third, the exemption may have been reduced by law. Several proposals in the Congress have been made in recent years to that effect and there is a strong likelihood that eventually one of those proposals will be enacted. Fourth, your estate may be of such a size (generally, over $10 million) where the exemption, even under current law, is taken away from you. In that case, your children would receive nothing; your entire estate will pass to your spouse. Fifth, your estate will have an option of deducting administration expenses (such as fiduciary commissions and attorney fees) either for estate tax or income tax purposes. Usually, those expenses will be deducted where they save the most tax. But the effect of deducting them for one tax purpose has other ramifications. For example, if the fiduciary commissions and attorney fees are $100,000, and they are deducted on the estate's income tax return rather than the estate tax return, the effect will be for your children to have to pay them all because of the way the tax-oriented formula clauses work. On the other hand, if these expenses are deducted for estate tax purpose, their effect will be to have your spouse bear the entire burden.

The moral is that you should not use tax-driven formula clauses unless you are dedicating your entire estate to your spouse and the people you want eventually to receive your property are the same people to whom your spouse wants to leave his or her property. Unfortunately, few lawyers realize the detriments of using tax-oriented formula clauses to divide an estate in a subsequent marriage circumstance. The lawyers have been conditioned to minimize taxes to such a degree that sometimes they lose sight of the greater goal of doing what is fair and less likely to produce conflict.

TRY TO SEPARATE ASSETS CLEARLY

A better plan in a second marriage situation is to provide for the beneficiaries to receive legacies of specific items of property, fixed sums of money bequests or fractional shares of your probate estate (not dependant upon tax-oriented concepts). Although it is possible for conflicts to arise with those types of legacies, the probability of them arising is much diminished.

In some cases, an even better plan will be to separate the inheritances for the descendants from the inheritances for your spouse. For example, pre-death gifts to a trust for your spouse which purchases, for example, a life insurance policy on your life to provide an appropriate inheritance for your spouse and leaving the balance of your estate to your children may greatly reduce conflicts. However, if your spouse will have a minimum share right, or similar claim to your estate, such pre-death gifts to a trust for your spouse may not satisfy your spouse's claims to the minimum share. You should discuss the matter thoroughly with your attorney and decide on the most appropriate method of funding the inheritance for your spouse and funding the inheritance for your children.

One plan, which has considerable merit to it, is to leave one-half of your estate to (or in trust for) your spouse and one-half to your children. That way all the beneficiaries share proportionately in fortunes or misfortunes of your property. Nonetheless, even if that is the case, conflicts sometimes can arise. For instance, your spouse may not wish to receive interests in your closely-held business but rather to receive cash or marketable securities to satisfy her or his one-half interest. Sometimes, that will fit in exactly with what everyone wants but sometimes it will not.

SOLVING THE UNPRODUCTIVE TRUST PROBLEM

As discussed earlier, if you place assets into most forms of marital deduction trust, your spouse must have the right to force the trustee to generate a reasonable level of income—that is a tax rule. Even if you do not care whether or not the trust qualifies for the marital deduction (because the marital deduction usually only postpones the tax), your spouse nonetheless may have the right to complain that the trust is not adequately productive of income if he or she is a beneficiary of the trust. Certainly, you can specify that your spouse has no rights to question the level of income produced by the trust, but that invites a trustee to give your spouse nothing. Moreover, if you want to use interests in a trust (in those states where it can be done) to satisfy your spouse's right to a minimum share of your estate, your spouse generally will have to hold the right to make the trust reasonably productive of income.

One way to resolve the unproductive property dilemma, from a somewhat practical perspective, is to provide for your spouse to receive a minimum sum of money each year. You might provide, for example, that your spouse is to receive from the trust at least a minimum annuity. The annuity could be based on a percentage (such as 5%) of the initial value of the trust. (Because in all likelihood there will be a tax audit of your estate, you will have a solid number for the initial value.) You may even wish to provide that the sum is to be adjusted for some cost of living factor. In such a case, your spouse will be entitled to receive that annuity even if accounting income is so low that your spouse otherwise would be entitled to force the trustee to make the property produce a greater return. Five percent is probably a safe threshold in most states but you should discuss the matter with your attorney. In addition, although providing the minimum annuity may effectively prevent your spouse from forcing the trustee to sell the assets in the trust to make the trust more productive of income, the trustee nonetheless probably will have to raise the cash in order to pay the annuity. That may or may not be easy to do. A regular redemption program by the company of business interests held in the trust may provide the cash necessary to fund your spouse's annuity. On the other hand, it may be that the business will not do that or there are adverse consequences to such action for the business or for the trust. Generally, however, the "worst" circumstance is that the company will have to borrow money (or sell assets incurring a capital gain) to make the redemption of business interests held by the trust and the trust will have to treat the redemption proceeds as a taxable dividend (rather than as capital gain or as a return on investment). However, providing your spouse with a fixed annuity (coupled, perhaps, with a cost-of-living adjustment) with regular redemptions of the business interests in the trust may prevent the "unproductive property" problem from becoming a real one for your family.

An alternative to an annuity is a unitrust payment. A unitrust is one which pays a fixed percentage (such as 5%) each year of the value of the trust for that year. Hence, if the trust increases in value, the unitrust amount increases with it. That can eliminate the need to use a cost-of-living adjustment. However, the requirement of an annual valuation of closely-held business interests may make the unitrust an impractical vehicle for payments to your spouse.

Choice of Fiduciaries

The choice of the executor and trustee is always one of the most critical decisions in the estate plan. Few property owners appreciate the importance of that choice or recognize that the fiduciary becomes the substitute decision-maker for the property owner after death.

Your choice of the fiduciary (discussed in more detail in Chapter 13) may depend, in part, on how you divide up your estate. As indicated above, where (contrary to the advice given earlier) you decide to use a tax-driven formula bequest the size of which is dependent upon tax elections, and if you name either your spouse or your children (or all of them) as the fiduciaries entitled to make the tax elections, you enhance the probability of conflict and litigation. You are much better off naming an independent third party, such as a bank or trust company, as the fiduciary. If your attorney, in addition to representing you, also represents your spouse or your children, your attorney may not be a good choice as the fiduciary since your lawyer's obligation to do what is in the best interests of the estate may conflict, in many circumstances, with his or her duty as the legal advisor for other members of your family.

In any case, you should discuss with your attorney which attributes of a fiduciary are likely to reduce the probability of conflict among surviving members of your family.

If you separate the assets of your estate for your spouse (for example, by funding your spouse's share with life insurance) from the assets passing to your children, the probability of conflict is substantially reduced. In such a case, choosing your children, for example, as the executors may not be an inappropriate choice. Similarly, if you decide to fund your children's inheritance with separate assets and leave the balance of your estate to your spouse, your spouse may be the appropriate fiduciary.

Even if you divide your estate on a 50/50 basis between your spouse and your children, conflicts with the fiduciary can arise. For example, under most Wills (and other estate planning documents) and under the laws of several states, even if the estate planning documents are silent, the executor can allocate a different class of assets to one beneficiary and another class to a separate beneficiary. For example, if your spouse is named as the executor, your spouse may decide to allocate to himself or herself the more highly-liquid and more-productive assets and give your children assets of allegedly equal worth but which are not marketable or less likely to produce income.

How You and Your Subsequent Spouse Can Help Each Other with Your Estate Planning

Often and to a significant degree, husbands and wives can help each other with their own estate planning. For example, your spouse is permitted to pretend (under a concept known as "gift-splitting") that he or she has made one-half of all gifts you make during the year. For example, you are permitted to give as many individuals as you wish $10,000 a year free of gift tax. Your spouse can do the same. If your spouse has children of his or her own, it is unlikely that your spouse will want to give $10,000 to each of your children each year even though that can be done free of gift tax. On the other hand, the law permits your spouse to gift-split with you on gifts you make to your children. That means that you could give each of your children $20,000 a year and your spouse could gift-split so that she or he is treated as having made $10,000 or one-half of each such gift. No gift tax will be payable on those gifts. You can do the same for gifts your spouse makes to his or her children.

Unfortunately, when you gift-split, it applies to all gifts during the year. The tax law does not allow you and your spouse to pick-and-choose the ones with respect to which you want to gift-split and which ones you do not.

Also through gift-splitting, your spouse can agree to use his or her other exemptions under the tax law as well. For example, your spouse can agree to use his or her $600,000 gift tax exemption for gifts to your children. If your spouse intends to leave his or her property to charity so that no effective use of his or her exemption is made, there is some chance your spouse would agree to allow his or her gift tax exemption to be used on transfers to your children. Again, your spouse does not have to transfer property. Your spouse can use her or his exemption by gift-splitting. Similar use can be made of your spouse's exemption with respect to transfers to grandchildren and which can be protected from the second tax on transfers to grandchildren (known as the generation-skipping transfer tax and which is discussed in more detail in Chapter 14).

You and your spouse should be aware of conflicts that could arise between the two of you by gift-splitting. Generally, each of you will be liable for any gift tax (including penalties or interest) which later arises where you have agreed on gift-splitting. For example, you make a gift of interests in your business to your children. You claim that the gifts are only worth $20,000 and your spouse agrees to gift-split with you. Later, it is determined that the gifts were really worth $50,000. Your spouse will have been deemed to have gift-split with respect to the entire $50,000 and your spouse will owe gift tax (or have to use gift tax exemption) with respect to the $15,000 excess above the $10,000 annual exclusion amount. Of course, you and your spouse could agree that if something like that happens you will be responsible for any gift tax, interest and penalties. Sometimes, however, it is difficult for spouses to negotiate with each other on such matters. In fact, some spouses in subsequent marriages refuse to gift-split because they want to maintain some privacy and because of the difficulties which could arise in the event that a tax problem later arises on such gifts.

Adopting Your Spouse's Children and Your Spouse Adopting Your Children

Not infrequently, especially where the other parent of your children is deceased, a new spouse will adopt the children of the other spouse. Generally, if the other parent is still alive, one cannot adopt someone else's children unless that other parent consents in a formal court proceeding. That sometimes happens when the other parent (typically the father) has not been part of the family unit for a long period. In addition, the other parent's obligation to support generally terminates when someone else adopts the child. Hence, there may be a financial incentive for the other parent to consent to the adoption.

In most circumstances, if your spouse adopts your children while they are young (or you adopt your spouse's children when they are young) the adopted children will grow to be treated in the same manner as any other children in the family. In some (but not all) states, you can even adopt adult children.

Sometimes, people will attempt to adopt children to prevent interests in trusts which will end when they die from passing to collateral relatives. For example, suppose your grandmother creates a trust which is for your benefit during your life and which is payable at your death to your children, or if you have none, to your brothers and sisters or their children. Suppose further that you are likely to be childless when you die. You may decide you would like to adopt your spouse's children so they, rather than your brothers and sisters receive the trust property. Before you do this, you should check with your attorney as to the effect of adoption with respect to interests in trusts. Many states have rules (particularly with respect to old trusts) which provide that adopted children cannot take interests in trusts. Somewhat similarly, some states permit adopted children to take but only if they are adopted while they are minors.

It is interesting to note that some federal tax rules now treat your spouse's descendants (even if you have not adopted them) as your own. In some cases, the rules are beneficial to you; in other cases, those rules will be detrimental. However, not all federal tax and other laws treat your step-children as your own. You may find it appropriate to consult with your attorney about the effects of having step-children before you marry someone with children.

As indicated earlier, the estate and gift tax exemption (which can be as great as $600,000) and the exemption for transfers to grandchildren (which can be as great as $1 million) are personal and cannot be transferred from one person to another. Each of you and your spouse have your own exemptions and, through gift-splitting, can, as a practical matter, transfer the benefit of the exemption to each other during your lifetimes. However, if the less-wealthy spouse dies first, his or her estate tax and generation-skipping tax exemptions may be wasted.

The IRS has held that effective use of your spouse's exemptions can be made if you create a QTIP special form of marital deduction trust for your spouse during your lifetime. The trust, as explained earlier, must provide for your spouse to receive the income for life, but you can control where the property goes when your spouse dies. That trust will form part of your spouse's estate when your spouse dies, and your spouse's exemptions can be applied with respect to assets in it. That prevents waste of your spouse's exemptions if your spouse's own property is insufficient to take full advantage of her or his exemptions. In fact, the IRS has set forth a mechanism in which you can receive the income from the trust after your spouse's death and without having the trust form part of your tax estate when you die. The IRS has approved several methods of doing that, but you must receive the advice of a competent tax advisor to make sure you don't do it improperly. If you do it improperly, the trust will be includable, and therefore taxable, in your estate when you die whether or not you predecease your spouse. Properly structured, however, such a QTIP trust can be a favorable arrangement: You will provide an income interest for your spouse for life (something you may want to do anyway), be able to receive the income interest for yourself after your spouse dies without having the trust be part of your taxable estate and allow your spouse's exemptions to be applied against the assets in the trust when your spouse dies.

Family Residence and Personal Use Assets

Even if you are not obligated to do so, you may want to permit your spouse to remain in the family residence and to use its contents for at least a limited time after your death. Particularly, if relations between your spouse and your children are not good, your spouse may be pressured to vacate the home shortly after your death if the children succeed to ownership of it. You should decide what you want to happen with respect to the house. You can carve up its use almost any way you wish. For example, you could give your spouse the absolute right to live in the residence for six months or a year after your death with the estate funding the expenses. Although the value of the use of the home will not qualify for the marital deduction, it will not increase taxes, as a general rule, over what they otherwise would be if you left the house directly to your children without your spouse having any right to use it for some reasonable period of time after your death. Keep in mind that homes often are held by spouses in joint name with rights of survivorship. In such a case, your spouse will succeed to complete ownership of the home. Check to see how its ownership is held.

Burial Expenses and Health Care Decisions

Not infrequently, your spouse and your descendants of a prior marriage may disagree as to your funeral and burial arrangements. Those disagreements can be particularly difficult if your children and your spouse do not share the same religious beliefs.

The best case is for you to provide specifically in both your Will (and in another document which does not have to be established in court) exactly what your wishes for disposition of your body are.

Similarly, it is important for you to execute documents which specify your wishes for your health care if you are incompetent to make them known and to name one (and only one) person to make decisions for you. Chapter 11 discusses these documents which set forth your health care decisions and which name someone to make health care decisions for you (called, respectively, Living Wills and Health Care Proxies).

SUMMARY AND CONCLUSIONS

It is common for married persons to have descendants from prior marriages. In such cases, conflicts after your death are likely to arise unless your spouse has adopted your children while they are young. In any case, it is appropriate for you to consider what rights your spouse will have with respect to your property in making your estate plans. In some cases, you can provide for your spouse to receive less (such as providing for your spouse to receive property in trust) than what the law will provide if you do not carefully plan. In any case, you must eventually decide on the appropriate division of your property. Steer clear of tax-oriented formula provisions as the method of dividing your estate between your spouse and your descendants. Funding either your spouse's or your children's inheritance with separate assets (such as life insurance) may be the best plan of all. Alternatively, leaving each a fractional share (not determined by tax concepts) of your estate may be best even though it may not ultimately minimize taxes. Avoiding costly litigation may be more cost efficient than trying to squeeze out every possible dollar of tax reduction. Your choice of your executor and trustee will be an especially important decision in a subsequent marriage circumstance. Although you and your spouse can assist each other with your estate planning, sometimes conflicts will arise in doing so.

CHAPTER 13

WHOM SHOULD I CHOOSE AS MY EXECUTORS AND TRUSTEES?

INTRODUCTION AND OVERVIEW OF CHAPTER

The choices of the persons to be the executors of your Will and trustees of trusts you create, as well as certain other fiduciaries, are some of the most important decisions you will make. Generally, those fiduciaries become the legal owners of your property. They hold the authority, usually to the exclusion of the beneficiaries for whom they act, to decide when and if property will be purchased, sold, exchanged, abandoned, invested for high income, low income or no income at all. The law imposes restrictions, in some cases, as to whom you may choose to act as a fiduciary. Through planning you may be able to expand the class of persons whom you wish to act. Generally, fiduciaries are entitled to compensation for their services. Within limits, you can provide for a different level of compensation, or no compensation at all, although, in any case, a person may refuse to accept an appointment. The choice of the appropriate fiduciary may be complex. Certain individuals will have conflicts of interest in acting for the beneficiaries, and those conflicts may not be obvious. In some circumstances, adverse effects will befall a fiduciary who acts in certain capacities or choice of a particular fiduciary will cause adverse tax or other effects to the beneficiaries. This Chapter explores these matters and makes recommendations as to the selection and compensation of the fiduciaries who will act for you and for your family.

339

TYPES OF FIDUCIARIES AND THEIR DUTIES

Executors

Description

Usually referred to as the "executor of the estate," but more properly as the "executor of the Will," the executor is the one who "executes" the provisions of your Will. In fact, the duties and responsibilities of the executor are much broader than that. In some jurisdictions, the executor is known as the "personal representative" of the estate. Those terms will be used interchangeably in this Chapter.

If you have no Will, or no one whom you have named to be the executor serves, the person who administers your estate is known as the "administrator." Generally, the duties of an executor and administrator are identical. However, you can expand or restrict the duties and responsibilities of your executor, compared to those of an administrator if you have no Will, by placing appropriate provisions in your Will.

General Duties

Safeguard and Collect Assets Passing Under the Will

One of the primary duties of an executor is to safeguard all of your assets. Generally, that responsibility extends only to assets which do not pass at your death by other means, such as life insurance proceeds which pass directly to a named beneficiary pursuant to a designation form filed with the insurance company. In some states, the executor's duty with respect to some assets, such as real estate, is limited. Nonetheless, the executor has an affirmative duty to safeguard assets passing under the Will and, in some cases, even those passing outside of the Will. An executor who fails to safeguard those assets properly generally will be personally liable for any resulting losses. That is a factor you should consider in selecting the personal representative of your estate.

The executor also is responsible to collect the assets which pass under the Will. Some lawyers refer to that as "marshalling" the assets. All that means usually is that title to those assets is transferred to the executor, and the executor becomes their legal owner. Almost always, the executor's position is disclosed in the title. For example, the stock in your business will be re-registered, after your death, from your name to "ABC Bank, as Executor Under the Will of John Jones." Showing the executor's title in the ownership of the estate assets reduces the probability of the executor's own creditors attempting to attach them to pay the executor's personal obligations and, to some degree, retards the executor's ability to abscond with assets belonging to the estate and prevents confusion as to beneficial ownership.

Settle Claims and Pay Debts

Another obligation of the executor is to settle claims against your estate and to pay any debts properly owing. In many states, an executor who fails to pay your debts, to the extent they are enforceable against your estate, and to settle claims against your estate in a proper way, is personally liable to the creditors. The rules relating to claims against a decedent's estate and the obligation of an estate to pay the decedent's debts are complex. Generally, only attorneys who practice in the area of estate administration and professional fiduciaries are familiar with those complex rules. That does not necessarily mean that you should only appoint someone familiar with those rules as the personal representative. Through proper legal representation, the executor will be advised what action should be taken.

Make and Change Investments

Generally, a personal representative must make assets of an estate productive. An executor who fails to invest cash in your estate, such as by leaving a large sum in a non-interest bearing checking account, may be liable for loss of income even if you also had failed to invest the cash during your lifetime.

In addition, an executor is obliged to make only prudent investments and, as a general matter, to dispose of any investments which are not prudent. To some degree, that can be a problem in the estate of an owner of a closely-held business. The rules relating to what constitutes a prudent investment are complex. Generally, to be prudent an investment must be of the type which a prudent person (or, in some states, a prudent investor) would make desiring to achieve a reasonable level of income and to preserve corpus. Usually, prudent investments exclude speculative ones. Often, interests in a closely-held business will be regarded as speculative particularly if they represent a significant portion of the estate.

Generally, an executor will continue to hold the closely-held business interests which you owned at the time of your death. However, adverse conditions in the business may cause the executor to wish to sell those interests to avoid the personal liability which may result if the estate sustains losses because the assets are not sold.

In almost all circumstances, it will be appropriate for your Will to contain an express authorization for your executor to hold the business interest during the administration of your estate even if that interest would otherwise represent an imprudent investment. (A comparable provision should be contained in your revocable living trust if you dispose of your assets by that means.) In some cases, individuals have attempted to prohibit the sale of their business interests by the executor (and, in some cases, even by the trustees). Surprisingly, courts have generally refused to enforce such directions and have held fiduciaries liable who have held the business interests when it was certain that losses would be sustained. (In some states, it may be possible to obtain express court authority to hold on to the closely-held business interests.) Usually, it is best to provide as much protection to the personal representative as possible in holding the business interests after your death but not prohibit their disposition.

One method of attempting to ensure that the business interests will not be sold during the administration of your estate is to bequeath them specifically to someone, such as a child who will operate the business after your death. Such a specific disposition greatly reduces the executor's capacity to sell those interests although, in most states, the executor may do so if necessary to pay claims against the estate or to pay death taxes. Alternate ways to try to inhibit the sale of your business are discussed in Chapter 5.

In any event, it is generally best to discuss your wishes with respect to the disposition of your business interests with the persons whom you will name as the executors under your Will.

Minimize Family Disharmony

Often, the death of the central figure in the family will cause a change in family relationships. In some cases, family disharmony will result. In addition, the way in which the estate is administered may cause further disharmony. Even if you have named an independent third party, such as a bank or trust company, as the personal representative of your estate, your surviving family members may disagree as to what that executor should do. Some family members may want assets immediately sold while others may want them retained. Some family members may want your estate invested to produce high income while others may want no or low current income produced in favor of appreciation. The list of potential disagreements is virtually endless. Sometimes, even the most experienced and wise personal representative will not be able to prevent family disharmony from occurring. On the other hand, the selection of an insensitive person as the personal representative greatly enhances the probability of family strife occurring. That strife, unfortunately, often translates into legal action, and the result is often very high legal expenses.

Speed the Administration of the Estate

In certain cases, as will be discussed in Chapter 14 relating to the deferral of payment of estate tax, it will be appropriate to avoid closing the administration of an estate. Usually, however, beneficiaries will desire for the administration of the estate to be completed as quickly as possible. Almost by its nature, prolonging the administration of an estate will result in additional expenses, such as attorney's fees. Moreover, beneficiaries are often anxious to receive benefits from an estate and often the benefits are not paid, or are not paid in full, until the administration of the estate is closed.

Often factors beyond the control of the personal representative, and the personal representative's attorney, will prevent the administration of the estate from being closed quickly. That will occur, for example, where litigation arises with respect to estate taxation or other claims against the estate or the ownership of assets.

File Death Tax Returns and Pay Death Taxes

Generally, your executor will be personally responsible to make sure all death tax returns are filed and all death taxes are paid when initially due. Your estate faces potentially very heavy penalties if taxes or returns are not paid and filed on time—for example a late filing penalty equal to 5% of the total estate taxes due will be imposed if your federal estate tax return is filed one day late, even if the total tax is paid on time. Those fines are imposed on the estate although your executor, if at fault, may be required by the court having jurisdiction of your estate to pay those fines personally.

Every state imposes some type of death tax. The procedures for paying the tax and filing the return vary from state to state. In addition, if you die owning real estate or tangible personal property (such as a car, boat or furnishings) situated in another state or states, your executor probably will be required to file a return and pay tax in that other state or states as well.

As explained above, if the estate taxes, and in some cases gift or income taxes you owe for the period prior to your death, are not paid when due, your executor may be personally responsible for paying them. In some cases, the executor will be able to recapture assets held by others, such as beneficiaries who hold property included in your estate, to pay such taxes, but in some cases the executor may have to pay those taxes individually and not be reimbursed.

File Other Reports

Other reports or returns also may have to be filed. Many states require that an inventory of the assets which will be disposed of by your Will must be filed in local court within a certain time. Some also require reports about your estate during its administration. Failure to file those returns on time may result in fines imposed against your estate or the executor. In addition, your personal representative generally will be responsible to make sure that all state and local pre-death income and gift tax returns be filed. Both your estate and the executor may face penalties if they are not filed and any resulting taxes not paid on time.

Distribute Assets to the Beneficiaries

One of the most important duties is to distribute the assets to the beneficiaries. In some cases, executors fail to distribute all of the assets because a reserve for unpaid taxes or potential claims is maintained and then forgotten about.

In many cases, the personal representative will be able to distribute some assets to the beneficiaries well before the administration of the estate is complete. For example, if you make a gift of your antique automobile to your nephew, and the personal representative of your estate is confident that your estate holds adequate liquid assets to pay all taxes and all other potential claims, the executor may decide to distribute the title of the automobile to your nephew early during the administration of your estate. With proper planning, your executor may prudently distribute a significant percentage of your estate well before its administration ends.

Some professional fiduciaries follow a policy of not distributing much of anything until the estate is virtually closed. One of the primary reasons for that is to protect the executor from being personally liable if a shortfall in assets develops and taxes or other claims against the estate cannot be met. If it is important to you that your beneficiaries receive distributions prior to the completion of the administration of the estate, at a minimum you should consider placing such a request in your Will and also consider discussing that matter with the individual or institution you name as your executor.

Account

As a general matter a personal representative may have a duty or can be compelled to prepare a written statement of the activities which it has undertaken. That written statement is usually called an accounting. In some states, such as New York, it is common for personal representatives, as a matter of course, to prepare such a written account, submit it to the beneficiaries and/or the court and ask for approval of all actions the executor has taken. In other states, it is rare for a personal representative voluntarily to account or even be ordered by a court to account, which almost never occurs unless a beneficiary commences an action for an accounting. The costs of preparing such an account typically are borne by the estate (or trust) involved. In some states, you may be able to provide protection to your personal representative even if the representative does not present a written account to the beneficiaries or presents one in a form which is not the one prescribed under the normal rules of state law and procedure. The costs of administering your estate, and any trust you create, can be high, often exceeding 5% of your assets. You should discuss in some detail with your attorney how you can reduce those expenses.

Trustees

DESCRIPTION OF TRUSTS AND GRANTORS AND TRUSTEES

A trust is a legal relationship usually involving three persons: the grantor of the trust, the trustee of the trust and the beneficiary of the trust. The grantor is the person who transfers the assets, such as cash or other property, which are held in the trust. The grantor may be known by several other names, such as trustor, settlor or donor.

The trustee is the person who holds legal title to the assets in the trust, administers the trust, acts on its behalf although in all cases solely for the benefit of the beneficiaries. The beneficiary or beneficiaries are the persons for whose current or future benefit the assets are held in trust.

SIGNIFICANT DIFFERENCES BETWEEN TRUSTEES AND EXECUTORS

In many ways, the duties of an executor and a trustee are similar. Both are fiduciaries and must act in the best interests of the beneficiaries as opposed to themselves. In some cases, such as where a revocable living trust is used as a substitute for a Will, the duties of the trustee, after the death of the grantor who created the revocable trust, will be very similar to those of an executor during the first few years of administration of the formerly revocable trust.

Generally, however, the obligation of the trustee to invest and reinvest assets, as opposed to holding them for distribution to the beneficiaries or to liquidate them, is greater than that of an executor. In addition, the administration of a trust generally lasts for a longer time than the administration of an estate, although there are exceptions to that rule.

The duties of the trustee generally continue even after the trust comes to an end. For example, when your youngest child becomes age 35, the trust, by its terms, ends. However, the trustee will continue thereafter to arrange for legal title of the assets to be transferred to the beneficiaries, collect any fees due the trustee, pay any unpaid expenses of the trust and, perhaps, submit the statement of the trustee's acts during the administration of the trust (the accounting). Not infrequently, three years will expire between the time the trust, by its terms, ends, and the assets in the trust are fully distributed to the beneficiaries. If there is a dispute as to which persons are entitled to the trust property, as there often is, it may be many years after the trust ends before the assets, in fact, are distributed to the beneficiaries.

GENERAL DUTIES

The trustee accepts legal title to the trust assets, and, in some cases, as with an executor, must take action to collect such assets—that is, to make sure that assets which belong to the trust are legally registered in trust name. Because the tenure of the trustee may be longer than that of the personal representative, the trustee, perhaps, should have a greater propensity for furthering family harmony. Usually, an executor has little authority as to the disposition of assets. The Will, or if there is no Will, state law, generally makes it certain as to which beneficiary receives which assets. However, a trustee often is granted, and with good reason, broad discretion as to whether assets should be paid to one beneficiary as opposed to another, or as to whether no payments should be made to any beneficiary. A trustee who is insensitive to the consequences of the actions he or she takes may generate family disharmony which can result in the dissipation of trust assets as litigation among beneficiaries ensues.

Guardians

OVERVIEW OF TYPES

The law provides for several different types of guardians. Guardians act on behalf of individuals who do not have legal capacity to act on their own. Guardians may be appointed for minors, persons who are incompetent, persons who are incarcerated or others unable to act on their own behalf. Parents, for example, are sometimes referred to as the "natural guardians" of their children. Also, sometimes when a minor is involved in a lawsuit, the court will appoint a guardian for that person solely for purposes of the litigation. Sometimes, that fiduciary is called a "guardian ad litem" (guardian for the litigation). In arranging for the care of your children if you die while they are minors and for management of the minor's property, the law usually recognizes two types of guardians: a guardian of the person and a guardian of the property.

In some states, a guardian for an adult is called a "committee." The functions, however, are the same regardless of the name. As will be discussed below, however, a guardian is different from a "conservator."

GENERAL DUTIES OF A GUARDIAN OF THE PERSON

The guardian of the person typically is the one who is authorized by law to act on behalf of a minor, or an adult who is incompetent, on personal matters. For example, the guardian of the person usually will decide what school the minor will attend, whether certain medical procedures will be undertaken on behalf of the child, what religious instruction the child will receive, where the child will live, etc. Generally, but not in all cases, the child will live with the guardian of his or her person. Where the child is very young, the guardian of the person can have a significant impact during the child's formative years. Although it is rare for a child to be orphaned before majority, it occasionally happens and your selection of the appropriate guardian for your minor children will be an especially important one for you. You should choose an individual or individuals in whom you repose the greatest trust, who you are confident will act in the best interests of your child. However, you should be aware that taking your child into the guardian's home will impose a significant emotional and, perhaps, financial burden on the guardian. In one case, for example, the aunt and uncle of three orphaned children were named their guardians when the parents of the infants died in an automobile crash. It imposed such a burden on the aunt and uncle that they waited nearly 15 years before they had children of their own. The aunt and uncle had been married only three weeks at the time that the children's mother and father died.

In any case, you can name in your Will the guardian of the person of your minor children if the child's other parent does not survive. Also, in a growing number of states, you can name during your lifetime a "standby" guardian for your minor children, with the appointment becoming effective upon your incapacity (mental or physical) or death. Your failure to name a guardian may result in a significant dispute following your death as to who is the proper person. Typically, the other members of the mother's and father's family will literally fight over the children. Where both families are wealthy, the court may "split" the child between the two families which may not be in the child's best interest. It may be better, for example, for the child to have only one guardian of the person, to live in the guardian's home and visit with other family members only on the same basis that the child would have visited with them had the natural parents survived.

GENERAL DUTIES OF A GUARDIAN OF THE PROPERTY

The guardian of the property becomes the legal owner of the child's assets. In other words, the guardian of the property holds the purse strings. The guardian of the person need not be the same as the guardian of the property. In fact, in some cases, it will be appropriate to name different persons to each role. To some degree, forcing the guardian of the person to have to go to someone else (the guardian of the property) for funds may increase the probability that the child's property will be properly expended.

However, that may be an unnecessary procedure and it will result in additional expense which probably will be imposed upon the child's property. Under the law of many states, the guardian of the property must account in court (that is, submit a written statement of assets on hand, income and expenses) each year to ensure that the child's property is properly being managed and used.

The use of a guardian of the property, however, is usually a poor one. Guardians almost always have to post a bond to ensure they will act properly and in some states account at least once a year in court. In addition, their activities are very closely monitored by the court and the restrictions on a guardian of the property to spend funds on behalf of the minor are greater than those imposed upon other fiduciaries. In fact, you probably are better off ensuring that assets for any minor are placed into a trust or a similar arrangement. The flexibility in dealing with the property is much greater that way. The only circumstance in which you would want a guardian of the property is where you do not have confidence in the honesty or integrity of the person whom you would choose to manage the assets of the child. If that is your concern, choosing a prominent bank or trust company as trustee probably will ensure that your child's assets are safe-guarded. The trustee for the child will have much greater flexibility in taking action on his or her behalf, in paying funds over to the guardian of the person, and taking other action on behalf of the child than would a guardian of the child's property.

Appropriate Characteristics of Guardians

The appropriate characteristics for a guardian of the person is someone who is willing to take your child into his or her home or at least supervise the personal activities of your child. Usually, the appropriate guardian is a relative of the child or a close friend and confidant of yours. In all events, you should discuss ahead of time with the individual or individuals whom you wish to appoint the fact that you have named them in your Will as the guardians of your minor children. Not infrequently, parents discover that the person whom they wish to be the guardian does not wish to act. That person, for example, may not have children or is looking forward to the day that there will be no children in his or her home. Even if the person whom you would choose as the guardian has children of the same age that you do, the bur-den of having additional children in the household may be more than the individual wishes to take on.

If you have a child with a medical or dysfunctional prob-lem, you may find that few will "volunteer" to be the guard-ian of the person. Again, a critical matter is that you discuss the potential appointment with the individuals whom you would choose as guardians ahead of time.

Grandparents may or may not make an appropriate choice of a guardian. Naming a 70 year old grandparent as the guardian for a three year old may not be a wise choice even if the grandparent is the closest relative. It may turn out that the child is really more than the grandparent can handle. If you decide not to choose your parents or your spouse's parents as the guardians you may want to discuss that matter with them ahead of time. You reduce the probability of your parents and your parents-in-law objecting to the appointment you have made and you can let them know that even if they believe otherwise you feel it would be an undue burden to impose the guardianship on them.

You and your spouse should choose the same individual as the guardian. Failure to do so may result in a conflict between your Will and your spouse's Will as to the appointment of the guardian, and problems can arise if you and your spouse die at the same time or under circumstances in which the order of your deaths is not clear.

The guardian of the property, as explained above, may be the same person as the guardian of the person. However, they need not be the same. For example, you might appoint a bank or trust company as guardian of the property with a family member as guardian of the person. However, it must be emphasized again that you should attempt to avoid having a guardian of the property by using a trust for the child instead.

LIMITATIONS ON CHOICES OF GUARDIANS

If you fail to name a guardian of the person or property, the law usually specifies the people who can serve and the priority of their right to serve, generally starting with closest relatives. Those closest relatives, for example, are usually the child's grandparents. Because the grandparents may come from both the father's and mother's lines, there is some likelihood of a dispute where you fail to name a guardian with resultant ill-will and expense. Generally, you can choose any honest, adult competent person you wish to serve as the guardian. There is no requirement that you choose, for example, someone of the same religious beliefs that you hold and which your child is expected to adopt.

Conservators

DESCRIPTION

A person who is experiencing difficulty in managing his or her financial affairs may have a conservator of the property appointed as opposed to a guardian (or a committee). Conservator appointments are generally preferred over the appointment of a guardian because a conservatorship does not require a finding of total legal incompetency.

General Duties

A conservator generally manages the financial affairs for a conservatee. In most states, however, the conservator does not have control over the "person." For example, a conservator may not have the power to sign the conservatee into a nursing home or take similar actions. However, the law is developing in a way which would allow conservators, in certain cases, to take personal action on behalf of the conservatee. However, the difficulty is that under a conservatorship the conservatee has not been found to be incompetent and, therefore, is presumed to be able to make personal decisions on his or her own behalf.

Appropriate Characteristics of Fiduciaries

Integrity

Integrity is almost synonymous with the concept of fiduciary. If you have any question about a person's or institution's integrity, you probably should not consider appointing that person or institution in any fiduciary capacity. As stated before, the personal representative of your estate becomes the legal owner of your property. The opportunity to deflect assets to the executor's personal use may be too great a temptation for a person of less than the highest integrity. In many cases, when theft by a fiduciary is discovered, the fiduciary has inadequate assets to repay the estate or cannot be found. One of the advantages of a corporate fiduciary is that even if it, or one of its employees, unlawfully appropriates the assets, it will be personally liable and probably can be forced to pay.

Capacity

Even a person of the highest integrity may not have the capacity to act as the personal representative of your estate or as trustee of trusts you create. As explained above, the responsibilities of a fiduciary are many and complex. For example, decisions such as when, and at what levels, to compromise claims, including claims by tax authorities for additional taxes, are often complex ones beyond the capacity of certain persons. Nonetheless, an individual need not be a professional fiduciary or experienced in such matters. If your personal representative chooses a wise and experienced lawyer to represent the estate, the attorney probably can provide sufficient guidance to even an inexperienced person so that he or she can do an adequate job in administering the estate. However, you cannot direct the personal representative to choose a particular lawyer or law firm. In addition, the fiduciary is not required to follow even the most sage advice of the lawyer. Nonetheless, you may have confidence in the person whom you select as the executor or trustee to choose an attorney or law firm with adequate experience and judgment to be able to well represent your fiduciary.

Diligence

Probably the major complaint about lawyers is procrastination. Lawyers are viewed as being insufficiently diligent in completing work for their clients. To some degree, the charge is a fair one. Attorneys should complete their assignments diligently and, therefore, within a reasonable time. That is also true for the personal representative of your estate. An individual, or institution, which demonstrates a propensity toward procrastination may be a very poor choice. In addition, if you choose someone who is not experienced in fiduciary matters and will be relying on the attorney to accomplish the job, you best make certain that a non-procrastinating attorney will be chosen to represent the fiduciary. Because you cannot dictate the choice of an attorney, you should discuss the matter with the person whom you select as a fiduciary ahead of time.

Availability

You may know someone who would be the ideal executor or trustee. Perhaps, that is the person whom you were closest to in college and who has had substantial experience in fiduciary-related matters, knows your family well, shares many of your values, is hard working and of the highest integrity. A person such as that, however, may not have the time to act as the personal representative of your estate or as trustee of trusts you create. Sometimes individuals will choose persons in another part of the country to be the fiduciary. Even in those states where such an appointment is valid (and in some states, such as Florida, it usually is not), the selection of a person far away may not be appropriate. Although with express delivery services, facsimile devices and conference calls, personal meetings may not be necessary in order to adequately carry out the administration of an estate, a person who is far removed from where the administration will occur often will not do the best job.

Lack of Conflict

An actual or potential conflict of interest may render someone who otherwise would be a good choice as a fiduciary completely inappropriate. As explained in more detail in Chapter 12, choosing one of your children as the executor where you leave a significant portion of your estate to your spouse who is not your child's other parent may put your child into a position of conflict of preferring himself or herself over your spouse.

Owners of closely-held businesses often face such potential conflicts in choosing a fiduciary. For example, you may believe that your partner, co-shareholder, president of your company or someone else involved in your business would be an excellent choice as the personal representative of your estate. Often, however, such people have conflicts of interest. For example, can you really expect the successor president of your company to recommend that the company be sold or liquidated, which will result in the loss of his or her job, even if that is in the best interests of your family? Similarly, how is your surviving partner or co-shareholder going to set his or her salary once you are gone and your family succeeds to your interest in the business?

The choice of such individual may well be appropriate but it often requires careful consideration of potential conflicts. In some cases, you may want to eliminate such a person from participating in certain decisions with respect to certain assets in your estate just to make certain that all factors, including your family's best interests, are taken into account. You usually can accomplish that by appointing co-executors or co-trustees and specifying in which decisions some of them can or cannot participate.

SPECIAL CHARACTERISTICS OF A TRUSTEE

All of the characteristics of a fiduciary listed above (integrity, diligence, capacity, availability, responsibility, lack of conflict, experience and dedication) are also the appropriate characteristics for a trustee. However, a trustee, perhaps more than a personal representative, must possess a higher degree of sensitivity to the needs of the beneficiaries and the capacity to take action which minimizes rather than promotes family disharmony. Also, investment experience and capacity usually play a greater role with a trustee than with an executor, the latter's duties generally being ones of short-term investment and prompt distribution of assets to the beneficiaries.

In other words, a good personal representative may not necessarily be a good trustee. For example, your brother or sister may make an excellent personal representative of your estate because of his or her integrity and availability and the fact that you are confident your sibling will choose a competent attorney to assist in carrying out the executorial duties which probably will be completed in a short time after your death. Your brother or sister may not, however, be a good trustee of a trust which is a more long term undertaking. First, your sibling may not possess the requisite objectivity in determining how certain discretionary powers, such as the right to distribute income among a class of beneficiaries, should be exercised. Moreover, although a sibling might be capable of hiring an investment counselling firm to advise how trust assets should be invested, that may result in additional charges to the trust compared to hiring a trustee who already possesses significant investment capacity. In fact, a family member or friend may not be able adequately to monitor the performance of an investment advisor so that he or she will change investment advisors at appropriate times under a trust agreement.

One reason for selecting a corporate fiduciary as trustee as opposed to an individual is where the trust will last a long time. The administration of your estate probably will not last for more than 15 years or so, and may be completed, as a practical matter, within four years of your death. An individual you choose to act as the personal representative probably will live through the administration of your estate. However, if you create a long-term trust, and there are many good reasons to do so, any individual you would name as the trustee may not survive the administration of the entire trust. A bank or trust company probably will.

TYPICAL CHOICES OF EXECUTORS AND TRUSTEES

Limitation of Choices

Many states limit the persons who can act as an executor or trustee. Most states limit the choices for a trustee under a decedent's Will to individuals and banks and trust companies. Some states also prohibit non-residents, or out-of-state banks and trust companies, from acting as trustees under Wills.

In contrast, your choice of a trustee is generally much greater where the trust is created by contract—that is, by an agreement of trust rather than by Will. For example, if you reside in a state which prohibits non-residents of your state from serving as trustee under your Will, you can either direct the original probate of your Will in another state which does not so discriminate against non-residents of your state or, alternatively, use a revocable living trust agreement as the substitute for your Will. In almost all cases, anyone you wish, including, in some cases, an entity which is not an individual or a bank or trust company, may act as trustee under a trust agreement.

A Business Associate

As discussed in more detail under Chapter 3 relating to planning for successor managers of your business, it usually is desirable to have someone familiar with your business, or at least its industry, involved in the administration of your estate and any trust which holds interests in your business. However, as just pointed out, many of those individuals could be in a position of conflict of interest. One of your competitors may eventually become a close and respected friend of yours. That person may know better than anyone else the best way to operate your business. However, appointing such a person as your personal representative or trustee necessarily will result in a conflict of interest at least between your company and his or hers.

A Better Alternative

A better alternative may be to appoint others as the personal representatives and trustees but expressly authorize them to retain the services of advisors who might include the person who becomes the CEO of your business after your death, the surviving co-owners of your business and others in your industry, even though they may be competitors in many senses. As will be discussed in more detail below, a committee, especially with certain "checks and balances", may be an appropriate choice for you to consider.

FAMILY EXECUTORS AND TRUSTEES

Naming certain members of your family as personal representatives of your estate and trustees of trusts you create may be an appropriate choice. Not infrequently all adult and competent children are appointed as fiduciaries to serve, perhaps, with others. In other cases, the oldest child is appointed with the next eldest becoming the successor in the event the oldest cannot act, and so on to the youngest. In some circumstances, a child will resent not having been appointed if a sibling is. Those attitudes may be especially likely to arise where the children who are not chosen do not understand why others were. At a minimum, it will be appropriate for you to consider explaining your choice in your Will. (For example, "I have chosen only my daughter, Mary, to serve as a personal representative of my estate because I believe Mary has the requisite time to devote to the administration and I do not wish to burden my other children with the responsibilities of serving. My failure to appoint my other children should not be regarded by them, or anyone else, as an indication that I hold them in any less esteem.") In fact, you may wish to discuss your choice with your children during your lifetime. That way, you can determine in advance whether you will be causing ill-will among some of your children if you fail to appoint one or more of them.

As explained in more detail in Chapter 12, choosing your spouse who is not the parent of all your children as executor may not be a sensible decision. Similarly, having your children from a prior marriage serve alone or even with your spouse may not be a good choice.

In a few circumstances, having a child or children serve alone may cause problems for them. For example, if you allow your executor to allocate your tangible personal property (such as your furniture and furnishings and objects of art) among all of your descendants in such shares as your executor chooses and you name one or more of your children as the personal representative of your estate, the IRS almost certainly will take the position that your child, as executor, could have chosen all the assets for himself or herself and by failing to do so has made taxable gifts to the other descendants. Your lawyer should be able to advise you whether circumstances dictate a compelling reason why one or more family members should not serve alone.

INDEPENDENT EXECUTORS AND TRUSTEES

Individuals

Many persons find it appropriate to appoint a non-family member and a non-beneficiary as a personal representative or trustee. Some individuals, by reason of their closeness to the family, their common sense, investment experience and other qualities are appropriate choices for consideration.

Certain professionals with whom you have worked, such as your lawyer or accountant, may be appropriate individuals to appoint. On the other hand, the services of such professionals generally can be made available to your estate or trust by their being hired by the personal representative or trustee. Of course, as stated earlier, neither your personal representative nor your trustee can be required to hire your lawyer or accountant, but usually such individuals are chosen and you can increase the probability of that happening if you speak to your executor or trustee about the matter yourself.

In some circumstances, it will not be necessary to name a person as a "full blown" executor or trustee. For example, you may want the family business to be sold only if your roommate from college, in whom you repose great trust, approves. Your roommate could be made a special fiduciary for just that purpose and would not otherwise have to participate in the administration of your estate or any trust.

To a significant degree, there is nothing especially fulfilling about being a personal representative. Professionals do it in order to be paid for the services. Hence, in many circumstances, it may be better merely to authorize those you do appoint as personal representatives and trustees to be able to hire those individuals whose judgment may be needed on special matters rather than making those individuals fiduciaries themselves.

Corporate Fiduciaries

Many people have very strong feelings about banks and trust companies as personal representatives or trustees. Many of the stereotypes given them are deserving. Banks tend to be conservative and cautious. On balance, however, the positive attributes of many banks and trust companies far outweigh the perceived detriments. In addition, conservative and cautious approaches to trust and estate matters tend to prove to be appropriate ones. Moreover, banks do not get sick and die as individuals do, although in rare circumstances individual trust officers may change rather frequently. In most circumstances, the bank or trust company will act impartially although conflicts can arise.

Banks generally have a "deep pocket" and carry insurance to cover their liabilities. That means that if mismanagement occurs, the estate or trust can readily be made whole. Generally, that is not true for individuals. Although you can require any individual you name as fiduciary to carry a bond to insure your estate or trust will be repaid for the individual's impropriety, almost always such bonds are waived. Hence, as a practical matter, the only way you can be assured of your estate or trust being made whole for fiduciary misconduct is to name a financially secure and/or well insured bank or trust company.

Some banks have consistently better investment performance than others. Contrary to the belief of some, certain banks consistently achieve very superior investment returns for trusts and estates they manage. Some banks have much greater expertise in the administration of estates and trusts involving closely-held businesses than others do. In fact, some banks tend to specialize in certain areas of estate and trust administration. You will not commonly find banks in Manhattan administering an estate where the major asset is a family farm. A bank in a rural area with such experience might be a better choice for such an estate.

Of course, banks and trust companies, like all other institutions, change over time. One matter you probably should consider is to build in flexibility so that the bank or trust company, or any other fiduciary, can be removed if that is in the best interests of your estate or trust. A Trust Protector or Trust Protector Committee, discussed later in this chapter, is an excellent means of arranging for that. The possibility of removal will tend to keep the bank "on its toes." Unfortunately, many individuals do not provide for a bank's removal and its responsiveness to the needs of the estate or trust and the beneficiaries may wane.

Although banks and trust companies are rarely regarded as perfect choices, they do tend to be relatively impartial. A fiduciary who is tempted to do something for himself or herself at the expense of the beneficiaries may do so because it is a once-in-a-lifetime opportunity. Banks and trust companies cannot afford to be criticized where they put the interest of the institution first.

Special Considerations in Choosing Trustees

TYPICAL CHOICES OF TRUSTEES

Whom you should choose as trustee of the trust depends upon the terms of the trust and the purposes for which it is created. For example, if you create a marital deduction trust for your surviving spouse which upon your spouse's death will terminate and be paid outright to your descendants, you might allow your spouse, in those states where it is permitted, to be the sole trustee if your spouse has the capacity to invest or the investment choice will be limited, such as to municipal bonds only.

Where the trust will be large, it may be beyond the capacity of one individual to manage the entire trust. That may also be true where the trust is expected to last beyond the life or competency of the individual whom you would otherwise choose as the trustee.

Common choices are family members, trusted individuals, not infrequently an investment advisor, attorney and/or accountant or a bank or trust company in whom you have confidence. Such choices may not be appropriate ones, depending upon the terms of the trust, the identity of the beneficiaries and the purposes for which the trust is formed. For example, if you create a trust where the trustee has broad discretion to accumulate income, to pay income or principal among a class consisting of all of your descendants living from time to time, or apply assets for their use, the choice of a family member as trustee may be disastrous. First, in some states the individual family member cannot hold the power to pay income or principal to himself or herself. Second, tax problems will almost certainly arise for the beneficiary who holds that power and possibly for others as well. For example, any beneficiary who holds the power to pay principal to himself or herself is deemed to own such property for tax purposes; the power may also make such assets subject to the claims of the beneficiary's creditors. Third, no family member, no matter how objective he or she usually is, may be able to make objective decisions with respect to the application or use of assets in the trust in all cases. The family member may well be unable to determine the proper share which those individuals closest to the trustee are to receive.

However, in many cases, a family co-trustee, including one who is a beneficiary, can be a good choice in monitoring the actions of the other trustees and in making or at least monitoring investment decisions. In fact, naming an individual as trustee may force that person to participate more fully in the trust and ensure that more attention is paid to the trust. It also may help a beneficiary mature and learn about important financial matters and how a trust operates. Some individuals, however, are not appropriate choices even if they are beneficiaries of the trust. Putting aside obvious points like incapacity to act because of minority or other disability, some individuals tend to be disruptive or may tend to make imprudent investments.

Where the trust will consist of interests in your closely-held business, choosing family members who will operate the business to be trustees may or may not be a good choice. If you name your son, for example, as the investment trustee, he alone, presumably, will decide who operates the family business. As long as he has confidence in himself, he may choose to operate the business. He may or may not make the best decisions for the business or for other members of the family. It might be better, for example, to name him as only one of three trustees so that he alone can exercise the powers as to the operation of the business, including who will manage the business or veto certain decisions relating to it or the administration of the trust.

In such a case, the right choice depends largely on your perspective. Even if your child, for example, has demonstrated outstanding skills to manage the family business, his or her capacity or interest to do so may change over time. If you put your child in a position alone to make all decisions with respect to the business, it may be impossible, as a practical matter, to prevent him or her from doing so even when his or her actions are not in the best interests of the business, the trust or its other beneficiaries. A system of "checks and balances" among the trustees may be an appropriate system to implement. For example, choosing your child who in all probability is going to operate the family business with at least one other family member and perhaps an outsider, which might be a bank or trust company, as co-trustees might be a good choice.

As explained later in this Chapter, empowering a disinterested Trust Protector or Trust Protector Committee to remove your child or anyone else as trustee in the event that he or she fails to carry out his or her fiduciary duties probably is appropriate for you to consider. No matter how much confidence you repose in a certain family member today, your confidence may change in the future. At some point, that individual may no longer possess the requisite skills to carry out actions which are in the best interests of the business, the trust which owns it and the other beneficiaries. Your failure to consider that prospect realistically, and provide a mechanism to permit change, will almost certainly result in financial losses and litigation. Almost everyone loses in litigation when you realize that the litigation could have been avoided and the correct result for the business, the trust and its beneficiaries achieved in a more expedient manner.

INDEPENDENT TRUSTEES

Independent trustees are usually those who are not beneficiaries. An independent trustee can include a family member who is not a beneficiary and probably will not become one in the future. For example, a sibling or cousin of yours might be an appropriate choice. However, if your sibling will become a beneficiary at some time, such as if all your children die, your sibling is not really independent. In fact, arming that person with certain powers can cause tax problems for him or her.

If the trust is for your descendants, you could name a child-in-law as a trustee. Such a choice probably will prove to be a poor one, however. First, more American marriages end in divorce than in death. If you name your son-in-law as trustee of the trust for your daughter, undesirable consequences may result if the marriage breaks down. In addition, you may be giving your son-in-law inappropriate authority over the financial affairs of your daughter. In addition, although your daughter might well and, perhaps, should complain if certain imprudent investments were made by the trustee, the probability that she would complain about imprudent investments made by her husband as her trustee is slight. As a consequence, you should not appoint a child-in-law as a trustee unless you provide a simple-to-implement mechanism to have that person removed (with automatic removal if the marriage breaks down) or there are sufficient other trustees that the actions of your child-in-law as trustee can be overridden by the others.

Banks and trust companies are in the business of being independent trustees. There are thousands of such institutions throughout the United States. Some are better at certain tasks than others are. For example, if your estate or trust will consist of farm land, appointing a small bank in Manhattan which has no experience in administering such assets may be a poor choice.

The choice of a bank or trust company may be an excellent one. However, some mechanism for the removal of the bank or trust company is appropriate to consider especially if the trust is scheduled to last a long time. A Trust Protector or Trust Protector Committee, discussed later in this chapter, may be the most appropriate choice.

SUMMARY ON CHOICES OF TRUSTEES

Probably, it is best for you to consider as trustee the type of individual whom you would consider for an independent board of directors of your company. The word "independent" connotes that at least some of the trustees will not be officers and directors of the company and not all of them will be family members. If you name those who act as officers and directors of your company as the board and also the trustees (and therefore the owners), they can perpetuate themselves regardless of how well they perform for the business or for the trust or for its beneficiaries. Family members may not be appropriate choices acting alone because of their inability to make objective decisions.

As a consequence, you must consider some independent persons including, for example, a bank or a trust company. However, a bank or a trust company under certain circumstances will "go along" with certain wishes of the family.

ONE POSSIBLE SCENARIO

Although it is impossible to set forth the remedy for all circumstances, many individuals have discovered that choosing three trustees or executors is appropriate. One is a family member, another is a trusted independent individual and the third is an independent bank or trust company. Having a Trust Protector, or a Trust Protector Committee, who has the power to remove and/or replace any or all of those fiduciaries may be appropriate. Sometimes, it will be appropriate to authorize the fiduciaries, or some of them, to add additional fiduciaries, but you may also wish to require the consent of some third party, such as the Trust Protector, to prevent inappropriate persons from being selected as co-fiduciaries.

SUCCESSOR TRUSTEES AND EXECUTORS

Many individuals are unable to find satisfactory independent persons to act as fiduciaries for their estates and trusts. In addition, even if you have individuals who seem ideal for those positions now, they may cease serving well before the administration of the estate or trust ends. That brings up the perplexing problem of providing for successor fiduciaries. The following are typical ways of choosing successors:

a. *Self-Perpetuating Selection.* Sometimes the last individual who acts is authorized to name his or her successor. You can control the selection by setting forth criteria. For example, you might require that after the last named individual serves, a bank or trust company be appointed. Alternatively, you can require that the individual be at least of a certain age (but not more than some other age), reside in a certain location, have specified experience or a certain educational background, etc.

b. *Choice By Position.* Some clients specify that after all named individuals cease serving a person in a certain position shall serve. For example, you might provide that the president of your *alma mater* serve as the fiduciary. Not infrequently, the person who is head of a bar association is chosen. However, merely because you choose by position does not guarantee that the individual will accept the appointment or would be an appropriate choice. Sometimes, positions in organizations are filled for political reasons rather than strictly on the basis of competence. Even in a circumstance where you are certain that the person chosen for an independent position will be selected on the basis of competence in his or her field, it does not mean that the person necessarily will be an appropriate fiduciary for your beneficiaries.

c. *Selection by Position.* One alternative which has proved to have merit in many cases is to allow a person in a certain position to choose the successor fiduciary. For example, you might provide that the three senior partners of a particular accounting or law firm are to select the successor fiduciary. If you choose a large, long-standing firm, there is a reasonable probability that a thoughtful decision will be made. A prominent firm probably has much to lose if it makes a selection in an inappropriate manner. In addition, there may well be liability to the individual or committee which selects a person who violates the trust reposed in him, her or it in the fiduciary position.

Although the head of your *alma mater* may not be an appropriate choice for fiduciary, perhaps, that person would be willing to select a successor fiduciary, especially if you have been a significant supporter of your college. However, as explained above, any selector may have liability if the selection turns out to be a poor one.

In many circumstances, it will be appropriate to direct that the committee that chooses successor fiduciaries cannot select any of its members or certain persons affiliated with it as a successor executor or trustee. The purpose of excluding members from selection, of course, is to attempt to increase the probability of an objective and reasonable decision being made. Nonetheless, abuses in the selection process can occur. In some cases, clients insist that the selection by the committee be subject to a veto by another. Obviously, you should attempt to ensure that the person, or groups, holding the veto power is independent of the person, or committee, which makes the selection of the successor fiduciary. By providing someone with a veto power, you provide a type of "checks and balances" system. Again, you may want to choose a position where the selectors, or vetoers, would have their reputation damaged if the process is abused and their reputation in such matters is important to maintain.

Another alternative is to allow a judge or a former judge to select. Although it is true that certain judges will choose political colleagues for lucrative fiduciary positions, some judges have demonstrated such independence that the probabilities are great that an objective, non-political appointment will be made by them.

Regardless of the method your choose, you must be relatively certain that those who are designated as the selectors, or vetoers, will act. The possibility that they might be liable for a poor selection (or a failure to veto) may mean that the person or committee authorized to select will not act. Providing a fee for such persons to act may be appropriate. On the other hand, the probability is likely that an entity with whom your family has a close affiliation (such as an accounting firm which has represented your family or business for a long time) will make a selection. Again, one reason that allowing your accounting or law firm to select successor fiduciaries may be appropriate is because the firm may suffer damage to its reputation if it abuses the process or refuses to act when the need arises.

YOUR OWN PERSONAL CORPORATE FIDUCIARY

Trust companies, like banks, often are significantly regulated by the government. Usually, in order to offer services as a corporate fiduciary under state law, minimum capitalization, special regulation and control requirements will apply to the corporation. In many states, however, a "special purpose" trust company may be formed. A special purpose trust company usually is formed to act only as a fiduciary in relationships created by members of your family, or the family of your parents so that it would include your brothers and sisters and their families. In many circumstances, you are permitted to form such special purpose trust companies under the general business laws of the state rather than the more regulated and costly provisions relating to banks and trust companies.

A special purpose trust company offers several advantages to some families. First, it provides continuity of fiduciary relationships. You need not be concerned that the named fiduciary will die, move away, or become incompetent, as you should be if you name individuals as fiduciaries. Of course, the employees of the trust company will be individuals, who eventually will die, move away, retire, resign or become incompetent. Second, the commissions which the trust company earns can be shared by all members of your family to the extent they own or have a beneficial interest in the special purpose trust company. For one family, for example, which had a member who was incapable of serving as a fiduciary, a special purpose trust company was formed which acted as the fiduciary and received substantial commissions. The special purpose trust company was owned by a trust which had been formed for certain members of the family, including the one who could not serve as a fiduciary. The fees paid to the special purpose trust company were, in turn, distributed to the trust which owned it. The trust, in turn, used that income for the beneficiaries. Hence, the family member who could not serve as a fiduciary was able to participate in fees which the trust company received while acting as fiduciary. The fee income was not taxed to the trust company because it was an S corporation.

Although, as a general rule, banks cannot be S corporations, a special purpose trust company can be one. Thus taxation at the corporate level can be avoided. Under current law, certain trusts can be shareholders of S corporations so that minor, disabled or certain other family members can have their ownership interests in these special purpose trust companies held by a trustee. Of course you must, in turn, find an appropriate trustee of that trust which owns the stock in the corporation. It is unclear what the effects will be if the trust company is the trustee of the trust which owns the stock in the trust company. Generally, families form a committee of individuals (discussed in more detail below) to act as the trustee of the trust which, in turn, owns the shares in the special purpose trust company.

The special purpose trust company, to some degree, also eliminates the sometimes perplexing problem of choosing non-family/non-beneficiary fiduciaries. As explained above, non-family or, at least non-beneficiary trustees, and sometimes executors may be required to avoid tax and creditor problems for the family members and other beneficiaries. The special purpose trust company can be used for that non-beneficiary position as well, at least as long as the beneficiaries do not control the trust company.

REMOVAL OF FIDUCIARIES— TRUST PROTECTORS

Not infrequently, it will be appropriate for certain fiduciaries to be removed or for the beneficiaries to think they should be. Unfortunately, few Wills and trusts are prepared with adequate thought given to the removal of fiduciaries. The administration of the estate of an owner of a closely-held business often will last for more than 15 years. Trusts often are designed to last for 100 years or more. Regardless of how appropriate the individual or entity named as the fiduciary was at the time of its selection, circumstances may develop which make the choice an inappropriate one.

Often, proceedings are commenced in court seeking to

have a fiduciary removed. Such proceedings almost always are expensive and are rarely successful except in cases where there is a clear breach of fiduciary duty. Even in those circumstances, the legal complexities may result in such delays that, as a practical matter, they are unsuccessful. That suggests that a more expedient and rational method of providing for the removal of certain fiduciaries should be provided.

One way, which probably is legally enforceable in most states, is to allow the competent adult beneficiaries, either by majority or unanimous vote, to remove the fiduciary. Unfortunately, the IRS has taken the position that severe tax problems can arise for beneficiaries who have the power to remove one fiduciary and name another. Although the position has been severely criticized by many professionals, and although some decisions suggest it would not be supported in court, it probably would be unwise to structure the removal and replacement process in a way that violates current IRS pronouncements. At a minimum, your family may have to bear the financial and emotional expense of doing battle with the IRS and may decide to compromise the matter which could result in the payment of significant taxes.

Although the parameters of the position have never been entirely set forth, or tested in court, it appears almost certain that if the removal and selection process is granted to a person other than the beneficiaries, even if that person is, in turn, a close friend or relative of the beneficiaries, the IRS would not contend that adverse tax consequences will befall the beneficiaries. As a consequence, you should consider, again by name and or position, designating someone who can remove and replace fiduciaries. Such individuals are sometimes called "Trust Protectors." (In fact, some individuals appoint several individuals to constitute a Trust Protector Committee.) The reason is that their job is to protect the trust, or the estate, from an inappropriate fiduciary. You can specify the reasons for the removal, such as a conclusion by the Trust Protector that investment performance has been inadequate or that dealings with the beneficiaries have been unfair. However, setting forth a standard may provide an opportunity for any fiduciary whom the Trust Protector attempts to remove to go to court to contend that the standard or condition for removal has not been met. It probably is best to provide that the Trust Protector can remove and replace fiduciaries for any reason or for no reason at all. Again, as indicated above, you can reduce the incentive for the Trust Protector to act precipitously by eliminating any financial benefit in so acting, by prohibiting the Trust Protector from being able to appoint himself or herself or a close relative or affiliate of the Trust Protector as the successor fiduciary.

An alternative, which probably is safe, is to allow the beneficiaries to remove the fiduciary and allow someone else, such as the Trust Protector, to select the successor. The reasoning as to why the power to remove and replace can cause tax problems for the beneficiaries would not appear to apply where the beneficiaries can only take one of those two steps but not both. However, it is appropriate to note once more that the parameters of the Service's position have not yet been set forth. As a consequence, it is still not absolutely certain whether arming the beneficiaries with only one of the two powers will cause them problems.

A second reason not to give the beneficiaries the power to remove and replace relates to potential creditors' rights. As is explained in more detail in Chapter 16, trust interests generally are not attachable by the creditors of beneficiaries who have not contributed property to the trust. A wall of protection is built up around the trust assets for them. However, a beneficiary who can distribute assets to himself or herself may be treated as owning those assets, thus making them attachable by his or her creditors. Giving a beneficiary the right to remove and replace trustees might make such assets attachable by creditors—the theory being that the beneficiary can always find someone who will do his or her bidding for the fiduciary fee and, as a consequence, the power to remove and replace puts the beneficiary in the position of being able, as a practical matter, to take anything out of the trust which the beneficiary wishes.

A third reason not to allow a beneficiary to remove and replace is one of common sense. Sometimes, a beneficiary will not do what is in his or her own best interests. Allowing the beneficiary to remove and select fiduciaries may give the beneficiary inappropriate power at an inappropriate time, such as where he or she is unduly subject to the suggestions of others. For example, a beneficiary who is subject to undue influence by others might be influenced to remove and replace an appropriate fiduciary and appoint someone less capable as the successor. Giving the beneficiaries no more than the power to remove, or the power to name successors, but not both, provides a type of check and balance which may be better for the beneficiary. Obviously, some alternative methods of removal or selection must be in place when the beneficiaries are incapable of acting, because, for example, they are all minors.

In any case, you should discuss in detail with your attorney processes for the removal of fiduciaries. Failure to provide for removal means that your beneficiaries, even in the most egregious circumstances, will be forced, almost certainly, to go to court. That will be expensive and the probability of success usually is not good.

COMPENSATION

Some states provide specific formulas for compensating personal representatives and trustees. For example, in New York, each executor, up to a maximum of three and provided the estate is of a certain minimum size, is entitled to a commission of at least 2% of the estate. In most states, the personal representative or trustee is entitled to "reasonable compensation." Most banks and trust companies in reasonable compensation states provide a fee schedule of what they will charge. Although the court having jurisdiction of the estate or trust may have the power to award compensation less than that which the bank has determined pursuant to its published fee schedule, such reductions are rare and almost never occur unless a beneficiary objects to the fee sought by the corporate fiduciary. To some degree, competition among the corporate fiduciaries in the geographic area where your estate or trust will be administered may tend to keep the fees at a reasonable level. However, in some circumstances, the fees may not be fair.

As a general matter, you can condition the appointment of any person or corporation as a personal representative or trustee on its accepting different compensation from that provided under the controlling statute or in the fee schedule published by the bank.

On the other hand, you can provide for extra compensation should circumstances justify it. Many banks add on an hourly charge for work performed by bank personnel where litigation, a public offering of a private company, or certain other extraordinary events happen which do not ordinarily occur in the administration of an estate or trust.

You should discuss with your attorney how you should set the compensation of the personal representatives of your estate. Some very wealthy individuals specify a fixed amount, such as $100,000 to be paid $20,000 yearly during the first five years of administration of the estate with any unpaid balance to be accelerated if the administration is completed faster than that. Some individuals provide for a small percentage, such as 1/2% of the value of their estate. Still others specify that the compensation shall be determined from time to time by the adult, competent major beneficiaries of the estate, such as the property owner's children, with a "cap" of not more than what the applicable rates would produce in the absence of such an agreement. Sometimes, when a professional individual, such as an accountant or a lawyer, acts, the professional will be paid his or her standard hourly time charges for time spent as an executor or trustee.

Commissions for Family Fiduciaries

In some cases, it will be suggested that family members serve as fiduciaries without compensation. That may or may not be wise. For example, if you are leaving your entire estate to your spouse free of estate tax under the protection of the marital deduction, having your spouse receive commissions for serving as executor may not be appropriate. Although such commissions are deductible for estate tax purposes, your estate will pay no estate tax anyway. In addition, the commissions your spouse, or anyone else, receives are includable in taxable income. If that amount had passed instead as an inheritance to your spouse no income and no estate tax would be imposed on it. Those reasons suggest that it would not be appropriate in such circumstances for your spouse to receive commissions as a personal representative of your estate. However, circumstances may occur where it would be appropriate for your spouse to receive that compensation. One circumstance may be where claims against your probate estate exceed that estate, meaning your spouse would inherit nothing from it. An executor's entitlement to commissions is almost always superior to a creditor's entitlement to be paid on the claim. In any case, if you have confidence in your spouse's ability to do what is in your estate's overall best interest, it probably is best to allow your spouse to decide whether to take that compensation. It is the position of the IRS that your spouse must decline any entitlement to commissions within six months of his or her appointment as the personal representative of your Will. If you do not have confidence that your spouse will make the appropriate decisions as to commissions, it is questionable whether you should consider appointing your spouse as a personal representative at all.

In some cases, it will be appropriate for you to consider providing that your children will not receive commissions for acting as executor (or trustee). That may be the case, for example, where not all of your children are appointed. There may be some resentment by those who were not nominated and that resentment may be exacerbated if those who serve are entitled to commissions as well.

However, it probably will be less costly from a tax perspective for your child or children to receive commissions than an inheritance subject to estate tax. The estate tax rates are often much higher than effective income tax rates are. By allowing your child to receive commissions, which almost always are deductible for estate tax purposes, you can shift their taxation from the higher estate tax rates to the lower income tax rates. What is best to do may involve a complex decision-making process. Obviously, it is impossible to foresee all the events which will arise after your death and which should be considered in making the decision. However, as indicated above, even the IRS will respect the waiver of commissions by a fiduciary if the waiver is signed within six months of the fiduciary's appointment.

LIMITATION OF CHOICES OF EXECUTORS

Almost all states put some restrictions on whom you can select as an executor. Many states exclude, for example, individuals who are not United States citizens or corporations. Others, such as Florida, prohibit appointing non-residents of the state except for certain close relatives. Your attorney should be able to advise you as to whether the persons whom you wish to serve may do so. If your choice of executor is foreclosed, you may be able to arrange for that person nonetheless to act either by naming the person as the trustee of a revocable living trust which you will use as a Will substitute and/or by directing the admission of your Will to original probate in a state where that person can act.

RESIGNATIONS BY EXECUTORS AND TRUSTEES

Your nomination of an individual or corporation as an executor or trustee in your Will usually is not effective until that appointment, in effect, is confirmed by the court having jurisdiction over your estate. That is not true, however, for a person appointed as a trustee of a revocable living trust which acts as a Will substitute or any other trust created by an instrument other than a Will. Similarly, in almost all circumstances, the executor or trustee named in a Will needs the permission of the court to resign through a formal and sometimes costly legal procedure. However, with trusts created other than by Will usually you can authorize that as it can save considerable legal expense when a fiduciary does wish to resign.

SUMMARY AND CONCLUSIONS

Regardless of how you dispose of assets at your death, you should have a Will which means that you will need to appoint an executor of your Will or personal representative of your estate. Even if the assets disposed of by your Will are limited, an executor almost always plays a critical role in the administration of your estate, such as making certain tax elections. Whether you create a trust under your Will or by a trust agreement, you will have to appoint a trustee if you create a trust. Almost certainly, you will create a trust to cover a circumstance of property being inherited by a minor or incompetent. In addition, because trusts can serve so many purposes, including protecting assets from claims of creditors, you may wish to consider a long-term trust and provide the trustee with significant discretion. In such a case, the trustee will have significant authority over the disposition of property. In any case, in choosing executors and trustees, consideration should be given only to choosing individuals and institutions which have demonstrated integrity, diligence, capacity and availability to act, will not engender conflicts of interest and have an appropriate level of experience for the job. Where the estate or trust will consist of interests in a closely-held business, choosing those whom you would select as independent members of the board of directors may be appropriate choices as executors and trustees. In any case, a system of checks and balances should be placed into effect to try to reduce the probability of imprudent and improper decisions being made with respect to your assets. Regardless of whom you choose, a mechanism, other than going to court, for the removal of certain fiduciaries should be used. The appointment of a Trust Protector or a Trust Protector Committee will be appropriate to consider.

One of the most important decisions you will make if you have minor children is the selection of the guardian of the person and property of the minor child in the event that the child's other parent does not survive. Although children are rarely orphaned before reaching adulthood, the effects of failing to name the person whom you want to act as guardian for your minor child can be so adverse that the decision should be made with great care.

CHAPTER 14   HOW CAN I SAVE ESTATE AND RELATED TAXES?

INTRODUCTION AND OVERVIEW OF CHAPTER

Could your business survive if it had to pay in cash nine months from today a judgment equal to 55% of its net worth? That question, as a practical matter, will be asked at your death. If you cannot answer it with a resounding "yes", estate planning during your lifetime will be critically important if you want your business to survive you.

The United States estate, gift and generation-skipping transfer taxes (collectively called "wealth transfer taxes") are the highest taxes imposed in this country. Each can reach rates of or in excess of 55%. Sometimes, all three, and very often two of the three, can be imposed on the same property, resulting in an effective combined rate of taxation of over 80%.

However, for three reasons, individuals spend more time trying to avoid the less onerous income tax than planning to avoid the higher wealth transfer tax. First, the owner of property usually does not have a wealth transfer tax problem; rather his or her descendants or other beneficiaries do. It is human nature to do things for yourself and not for others. Saving income tax helps you; saving estate tax helps someone else. Second, because it is beneficial to postpone income tax, many individuals also believe that postponing wealth transfer tax must be beneficial. But, postponing wealth transfer tax usually does not reduce the tax burden. In fact, it usually increases it. Third, there is a normal human

379

propensity to avoid dealing with matters relating to one's own death.

This Chapter discusses wealth transfer taxes and presents approaches to reduce or avoid them.

AN OVERVIEW OF THE FEDERAL ESTATE AND RELATED TAX LAWS

Estate, Gift and Generation-Skipping Transfer Taxes: Supplements to Each Other

In almost all cases, the three wealth transfer taxes (estate, gift and generation-skipping) supplement each other. If you attempt to avoid the estate tax, you run into the gift tax. If you try to avoid the generation-skipping transfer tax you probably will face the estate tax. To a large degree, these three tax systems also are similar to each other, but many important differences remain. Sometimes, a property owner can reduce taxes by exploiting those differences.

Gift Taxes

ANY TRANSFER FOR LESS THAN FULL VALUE: DONATIVE INTENT IS NOT REQUIRED

Any transfer you make during your lifetime where you get back less than what you transferred potentially is subject to gift tax. Usually, when people think of a gift they think of a donative intent (that is, an intention to benefit the recipient of the property). However, with certain limited exceptions (discussed below) a donative intent is not necessary in order for a transfer to become subject to gift tax. All it takes is that you transfer property worth more than what you get back.

GIFT TAX RATES

The stated federal gift tax rates run from a low of 18% to a high of 55%. In fact, the way the tax is calculated, you reach an effective rate of taxation of 60% for gifts above $10 million (and up to about $20 million). Hence, in some cases, if you give $100,000 to a child, you may pay $60,000 in gift tax. In determining the rate of gift tax, you must look at your cumulative taxable transfers during your lifetime. As a consequence, a gift you make in 1990 will be taxed at a higher rate if you previously made a taxable gift in 1970 than if you never before made a taxable gift.

LIFETIME VERSUS DEATHTIME GIVING

There is a distinction between gift tax and estate tax that is one of the most important factors in tax planning: You *do not* have to pay a gift tax on the gift tax you pay to the government. You *do* have to pay an estate tax on the estate tax you pay to the government. (This "tax on tax" is discussed further later in this Chapter.) Although the stated estate and gift tax rates are the same, that means the gift tax rates have an effective impact of only about two-thirds of the estate tax.

Other factors, however, may bring the taxes on lifetime gifts to about the same (and in some cases a higher) level as the estate tax. One of those factors is state gift taxes. Currently, six states impose a gift tax: New York, Delaware, South Carolina, North Carolina, Tennessee, and Louisiana. Although it is true that all states impose a death tax, because of special credits most of the state death tax (and in some states, all of the state death tax) is paid for, in effect, by the federal government. There is no similar state gift tax credit. Hence, state gift tax (where it is imposed) can have the effect of increasing the gift tax rates to about the level of the estate tax rates.

Another important distinction between lifetime and deathtime transfers is the resulting income tax basis of the property in the hands of the recipient. As a general matter, if you make a gift of property during your lifetime your basis in the property will be carried over to the recipient. For example, if you buy stock for $10,000 in 1970 and give it to your daughter in 1990 when it is worth $45,000, your daughter's basis in the stock will be $10,000. (In some cases, you can add part of the gift tax paid to the basis of the property in the hands of the recipient and certain other special rules may apply.) On the other hand, as a general matter, if you leave the stock to your daughter when you die and it is then worth $45,000, your daughter's basis will be $45,000 rather than $10,000.

Needless to say, comparisons between lifetime and death-time giving are complex and you should obtain the advice of a competent advisor before making any significant lifetime gifts.

EXCEPTIONS AND EXCLUSIONS

OVERVIEW

Effective lifetime gift tax planning generally revolves around using exceptions, exclusions and special rules under the gift tax system. There are more exceptions, exclusions and special rules available for lifetime transfers than for deathtime ones. On account of that, it is important for you to work with your advisors as early in your life as possible if you wish to achieve effective wealth transfer tax reduction.

ANNUAL EXCLUSION GIFTS

You can give as many individuals as you wish, free of gift tax, up to $10,000 a year. That is known as the "Annual Exclusion." For example, if you have 15 friends and relatives you want to benefit to the maximum extent possible each year without paying any gift tax, you can give each one $10,000, or a total of $150,000, each year, entirely free of gift tax. (Those annual exclusion transfers are usually exempt from generation-skipping transfer tax as well.)

Your spouse can make annual exclusion gifts and can make them to the same persons you do. The law also allows your spouse to pretend, under a concept known as "gift-splitting", that your spouse made one-half of all gifts which you made to persons other than your spouse. For example, if you give $20,000 to a friend, the law allows your spouse to pretend that he or she made one-half of that gift to your friend. Because each of you and your spouse can give the friend $10,000 a year, your gift of $20,000 will be treated as two separate gifts (by you and your spouse) of $10,000, and no gift tax will be imposed.

Whether or not you are married, over time, maximizing the use of the annual exclusion can effect significant overall tax reduction. For instance, if you are married and have two children and four grandchildren, you and your spouse can transfer up to $120,000 each year to your children and grandchildren entirely free of wealth transfer taxes. Over a ten year period, you will have transferred $1.2 million entirely free of tax. However, that does not demonstrate the full impact of the savings. In addition to the value of the gifts, you will also avoid wealth transfer taxes on any income and appreciation which the property generates after the transfer. For instance, if the property produces 8% a year in income and/or appreciation, at the end of the ten year period, you will have removed approximately $1,875,000 from your estate without wealth transfer tax.

Certain transfers do not qualify for the $10,000 annual exclusion. In particular, that may be the case for transfers in trust. Often, however, it is possible to rearrange a transfer in trust so as to qualify for the annual exclusion. Your tax attorney or other advisor will be able to tell you whether transfers you propose to make qualify for the annual exclusion, and assist you with appropriate planning in that regard.

TUITION AND MEDICAL CARE TRANSFERS

In addition to making transfers under the protection of the annual exclusion, you can pay for the medical care and tuition of another person (even if you are not obligated to support that person) without liability for gift tax. For example, if you have an adult child, you are usually not obligated to support that child. However, you may pay the child's tuition without making a gift. Similarly, a friend of yours (or just someone you have read about in the newspaper) desperately needs an expensive operation to save his or her life. Paying for the medical care will not be treated as a gift.

It is appropriate to emphasize, however, that the exception for tuition and medical care applies only if you make payments directly to the educational institution or to the health care provider. Reimbursing your child for tuition (or giving cash to your child to enable the child to pay tuition) or paying health insurance premiums for someone will not fall under the exception (although such payments may qualify under the $10,000 annual exclusion).

The tuition/medical care exception provides an important and often neglected opportunity for you to transfer wealth tax-free above the annual exclusion amount. For example, paying for nursery school for your grandchildren will benefit your children but will not be considered a taxable gift. In some areas of the United States, such as New York City, private schooling, even at the nursery school and grammar school level, costs many thousands of dollars a year. Over time, your paying (again, directly to the educational institution) for the education of family members will transfer significant wealth to your loved ones.

Paying for medical care for family members also can transfer significant wealth over time. As indicated, the medical care exception does not apply to the payment of health insurance premiums. Usually, however, health insurance does not cover all expenses. One practical method of funding such expenses is to create a bank account in your own name, grant your children signatory authority over the account and authorize the children to make the checks on the account payable to health care providers (such as their own family doctor or dentist). Pursuant to your agreement with the children, they will replenish the account to the extent of their insurance reimbursement. The amount which is not replenished should qualify under the medical care exception.

THE MARITAL DEDUCTION

Under current law, you can give as much property to your spouse as you wish, if the gift is in proper form, without paying any gift tax at all. This is the so-called the "marital deduction." Almost all outright (direct) gifts to your spouse will qualify for the marital deduction (unless your spouse is not a U.S. citizen, in which case special rules apply). Certain transfers in trust will also qualify for the marital deduction. One of the most popular methods of giving significant property to a spouse (especially when either or both of you have descendants of a prior marriage) under the protection of the marital deduction is through a special form of trust known as "qualified terminable interest property" and typically referred to as a QTIP.

Transferring property to your spouse can serve many purposes but, as a general rule, ultimately it does not prevent the property from being taxed. Any asset you transfer to your spouse under the protection of the marital deduction (whether outright or in trust) will be includable in your spouse's wealth tax base, and therefore subject to gift or estate tax in your spouse's hands, unless your spouse dissipates the property before his or her death.

However, as will be discussed in more detail below, making transfers to your spouse under the protection of the marital deduction can postpone the imposition of tax, can provide an opportunity to use your spouse's exemptions and exclusions and, if your spouse survives you for a long time, can permit your spouse to engage in lifetime planning.

THE CHARITABLE DEDUCTION

Believe it or not, when you transfer property to charity, the transfer may be subject to gift tax! The tax law severely restricts the ways in which you can transfer property to charity without gift tax. Generally, any transfer you make which qualifies for an income tax deduction will also qualify for the gift tax deduction. However, those two tax systems are not completely identical and it is appropriate, as a consequence, to consult with your tax advisor before making any significant charitable gifts. In particular, if you or another individual retain or receive (or possibly could receive) a benefit from the property transferred to charity, there is a strong likelihood that the transfer will not qualify, in whole or in part, for the charitable deduction, unless it is in a special form. It is pretty discouraging to learn after the fact that not only is there no income tax deduction for the transfer to charity but the donor is required to pay gift tax on the transfer as well.

THE LIFETIME/DEATHTIME "EXEMPTION"

IN GENERAL

Under current law, almost all individuals can transfer up to $600,000 free of gift or estate tax to any other person. That is referred to as the gift and estate tax "exemption" (or the "unified credit"). The exemption is in addition to other exceptions, deductions and exclusions, such as the annual exclusion and the marital and the charitable deduction.

There is only one exemption during life and at death. To the extent that you use the exemption to protect lifetime gifts from gift tax, the exemption is not available to protect death-time transfers from estate tax. It is the position of the IRS that you must use the exemption against the first taxable gifts you make during your lifetime. You cannot preserve it for later transfers. That means if you want to save the exemption until you die so you can, for example, make a transfer at your death to a special friend free of all death tax, you will be unable to do that if you make significant taxable gifts during your lifetime.

WHY MANY WILL LOSE THEIR EXEMPTIONS

One of the most effective planning steps you can take is to use your $600,000 exemption as early in your life as you can reasonably afford to do so. There are several reasons for that.

First, over time, your exemption, as a practical matter, will grow by the amount of additional income and appreciation it protects from tax. For instance, if you transfer $600,000 30 years before you die and the property earns 8% a year after the transfer, at your death approximately $6 million will be protected from tax. Similarly, if you fail to use the exemption, inflation will erode its worth in terms of a present value. For instance, over that same 30-year period, if inflation occurs at 5% a year, the exemption will be eroded, in terms of current dollars, down to about $130,000.

Many politicians have attempted to reduce the amount of the exemption down to a level of $250,000 or less. If you use your exemption for lifetime transfers before that change in law occurs (and there are many who are certain it will happen) you will be able to preserve it, as a practical matter, at the $600,000 level.

In addition, if you hold significant wealth, the tax law takes the $600,000 exemption away from you. If your total base of wealth exceeds $10 million, the exemption will begin to be phased out and will be entirely phased out when you have made total deathtime and lifetime transfers of about $20 million. One of the most effective ways to avoid that impact is to use the exemption early in your life and to postpone making taxable transfers above the $10 million level for as long as possible. Let's go back to our prior example of your transferring $600,000 thirty years before your death. As explained, if the transferred property produces income and appreciation of 8% a year, it will grow to $6 million by the time you die in 30 years. At that time, your $600,000 exemption may be recaptured. However, because you used it early in life, you will have protected $5.4 million ($6 million less the $600,000 exemption recaptured) from wealth transfer tax.

HOW TO USE THE EXEMPTION BUT REGAIN THE PROPERTY (MAYBE)

People hesitate to transfer significant property during their lifetimes for many reasons. One of the most common is fear that they will need the property later in life. Although it usually makes good sense from a tax perspective to use your gift tax exemption as early in your life as you possibly can, concern that you may need that $600,000 later in life may well inhibit you from doing so.

You cannot effectively transfer property out of your estate and yet have the right to recapture the property. Nonetheless, there are some ways in which you can transfer property but, perhaps, get that property back if you need it.

One way is to create a trust for the benefit of your children and give your most trusted child the right to appoint the property to anyone he or she wishes in the world (other than himself or herself, his or her estate or the creditors of either) during his or her lifetime. If it should become essential that you receive the property back, the child may exercise that power and direct the trustee to pay the property over to you or otherwise provide you with the use of or income from the property. Although it is not absolutely certain, it is highly probable that the mere possibility that you could get the property back at the direction of one of your children who is a beneficiary of the trust will not cause the property to be included in your estate except to the extent the child, in fact, exercises the power in your favor.

Alternatively, you can name your spouse as a beneficiary of a trust and give the trustee discretion to distribute all or part of the trust property to your spouse. Your spouse, in turn, can give the property back to you entirely free of tax by reason of the gift tax marital deduction. Again, it is highly improbable that the property will be includable in your estate on account of that mere possibility. By the way, if you wish, it appears that you can define your spouse as the person to whom you are married from time to time rather than naming your current spouse.

Of course, if you do get the property back from the trust by reason of the exercise of a child's power of appointment or from your spouse, you will have wasted your $600,000 exemption. Hence, it probably would not be appropriate to use your exemption to create such a trust if you believe it is highly probable that you will need the property back at a later time in your life.

THE POOR BARGAIN RULE

Although a transfer for less than full value in money or money's worth may be subject to gift tax, there is an exception, basically, for striking a poor bargain. For example, if you paid a dealer $80,000 for a boat which is worth only $50,000, the $30,000 excess is not considered a gift. It falls under an exception for "business transactions." The exception can apply even in a family situation, so that if you overpay your child for doing work for you, the excess above what you should have paid will not be considered a gift—but only if you can prove that there was no donative intent and you simply struck a poor bargain. Family transactions are closely scrutinized by both the IRS and the courts. In fact, there is a presumption that any transfer to a family member in excess of what is received is a gift.

Estate Tax

ANY TRANSFER FOR LESS THAN FULL VALUE: DONATIVE INTENT IS NOT REQUIRED

Just as, in general, any transfer for less than full value in money's worth during lifetime may be subject to gift tax, so too is a transfer at death for less than full value in money's worth subject to estate tax. For example, you promised your daughter that you would give her $25,000 when and if she graduated from college, and under applicable state law her claim against you is enforceable because she has graduated. However, it is not regarded as a claim based upon money's worth because you did not receive an asset or other property interest of equal value. Hence, the payment to your daughter at your death would be subject to estate tax.

ESTATE TAX RATES: TAX-ON-TAX

The federal estate tax rates are listed as identical to the gift tax rates. However, as noted above, you do not have to pay gift tax on gift tax you pay to the government, but, you are required to pay estate tax on estate tax. For example, if your estate is $20 million, your estate will owe $11 million in estate tax unless some exception, deduction or special credit applies. Although the stated top estate tax rate is 55%, it is 55% of the entire $20 million estate. That means the tax is $11 million and your family will receive only $9 million. From the perspective of how much your family receives and how much the government receives, the tax rate is 122%, not 55%. By contrast, with your $20 million you could give your children nearly $13 million during your lifetime, by paying a 55% gift tax of about $7 million. Hence, you can increase what your children receive by almost 45% by making lifetime rather than deathtime transfers. (Estate tax is due on any gift tax paid on any gift made within three years of death.)

EXCEPTIONS AND EXCLUSIONS

FEWER AVAILABLE THAN FOR LIFETIME TRANSFERS

Many of the exceptions or exclusions which are available to protect lifetime transfers from gift tax are not available for deathtime transfers. For example, there is no annual exclusion, or tuition or medical care exception under the estate tax. That is why you should use those special exemptions during lifetime.

THE MARITAL DEDUCTION

Just as one spouse may transfer all of his or her assets, subject to very few exceptions, to his or her spouse free of gift tax during lifetime, spouses may transfer all their property at death to the survivor without any estate tax (again, subject to special rules if the spouse is not a U.S. citizen).

Also, just as in the case of the lifetime marital deduction, the estate tax marital deduction only, in effect, postpones tax, because any property which qualifies for the marital deduction is includable in the estate (or gift tax base) of the surviving spouse who receives the property unless it is dissipated by the surviving spouse prior to his or her death. The same types of interests which qualify for the marital deduction, such as most outright transfers, and certain transfers in trust, such as a QTIP trust, apply equally to both deathtime and lifetime transfers.

The marital deduction is discussed in more detail later in this Chapter.

THE CHARITABLE DEDUCTION

No estate tax is payable upon bequests to charity made at death. As explained above, however, with respect to lifetime gifts, transfers at death to charity must be in a proper form to be deductible. If they are not in a proper form, no charitable deduction will be allowed even though the property is, in fact, transferred to charity. No income tax deduction is permitted for a bequest to charity taking effect at death. However, a type of charitable income tax deduction can be obtained where certain assets "pregnant" with income at death are bequeathed to charity.

The charitable deduction is discussed in more detail later in this Chapter.

BONA FIDE, FULL VALUE DEBTS AND EXPENSES

In computing the estate tax, a decedent's estate is entitled to a deduction for debts owed and for the expenses of administering the estate. Deductible debts include only those which are based upon consideration in money or money's worth. For example, if you owe money to a bank, that debt will be deductible for estate tax purposes regardless of the use you made of the borrowed funds. You owe the debt because you received money from the bank. If the debt is not enforceable against your estate, however, it may not be deductible. For example, if the time to enforce the debt under the statute of limitations has expired, even if the debt is paid, the deduction may not be allowed.

On the other hand, a claim which is enforceable under state law but was entered into for less than full consideration in money or money's worth is not, subject to one exception, deductible for estate tax purposes. The example given above is an illustration: You promised to give your daughter $25,000 if and when she graduated from college. She graduated shortly before you died. She makes a claim against your estate for the $25,000. That type of claim probably is enforceable under state law. In other words, your estate is obligated to pay it. However, you received nothing by your daughter's graduating from college except, perhaps, some emotional relief. An argument that it means that you would not have to support your daughter because now she can support herself because she is a college graduate will not sustain the deduction: You would not have been obligated to support her anyway.

The one exception to the rule that the debt must have been contracted for full consideration in money's worth relates to charitable pledges. Sometimes, a pledge you make to charity will be enforceable under state law against your estate. A special provision of the tax law allows such enforceable pledges to be deducted as debts for estate tax purposes.

The expenses of administering your estate also are deductible. Those expenses will include court costs, appraisal fees, fiduciary commissions, attorneys' fees and any other related expenses. In some cases, however, the expenses will be found to be unreasonable or not allowable under local law and, therefore, may not be deductible even if paid. For example, one recent case held that expenses paid to the attorney representing the personal representative may not be deducted to the extent they are unreasonably high or do not relate to work done in administering the estate (e.g., they represent personal work done for beneficiaries).

The ability to deduct the expenses of administering your estate is important. Where your estate is in a very high tax bracket (such as 60%), the ability to deduct those expenses causes, in effect, 60% of their cost to be borne by the government. For example, if the cost of administering your estate equals 5% of your estate but is deductible in a 60% estate tax bracket, the effective cost drops to 2%.

THE LIFETIME/DEATHTIME "EXEMPTION"

As explained above in connection with gift taxes, almost all individuals have a $600,000 exemption which may be used against taxable transfers either during lifetime or at death. Because of the marital deduction and charitable deduction, the exemption is not used for qualifying transfers to your surviving spouse or to charity. As also is explained above, if the total of your taxable lifetime transfers and your estate exceeds $10 million, your exemption will be phased out and will be entirely taken away when those total taxable transfers reach about $20 million.

Generation-Skipping Transfer Tax

ANY TRANSFER TO OR FOR GRANDCHILDREN OR MORE REMOTE DESCENDANTS IS SUBJECT TO TAX

In addition to estate and gift taxes, a further tax is imposed, as a general rule, when property is transferred to or for the benefit of a grandchild or more remote descendant (or someone of an equivalent generation, such as a great-niece). The tax applies to direct transfers, such as a cash gift you make to a grandchild, and also to transfers from a trust to a grandchild. For example, the generation-skipping transfer tax or "GST" will be imposed when the trust you created for your daughter becomes payable to your daughter's children (your grandchildren) when your daughter dies.

It is worth emphasizing that the generation-skipping transfer tax is imposed *in addition to* estate and gift tax on any gratuitous transfer to a grandchild (or more remote descendant).

TAX RATE

Unlike the estate and gift tax rates which start at 18% and increase to 55% (and eventually 60%), the generation-skipping transfer tax is always imposed at the top stated estate and gift tax rate, currently 55%. As a general matter, however, the generation-skipping transfer is imposed only on the net amount after any gift or estate tax has been paid. For example, you leave $500,000 to your granddaughter at your death. The bequest generates a $275,000 estate tax, meaning that your granddaughter will net $225,000. The 55% generation-skipping transfer tax is imposed upon that net $225,000 (reduced by the GST tax). By the way, after that tax also is imposed, your granddaughter will net only $145,161 of the original $500,000 bequest.

EXCEPTIONS, EXCLUSIONS AND EXEMPTIONS

MOST GIFT TAX EXCLUSIONS APPLY BUT SOMETIMES IN DIFFERENT WAYS

Most of the exclusions and exceptions which apply for gift tax purposes, such as the $10,000 annual exclusion, and transfers for tuition and medical care, also apply for generation-skipping transfer tax purposes. However, in certain cases, they apply in different ways. One of the most important parts of planning to reduce the impact of generation-skipping transfer tax, which can be crippling, is to use the exemptions and special rules to the maximum extent possible.

THE $1,000,000 EXEMPTION

Every individual has a $1 million exemption for generation-skipping transfer tax purposes. It is called the GST exemption.

In a sense, it is a true exemption in that you can transfer, for example, $1 million to a grandchild (or more remote descendant) entirely free of generation-skipping transfer tax (although gift tax or estate tax might be payable on the transfer; remember, they are separate taxes). However, in a more global sense, the GST exemption is only a rate reducer. For example, if you transfer $4 million to a trust and apply your entire $1 million GST exemption to the trust, the effect will be to reduce the generation-skipping transfer tax rate from 55% down to 41.25% (that is, 75% of the top rate).

Effective use of the $1 million GST exemption is one of the most important planning steps a property owner can take. You should be aware of three important aspects of using it.

First, you almost always will be better off creating a separate trust which is entirely exempt from taxation rather than merely using the exemption to reduce the effective rate of taxation. Second, planning for a well-to-do person, including the owner of a closely-held business, is complicated because the GST exemption of $1 million is larger than the $600,000 estate/gift tax exemption. Special planning may have to be undertaken to make sure that taxes are not unnecessarily paid because of this difference in exemptions. Third, just as the $600,000 exemption if used early in lifetime can protect much more property from tax than that stated amount (or, conversely, avoid having its worth eroded by inflation), so too can the GST exemption be used to protect, over time, much more property from tax than $1 million (and, conversely, avoid being eroded by inflation). In fact, as explained in Chapter 9, using your $1 million GST exemption in a Megatrust℠ can result in protecting more than $10 billion from tax.

The Combined Effect

ASSETS DOUBLY (OR TRIPLY) TAXED

Unless planning is undertaken, transfers to grandchildren or more remote descendants will be subject to at least two layers of tax: first, an estate or gift tax, and second, a generation-skipping transfer tax. If the assets are subject to the highest federal estate and generation-skipping transfer taxes, approximately 82% of their worth will be eroded by those taxes. In effect, that means that for every $1 transferred to the grandchildren, $4.55 must be transferred to the government. One way to view that is that the combined effect of the two tax systems is 455%! It is unlikely that your business will be able to survive the impact of such taxes. Accordingly, if you wish to see it continue (or your family be able to derive benefits from the wealth you have built), significant planning, especially early in your lifetime, will be critically important.

By the way, as horrible as that level of taxation appears, in some cases, the tax rates can be worse. For example, if you die a resident of a state which imposes an extra estate tax (such as New York), combined death and generation-skipping transfer taxes can erode 85% or more of your wealth. Moreover, with respect to one category of assets, so-called "income in respect of a decedent", discussed below, the effect of taxation can even be greater because property can be subject to a third (and, sometimes, a fourth) level of tax.

The Major Tax Saver in Estate Planning: The Tax-Free Step-Up in Basis at Death

Subject to certain rather modest adjustments, the recipient will take over your basis in property you give away during your lifetime. This is called the "carryover" basis. For example, if your basis in your company's stock is $100 a share, and you give the stock to your children when it is worth $15,000 per share, your children's basis will be your basis of $100 per share. There will be some adjustment upward because, if gift taxes are paid on the gift, a portion (but only a portion) of the gift tax paid may be added to your children's basis. However, even with that addition, the basis of the property in the hands of your children will be well below its current fair market value.

However, a remarkable event occurs when a property owner dies: Almost all assets receive an automatic change in income tax basis to their estate tax value. This is normally referred to as the "step-up" in basis (although it may be a "step-down" if the estate tax value is less than the decedent's basis).

That change in basis occurs *whether or not* estate tax is paid. For example, if your basis in your company's stock is $100 per share and the stock is worth $15,000 a share at your death and you leave the stock to your spouse, your spouse's basis will be $15,000 a share even though no estate tax was paid because the transfer to your spouse was protected by the estate tax marital deduction. In addition, when your spouse later dies, and the value of the stock may have further increased, an automatic change in basis will again occur when the stock is inherited by your descendants. (Of course, in the latter case, estate tax probably will be paid.)

The income tax-free step-up in basis at death is the major tax saver in estate planning. It also is a major factor that prevents many property owners, especially many owners of closely-held businesses, from making gifts of their property (such as interests in the business) during lifetime. They understand that upon death all of the inherent gain in the asset will be forgiven for income tax purposes. That permits much more flexibility in disposing of the asset and is a major reason to "hang on" to the asset until death.

At one time, the Internal Revenue Code provided that the basis of even inherited assets would be carried over to their recipients. It was an extraordinarily important change in the law. (In fact, I wrote a book about it.) Fortunately, however, that provision was repealed retroactive to its original effective date. There is some danger, however, that a similar law may be enacted again in the future to feed the government's constant hunger for new sources of revenue.

ASSETS DENIED THE BASIS CHANGE

IN GENERAL

Although most inherited assets receive the tax-free step-up in basis at death, there are some exceptions to that general rule, the most important of which relates to a category of assets known as "income in respect of a decedent."

EFFECT

Assets which constitute the right to "income in respect of a decedent" (commonly referred to as IRD) usually are subjected to *both* income tax *and* estate tax. Although a partial income tax deduction is allowed for any estate tax paid on the IRD, the overall effect will be to erode, in many cases, 80% or more of the IRD asset by tax, even if the IRD is only subjected to one wealth transfer tax (and not a second one, such as the generation-skipping transfer tax). Where the IRD is subjected to estate tax, generation-skipping transfer tax and income tax, often over 90% of the asset's worth will be eroded. If additional state death taxes and/or state and local income taxes are also imposed on the IRD, the effective rate of taxation can exceed 100%!

MEANING

Because IRD can be exposed to such tremendously high levels of taxation, it is important to know what IRD is. Unfortunately, the definition provided by the tax law (tax income to which the property owner was entitled at death but which is not properly includable in the property owner's final or a prior income tax return) is not very enlightening. Generally, IRD refers to receipts which would have been taxable income had the decedent lived long enough to collect them. IRD includes, for example, virtually all forms of deferred compensation, whether in a qualified retirement plan, an individual retirement account, a Rabbi trust or any other arrangement. It also includes interest which is accrued at death, including interest on Series E and EE savings bonds (which interest often represents a significant portion of their worth because the taxation of the interest may be deferred until they are redeemed). IRD includes also the inherent gain on any note held at death which represents entitlement to proceeds of property sold on an installment basis.

THE SUCCESS TAX ON QUALIFIED PENSION PLAN PROCEEDS

As discussed in more detail in Chapter 8, if your qualified retirement plan (or similar tax-benefitted arrangement) has more than mediocre investment success, it will be subject to a non-deductible 15% excise tax on the better-than-average performance. As a general matter, if the tax has not already been imposed during your lifetime, it will be imposed upon your death. This extra 15% estate tax is an excise tax, in effect, on successful investment performance. The tax is due *in addition to* the regular estate tax, any generation-skipping transfer tax and the income tax which is imposed upon the plan proceeds because the plan proceeds will represent IRD.

OVERALL IMPACT

When all of those taxes are combined, the rate of taxation can, in extreme circumstances, exceed the amount subject to tax! Therefore, if your estate will include significant amounts of IRD, and especially qualified retirement plan proceeds, special planning during lifetime is crucial.

A REAL EXAMPLE

I represented a professional who advised me that he wanted to leave his entire estate to his girlfriend (whom he could not marry for religious reasons). His estate consisted almost entirely of approximately $8 million in qualified retirement plan benefits. I completed a calculation for him and advised him that within one year of his death the $8 million would be eroded down below $800,000. Needless to say he was astounded and asked how that could be.

I explained that approximately $4 million in estate tax would be due (actually it would be somewhat more than that). The only source of payment for that $4 million in estate tax was the qualified plan proceeds. Once his estate took out $4 million in plan proceeds to pay the estate tax, the estate would have generated $4 million in income (because the proceeds represented IRD). In a 50% income tax bracket, the estate had now generated a $2 million income tax liability. The only source of payment for those income taxes also was the qualified plan. Taking out another $2 million in cash from the qualified plan (to pay the income tax on the first $4 million taken out to pay the estate tax) generated another $2 million of taxable income, producing another $1 million in income tax liability which also had to be funded by further withdrawals from the qualified plan. By the time I finished my calculation, less than $800,000 was available for the girlfriend.

Through careful planning, however, we were able to greatly reduce the impact of taxation in that case.

WHAT TO DO WITH IRD

BEQUESTS TO CHARITY

If you have any thought about benefitting charity as part of your estate plan, doing it with a right to IRD will cost your family the least. Assets which are entitled to the income tax-free step-up in basis probably will not face an effective rate of taxation of more than 60% (or possibly 65% in certain states). That means that your family will net 40% or more of each of those assets (assuming generation-skipping transfer tax also does not apply). But if those assets are IRD, they will be eroded by about 85%, down to 15% of their worth. As a consequence, bequests of IRD assets to charity can be an extremely inexpensive way for you and your family to support charitable causes you care about.

Your family loses little, because they would receive little if the IRD passed to them. Meanwhile, charity receives the full benefit of the IRD, because charities normally are exempt from income tax. Unfortunately, the 15% extra estate tax on certain qualified retirement plans (and similar tax-benefitted arrangement) cannot be avoided by making them payable to charity; nonetheless, because they almost always represent IRD, they may still be a good asset to leave to charity.

YOU CAN DO IT ALL WRONG TOO

Even if you decide to fund your charitable bequests with IRD it is possible for the bequest itself, in effect, to explode in your estate and cause horrendous tax problems. In one circumstance the estate consisted almost entirely of installment notes representing IRD. Charity was left about one-half of the estate, but the structure of the Will effectively blocked having the IRD allocated to charity. As a consequence, charity was entitled to a significant portion of the property owner's estate but all of the income tax on the IRD, as well as the estate tax it generated, was borne by the individual beneficiaries of the estate. They would have wound up with virtually nothing except that a compromise was reached with the charity. The moral is that you should ensure that you receive competent advice in dealing with IRD.

A NOTE ABOUT CHARITABLE REMAINDER TRUSTS

As explained in more detail in Chapter 8, a charitable remainder trust, as a general rule, is entirely exempt from income taxation. A charitable remainder trust is one which makes annual payments to an individual or individuals for a period of time or until the individuals die, at which time the balance left in trust (or the "remainder") passes to charity. A charitable remainder trust can, as a general rule, receive unlimited quantities of income, including IRD, and avoid paying any income tax. As a result, leaving IRD to a charitable remainder trust may provide a significantly greater wealth base for your family members than if you left the IRD to them directly. In addition, there may be a modest reduction in estate taxation because a deduction is permitted for the tax value of the remainder in the trust committed to charity. However, just as the funding of a charitable bequest with IRD can be done incorrectly and produce extremely adverse income tax consequences, so too can the funding of a charitable remainder trust with IRD. Again, it will behoove you (and your family) to discuss those matters with a competent tax advisor.

HOW STATE TAXES ADD TO THE TAX BURDEN

State Gift Taxes

Only six states—New York, Delaware, North Carolina, South Carolina, Tennessee and Louisiana—have a gift tax. Residents of such states must, therefore, consider such taxes in their estate planning. Moreover, if you own real property or tangible personal property located in a state that imposes a gift tax, even if you reside in a different state, a transfer of such property will be subject to gift tax based on its location in the state.

Every State Has a Death Tax

For largely historical reasons, the United States government permits a dollar for dollar credit against its estate tax, subject to a limit, for death taxes paid to a state. For example, if your estate is in the 55% federal estate tax bracket, your estate will not pay 55% to the IRS but only about 39%. The other 16% will actually be paid to one or more of the states. Generally, the only exception to that rule is if you are a United States citizen not residing in the United States. Then the whole tax might go only to the IRS.

Some states, such as Florida, advertise that they have no death tax. In fact, every state, as well as the District of Columbia, has a death tax. However, about one-half of the states impose a death tax only equal to the credit which the government allows against the federal estate tax, without increasing the overall tax burden on the estate (e.g., the 16% discussed above). Florida is an example of such a state. The other states impose higher taxes, ranging from 1% (or less) to up to 20% or more.

A few states impose an "inheritance" tax. The major difference between an inheritance tax and an estate tax is that the amount of tax which is imposed under an inheritance tax system is dependent upon who inherits the property. Typically, inheritances received by closer relatives (such as a spouse or a child) are taxed at a lower rate than inheritances received by others. (For example, the Montana inheritance tax can reach 32% for transfers to unrelated persons.) With an estate tax system, the tax is imposed upon the full value of the property being transferred at death regardless of whom the inheritor is. However, the distinction between an inheritance tax system and an estate tax system is often blurred. For example, under the federal, and many state estate tax systems, transfers to spouses are exempt from taxation or are taxed at lower rates. At one time, under the federal estate tax law, certain transfers to minor children also were exempt from taxation.

How Some State Death Taxes Cause Federal Estate Taxes

Many states follow the same rules for imposing their state death taxes as the federal government. Some states, however, have different tax systems. For example, some states do not provide an unlimited marital deduction or the same level of estate tax exemption as does the federal government. That means more property may be subject to tax by the state than it is by the federal government. In some cases, that can cause federal tax to be due (or increased) where no tax would otherwise be due.

For example, if you leave your entire estate to your spouse, no federal estate tax should be due by reason of the estate tax marital deduction. However, if a state does not provide a similar exemption from taxation for transfers to your spouse, the state may impose its death tax. If that death tax is greater than the available exemption under federal law, federal tax itself will become due. The reason is that the funds used to pay the state death tax do not qualify for the marital deduction. That reduces the marital deduction, increasing the federal taxable estate potentially to the point where the taxable estate exceeds the federal exemption. In that case, federal estate tax will be due. In turn, the federal tax fails to qualify for the marital deduction and it, in turn, causes more federal tax to be paid. In fact, in many estates, each dollar of state death tax will cause a dollar and one-half of federal tax to be paid.

The important point is for you (and your advisors) to be aware of that potential problem in planning your affairs. For instance, even if you are very confident that your spouse will survive you, you should take steps to ensure that your estate will have adequate liquidity to pay any state death tax (and any resulting federal estate tax) which may become due if the state does not exempt transfers to your spouse to the same extent as does the federal tax law. In some cases, the state death tax impact may be so adverse that you may consider changing your tax domicile.

Why Part (Or Even All) of Your Estate May be Subject to Death Taxes in Another State

Although the Supreme Court's decisions are not models of clarity or consistency, it appears that a state can impose its death tax only on real and tangible personal property physically located in the state regardless of where its owner resides, and on other assets (such as stocks, bonds and cash) can be taxed only by the individual's domicile (primary residence) state at the time of death. For example, if you reside in New York and own a summer home in Connecticut, the summer home and its contents will be subject to Connecticut's death tax (and not New York's).

The states, in their never-ending quest to collect more taxes, generally try to impose the death tax at the highest rate possible. For example, rather than computing the tax on real estate owned by a non-resident of the state at the lowest tax rates, or even at the average rates, some states attempt to tax the property at the highest rates that would apply if the property owner had died a resident of the state.

Thus, even if you reside in a state with no "extra" state death tax, your estate may face extra death taxes if you own real or tangible personal property in another state.

Domicile and the Importance of Domicile

In addition, your estate may be subjected to full estate tax by several states if each one is able to establish that you were domiciled there at your death. Although you may have been advised that each individual has one and only one domicile, in a famous case involving the Campbell™ Soup fortune, the United States Supreme Court held that both New Jersey and

Pennsylvania could consider the property owner to be a domiciliary and subject the entire estate to tax.

Domicile, as a theoretical matter, depends on two factors: presence in the state, and an intent to make that state your primary home or "nest." For some their domicile will be clear. Many of us, unfortunately, face circumstances where there is no clear evidence of our domicile. For example, not infrequently, individuals who retire begin to spend considerable time in more than one state. Often, the individuals are prone to claim domicile in the state with the lowest income tax burden, but continue to spend considerable time in the state in which they were originally domiciled.

Because a person's intent to make a permanent home cannot be proved absolutely, the law has developed factors which it looks to as evidence of that intention. Chart 14.1 sets forth some of the steps which you can take to show your intent to establish domicile. However, the center of your social, family and business activities usually is the most important factor by which the determination of domicile is made. Merely following the "mechanical" steps (such as filing a declaration of domicile, obtaining a resident driver's license, etc.) will not carry the day in many cases. Generally, I counsel individuals to spend a majority of their time in the jurisdiction which they claim to be their domicile. Having at least as elaborate and expensive a home in that jurisdiction as in any other is extremely important as well. If other members of your immediate family, such as your spouse and minor children, reside in another jurisdiction, your ability to prove that the place you contend to be your home is really your domicile will be much more difficult.

In addition, the following practical advice is offered. First, if you decide to change domicile, attempt to take all of the steps you possibly can simultaneously. Doing some of them, but less than all of them, creates, perhaps, the worst of all possible situations. Do not take risks unreasonably. For example, if you cannot switch to a non-resident membership in a club, church or synagogue, because no non-resident membership is offered, consider resigning, attending only as a

CHART 14.1
Proving Your Domicile

- Spending a significantly greater portion of each year in the new (or established) domicile state.
- Acquiring a more substantial home in the new (or established) domicile state.
- Disposing of any home in the former domicile (or non-domicile) state.
- Registering and voting in the new (or established) domicile state.
- Revoking any declaration of domicile made in any other state.
- Declaring the new (or established) domicile to a United States census taker.
- Filing all tax forms at the IRS service center for the new (or established) domicile state.
- Filing a final (so marked) resident tax return in the former domicile state (and city, if applicable).
- Signing a new Will (and other documents) declaring the new (or established) domicile.
- Paying all taxes as a resident of the new (or established) domicile state.
- Registering cars, boats, etc. in the new (or established) domicile state.
- Acquiring a driver's license in the new (or established) domicile state and surrendering any issued in other states.
- Obtaining non-resident license privileges (e.g., fishing license) in non-domicile states.
- Resigning from, or changing to non-resident status for clubs, churches, etc., in non-domicile states.
- Changing all documents, subscriptions, passport, listings (e.g., in *Who's Who*) etc., to reflect the new (or established) domicile state.
- Taking all other steps to show that the center of his or her activities has been changed to the new (or is established in the) domicile state.

guest and/or making whatever contributions you think are appropriate. Make sure that all important correspondence is addressed to you in the location which you claim to be your domicile. Pay all taxes required of residents of the state you claim to be your domicile. Prepare a "canned" obituary if it is likely that a significant obituary will be carried in newspapers when you die, reciting as your home the place you claim to be your domicile.

Second, attempt to claim a new home as a domicile only if you are willing to spend a clear *majority* of your time there. Generally, a plurality of time (that is, more time in the new state than anywhere else but less than half of the time) will not suffice to prevent tax authorities in the state in which you were previously domiciled from trying to tax you.

Third, remove all real and tangible personal property from the state in which you were formally domiciled. If you own real or tangible personal property there when you die, your estate will be required to file a non-resident death tax return with that state. That will provide the state with an opportunity (and it will take that opportunity) to investigate whether you were still domiciled there when you died. In New York, for example, a very lengthy affidavit must be completed by the estate of anyone who owns real or tangible personal property in that state at death but claims that he or she was not domiciled there at death. Often, answering the questions will be uncomfortable. The state will inquire with respect to many or all of the items listed in Chart 14.1.

Fourth, keep a diary (or have someone keep it on your behalf) together with independent proof as to where you spent each day of the year. Such a diary also may be kept for your family members (such as your spouse). The burden is on you to establish that you did not spend time in the state. Airline tickets, telephone bills (which show that telephone calls were made from the home you claim to be your domicile) and similar documentation should be retained for at least "rolling" three-year periods.

Even if you decide you do not really care what happens to your property when you die and just simply are not going to adjust your lifestyle to reduce taxes on your children's behalf, being sloppy about establishing clear evidence of your domicile may come back to haunt you during your lifetime with respect to gift tax and income tax.

Each state constitutionally may impose its income tax on your world-wide income if you either (1) spend more than 183 days there in any calendar year and have a home there available for your use or (2) you are domiciled in the state during the year. Not infrequently, for example, when one spouse dies owning real or tangible property situated in New York State, the family will act as though it does not care about the domicile issue because the entire estate is passing to the surviving spouse under the protection of the marital deduction. However, New York State may then take the position that back income taxes are due. In one case, New York State attempted to go back and impose over 30 years' worth of back income taxes contending that the person had been domiciled in New York State for 30 years but had failed to file tax returns.

That brings up another practical pointer: For every year after you change domicile from one state to another you should file a non-resident income tax return with the tax authorities of your prior home state unless you are absolutely confident that you have no connection whatsoever with that state. Usually, filing a non-resident income tax return will start a statute of limitations which will prevent the state from taxing you as a resident for more than three (or in some cases six) prior years.

If there is any question as to your domicile, it is important for you to seek the advice of an attorney. You may have to adjust your lifestyle to avoid certain state and local taxes or other problems. However, failure to heed your advisor's counsel may cause you to incur significant taxes.

Changing Domicile for Incompetents

Often, considerable taxes can be saved by changing domicile prior to death from a high tax jurisdiction to one which imposes a death tax only equal to the amount which the federal government allows as a dollar-for-dollar credit against the federal estate tax. A New Yorker, for example, who changes domicile to a state, such as Florida, Texas, California or Alaska, which imposes the lower estate tax, will avoid state death tax equal to 5% of the entire estate. On a $20 million estate, the savings can be as great as $1 million.

Individuals often do not take all the appropriate steps to change their domicile to a state with a lower death tax burden. And, even though they (and their family) may want to do that shortly before death, they may no longer have the legal capacity. As explained above, a change in domicile not only requires physical presence in the new state but it also requires an intention to make that state the new home. If you are under a legal disability you may not be able to form the requisite intent.

Fortunately, there is an almost fool-proof way to change domicile in such a case, although few advisors are aware of it. A proceeding can be commenced in court in the state of current domicile for an order allowing the person's domicile to be changed to another jurisdiction. Typically, the reason recited for the change is greater convenience for the person under disability (because he or she will live near a relative), lower nursing home costs, better weather, and lower income taxes. It appears that once the court's order is entered, it is absolutely binding on the state tax commission of that state. Of course, some families will be hesitant to commence a proceeding in which it must be alleged that the individual is incompetent. However, overall, the potential savings in state death taxes may establish that it is an appropriate step to take.

More on Removing Real and Tangible Personal Property from Your Former Domicile

As noted, it is appropriate to "remove" real or tangible personal property from a state if you do not wish your estate to be required to file a state death tax return there. Obviously, one way to do that is to sell the assets prior to your death. However, that may incur taxes. Moreover, you may want to continue to use an asset, such as a weekend home, in another state.

One method, which has been used with considerable success, is to transfer the real or tangible personal property located in the other state to a corporation. That will prevent you from owning real property or tangible property in the state at death; rather, you will own an *intangible*—corporate stock, which is not taxed to a non-resident. Not infrequently, ownership of a home is evidenced by corporate stock—there are literally thousands of apartments in New York City, for example, which are "co-operatives." In that case, the owner of the home does not own real estate (which is the case with a condominium, for example) but owns shares of stock. The shares of stock, because they are an *intangible*, are not subject to estate tax by New York State when they are owned by a non-domiciliary of the state.

There may be further ramifications (including corporate level income taxes) of incorporating some of your assets. Also, the corporate formalities must be observed. You will need to discuss these matters in detail with your advisor prior to seeking to form such a corporation.

AVOIDING TAX ITSELF USUALLY IS NOT A PRIMARY GOAL

A Common Misconception

Many individuals believe that the goal of estate planning is to avoid as much death tax as possible. If that were really your goal it would be as simple to achieve as leaving your whole estate to charity. However, that is not your goal. Rather, your goal is to transfer the maximum possible property to your loved ones. The reason you want to avoid tax is to maximize what they will receive.

Why the IRS, Without Planning, Will be Your Major Beneficiary

Without proper planning, the IRS probably will be the major beneficiary of your estate. Even Americans of rather modest wealth will have 50% or more of their wealth eroded by taxes at death. Few professionals, such as lawyers, physicians and accountants appreciate that, in many cases, a majority of their wealth will be represented by the right to income in respect of a decedent (IRD). As discussed earlier, IRD can be subject to both estate tax and income tax, resulting in an approximate 80% rate of tax. Hence, a professional with even a modest estate may see over one-half of his or her wealth eroded by taxes unless proper planning is undertaken well prior to death.

Why Tax Reduction Really Has to Be a Primary Estate Planning Objective

That brings us back full circle: Tax reduction has to be a primary estate planning objective, but only as it can maximize what will pass to your loved ones. That type of tax reduction is not so simple. Not only are the wealth transfer taxes the highest taxes imposed in the United States, they are among the most complex. The auditing agents of estate and gift tax returns must be attorneys licensed to practice law. (That is not the case, for example, for the income tax.) Those agents devote all of their time to the collection of taxes. They are extremely efficient, and it is understood that the IRS collects more taxes in audits of estate tax returns than any other type of audit. The only way you will be able to achieve significant estate tax reduction is to begin planning as early in life as is reasonably possible.

In fact, with proper and early planning, you should be able to reduce the estate tax burden by 50% or more. Few individuals, however, achieve that much of a savings. There are many reasons for that, but lack of motivation is certainly one: Individuals realize that they do not have an estate tax problem, but rather the problem is one for their surviving family members or loved ones. No one can force you to plan but, as explained below, the opportunities are there for you to take.

THE FOUR MAJOR FACTORS WHICH DETERMINE THE LEVEL OF DEATH TAX AND HOW TO USE THEM FOR YOUR BENEFIT

Factor Number One: What Is in Your Estate and How You Can Reduce It

It Is Probably More Than You Think

The death tax is imposed upon much more than property you own at the time of your death. It can include property you have given away (or even sold) long before you die. For example, if you transfer your home to your children and retain the right to live in there, the home will be included in your estate. Your estate may also include assets you have never owned, such as death benefits payable by your company to your surviving family members and property over which you have a broad power of disposition (a so-called "general power of appointment"). Contrary to popular belief, life insurance generally *is* subject to estate tax in the estate of the insured unless proper planning is undertaken well before death.

KEEPING ASSETS OUT OF THE ESTATE IN THE FIRST PLACE

It is much more difficult to effectively remove an asset from your base of wealth once you have acquired it than to avoid accumulating that wealth in the first place. Thus, as will be discussed in more detail below, when new opportunities to enhance wealth are available, arranging for them to be undertaken by other members of your family (such as children or trusts for their benefit) will reduce overall taxation.

A REMINDER THAT LIFETIME GIFTS SHOULD BE MADE EARLY

One of the most effective ways to avoid estate tax is to transfer assets prior to death as gifts. As explained above, there are several opportunities to transfer property free of gift tax, such as under the protection of the gift tax annual exclusion, to prevent property from being includable in your estate. As also explained above, it will be more efficient, as a general matter, if you use your $600,000 exemption equivalent as early in your lifetime as possible.

Even if you made transfers and paid gift tax, that usually will be more efficient than subjecting the property to tax at death for two basic reasons. First, as explained above, gift tax is not itself subject to gift tax whereas estate tax is itself subject to estate tax. You should also note that any gift tax you pay on gifts made within three years of death is itself subject to estate tax. That is another reason to make gifts early in life. Second, all future income and growth on the property given away, if properly structured, will escape gift and estate taxation in its entirety. Indeed, the most efficient way to give is to give away those assets (even paying taxes on them) which have the greatest potential for appreciation. In effect, whenever the anticipated appreciation (including income) on a particular asset is greater than the anticipated appreciation (and income) on the assets which would be used to pay gift tax, the high appreciation asset should be given away and the taxes funded as early as possible. The principle is simple: Impose the wealth transfer tax as early as possible on an asset which is expected to have the greatest appreciation.

PRACTICAL LIMITS ON LIFETIME TRANSFERS

Maintaining Your Lifestyle

Wealth transfer tax reduction usually can occur only if significant lifetime planning, including significant lifetime transfers, are made. However, you should never give away so much property that it could jeopardize the lifestyle which you currently enjoy or which you wish to enjoy in the future. Despite any understanding you may have with your children, once the property is transferred, they will regard it as theirs and no longer yours.

The King Lear Effect

In Shakespeare's play *King Lear*, King Lear gives his kingdom to his daughters who then turn against him. His "fatal flaw" was that he believed he could continue to enjoy the benefits of his wealth and office without owning them. Instead, of course, the relationship he had with his children was, in effect, reversed. They were no longer dependant upon him; he was dependant upon them.

Although the tragedy of *King Lear* is fiction, like so many of Shakespeare's works, it rings true. To some degree, the tragedy of *King Lear* has occurred in modern time with respect to great family fortunes. In one of the widely publicized will contest cases in America, the patriarch bestowed significant wealth upon his children at very young ages. In part for that reason, his relationship with his children virtually evaporated. As indicated, the matter culminated after his death in one of the most expensive and highly-publicized Will contests ever.

The relationship between you and your children (and other loved ones) is based upon many factors, which may include your position in the family as the one who controls the family's wealth. Perhaps, sharing a significant portion of that wealth with your children or other loved ones early in your lifetime may strengthen and enhance an appropriate relationship with them and with your spouse after your death. However, you should consider the matter carefully. You do not want to suffer the same tragedy that King Lear did.

One of the practical ways that you can avoid suffering the tragedy of King Lear in your own family is to make certain that transfers are meted out to family members only if they maintain an appropriate lifestyle. There is, in effect, only one real way to do that, and that is to place the majority of any transferred wealth in a flexible trust for the benefit of your family members or other loved ones. The Megatrust^{sm}, discussed in detail in Chapter 9, has been specially designed to allow a trustee to take whatever action is appropriate to increase the probability of your children leading proper lifestyles.

The bottom line is that you can avoid the *King Lear* effect on you (and on your spouse after your death) and yet take action during your lifetime to reduce wealth transfer taxes significantly if you plan accordingly.

Specific Tax Reduction Arrangements

Congress has spent considerable time attempting to foreclose legitimate arrangements which may reduce estate tax. The IRS and the Treasury Department regard "planning" as inappropriate. Both of those agencies want you to pay the maximum conceivable tax and continuously lobby with Congress to shutdown virtually every planning opportunity (including the $10,000 annual exclusion) which could possibly reduce tax and increase the amount of wealth your family members receive. At the end of this Chapter I describe some estate planning techniques that are effective as of the time of the printing of this book. However, it is likely that many of them will be attacked and foreclosed, at least in part, in the relatively near future. They are discussed in order to present you with an overview of estate planning and to allow you to determine whether you wish to explore using them with your own advisors.

Factor Number Two: Valuation: A Key Element in Estate Planning

OVERVIEW OF THE CRITICAL IMPORTANCE OF VALUATION

Over the past several years, valuation has become a more important factor than ever in estate and financial planning. The reasons are fairly obvious. First, if you can increase the value of an asset, you increase your base of wealth and therefore your financial security. On the other hand, if you can reduce the tax value of an asset at the time it is subject to tax, the taxes will be reduced.

THE CRITICAL FACTOR: THE MEANING OF FAIR MARKET VALUE

In General

In almost all circumstances, the estate, gift and generation-skipping transfer taxes are imposed upon the fair market value of an asset at the time it is transferred. Fair market value means the price at which the asset would change hands between a willing buyer and a willing seller, both of whom have reasonable knowledge of the factors affecting the worth of the asset and neither of whom is acting under a compulsion. The determination of fair market value of items such as publicly-traded securities is simple: It is based upon the value at which the property traded hands in the market place on the date of the transfer.

Most assets, however, do not lend themselves to such precise valuation. Rather, the value must be determined by appraisal pursuant to the "willing buyer/willing seller" valuation methodology. Real estate, interests in closely-held businesses, works of art and other items of tangible personal property usually must be valued by appraisal pursuant to the willing buyer/willing seller methodology.

Usually, a sale on or near the valuation date between third-parties is used as the best evidence of the asset's value. If the asset itself was not sold within a reasonable time of the valuation date, appraisers typically look at sales near that time of comparable property. For example, you may have owned your home for 30 years prior to your death. Unless the home is sold soon after your death, there will be no sale near your death to determine its value. However, there may be other homes in your neighborhood (or a comparable neighborhood) which were sold at or about the time of your death. Usually, the fair market value of your home will be based upon the sales of those other homes adjusted for different factors such as size, quality and precise location.

The One Exception: Special Use Valuation

There is one exception to the rule that taxes are imposed upon the fair market value of an asset. That exception, which applies for estate and certain generation-skipping transfer tax purposes, but not gift tax purposes, relates to real estate which is used in a farm or another closely-held business, if certain conditions are met. Rather than imposing the estate or generation-skipping transfer tax on the real estate's fair market value, the tax is imposed on the value of the real estate in the business as determined under special valuation rules. Your estate must meet certain requirements in order to be eligible for such so-called "special use" valuation. Among other conditions, the closely-held business (including the real estate) must comprise about 50% of your estate, the real estate must comprise about 25% of your estate, the real estate must have been used in the business for a certain time prior to your death and it must be inherited by and the business must be operated by certain close family members for a certain period after your death. Overall, special use valuation can reduce your taxable estate by as much as $750,000. That can reduce overall estate taxes by about $400,000 (and possibly more if there is potential generation-skipping transfer tax). For many families, such a reduction in taxation will be critically important; for others, it will not be important. If it will be important to your family, it is necessary for you to plan with your advisors during your lifetime to assure that your estate will be entitled to special use valuation.

Discounts in Valuation

As mentioned above, determining the value of marketable securities is relatively simple: It is the price at which they traded hands between third parties at or about the valuation date (usually, the date of the gift or your date of death). However, closely-held business interests, by their very nature, are not sold on a marketplace and, therefore, cannot be valued in that way. Often, reference to sales of interests in comparable publicly-traded companies is used to determine the value of a closely-held business. However, non-marketable securities (that is, interests in a closely-held business) generally sell at a significant discount from their publicly traded counterparts. One study, for example, found that the discount averaged 35%. That discount in valuation can significantly reduce taxes when you transfer an interest in your closely-held business to others.

For example, assume that another company, comparable to yours, is publicly traded. Its stock sells for ten times earnings. The initial indication is that your company also should sell for ten times earnings. However, because interests in your business are not as freely saleable as those of the publicly-traded company, on an average interests in your company are worth less. They may not be worth less to you or members of your family—but that is unimportant. The tax law does not value property based on what it is worth to you or members of your family; rather, it values the property for tax purposes at its worth to an independent third party. That independent third party is certainly going to pay less for an interest in your business, all other things being equal, than one in which he can merely call a stockbroker at any time and have the interest sold.

Although the government studies indicated that 35% was the average discount for "lack of marketability", the IRS attempts to apply much smaller discounts. In certain circumstances, however, interests in your company may be valued at even steeper discounts. And from a tax perspective, that is beneficial: The steeper the discount, the lower the value; the lower the value, the lower the tax.

The second discount, which some appraisers do not distinguish from the first, is a discount for a minority interest. Again, the government's own studies indicate that a minority interest in a business is worth less than a proportionate part of the value of the business as a whole. That is true even for publicly-traded securities. The reason is lack of control. In a closely-held business, the discount for a minority interest may be even greater. As a rather insignificant (minority) shareholder in a closely-held business, you will have little impact on the operation of the venture including decisions to make payments to shareholders. In fact, where the closely-held business is controlled by a family group, a minority interest may be almost worthless to third parties.

In the "real world", third parties who are asked to make minority investments in closely-held businesses often seek certain protections. It is common, for example, for such investors to have the right to cause the corporation to buy out their stock within a certain period of time unless certain events occur (such as dividends being paid at a certain level and/or the company registering the stock so it can be sold in the public market, etc.). Without those additional protections, the minority equity interest in such a case probably has little worth. In other words, the discount may be as great as 70% or more. The IRS resists such significant discounts.

It is important for you to be aware of the level of potential discounts in planning your financial affairs.

A Most Important Planning Strategy: Changing the Nature of the Asset So as to Change Its Value

As can be seen, certain property interests may have a significantly different value than others which, in some ways, are comparable to them. For example, if the interests in your business are non-marketable they will be worth less than if they are marketable. As discussed at the end of this Chapter, in some cases you can exploit those valuation rules to change the tax value of an asset by changing its nature.

You will see that there are ways of avoiding having your assets valued for wealth transfer tax purposes at their full fair market value. One method is to divide a majority interest in your business into minority pieces. The rules about minority discounts and how the nature of an asset can be changed so as to minimize the asset's value are complicated. It is advantageous to consult an experienced tax advisor and obtain an independent third-party appraisal. Another method that will be discussed in more detail later is to form an investment company, in corporate or partnership form, with other family members and, if possible, with non-family members as well.

A Note About Appraisers

No valuation you obtain (even from an independent third-party appraiser) is binding upon the IRS or the courts. Nonetheless, an independent third-party appraisal, reasonably relied upon by you and your tax advisors, should prevent the imposition of certain penalties if it is determined that the property was incorrectly (even if innocently) undervalued. In addition, by obtaining an independent third-party appraisal at the time that you make the transfer, you can select the best appraiser, thereby foreclosing the IRS from hiring that appraiser to work against you. In some circumstances, that will be a major tactical advantage in dealing with the IRS.

In fact, some recent decisions indicate that taxpayers cannot avoid the incorrect valuation penalties if they rely on persons who are not qualified appraisers. Your lawyer or accountant, no matter how gifted and experienced, may not be regarded as a qualified appraiser and that means that you may face penalties if you rely on his or her valuation unless that professional also is a recognized expert. Hence, you should use a qualified appraiser whenever the tax consequences of a transaction (including gifts or bequests you make) are dependent on value. Your lawyer or accountant, if not a qualified appraiser, can obtain a list of appropriate professional appraisers for you.

Factor Number Three: What Comes Out of the Taxable Basket of Assets

DEBTS AND EXPENSES

As discussed above, debts, such as unpaid medical bills or mortgages on property, the expenses of administering your estate, and funeral expenses are deductible for estate tax purposes. However, remember that in order to be deductible, a debt must be founded on consideration in money or money's worth.

MARITAL DEDUCTION TRANSFERS

Overview

As noted above, you can transfer unlimited quantities of property to a spouse free of gift or estate tax by reason of the marital deduction. As a general matter, however, any asset transferred under the protection of the marital deduction will be includable in your spouse's estate or be subject to gift tax if your spouse transfers it during his or her lifetime. Hence, to a large degree, the marital deduction does not eliminate or reduce taxes but only postpones them. Although postponing tax generally is beneficial, you must remember that if the assets you transfer to your spouse under the protection of the marital deduction increase in value, even more will be subject to tax when your spouse dies. Therefore, you must consider whether that potential increase in estate tax on the asset will be more than offset by postponing the tax from the time you die until the time your spouse dies, and by the step-up in income tax basis for the asset at your spouse's death. As will be explained in more detail below, after analyzing these factors, you may well conclude that using the marital deduction in your circumstances will not reduce overall taxation.

Requirements

Usually, only two types of transfers will qualify for the marital deduction. First, almost all outright transfers to your spouse will qualify. The exceptions are relatively rare although obviously they can be important—your attorney should be able to spot them and recommend appropriate planning. (One important exception is transfers to a spouse who is not a U.S. citizen.) Second, transfers in trust for your spouse also can qualify for the marital deduction, provided that you comply with special tax law requirements.

Basically, three types of trusts qualify for the marital deduction. The type most commonly used today is "qualified terminable interest property", usually referred to as QTIP.

In order for a trust to constitute a QTIP, your spouse must be entitled to all of the "accounting income" which the trust generates each year. Accounting income may be different from tax income. It includes interest (including tax-exempt interest), dividends, rents and royalties, and excludes capital gain, under most circumstances. Your spouse must be given the right to make the trust produce a reasonable amount of such accounting income. What constitutes a reasonable level of accounting income has never been determined absolutely. It does not, however, mean that all or even a significant portion of the assets must be invested in fixed-income obligations (such as bonds). Moreover, the trust is usually not required to produce the accounting income in all events, but only upon the demand of your spouse.

When your spouse dies, the remaining QTIP trust property will go wherever you have specified, after payment of the estate taxes which the trust will generate in your spouse's estate at your spouse's death (remember—the marital deduction means property is *not* taxed in your estate but *is* taxed in your spouse's estate when your spouse dies).

A QTIP trust gives you the most control over the assets and gives your spouse the smallest interest that is possible under the federal tax law while still qualifying for the marital deduction. Of course, you can give your spouse greater rights, such as more than income under certain circumstances, or a limited power to control the disposition of the trust assets at her death, and/or you can authorize the trustee to pay principal to your spouse under certain conditions or in the trustee's sole discretion. However, if you wish, you can limit your spouse to just the income interest (and right to make the trust productive) as described above.

A QTIP trust is often used where your spouse is not the parent of your children. That matter is discussed in Chapter 12. However, as discussed in that Chapter, the requirement that your spouse must have the power to make the trust reasonably productive of income may cause a problem if the trust is funded with an interest in your closely-held business which is not generally productive of income. In such a case, if your spouse demanded that the trust be made reasonably productive, the business would have to pay income or, possibly, the trustee would have to sell part or all of the trust's interest in the business (or ask the business to redeem the interest) in order to generate income. Any of those alternatives may cause problems for your business.

The second type of marital deduction trust is almost identical to a QTIP except that your spouse is given the absolute power to control where the trust property goes when he or she dies. That power must include the power to cause the trust property to be paid to the spouse or the spouse's estate—a so-called "general power of appointment."

The third type of marital deduction trust is known as an "estate trust." Your spouse need not be given the right to any of the trust income during his or her lifetime. However, the trust must terminate in favor of your spouse's own estate. That means that your spouse can control the ultimate destiny of the property by his or her own Will. Estate trusts are rarely used today.

Why Using the Marital Deduction May Increase or Decrease Taxes

Although usually the marital deduction does not eliminate, but only postpones, the estate tax until your spouse dies, in some cases it may reduce tax. For example, if your spouse does not have enough property to use his or her own $600,000 estate tax exemption (or the $1,000,000 generation-skipping transfer tax exemption), transferring property to your spouse under the protection of the marital deduction may provide your spouse with an adequate base of wealth to absorb your spouse's exemptions. Similarly, you may have so much property that a significant portion of your estate may be subject to tax at the highest estate tax rate, while your spouse may have little property. In such a case, much of what you leave to your spouse under the protection of the marital deduction will be subject to tax at lower than the top rates when your spouse later dies. Moreover, property you leave to your spouse can be used by your spouse during his or her lifetime to undertake planning which is available for lifetime transfers but not for deathtime ones. In such circumstances, using the marital deduction (either during your lifetime or at your death) may reduce overall taxation.

On the other hand, in some cases using the marital deduction may increase overall taxation. For example, if you leave your entire estate to your spouse under the protection of the marital deduction, you may fail to use your own $600,000 estate tax exemption equivalent or fail to take advantage of the opportunity to expose property to tax in your estate at a lower rate than that which may apply to your spouse's estate.

Look at it from Your Children's Perspective

Even if using the marital deduction for all or a significant portion of your estate may reduce overall taxation, it probably is best from your children's own selfish perspective if you do not utilize the marital deduction at all but leave all of your property to your children when you die. If you use the marital deduction, your children will not receive any property until your surviving spouse dies. Your children may be better off receiving less property when you die as opposed to more property at your spouse's later death.

Children traditionally do not mind waiting to receive their inheritance until their mother and father have both died. However, if your spouse is not the parent of your children, you may find significant resentment by your children if you leave most of your estate to your spouse, especially if your spouse is considerably younger than you are (or, as is sometimes the case, younger than your children).

Why You Should Consider Using the Marital Deduction Even If You Want to Benefit Your Children or Others

Sometimes, a property owner will wish to leave property to children, grandchildren, charities or others upon his or her death rather than having such gifts made only when both spouses have died. However, from a tax perspective, it almost always is better to leave the amount which you would have left to your children, charity or others to your spouse, and allow your spouse to make those transfers "for you."

For example, if your estate is in the 50% effective estate tax bracket and you leave $100,000 to your children, half of that amount, or $50,000, will have to be paid in estate tax. If, instead, you left the $100,000 to your spouse free of estate tax by reason of the marital deduction, your spouse could then give those funds to your children. It might be possible for your spouse to use lifetime planning arrangements (such as making gifts under the protection of the annual exclusion) so that no tax would be paid at all on such transfers. However, even if your spouse could not do that, your spouse could increase the net amount your children would receive from $50,000 to $66,666. The reason is that a lifetime gift of $66,666 will produce a gift tax (at the 50% bracket) of only $33,333. The sum of the gift and the gift taxes still totals $100,000, but now by reducing estate taxes you have increased the net amount your children receive. Of course, you must be confident that your spouse will follow your wishes. Even then, I recommend that you spell out your hope and expectation that your spouse will use the special gift to him or her to make gifts to your children. (Unfortunately, if you go so far as to impose a legal obligation on your spouse to make the gifts to your children, you will lose the tax savings.)

You can transfer property to charity, just as you can to your spouse, free of estate tax. Nonetheless your family may be better off if you leave the amount which you would have given to charity upon your death to your spouse and allow your spouse to make the charitable transfers for you. (The transfers by your spouse still can be made in your name.) As a general matter, no income tax deduction is generated by leaving property at your death to charity. However, if you leave property to your spouse, your spouse will receive an income tax charitable deduction if he or she gives the property to charity. Again, you must have confidence that your spouse will carry out your wishes. As indicated above, I usually recommend that the special gift to your spouse be accompanied by words of hope and expectation as to what your spouse will do with those funds.

CHARITABLE TRANSFERS

The Responsibility to Give

The government encourages each of us to make transfers to charity by providing two tax benefits. First, as a general matter, we are entitled to an income, gift or estate tax deduction on transfers of assets to charity. That reduces the cost of giving. In fact, to the extent of the effective tax bracket (and to a greater extent the higher that bracket is), we have shifted the cost of the charitable gift to the government. The second benefit is the exemption from taxation which charities enjoy. As a general matter, a charity can receive unlimited income and pay no income tax at all.

The government's encouragement of charitable giving is not just detached generosity. Rather, it reflects the fact that charitable activity alleviates part of the responsibilities of government. Were it not for private schools, for example, almost all of which are charitable institutions, the government would have to incur additional expenditures for education. The same is true for medical services and almost all areas of charitable endeavor. It is also appropriate to note that not only are charities reducing the burden of government but they are carrying out those activities in a much more efficient manner. The government is one of the most inefficient organizations, while charities tend to be as efficient as for-profit businesses.

Because the law assists you in making charitable transfers by reducing the tax burden on you or your estate, you may find it even more appropriate to give back to the community some payment for the success which the community helped you to achieve. Moreover, through careful planning, you can increase the part which the government bears of each charitable transfer you make and benefit your loved ones as well.

Keep the Tax Rules in Mind

The tax rules relating to charitable giving are among the most complex in the Internal Revenue Code. Although most outright transfers to charity will generate a deduction of one type or another, in some cases, no deduction will be permitted. For example, usually, an income tax deduction is permitted only to the extent of your basis in the property (i.e., what you paid for it) plus any untaxed gain to the extent it represents long-term capital gain (as opposed to ordinary income). And even that rule is subject to several exceptions and limitations. You should not make significant charitable transfers without the advice of a competent counsellor. Such advice can reduce the cost to you of giving, or can increase the amount charity receives, or both.

A Reminder About Income in Respect of a Decedent

As discussed above, income in respect of a decedent (IRD) usually is subject to both estate tax and income tax, often bringing the effective rate of taxation to 80% or more. The most inexpensive bequests you can make to charity at your death are those which consist of the right to IRD. If you left the right to IRD to a family member, such as a child, the child would net 20% or less of the asset, in many cases. For non-IRD assets, the child may wind up with 45% or more. That means that to the extent possible all charitable bequests should be funded with the right to IRD.

Special Charitable Transfers

Charitable Remainder Trusts

Not infrequently, an individual will make a transfer which benefits himself or herself (or another individual) as well as charity. Usually, those are called "split-interest" transfers because the transfer is split between charity, on the one hand, and an individual or individuals, on the other. A common example is a charitable remainder trust. One or more individuals may receive payments from the trust for life (or a fixed term of years) and then the property will be transferred to charity. Usually, the payment to the individual or individuals must be an annuity or a unitrust amount. An annuity, of course, is a fixed dollar amount which does not vary from year to year. A unitrust payment is a fixed percentage of the annual value of the fund. If the fund increases, the unitrust recipient will receive more than in the prior year; if the fund goes down, the unitrust recipient will receive less than the year before.

Charitable remainder trusts offer two potential tax advantages. First, a deduction is permitted for the value of the remainder committed to charity. Actuarial computations are made to determine how big the deduction will be. Basically, the longer the trust will last for individuals and the higher the payout is, the smaller the deduction will be. Often, it represents a relatively small percentage of the assets placed in trust. Nonetheless, to the extent of the deduction, it reduces taxes and thereby increases the amount which is available for the individual beneficiary or beneficiaries.

The second benefit relates to the exemption from taxation which the trust enjoys in most circumstances. The trust, like charity itself, usually can receive unlimited quantities of income without paying tax. The individuals are taxed only as and when the trust makes the annuity or unitrust payments to them. Whenever the amount of taxable income received by the trust exceeds the current payout to the individuals, income can accumulate in the trust on a tax-deferred basis. In the case of a unitrust where the payments to the beneficiaries change with the value of the trust, that means that more will be available in the trust to generate payments to the individual beneficiaries. Over time, the trust's exemption from taxation can produce a much larger base of wealth.

Moreover, the charitable remainder trust provides an excellent alternative, in many circumstances, for disposing of the right to income in respect of a decedent (IRD). Although you should ask your tax advisor to prepare some calculations for you, in almost all circumstances your children will be better off if the IRD is paid to a charitable remainder trust for their benefit rather than outright to them at the time of your death. In some cases, that strategy can increase the economic benefit to your children from the IRD by a significant multiple.

Charitable Lead Trusts

A charitable lead trust, in a sense, is the "flip side" of a charitable remainder trust. Charity receives the first or "leading" interest in a trust with the remainder then passing to or in further trust for individuals. Like a charitable remainder trust, a charitable lead trust must provide for payments of an annuity or unitrust amount, in this case to charity. Because the value of charity's interest is determined based on the size of the payments to charity and the period for which those payments will be made, in some cases virtually all of the value of the trust may be deemed to have been transferred to charity. Therefore, gift or estate tax (and in some cases generation-skipping tax) can be reduced. In fact, it is possible, with a charitable lead annuity trust, to reduce the amount subject to gift or estate tax to zero.

Basically, the IRS assumes that the charitable lead trust can earn no more than 120% of the rate currently being paid on three-to-nine year Treasury obligations. Where the nature of the assets (or their low tax value, such as by discounts, discussed above) suggests that a higher rate can be earned, it may be possible, with a charitable lead trust, not just to benefit charity but to enhance the amount of wealth which your family ultimately receives. On the other hand, the trust must make the required payment to charity each year. If the trust property fails to produce an adequate rate of return to fund that annual obligation, the trust will be eroded over time. In fact, in some circumstances, the entire trust will be depleted by payments to charity so that nothing is left at the end of the charitable term.

If you use a charitable lead trust, the time at which your family will receive property from you may be postponed (but keep in mind that you can also create a charitable lead trust during lifetime). A charitable lead trust will also let you pinpoint exactly when the assets will be received. For instance, you have a ten-year-old child (or grandchild). You would like that child (or grandchild) to have a certain level of wealth when he or she is 35. By creating a 25-year charitable lead trust, you can ensure that the property will be available to the child at age 35.

Charitable remainder and lead trusts are complicated arrangements. They may or may not be appropriate for you. Special rules apply when such trusts are funded with interests in a closely-held businesses. Use one only after consultation with your tax advisor.

Conservation Easements

The tax law allows an income and gift tax deduction, if the transfer is made during lifetime, or an estate tax deduction, if the transfer occurs at death, for a gift of a conservation easement over real estate. A conservation easement is a restriction which prohibits certain activities and development of real estate. Usually, the property must be either environmentally or historically significant. For example, prohibiting the development of a vacant lot in a crowded city may entitle its owner to a deduction. On the other hand, prohibiting the development of a farm in a highly-rural area (where there is virtually no development activity) may not produce any deduction at all.

The restriction takes effect by your transferring the development and similar rights either to the government or to a qualified charity. (A transfer of the easement to a family foundation will not generate the deduction.) Usually, it is a mistake to ever involve the government in such a matter. Even if the current "administration" of the government seems reasonable, you can be assured that the administration and the attitude of the government will change over time. The entity which holds the conservation easement will have certain rights with respect to your property (such as the right to inspect it from time to time). Almost always, you will be better off granting the easement to a charity.

A conservation easement can produce several benefits. First, it can assure the preservation of property which is important to you. For example, a number of ecologically important parcels of property have been preserved permanently through the grant of conservation easements. Second, the owner is entitled to what may be a significant income tax deduction (equal to the difference between what the property was worth before the restriction on development was imposed and its value thereafter). Third, the value of the property is reduced for gift and/or estate tax purposes.

If you own a piece of real estate which is potentially important, historically, ecologically or for the scenic enjoyment of the public, and you do not want it to be developed commercially (including for multiple residential home construction), you might discuss conservation easements with your tax advisor.

Private and Community Foundations

The federal tax law and state property and related laws encourage charitable giving. The tax law generally provides a deduction for contributions to charities and grants them a total exemption from taxation. State law usually allows charities exemptions from real estate and other taxes, and affords other privileges which are not available to for-profit businesses or to individuals. State law often provides different rules for different types of charities. For example, charities which operate schools may be required to operate under a somewhat different set of rules than charities which merely make grants for other charitable purposes. The federal tax law also distinguishes among different types of charities. As a general rule, the tax law divides charities into two categories: private foundations and public charities. Generally, the classification of a charity as a private foundation or a public charity depends upon the sources of the charity's support, and is not dependent upon its size or the type of its charitable activities. (There are exceptions to that rule. For instance, all churches are regarded as public charities even if their support is from only a small segment of the general public.) Generally, a charity is regarded as a private foundation if its support is derived in large measure from investment income and/or a small group of individuals or businesses.

Many families and businesses create, fund and operate private foundations. There are advantages and disadvantages of creating and using a private foundation as a vehicle for your charitable giving. On the plus side, private foundations permit a more "focused" charitable program. Rather than merely responding every time you or your business is asked to make charitable contributions, you or your business makes contributions to the foundation. The foundation in turn, through a regularized procedure, receives applications and distributes funds or assets either directly for charitable purposes or to the charitable institutions it wishes to support. Usually, the tax deduction permitted for contributions to charity is allowed at the time contribution is made to the private foundation, even where the contributor (such as you or your business) continues to control the ultimate destiny of the funds.

Another advantage of a private foundation is that it can be used as a mechanism to keep your family together if members of your family serve on the board of directors or as trustees of the foundation. Generally, the next best thing to owning a lot of money is controlling a lot of money. Being able to participate in the disposition of significant funds to charity generally places an individual in a good light in his or her community. In addition, younger members of the board often learn the importance of cooperation and compromise. Your children, for example, may learn that if they want to fund a particular type of charitable program, they will have to come up with persuasive reasons to convince their siblings (as well as you and your spouse if you and your spouse are on the board) why their program, as opposed to others, should be supported.

There are negative aspects of private foundations as well. In a few cases, the income tax deduction for contributions to private foundations may not be as beneficial as that for contributions to public charities. However, through proper planning with your advisors, you may be able to obtain the same benefits. In addition, as a general rule, the reporting requirements for a private foundation (including having to make the records of the foundation available to the public) are greater than for a public charity. Also, as a general matter, neither you, nor members of your family nor your business may have any economic dealings with any foundation created and funded by you or the business. For example, you may not buy or sell property to or from the foundation nor may you own property with the foundation even where such transactions are advantageous for the foundation. Also, in many circumstances, your foundation will be able to own only two percent of your company's stock. In some cases, it may be possible for it to own as much as thirty five percent of your company's stock.

If you are charitably inclined, it may well be worthwhile to consider creating a private foundation to provide a more professionally oriented charitable giving program, to permit your children to become philanthropically oriented at relatively young ages and to enhance the recognition of your family and your business in the charitable community.

An alternative to running your own private foundation is to create a fund at a Community Foundation. Community Foundations are treated as a public charity for tax purposes. They usually serve a particular "community" (such as the greater Cleveland area or the entire state of Texas) by granting funds to operating charities (such as schools, museums, centers for developmentally disabled children, etc.) in that location. They permit individuals and businesses to maintain a fund at the Community Foundation in the name of that person, his or her family or his or her business. The assets contributed by you or your business fund are professionally managed by banks in your area and the professional staff of the Community Foundation completes all administrative work and reporting requirements for your fund. You or your business can either specify an area or areas of charitable pursuit to where the contributed assets are to be devoted or you or your business can advise (but not direct) the Community Foundation each year as to which other charities you or your company wishes to have funds distributed that year.

In many cases, using a fund at a Community Foundation will be preferable to creating and operating a private foundation. If you are charitably inclined and especially if you wish to explore how benefitting charity may be able to assist in achieving financial and estate planning goals, you probably should discuss both private foundations and Community Foundations with your advisors.

Factor Number Four: When Taxes Are Due

ASK THE RIGHT QUESTION: COULD YOUR BUSINESS SURVIVE IF IT HAD TO PAY A CREDITOR 55% OF ITS NET VALUE NINE MONTHS FROM TODAY?

As a general matter, federal (and most state) death taxes are due nine months after death. For individuals who are moderately well-to-do, 55% (or more) of their estates will be eroded by taxes. If your estate consists, in significant part, of interests in a closely-held business, the effect is to impose the burden of the tax on your business.

Few businesses could survive if they had to pay 55% of their net value nine months from today. Yet, that is exactly what owners of closely-held businesses face. Fortunately, planning usually can reduce the burden and, for many closely-held business owners, a special opportunity to defer the estate tax is available.

SPECIAL OPPORTUNITY FOR AN OWNER OF A CLOSELY-HELD BUSINESS: PAYING THE TAX OVER 15 YEARS

How It Works

A special provision of the federal tax law permits the estate of a closely-held business owner to pay a portion of the estate tax over an approximately 15-year period following death.

Interest only is paid for about the first five years after death and then one-tenth of the tax (together with interest on the unpaid balance) is paid from year five to year 15. Only the estate tax attributable to the closely-held business interest can be postponed. The portion of the estate tax attributable to other assets, such as cash, real estate not used in the business and marketable securities, will still be due nine months after death.

It is appropriate to note, however, that not all states offer the same type of deferral. Yet, as discussed above, each state has a death tax which usually will represent about 30% (or more) of the total tax bill. You may wish to check with your tax advisor to determine whether or not your home state has the deferral privilege. Using the federal deferral privilege may provide significant relief, but if 30% of the tax attributable to the closely-held business still must be paid shortly after death, that relief may not be adequate to prevent destruction of the business.

Requirements

Not all estates qualify for the deferral privilege. Basically, the tax law imposes three requirements.

First, more than 35% of your estate (as specially defined) must be comprised of qualifying business interests. For many business owners, that part of the test is relatively simple to meet.

Second, the business must be "closely-held." Here, your estate can qualify in one of two ways. Either you must have 15 or fewer shareholders or partners, or you must own 20% or more of the equity interest in the business. The latter rule often is the more generous one. In fact, if you own more than 20% of all of the outstanding stock of even a publicly-traded company your estate can qualify for the 15-year deferral privilege. If, on the other hand, you own less than 20%, you can still qualify if there are 15 or fewer shareholders or partners. In some cases, one family member is deemed to own the interests held by another. Hence, even if you are somewhat over the 15-owner limit, check with your tax advisor as to whether or not one of the special attribution rules might cause the business to be treated as having no more than 15 owners. If you still do not meet the ownership test, it is possible that steps can be taken (such as buying out the interests of some of the other owners) so that you meet the 15-owner limit at your death.

The third requirement is that the business must be an active business enterprise and not just a vehicle for managing investments. That test might seem very simple to meet, and it is for some. However, if you operate your business through a holding entity your estate may not qualify. For example, if you own a holding partnership which, in turn, owns other businesses, the holding partnership may not be regarded as an active business. The law in that regard is not entirely clear. If you use a holding entity (whether in partnership or corporate form), check with your advisor to see whether your enterprise will be regarded as an active one.

A special warning should be added here. For technical reasons, you usually cannot go to court if the IRS denies you the right to defer the estate tax over 15 years. Hence, it is important to take steps so that it is as clear as is reasonably possible that you meet the requirements for deferral. In this case, falling into a "grey" area or having a colorable claim is not enough.

The Cost of Borrowing from the Government

Interest must be paid on the estate tax deferred. However, although the interest rate is tied to market rates, the cost of borrowing generally is very low. That is because the interest paid on the deferred tax is deductible for estate tax purposes. Your estate probably will be in a 55% effective estate tax bracket, which means that most of the burden of the interest will be borne by the government.

How to Increase the Percentage Deferred

As noted, the 15-year deferral privilege only applies to that portion of the estate tax which is attributable to the qualifying closely-held business interest. For example, if 60% of your estate consists of qualifying closely-held business interests, then 60% of the federal estate tax may be deferred. (As mentioned above, your home state may or may not have a comparable deferral provision.)

You may be able to increase the percentage of your estate which is deemed to consist of closely-held business interests and thereby increase the percentage of tax which can be deferred. Contributing additional assets to your closely-held business to increase your equity interest may be effective, if those assets are then employed in the actual operation of the business. Another way to increase the percentage of your estate which is deemed to consist of a qualifying closely-held business interest (and/or possibly to push your estate over the minimum 35% threshold) is to convert charitable bequests you would otherwise make at death into binding charitable pledges. For the purpose of determining the percentage of your estate which consists of qualifying closely-held business interests your estate is reduced by, among other things, all debts you owe at the time of your death. Legally enforceable charitable pledges count as debts for this purpose. It is usually possible to cause charitable pledges to be legally enforceable under state law. Thus, as long as you are absolutely certain that you will make certain charitable bequests, if you wish to increase the percentage of your estate which is deemed to consist of a qualifying closely-held business interest (thereby increasing the percentage of estate tax which can be deferred), you should explore with your legal counsel the conversion of charitable bequests into binding charitable pledges.

OTHER OPTIONS

Apart from 15-year deferral under the special rule for qualifying closely-held business interests, the IRS is permitted to (and generally will) grant your estate an extension, of up to ten years, to pay estate tax if the extension is for a reasonable cause. Probably, the most common example of reasonable cause is illiquidity of estate assets. If your estate consists significantly of closely-held business interest (but, perhaps, does not meet all the requirements for 15-year deferral), your estate almost certainly will have liquidity problems. Usually, the IRS is sympathetic in such circumstances and will grant an extension of time to pay. Sometimes, however, the IRS will grant the extension year by year rather than for the entire ten-year period.

Almost always, I advise estates to request the reasonable cause extension to pay even if the estate appears to qualify for 15-year deferral. There are two reasons for that. First, the IRS may determine that the estate, for a variety of substantive or technical reasons, is not, in fact, entitled to 15-year deferral. (Keep in mind, as stated earlier, that the IRS's determination is, as a practical matter, one which you cannot appeal to any court.) Second, under 15-year deferral, tax payments must be made in installments, usually commencing no later than the fourth anniversary of nine months after death. The reasonable cause extension, however, can defer payment of the entire tax (or any portion of it) for the full ten years after the normal payment date (nine months after death).

If for any reason you anticipate that you may not be able to use either of these deferral provisions, or may not be able to use them to the extent you believe will be necessary, it may be appropriate for you to discuss with a commercial lender prior to your death the possibility of loans to your estate to fund estate taxes. You will find, however, in almost all circumstances, that the commercial lender will grant you less favorable terms than will the IRS.

Chapter 15 discusses life insurance in detail. It is appropriate, however, to make a few comments about life insurance in connection with the timing of payment of estate taxes attributable to a closely-held business.

No doubt, you carry several different types of liability insurance. To some degree, you may view life insurance as liability insurance for death taxes. The imposition of death taxes is a virtual certainty. The time of payment usually is the primary unknown factor. Although, through proper planning, the tax burden can be reduced, and often funded by alternative means, acquiring life insurance until those steps are in place may be appropriate. That may be especially true if it is uncertain whether your estate will qualify for any deferral of payment of estate tax, or if your home state has no such deferral provision. In any case, the moral is clear: You should develop a plan well ahead of time with your advisors to fund your estate taxes.

A Word About Section 303 Redemptions to Take Money Out of a Business

Under the Internal Revenue Code, almost all distributions from a corporation to its shareholder are treated as taxable dividends. As a result, the earnings of the corporation are subjected to two layers of tax: one imposed upon the corporation on its earnings and another to the shareholder when dividends are received.

Although even distributions from the corporation in redemption of stock typically are treated as taxable dividends to shareholders, the amounts received in redemption of the shares are treated, in certain limited circumstances, as payment for the stock so that the taxpayer is permitted to recover basis (usually purchase price of the stock) and treat any additional proceeds as capital gain rather than as ordinary income. Even when capital gains tax rates are about equal to ordinary income tax rates, there are often advantages to receiving capital gain income—for example, it can be offset without limitation by capital losses. In the case of an estate, which normally will have received an income tax-free "step-up" in the basis of the shares at death to the estate tax value, the difference between dividend and capital gain treatment is extremely significant. If a redemption of the shares at their estate tax value is treated as a purchase rather than a dividend, the estate will experience no taxable income or gain.

A special provision of the Internal Revenue Code (Section 303) permits the redemption of shares owned by a decedent's estate to be treated as a purchase of the stock in circumstances where the redemption proceeds otherwise would be treated as dividends.

For example, in almost no circumstance would a redemption of shares from a person who owns all (or almost all) of the stock in a closely held business be treated as a purchase of the shares rather than a dividend unless all of that shareholder's stock were redeemed. However, this restriction does not apply under Section 303. This means a person who owns all of the stock in a closely-held business may have the shares redeemed after his or her death and may continue to have the estate own 100% of the shares (even after the redemption), and yet may still have the proceeds received in redemption treated as sales proceeds (resulting in no gain except to the extent that the proceeds are in excess of the estate tax value of the stock). Of course, because the owner owns 100% of the shares there is no reason to attempt to obtain a price in excess of estate tax value which, as a practical matter, means that the redemptions may occur without any income tax consequences at all. Similarly, if a husband, wife and their children own all of the stock of a company, and if the husband dies leaving all of his stock to the wife, Section 303 permits sale treatment upon a redemption of shares from the estate where such treatment would probably not otherwise be possible.

The criteria for qualifying for redemption under Section 303 are similar to those for qualification for the 15 year estate tax deferral provisions under Section 6166. (The requirements relating to Section 6166 are discussed, in some delay, earlier in this Chapter.) In order to be eligible under Section 303, the decedent's stock interest must have a value that exceeds 35% of the gross estate less certain allowable deductions. Like Section 6166, interests in 2 or more closely held businesses can be aggregated if 20% or more of the total value of each business is included in the decedent's estate. Unlike Section 6166, there is no requirement that the business be an "active" one, or that the stock be "closely held." Most important, unlike Section 6166, the redemptions which are entitled to sale treatment under Section 303 are an amount equal to the sum of (1) federal and state (and foreign) death taxes imposed upon the estate, (2) administration expenses and (3) funeral charges. The amounts received in the redemption do not, however, have to be applied in payment of those items. Thus, Section 303 is useful not only as a means of obtaining needed cash to pay estate obligations at little or no tax cost, but also simply as a means to remove cash from a corporation with little or no tax cost at the shareholder level. (If the corporation has to sell appreciated assets to generate the cash for the redemption, there will, of course, be a corporate level tax on that gain.)

Generally, a redemption under Section 303 must take place within 3 years and 90 days of the date that the federal estate tax return is filed (or the due date if the return is filed early). However, if an estate has qualified for deferred payment under Section 6166, Section 303 redemptions can occur, in effect, without them being treated as "dispositions" under Section 6166. Usually, a disposition of more than 50% of the estate's interest is a closely held business. This will cause the estate to lose its eligibility under Section 6166.

ESTATE PLANNING STRATEGIES

Introduction

The number of tax savings strategies is almost without limit. Whether any is appropriate for your use can only be determined in consultation with your advisors. Some techniques are more aggressive and, therefore, involve more risk than others.

"Grantor" Trusts

Generally, two taxpayers who earn $25,000 each will pay less in combined income tax than one taxpayer who makes $50,000 a year. The reason is that income rates are progressive: Each additional dollar you earn is subjected to an ever-increasing rate of taxation until the top rate is reached.

At one time, federal income tax rates could exceed 90%. The ability to divide income with other family members or trusts for their benefit was compelling because it reduced overall taxation and thereby increased the family's wealth. To prevent taxpayers from being able to shift income to a trust, without in fact relinquishing control over and/or interest in the assets, certain special rules were developed under which the income of a trust was taxed back to the person who created it. Those rules are known as the "grantor trust" rules because they tax the income of the trust to the grantor—that is, the person who created the trust.

In many cases, taxpayers continue to attempt to avoid application of the grantor trust rules so that they are not taxed on the income of a trust. However, in some cases, it will be beneficial to create a trust in which the income is taxed back to you. Because tax on the income earned by the trust (including capital gain) will not be paid by the trust (or its beneficiaries), the trust can grow on a pre-tax basis. Although you will pay the income tax, it is widely believed among experienced estate planners that your payment of the tax on income and gain of grantor trust is not a gift.

Your ability to pay that income tax can be significant over time. For example, you create a trust for your children with $100,000 which earns a 10% taxable return each year. The trust is in an effective 35% tax bracket, meaning that the net return to the trust each year is 6.5%. Assuming all after-tax earnings in the trust are accumulated, the trust will have $661,000 in it after 30 years. If, however, the trust is a grantor trust for income tax purposes so that you pay the income tax, the trust will grow at 10% a year. That means after a 30-year period, the value of the trust will have grown to $1,744,000 rather than $661,000. (As noted above, it appears relatively certain that the additional $1,083,000 in the trust is not subject to gift tax.)

However, the trust must be properly structured so that it is not includable in your estate when you die. To some extent, the rules which cause income of a trust to be taxed to its grantor and the rules which require that the trust corpus be includable in the estate of its grantor overlap. As a consequence, structuring the trust as a grantor trust (so that its income is taxed to you rather than to the trust or its beneficiaries) while avoiding inclusion in your estate is a complicated matter and great care must be used to achieve that result. Be sure that you seek the advice of an experienced tax counsellor before creating such a trust.

You must also consider that if you are in a higher effective tax bracket than the trust (or its beneficiaries), structuring the trust as a grantor trust so that its income is taxed to you will increase the overall income tax burden on the family. Whether that outweighs the benefit of pre-tax growth in the grantor trust, as described above, depends upon the circumstances. In considering this question, it should be kept in mind that if a trust is not a grantor trust, any trust income that is distributed will normally be taxed to the beneficiaries who receive it. If the beneficiaries are minors, also keep in mind that income of persons under the age of 14, as a general rule, is taxed at the highest income tax rates because it must be cumulated with the minor's parents' income.

Another factor that should be considered is state and local taxation. If you reside in a jurisdiction which has high state and local taxes, those taxes generally can be avoided by creating a trust in another jurisdiction and having the income of that trust accumulated, unless it is a grantor trust for income tax purposes. Often, state and local taxes will have an effective rate of 10%. Avoiding that 10% rate of taxation over a long term can mean considerable additional money in the trust for the family. In such a case, avoiding income taxation to you by use of a non-grantor trust may be appropriate.

It is true that, currently, the federal income tax structure is such that many individuals reach the top tax bracket at relatively low levels of income. As a consequence, at the present time, having income of the trust taxed to its grantor, by reason of the application of the grantor trust rules, probably will not increase the overall federal income tax burden. However, that has not always been, and may not always be, the case. Therefore, if you choose to create a grantor trust, it should be structured so that it can cease to be a grantor trust at some future time, if that should become appropriate.

Qualified Personal Residence Trust to Transfer Homes at Reduced Tax Cost

A special type of trust can be used to transfer a home to family members at significantly reduced gift tax cost and with no estate tax. This special type of trust is known by a variety of different names including "qualified personal residence trust" and "House GRIT." Each person can create such trusts to transfer up to two homes. However, if a person transfers two homes, one must be his or her principal residence. Therefore, except in that rare case where you and your spouse have separate principal residences, you two together will be able to transfer only three homes. For most taxpayers, however, three homes would represent a significant level of wealth which, if properly transferred through qualified personal residence trusts, could effect significant tax savings.

HOW THE QUALIFIED PERSONAL RESIDENCE TRUST WORKS

During lifetime, the owner transfers the home to a trustee. The trustee is required to allow the grantor of the trust (that is, the former owner) to continue to use the home as a personal residence for a fixed number of years specified in the trust instrument (the "fixed term"). When the fixed term ends, the right of the former owner to use the house as a personal residence ends. The home is then either distributed to designated family members, such as children, or remains in trust for them.

WHY THE GRANTOR CAN HAVE THE RIGHT TO USE THE HOME ONLY FOR A FIXED TERM

If you transfer an asset to others, such as your children, during your lifetime with an understanding (whether or not legally enforceable) that you can use the property for the balance of your lifetime, the asset comes back into your taxable estate as though you never gave it away. However, if you retain the right to use the property for a term which ends before your death, the property will not come back into your taxable estate. That is why the grantor of the trust retains the right to use the property as a residence only for a term of years and not for his or her life. The term chosen should be one which it is anticipated that the grantor can survive. If the grantor dies before the term expires, the home will be brought back into the grantor's estate for tax purposes. A term of one-half or two-thirds of an estimated normal life expectancy may be an appropriate maximum.

Why the Qualified Personal Residence Trust Saves Taxes

Sometimes, a transfer of an asset to a trust is ignored for gift tax purposes. For example, a transfer to a revocable trust is not a taxable gift. By the same token, such a transfer (often termed an "incomplete gift") does not remove assets from your estate.

If, on the other hand, you transfer an asset in trust constituting a completed gift, you are deemed to have made a gift of the entire value transferred to the trust, except to the extent that you retain certain special types of interests in the trust. For most purposes, any right you retain to the income from or use of an asset in trust is valued at zero, so that you are still deemed to have made a gift of the entire value of what has been placed in trust. However, a special rule applies to homes. In effect, the Internal Revenue Code allows you in computing the gift to subtract from the value of the home the rental value for the term you have retained. For example, if you are 50 years old, and you transfer a home worth $500,000 to a qualified personal residence trust retaining the right to use the property as a personal residence for 20 years, you will be deemed to have made a gift of only $77,000 if the annual rental value of your home is deemed to be about 8% of its value when you created the trust.

The good news is that you do not have to establish the rental value. The IRS publishes rates each month which are used for that purpose. Actually, the rates have nothing to do with the rental value of homes but are tied to what is being paid on Treasury obligations for the month you create the trust. Usually, those rates are relatively high compared to prevailing rates in the marketplace. For example, for June 1990, the rate was 10%. For November 1992 it was 6.8%.

The higher the interest rate, the higher the deemed rental value, and the smaller the gift. Chart 14.2 sets forth examples of the amount of the gift at different interest rates, different terms and different ages.

By the way, the gift in a qualified personal residence trust

CHART 14.2
Amount of Gift Made Through a
Qualified Personal Residence Trust

Age	IRS ASSUMED INTEREST RATE	
	6.8%	10%

5 YEAR TRUST		
35	71.3%	61.5%
50	69.4%	59.9%

10 YEAR TRUST		
35	50.6%	37.6%
50	47.4%	35.3%

15 YEAR TRUST		
35	35.6%	22.8%
50	31.4%	20.1%

is not eligible for the annual exclusion but can be protected by any available $600,000 exemption.

WHAT HAPPENS IF THE HOME IS SOLD DURING THE FIXED TERM

Actually, there are two types of house trusts. One is known as a qualified personal residence trust and the other as a personal residence trust. There are several differences between the two and one relates to what occurs if the house is sold during the fixed term (i.e., during the term for which the former owner has retained the right to use the home as a personal residence). In that event, a qualified personal residence trust offers much more flexibility. Basically, if the property is sold, the trustee has two choices: (1) buy a new home for the use of the grantor, or (2) begin paying an annuity to the grantor. The amount of the annuity is based upon certain factors which existed at the time the trust was created, but basically if the property is sold, to the extent of any proceeds that are not reinvested in a new home, the qualified personal residence trust is converted into a Grantor Retained Annuity Trust (GRAT), another special type of trust which is discussed later. Therefore, I recommend use of the qualified personal residence trust (rather than the personal residence trust) in most cases.

HOW THE FORMER OWNER CAN CONTINUE TO USE THE HOME

Even after the fixed term ends, the grantor may be able to continue to use the home in one of three ways.

First, the grantor could rent the home from the new owners (*i.e.*, the children or a trust for family members). Full and fair rent must be paid. Also, there should not be any agreement when the trust is created that the home will be leased back to the grantor after the fixed term. As discussed earlier, such an agreement may cause the property to come back into the grantor's taxable estate.

Generally, the payment of rent generates taxable income and if the property is a personal residence the rent payment is not deductible for income tax purposes. However, if the home remains in trust after the fixed terms and the trust is a so-called "grantor trust" for income tax purposes, it appears that no one (not the trust, not the beneficiaries and not the former owner) is taxed on the rental income. As discussed above, a grantor trust is one in which all of the income of the trust is attributed to the trust's grantor. The IRS has ruled that transactions between a grantor and a grantor trust are not reportable for income tax purposes. That should mean that rent the grantor pays to such a trust is not subject to income tax. Obviously, to get the benefit of that rule, the trust must continue after the fixed term. If the house has been distributed directly to other family members, the special grantor trust rule to avoid the taxation of the rent would not apply.

A second way in which the grantor might continue to use the home even after the fixed term is to buy the home from the trust. If the home has been distributed to other family members after the fixed term and is worth more than its income tax basis, such a sale will result in gain and income tax will have to be paid. However, the same rule which appears to prevent rent from being subject to tax if the rent is paid to a grantor trust also should prevent the gain from being taxed if the seller of the home is a grantor trust and the buyer is the grantor.

Buying the home from a grantor trust after your term ends has another potential benefit. When the "dust clears", you will have transferred cash to the trust and you will have reacquired the home. When you die, the income tax basis of the home will be increased to its value at the time of your death. If the home had remained in the trust or been distributed to your children, your children would instead take over your original basis in the home (subject to certain minor adjustments under the tax law). Meanwhile, the cash you transferred to the trust can be invested and the basis of those new investments (which, presumably, will be much higher than your original basis in your home) will eventually be distributed to your descendants.

Obviously, the grantor must anticipate having sufficient assets to be able to rent or buy the house back if he or she wishes to be able to use the house as described above after the fixed term ends.

It does not make sense to have a qualified personal residence trust terminate in favor of your spouse. You could have transferred the property to your spouse without using a qualified personal residence trust, entirely free of gift tax, by reason of the marital deduction. Nonetheless, you may want your spouse to have the right to use the property during the balance of his or her lifetime (or at least as long as you two remain married), because that may provide a third way for you to use the home while you are married. The best way to arrange that is to have the home continue to be held in trust after the fixed term until both you and your spouse die. The trustee can be authorized to give your spouse the right to occupy the home even though it is in trust. The law appears relatively certain that if you continue to use the home only as a guest of your spouse, the home should not be includible in your estate. And even if the trustee allows your spouse to use the home as his or her personal residence for his or her own life, the home should not be included in your spouse's estate either. It appears that you can define your spouse as the person to whom you are married from time to time. Hence, should you become divorced from your present spouse or should your present spouse predecease you, the trust would allow any future spouse of yours to use the home (and your future spouse may, in turn, allow you to use the home as his or her guest).

If you provide for the home to be distributed outright to your children at the end of the fixed term, you will probably be able to use the home, at least on an occasional basis, with the consent of your children. As indicated above, however, it is important to be able to establish that you had no understanding with your children at the time you created the trust that you would be able to use the home after it was transferred to them. Otherwise, the home may be brought back into your taxable estate. If your children continue to allow you to use the home on virtually the same basis as you did while it was held in trust for your benefit during the fixed term, you can anticipate that the IRS will contend that there was such an understanding and, therefore, that the home is includible in your taxable estate. The IRS and the courts will also look carefully at who is really paying for the upkeep of the property. If you continue to pay the upkeep, you can expect the IRS to attempt to include the home in your estate even if your use is significantly less than it was while the home was held in the trust.

Summary About Qualified Personal Residence Trusts

A qualified personal residence trust permits a homeowner to transfer a home through a trust to family members at relatively low gift tax cost. In fact, no gift tax may be due if sufficient gift tax exemption is available (which can be $600,000). However, to be effective, the property owner must live until the end of the term for which he or she has retained the right to use the home as a personal residence; otherwise, the property will be brought back into the grantor's taxable estate (although a credit will be allowed against the estate tax for any gift tax paid when the home was placed in the trust). In addition, the property owner must have sufficient resources so that he or she can afford to give up the use of the home when the fixed term ends. That means that the former owner must have sufficient resources to be able to rent or buy the home back, acquire a substitute home or give up the use of the home altogether.

Split Purchase of a New Residence

It appears that, for a new home, you can go "one better" than a qualified personal residence trust. The qualified personal residence trust may be viewed as having two (or more) potential disadvantages. First, if you die while you have the right to use the home, the home is brought back into your taxable estate. Second, your absolute right to use the home, therefore, must end before your death. In many cases, you may wish to continue to use the home until you die.

If you are going to acquire a new residence there may be a better way: a "split purchase" or "SPLIT" of the home with one or more of your descendants or a trust for their benefit.

The rule which includes property in your taxable estate if you have the right to use it at death applies only if you previously transferred that property during your lifetime for less than full value. It appears that if you initially purchase from a third-party only the right to use the property for your life (which lawyers call a "life estate"), while your children, for example, buy the remainder (i.e., the right to own the property after you die) from the third party, the property should not be includible in your estate when you die because you did not transfer the remainder (or any other interest in the property) to your children.

How much you pay, and how much your descendants pay, for your respective life estate and remainder interests again depends upon monthly tables which the IRS publishes and other factors, such as your age. In many cases, your children will have to pay only a small part of the total purchase price. Chart 14.3 sets forth some examples for taxpayers at certain ages and at certain IRS interest rates.

The split purchase allows you to use the house for your lifetime without having to move and, it appears, without causing the home to be includible in your estate. It appears that you can also acquire an initial life estate, with your spouse acquiring a successor life estate (just in case he or she survives you and wants to continue to use the home), and your descendants purchasing the remainder. It is possible for a trust for your descendants to purchase the remainder; however, as discussed below, you should not supply the funds for that purchase.

SOME WARNINGS ABOUT SPLITS

Some warnings about split-purchases are in order. First, the SPLIT of a home is a relatively new concept. Recently issued Treasury Department regulations, which normally have the force of law, strongly support the conclusion that no part of a split-purchased home should be includible in your estate, as a general rule. However, no court has yet ruled on the matter.

Second, it appears that the IRS will contend that the split-purchased home is includable in your estate for tax purposes

CHART 14.3
Split Purchase of Home—Percentage of Cost of the Home Paid by the Parent and by the Child

Age	IRS ASSUMED INTEREST RATE	
	6.8%	*9%*
45	83%/17%	88.6%/11.4%
55	73%/27%	80%/20%
65	60%/40%	69%/31%

if you supply your children (or a trust for their benefit) with the funds to purchase the remainder interest. Hence, to be on the safe side, your children (or the trust for their benefit) should come up with "clean" funds—such as money they have earned, or which was supplied to them by someone other than you. Funds your spouse supplies should be regarded as "clean" for such purposes provided you did not transfer the funds to your spouse and that your spouse will not also acquire a successive life estate in the property. It may be best if there are other relatives (such as your parents) who can supply the children (or a trust for their benefit) with the funds to purchase the remainder.

Third, although there is virtually no law to support it, there is some possibility that the IRS might contend that your children must recognize income when your life estate in the home ends and they succeed to full ownership of the property. Again, no court has ruled on this matter, although strong arguments can be made that no such taxable income should be deemed recognized by your children.

SPLITTING YOUR BETS WITH A FIXED TERM SPLIT OF A NEW HOME

A SPLIT also can be used to "split your bets" in a sense. Rather than purchasing a life estate, you could purchase a term of years (that is, the right to the exclusive use of the property for a fixed number of years). That puts your ownership in the same position as if you already owned the home and created a qualified personal residence trust. Your descendants (or a trust for their benefit) would acquire the remainder. If you live until the end of the term, the home should not be includible in your estate; that is the same effect as if you had purchased the home and put it into a qualified personal residence trust. If you die during the term, your estate would have the "backup" argument that only the value of the right to use the home for the remaining fixed term should be includible in your estate and not the full value of the home.

Transferring Property at Reduced Tax Cost Through a GRIT to More Distant Relatives or Non-Family Members

As noted above, if you create a trust and retain the right to receive the income from the trust or the use of the trust property, you will be deemed to have made a gift of the full value of the property, unless the property you contribute is a personal residence. However, that rule applies only if the property is destined to go to your spouse, your brothers and sisters or your or your spouse's descendants (including your stepchildren). That rule does not apply if the trust property will pass only to more distant relatives such as nieces and nephews, or people who are not related to you, such as a boyfriend or girlfriend. As a consequence, if you want to make a gift to a more distant relative, such as a niece or nephew, or to a friend, such a trust, known as a grantor retained income trust (GRIT) is an excellent tool.

In order to create a GRIT, you transfer property to a trust but retain the right to receive the income from the trust for a fixed number of years. Income generally includes dividends, interest, rents and royalties but not capital gains. When the fixed term ends, your right to the GRIT income ceases and the property is transferred to or is held in further trust for the other beneficiaries (who, again, cannot include your spouse or other close relatives) free of estate tax and without any additional gift tax. However, like the qualified personal residence trust, discussed above, if you die before the fixed term ends, the property in the GRIT will be brought back into your taxable estate.

The gift you make when you create the GRIT is equal to the value of what you put in the trust less the present value of the income interest you retain. In most cases, the present value of that income interest will be determined based upon the IRS estimate of what property is supposed to earn at the time you create the trust. Generally that it is a relatively high rate of return equal to 120% of the rate on mid-term Treasury Department obligations for the month you create the trust. The higher the presumed rate of return, the higher the value of your retained income interest, and the smaller the gift. In many cases, you will be able to transfer property at a gift tax cost of about ten percent of what the estate tax cost in a GRIT would be. Chart 14.4 illustrates the gift a grantor would make by transferring property through a GRIT under various assumptions.

POTENTIAL PROBLEMS WITH GRITs

As noted, if you die while you are entitled to the income from the property in the GRIT, the GRIT property will be includible in your estate. In addition, one recent tax case indicates that, if you fund the GRIT with property which is almost certain to produce an extremely low rate of return and which probably will not be sold to produce more income, you may not be able to value your retained income interest by reference to the IRS tables. In that case, the GRIT was funded with closely held stock which paid an annual dividend of about 2/100% at a time when the IRS tables assumed a return of 10% a year. Although the court did not state how the value of the income interest would be determined, it held that the 10% tables produced a "wildly" unreasonable value on those facts and could not be used.

It seems that if you fund a GRIT with an asset which produces a reasonable rate of return, you can use the IRS tables to value your retained income interest even if the actual rate of return on the GRIT property is less than the table rate. Although sometimes the return on closely-held

CHART 14.4
Amount of Gift (as a Percentage of Value) through a GRIT

10 YEAR TRUST

Age	IRS Assumed Interest Rate	
	8%	10%
40	44%	37%
50	42%	35%
60	37%	31%

business interests is not high, because earnings either are distributed only as salaries or are reinvested in the company, non-taxable distributions which are allocable to the income account should be satisfactory. For example, if your company begins to pay a reasonable level of stock dividends, that should be treated as a satisfactory return if, under the terms of the trust, stock dividends are treated as income. Those stock dividends usually can be structured so that they are not subject to income tax.

If you wish to transfer property to nieces and nephews and other more remote relatives, or to non-relatives, you probably should discuss using a GRIT with your advisors.

Transfers to Close Relatives through a GRAT

You cannot use a GRIT to make transfers to close relatives, such as your descendants, at low tax cost, except in the case of a qualified personal residence trust, discussed above. The reason is that the tax law will value the income stream you retain at zero, meaning that the gift will equal the full value of what you place in the trust. However, you can attempt to transfer property to close relatives at low gift tax act through a Grantor Retained Annuity Trust (GRAT).

Rather than paying you income for a fixed period of time, a GRAT pays you an annuity. The annuity usually is expressed as a percentage of the initial value of the trust. For example, if the assets you contribute to the trust are worth $400,000 and you retain the right to receive an 8% annuity for 10 years, you will be paid an annuity of $32,000 (8% of $400,000, the initial value of the trust) each year for 10 years. At that time, your right to payments from the trust will cease and the property will pass to or be held in further trust for other persons, such as your children.

In determining the value of the gift you make through a GRAT, you are permitted to deduct from the value of what you transferred to the trust the value of the retained annuity stream. The value of the retained annuity stream will depend not only upon the value of what you contribute but on the size of the annuity (as a percentage of the initial value of the fund) compared to the IRS assumed earnings rate for the month in which you create the GRAT, the period for which the annuity will be paid and your age. Chart 14.5 illustrates how small the gift could be for transfers to an eight-year GRAT based upon different ages of grantors and IRS assumed earnings rates. (If the grantor is married, the gift may be smaller in some cases.)

In theory, it may be possible to retain a sufficiently high enough annuity for a sufficiently long period of time that you can reduce the value of the gift you make through the GRAT to zero. Whether or not that is possible, you probably should not attempt to reduce the value of the gift to zero. Were you to structure the GRAT in such a way that the gift will be zero, the IRS might contend that it cannot administer the tax law effectively because even if you have undervalued the property (and therefore the annuity) it cannot collect any money—in all cases, the value of the gift will be zero. Although it seems questionable whether that policy argument

CHART 14.5
Illustration of Approximate Minimum Possible Gift
in Eight-Year GRAT of $100,000
for Grantors of Various Ages
at Different Interest Rates

Age	IRS ASSUMED INTEREST RATE				
	6%	7%	8%	9%	10%
35	$ 690	$ 680	$ 670	$ 660	$ 651
45	$ 1,657	$ 1,632	$ 1,608	$ 1,585	$ 1,561
55	$ 3,908	$ 3,851	$ 3,795	$ 3,741	$ 3,687
65	$ 8,549	$ 8,428	$ 8,310	$ 8,192	$ 8,077
75	$17,755	$17,512	$17,273	$17,037	$16,804
	ANNUITY				
	$15,752	$16,324	$16,904	$17,488	$18,080

would prevail in court, it usually is unwise to structure a transaction which is likely to be contrary to an IRS position. Hence, in creating a GRAT, you may be able to reduce the value of the gift to a small amount, but you should not reduce it to zero. The last illustration in Chart 14.5 shows how you can reduce the taxable portion of a $400,000 transfer for a 45-year-old grantor at a 10% IRS assumed earnings rate down to approxmately 1% of that amount, or only approximately $4,000.

Like a qualified personal residence trust, the gift made through a GRAT cannot qualify for the annual exclusion. Hence, you will have to pay gift tax on it unless you have remaining gift tax exemption equivalent available.

WHEN A GRAT WORKS

In effect, the IRS tables assume that the property you contribute to the GRAT will produce a certain rate of return each year. That rate is based, again, on the mid-term Treasury Department bond rate for the month you create the GRAT. If the annuity is based exactly on that rate of return, it will be assumed, as a practical matter, that the original property contributed to the trust will remain in it and no part of it will be returned to you and no income will be accumulated in the trust. In effect, the gift you make in that case is equal to the present value of the property, discounted for the time during which you are entitled to the annuity. If the annuity is higher than the IRS assumed rate of return, it will be assumed that part of what you put in the trust must be returned to you each year to pay the annuity in full. That has the effect of reducing the amount of the gift because it is assumed that there will be less value in the trust when your annuity term ends and the assets are distributed to or held in further trust for others. On the other hand, if the annuity rate is less than the assumed IRS earnings rate, it will be assumed that excess income will be accumulated in the trust and more than what you originally contributed eventually will pass to others. That will make the gift larger than if the annuity rate were exactly equal to the IRS assumed rate of return.

Obviously, the annuity rate compared to the IRS assumed

earnings rate is important in determining the size of the gift. Of equal, and perhaps even greater, importance is what really happens in the trust. Reference again should be made to Chart 14.5. In the circumstance where the IRS assumed interest rate is 7%, the annuity is 16.3%, the grantor is 55 years old and retains a right to receive the annuity for eight years, the value of the gift is only 3.5% of the amount originally contributed to the trust. If, in fact, the property produces only the IRS assumed rate of return of 7%, virtually all of the property will have been returned to the grantor by the time the annuity term ends. Hence, the GRAT usually is effective only where the actual rate of return on the property exceeds the IRS interest rate (and taking into account the grantor's mortality). Not infrequently, closely-held business interests produce or can be made to produce such a high rate of return, because of the discounts commonly used in valuing such interests. Thus, such interests may be suitable for transfer to a GRAT.

AN EXAMPLE OF A GRAT FOR A CLOSELY-HELD BUSINESS INTEREST

A property owner, age 55, had inherited a business several years before from his mother. The business had a current worth of about $10,000,000. The business was in the form of an S corporation so all of the income was taxed to the shareholder even if not distributed. The effective rate of income tax imposed on the income was about 33%, considering state and federal taxes. The business was a stable one producing a current rate of return, based upon the $10,000,000, of about 11% a year (annual earnings were $1,100,000—no corporate tax was payable because it was an S corporation).

The property owner wished to transfer 30% of the stock to his son at the lowest possible gift tax cost. The 30% block of stock had been appraised at $2.25 million. Although the business, as a whole, was worth $10 million, the appraiser, using standard valuation methodology, valued the 30% block of stock with a 25% minority discount at $2,250,000.

The shareholder contributed the 30% block of stock to a

GRAT retaining the right to receive an annuity for eight years equal to 16.3% of the value of stock when it was contributed to the trust. The assumed IRS interest rate was 7%. At a value of $336,750 for the block of stock, the annuity was $270,000. If the grantor were living at the end of the eight years, his interest in the GRAT would terminate and the property would be distributed to his son without any further gift tax and no estate tax. However, if the grantor died during the ten-year term, all or a portion of the trust assets would be includible in his estate.

The pro-rata share of earnings of the corporation attributable to the 30% block of stock was $375,000 (30% × $1.25 million estimated annual earnings). Of course, there was no guarantee that all the earnings would be distributed, but it was anticipated that such a distribution would occur each year. If it did, the trust would receive $375,000 each year, more than adequate to pay the $366,750 annuity. Hence, the entire 30% block of stock together with income paid to the GRAT in excess of the annuity amount would be held in the GRAT for eventual distribution to the son.

Based upon an initial value of the 30% block of stock at $2.25 million, the grantor would make an $80,000 gift upon creation of the GRAT. If the IRS were able to establish a higher value for the stock, two adverse effects would occur. First, the size of the gift would increase, although the increase would be proportional. For example, even if the IRS were able to establish that the 30% block of stock was worth twice as much as the taxpayer contended, the gift would rise from only $80,000 to $160,000. The more serious problem is that the amount of the annuity required to be paid also would have to double from $366,750 to $733,500.

WHAT HAPPENS IF THE TRUST DOES NOT HAVE ADEQUATE INCOME TO PAY THE ANNUITY

If the trust does not have adequate income to pay the annuity, other assets of the trust must be distributed in satisfaction of the annuity. It appears, however, that even if appreciated assets are distributed in satisfaction of the right to the annuity no taxable income is generated if the trust is structured to be a grantor trust for income tax purposes, as discussed above. Usually, it is simple to make a GRAT a grantor trust. Moreover, a grantor trust usually can be a shareholder in an S corporation.

A WORD ABOUT THE GRAT TERM

For a variety of reasons, some practitioners recommend the use of only very short term GRATs, such as for two years. The grantor can recontribute the assets to another short-term GRAT after the two years, and can repeat that process several times, each time distributing anything left in the GRAT after the fixed two year term to the other beneficiaries. Among other risks, the grantor who intends to keep rolling assets over into short-term GRATS may discover that GRATs have been, in effect, prohibited under the Internal Revenue Code. Nonetheless, where it is anticipated that an asset will produce a spectacular return in a very short time, a short-term GRAT for that asset may be ideal.

SUMMARY ABOUT GRATS

GRATs are complicated arrangements but can be used in some cases to transfer assets to close family members at reduced gift tax cost. However, usually, they are effective only if the property contributed to the trust produces a rate of return (income and appreciation) in excess of the IRS assumed interest rate (as adjusted to reflect the grantor's mortality). It appears that if income is inadequate in any year to pay the annuity, other assets must be distributed to pay the annuity in full. If the GRAT is a grantor trust for income tax purposes, the distribution of even appreciated assets in satisfaction of the annuity should not cause gain to be recognized for tax purposes. If the grantor dies while entitled to the annuity payments, all or a portion of the GRAT will be includible in his or her estate. Thus, it is appropriate to retain an annuity for a period expected to be considerably shorter than the grantor's life expectancy.

Split Purchase Annuity

Just as a split purchase of a new personal residence may provide better overall benefits, in some cases, than a qualified personal residence trust, so may a split purchase annuity (SPAT) sometimes be better than a GRAT. Rather than transferring assets you own to a GRAT from which you would retain an annuity for a fixed number of years, you and a descendant (or a trust for descendants) would buy assets in such a way that you are entitled to an annuity stream from the property for life (or a term of years) and your descendants (or a trust for your descendants) is entitled to receive all of the property thereafter.

Although part or all of a GRAT will be includible in your estate if you die while you are entitled to annuity payments from the GRAT, no property should be includible in your estate if you effect a SPAT except to the extent that there are unpaid annuity payments due you at the time of your death. Hence, if your right to the annuity payments ends with your death, it seems that nothing should be included in your estate.

The potential problems with SPATs are similar to those for SPLITs. For example, your descendants should use funds not supplied by you to buy their interest in the SPAT. Also, obviously, you must not already own the asset which forms the basis of the SPAT. Hence, you could not use current interests in your business. For those, you would have to use a GRAT. A SPAT may also raise difficult income tax issues. In any case, a SPAT will be effective only if you anticipate that the asset will generate more than the IRS's assumed rate of return (as adjusted for your mortality). If the assets in the SPAT produce less than that rate, the investment your descendants make in the arrangement will actually be transferred to you in payment of the annuity, thereby diminishing their wealth and increasing your estate. In any case, you should discuss the arrangement in detail with your advisor before attempting to create a SPAT.

Using the Extra-Crummey℠ Trust for Annual Exclusion Transfers

Over time, significant property can be transferred free of estate, gift and generation-skipping transfer tax under the protection of the $10,000 annual exclusion. For example, if you are married, and have two children and four grandchildren, you can remove over $1.7 million from your taxable estate by making the maximum annual exclusion transfers for ten years if the property you transfer thereafter earns 8% a year.

Most outright transfers qualify for the annual exclusion. That is the obvious way to make such gifts, unless (as is often the case) the recipient is a minor (or is incompetent). In that case, the transfer has to be made, as a practical matter, to a fiduciary, such as a trustee, for the minor (or incompetent). However, not all transfers to trustees and other fiduciaries qualify for the annual exclusion.

There are two commonly used arrangements to qualify transfers in trust for a minor for the annual exclusion. One is known as the Uniform Gifts to Minors Act (or Uniform Transfers to Minors Act in some states). The other is a Section 2503(c) Trust, a special type of trust for minors authorized in the Internal Revenue Code. Millions upon millions of dollars are transferred to minors each year under those two arrangements. They work well and, properly structured and administered, are relatively inexpensive to create and maintain. However, both of them suffer from a major defect: Upon reaching age 21 (and, in some cases, 18), the child will be absolutely entitled to the property.

Few property owners wish their children (or grandchildren) to receive large sums of money at age 18 or 21. Yet little thought is given to that when the recipient is very young. Although the child (or grandchild) voluntarily can transfer the property in further trust for his or her benefit upon reaching majority, often the former minor decides that gaining control of the property is better. In fact, those minors who want the property upon majority are probably exactly the ones who should not have it.

To furnish a bit more of a restriction, some trusts provide for the property to continue in trust after the child reaches age 21, but in that case the child must have the right to withdraw the property for 60 days or so after reaching that age. If the child is not expressly informed of that right upon becoming an adult, he or she probably has a continuing right to demand the property even after the 60 day period expires. Therefore, that is far from a perfect solution.

To avoid this problem, a special type of trust has been developed which permits transfers to qualify under the annual exclusion and also allows the property to remain in trust for the beneficiary's entire lifetime or until an appropriate age or event (such as graduation from college). It is called the "Extra-Crummey^sm Trust" because it is based upon a famous case known as *Crummey* v. *Commissioner* to which I have added something extra.

In the Extra Crummey^sm Trust, as much as can possibly qualify under the annual exclusion can be transferred to the trust each year without fear of causing tax problems to the beneficiary. The beneficiary is given the right, for 30 days after a contribution in the trust is made, to withdraw property from the trust (that is the so-called Crummey withdrawal power, based on the *Crummey* case). Where the beneficiary is a minor, his or her parent determines whether to exercise that power. Thereafter, the beneficiary retains the right to withdraw the property but only with the consent of the trustee, who should not be anyone who has contributed property to or has an interest in the trust. The transfers will qualify for the annual exclusion and yet the property, as a practical matter, can remain in trust for the lifetime of the beneficiary, or until an age specified in the instrument.

An Extra Crummey^sm Trust can be structured to receive contributions over many years and even for new beneficiaries, such as children and grandchildren, born after the trust is set up. Hence, with one trust, you can cover all annual exclusion gifts to your descendants. In fact, the trust can be used even for adults. Although, obviously, there is a greater probability that an adult will exercise the withdrawal power than that one will be exercised on behalf of a minor, it is exceptionally rare, in my experience, for anyone to exercise a withdrawal power which has been designed so that transfers to a trust qualify for the annual exclusion.

In summary, the Extra Crummey^{sm} Trust can be used to qualify transfers for the gift tax annual exclusion and yet permit the property to remain in trust for as long as you wish, and it can be structured to receive future gifts for later born children or grandchildren.

What to Do to Keep Control of the Assets

If you have already made transfers under a Uniform Gifts to Minors Act arrangement or a Section 2503(c) trust, and you would now like to prevent the property from being distributed at age 18 or 21, you may wish to consider one of the two following ideas. First, if you have some influence with the recipient, you may be able to persuade him or her, upon receipt of the property, to transfer it to a trust that is revocable but only with the consent of another person (which person should not have any interest in the trust). Second, you might consider whether, under applicable state law, the custodian under the uniform gifts to minors act or the trustee of the Section 2503(c) trust is authorized to invest the assets in a partnership. If so, you could form a limited partnership of which you would be the general partner and the custodian or trustee would be a limited partner (acquiring that limited partnership interest in exchange for the assets). By providing that the general partner shall control all investments and distribution of partnership assets, you can effectively maintain control over the property even when the limited partnership interest is distributed to the beneficiary at age 18 or 21. As discussed below, such a "holding company" arrangement should not cause the trust assets to be included in your estate.

Breaking Up Interests to Change Their Tax Value

One of the most effective ways to change the value of an asset is to divide a majority interest into minority pieces. For example, the law is relatively well settled that even if you own 100% of your closely-held business, lifetime gifts by you of minority interests will be valued at a discount. For instance, if your business is worth $10 million (taking into account that interests in it are non-marketable), and you give away 10% of the stock to your children, the value of that stock should not be treated as $1 million but something less to reflect the fact that you are transferring a minority interest.

The IRS sought many times to eliminate the minority discount. To date, the IRS has been unsuccessful and recent statements from Congressional committees acknowledge the existence of such discounts even in family transfers. In fact, the IRS recently threw in the towel.

The rules about minority discounts and how the nature of an asset can be changed so as to minimize the asset's value are complex. Before making such gifts, it will behoove you to work with an experienced tax advisor and obtain an independent third-party appraisal.

Use of a Holding Company

WHY HOLDING COMPANIES ARE FORMED

To some degree, family holding companies are formed for the same reasons people purchase mutual funds. By acting together, property owners are able to obtain opportunities to invest and/or to invest on better terms than if they acted alone. Many financial advisers (often called "money managers") offer their services only to property owners who have a certain minimum amount to invest. By banding together through a holding company, those with less than the minimum can obtain those investment services. In addition, a holding company also permits more centralized management and administration of family wealth. A third reason for the use of a holding company is to change the nature of what is owned so as to reduce its tax value.

THE FORMATION SHOULD BE TAX FREE

As a general matter, the formation of a holding company, whether in corporate or partnership form, can be done income tax free. In other words, you usually do not recognize gain or loss upon contributing assets to a holding company. However, gain will be recognized if you contribute appreciated marketable securities and the holding company is regarded as a "swap fund." A swap fund is one in which the transfer results in diversification of interests and, among other things, more than 80% of the assets are readily marketable securities or similar publicly traded investments. There may also be other circumstances in which gain will be recognized upon contributing assets to a corporation or a partnership. But by working closely with your advisors, you should be able to avoid recognition of gain in forming a holding company, in most cases.

Tax Values of Interests in Holding Companies

Transfers of interests in your closely held business may be valued at a discount, as discussed above. In some cases, however, you will wish to transfer other assets, such as marketable securities or cash equivalents. Usually, those assets will be valued for wealth transfer tax purposes at their full fair market value. However, by changing the nature of the assets you own, you may be able to change their value for tax purposes. One of the most effective ways to do that is by forming an investment company, in corporate or partnership form, with other family members and, if possible, with nonfamily members as well.

Once a holding company is formed, you will no longer own the assets (such as cash) which you previously held. Rather, you will own non-marketable equity in a closely-held holding company. If the company is formed so that you never acquired a right to force liquidation of your interest, it appears that your holdings should be valued with the lack of marketability discussed in more detail earlier in this Chapter. Moreover, if you transfer minority interests in the holding company to others (such as your children), those interests should be valued with appropriate discounts.

Without much doubt, you will greatly reduce the value of your interest in the holding company if persons who are not members of your family also are investors and the company can be liquidated only with their consent. Although the restriction on you ability to cause the liquidation may be no different in theory whether outsiders need to consent or not, the tax law developed over many decades suggests that the courts apply larger discounts when persons who are not family members have significant control over the property. Moreover, under specific Internal Revenue Code provisions in some cases, restrictions which can be removed by the family are ignored for valuation purposes.

You Will Need Expert Advice

Although it is not difficult to form a holding company, in order to obtain the potential tax and other benefits described, you will need the advice of one or more competent advisors. For example, interests in holding companies can be restricted so they cannot be transferred to outsiders without the consent of the holding company, or its co-owners, but such restrictions on transferability can have tax and other consequences. The cost of forming such a company may be somewhat higher than you might expect but it is worth the additional cost to obtain the desired results.

Making Gifts of Interests in the Holding Company

You may wish to transfer the shares of stock or partnership units in the holding company to others, such as your children. In most circumstances, those interests should qualify for the gift tax annual exclusion, although sometimes they may be so restricted that they will not qualify. You should confirm with your advisors that the shares of stock or partnership units in a holding company will qualify for the annual exclusion if transferred during your lifetime.

Recently, the IRS indicated that even if you retain the power to control the management of the holding company (including controlling when distributions of income to the partners or shareholders are made), for example by owning the voting stock or being a general partner, shares of stock or partnership units you give away during your lifetime will not be includable in your estate. For over 70 years, the tax law has required that any property you give away must be included in your estate if you hold the power at your death to control the beneficial enjoyment of that property. Some tax accountants and lawyers have expressed concern that if you hold the power to control the flow of distributions from a holding company, any stock or units you give away will be includable in your estate. Although the matter has not been finally resolved, it now appears that the IRS will not attempt to take that position in most circumstances. Because this is an area of law which is not well developed, you should discuss the matter carefully with your tax advisor before deciding whether or not you wish to control distributions and other aspects of the holding company.

PARTNERSHIP VS. CORPORATE HOLDING COMPANY

As indicated above, a holding company can be in corporate or partnership form. In some states, it can also take the form of a limited liability company, which has some attributes of both but usually is treated as a partnership for federal tax purposes. Which form is best depends on many factors. However, under current tax law, it probably is considerably better to form a holding company as a partnership (or a limited liability company which is treated as a partnership for tax purposes). Among other advantages, a partnership, unlike a regular corporation, is not itself taxed; the income is taxed directly to the partners. Although income of an S corporation generally is taxed directly to its shareholders, S corporations can have only 35 shareholders, can have only certain trusts as shareholders, can have only one kind of equity (common stock) and are subject to other restrictions which do not apply to partnerships. In addition, the income tax consequences for partnership units held at death can be much more favorable than for shares of stock held at death.

Valuation Freezes

OVERVIEW

Every additional dollar of wealth you accumulate during your lifetime may be subjected to estate tax when you die. Estate planners, therefore, sought to devise ways in which the value of property could be stabilized or "frozen," with future growth inuring to the benefit of younger members of the family, such as children or grandchildren. Often, such stabilization arrangements occurred in connection with closely-held businesses, and commonly were referred to as "preferred stock valuation freezes" although they were employed for businesses in partnership, as well as corporate, form. Basically, the equity in a business was restructured so that more senior members of the family held preferred stock and more junior family members held common stock (or equivalent interests in a partnership). The expectation was that the preferred stock would be "frozen" at its then value while the common stock would receive the benefit of all future growth in the business.

The IRS waged a vigorous campaign against valuation freeze. Although it largely failed in court, eventually it had legislation enacted. Some of this "anti-freeze" legislation was impracticable to administer for both taxpayers and the IRS. Recently, Congress sought to clarify the situation by enacting complex new rules, embodied in what is referred to as Chapter 14 of the Internal Revenue Code. Although it is an effective law, some opportunities still remain to significantly reduce estate and gift taxes.

The Fundamental "Anti-Freeze" Rule of New Chapter 14

The basic rule of Chapter 14 of the Internal Revenue Code is that if you (or anyone in your generation or an older generation of your family) transfers, by gift or sale, common stock (or a comparable interest in a partnership) to someone in a younger generation of your family (such as a child), you will be deemed to make a gift of any preferred stock which you, your contemporaries or older family members own. In other words, if you give all of the common stock in your business to your daughter and you continue to own preferred stock, you will be deemed to make a gift to your daughter equal to the value of the preferred stock as well as the common stock. If you sell the common stock to her for its fair market value, you will still be deemed to make a gift to her equal to the value of the preferred stock you (or senior family members) retain.

For example, your business is worth $5 million. The common stock is worth $3 million and the preferred stock is worth $2 million. If your children purchase the common stock from you for its full fair market value of $3 million you will be deemed to have made a gift to them of the $2 million value of the preferred stock even though you continue to own that stock. Similarly, if you in fact give the common units worth $3 million to your children, you will be deemed to have made a gift to them not just of that $3 million worth of common stock but also of the $2 million worth of preferred stock, even though you continue to own the preferred stock.

There are some important exceptions to this rule. One is where either the preferred interest retained or the common interest transferred is traded on an established securities market. Another is where the common units are transferred to someone who is not closely related (or is unrelated) to you or your spouse.

KEY WAYS TO AVOID CHAPTER 14

There are several key ways to avoid the impact of Chapter 14. The first, and perhaps the most obvious, is to give away (or sell) to your children or grandchildren the same type of interest which you continue to hold. For example, if you own only common stock and you give or sell that stock to your children or grandchildren, the new anti-freeze rules will not apply. Of course, you will not effect a classic freeze transaction although all future income and growth with respect to the common interest transferred to your descendants should be removed permanently from your estate.

The second key relates to what is really the golden rule of new Chapter 14: You can transfer property at reduced, and in some cases no estate or gift tax cost, to your descendants if the property involved produces more than a market rate of return.

If, for example, your business produces, based upon its current net worth, a rate of return in excess of a "market rate of return," you might consider a type of "classic" preferred stock freeze transaction (or a comparable transaction involving partnership interests). The deemed gift rule of Chapter 14, described above, does not apply if you (or other senior family members) retain a cumulative preferred stock that bears a market rate of return. Cumulative, of course, means that even if the required distribution (e.g., the preferred stock dividend) is not made when due, the right to it accumulates so that is must be paid at a later time. All distributions must be paid within four years of their original due date, in order to avoid falling under another complex set of Chapter 14 gift tax rules.

A critical element, obviously, is the meaning of "market rate of return." In most circumstances, there is no definite market rate of return (it is not defined with reference to any IRS or government table). Almost certainly, it is significantly in excess of the return on risk-free investments (such as Treasury obligations). In fact, because your business is closely-held, it may be considerably greater than that. If the prime lending rate were 8%, for example, the market rate of return on your business might be 12%, 14% or even higher. Basically, it is the rate of return which independent third parties would demand to receive on fixed obligations (such as preferred stock) in your business. If your business, based upon its current net worth, is expected to produce rates in excess of that, you may wish to consider discussing with your tax advisor a classic freeze transaction if you believe that would help achieve your financial and estate planning goals.

A third key is to turn the Chapter 14 rules in your favor by effecting a "reverse" freeze. Rather than your holding the preferred interest in your business while your children hold the common interest, you can arrange for your children to own the preferred and for you to own the common. As indicated above, the market rate of return on a preferred interest in your business may be relatively high compared to the rate of return on risk-free investments (or investments which would be regarded as less risky than investing even in a successful closely-held business). In addition, interests in your closely-held business are likely to "suffer" from two valuation discounts: lack of marketability and minority discounts. What that means, of course, is that you will have to pay a relatively high rate of return on preferred stock in order to provide a market rate of return. By holding the preferred interest, your descendants will be entitled to receive earnings at that market rate before you receive any income on the common equity. Over time, that preferred return can be significant.

Assume, for example, that your business is worth $4 million and the rate of return on a preferred interest must equal twice the current rate on mid-term Treasury Obligations in order to support a $2 million par value for the preferred interest. If the mid-term Treasury rate is 7%, the preferred units would have to be entitled to a preferred return of 14%. In effect, that means that the first 7% of earnings in the entire enterprise (not just on your child's $2 million, but your $2 million as well) will be payable to your child. Of course, to the extent that earnings exceed 7%, the value of your common units will increase. Often, however, the return to which the preferred interest is entitled will absorb virtually all of the earnings of the enterprise, especially in its early years, meaning the value of your common units, in fact, will be frozen, if not depressed. In addition the preferred units can be converted into common ones, usually without income tax and, presumably, that conversion will occur when it is determined that the rate of return to the holders will thereby be higher.

In fact, where the enterprise fails to produce an overall return sufficient to make the payment each year on the preferred units, there will be a shift of wealth from the common equity holders to the preferred holders. In some cases, over time, the preferred units may come to represent virtually the entire value of the business and, properly structured, all of that shift in wealth may have occurred entirely free of gift tax.

A reverse freeze is a complicated arrangement. What form the business should be in and the attributes of the preferred and common units depend upon a variety of circumstances. If you can restructure your business without adverse income tax effect to permit younger members of your family to acquire high-yielding preferred units, that may be an appropriate way to shift value to them, unless you anticipate that the business will grow faster than the market rate of return which would have to be paid on the preferred interests so their fair market value is equal to their par value. If it is anticipated that the company's overall earnings will be greater than the market rate of return a classic freeze with cumulative preferred being retained by the more senior members of the family, as discussed earlier, might be considered instead. In any case, your financial and legal advisors should be consulted in determining whether any type of freeze is appropriate. It should be noted that an S corporation cannot be used to effect a classic freeze or a reverse freeze because an S corporation can have one type of stock (only differences in voting rights are permitted).

Effect a "Death-Time Freeze"

Under Chapter 14, if you or your spouse transfer a common interest to your children while either of you retain a preferred interest, the value of the retained preferred interest will be treated as an additional gift to your children (unless an exception applies, such as for cumulative preferred units carrying a market rate of return). However, you may be able to effect such a freeze transfer at your death. In effect, if you are survived by your spouse, you can provide for preferred units to pass to your spouse (or a trust for your spouse's benefit) under the protection of the marital deduction and for common units to be transferred to or in trust for your descendants. Historic methods of valuing those interests, and not the new anti-freeze rules of Chapter 14, should apply in such a case. You will thereby have effected a freeze for the balance of your spouse's lifetime. Moreover, your spouse (or the trust for your spouse) may receive more of the current return from the business by virtue of holding the preferred interest, which may be appropriate.

The value of the common interests passing to your children obviously will not qualify for the marital deduction. Thus, to the extent the value of those common interests (together with any other taxable bequests made at your death) exceed the value of your remaining estate tax exemption, estate tax will be due. It may, however, be possible to structure the preferred and common interests so that the value of the common interests is relatively low, thereby minimizing the amount of estate tax which will be payable at your death.

The death-time freeze can be an excellent tool to reduce taxes on interests in your business and to effect a freeze during the balance of your spouse's lifetime. However, it is a complicated transaction and should be considered only with the advice of your tax advisors.

Low Interest Loans

The Internal Revenue Code contains rules about the effects of interest-free and low-interest loans to family members or entities in which they have a significant interest. In particular, the tax law provides certain safe-harbor interest rates. Those safe-harbor rates are often much lower than comparable commercial loan rates, because the safe-harbor rates are determined by reference to the rates on United States Treasury obligations. Your ability to loan funds to members of your family at the low safe-harbor rates is an excellent way of freezing your wealth and allowing the younger generation to obtain the fruits of higher rates of return.

For example, you see a business opportunity and you would like a corporation or a partnership owned by your descendants to invest. (It might be a new product or service which your own company might otherwise provide.) However, the new business needs capital to create/manufacture/market/etc., the new product or service. You can provide that capital by loaning funds to the new business at the low safe-harbor rate. If your children (with appropriate advice and guidance) can't earn more than the rate being paid on Treasury obligations, your children probably should not be in the business at all. Subject to very few restrictions (about which your own tax counsellors can advise you) you can make unlimited loans to the new enterprise owned by your descendants at the safe-harbor interest rate, and you may make those loans in some cases without guarantees by or personal liability of your descendants to pay off the loans if the venture fails. Moreover, if you use a grantor trust (discussed in more detail above) to hold the business interest for the benefit of your descendants, you will not even have to include the interest on the loan in your income. (The interest must, however, be paid or accrued in order to avoid gift tax problems.)

In some circumstances, the IRS may contend that a loan is actually equity. Where the service can establish that your loan was, in whole or in part, equity, and that equity represents preferred equity interest, with your children owning common equity, the "anti-freeze" rules contained in the 1990 tax legislation, discussed earlier, might apply. Your advisors can tell you how to capitalize the structure of the business to help avoid the IRS successfully being able to contend that your loan really is equity. In any event, safe harbor interest rate loans to enterprises on behalf of your children may be an especially effective tool when interest rates are relatively low. In fact, such loans may be appropriate whenever you anticipate that your children can earn more on funds borrowed from you than the safe harbor interest rate you must charge them to avoid being deemed to have made a taxable gift.

DO NOT BE TEMPTED TO PLACE YOUR FAMILY IN A POSITION TO PERPETUATE FRAUD

In General

No one enjoys paying tax, and estate taxes are among the most unpopular and highest taxes imposed in this nation. Not infrequently, individuals will be prone to evade taxes by hiding the transfer of wealth.

Most practitioners have had surviving family members approach them about the fact that the property owner arranged his or her affairs in such a way that the taxing authorities would be unaware that certain assets were transferred to them either during life or at death. The individuals often feel embarrassed and uncomfortable. Moreover, they usually understand that criminal charges are possible if the fraud is discovered, as it often is. The family is on the horns of a dilemma: On the one hand, the family does not want to take the risk of perpetuating a fraud but, on the other hand, they do not wish to have their inheritance eroded by expenses and potential penalties which might be imposed if they try to rearrange the transaction to avoid perpetuating the fraud.

Do not be tempted to perpetuate a fraud, no matter how foolproof or modest it seems. In fact, through proper planning, you may be able to save more legitimately than you possibly could by trying to accomplish your estate and financial planning through fraudulent transactions.

A Note About Expatriation: The Ultimate Estate Plan?

The United States is virtually the only major country which imposes its death tax not only on the basis of residency in the United States but on the basis of United States citizenship as well. That means that even if you are willing to leave the United States to avoid exposing your property to a death tax, your efforts will be unsuccessful if you remain a United States citizen. In fact, even if you are willing to renounce your citizenship, your efforts at avoiding estate tax may be unsuccessful for ten years after you do so. However, through proper planning, a person who renounces his or her United States citizenship and changes permanent residency to another country, may be able to avoid any gift taxation or estate taxation.

Renouncing one's citizenship is an exceptionally weighty decision. It should only be undertaken if you are able to obtain citizenship in another first-world country. At the present time, it appears that only Ireland, Canada, New Zealand or Australia represent viable alternatives to United States citizenship. Other first world countries have tax systems which are as onerous as those of the United States or have procedures for becoming a citizen which are impracticable to implement.

It is understood that several hundred people each year renounce their United States citizenship for tax reasons. The small number who do so reflects the fact that for most of us saving taxes at all costs is not our greatest priority.

EARLY LIFETIME PLANNING IS THE KEY TO ESTATE TAX REDUCTION

It Is Far Easier to Deflect Future Growth Than to Disgorge It

It is easier for you to deflect future growth to family members than it is to disgorge it once it is earned. For example, if you form a new business, it may be much less expensive, from a tax perspective, for you to arrange for your children to own all or a significant portion of the equity (through trusts, if that is more appropriate) than to transfer it to them after the company has been operated successfully for a time. Similarly, if you see opportunities to make investments which may produce a greater-than-average return, it may be appropriate for you to arrange for other members of your family (or trusts for their benefit) to make the investment rather than making it yourself.

An example will illustrate how effective such a strategy can be. One of our clients formed a business, investing only a few thousand dollars. He had one-half of the stock placed in trust for each of his children. He and his wife purchased the other half. The business is now worth tens of millions of dollars. The children's base of wealth is secure. The family has avoided millions of dollars of wealth transfer tax because the future growth was deflected rather than having it accumulated and then attempting to transfer. There is an additional benefit which the family enjoyed: greater flexibility in the disposition of wealth. The family is charitably inclined. Because the children (and grandchildren) have adequate resources for their personal needs, the parents are free to devote a greater portion of their estate to charity and to use other estate planning arrangements which can reduce tax but involve the delayed receipt of property by their children and grandchildren. Those opportunities would not be available (or would be available only to a lesser extent) if the children and grandchildren's personal needs were not already so well taken care of.

Adopt a Tax Plan Even If You Do Not Implement It

Giving away property can be difficult. However, it is appropriate for you to adopt a tax plan even if you do not immediately implement it. First, it will show you the scope of the tax problems which your family will face upon your death.

Second, it will familiarize you with planning techniques and let you weigh various options. Third, it may provide others with an opportunity to carry out your plans in the event that you become unable to do so.

Arranging for Others to Take Action You Have Failed to Take

POWERS-OF-ATTORNEY

The best estate and financial planning occurs as early in life as possible. Nonetheless, significant tax and other savings can still be achieved by action taken shortly before death. However, many individuals become legally incompetent to take action immediately prior to death because of pre-death illnesses and other conditions. It is not uncommon, for example, for a person who suffers a stroke or heart attack to survive for several hours or even weeks before death.

You should act now to ensure that steps can be taken to ease the administration of your estate, assist in the continuity of your business and reduce taxes, even if you become incompetent. One way to attempt to accomplish that is for you to execute a so-called "durable" power-of-attorney. That document (which forms an important legal relationship) is discussed in more detail in Chapter 10. You should ensure that it is properly drafted to survive your mental incapacity, and that it names at least one trusted individual other than immediate family members. However, as explained in more detail in Chapter 10, individuals acting under a power-of-attorney may encounter difficulty because, among other things, powers-of-attorney are narrowly construed. Alternatives, or supplements, to powers-of-attorney, are needed, and one of the most powerful is the Master Living Trust^{sm}.

THE MASTER LIVING TRUST©

Many individuals dispose of most (if not all) of their wealth not by a Will but by a revocable living trust. In some states, such as California, a revocable living trust is the norm. Generally, the revocable living trust has little practical impact during lifetime. However, properly structured, it can be used to mastermind the final estate planning. The Master Living Trust^{sm} has been designed especially for that purpose.

Among other things, it provides for an independent trustee to take action immediately prior to your death so as to implement important business, tax and financial planning. For example, your estate plan may provide for property to pass into a trust for your spouse which is intended to qualify for the marital deduction. Recently, a Tax Court decision held that a significant number of trusts, which lawyers throughout the country thought clearly qualified for the marital deduction, did not qualify. It was possible, of course, for all competent individuals to execute new documents conforming to the change which the Tax Court recommended. However, that would be impossible for most property owners who were legally incapacitated. The trustee of the Master Living Trust© would be able to effect that change for an incompetent person because of the express authorization to do so in the trust instrument.

Even if you do not wish to use a revocable living trust, you might consider a "standby" revocable living trust (in the form of a Master Living Trust© with an express authorization under a durable power-of-attorney for the attorney-in-fact to transfer your assets to the Master Living Trust© if you become mentally disabled.

SUMMARY AND CONCLUSIONS

Federal and state wealth transfer tax systems are complex. In addition, the rates of taxation imposed are the highest in the country. For most individuals of moderate wealth, at least one-half of their estate will be eroded by taxes when they die. In some cases, more than 80% will be eroded, and for some types of assets, the erosion can approach their entire value. Although estate and related tax planning also is complicated, opportunities to effect significant reduction in taxation are available for those who will begin implementing them early in life. For owners of closely-held businesses, such planning is critically important because for many of them the estate tax burden will be imposed, as a practical matter, on their business. Few, if any, businesses could survive if within nine months, more than half of their net worth had to be paid in cash to a creditor. Yet, for the unplanned estate of a closely-held business owner, that is what the enterprise may face. The tax law also offers estates of owners of closely-held businesses some special opportunities. It is usually possible to structure ownership so as to defer payment of a significant portion of the estate tax. Moreover, properly arranged, interests in a closely-held business can be valued at a significant discount, which can translate into significant tax savings. In order to ensure that you and your family take full advantage of all of the benefits which are available to owners of closely-held businesses, expert advice and early action are the key.

CHAPTER 15

SHOULD I ACQUIRE LIFE INSURANCE?

INTRODUCTION AND OVERVIEW OF CHAPTER

A significant portion of wealth transferred at death is represented by proceeds of life insurance. Life insurance long has been, and probably will continue to be, a major part of financial and estate planning for many. It is sometimes a necessary ingredient to complete an estate plan for the owner of a closely-held business. However, it is one of the least understood types of property. In order for you to determine whether, how much, and what kind of life insurance you should acquire, it is appropriate for you to become familiar with the financial aspects of life insurance and the property and tax rules which apply to this unique asset.

WHY LIFE INSURANCE IS SOLD AND NOT BOUGHT

Traditional Reasons for Acquiring Insurance

Most of the time, you are urged to acquire life insurance for the benefit of other people. By its very nature, life insurance is designed to ripen when you are dead. The usual reasons you are told to acquire it include: To replace your salary (or other earnings) which will disappear or be reduced upon your death; to fund estate taxes (so that your base of wealth will not be eroded for your surviving family members); to build wealth for other family members (so that, for example, your children can complete their college educations); to allow your business to continue operating after your death (by providing the company with cash to hire an expensive new chief operating officer or to meet other business needs which are likely to arise on account of your death).

479

You will note that all of those reasons have one thing in common: None of them benefits you personally because all of them relate to events after your death. In other words, life insurance is something for somebody else. (The same is true for much of estate planning and is a prime reason it is neglected.) Spending money for other people often runs counter to our nature. Human beings survive because they tend to do things which are in their own personal best interest; however, when we spend our funds for someone else, we at least enjoy some psychological benefits during our lifetime. Buying life insurance provides us with peace of mind and should also give our dependent family members a feeling of security. (Of course, because the payoff is likely to be so far off in the future, their appreciation of the benefit of the insurance is diminished by the waiting time involved.)

Many people use excuses like "I don't believe in life insurance" or "I don't need life insurance."

However, each year, you acquire other types of insurance. For example, you probably carry more automobile insurance than the minimum required by your state. Similarly, each year you carry household insurance. There is a good chance, also, that you went out of your way to apply for and now carry liability insurance (an "umbrella" policy) in addition to that which may be provided under your household insurance policy. Your business also carries various kinds of insurance. In other words, you insure your most valuable assets.

You may be your family's most valuable asset and yet there is an excellent chance that asset is significantly underinsured. Like it or not, the reason is probably that expressed earlier: You perceive that you get no present benefit from carrying the insurance on your life because it does not pay off until you die; hence, you don't want to expend your assets to acquire it. As an owner of a closely-held business, it is likely that your death will represent one of the most adverse financial events in your family's and in your business' history. You owe it to your family and your business to consider taking some steps to protect them when that event occurs. In fact, there are special reasons why owners of closely-held businesses should consider and, in many cases, acquire life insurance.

Other Reasons for Acquiring Life Insurance

CREDITOR PROTECTION

Although creditor protection will be discussed in more detail in Chapter 16, it is appropriate to mention it here in connection with life insurance. In some (but not all) states, it appears that your interest in a life insurance policy, including its cash value, cannot be attached by your creditors. For example, even if you could demand the entire $1 million cash value of your life insurance policy at any time, your creditors, even in a bankruptcy proceeding, would be unable to attach the policy or that $1 million in several states.

As a practical matter, other than interests in qualified retirement plans, life insurance may be the only asset which may have significant liquid value which is so protected. (Some states, such as Florida, protect your principal residence from claims of creditors. Obviously, that exception can be very important but it is not a liquid asset.)

As mentioned, not all states offer that creditor protection for life insurance policies, including cash value, from claims of the owner's creditors. It appears that the question of whether you will have that protection depends upon your residence at the time the creditor attempts to attach the property. Moreover, if you acquire a policy or add cash to it in defraud of creditors (discussed in more detail in Chapter 16), the policy probably will not be protected from the claims of your creditors.

Although the protection offered by the policy of insurance can be of extreme importance, it is likely that your advisors will recommend that the insurance on your life be owned by someone other than you (to avoid estate taxation of the proceeds and, perhaps, for other reasons). In fact, in many cases, a trust for your family will own the policy. As is discussed in more detail in Chapter 16, that trust will provide its own protection from claims of both your creditors and creditors of the trust beneficiaries. As a consequence, in many cases, the protection which is afforded against claims of creditors of a policy of insurance in some states may not be of importance because the life insurance policy will be protected because it is owned by a trust. However, the creditor protection provided by using a trust and creditor protection afforded by the policy can be different and can have different ramifications. For example, in the United States, you can usually protect assets from clams of creditors by creating a trust only if you exclude yourself from being a trust beneficiary. Where state law protects a life insurance policy from claims of creditors, you can continue to own the policy directly—and that will allow you direct access to its cash value (something you cannot access if you have transferred property in a trust for others).

TAX BENEFITS

Life insurance is uniquely treated under the Internal Revenue Code. The treatment is, in almost all respects, beneficial. First, it is relatively simple to avoid the estate taxation of life insurance proceeds. That is discussed in more detail later. Second, dividends received on a policy of insurance are not subject to income tax except to the extent that they exceed the total premiums you have paid. Third, the increase in value of the cash value component of life insurance is not subject to income tax until the profit is withdrawn from the policy. Fourth, except for certain single premium and other "modified endowment contract" policies, the owner may withdraw profit earned on the cash value, up to the total premiums paid, without paying any income tax on such profits. In other words, the owner can withdraw his or her investment (or basis) first from the policy and be treated as though he or she left the profit in the policy (thereby keeping it from being taxed). Fifth, again except for a modified endowment contract policy, the owner can borrow the entire cash value of the policy, including the profit element, without causing the profit to be subjected to income tax. Sixth, in almost all cases, all the inherent income tax liability with respect to the policy disappears when the insured dies.

Those special tax benefits which a life insurance policy

offers are discussed in more detail later in this Chapter. They are extremely important to consider in structuring your insurance program because they can be used to reduce the cost of insurance. However, the tax benefits alone probably do not justify acquiring insurance. (If someone else in your family, such as an adult child, is acquiring insurance on his or her life, you may be able to access that policy's tax benefits for yourself.) Nonetheless, as indicated, it is important for you and your advisors to understand the unique tax benefits which an insurance policy can offer. Then, when a decision is made to acquire insurance, its ownership and maintenance can be structured to minimize cost by taking maximum advantage of the tax benefits which the policy offers. Unfortunately, many advisors do not fully understand the tax benefits which life insurance products can offer and how to maximize those benefits.

SPECIAL TEMPORARY REASONS—ESTATE PLANNING STRATEGIES

As explained in more detail in Chapter 14, the tax law appears to allow property owners to transfer wealth to their family at low or even no effective estate and gift tax cost if the assets involved produce more than a market rate of return. However, that strategy usually takes a long time to be effective. Other strategies allow you to deplete part of your estate for tax purposes but, again, often only if the strategy is carried out over a considerable period of time. If you die in the interim, the program may not produce the results sought and the need for liquidity to pay estate tax will be undiminished. That is one of the special temporary reasons to acquire insurance.

For example, if you decide to transfer a residence of yours to your descendants through a house GRIT (discussed in Chapter 14), at significantly reduced gift tax cost, by retaining the right to use the home as a personal residence for ten years, your death any time during that ten-year period will foil your plan: The full value of the home will be includable in your estate as though you never gave it away and estate taxes will be due. If you live for the ten years, the house will be removed from your tax estate and no death taxes will be payable on its value. Many individuals, when engaging in such an estate planning strategy, acquire life insurance to shift the risk of a premature death (such as within the ten-year term) over to an insurance carrier.

Similarly, many individuals who create charitable remainder trusts (discussed in more detail in Chapter 8, relating to retirement planning) acquire insurance so that, if they die prematurely and the property in the trust is transferred to charity much earlier than expected, the base of wealth the family loses is replaced by insurance proceeds.

The bottom line is that you may wish to consider acquiring life insurance on a temporary basis when the estate or financial planning strategies you have chosen to use are likely to achieve their goals only if you live for a certain period of time.

Summary

Despite needs for insurance which objectively may be present, the fact that it is almost always acquired for the traditional reasons of benefitting persons other than the insured makes it one of the most difficult financial products to be sold. Almost no one ever affirmatively seeks out the acquisition of life insurance (although, sometimes, after a decision to acquire life insurance is made, comparative shopping does occur). Some successful life insurance sales representatives sell their products by emphasizing the benefits to the insured which the policy can offer rather than the benefits which it can offer to surviving family members. In any case, properly structured, the tax benefits which apply to life insurance can be used to reduce its cost.

HOW TO CHOOSE A PRODUCT

Introduction on Need

Almost always, the need for liquidity or capital at death must be present for there to be a need for life insurance. Sometimes, individuals will perceive that life insurance will reduce the costs of providing liquidity or capital compared to other arrangements. On average, the insurance company pays back to you exactly what you paid it (plus some earnings factor). Certainly, if you die much earlier than anticipated, the return on your investment will be very high. If your death occurs in the first year, for example, the rate of return may be 1,000% or more. However, if you live to your approximate life expectancy, the return to you will be about an average portfolio return. Of course, the portfolio approach introduces factors of risk and timing. If you live for much longer than expected, the return will decrease and probably will be less than the average return provided by a well-balanced portfolio. (The reason for that is that you have had the benefit of having your life insured during your lifetime; those in your group who died early got a greater-than-average return, and that means someone else in the group has to get a lower-than-average return.) But averages may be meaningless if you have a need for insurance. For example, if an analysis shows that at the present time you cannot fund the estate taxes which will arise on your death, you almost certainly need to acquire insurance—at least on a temporary basis. Even if you are certain that you and your advisor will be able to fund the estate taxes from an alternate source later, it probably is prudent (if not imperative) that you acquire adequate insurance now—just in case you don't live for the "average" life expectancy for people your age or you and your advisors do not meet your liquidity or capital needs goals in other ways.

What that means is that you should acquire insurance if you have a need for it and it does not significantly detract from your lifestyle. For many of us, our base of wealth is insufficient to allow our families to maintain the economic lifestyle we want them to continue after our deaths. Life insurance is especially suited in that kind of circumstance. As mentioned above, and as will be explained in more detail later, life insurance does offer some unique benefits under the tax law. A well-to-do, highly-liquid individual might decide to acquire insurance primarily for that reason.

The reason you acquire life insurance should be similar to the reason you acquire other forms of insurance, such as casualty, automobile and household insurance. The primary reason you acquire those is that you cannot afford (or would find it horribly disruptive to have to afford) the damage or expense which would result if what you have insured against occurs. You should acquire life insurance if the financial consequences of your death are such that your survivors (which, in some cases, will include your business) cannot afford the effects of your death. However, on an average, over time, the insurance company will pay out upon your death only the premiums which have been paid during your lifetime plus an earnings factor. Nevertheless, if you have a need for insurance, averages may be meaningless to your survivors.

SHORT-TERM NEEDS

Many individuals have a relatively short-term need for insurance. Sometimes, a lender will insist that insurance be carried on your life until the loan is repaid. Another circumstance where the need of insurance may be relatively short-term is where you decide to acquire insurance to guarantee that your children's education can be finished. You may not even consider that until your son or daughter goes to college. You then realize that they might be unable to finish if you die before they graduate. In that case, you might acquire insurance for the remaining three or four years they will attend college.

In such cases, term insurance almost always is the least expensive type of insurance to acquire. The reason is that the commissions and other costs which are imposed are lower, in part, because the premium is lower. However, in some cases, obtaining a universal or variable policy (defined later) may provide you with term rates as inexpensive as those provided by a policy which only has a term feature. Yet the universal or variable policy will have the flexibility to be used as a cash value policy if the need for that type of insurance develops.

In addition, as will be explained more completely later with certain policies which have cash value, you can pay for all but the first year's term premium with income which will never be taxed. Where such a policy provides a real term cost no greater than with a policy which has no other feature, that may be a better choice even if the need for insurance is relatively short-term.

LONG-TERM NEEDS

Where the need for the insurance is long-term, it will be appropriate to consider a cash-value policy. An analysis should be made, however, of (1) the cost of acquiring a term policy which you can renew without examination each year for the time which you believe you will need the insurance and (2) a cash value policy providing a comparable total benefit paid at death. Almost always, the cash value policy (whether of the tradition type or a universal or variable one) will be less expensive over the long haul unless you are positive you can outperform the insurance company's investments. But outperforming the insurance company may not be easy. One of the reasons is that the investment of the cash in your policy will build on a tax-deferred or tax-free basis. For example, if you are in a 50% annual income tax bracket on your investment returns, you will have to double the return which the insurance company makes if all other things are equal. Of course, they may not be equal. (For instance, as a practical matter, you will be able to make more speculative investments than the insurance company or its fund managers will. Of course, the more speculative the investment the greater the risk.) Nonetheless, the tax-deferred environment under which the cash in your policy will be invested is a major advantage.

PERMANENT NEEDS

Some individuals conclude that they have a permanent need for insurance. If the individual lives for a long time, the cost of term insurance becomes virtually prohibitive because, at advanced ages, the premium will approach the amount of death coverage provided. In addition, the insurance carrier almost always will stop offering term insurance when you reach a certain age. Where the need for insurance is regarded as permanent, you will have little choice but to use a cash value type policy. Where you perceive a permanent liquidity need existing at your death, you may wish to explore alternative methods of providing liquidity rather than by carrying insurance for your entire life. However, few individuals find them and carry them out.

More long-term needs include providing a base of wealth to generate income for surviving family members. That need may never disappear but, for many, becoming vested in significant retirement benefits may reduce or eliminate the need for insurance. Many owners of closely-held businesses carry insurance to fund estate taxes. The need for that insurance may be long-term but not permanent, such as where it is intended that the company will "go public" providing a ready market for the stock held by the owner's estate at death or where the business probably will be sold or liquidated after a period of time.

DETERMINE ALTERNATIVES AND THEIR COSTS

Life insurance provides instant liquidity to cover the costs associated with death. In many cases, over the long term, alternative methods of providing liquidity or eliminating the need for life insurance may be available. For example, building liquid wealth during lifetime through savings may dissipate the need for liquidity which life insurance will provide. For some, building that wealth through the life insurance policy's cash or investment component itself may be an appropriate method because of the tax-deferred investment environment which investments in life insurance policy provide.

Where the need for insurance relates primarily to funding estate taxes, lifetime estate planning may reduce a growing need for more insurance. For example, you may be able to transfer adequate wealth to other family members through special lifetime arrangements (some of which are discussed in Chapter 14) to reduce the need for additional insurance. Most individuals, however, do not adequately prepare for the liquidity needs which their business, their surviving family members and their estate will have upon their deaths. In fact, the successful business owner may constantly have a greater need for insurance. The base of wealth may continuously increase (and, perhaps, at a much higher rate than an average portfolio return) so that the need for insurance to fund death taxes increases. In any event, you will need constantly to seek additional insurance if you do not take those lifetime planning steps to limit the level or rate of growth of your estate.

One way that you may be able to limit permanently the amount of insurance you need is to decide that your family will receive a certain dollar amount from your estate and the balance will pass in a form (such as to charity) so that it will not be taxed. For example, you might decide that each of your children should receive a certain fixed sum (no more, no less). Based on current death tax rates, your advisors can tell you how much life insurance is needed so that estate taxes can be paid on the net inheritance amount you want your children to receive. Whether your estate goes up or goes down, you can be sure that the estate taxes will be covered by insurance proceeds. Over time, however, your decision may change and the amount you plan to leave your children may be so eroded by inflation that you will decide that they need more. When that happens, you may need more insurance.

In any case, appropriate estate and financial planning includes assessing the long-term liquidity needs your business, surviving family members and estate will face. Although insurance may be an especially suited tool to help achieve that result, it may not always, over the long term, be the single solution. As a consequence, it is appropriate for you to consider as early in the planning stage as possible alternative methods of providing liquidity or reducing the need for liquidity at your death.

Insurance You Just Can't Turn Down

As explained elsewhere, if you are in less-than-average health for your age, you will be charged a premium at a level which would be charged to a person who is older than you are or the insurance company will decline coverage altogether. Some companies, by the way, will write insurance when others will not.

If your death is anticipated to be imminent, no insurance company will provide you with insurance. However, in some cases, you can obtain what is known as guaranteed issue insurance. Some organizations, such as professional associations, from time to time offer certain levels of insurance which you may obtain without examination and will pay off in full even if you die within two years of acquiring the insurance. If you or a member of your family should become afflicted with a condition where it is known that death certainly will occur earlier than normal, you might ask your advisors to see whether you or that family member qualifies for any guaranteed issue insurance. However, almost always, the amount of guaranteed issue insurance will be limited.

WHAT IS LIFE INSURANCE

Basic Explanation— The Death Benefit Component

Life insurance is defined as a contract between the holder of a policy and an insurance company under which the company agrees, in return for premium payments, to pay a specified sum (the face value or maturity value of the policy) to the designated beneficiary upon the death of the insured.

In fact, life insurance is really **death** insurance. The event against which you are insuring is death. You do not buy "no accident" insurance for your car; rather, you buy "accident" insurance. Your auto policy pays off only if you have an accident and the name reflects that. Life insurance usually does not pay off if you live; it pays if you die. However, the industry discovered that the name "death insurance" really killed sales so the name was changed to "life insurance", and it does sell much better with that label on it.

In any case, types of life insurance have been around for about as long as human beings have walked the face of the earth. Early hunters, for example, used to agree that if one of them died while pursuing game, the survivors would take care of the deceased hunter's family. That is a rather crude form of life insurance. Today, life insurance works in a similar but more sophisticated way: Groups of individuals band together by buying life insurance from a company and agree in effect that the survivors will provide for the beneficiaries of any deceased member of the group.

How Life Insurance Works

In its most basic form, life insurance works the same way that all your insurance works. When you buy household insurance, for example, you usually pay a premium for a fixed term, such as one year. If the event you insure against occurs (such as the theft of your property at your home), the insurance company will pay the benefit provided under the policy. If the event you insure against does not occur, the insurance company keeps the premiums and the coverage ends. Of course, you and the insurance carrier often decide to continue the coverage for another year. However, in almost all cases, the insurance contract is for a term of one year.

Term life insurance basically works the same way. For a premium, the insurance company promises to pay a predetermined amount (usually the face amount of the policy) if the event you insure against (in this case, death) occurs during the term. If you do not die, the insurance company usually pays nothing and the coverage ends. Just as you and your household insurance carrier may agree to extend the coverage for another year, you and the life insurance company may agree to extend the coverage for another year. However, your household insurance company may refuse to renew the insurance and so may your life insurance company. Your life insurance company may refuse to renew the insurance because your health has deteriorated and the probability of the time of your death becomes sufficiently unsure (or in some cases, too sure that it will happen too soon) that the insurance company either will refuse to provide you with any life insurance or will do so only at a very high premium.

For that reason, individuals often seek to have an automatic right to renew the insurance for as long as they wish to be provided with life insurance coverage. Insurance carriers provide that option, but they charge more for insurance which is automatically renewable than if it can be renewed only if you undergo and pass another medical examination.

Cash Value Insurance Component

All life insurance contains a term or pure death benefit element. That is the amount for which the insurance company is at risk. For many cash value policies, the cash (or investment) value is substituted for part of the death benefit. In the early years, when the amount you pay is in excess of the cost of the term insurance being provided under the policy, the excess, plus its earnings, is accumulated under the policy. If the policy constitutes a life insurance contract within the meaning of the Internal Revenue Code, those earnings will not be taxed to the policy's owner unless those earnings are deemed distributed to the owner of the policy.

Modified Endowment Contracts

If the insurance policy constitutes a "modified endowment contract," any distribution or borrowing from the policy is treated as a distribution of the earnings (to the extent of such earnings) and will be includable in the tax income of the policy owner. (In some cases, non-deductible tax penalties also are imposed.) In other words, whether cash is distributed as a withdrawal or as a loan, the distribution is treated as consisting first of the earnings experienced in the policy rather than a non-taxable return of basis or investment in the policy (which is usually equal to the total premiums paid less dividends received).

Modified endowment contracts are those which are paid up by a single premium or in a very short period of time. Paid up means that it is anticipated that the policy has adequate cash value to generate sufficient earnings to keep the policy in force, without the payment of any additional premiums, until the insured dies.

As a general matter, it is desirable to avoid having a policy be a modified endowment contract. If the owner ever wishes to borrow against the policy or withdraw cash value from it, usually it will not be beneficial to have to pay tax on that withdrawal or borrowing. Although it may not be possible to avoid modified endowment contract status in all circumstances, usually you can achieve paid-up status over a very short term, such as four years, without having the policy be treated as one.

Tax-Free BuildUp

As indicated, whether the policy is a modified endowment contract or not, earnings inside the policy will build tax-free (until withdrawal) as long as the policy constitutes a life insurance contract under the Internal Revenue Code. In addition to being a life insurance contract under state law, the policy must also meet certain tests set forth in the Code. Although alternative tests are provided under the tax law, generally, only a maximum annual premium can be paid and the cash (or investment) value of the policy cannot exceed a certain level based upon the amount of insurance being carried. The older the insured, the more the value can be. If earnings are very high inside the policy, the contract may lose its status as a life insurance policy. From that point on, earnings will be taxed directly to the policy's owner as though the owner were maintaining, in effect, a brokerage account at an investment brokerage firm.

All life insurance contracts provide that the company can refuse to accept additional premiums from you if that would cause the contract to fail to maintain its status as a life insurance policy. In addition, if the earnings are so great that the policy would lose its status as a life insurance contract for tax purposes, the insurance company will sell you additional insurance, without medical examination, so that the policy can maintain its life insurance contract status under the law. Alternatively, the owner will have to withdraw cash value from the policy in order for the contract to maintain its tax status. If there is any possibility of that happening, it is much better, as a general rule, for the policy not to be a modified endowment contract. If it is a modified endowment contract, probably the entire amount withdrawn will be includable in gross income. If it is not a modified endowment contract, only to the extent the amount withdrawn exceeds total premiums paid (less dividends received) will it be includable in gross income.

Although the tax law places limits on the amount which can be invested in and built up in a life insurance policy, for many, the amounts are significant. Chart 15.1 provides an illustration of the amounts which can be built up under a policy taken out on the life of a 46 year old with a $2 million policy over 20 years.

Investment Flexibility

All other things being equal, your investments will grow much quicker in a tax-deferred investment environment. However, things are not likely to be exactly equal when you "invest" through a life insurance policy. First, unless you choose a variable product, the insurance company will decide how your cash is invested. Some individuals regard insurance company investment performance as good; others do not. With a variable policy, the owner has at least some choices. Usually, the owner can choose to invest in one or more mutual funds and money market accounts. Typically, these include a bluechip stock fund, a growth fund, an aggressive growth fund and a fixed income fund. However, the choices vary from insurance company to insurance company and, in some cases, from policy to policy with the same company. Usually, the insurance company retains the right to change investment advisors to a mutual fund even if it uses outside advisors. Some professional advisors recommend against variable insurance on account of what might be called "the risk of choice." That is, they perceive the owner of the policy faced with several choices will neglect to make the best one or even good ones. They perceive that some owners either do not have (and will not acquire) necessary expertise to make good investment selections or will not diligently exercise their expertise (or that of their advisors). It is a reasonable contention. It means that you probably should consider acquiring a variable policy in order to have greater investment flexibility only if you have (or will obtain) adequate expertise and will prudently exercise it. In any case, you must pay for the insurance in order to access the

CHART 15.1

Illustration of Maximum Premiums and Values for a $2 Million Policy on the Life of a 46 Year Old to Maintain Its Status as a Life Insurance Contract for Tax Purposes

Policy Year	Age (Beginning of Year)	MAXIMUM PREMIUMS PAYABLE TO AVOID LOSING LIFE INSURANCE CONTRACT STATUS		Maximum Cash Value Allowed to Avoid Losing Life Insurance Contract Status
		Per Year	Total Cumulative	
1	46	$478,567	$ 112,674	$ 1,834,862
2	47	0	225,348	1,941,748
3	48	0	338,022	2,061,856
4	49	0	450,696	2,197,802
5	50	15,840	494,406	2,352,941
6	51	98,881	593,287	2,564,103
7	52	98,881	692,169	2,816,901
8	53	98,881	791,050	3,125,000
9	54	98,881	889,931	3,508,772
10	55	98,881	988,812	4,000,000
11	56	98,881	1,087,693	4,347,826
12	57	98,881	1,186,575	4,761,905
13	58	98,881	1,285,456	5,263,158
14	59	98,881	1,384,337	5,882,353
15	60	98,881	1,483,218	6,666,667
16	61	98,881	1,582,099	7,142,857
17	62	98,881	1,680,981	7,692,308
18	63	98,881	1,779,862	8,333,333
19	64	98,881	1,878,743	9,090,909
20	65	98,881	1,977,624	10,000,000

tax-deferred investment environment which the policy can offer.

In any event, the purposes for which you acquire the insurance or your investment philosophy (or the lack of availability of cash to invest) may mean you choose not to use the tax-deferred investment environment which the policy offers. For example, if you acquire insurance to fund death taxes, you may "deposit" the minimum necessary to keep in force the insurance you believe your estate will need rather than attempting to make maximum use of the tax-deferred investment environment a policy can provide.

Insurance Company Management Fees

The insurance company charges fees for managing funds. In some cases, such as where there is an outside advisor to a fund, the fee may be shared with that advisor. The amount of the fee generally is a percentage of the value of assets under management. Typical charges run from 1.5% to 2.5% per year. Some may be less; some may be more. Obviously, the higher the annual charge for management, the smaller the return, all other things being equal. You and your advisors should be aware of those annual charges as well as the investment performance history of the funds in which you may invest.

How Life Insurance Policies Are Priced

BASIC DETERMINANTS OF COST

As will be explained in more detail later, term insurance is the only type of insurance really offered. However, it is packaged in so many special ways and with so many additional features that it appears as though there are a great variety of different types of life insurance. In its basic form, however, there is nothing but term insurance. One of the primary factors in pricing the term element of a policy will be the probability that you will die during the term of coverage. As you get older, the probability of your death within any term (such as the next year) will be greater than if you are younger, all other things being equal. All other things, however, may not be equal. One major difference is sex. Women tend to live longer than men. Companies take that into account; most charge higher premiums for men than women but a few do not. However, such unisex rates will result in higher rates for women and lower rates for men than gender biased rates.

Another primary factor is health. If you are average health for your age, you will be charged an average premium for the product. If you are less healthy than average, you will be charged a premium for an older person; the insurance company will make a determination as to what age your health represents. For example, if you are 45 years old but have a health problem, the insurance carrier may charge you the same premium which it would for a person of average health but age 50 years.

Other important factors include the sales representative's commission, the costs of operating the insurance company, the premium tax charged by the state involved, the profit the company seeks to make as well as the price of additional features.

GOVERNMENT CONTROL

Insurance companies are regulated by the states in which they do business. Compared to most businesses, insurance companies are very regulated. However, the amount of control in many respects is not total. The types of products offered, how they are sold and the prices which are charged are primarily left up to the insurance companies. Do not think that the policies, or the companies, are interchangeable. They are not. In fact, it is interesting to observe the wide disparity for term insurance charges for an insured of the same age from company to company.

Publicly-held insurance companies, just like other publicly-held companies, are subject to federal government reporting and disclosure requirements. These federal controls can be very important. So-called "mutual" life insurance companies are not "regulated" in the same way.

HOW LIFE INSURANCE SALES REPRESENTATIVES ARE COMPENSATED

Almost all life insurance sales representatives are paid a percentage of the premiums you pay on the life insurance product. For most policies sold, the agent (and others associated with the agent) usually will receive a percentage of the first year's premium. Different companies pay different percentages and, in some cases, different percentages on different policies. If you buy a so-called "cash value" policy, the illustrations which are presented to you may demonstrate that there is little or no cash value at the end of the first year but significant cash value (as a percentage of a premium paid) in the second year. The reason is that a significant part of the first year's premium was used to pay for the first year of insurance and sales and related costs. Sometimes, the commissions will be spread over the first several years so that there will be cash value "working" even in the first year. In such cases, if you cancel the policy and try to obtain the cash value, a surrender charge will be imposed so as to recover the deferred charges.

HIDDEN COSTS

Company and Product Quality

Although banking is one of the most regulated industries in the United States, we have all learned that the quality of banks varies widely. The quality of insurance companies varies widely, too, although, as indicated elsewhere, few insurance companies have experienced the severe problems that banks and savings institutions have. Some are much more efficient than others; some are more financially sound than others; some are more innovative and responsive than others. The financial position of the company will have a significant impact on the quality and financial security of the policy. The various states provide a type of insurance protection for a policy governed by that state, but only up to certain limits.

Many policyholders of some insurance carriers, such as those holding policies issued by Executive Life, have learned that they may not get what they paid for. (However, in modern times, no American insurance company has failed to pay a death claim although not all payments required under annuity contracts have been paid.) Hence, the quality of the insurance company is very important. Ratings of insurance company quality are available. However, the ratings often are inadequate. For example, immediately prior to the state take-over of one of America's large life insurance companies because of its terrible financial problems, it was carrying the highest rating from one rating service. That is not to say that you and your advisors should not consider the ratings. There are four major insurance rating services (A.M. Best, Standard & Poor's, Moody's, and Duff & Phelps) and you or your advisors should check all of them before buying a product from a particular carrier. Your professional insurance advisor can supply you with that information.

Unfortunately, the ratings of companies and their products are sometimes so complex and so contradictory that it is often difficult for a purchaser to be able to discern comparative company quality. Moreover, sales representatives of less well rated companies will point to alternative rating services in which their company has a better rating. Alternatively, they will point out that ratings change over time and that even if you choose a company with the highest rating today it may not have that rating at the time when the death benefit becomes payable to your family. In any case, you probably should choose a product from a company only if it has a top rating from at least two of the rating services.

The quality of products also varies widely even if the insurance companies offering those products are in the same financial position. In fact, the quality of products varies even within the same company. One company, for example, may offer a very high-quality term product but a poor quality cash value policy. Again, if you are going to make a significant investment in a life insurance policy or policies, it may pay you to hire an independent advisor to assist you with the analysis and to make recommendations to you. Also, if you are going to buy a considerable amount of life insurance, you may wish to consider acquiring policies from more than one carrier. That allows you to spread the risk of insurance company financial problems.

State Premium Taxes

The several states and municipalities impose a tax on premiums. Some are approximately four times greater than others. Usually, the tax is imposed based upon the principal residence of the insured. Some states discriminate against products sold by companies whose headquarters are not within the state. For example, at the present time, New York charges a .8% premium tax if the company is a New York-based life insurance company. If it is an out-of-state company, New York charges 2%. In any case, it is a factor for you to consider in choosing a particular type of product.

Surrender Charges

As explained earlier, some policies will show the presence of considerable cash value even in the early years of the policy's life. However, many policies provide that if you attempt to surrender the policy, you must pay a so-called "surrender charge." That charge is to repay the company for "front-end" sales and related charges incurred at the time of issuance of the policy. You should be aware whether and under what circumstances there are surrender charges.

Other Factors Which Affect Cost and Quality

Many other factors will affect the quality and cost of your product. The illustration presented by your sales representative cannot accurately reflect what the performance of your policy will be. For example, on any cash value policy, an assumption will be made as to earnings.

One step you can take to help determine the expected performance of your policy is to request all competing sales representatives to present their illustrations using the same rate of return. More important, it will be almost impossible for you to determine whether or not each carrier, in fact, can produce the same rate of return. Regardless of how the illustrations come out, the thing that really counts is whether or not one company outperforms another. If you choose 8% as the annual rate of return for purposes of illustration, and Company A looks better than Company B, the comparison may be meaningless if Company B, in fact, outperforms Company A. In addition, different companies have different charges for the term insurance (which is present even with a cash value policy). That also affects the illustration. Those term changes usually can change during the course of holding a policy and, therefore, the estimates used may not be correct.

In other words, in presenting illustrations, the company will make certain assumptions as to earnings and certain assumptions as to the cost of the term insurance element of the policy. Some companies may assume higher earnings and higher costs of insurance; others may assume lower costs for insurance but lower earnings. Other factors also are considered in the illustrations. For example, some illustrations fail to take into account recent tax law changes which, in effect, require sales commissions to be deducted by the company over a longer term, thereby, in many cases, increasing insurance company costs, as a practical matter. Of course, the actual premiums you pay may be a most important factor in determining performance. What that means, in large measure, is that analyzing illustrations is, to some degree, much more an "art" than a "science." You probably will find it helpful to have the illustrations of different policies using the same rate of return. However, you will probably need the assistance of a well-trained and experienced insurance field representative to assist you in making the best choice. But, in any event, make sure you see more than one company's illustrations.

Nonetheless, comparisons at a fixed, stated rate for each carrier can be helpful in showing certain other assumptions made by the company and the costs it makes for managing the cash value, delayed or extra commissions paid and similar factors.

How to Reduce Costs

Shop Around

Most business people, as well as other customers, do comparative shopping when acquiring a product where a significant investment will be made. Over time, the amount invested in a life insurance policy may be considerable especially if you live as long as you hope to live. Although you may find it difficult to do the comparative shopping for life insurance, your professional insurance and other advisors should be able to do so for you. However, it will be impossible for them to be able to forecast the future and that ultimately will turn out to be one of the most important factors. However, knowing current costs, the financial condition of the insurance carrier, and both the short-term and long-term investment performance history of the company (or its investment advisors) are definitely important factors for you and your advisors to consider in choosing a policy. Some advisors believe that you are better doing comparative shopping of life insurance agents rather than companies. You probably should do both—and a good agent can be of invaluable assistance in comparing companies and products.

Choose the Right Product for the Job

Perhaps, more important, make sure you choose the right type of product to cover the need for insurance. A cash value policy almost certainly is the wrong choice for a truly short term need for insurance. You probably will overpay for doing that. Similarly, buying term insurance when the need for insurance coverage is long-term or permanent will cost you more than a good quality cash value product.

HOW TO PAY FOR LIFE INSURANCE

"Tax Deductible" Life Insurance

THE MYTH OF PENSION PLAN LIFE INSURANCE

As is explained in detail in Chapter 8, contributions to qualified retirement plans are income tax deductible. Sometimes it will be recommended that the plan acquire life insurance. The contention made is that you are really buying life insurance with tax deductible dollars. Life insurance premiums are not deductible for income tax purposes, except in the case where one person, such as an employer, deducts the cost of them, but someone else, such as an employee, must include the cost of premiums in income. Hence, the contention that you have made the premiums on life insurance deductible sounds inviting. However, such a contention misrepresents what really occurs. The investment in an insurance policy is not tax deductible.

On the other hand, any investment, whether it is in life insurance, municipal bonds or stocks is not deductible. Funds contributed to a qualified retirement plan are. What happens to the funds after they are contributed in no way affects whether or not the deduction is permitted. The same dollars are available for investment whether the investment is made into a life insurance policy, bonds, stocks or any other investment which may be lawfully made by the retirement plan. Hence, the cost of insurance is not really made tax deductible at all.

Moreover, the tax law imputes taxable income to an employee to the extent of the cost of the term insurance element of the policy which is acquired by a retirement plan. Although the amount imputed to the employee as taxable income where the employee's retirement plan acquires insurance on the employee's life usually is less than the real cost of insurance, there is no absolute "free ride" for acquiring insurance through a retirement plan.

However, some qualified plans can be structured so that more can be contributed, on a tax deductible basis, to provide, in addition to retirement benefits, a pre-retirement insurance coverage feature. The value of the term insurance coverage provided under the plan will be imputed to the employee whose life is insured. However, in some cases, it may be possible to receive a deduction (in the early years of funding for the insurance) in an amount greater than that imputed back to the employee. There may be three reasons for that phenomenon. First, the funding for the death benefit may be based on the higher "guaranteed" insurance rates; the value imputed as income will be lower. Second, as a general rule, the amount imputed to the employee for the insurance carried on his or her life is less than the rates actually charged by the insurance company (which themselves are lower than the guaranteed rates). Third, in some cases, it is possible to "accelerate" the funding over a shorter period of time than the period for which the insurance will be carried (until retirement). In a "strict" sense, taxable income does not disappear because the employee has imputed income for the coverage provided by the employer, the cost of which is income tax deductible to the employer. However, the amount deductible by the employer may be greater than the employee includes in income and the time that the employer gets to deduct the contribution attributable to the insurance may be earlier than when the employee must include the entire amount in income. Your pension consultants can advise you as to whether or not such a program can be used in the qualified plans you maintain and help you decide whether it would be efficient to do so.

Insurance may be an appropriate investment for your retirement plan or it may not be. In any case, it may not be more efficient to buy it through your plan, as a general rule, than any other way. However, having the plan acquire insurance appears attractive. The reason goes back to the fundamental reason for resisting acquiring insurance in the first place: You perceive that there is no benefit to you in having the insurance but only a benefit to those who survive you; because you cannot currently access the funds in your retirement plan (without significant income tax and penalties at least), you can fulfill your "moral" obligation to get the life insurance by using retirement plan funds rather than expending assets which you could otherwise use for your own current benefit.

In any case, your survivors will probably suffer a disability if you acquire insurance in your retirement plan. Almost always, the ownership of life insurance can be structured so as not to be includable in your estate for estate tax purposes. Subject to a possible exception (one promoted technique which has never been tested in court and which some advisors feel does not work), life insurance proceeds received by your plan upon your death almost certainly will be includable in your estate for estate tax purposes. Where your estate tax rate is 60%, as it is for many owners of closely-held businesses, your family will only net 40% of the proceeds because it was acquired by your retirement plan rather than outside of the plan.

Overall, you and your advisors may well conclude that acquiring insurance through your retirement plan is not an appropriate way to fund the cost or to acquire insurance on your life. Nonetheless, at least in some cases, there is a way in which you can make the real cost of term life insurance better than fully tax deductible.

A Way That Works and May Work for You

As mentioned above, the profit earned on the cash value component of a life insurance policy generally is not subject to income tax until the profit is withdrawn. By using those earnings to pay for the term cost of the insurance, you will be able to pay for life insurance with income which will never be subject to tax. That is as good, if not better, than making those premiums tax deductible.

Perhaps, the best way to understand what occurs is to consider something that is not really true. Suppose I went to the IRS and got it to agree that if a property owner invested in a savings account in the Blattmachr Savings Bank and directed that the interest in that account had to be used to pay for life insurance on the depositor's life, the interest would never be taxed to anyone. I think we would all agree that the Blattmachr Savings Bank would have a lot of deposits. Because the interest would never be taxed, we would cut the cost of the insurance by the effective rate of taxation. For example, if you deposited $100,000 and the Bank paid you 5% or $5,000 a year in interest, but the Bank used the funds to pay a $5,000 term insurance premium on your life, the real cost of that insurance has now dropped to $3,000 if you are in an effective 40% income tax bracket. The reason, of course, is that without the special arrangement made with the IRS the $5,000 would be taxed to you and after the 40% income tax, you would be left with only $3,000. However, because you invested through the Blattmachr Savings Bank, you got the full economic benefit of the entire pre-tax $5,000. Effectively, you can accomplish the same result with certain life insurance policies.

Some policies are structured so that if you do not pay the term insurance element each year, the cash value is charged with the cost of that premium. You can structure the cash value so that the earnings equal the amount of the term insurance. That way, the earnings are charged with the cost of the term insurance. However, your basis in the policy will equal the full amount of premiums paid (including that part of premiums allocated to the cash value component of the policy). That means that you can withdraw from the policy an amount equal to your basis (or total premiums paid), and no part of the income earned on that will ever be taxed to you. In fact, I arranged for that when I acquired a policy when I was 46 years old. I decided I needed insurance between ages 46 and 66 because by age 66 my wife and I will become vested in my firm's non-qualified retirement plan and my need for insurance will go down or disappear. For that, and other reasons, I determined that I might not have to continue to carry the insurance beyond age 66. Based upon current estimates, the total premiums paid for the 20 years for the $2 million of term insurance coverage would be $183,547. (The present value of those payments over 20 years was $79,362 using a 7.5% discount rate). I assumed that the cash I invested in the policy would earn 7.5% a year. On that basis, I needed an initial cash value of $108,356. At 7.5% a year, that amount would produce enough to pay the $183,547 over the 20-year term and have a cash value, as it did in the beginning, of exactly $108,356. At that time, I would be able to withdraw all cash from the policy (for example, by canceling it). Because total premiums paid would be $108,356, my basis would be $108,356 and I would have no gain (or loss) by withdrawing the $108,356. That is illustrated in Chart 15.2.

Of course, what I expect to happen during the 20 years is that the income earned by the cash value in the policy will be used to pay the term insurance costs. But that $183,547 of income earned will never be taxed. If it had been taxed, for example at a 50% effective income tax bracket, I would have received only $91,773 and, as a consequence, I would have only been able to obtain 50% as much insurance. However, I was able to arrange the funding of the term insurance component of the policy (which pays for the actual death benefit)

CHART 15.2

**Illustration of Paying for the Term Insurance
Element with Pre-Tax Policy Earnings**

Policy Year	Age (Beginning of Year)	Insurance Amount	Premium	Projected Earnings on the Cash Value at 7.5%	Cost of Term Insurance
1	46	$2,000,000	$108,356	$ 7,787	$ 6,323
2	47	2,000,000	0	8,064	4,266
3	48	2,000,000	0	8,329	4,636
4	49	2,000,000	0	8,583	5,116
5	50	2,000,000	0	8,830	5,433
6	51	2,000,000	0	9,069	5,816
7	52	2,000,000	0	9,296	6,256
8	53	2,000,000	0	9,504	6,756
9	54	2,000,000	0	9,687	7,316
10	55	2,000,000	0	9,838	7,996
11	56	2,000,000	0	9,949	8,676
12	57	2,000,000	0	10,013	8,436
13	58	2,000,000	0	10,024	10,256
14	59	2,000,000	0	9,973	11,096
15	60	2,000,000	0	9,851	12,036
16	61	2,000,000	0	9,654	12,856
17	62	2,000,000	0	9,382	13,636
18	63	2,000,000	0	9,034	14,376
19	64	2,000,000	0	8,603	15,116
20	65	2,000,000	0	8,079	16,016
Total			108,356	183,547	183,547

using income which will never be taxed (which is as good if not better than making the term premiums income tax deductible). Overall, that strategy will save me about $90,000.

Of course, if the cash earns less than 7.5%, the entire $108,356 I have paid in premium will not be there at the end of 20 years. In fact, it might be entirely eroded. Still, I will have never been taxed on the income of the policy which was earned to pay for the insurance. If the cash earns more than

7.5%, more will be in the policy than $108,356 at the end of 20 years so that if I canceled the insurance at that time I would have some taxable income (to the extent I got back more than the $108,356 in premiums I paid). Furthermore, if the term premiums turn out to be more (or less) than the insurance carrier has projected, I will have less (or more) in cash value at the end of the 20-year term. Certainly, I may indeed have a need for life insurance once I am 66 years old. My policy is structured so I can continue it from then on (regardless of my health). If I do choose to continue the insurance, I can again structure the premium payments in a tax favorable way (unless the law changes so as to prevent me from doing that).

You can do the same with certain other life insurance products as well. To be able to reduce the cost of carrying the death benefit for any given period of time (including for your entire life) can save quite a bit of money.

Other ways to benefit from the tax deferred investment environment which a life insurance policy offers are discussed in more detail later. Those are in addition to being able to pay for the term insurance component with income which is never taxed.

Tax-Favored Life Insurance Arrangements

IN GENERAL

In certain circumstances, the tax law provides for the cost of insurance coverage to be reduced, in effect, by tax benefits. As a practical matter, these benefits reduce the cost of acquiring and maintaining the insurance.

GROUP TERM SECTION 79

Section 79 of the Internal Revenue Code provides a special rule for certain group-term insurance provided by an employer. Basically, it provides that, if the requirements of the section are met, an employee has no imputed income by reason of the employer providing him or her with up to $50,000 of life insurance coverage each year. Income is imputed to an employee to the extent that the group term coverage exceeds $50,000 a year. However, the amount imputed is very low compared to the real cost of the insurance coverage, and that, of course, is beneficial. The employer will get a deduction for whatever the insurance costs, but the employee will have to include in income only the value of coverage in excess of $50,000. That amount will be much less than the real cost of the insurance.

As with many tax benefits, the Internal Revenue Code sets forth several conditions in order to obtain group-term section 79 benefits and limits the benefits which can be provided under such a plan. As a general matter, all employees must be covered and discrimination among employees is prohibited. Although the benefits of group-term section 79 vary from business to business, you may find that trying to "style" your insurance as a group-term section 79 plan is not cost effective. You may be better off just buying the best insurance you can for your employees, if you want to provide them with that benefit, and acquire individual (non-group) insurance for yourself.

If your business operates as a partnership, the partners will not be entitled to the tax benefits which section 79 plans can provide. The section applies to owners only if the owners are employees of a corporation. In any case, as indicated, many companies have discovered that the potential income tax favorable benefits of section 79 are not worth the costs of complying with it.

Company "Split-Dollar"

EXPLANATION

Not infrequently, an employer and an employee (and sometimes a corporation and a shareholder) will agree to split the benefits of a life insurance policy. Such arrangements are usually called "split-dollar" plan arrangements or contracts.

Usually, the employer and the employee agree to own a life insurance policy in such a way so that, if the employee dies, the insurance proceeds will be split so that the employer receives an amount equal to the premiums it has paid (or the cash value of the policy immediately before the employee's death), and the employee's beneficiaries receive the balance. If the employer pays the full cost of the insurance, it is the position of the IRS (and at least one court) that the employee has imputed income equal to the cost of one year's worth of term insurance in the amount of the death benefit which the employee's beneficiary would receive if the employee died.

For example, your corporation and you as its CEO, acquire a policy of insurance on your life in the amount of $2 million. In the first year, the employer pays total premiums of $100,000. The first year cash value is less than that, and pursuant to the agreement between you and the corporation, if you die, it gets the $100,000 premium it paid back, and your beneficiaries would receive $1.9 million. In that case, because the employer paid the entire premium, you are treated as receiving compensation equal to the cost of $1.9 million of term insurance coverage for the year.

A special government table is used to determine how much the insurance coverage is worth to you and, therefore, how much you must include in income. It is called the "PS 58" table. The IRS has agreed that if the insurance company which writes the policy offers a one-year insurance policy with a premium less than the PS 58 amount, and almost all companies do, that amount can be included in income instead of the PS 58 amount. In any case, the split-dollar imputed amount (that is, the lesser of PS 58 or one-year term premium charged by the insurance company) almost always is significantly below what the insurance company is actually charged for the term coverage provided under the policy. As a consequence, you may view yourself as benefitting to the extent the income tax on the imputed income is less than what you would have to pay for the insurance coverage the employer is providing. (Even though the insurance company may offer a very inexpensive one-year policy, the term cost of which is used to determine the split-dollar insurance amount, such insurance is rarely acquired and never is used in a split-dollar arrangement, which always involves a cash value policy.)

There may be additional benefits as well. First, you include in income only the split-dollar imputed income amount for a person your age even if you are "rated" so that the actual insurance premiums are being charged as though you were much older than you are. Second, although the law imputes income as though the insurance were cancelable each year (and, therefore, represents only one year's worth of term insurance), in many circumstances you will be confident that the insurance will last for a much longer period of time.

If the employee pays the portion of the premium equal to the split-dollar imputed income amount, then the employee has no imputed income. Some employers, in fact, provide as a bonus a sufficient amount to the employee so that the employee can pay the income tax on the bonus and have enough left over to pay the split-dollar imputed income amount.

PROBLEMS AND UNCERTAINTIES OF SPLIT-DOLLAR

One of the problems with split-dollar insurance is that with a traditional cash value policy, the amount of coverage which the employee receives each year goes down as the premiums paid by the employer (and the cash value) increase and the death benefit remains level. See Chart 15.5. For instance, in the example above, it was assumed that of the $2 million policy your beneficiaries would receive $1.9 million if you died the first year. By the tenth year of coverage, your beneficiaries may receive less than $1 million. By the twentieth year, your beneficiaries may receive less than $100,000 of the $2,000,000 paid at your death. The reason is that by that time the cash value has grown to $1.9 million; pursuant to the split-dollar contract the employer is to receive the amount if you then die.

Some policies are designed so that the term coverage (and, therefore, the amount the employee's beneficiaries would receive) remains constant. However, the amount of imputed income (or the amount the employee must pay to avoid imputed income) goes up each year because the employee is older each year. Where the death benefit goes down, the overall amount imputed each year may not increase dramatically. However, where the amount of coverage provided to the employee remains more or less constant, there will come a point where the cost of the insurance will be very high. In some cases, it may have been more efficient to have provided insurance coverage to the employee in a way which will not result in imputed income to the employee later in life when the amount of imputed income will be high.

As indicated, the current rules relating to the tax consequences of maintaining a split-dollar contract have been developed by the IRS and do not necessarily reflect the law. Although widely accepted, and approved by at least one court, there is no definitive law approving that treatment. In fact, the IRS has given some indication that it may change its position in regard to the consequences of maintaining a split-dollar contract between an employer and an employee (or a corporation and a shareholder). Originally, the IRS treated the split-dollar arrangement as an interest-free loan by the employer to the employee. When the IRS lost a case which stated that an employee did not have to include in income anything on account of an interest-free loan made by his or her employer, it changed its position and theorized that the benefit which is provided the employee was equal to the value of one year's worth of term insurance. In 1984, however, the Internal Revenue Code was amended to provide that an employee does have imputed income by reason of an interest-free loan from the employer. Recently, the IRS has indicated that those changes to the Internal Revenue Code may affect the consequences of a split-dollar agreement. For many, that would significantly reduce the benefits which a split-dollar arrangement may provide. For some (especially those who are older and/or while interest rates are low), the change in treatment could be beneficial. Nonetheless, where a split-dollar contract, as it is currently treated by the IRS, is regarded as beneficial, it may be appropriate to enter such an arrangement. If the IRS does change its position about the tax consequences, the arrangement probably can be terminated. It is likely, in any case, that any change by the IRS would be prospectively only and pre-existing split-dollar arrangements would be "grand-fathered."

There are several variants of split-dollar arrangements. Many of them result in additional benefits to the employee. Some advisors believe that there is no additional imputed income by reason of providing such additional benefits. Several lawyers, however, believe that there will be additional tax consequences to such extra benefits. You should be aware of the potential additional consequences of any special split-dollar arrangement which your company enters into either with you or other employees.

There is one additional potential adverse consequence of a split-dollar arrangement between you and your corporation if you own the majority of voting stock in it (or, if your company is a partnership, and you are a general partner in it). It appears to be the position of the IRS that if you own a majority of voting stock in any corporation which owns (or you are a general partner in a partnership which owns) even a portion of a policy of insurance on your life that all of the proceeds will be subject to tax in your estate. That will be the case even if, for example, the death benefit portion is owned by a member of your family. (In the usual case, the insurance owned by another family member would not be in your estate.) Almost always, individuals want the death benefit to be excluded from their estates for tax purposes. Usually, that can be accomplished by having someone other than you own the insurance. However, if you wish to accomplish that result but also enter into a split-dollar insurance arrangement with a corporation of which you currently own a majority of the voting stock, you should consider the estate tax effects with your tax advisors.

If your company operates as an S corporation, additional and potentially devastating consequences may occur if it enters into a split-dollar arrangement with you or any other shareholder. The IRS once announced (although somewhat unofficially) that a split-dollar arrangement between an S corporation and one of its shareholders constituted a second class of stock. Because an S corporation can have only one class of stock, a split-dollar contract between the company and a shareholder, according to the IRS, would cause the corporation to lose its S status. Although the IRS has somewhat mellowed on its position, it seems as though it has not dropped it altogether. Hence, before you let your S corporation enter a split-dollar contract with any person who is a shareholder (even if it is claimed that the arrangement only is being entered with that person in his or her capacity as an employee), check with your tax lawyer or tax accountant. In fact, you should consider getting a ruling from the IRS on the matter.

Family "Split-Dollar"

On an increasing basis, the benefits (and ownership) of a policy of insurance are divided or split between family members in a way similar to that involving employers and employees (or corporations and shareholders). Such an arrangement is sometimes referred to as "family split-dollar." It appears that rather than resulting in imputed income, a family split-dollar arrangement could result in an imputed gift where the cost of a benefit made available to one family member is provided by premiums paid by another. Although not absolutely clear, it appears that the tax consequences would be similar to company split-dollar arrangements—that is, the amount of imputed gift benefit will be the lower of the PS 58 cost or the one-year term insurance cost charged by the insurance carrier.

Family split-dollar, it appears, if properly structured, may be used to keep the term insurance element from being subject to death tax while allowing the insured or someone else access to the income tax-deferred investment environment of the cash value component of the policy. That arrangement, however, may be dependent, in part, on the type of product used and other factors. If you or any member of your family have a need for insurance, owning through a family split-dollar arrangement may be especially effective. You should explore this concept with a tax advisor and an insurance representative who are experienced with it; unfortunately few are.

How Split-Dollar Insurance Can Leverage Gift Tax Exclusions

As mentioned earlier, although it is not entirely free from doubt, it appears that whether the split-dollar contract is one entered into with a company (such as the insured's employer) or a family member, the amount of imputed benefit is equal to the split-dollar amount (which is the lower of the PS 58 amount or the term cost of insurance quoted by the insurance company). That split-dollar imputed amount is almost always less than the real cost of the term insurance charged under the insurance contract owned in the split-dollar arrangement. Where the person or entity holding the term insurance (death) benefit component pays that amount, there should be no imputed income or gift as a result of the split-dollar arrangement. However, in fact, the cash value component (owned by the other party to the split-dollar contract) provides, in effect, a subsidy to the person or entity owning the death benefit component. That means that more insurance can be provided for the same gift tax cost or the same level of insurance can be provided at a lower gift tax cost.

For example, the insured's spouse and three children are beneficiaries of the irrevocable life insurance trust which owns the death benefit component of the policy. The insured may make total transfers each year free of gift tax to the trust under the protection of the $10,000 annual exclusion of up to $70,000 ($10,000 for the insured's spouse and $20,000 for each of the insured's children assuming the insured's spouse will "gift split"). Of course, the amount available for transfer under the protection of the annual exclusion has to be reduced by other gifts made during the year to the family members.

That means, in effect, that the insured can pay $70,000 a year in premiums with respect to the term insurance element owned by the irrevocable life insurance trust without paying any gift tax. However, if the irrevocable life insurance trust only has to pay the split-dollar imputed amount, the amount needed to be transferred each year to the trust will drop. For some policies, it will drop to about $40,000. Alternatively, it means that the amount of total term insurance cost could increase to about $110,000 a year with some insurance contracts. Yet, under the split-dollar arrangement, it appears that the trust only has to pay at the split-dollar imputed amount which would be only about $70,000 a year. As indicated, under the example, it is assumed that the insured can transfer that amount each year to the trust free of gift tax. The difference between the actual cost of the insurance of $110,000 and the split-dollar imputed amount of $70,000 is charged to the cash value component owned by, perhaps, the family business, a special investment company, the insured's spouse or the marital deduction trust for the insured's spouse, and it appears that subsidy will occur without imputed income or imputed gift tax liability.

That leverage of annual exclusions through split-dollar insurance can also occur with respect to the insured's gift tax exemption equivalent. It also can reduce the amount of gift tax paid where the amounts given or deemed given to the trust exceed exclusions and exemptions.

Potential Ultimate Problem with Split-Dollar

Even though the amount imputed as income or as a gift on account of a split-dollar arrangement is less than the real cost of insurance being provided, the projected amount of income or gift increases over time. At older ages, it can be very large. If you anticipate maintaining the insurance for a long time, some consideration should be given in the early planning stages for "exit strategies." One commonly used is for the employee (or family member or trust) who owns the death benefit component to buy out the cash value component from its owner. Some life insurance representatives believe that the purchase price only has to equal the premium paid by the owner of the cash value component even if that component is worth much more. Others believe the purchaser will have income in that case if the cash value exceeds the premiums which have been paid for the cash value component. To be conservative, you should explore other exit strategies with your advisors.

One plan to consider is having the owner of the death

benefit component fund and own part of the cash value component. That cash value should build on a tax-deferred basis and eventually can be substituted as part of the liquidity for which the death benefit was being maintained.

HOW TO PREVENT LIFE INSURANCE PROCEEDS FROM BEING SUBJECTED TO TAX

How Life Insurance Is Taxed

DEATH TAX

Life insurance proceeds are includable in the estate of the insured if one of two conditions exist. If you provide for the insurance to be paid to your estate, the proceeds are includable in your estate for tax purposes. The insurance is treated as paid to your estate not just by naming your estate as the beneficiary but by arranging for the proceeds to be used to pay off an obligation your estate otherwise would have to pay. For example, if you are indebted to a lender and insurance is payable to the lender so that your estate is not obligated to pay off the loan, the proceeds will be treated as payable to your estate and they will form part of your tax estate. Similarly, the proceeds will be included in your taxable estate if you require the beneficiary to use the proceeds to pay your estate taxes.

Even if the proceeds are payable to someone other than your estate, they will be includable in your estate if you hold at or within three years of death any ownership interest in the policy. That ownership interest is called "incidents of ownership" under the tax law. Basically, incidents of ownership include your right to receive or your right to control the economic benefits of the policy, its cash value (if any) or the death proceeds.

In some cases, that ownership is imputed to the insured and that often can be a problem for the owner of a closely-held business. For example, your company owns a policy of insurance on your life which is payable to your spouse. If you own more than 50% of the voting stock of the company, the ownership held by the corporation will be imputed to you for estate tax purposes. Moreover, if you are a general partner in a partnership, even if you own less than a majority interest in it, the IRS probably will attempt to tax in your estate any insurance on your life which is payable to someone other than the business itself. (There is an exception for group term section 79 insurance, discussed earlier.)

Different states provide different rules with respect to the death taxation of life insurance proceeds. Sometimes, the rules are more favorable to taxpayers. In any case, if you structure the ownership of the life insurance policy so as not to be includable in your estate for federal estate tax purposes, you almost certainly will avoid state death tax as well.

GIFT TAX

Designating someone as the beneficiary of a policy is not considered a completed gift for tax purposes. Hence, no gift tax is paid merely by naming a beneficiary regardless of the size of the policy or how likely death may be. On the other hand, if you irrevocably designate someone as the beneficiary of a life insurance policy, if you assign ownership of the policy to someone else or if you pay premiums on a policy which is owned by someone else, you will be deemed to be making a gift.

Almost always, when you attempt to avoid estate taxation of life insurance, you face gift taxation. The reason is simple. If you own the insurance policy when you die, the proceeds will be taxed as part of your estate. To avoid that, you probably will arrange for someone else to own the policy. However, if you continue to pay for the insurance owned by someone else you will be making a gift. That will be discussed in more detail later.

INCOME TAX

As a general matter, proceeds of life insurance paid upon the death of the insured are not includable in gross income. However, those proceeds paid to a corporation can be subject, at least in part, to the corporate alternative minimum tax. (That problem does not occur for an S corporation.) If you have arranged for insurance on your life or the life of someone else to be paid to your corporation, you should discuss the matter with your company's tax advisor to determine whether alternative minimum tax may be due on the proceeds and, if so, what action may be appropriate to avoid that result.

In addition, if the policy has been acquired "for value" other than from the insurance company the proceeds in excess of what has been paid for the policy are subject to ordinary income tax. As indicated, that transfer-for-value rule does not apply where the policy is acquired directly from the insurance company. Hence, if your child acquires a policy on your life from an insurance company, the proceeds paid at your death to him or her should not be subject to income tax even though he or she acquired the policy for value from the insurance company. On the other hand, if your child bought the policy from anyone else after its original issuance, a portion of the proceeds probably will become subject to income tax in his or her hands. The transfer-for-value rule does not apply to a policy you transfer to someone by gift.

The tax law provides some exceptions to the rule that proceeds may be subject to income tax if the policy is acquired for value. Some of those exceptions can be used effectively by owners of closely-held business. The acquisition of the policy by the insured himself or herself falls under the exception. A corporation in which the insured is a shareholder or an officer also falls under the exception as does an acquisition by a partnership of which the insured is a partner.

It appears that if you structure a trust so that its income is attributed to yours, the purchase of the policy by the trust on your life will fall under the exception provided for acquisitions by the insured himself or herself. For example, your company owns a policy of insurance on your life. You are in the process of selling your business and wish that policy to be owned by your children. You could acquire the insurance and then give it to your children but if your death occurs within three years, the proceeds will be includable in your estate. If your children buy the policy from the company, the proceeds may be subject to income tax when they are paid. If, however, you create a trust so its income is taxed to you, the proceeds should not be subject to income tax when you die even if the trust buys the policy. That is because for income tax purposes (but not estate tax purposes) you should be treated as the one buying the policy and that falls under an exception to the transfer-for-value rule.

It is important to emphasize that the transfer-for-value rule which causes a portion of the proceeds to be subject to income tax does not apply where the transfer is made by gift. Also, as stated, it does not apply where the policy is acquired directly from the insurance company by someone other than the insured. However, only someone with an "insurable interest" in the life of the insured can acquire a policy on someone's life directly from the insurance carrier. Insurable interest means having an economic stake in the life of the insured person. Members of the immediate family, the insured's business or a business in which the owner is a key employee are common examples of persons or entities who have an insurable interest. The IRS has taken the position that where someone without an insurable interest acquires a policy, the proceeds will be subject to income tax. In any event, you should be sure, if there is any doubt about it, that a direct acquisition from the insurance company does not violate the insurable interest laws of your state.

How to Avoid or Reduce Estate and Related Taxes Associated with Life Insurance

IN GENERAL

As explained above, if the proceeds are payable to your estate or you hold at or within three years of death any ownership interest in the policy, the proceeds will form part of your taxable estate. If you are married, and the proceeds are paid to your spouse, or to a qualifying form of trust for the benefit of your spouse, the proceeds may not be subject to tax by reason of the estate tax marital deduction. However, if your spouse does not survive you, the marital deduction will not be available. Even if your spouse does survive, the unexpended proceeds will be includable in your spouse's estate when your spouse later dies.

In any case, if you make the proceeds payable to someone other than your estate and you do not hold at or within three years of death any ownership in the policy, the proceeds will not be subject to estate tax when you die regardless of the identity of the recipient. If you already own a policy, usually the only practical way to avoid that ownership is to assign it to someone (and hope that occurs more than three years before your death).

On the other hand, if you do not already own the policy, you usually will be able to arrange for someone (with an insurable interest) to be the initial owner of the policy. In that case, the proceeds will not be subject to estate tax (unless they are payable to your estate) even if you die within three years of the issuance of the policy.

DETERMINING THE OWNERS OF INSURANCE ON YOUR LIFE

Arranging for your children, for example, to acquire the insurance on your life, if they are adults, is usually a relatively easy matter. You will not cause the proceeds to be includable in your estate even if you pay the initial premium or all of the premiums.

Having your children, however, acquire the insurance on your life may not turn out to be a wise decision. If a child of yours predeceases you, the child's own family members probably will inherit the child's ownership in the policy. That may include a former child-in-law of yours and you may not wish that person to be a participant of the insurance proceeds. Indeed, you may feel uncomfortable in having someone who is no longer related to you own insurance on your life and, therefore, be benefitted by your death.

Where significant amounts of insurance are involved, it may be best to have a trust for the benefit of your family acquire the insurance. The administration of insurance in such a case generally is simpler. Moreover, you can designate who the beneficiaries of the trust (and therefore, the insurance proceeds) will be if your children or other descendants of yours predecease you. The trust also can be structured so your surviving spouse can benefit from the proceeds (such as receiving income which the proceeds generate) without causing the proceeds to be includable in your spouse's estate. Thus, the proceeds will not be eroded by estate taxes when your spouse dies.

MINIMIZING GIFT AND GENERATION-SKIPPING TRANSFER TAXES

Whenever you arrange, however, for someone else to own insurance on your life which you pay for, you will be making a gift. In most cases, the amount of the gift will be the amount of premiums paid (or the approximate cash value of the policy if you already own it and transfer it to someone else). If you transfer the policy directly to another individual (or pay the premiums on a policy owned directly by another individual), those transfers can qualify under the protection of the $10,000 annual exclusion.

Special rules, however, apply where life insurance is owned by a trust. Special provisions must be contained in the trust which permit the beneficiaries to demand property from the trust in order to allow transfers to it to qualify for the $10,000 annual exclusion. Sometimes, the insured fears that the beneficiaries will demand property from the life insurance trust and thereby ruin the purposes for which the trust was created and the insurance is carried. That very rarely has happened. Usually, the family understands the purposes for the arrangement and will not exercise any rights of withdrawal. Moreover, almost always, the family is aware (or can be made aware) that the trustee holds the power to cut off additional rights to the trust, and that may happen if a beneficiary takes inappropriate action. Moreover, if beneficiaries do withdraw property from the trust, you can stop providing the funds to pay for the premiums.

Life insurance trusts are somewhat complex. You should seek the advice of a tax advisor before creating one. In almost all cases, it will be appropriate for you to discuss the acquisition of insurance with your advisor well before anyone applies for the insurance. If you acquire the insurance, you will have to live at least three years after you transfer it, in almost all cases, to avoid having the proceeds form part of your tax estate. If you arrange, however, for someone else to acquire the insurance (such as a trust for members of your family), you can avoid the transfer-within-three-years-of-death rule if you follow the advice of a competent practitioner.

Whenever the beneficiaries of insurance may include grandchildren or more remote descendants, consideration must be given to the special (and onerous) generation-skipping transfer tax which can apply to transfers to them. That tax is discussed in detail in Chapter 14. How you can minimize that tax will be important for you to consider. You should seek advice about avoiding that tax long before you acquire a policy or assign a policy you already own.

WHY GIFTS WITH RESPECT TO LIFE INSURANCE OFTEN MAKE SENSE

Not infrequently, the level of gifts made with respect to maintaining a life insurance policy owned by another may be considerable. Sometimes, the gifts will be so large that gift tax will be due. Using annual exclusions and your $600,000 gift tax exemption to avoid paying gift tax on life insurance transfers may be cost effective only if the insurance is carried to your death. Not infrequently, insurance is terminated before the insured dies. In that case, you will have paid gift tax (or used annual exclusions or your gift tax exemption) on transfers to keep the insurance out of your estate to no avail. You may have been better off using the exemption, annual exclusions or paying gift tax with respect to other transfers.

Life insurance is very often uniquely suited for ownership by another person to avoid having the proceeds eroded by death tax. Almost always, one or more of the reasons for carrying the insurance relate to fulfilling needs which arise after death. In most cases, preventing the proceeds from being eroded by death tax will help fulfill those goals and will reduce the need for insurance.

For example, your insurance representative convinces

you that you need $10 million of insurance in order to pay the $10 million of estimated estate taxes which will arise at your death on the value of your business. If you do not arrange for someone other than yourself to own the insurance, the proceeds will be eroded by estate taxes probably down to no more than $4.5 million. That means, in effect, that to provide your estate with $10 million net proceeds, you would have to carry about $22 million of insurance so that after death taxes your estate would have $10 million. It also means that you will be paying more than twice as much for insurance—gift tax almost always will be less expensive. For example, if the $10 million of insurance is costing you $100,000 per year, $22 million of insurance will cost about $220,000. Even if you have to pay a 55% gift tax on each premium, you can arrange for the proceeds not to be subject to estate tax, and it will cost you only $55,000 a year in gift tax to do that. Hence, for a price of $155,000 per year (a $100,000 premium and a $55,000 gift tax) you can have your survivors net $10 million of proceeds. If you do not arrange for the insurance to be owned by someone other than yourself, you will have to pay $220,000 a year (all premiums, no tax) to have your survivors net $10 million at your death. (By the way, your survivors, or the trust which owns the policy, can make the insurance proceeds available to your estate for the payment of taxes, etc., by buying assets from your estate, almost always without income tax consequences, or by lending funds to your estate.)

In some cases, other members of your family, such as your children, can acquire the insurance and pay the premiums. That will avoid gift taxation but few children are in a financial position to do that. Overall, it usually is best, if it is anticipated that insurance will be carried for a long time, for you to arrange for someone else to own the insurance and for you to pay the premiums. In some cases, such as with company and family split-dollar, the amount of the gift being made by paying for insurance owned by another can be reduced because of the relatively low amount imputed as the cost of the insurance when a split-dollar arrangement is used.

TYPES OF PRODUCTS

Two Types Are Really Only One

If you ask most people in the industry, you will be advised that there are two basic types of life insurance: term and cash value. In fact, the management of some insurance companies is aligned on the basis of term products and cash value products. Often, there is considerable rivalry between the two with the cash value side referring to those on the term side as "termites."

In fact, there is only one real type of life insurance: term insurance. A cash value policy is a coupling of a term policy with an investment feature. Although the investment component is treated as life insurance for certain state law and tax purposes, from a financial and risk perspective it is not really insurance.

Term

MOST OF YOUR OTHER INSURANCE IS TERM INSURANCE

As explained above, almost all the insurance you ever acquire is term insurance. Your household, automobile, liability, casualty and other types of insurance are written for a specific period of time, or term. Usually, that term is one year. If the event you insure against (such as an accident with your automobile) occurs, the insurance company will pay you as provided under the policy. Life insurance works the same way.

HOW IT WORKS

When you acquire a term policy, you are provided with coverage for that term (almost always, one year). If you die within that term, your beneficiaries will be paid as provided under the policy. If you live for the term, usually no payments are made although some companies pay dividends or provide additional types of payments in the event you become disabled, etc.

Chart 15.3 illustrates a typical one year term policy. You pay a premium, the coverage lasts for the term and the coverage then ceases, unless you die, in which case the death benefit is paid.

CHART 15.3
**A Chart Illustration of an Example of Term Insurance
(e.g., for one year)**

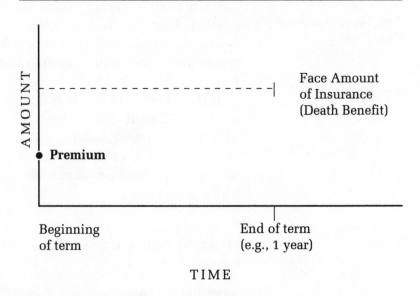

Face Amount
of Insurance
(Death Benefit)

● **Premium**

Beginning
of term

End of term
(e.g., 1 year)

TIME

Other Types of Term Life Insurance

Individuals sometimes have need for insurance for one year only. For example, you might be required by a lender to carry insurance on your life (payable to the lender) while the loan is outstanding. If it is a one-year loan, the lender may insist that you get only a one-year policy.

Most of us, however, who have a need for insurance usually conclude that it is going to be needed for longer than one year. As explained earlier, I determined, for example, that my need for insurance probably would last for at least 20 years, until my wife and I become vested in the retirement plan at my law firm. In effect, I wanted insurance for at least a 20-year term. Insurance companies make 20-year term insurance available by allowing you to renew the insurance each succeeding year without medical examination. Generally, that type of insurance is more expensive than one which automatically expires at the end of each year and can be renewed only if you undergo (and pass) a new medical examination each year. Few individuals want to take that risk, so most acquire term products which allow automatic renewal without further medical examination. Chart 15.4 contains an illustration of such a policy. However, you do have the alternative of not renewing and instead undergoing a new medical exam each year and, if you pass it, acquire a new term policy each year which also contains a renewal feature. Over time, that may reduce the cost of carrying the insurance. However, comparative shopping will show whether or not the savings will be significant.

Generally, there are three ways in which insurance companies charge for term rates. In fact, you can consider them three types of term insurance. One is known as "annual renewable term." With such insurance, all persons of the same age pay the same rate regardless of how long each has held the policy. For example, all 50 year olds pay the same rate. In other words, a 40 year old, who acquired the policy ten years ago, pays the same rate (now that he or she is 50) as another 50 year old who "passes" a medical examination now and acquires a term policy. The second type is known as "select and ultimate." Generally, with "re-entry" term, once you pass the medical examination, you pay a certain rate but if you agree to undergo and pass another medical at a later time, you get a (new) lower rate. The third is know as re-entry term (a subset of select and ultimate). Typically, these term policies provide very inexpensive rates for the first year or so, but the rates then significantly increase. Not all companies provide all three types. Indeed, the three types of insurance reflect different philosophies.

The key point is that even though it may seem that purchasing term insurance must be the easiest of life insurance product selection decisions to make, it shows that even acquiring term insurance can be a complex matter. Probably, you should obtain the services of an experienced and well-trained life insurance field representative who can provide you with illustrations from various carriers representing various different types and help you choose the one which is best for your circumstances. Furthermore, when selecting an insurance field representative, you should look for one who

CHART 15.4
**A Chart Illustration of an Example of Renewable
Term Insurance**

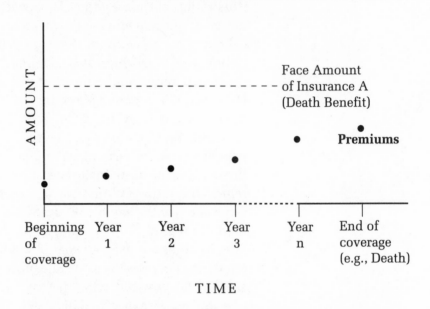

TIME

has a track record of servicing his or her client's needs over the long term; you may not be well served by choosing a sales representative merely because he or she appears to offer the "cheapest" product but is the type of person who is not willing to continue to service your insurance needs.

In any case, with a typical term policy, whether or not it can be renewed without medical examination each year, the premiums increase (because each year there is a greater probability that you will die) and the amount of death benefit remains level.

Most insurance companies will only write pure term life insurance through a certain age, such as age 70. If you live longer than that, the insurance coverage ends.

When an individual reaches advanced ages (such as over the age of 90), the probability of death, on average, is so great that the premiums become very large. It does not mean, however, that the insurance is any less of a bargain at that age than at an earlier age. A 25 year old, for example, can acquire insurance at a very inexpensive price. However, the probability that the insurance company will have to pay a death benefit is very remote. For a 90 year old, the premium will be high but the probability is relatively great that the individual will die within the year.

Keep in mind that the anticipated mortality for all individuals of a particular age (or those who are treated as of that age) is a major factor in determining the cost of the insurance. If you are at an age where 1% of the population will die before reaching the next birthday, the insurance carrier needs to charge you 1% of the face benefit just for the mortality cost. If there is a 5% probability that individuals of your age will die, the carrier must charge five times as much for the same amount of death benefit. You should be aware, however, that in setting term premiums, different companies use different data. Some use historic data, while others project into the future. Usually, the rates quoted in the policy are not guaranteed, although there may be a maximum guarantee charge. The fact that the rates usually are not guaranteed makes comparisons somewhat difficult. Working with comparative guarantees may not be helpful because companies rarely, if ever, use them.

Cash Value Insurance

WHAT REALLY IS HAPPENING

A cash value policy has two components: a term (or death benefit) component and a cash value (or investment) component. Usually, the sum of the death benefit plus the cash value equals the stated death benefit. Chart 15.5 illustrates what happens with a typical cash value policy.

You will note from Chart 15.5 that the amount for which the insurance carrier really is at risk goes down each year and cash value is substituted. In other words, the amount of real insurance that you are provided each year goes down. By the thirtieth year of coverage, for example, the amount of real insurance coverage is very small and almost all of the coverage is provided by cash. Because you already own the cash (and usually can demand it at any time), there is very little for which the insurance company is at risk. Even though you are much older at that time, the premiums for the death

CHART 15.5
A Chart Illustration of an Example of Traditional Cash Value Insurance

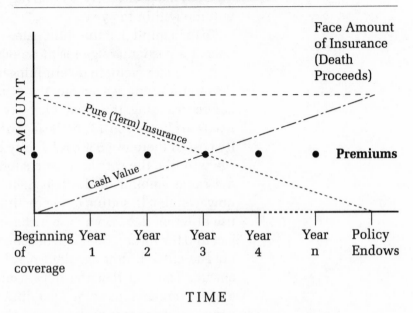

benefit are not very high because the amount of real death benefit coverage is very low. In fact, if you live long enough, the policy's cash value will equal the death benefit and, in many cases, at that time the face amount of the policy will be paid to its owner.

Many cash value policies provide for a level premium. For example, you pay the same premium at age 72 that you paid when you acquired the policy at age 30. Obviously, there is a much greater risk when you are 72 that you will die in the next year than when you were 30. Yet the insurance carrier appears to be charging you the same premium. As indicated above, however, you are not being provided the same amount of insurance. The amount of real insurance coverage is reduced (and substituted with cash). Because there is less real insurance (that is, the amount for which the insurance carrier is at risk), the amount it has to charge you for insurance goes down. In addition, the cash value will be producing income itself which the insurance carrier, in effect, uses to pay part of the cost of the term insurance coverage, in some cases. As explained earlier, it is efficient from an income tax perspective to allow income earned on the cash value component to be used to pay the term insurance element; that produces, in effect, tax deductible life insurance. Traditional cash value policies, however, are not usually designed to maximize that potential benefit.

You may have heard of the phrase "buy term and invest the difference." In other words, some people claim that what you should do is buy term insurance, save on your own the amount of extra premium which you otherwise would have had to pay for a cash value policy and, over time, self-insure. However, that is what happens when you buy a cash value policy: You are buying term (although the amount of term coverage decreases) and the difference is saved for you by the insurance company in the cash value component of the policy.

VARIANTS OF CASH VALUE INSURANCE

Whole Life

Sometimes, cash value insurance is called whole life insurance or by a somewhat similar name. Usually, in the industry, whole life refers to a policy which is "paid up" (that is, no further premiums need to be made to carry the insurance) at a certain age. Paid-up insurance only means that, based upon estimates, the policy will have adequate cash value so that its expected income will be sufficient to pay for the term insurance component at such a level that the death benefit will remain level even though no additional premiums are paid. Almost always, if the investment performance is less than forecasted, the owner will be required to make additional premium payments in order to maintain the original death benefit.

Universal Life

Universal life more classically illustrates the separate term (or death benefit) component and the cash value (or investment) component of a policy. Usually, it allows the policy owner to vary the level of death benefit and vary the amount of cash value. Generally, premiums can be paid so as to maintain the death benefit (or term insurance component) constant. Any cash value can be in addition to the face amount of term insurance coverage. In other words, if the insured dies when there is positive cash value, the term element plus the cash (or investment) value will be paid if that structure is chosen. (Both components, generally, are treated as life insurance proceeds for tax purposes and neither, in the usual case, is subject to income tax). In contrast, with the more traditional cash value policy, the sum of the term benefit and cash value equals the face amount of the policy; the policy does not pay the face amount plus the cash value.

Chart 15.6 presents an illustration of a universal policy. It assumes that there is a level death benefit and there is a significant cash value (or investment) component. You should be aware that the amount of death benefit can be reduced and the cash value kept very small.

Some sales representatives recommend universal life because there is greater flexibility than with a traditional cash value policy. While the insured is young, the insured can pay the term premium, because the cost is relatively low. The insured may not have adequate resources to pay additional premiums which will be credited to the cash value component. As the insured ages, and the cost of term insurance goes up but the financial wherewithal of the insured increases, the insured can pay premiums in excess of the cost of term insurance, thereby building cash value and allowing the owner to reduce the level of term insurance, the cost of which increases each year.

Variable Life

Variable life insurance is similar to universal in that the policy separately illustrates the death benefit (or term) component and the cash value (or investment) component. See Chart 15.6. One unique difference, however, between the two is that with a variable policy the owner usually gets to

CHART 15.6
A Chart Illustration of an Example of
Universal/Variable Insurance (One Mode)

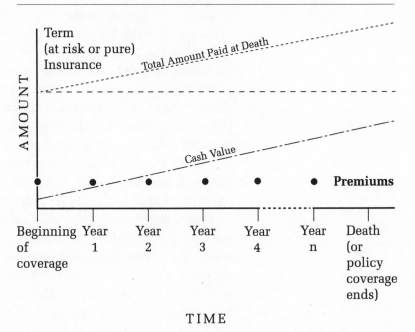

TIME

choose among a complex of mutual funds and money market accounts as to how the cash value component will be invested. (Usually, the insurance carrier also offers an account which it manages.) The insurance carrier may manage the funds or accounts itself, or it may hire outside investment advisors. Some policies make charges for shifting investments from one type of fund or account to another. However, in almost all cases, such transfers from one type of investment can be done income tax free. In other words, you and your advisors can choose how to allocate the cash value among funds rather than allowing the insurance carrier to do so and make changes without income tax consequences. Usually, individuals prefer choosing among investments rather than having no choice. Only a variable product, as a general matter, provides the owner with a choice.

The fact that the owner has a choice produces other ramifications. First, a variable product is regarded as a security under federal securities law. That means that the sales representative must have an appropriate securities license to sell the product. It also means that more disclosures will be made to you as compared to the disclosure made with respect to other types of life insurance policies. Not all sales representatives are licensed to sell such security-based products and, therefore, may not recommend them.

Another major difference between variable products and other types of life insurance relates to the security of the cash value component. Unlike the cash value in other policies, the cash value (or investment) component of a variable product is not subject to the claims of the insurance company's creditors (unless it is in the company's own account). As mentioned above, although certain states provide some insurance protection for the cash value of your policy, it may not provide complete protection. You can protect the cash value (or investment) component of your insurance by choosing a variable product and not having it invested in the account which will allow the insurance company's own creditors to attach the property. Because insurance often is carried for long periods of time, and because the financial strength of a carrier, therefore, may change dramatically over that time, protecting the cash value component (which usually becomes the most significant part of the insurance coverage) from the claims of the insurance company's creditors may be an especially appropriate factor for you to consider in choosing a policy. In fact, for that reason alone you may choose a variable policy rather than any other type of cash value product.

Accidental Death, Travel and Similar Policies

Most other forms of life insurance are merely variants of term (or term plus cash value) insurance. An accidental death policy, for example, merely provides an additional benefit if you die accidentally. Again, the insurance company's own studies indicate the probability of that happening for a person with your particular profile and at your age. Many advisors recommend against acquiring accidental death insurance. The reason is a simple one: Why should your family need more if you die accidentally than if you die from natural causes? In fact, the costs associated with your death probably will be less if you die accidentally than if you die from natural causes. Usually, when people opt for the accidental death rider they do so because it appears to be so inexpensive. However, from an actuarial perspective, it is just as expensive as any other type of insurance. The insurance carrier knows exactly the probability of your death by accident and it is using that as a factor in determining the cost. In fact, each dollar of accidental death premium you pay may produce a bigger profit for the insurance company than for each dollar of regular term insurance premium.

Travel policies typically are term policies but for very short periods of time, such as two weeks or a month. However, in substance, they are just another form of term insurance although, occasionally, different features are added.

Mortgage insurance is nothing but decreasing insurance, usually. In most cases, the amount of debt remaining on your mortgage loan goes down each time you make a mortgage payment. The policy provides a death benefit which parallels the remaining unpaid mortgage debt. Almost always, you can obtain less expensive insurance coverage than that provided by mortgage insurance.

Other Special Features

Policies may provide additional features. Some policies, for example, provide for payment of the death element if you become terminally ill or if you need a life-saving operation such as a lung transplant. Generally, to the extent that the amount paid under the policy during the insured's lifetime exceeds the premiums paid, the excess is taxed as ordinary income. However, the IRS is considering creating an exception if the insured is expected to die within 12 months of the payment of the proceeds.

Some policies provide for a waiver of premiums if you become disabled. Again, you will be charged an additional premium for that feature. The insurance company will determine the cost of that feature by a variety of factors including the probability of someone with your profile (such as whether you skin dive as a hobby) and at your age becoming disabled.

SECOND-TO-DIE INSURANCE

Introduction

Beginning in 1982, property owners were permitted to leave their entire estates to their surviving spouses free of estate tax by reason of the "unlimited" marital deduction. Up until that time, usually only one-half of the property owner's estate could qualify for the marital deduction. Since then, individuals have had an opportunity, as a general rule, to postpone all estate tax until both spouses die. Most couples take advantage of the marital deduction so no federal estate tax is paid when the first of them dies. One of the primary reasons for doing this is that avoiding tax when the first spouse dies means there is a larger base of wealth for the surviving spouse.

However, from the perspective of the couple's descendants (or other ultimate beneficiaries), postponing estate tax until both spouses die may not make good economic sense. One reason is that the estate of the first spouse to die would then be failing to use the lower estate tax brackets which could apply to it. The major reason, however, is that not only will the property which qualified for the marital deduction be subject to tax in the estate of the survivor (unless it is dissipated before the survivor dies) but its growth may be subject to estate tax as well. Where some of the assets which the surviving spouse inherits are anticipated to grow or continue to grow at a rapid rate between the deaths of the spouses, it almost always will be best to intercept the estate tax when the first spouse dies. In fact, it probably is best to intercept the tax while both spouses are living so that the lower gift tax rates can be used.

Because of the ability to postpone taxes until both spouses die, the life insurance industry has developed what are commonly called second-to-die or survivorship policies. (Actually, second-to-die policies were available before 1982 but they were rarely used for a husband and wife. In any case, the number of such policies has proliferated since then.) These policies pay a death benefit, as a general rule, only when both spouses have died. The real selling feature of such policies, however, is the **apparent** low cost of the insurance. Not infrequently, the annual premiums on a second-to-die policy will be a small fraction of what the premiums would be on a policy in which the life of only one of the spouses is insured. Make no mistake about it, however. The second-to-die policy is no less expensive than the single life policy. In fact, it may be more expensive. The key to understanding why is understanding that the insurance company, on average, only pays you back the total premiums you paid plus an interest factor.

Why Second-To-Die Insurance May Cost More

The reason why the annual premiums on a second-to-die insurance policy are lower than those on a single life policy is that the insurance company knows (with certainty) that, on average, it will not have to pay anything for a much longer period of time. It will not have to pay until both you and your spouse die. In fact, in some companies, the **present value** of the cost of second-to-die policies is more than the cost of the same type of single life policy. One of the steps you and your advisors should take is to do a present value cash and benefit analysis of a single life policy and second-to-die policy, both of which appear to be appropriate choices for you.

Several questions or concerns may arise with respect to second-to-die policies. First, fewer companies carry them and, therefore, product choices are fewer. For example, virtually no company offers a variable second-to-die policy although some are in the process of trying to develop one.

Second, certain tax questions arise with second-to-die policies which do not arise with respect to single life policies. For some individuals, those questions can become important. For example, it is unclear whether your spouse alone or both of you are the "insured" for purposes of the transfer-for-value rule, discussed earlier in this Chapter. Also, it is unclear whether you alone, your spouse alone or both of you are the insured shareholder for purposes of imputing incidents of ownership to an insured majority shareholder of your corporation. Several other questions about second-to-die insurance are unanswered because it is of such recent development. Your advisors should be able to tell you whether any could apply to you and might suggest that a second-to-die policy is an inappropriate choice.

Remember, the need to pay premiums will not end with your death but must continue until both you and your spouse die. Even if you acquire a "paid-up" policy, premiums may become due after you die and your spouse lives because the earnings on the cash value of the policy are lower than forecast. Moreover, not infrequently, the surviving spouse will be unable to maintain the insurance premium schedule. In any case, you should be sure that your spouse will be able to continue to pay comfortably the insurance premiums after you die. Usually, it is not cost efficient for you to buy another policy on your life alone to provide cash to your spouse to be able to do that.

The cost to your surviving spouse of maintaining a second-to-die policy after your death may be illustrated with respect to company split-dollar insurance. Some employers buy a policy insuring not only the life of an employee but also the lives of both the employee and the employee's spouse on a split-dollar basis with the employer. The amount of imputed income, in such a case, usually is vastly reduced while both spouses are alive. Rather than using the so-called PS 58 imputed income amount, it appears that the taxpayers may use the PS 38 amount, which, except at advanced ages, is a small fraction of what the PS 58 amount would be. However, once one of the spouses dies, the imputed income (and any gift) will be based on PS 58 rather than PS 38. Moreover, by that time, the surviving spouse may be much older. The jump in imputed income (or imputed gift if the policy is owned by someone other than the insured) can be enormous. That is not to say that using a company (or family) split-dollar arrangement is inappropriate for a second-to-die policy. Rather, it is only to point out that the costs of carrying the insurance through a split-dollar arrangement may increase dramatically at some point although, overall, it still may be the most efficient method of carrying the insurance.

A cost of a second-to-die policy that is often hidden is that taxes almost certainly will be paid at estate tax rates rather than gift tax rates. If you leave your assets and the proceeds of insurance on your life to your spouse under the protection of the marital deduction, your spouse will have the cash to pay the gift tax if he or she transfers your wealth to your children after you die. Generally, the gift tax rates are only about two-thirds of the estate tax rates.

Even if it is inappropriate for your spouse to make a gift of the inheritance received from you shortly after your death, you may nonetheless choose not to use the marital deduction but have the assets placed into a trust for the benefit of your spouse for life so the property will not be includable in your spouse's estate. In any case, if you forego the marital deduction in your estate, the assets can pass free of additional tax when your spouse dies. Although in that case estate taxes will be due at your death, the amount subjected to tax may be significantly less than what would be subjected to tax when your spouse later dies. If your assets are likely to grow faster than the portfolio return which will be produced in a policy of insurance on you and your spouse's life, your family almost certainly will be better off if you subject the property to death taxes when you die and have a policy of insurance on your life alone.

For example, it is anticipated that your business will be worth $10 million at your death. Assuming you arrange for the proceeds not to be subject to estate tax when you die, your advisors tell you that you will need $6 million of insurance proceeds to fund the estate tax when you die. (The $6 million is 60% of the value of your business.) It is anticipated that your spouse will survive you for eight years. If your business is expected to continue to grow at 20% a year after your death, it means that when your wife dies (eight years later) your business will be worth approximately $40 million. That also means that you will need $24 million of insurance to cover the death tax on what is expected to be the value of your business when your spouse dies. Hence, you will wind up needing **four** times more insurance by postponing the tax until your spouse dies. If you and your spouse are of the same age and health, the present value cost of the $24 million survivorship insurance will be about twice as much as the $6 million policy on your life alone.

On an average, if the husband and wife are of the same age, you can acquire twice the face amount of coverage on second-to-die insurance for the same present value of premium cost. (Again, that is attributable to the fact that the insurance company knows, on average, that it will not have to pay the proceeds for a much longer period of time.) On average, one spouse survives the other, of the same age, by about eight years. Hence, if you anticipate that your business will grow at a pace faster than what the insurance company is earning on its investments, it will be appropriate for you to consider acquiring a policy only on your life.

However, the foregoing advice must be tempered by other factors. As explained in more detail in Chapter 14, your surviving spouse may have opportunities to effect greater tax savings if your spouse inherits assets from you free of estate tax than you can achieve if you transfer assets to your children when you die. Nonetheless, very often, it will be beneficial for you to forego a significant portion of the marital deduction at your death. One reason for that is a special credit which may be available to your spouse's estate if your spouse dies within ten years of you and you do not use the marital deduction but place assets in trust for your spouse's benefit. Where it is anticipated that you and your spouse may die within ten years of each other, you should consult with your advisors as to how that credit may be used for your family's benefit.

HOW TO USE LIFE INSURANCE TO ENHANCE INVESTMENT YIELD

Investment Returns

In General

Although many individuals hold funds uninvested (such as in a non-interest bearing checking account), most investors seek as great a return as possible consistent with the risk they are willing to undertake. Failure to invest so as to obtain a return means, conversely, that the value of any account will be eroded by inflation.

THE POWER OF COMPOUNDING

Chapter 8, dealing with retirement planning, discusses the effect of compounding in detail. In any event, over time, a somewhat lower return which compounds usually is better than a somewhat higher return which does not compound. Failure to obtain earnings on earnings reduces effective yield. See Charts 8.1 and 8.2 for examples of the effect of compounding.

THE GREATER POWER OF TAX-DEFERRED OR TAX-FREE COMPOUNDING

As is also explained in more detail in Chapter 8, earnings which compound on a tax-deferred or tax-free basis, over the long term, greatly enhance effective yield. At an income tax bracket of 40% and a 10% return, more than three times the base of wealth will be built if the income tax can be deferred for 30 years (perhaps, a working lifetime) than if the income is taxed each year.

The important point is that tax-free compounding, or even tax-deferred compounding, has the effect of significantly enhancing yield. If the tax rate is 40%, and the return is 7%, avoiding tax has the effect of increasing your return by 280 basis points. By almost anyone's account, that is a substantial increase. As is discussed in more detail in Chapter 8, that is one of the primary benefits of and reasons why people create and fund qualified retirement plans.

Unfortunately, the tax law jealously guards the right to make investments which produce tax-deferred or tax-free returns. Although the taxpayer can acquire tax-free municipal bonds, their yield usually is pared down to just slightly over the after-tax return on comparable risk taxable bonds. Qualified retirement plans and individual retirement accounts are one of the few opportunities to invest on a tax-deferred basis. As indicated, the tax is only deferred with a qualified plan or similar arrangement. Even death will not remove the inherent tax liability. Similarly, the law permits you to acquire a tax-deferred annuity from insurance companies. However, as with qualified retirement plans, the inherent income tax liability never goes away, not even at the owner's death. Moreover, the "loads" for the privilege of investing on a tax-deferred basis with such annuities are relatively high. The insurance company, in effect, prices the product so that it shares in the benefits of tax-deferral with you.

Use of the Tax Favored Investment of Life Insurance

Life insurance may represent one of the best opportunities for investing on a tax-favored basis. Although it may not be a reason alone to acquire insurance, you may wish to consider, with your advisors, using the tax-deferred (and in some cases, tax-free) investment environment which a life insurance policy uniquely offers under the tax law. Also, the fees imposed on investment in life insurance contracts are generally lower than on tax deferred annuities. The problem, however, has been that it seemed that you could not keep the life insurance death benefit out of your estate if you wanted to benefit by investing in the cash value of the policy. However, family split-dollar arrangements, discussed earlier, may let you achieve both goals.

SUMMARY AND CONCLUSIONS

Life insurance is a unique property. It is specially treated for property and tax purposes. Often, that treatment is beneficial. No matter how it is "labelled," life insurance typically consists of a term insurance component and, in some cases, a cash or investment component. Which type of product is best to use, depends upon the particular circumstances and goals to be achieved. In many cases, the need for insurance can be reduced by alternative action. In any event, opportunities to structure the ownership of insurance so as to pay for the term insurance component with income which will never be taxed and to reduce the gift tax costs of paying for insurance are available. Owners of closely-held businesses should consider, in appropriate cases, both company split-dollar insurance and family split-dollar insurance.

CHAPTER 16

HOW CAN I PROTECT MYSELF, MY BUSINESS AND MY FAMILY FROM CLAIMS OF CREDITORS?

Americans are regarded as the most litigious people in the world. Each year, the number of lawsuits increases as does the total size of awards. Jury awards involving billions of dollars have been entered against businesses and upheld by the courts. Damages of tens of millions have been assessed against individuals and upheld by the courts. In addition, government actions can result in civil damages which, by law, can be or must be trebled. In recent years, federal, state and local governments have added automatic penalties, in many cases, where taxes are even innocently underpaid. The law provides little protection to companies and individuals who have large judgments rendered against them. However, through carefully structuring affairs for yourself, your business and your family, you can greatly reduce the prospects of having your wealth eroded by such claims. In fact, in some cases, you can completely immunize assets from claims of all creditors, including claims of the United States Government. This Chapter discusses some of the ways in which liabilities may arise and some of the things you can do to reduce the chances of your base of wealth, and that of your family and your business, being eroded by such claims.

HOW LIABILITY ARISES

Introduction

Liabilities can arise in almost any manner imaginable. In some cases, in fact, the law imposes strict liability. That means if you undertake an activity, you will be held liable for any damage which occurs to another person or to property no matter how careful you were and no matter how reckless the injured party was. Almost always, the liability is enforceable only through a legal action. Knowing how liability can arise and the reasons why you, your family or your business may be a target of claims, provides a base of knowledge which may then be used to protect property from claims.

Motivation to Make a Claim

Claims almost always are founded upon a desire to obtain money or property. Monetary loss, however, is not always the basis of the claim. Sometimes, certain activities provide someone else an opportunity to sue and collect an award even if the suing party is unable to establish actual financial damage or to claim specific property. In many cases, the financial damage cannot be proved directly. In suits for personal injury, for example, the worth of the often claimed "pain and suffering" is extremely difficult to measure. Juries often award damages based upon emotion, because it is impossible to measure the "value" of the pain and suffering which the suing party has experienced.

With rare exceptions, individuals who sue in the United States whether on personal injury, commercial or any other ground have a "heads I win, tails I really can't lose" situation. Unlike lawyers in many other countries, American lawyers, by and large, may accept representation on a contingency fee basis. That means that the lawyer is paid only if and to the extent that an award is made (or a settlement is reached); the fee is equal to a percentage of the amount recovered. Although contingent fee arrangements are governed in certain states, usually they are one-third and sometimes are one-half (and occasionally more) of the amount of the recovery.

The lawyer in analyzing a contingent fee case need not determine whether or not the client's case is a winning one.

All the lawyer needs to know, based upon experience or sometimes a guess, is that it is likely that some recovery (usually by a settlement) can be obtained.

Lawyers, and the public, have learned that certain entities tend to settle cases rather than litigate. Insurance companies make a business out of settling claims either on behalf of policyholders or on the claims made by policyholders. The insurance company often negotiates on behalf of policyholders who are sued and who have a right of indemnification from the insurance company. Lawyers, and the public, have learned to present claims in a way so that the probability of the insurance company offering a payment in settlement is increased. Again, it does not really matter whether the claim is an enforceable one, or, perhaps, even bona fide or brought in good faith; all that matters is that it is presented in a way that it is likely to result in a significant settlement.

Almost all prudent businesses and individuals carry one or several types of liability insurance. Your homeowner's policy, for example, usually provides for your insurer to pay for any damages (and related costs, such as attorney's fees) if someone is injured, claims that you are responsible, and the claim is of the type covered by your homeowner's policy. Both the public and lawyers know that virtually anyone who owns a home will have a homeowner's policy so that if the claim is made against the owner, an insurance company will defend the action on behalf of the homeowner and may settle the claim. In fact, it is commonly known by the public as well as by lawyers (collectively, called the "Bar") that owners of almost all valuable property insure that property.

What that all means is that if you, members of your family or business own significant property, you are likely to be a target of a lawsuit whenever you are connected with damage. Business owners, of course, suffer special danger on account of their employees. Under a special doctrine of the law, employers usually are liable for the actions of their employees.

It sometimes seems that today anyone who is injured is looking for an indemnitor. In many cases, the government provides causes of action. Legislation, for example, granting rights to sue for harassment in the workplace has recently provided a new base of bringing suit where none existed before. Similarly, new federal (and state) legislation providing for almost automatic liability against owners of property or operators of facilities which contain or produce toxic waste has created a new base of liability.

Even if no legislation is enacted to provide a remedy, the courts can develop theories to make one person liable for another. Perhaps, not surprising, even judges (and lawyers) are the subject of lawsuits. For example, the losing party in a lawsuit may sue the presiding judge claiming that the judge rendered the wrong decision (even if it has been upheld on appeal) or that the judge was prejudiced, etc. Several lawyers have been sued by the losing party of lawsuits where the lawyer did not represent that party but represented the winning party.

Even though such suits often are unsound, the procedures under which our American court system operate mean that they are difficult to dismiss and often are extremely costly to defend. One lawyer, for example, incurred over $800,000 in defending himself against the losing party in a lawsuit where the lawyer successfully defended the winning party in a contest over the results of an election in which the two parties to the lawsuit each ran for a local office. The attorney received a rather modest fee for successfully defending the election challenge and could have been financially ruined by the suit brought against him by the loser.

You May Lose Even If You Win

The cost of defending a lawsuit is not just the fees you will have to pay your attorney. Lawsuits can involve a tremendous amount of your personal and professional time. You may be required to give testimony under oath, provide written answers to written questions and make court appearances, as well as discuss matters with your lawyers and others, long before trial is even scheduled. The lawsuit can be emotionally consuming and, if it is against your company, disrupt the flow of business tremendously. Even where you could successfully defend the action, the time may come when almost anyone will consider a settlement.

Not infrequently, parties to a lawsuit will each believe fervently in the correctness of their positions. Over time, lawyers begin to suffer from what might be called "litigator's euphoria." The lawyer works on the matter so long and hard that he or she begins to believe the correctness of the positions taken on behalf of the client even if an objective analysis shows that the suit probably stands little chance of being successful. In such circumstances, it sometimes is best to settle.

Nonetheless, it may behoove you not to settle lawsuits which are frivolous. Allowing your business to develop a reputation as a settler may mean that suits are more likely to be commenced and demands for settlement awards to be higher. The risk you take, of course, in not settling is running up very high levels of legal fees and losing cases which your legal counsellors were confident you would win. It is often difficult, if not impossible, to forecast what a jury, or even judge, will do. You must keep in mind that the jury and the judge will not the know the truth of matters: They will know only what they hear in the courtroom.

Some government agencies, such as the IRS, also know that even weak claims can result in large rewards. The IRS and other tax collection authorities are, virtually by definition, only in it for the money. They are armed by the government with many more weapons to use than taxpayers have defenses. The tax agencies are aware of that and often obtain awards because of taxpayer's fear of such agencies, the agency's virtually unlimited resources and the expense of defending claims they bring.

Contract Liability

Liability can arise for an individual or for a business by reason of entering into a contract and failing to carry out its terms. An obvious example is where a company has paid for a product based upon the promise of another to deliver it at a certain time and the product is not delivered. The contract has been breached by the party who has failed to make delivery and that party, in most cases, is liable for the amount paid for the goods which are not delivered. In fact, in some cases, the party who fails to make delivery may be liable for the value of the product (if worth more than the amount paid) or the value of a substituted product, even if it costs more than the one which was ordered.

Contract liability can arise in more subtle ways as well. Often, individuals and even businesses do not understand that a contract usually does not have to be in writing and that even a course of conduct by parties can constitute a contract. For example, your company delivers fuel to single engine aircraft at a local airfield. You have had difficulties with one of the airplane owners and you decide that you will no longer deal with him. You order your employees that they are not to fulfill his request to put fuel in his plane. The owner leaves a note on your fuel truck saying that his aircraft is to be filled. Your employee, following your instructions, does not fill the plane. The next day, the owner takes off in his aircraft, runs out of fuel, crash lands and is injured. Almost without question, your company will be sued on the theory that the course of conduct you two previously followed constituted a contract under which you promised always to fill his plane upon his request.

Unfortunately, disputes often arise as to what the terms of the contract were. For example, your company sells stocks and bonds. A customer of yours learns that an investment he or she has made has been a loser. Your company is sued because the customer claims that your representative guaranteed that the stock would go up. Even if your employee denies that he made the guarantee, a jury may find otherwise.

Damages for breaches of contracts can be extremely high. For instance, your failure to deliver an inexpensive part, but one which is necessary for another business to complete its work, may make you liable for a large amount where you knew the large damage which the other company would suffer if it was unable to perform.

Tort Liability

Torts comprise a broad category of claims which arise on account of, in effect, a breach of a duty of care other than that which arises by contract. It includes damage caused by negligence (failure to exercise reasonable care), defamation (uttering or printing inaccuracies about a person), certain interferences with contracts other people have made, trespassing on someone's property, appropriating property belonging to someone else for your use and a variety of other claims. The list even includes, in some jurisdictions, the "intentional infliction of emotional distress." Although an innocent and harmless practical joke is not likely to give rise to a claim of intentional infliction of emotional distress, what you believe was just innocent funmaking may be regarded by the person who is the butt of the joke as so horrendous that your actions form the basis of a claim for significant damages.

Common examples of tort claims include injury caused by another's negligence. Damages caused by automobile accidents frequently lead to tort claims. Many states have passed statutes limiting the ability to bring such actions. However, thousands and thousands of tort suits are commenced every year.

Very often, and contrary to most breach of contract claims, damages in tort cases are impossible to measure with precision, although some measure may be possible. For instance, if a person dies as a result of negligence of another (such as in an automobile accident), the surviving family members of the decedent may be entitled to an award equal to the estimated value of the future earnings of the decedent. Often, expert witnesses are used to testify as to the proper measure of damage, and the experts often disagree, but the scope of damage can be determined with some precision. Many tort claims, however, involve damages which are, as a practical matter, impossible to measure with precision. Common ones are claims of pain and suffering, disfiguration, ridicule, etc. Awards in the tens of millions by juries in such cases are not uncommon.

PUNITIVE DAMAGES

In addition, in almost all tort claims, the plaintiff can request what is known as "punitive damages." Even if the actions of the defendant are not criminal, it may be possible to convince a jury, or a judge, that the activity which gave rise to the damage was so outrageous or condemnable that it is appropriate to impose additional damages to serve as a punishment and a deterrent to others. Although in some jurisdictions, and in some types of suits, punitive damages are not permitted or are limited, in many cases there is no limit and they may exceed many times the actual damage which the plaintiff can establish was inflicted.

Statutory Liability

In addition to liability for breach of contract or committing torts, liability may arise under statutes. For example, treble damages can be assessed against a business which violates certain of the so-called "anti-trust" (anti-competitive) laws. In effect, those, and many similar laws, are designed to permit private citizens, who are damaged by certain actions, to bring suit to recover damages. Often, the government also may sue under these laws. Sometimes, as in the case of anti-trust laws, the damages may be trebled and attorney's fees may be awarded. You may wish to discuss with your company's counsel whether the activities your company engages in are uniquely targeted by statute which could make the company (or you or other officers of it) liable for engaging in certain proscribed activity.

It is important to appreciate that liability arising under statutes, and even that arising with respect to torts, does not necessarily mean the activity was immoral. It is simply that the law wishes to either inhibit or eliminate certain activities, and allowing private citizens to brings suits under those statutes is permitted. For torts, wrongdoing is not necessarily the basis of liability. Statutes may impose "strict liability" for certain types of activity which are inherently dangerous. To some degree, the law searches for the party best able to absorb damage caused. For example, in some urban areas, injury caused by certain construction activity automatically entitles the injured party a recovery for certain damages, regardless of the care the construction company exercised or the lack of care which the injured party exercised, in certain cases and subject to certain limits.

Family Obligations

Under the law, you have an obligation to support your spouse and your spouse has an obligation to support you. In addition, both parents have an obligation to support minor children (and in some states even adult children in certain circumstances where there is special need). Usually, in an amicable family setting, no member thinks about the respective obligations of support which are owed.

If the marriage breaks down, however, obligations of support will be considered carefully and may result in the imposition of award for such matters as child support or alimony. Moreover, and as discussed in more detail in Chapter 12, the breakdown of your marriage may result in your spouse having a claim against your property (or a claim that your spouse had an ownership interest in it from the time it was acquired during the marriage).

The financial obligations owed to family members are some of the most rigorously enforced ones under the law. In fact, immunization from the claims of certain creditors often has an exception for obligations owed by reason of family relationships, such as child support.

Taxes, Penalties and Other Government Extracted Payments

Liability for taxes is certain to arise for virtually every American citizen, resident and business. The government, in its own self-interest, rigorously enforces claims for taxes. Although enforcement of taxes usually requires a court judgment, the government's ability to assess taxes and collect them can occur, in some cases, with little if any court supervision or recourse by the taxpayer to the courts.

In addition to private rights of action, some statutes also impose fines or penalties for disfavored types of behavior. These are not necessarily criminal penalties, but they can be very large. Government fines and penalties can be imposed for a myriad of activities. Often, the government will not be required to prove any measure of damage but just establish that the proscribed activity occurred. For example, under the Internal Revenue Code, the intentional failure to file a tax return (even if no tax is due) can result in the imposition of a fine of $20,000 (as well as incarceration). Operating equipment or engaging in other activities in violation of government regulations or rules (such as operating a vehicle without proper registration or the payment of all taxes) can result in automatic and often extremely high fines.

HOW CLAIMS ARE ENFORCED

Introduction

The determination of who is liable for a particular damage is not always certain. Often, more than one party is liable. In some cases, there is an order of liability. However, if one is unable to pay, those who are secondarily liable nonetheless are responsible to pay the claim.

Except for certain taxes and government penalties, where the government agency may be able to proceed even without authorization from a court, usually claims for damages can be enforced only after a judgment of a court. Procedures for when the judgment can be enforced vary widely from jurisdiction to jurisdiction, and in some cases, from court to court within a particular state. However, it usually takes an order of the court for it to be enforced. Except in limited circumstances, a judgment cannot be obtained without notice to the defendant, who must be given the chance to oppose it.

Under the United States Constitution, judgments from one state must be enforced by another. In addition, courts of one country may enforce the judgments of another. Occasionally, pursuant to treaties, one country will be obliged to enforce judgments obtained in another. That does not mean that a lawsuit can be successfully commenced against you or your company anywhere someone wishes. There are rules as to whether or not a court has valid jurisdiction over someone who is sued. However, once a judgment has been entered, it usually can be enforced anywhere in the United States and, in some cases, in other countries.

How Judgments Are Enforced

Different states have different rules for the enforcement of judgments. Occasionally, but only occasionally, the judgment will be against a particular piece of property. However, in the vast majority of cases, the judgment is entered against an individual, a corporation, a partnership or some other legally recognized separate entity, such as a government unit (for example, an incorporated village). In some cases, persons other than the one against whom the judgment was entered may be liable for it. For example, a general partner in a partnership usually is liable for all judgments against the partnership. However, in most circumstances, the party holding the judgment cannot enforce it against the general partner, if the judgment has been rendered against the partnership. Rather, the party holding the judgment against the partnership must commence a lawsuit against the general partner so that the judgment can be enforced against that partner as well as the partnership.

In any case, the enforcement of the judgment actually is made against the property of the person who is liable for the judgment rather than the person himself, herself or itself. Often, it is unclear as to which property is considered as belonging to the person liable for the judgment or which assets of that person are liable for that judgment. In fact, the limitations on what property is liable for a judgment often forms the basis of action to protect property against claims of creditors.

Assets Which Are Liable for Judgments

Federal and state laws prescribe rules as to what assets are liable for judgments rendered against an individual or another entity. Usually, assets which are directly owned are liable. However, various jurisdictions provide exemptions. Common ones include a home, although, in most states, the amount is limited. In some states, such as Florida and Texas, the exemption for a home is either complete or extremely generous.

Property which you own with another person, such as assets you own in common with your spouse, are subject to special rules. Usually, assets owned with another are liable for claims against one of the co-owners only to the extent of that co-owner's interest in the commonly owned asset.

In any case, the exemptions provided by law provide a special opportunity to protect yourself, your family and your business. Nonetheless, the exemptions may not be complete. Exceptions often are made for claims of spouses or other family members to support and to certain government agencies, such as tax authorities.

LIABILITIES FOR CLAIMS AGAINST BUSINESSES

Businesses typically operate in one of three forms: proprietorships, partnerships and corporations. A proprietorship is one in which an individual (or another entity) owns all of the interests in the business directly. Such a form of ownership is sometimes shown as "Jack Jones, doing business as Jack's Emporium" or similar phrases such as "Sarah Smith seamstress." Many businesses in America start, and often continue, as proprietorships.

Liability for Business Operations

PROPRIETORSHIPS

The law does not recognize a proprietorship as a separate legal entity, as a general rule. The owner/operator of the business is directly responsible for claims which arise out of the business, including those to the tax authorities, customers and persons who are damaged by the operation of the business. In that sense, it is the most risky form of business through which to operate. In fact, as indicated, for liability purposes, the business does not exist at all as a separate entity. Again, it has to be emphasized that your personal "fault" is not usually a basis for your liability when it comes to damages which arise in your business. The law simply makes the owner/operator directly responsible for all activities of the business, including activities of employees within the scope of their employment (even, in many cases, if the activity is directly contrary to an enforced set of rules).

PARTNERSHIPS

A partnership exists where two or more individuals (or other entities) join together for profit. Partnerships may be very formal in that they are formed pursuant to a detailed written agreement, acknowledging that the relationship is a partnership, with all appropriate filings. (Many states require that partnership agreements or other documentation with respect to them be filed with the government.) Partnerships, however, more often than not, are formed and carried out through an oral agreement and a course of conduct. In fact, in many cases, the law will imply the existence of a partnership even where the parties have not signed a written partnership agreement, made required government filings for partnerships or filed partnership tax returns.

Partnerships are contractual arrangements. The type of liability which can arise under a breach of contract discussed earlier can occur among the partners. In addition, the partnership gives rise to fiduciary responsibility among the partners to each other and to the partnership. Not infrequently, one individual will sue another claiming that an oral (or implied) partnership has been violated. For example, you have several discussions with a friend of yours about a new product which your company might produce and your friend gives you some suggestions about it. In time, your company produces that or a similar product. Your friend (or now actually a former friend) claims that he or she is entitled to part of the ownership of the product and the profits it produces pursuant to the partnership which the two of you formed.

The law recognizes two types of partnerships: general partnerships and limited partnerships. The primary difference relates to the lack of liability of and control by limited partners. All partners in a general partnership and the general partners in a limited partnership are liable for all claims, as a general matter, entered against the partnership. Most law firms, for example, are operated as general partnerships. Damage caused by any employee of the partnership may make every partner in the law firm personally liable for it even though no partner was aware of the activity which caused the damage.

In a limited partnership, however, the limited partners' liability is limited to the amount which is invested in the partnership (including any additional amount the limited partner has agreed to contribute or for which that partner is otherwise contractually obligated). The liability of limited partners is limited, in part, because their control of the day-to-day activities of the partnership is limited. Labeling a person (or entity) as a limited partner pursuant to a partnership agreement will not in and of itself provide the immunization from liability which a limited partner is entitled to. Rather, the limited partner's activities must be limited pursuant to the terms of the governing instrument and, in fact, the limited partner must not act like a general partner; otherwise the limited partner may be found to be a general one and limited liability may be lost. Usually, a limited partnership may be formed with an entity other than an individual being the general (and, therefore, the liable) partner. Not infrequently, a corporation (which itself usually provides limited liability for its owners) will be the sole general partner in a limited partnership with any individual owners being limited partners only.

In fact, a limited partnership is a superb form of operation for many closely-held businesses. The tax effects, under present law, of being a limited partnership are superior in many ways to any other form or entity, including an S corporation. There is no limit, as a practical matter, on the number or types of partners and, properly structured and operated, the limit of liability of limited partners is as complete as that for shareholders of a corporation. Moreover, estate planning is often facilitated (as discussed, in part, in Chapter 15) if an investment company is in partnership rather than corporate or proprietorship form.

The potential uses of a limited partnership to immunize some of your business's assets from liability are discussed later in this Chapter.

CORPORATIONS

The third usual form of operating a business is through a corporation. As a general matter, shareholders are not liable for claims against a corporation except to the extent of investment already made in it or an obligation to contribute to the corporation. Exceptions to that general rule sometimes arise but your legal advisors should be able to tell you what steps need to be taken to assure limited liability for all shareholders.

It is appropriate to note that although a limited partnership or corporation may limit liability of owners, an individual who actually causes damages is primarily liable for it. For example, if you commit a tort in the scope of your employment as the president of the company and the company is sued you may also be personally liable (if you are sued individually). In fact, your liability will be primary and the company's only secondary. Similarly, if an employee in a proprietorship injures someone, the employee may be primarily liable and the owner of the proprietorship only secondarily liable. As a practical matter, employees rarely are made to pay for damages for injury they cause. Nonetheless, you should be aware that if you actually operate your business, the limited liability which a limited partnership or corporation may provide its owners will not protect you if your activities caused the injury.

LIMITED LIABILITY COMPANIES

Many states recently have passed legislation authorizing businesses to operate through "limited liability companies." These entities have some attributes of corporations and some attributes of partnerships. In any case, they are intended to provide immunization from liability for their owners. They are extremely flexible entities and, to date, the IRS has recognized them as partnerships (generally, the preferred form of operating a business under the Internal Revenue Code). However, the limited liability enjoyed by the owners of a limited liability company in one state may not be available under the laws of another state. As a consequence, limited liabilities companies, although apparently attractive, may not be used widely except for limited purposes and where it is certain the activity of the entity will occur only within the jurisdiction in which the limited liability company is formed. Over time, however, if a nationwide uniform limited liability statute is enacted granting limited liability for its owners, the number of limited liability companies will greatly proliferate as they appear to be extremely flexible vehicles.

By Business Indebtedness

Not infrequently, liability arises on account of indebtedness relating to borrowing by another. Many owners of closely-held businesses are regularly asked to and agree to be liable for loans or other extensions of credit made to their businesses. That is the case even if the owners would not otherwise be liable, because, for example, the business is in the form of a corporation. (As noted above, in a sole proprietorship and a general partnership the owners are already liable for the debt obligations of their business.) In most cases, when an individual borrows directly from a lending institution, the individual will be liable to repay the indebtedness. In addition, an individual (or an entity) may be liable where repayment of an extension of credit is guaranteed by the individual (or entity). Parents, for example, are often asked to guarantee loans made to adult children who do not have a lengthy credit history because they are just beginning to work, etc. Liability for indebtedness generally arises by reason of contract. There are, however, exceptions to that general rule. For instance, if you take over another company or acquire all of its assets, you may become liable for its debts even though you did not expressly sign an agreement to assume that indebtedness. In that case, in effect, the indebtedness is shifted to you as a matter of law.

SOME STEPS TO CONSIDER TO PROTECT ASSETS FROM CLAIMS OF CREDITORS

Protecting Your Business from Claims

THE INSURANCE DILEMMA

Some businesses (such as medical practices or law firms) have "gone bare." That means that they no longer carry insurance for acts of malpractice. The reasons are two-fold. First, some professionals have discerned that they are more likely targets of malpractice claims if they have malpractice insurance. It is very easy for a claimant to find out if a firm carries it. As mentioned above, the public and lawyers know that insurance companies often are anxious to settle claims, in part, on account of the high cost of defending them and the vagaries of jury verdicts and the damages juries may assess. Even though the insurance carrier may be primarily responsible for any such claim, some professionals realize that their own personal assets are also on the line (to the extent that any award or settlement exceeds the insurance coverage). Also, in some cases, the insurance may not cover the claim at all (for any number of reasons) and professional reputations may be injured by such claims especially where payments and settlement are made. The second reason relates to cost. Malpractice insurance cost for almost all professions has increased dramatically—several fold over the past decade. Paying out a significant portion of gross receipts in professional liability insurance substantially reduces (or eliminates) profit.

Some other forms of businesses also have decided not to carry liability insurance. That may, or may not, make good sense, depending upon your industry and your position in it. If your company becomes the target of a significant claim, you may discover that lenders are hesitant to lend your business money unless they can get priority liens on certain of the company's assets (so that they would be paid before any claimant is at least if the assets securing the loan are sufficient to pay it off in full). Similarly, you may discover that suppliers and customers may not wish to deal with your company if they perceive that claims will affect the financial soundness of your business.

Often, businesses seek a general line of credit as "working capital" and for other reasons. Usually, that type of loan is not secured but is made on the general credit-worthiness of the borrowing company. Again, a substantial claim against your company if it has no insurance may significantly reduce your company's ability to borrow.

On the other hand, just as with many professionals, carrying liability insurance may enhance the probability of your company being a target of a claim. However, your business may be very different from that of the traditional professional. Most professionals have little "hard" capital in their businesses. They are primarily service providers. Although law firms, accounting firms, medical practices, engineering firms, etc., often have a much greater investment in capital (such as with computers or with other specialized equipment) than their predecessors did, they still operate primarily based upon the individual efforts of the professionals in the organization. Hence, there is little to attach (other than accounts receivable) in such organizations.

In any case, if your business has a significant base of capital (such as land, patents or equipment), the risk of significant claims being made against your company may be just as great whether or not you carry liability insurance. If that is so, it is probably appropriate for you to carry insurance if you can acquire it at any reasonable cost. (Reasonable, by the way, means that the cost is not so high as to make your company uncompetitive or to reduce your profits to such a degree that the value of your company clearly would be better devoted to other enterprises.)

There is at least one other additional reason why you should consider carrying liability insurance. A significant claim against your company, even if no award is ever entered, can be tremendously disruptive to the operation of the business itself. The top executives often become obsessed with the claim, especially if it could be so large as to put the company out of business. Those executives who do not have equity in the business may look for positions with other companies. Even those with modest equity positions may leave because they figure that their equity, on account of the claim, has little real worth. Even if your company will have to devote significant efforts to any matter involving a claim, usually the attention devoted to it by the managers of the businesses will be less if an insurance carrier is responsible for any damage and related costs.

TRY NOT TO MAKE GUARANTEES

Almost all closely-held business owners find that when they approach a lender it automatically expects the owner of the business (and, usually, the owner's spouse) to guarantee any loan made to the business, even if the company is a separate legal entity (such as a corporation). In some cases, you will only be able to obtain the loan you want by guaranteeing it. In other cases, you will receive better terms, such as a lower interest rate, if you guarantee the loan to your business.

As mentioned earlier in this Chapter, there may be great danger to your personal assets if you make such a guarantee. You may find that having another officer of your company apply for the loan and negotiate with the lender on behalf of the company may reduce the probability of the lender insisting that you make the guarantee. Similarly, if you fragment the ownership of your business (even among family members, for estate planning purposes or other reasons), it becomes much more difficult for the lender to ask that you, as one of only many owners, guarantee the loan. It usually becomes impracticable for the lender to insist, for example, that more than a dozen people make the guarantee.

In any case, if your company is financially sound, you may find that you can avoid personal guarantees without a significant impact on the terms of the loan. Alternatively, you may find that allowing the lender recourse not against you personally but against a limited group of your assets (perhaps a portfolio you have or one home) also may secure the loan on approximately the same terms as if you made a full personal guarantee.

USE SEPARATE BUSINESSES FOR SEPARATE FUNCTIONS

Very often, owners of a company will have all operations under one entity, such as a general partnership or a corporation. If a claim is made against the company, each and every asset of the business is liable for the claim. Sometimes, practical, tax and legal requirements compel that all operations be carried on under one entity. However, it often is possible to separate some of the functions of the business into several different entities without significant adverse tax and operational effects while significantly increasing the immunization of some assets in business operations from claims brought with respect to others.

For example, it is very common for real estate operators to hold all assets (or most of them) in one partnership. (Worse, it is often a general partnership where the owners themselves are also personally liable to the full extent, as a practical matter, of their net worth.) For instance, you own five apartment houses or office buildings all within the same partnership. If a claim arises with respect to one of those buildings, not only is the value of that building subject to the claim but all the other buildings are as well. If, instead, each building had been held in a separate **limited** partnership, each building would be liable, in effect, only for claims brought with respect to it. The same protection can be provided by using separate corporations. Historically, however, and currently for sound income tax reasons, real estate usually is held by partnerships rather than corporations.

Holding the buildings in separate general partnerships usually will provide little, if any, immunization for the other buildings which are not involved in the claim. The reason, as explained above, is that the general partners themselves are liable and, accordingly, everything they own (including the general partnership interests they hold in the other general partnerships) also are liable. In other words, a claim arises with respect to the first building owned by the first general partnership which, in turn, is owned primarily by you. The award exceeds the value of the building. You are responsible for the excess judgment, in almost all cases. Almost all of your assets, including the general partnership interests in the other four partnerships, also are liable. In effect, because your general partnership interest in the other partnerships can be attached, the buildings in those other partnerships are liable for the claim which arose from the first one.

It is hard to believe in some cases that sophisticated and successful businessmen and businesswomen hold more than one piece of property in any single separate legal entity. Sometimes, as explained earlier, there are operational or other reasons to do that. Usually, however, it is a failure to recognize the potential danger involved, until it is too late to do much about it. Once the claim is commenced, separately incorporating each building, or putting each piece into a separate limited partnership, may provide little, if any, real protection.

What is stated with respect to real estate parcels is just an illustration. If your company has several different divisions, which are not held in separate entities (such as separate corporations), your entire operation is liable even if liability arises in only one division. You should explore, with your advisors, whether it is practical to attempt to separate the divisions into separate legal entities (other than general partnerships) in a way so that claims which arise with respect to one operation do not infect the others with liability.

For example, you operate a cement company. Your operations include taking orders, collecting accounts, providing expert advice (for which you render separate charges), manufacturing cement, operating a stone and gravel quarry and several plants, and delivering cement to customers. You may find that although your business is almost completely "integrated" (from the mining of the raw materials used in manufacture to delivery of cement to the final user), some of the operations and assets could be held in separate entities.

If your company is an S corporation, it may not own more than 80% of another corporation. However, it can become a limited partner in a limited partnership and, also, own up to 80% of the stock in the corporate general partner.

Whether such a "reshuffling" of assets will have tax or other effects can only be determined by experienced advisors. You should not commence such a reorganization without a thorough analysis of the operational, legal and tax effects of such activity. However, you may be in a good position to analyze whether it is practicable to have different operations held in different entities. As indicated, it does not have to be separate lines of business, it can be different operations which go into different entities.

The extent to which conducting different operations and holding different assets in separate enterprises will provide immunization for the others can be uncertain in some cases. Very often, in legal matters, lawyers attempt to "pierce" the separate entities and to aggregate them. The rules relating to when that may occur vary from state to state. Obviously, if you attempt to use separate entities to provide such immunization, you should seek the advice of a competent and experienced counsellor before doing so. Your advisor should be able to tell you, among other things, whether having somewhat different ownership of various operations (such as where you own 100% of some, you and your spouse own 50% of another, and you, your spouse and your children own varying different interests in others) will enhance the probability of the separateness of those enterprises being respected for creditor purposes and what the tax, operational and other effects of such differences in ownership may be. (One thing your commercial business advisor may not be aware of is that you can fragment ownership of property for liability purposes but yet, by using special trusts, have you continued to be treated as the sole owner for income tax purposes.)

FOLLOW SOUND BUSINESS PRACTICES

Obviously, following safe and sound business practices is one of the best preventive medicines for claims. It is beyond the scope of this book to discuss any of those practices in detail. Some, such as setting and enforcing policies against unlawful discrimination and sexual harassment, apply to every business. Others are unique to a particular industry or company. Experience often is an excellent teacher of the types of safe and sound business practices your company should follow to reduce the probability of claims. Your industry, or an industry expert, or even your insurance carrier, may be able to provide your company with advice with respect to those practices.

Obviously, taking steps to protect your business protects your most important base of wealth and what is likely to be the major source of wealth for future generations, whether your business is sold or continues to be owned by your family after your death.

Protecting Yourself and Your Family from Claims

Introduction

As explained above, although you may become liable for certain claims, your creditors will seek the ownership of your assets to satisfy those claims. Almost never in this country is someone incarcerated for failure to pay claims. In a broad sense, you should consider undertaking two steps to reduce the liability of your own wealth from claims. First, you should attempt to minimize the circumstances under which you (and, therefore, your assets) may be liable for claims. Second, you should take steps to immunize your assets from claims for any liability which may befall you. As discussed later, certain assets are immunized from claims of creditors, at least in certain circumstances. Also, changing the ownership of assets can immunize them from their former owner's personal liabilities.

Operate Your Business in an Entity for Which You Are Not Liable

As explained above, if you operate a business as a proprietorship, you and the proprietorship are considered one for virtually all purposes, including for claims of creditors. As a general matter, subject to some important exceptions (about which your company's counsel should be able to advise you) owners of a corporation are not liable for the corporation's claims. That is true even if the corporation is an S corporation, in which case the income of the corporation is not taxed to it, as a general rule, but directly to the shareholders, even if the income is not distributed.

Notwithstanding the general rule of limited liability for shareholders, there are many cases in which the owner of a corporation may be liable for claims the company owes. First, the corporate form sometimes is ignored by courts. A frequent circumstance where that happens is where you have ignored the corporate form in the operation of the business. All those bothersome "little" things such as holding regular directors meetings, registering title of company assets in the company's name (and not your own), etc., are the type of activities which will be carefully scrutinized and may result in a finding that the corporation does not exist for purposes of claims. If you are interested in protecting yourself from the claims made against the business, it is important that you respect the separate legal nature of the business. All filings, tax returns, taxes, reports, meetings, etc., which are supposed to be made and held should be made and held in a timely manner with your company making and retaining appropriate records. You should follow a practice, when you are asked about your business, to mention that it is a corporation, that you are an owner of the stock in the company and are its president, chair or other manager, if that is the case. Do not refer to the company's assets, employees, etc., as your own; rather, refer to them as the company's assets, etc.

A second way in which the separate nature of the corporation may be ignored is where you are responsible individually for the injury. For example, if you drive a vehicle on company business and you are involved in an accident, both you and the company may be liable. Similarly, if you engage in an act of sexual harassment, both you and the company may be liable.

Your personal liability because of personal "fault" can arise in less direct ways as well. For example, if you hire someone who injures another and it can be established that you were negligent in entrusting the person with the activity which resulted in the injury, you may make yourself personally liable. (Regardless of whether you should or should not have placed the responsibility on the other employee, your company will almost certainly be liable for that employee's actions taken during the course of his or her employment.)

As mentioned above, operating through a general partnership (which will involve at least one other owner) provides virtually no protection for you individually if the business is sued. Only if the partnership is a limited one can protection for the partners be obtained. As explained above, that protection extends only to limited and not general partners. However, the general partner may be a corporation which, in turn, may immunize its owners from claims of creditors, if the corporate form is respected.

Limited partnerships, for closely-held businesses, are superb entities, in many cases. Often, they produce better tax results and offer much greater flexibility than S corporations. As a general rule, they can provide limited partners with as great protection from liability as shareholders in a corporation. However, it is critically important that you respect the **limited** nature of the limited partnership agreement.

In some cases, claimants will contend that limited partners should be liable for a partnership's obligations. Usually, if the limited partner, in that capacity, did not engage in any activity as a general partner (such as being involved in day-to-day business decisions), the limited partner will not be treated as a general partner for that reason alone. There are other ways, however, where the entity will not itself be treated as a limited partnership. In some jurisdictions, for example, failure to file a copy (or description) of the limited partnership agreement may cause the enterprise to be treated as a general partnership until the filing is made.

Many differences between operating as a limited partnership and a corporation exist. Your advisors can tell you what those are. In addition, sometimes there are different federal, state and local tax, filing, security law and other differences between corporations and limited partnerships.

As explained above, limited liability companies are likely to become a preferred method of operating a closely-held business in the future. In fact, if the state (and the only state) in which you operate has a limited liability act, you might well discuss with your counsel whether it would appropriate for any new activity to be placed in a limited liability company formed under that state law.

Acquire Assets Which Are Exempt from Claims of Creditors

Determining whether certain assets you own (or in which you have an interest) are responsible for your personal liabilities sometimes is a complex matter and turns, in large part, on the bankruptcy laws. The bankruptcy laws will be considered in determining whether an asset can be attached, as a practical matter, whether or not you are actually in bankruptcy. Often, a creditor will prefer that you not go into bankruptcy in order to avoid delay and additional cost; that preference can be beneficial for you as well. In any case, as a practical matter, creditors generally respect the protections for certain property interests which are available in a bankruptcy proceeding even if you do not go through one; the creditors know you can always file for bankruptcy protection.

In a federal bankruptcy case, an individual can choose to use the exemptions provided under federal or state law. Some states provide much more generous exemptions than the federal law does. In Florida, for example, your home is entirely exempt from claims of your creditors in bankruptcy regardless of the value of the home. In fact, many states provide some sort of exemption for homes, but often there is a very low limit, providing no significant protection.

As is mentioned elsewhere, in some states, although creditors of one spouse may be able to attach the interest of that spouse in an asset which is held by both spouses in a tenancy by the entirety, it may not be a valuable interest especially if the asset is the married couple's primary home. A tenancy by the entirety is a form of joint ownership usable only between spouses. Under it the surviving spouse succeeds to the ownership of the entire asset. The right to succeed to the ownership of the entire asset when the first co-owning spouse dies is called a "right of survivorship." Unlike other jointly owned assets, a tenancy by the entirety can be terminated only with the consent of both co-owners. Under the law of some states, it seems that if a creditor of one spouse attaches his or her interest in the tenancy by the entirety property, the creditor cannot bring an action to sell or divide the asset. If the other spouse survives the spouse with the liability problem the creditor will lose its interest. On account of that, the tenancy by the entirety asset may be of little worth to the creditor and, therefore, the creditor may sell it for substantially less than one-half of the asset's value or not attach it at all. However, some bankruptcy lawyers believe that the federal bankruptcy rules may be used effectively to terminate this special form of joint ownership by allowing the court to order that it be sold and the proceeds distributed between the creditor and the co-owner spouse. However, if the asset is the couple's primary home, it seems doubtful that the court will order its sale, especially if there are minor children in the household.

In any case, your counsellor can advise you as to any special and valuable exemptions which are provided under the law of your state. By the way, it usually is the law of the state where you reside when the bankruptcy action is commenced which controls which state exemptions apply. Because the exemptions may be higher in another state, debtors occasionally attempt to move to a more favorable jurisdiction. Sometimes, they are successful; sometimes, they are not.

If claims of creditors are of great concern to you, you might consider changing your residence to a jurisdiction with more generous exemptions, at a time when you have no significant claims against you. However, disrupting one's business and personal life on account of hypothetical claims which might be brought in the future may not be an appropriate step, especially when there are other ways in which you can protect your assets.

As will be explained in more detail later with respect to transfers to and for family members (and others), transfers in defraud of creditors are "voidable." Therefore, the property (or its value) is subject to attachment by creditors. A similar rule may apply with respect to acquiring a home where the home would be immunized from claims of creditors or acquiring other exempt assets, such as life insurance in some states. The time to make such investments or transfer is well before the creditors are on the scene so that the exemption provided for the asset will be respected.

MAXIMIZE CASH VALUE IF YOUR STATE PROVIDES AN EXEMPTION FOR LIFE INSURANCE

Under some states, the entire value of a policy of insurance owned by a debtor is exempt from claims of creditors in bankruptcy. The cash value of many life insurance policies can represent very significant sums, often many millions of dollars. If you reside in a state where the entire value of an insurance policy is exempt from creditors, you might consider "investing" in the cash value of policies you own. (As explained in Chapter 15, there are tax advantages to your doing that as well.)

The result seems extraordinary and it is. You have, for example, $2 million "invested" in the cash (or investment) value of a policy on your life. A large judgment is entered against you personally. Once that judgment is discharged (through settlement or bankruptcy), you can withdraw the entire $2 million and your former creditors will not be able to attach it.

QUALIFIED RETIREMENT PLANS

Although the parameters of the case have not been ultimately determined, a recent decision of the United States Supreme Court holds, in effect, that interests in a qualified retirement plan are exempt from claims of the employee's creditors. Frequently, significant wealth can be built in a qualified retirement plan. Usually, tax savings (which enhances investment yield, as explained in Chapter 8) is the primary motive for maintaining qualified plans. The exemption which the Supreme Court states is available for such plans also may be a factor to consider and may suggest maximizing the contributions which may be made to the plan for yourself and other family members. It seems that the immunization from claims of creditors may not be available for individual retirement accounts and self-employed plans, such as HR-10 plans. However, many states provide partial or total immunization for them.

Trusts Others Created for You

As a general rule, any interest you hold in a trust which was created by someone else for you is not subject to the claims of your creditors. For example, if your parents created a trust for your benefit instead of leaving your inheritance to you outright, your creditors probably cannot attach any of the trust assets unless you have a current, unrestricted right to withdraw property from the trust for your own benefit. Even if you have a fixed right to all the income from the trust, your income interest usually cannot be attached by your creditors (although, until the debt is discharged by settlement or bankruptcy they can claim income as it is paid to you). In some states, special "spendthrift" language has to be added to the trust to provide that immunization from the claims of creditors of the beneficiaries. In other states, the immunization is automatic.

A Special Note on Transfers in Trust for Others

So long as you do not do it in defraud of creditors, you can transfer assets to someone else (including your spouse or other family member) and the asset will no longer be subject to the claims of your creditors. However, those assets may then be subject to the recipient's creditors. You can effectively prevent that from occurring by transferring the assets for the other person in trust. As explained in more detail in Chapter 9, in the United States (and several other jurisdictions), a trust can be used, as a practical matter, to immunize absolutely the assets in it from claims of both your and the beneficiary's creditors. If you have any concern about claims of creditors, for yourself and for members of your family, you should consider transfers in trust. In fact, you should consider using the Megatrust^sm format, discussed in detail in Chapter 9, as it was specifically designed to minimize "leakage" out of the trust in favor of creditors and yet to be able to provide significant benefits to the trust's beneficiaries.

Assets Owned by Others

As a general rule, assets owned by another person are not liable for your obligations. Under some special rules, however, that result may change. For example, your spouse's one-half interest in your community property may be subject to the claims of your creditors, in some community property states, if your activity which gave rise to the liability is attributed to the community. For example, the community property of the spouse of a professional, whose practice is a community asset, may be liable for claims against the professional for malpractice.

Assets held in the name of another also will be liable for your obligations, as a general matter, if that person is merely a nominee or agent of yours. For example, funds you transfer to a person who has agreed to return them to you at your command probably will be liable for claims of your creditors.

Trusts You Create for Yourself

IN GENERAL

As a general matter in the United States (with some possible exceptions, such as, perhaps, Missouri), a trust you create for your own benefit is subject to the claims of your creditors to the extent you are entitled to or eligible to receive property from the trust, even if the assets are held in the name of another as trustee. For example, you create a trust with a local bank as trustee. The trustee can pay income among a class consisting of you, your spouse and your children. In almost all states, it appears that the entire income interest is attachable by your creditors. Similarly, if you are an eligible recipient of corpus, your creditors probably can attach the entire corpus of the trust because you are eligible to receive it and you created the trust.

In some states, it may be possible to immunize the assets in the trust from your claimant even if you are eligible to receive the property but only if the trustee can give property to you with the consent of the other beneficiaries. If you wish to consider such a trust, make sure your advisor tells you it will produce the result you want. It does not appear to be well established law in any American jurisdiction.

Some interests in trust you create for your own benefit may have little worth to your creditors. For example, to reduce gift and estate taxes, you create a House GRIT (discussed in Chapter 14), retaining the right to use the home the trust holds for ten years or until your earlier death, at which time the home will pass on to your children. In many states, all your creditors could attach is your right to live there. Your creditors probably could not sell that right because the occupancy will end at your death. Hence, as a practical matter, your use interest may be of little real worth. That probably means that you can buy off your creditors as to that use for a rather nominal amount.

Foreign Asset Protection Trusts

INTRODUCTION

The rule in virtually all of the United States that your creditors can attach property you have placed into trust for your own benefit is not the law of all countries. Recently, many "offshore" countries (including the Cooke Islands, the Bahamas, and others) have passed legislation which appears to immunize property held in a trust you have created for your own benefit from the claims of your creditors. However, most such jurisdictions usually have a transfer-in-defraud-of-creditors rule meaning that if you transfer the assets to the foreign trust in defraud of your creditors they may be able to attach the property. In fact, many of the trust companies operating in those jurisdictions require verification that you are not completely divesting yourself of most of your assets and you are not making a transfer in defraud of current creditors.

GIFT TAXES WHEN CREATING TRUSTS

If you make a transfer to a trust for your own benefit and yet immunize it from the claims of your creditors, the income from the trust is likely to continue to be taxed to you (except in special circumstances). Yet, the transfer to the trust will be a completed gift for gift tax purposes and you will have to pay gift tax on that transfer even if you wind up getting the assets back and even though they are available for your use. (The IRS has stated that if your creditors can attach the assets of the trust the gift is incomplete even if the trust is irrevocable. Because the gift is incomplete, you need not pay gift tax on it.) You can keep the gift to the irrevocable trust for your own benefit from being subject to gift tax, even if your creditors cannot attach the property. One way to do that is for you to retain the power to control the beneficial enjoyment of the property. For instance, if you can veto any attempted distribution by the trustee, the gift should not be deemed complete upon your transferring assets to the trustee. However, if you permit the trustee to transfer the assets to someone other than yourself, the gift will be complete at that time and you may be liable for gift tax on the value of what was transferred out of the trust.

It appears that in virtually all of these offshore jurisdictions you can prevent the transfers to the trust from being subject to a completed gift tax by sharing, with the trustee, control over the beneficial enjoyment of the property. That would include having the right to veto any proposed distributions by the trustee to others.

OTHER TAX CONSEQUENCES

From an income and sometimes an estate tax perspective, the foreign asset protection trust created for your own benefit should not be treated as though it exists during your lifetime. Hence, the income earned by the trust will be taxed to you even if not distributed to you. Also, if the transfer of the assets to the trust is not a completed transfer for gift tax purposes, the trust will form part of your estate for estate tax purposes. After your death, the assets should be brought back into the United States for some important tax reasons; they can even be paid over to a United States trust at your death to avoid the adverse tax effects of foreign trusts—those adverse rules will not apply during your lifetime.

HOW FOREIGN TRUSTS MAY PROTECT ASSETS

The foreign asset protection trust provides protection to you because any person who holds a judgment against you and wishes to attach certain assets will have to bring suit in the jurisdiction where the assets are located. In the case of assets held by a foreign trust, that foreign jurisdiction will be the location. The claimant will have learned by the time it seeks to execute on the trust's property that the trust is not liable under controlling foreign law for your debts. Rather, the trust is treated as a separate and independent person for claims purposes in that jurisdiction. A claimant of yours may face other hurdles as well. Some of the jurisdictions will not enforce an American judgment. As a consequence, the claimant may be required to commence a new lawsuit. In other words, you may get to retry in the foreign jurisdiction the whole underlying lawsuit which formed the basis of the United States judgment against you. That may be time consuming and expensive because the claimant will have to hire an attorney in the foreign jurisdiction and may have to spend considerable time there as well.

Although foreign asset protection trusts are a new development, so far they appear to work well in insulating assets from claims against the trust's grantor where the transfers to the trust are not in defraud of creditors. Also, it may be possible in some foreign jurisdictions for your company, as a grantor, to create a foreign asset protection trust for itself to immunize some of the assets of the company from claims.

It is not yet known how the American courts will react, in full, to foreign asset protection trusts. It is possible that you will be unable to obtain a discharge in bankruptcy if American creditors are unable to attach the property. That means your creditors can continue to attach assets which come into your hands. The matter simply has not yet been decided. In any case, it appears that the absolute worst case is that to obtain the benefits of the assets held in the foreign trust it may be necessary for you to move there or to another jurisdiction outside of the United States. In the real world, however, it is likely that offering up a significant part of the assets in the foreign trust will satisfy virtually all creditors so that you can obtain whatever discharge is necessary for you to be able, in the trustee's discretion, to enjoy the assets remaining in the trust even though you remain in the United States.

It is important to emphasize that you will not hold the right to reacquire the assets in the foreign trust. The extent to which you receive assets from the trust, or benefits of those assets, depends upon the exercise of discretion by the trustee. It seems likely that a trustee will be prone to re-transfer assets back to you (or members of your family). A trust company which fails to do so may find that its level of business quickly evaporates. The foreign jurisdictions which have passed such laws are hoping that considerable American wealth will be transferred there. The trustees will be paid for holding such assets and that is good for the economies of those countries.

POLITICAL RISKS OF FOREIGN ASSET PROTECTION TRUSTS

Although it has not happened in any of the jurisdictions which have recently passed the legislation causing the proliferation of foreign asset protection trusts, and it may never happen, it is possible that political developments could occur which might, in some cases, jeopardize the assets in the trust you have created there. Special mechanisms can be used, as a general matter, to change the situs of such trusts, as well as the trustee, if such events occur or appear likely to occur. In any event, should you be interested in creating a foreign asset protection trust, you should do so only after considerable counselling and personally interviewing trust companies from several of the jurisdictions. Their representatives often are in the United States and usually will meet without charge.

TAILORING YOUR FOREIGN ASSET PROTECTION TRUST

One additional word of advice about the foreign asset protection trusts is offered. Most of the trust companies have standard trust forms which they would like you and your counsel to use. (You should hire local counsel in that jurisdiction—it is to your benefit to have your own lawyer there). The trusts are not tailor-made to your specific needs. You should consider having your American and your foreign lawyer change the document to fit your particular circumstances. For one thing, you probably should provide that the trust can acquire assets for your use or use of your family members. As explained in Chapter 9, the Megatrust^sm format was especially designed to provide that type of flexibility and to maximize the immunization of property from claims of creditors (as well as reduce taxes). You may wish to consider using all or a portion of that format even for a foreign asset protection trust if you decide to create one.

Avoid High Liability Activities

Experience demonstrates that certain activities you may undertake are more likely to result in liability to you than others. Certainly, driving while intoxicated is likely to result eventually in your being sued for damage or injury you cause. Unfortunately, alcoholism is not a voluntary condition and it seems that for many people driving while intoxicated also is almost involuntary. Nonetheless, there are a number of other activities which truly are voluntary and if you want to reduce the probability of claims exposure you should avoid them. These include activities such as operating or owning facilities which may produce toxic waste. Even if you operate such a facility through an otherwise limited liability entity (such as a corporation), you may be personally liable for damage caused.

BUSINESS DIRECTORSHIPS

Directors of a company owe a duty of care and duty of loyalty to the company and to its shareholders and, in certain circumstances, to its creditors. Under the law, the shareholders may bring suit against the directors if they fail to carry out their duties properly. Very often, directors are sued when anything significantly adverse to the corporation occurs. For example, the individual members of the board of Texaco were sued after a judgment was entered against it for many billions of dollars in favor of Pennzoil. Without question, serving on the board of a public company is one which involves high risk of personal exposure. If you are asked to serve on the board of any public company, you should approach the acceptance with caution.

At a minimum, if you are asked to serve on the board of a public company, you should ask for a history of suits brought against the company and its directors and have your own advisors consider whether it appears that there is high liability in your serving.

If you decide to serve, you should ensure that you are provided with the finest type of directors' liability insurance. Unfortunately, in some cases, the insurance company will cancel (or refuse to renew) a director's liability insurance coverage when it anticipates that claims are likely to be made. In some cases, if the cancellation occurs before the claim is commenced against the director, the insurance coverage will not be available. It may be impossible to find substitute insurance at a reasonable cost or at any cost at all.

As a consequence, you should also insist on the broadest type of indemnification allowable under the law from the company itself. In some states, the indemnification which the business may provide you may be limited. For example, if you are found to have engaged in certain activities, the company may not be permitted, as a matter of public policy, to pay any fines or related civil damages which are imposed against you.

In fact, if you are asked to serve on the board of a public company, you should step back, with your advisors, and weigh the rewards of such service against the risks. At a minimum, you must be willing to make a commitment to fulfill your duty. That includes not only being "honest", but completely fulfilling your fiduciary duties. It means that you must attend meetings, read all materials sent to you, and otherwise reasonably perform the duties of the office of a director of the company. These duties include selecting an appropriate management team for the company and seeing that the managers carry out their duties in managing the company. An excuse of "I was so busy with other matters I did not know what was going on with the public company" might keep you from being charged with criminal activity but you are setting yourself up for an admission that you failed to fulfill your fiduciary duty and, as a result, you may be setting yourself up for possible claims of civil damages by the shareholders.

You may also wish to keep in mind that a small reduction in the market value of a public company may result, collectively, in tens of millions of dollars of damage to the shareholders. Usually, when a suit is brought against directors by shareholders, it is brought on behalf of all shareholders. As a consequence, the typical shareholders' suit alleges enormous damage. Even if the probability of success is relatively small, the large amount of the claim no doubt will require careful attention to it. Even if your expenses, such as legal fees and possible civil damages, are covered by an indemnification by the company and/or insurance, you will, no doubt, have to devote considerable personal time to the matter. In some cases, you may not have an unrestricted right to choose your own law firm and have it paid by the insurance or the company but will have to use counsel chosen by a majority of the board to defend it. (Of course, you can always hire your own law firm and have it paid for by insurance or the company but you may have to pay its fees yourself.)

It may also be appropriate, if you agree to serve on the board of a public company, to consider asking the controlling shareholder, if there is one and if he or she has asked you to serve, for a personal indemnification. In some cases, such personal indemnifications may be granted. However, you may wish to keep in mind, that in some cases the law will not enforce the indemnification where it would violate public policy (which may be the case where you are convicted of committing a crime, even if it is a so-called "white collar" crime, such as violation of securities laws).

BANK DIRECTORSHIPS

If you really want high exposure, serve on the board of a bank or savings institution. The number of directors who have had actions brought against them by both shareholders and the government is staggering. (You may wish to recall the investigation of President Bush's son.) The Federal Deposit Insurance Corporation (FDIC) and the Resolution Trust Corporation (RTC) have extraordinary powers to take over banks and savings institutions and to bring suit against former directors. When a bank is taken over by the FDIC or the RTC, that government agency succeeds to virtually all of the rights of the bank including any attorney-client privilege which the officers or directors had with legal counsel to the institution. On account of the enormous cost of bailing out banks and savings institutions, the government has armed itself with extremely broad powers. In many cases, the federal courts have granted injunctions in favor of the government and against the individuals preventing the individuals from transferring assets. Some directors, for example, have found it almost impossible to hire legal counsel as the lawyers are concerned that they will not be paid because the charges of damages are so severe and the restriction on transferring property are so great.

Compounding that exposure is the possible threat of a suit by shareholders whether or not the government sues the directors and whether or not the government is successful in sustaining its claims against the directors.

Although it is certainly possible to seek directors' insurance while serving on a bank or savings institution board, the amount of insurance you will be able to obtain may be significantly less than the potential damage which a failed institution may generate. For instance, if the bank or savings institution has $300 million in deposits, some portion of that (and other damages) may be lost if the bank fails. It is doubtful if the directors can get insurance for themselves in an amount to cover the potential damage.

The bottom line is that you should approach an invitation to serve on the board of a bank or savings institution (or holding company holding a bank or savings institutions) with the utmost caution. The potential for liability is so great (even for an institution which is financially strong at the time you first go on the board) and the size of potential damage so large that an appointment should be accepted only with great care.

PRIVATE COMPANY DIRECTORSHIPS

You may also be asked to serve on the board of a private company. In that case, unless it is an institution such as a bank or savings institution, the possibility of significant liability often can be reduced to an acceptable level. For example, if the owner of another company asks you to serve on his or her board, you probably can receive a personal indemnification from that person and, perhaps, all other shareholders. To the extent that the indemnification is enforceable, the shareholders will wind up suing themselves should they bring suit against you as a director. In addition, you may be able to secure an indemnification agreement with a private company which is more favorable than you could negotiate with a public one. The indemnification agreement you receive from a public company may be a matter of public record and on account of "appearances" may not be as one sided in your favor as you can arrange with a private company where the agreement can be held in confidence.

Nonetheless, you should be careful in accepting any directorship in a private company. For example, you should check to see whether suits have been brought against the company or its directors by anyone or whether there are grounds, such as the possibility of toxic waste pollution, that suits will brought in the future by government agencies or others. Often, when suits are brought, the plaintiff will sue everyone in sight, including directors. As explained earlier, it often does not matter whether those claims ultimately can be enforced. All the plaintiff typically cares about is generating sufficient concern so that a significant settlement is reached. Even with a private company, if you are sued, you may wind up devoting such significant personal attention to the matter that you may well wish that you had not accepted the directorship.

CHARITABLE DIRECTORSHIPS

You also may be asked to serve on the board of a charitable organization. Being involved in charitable activities can be very fulfilling. Charities have an important impact in our country and throughout the world. Unfortunately, you can be sued as a director of a charity on a variety of grounds.

For example, in one suit, the man who founded and funded a large charitable institution with tens of millions of dollars of his own money and the other directors were sued by the attorney general of the state where the charity had been formed because the charitable program, which was intended in turn to raise money, failed. The attorney general contended that the directors had been reckless in expending the charitable funds and personally sued all of them for millions. The suit was settled but it was not all covered by insurance and resulted in significant personal hardship to the founder and the other members of the board.

In almost all states, the attorney general is the statutory representative of charities or otherwise is empowered to enforce charitable trusts or other charitable entities. The attorney general usually is empowered to bring suit to try to override virtually any decision made by the charity's own board and seek to enforce the attorney general's own judgment on the charity. Usually, the attorney general is specifically granted the power to sue the board and the officers individually if charitable assets have been wasted.

In addition, directors and officers of charitable institutions which are regarded as "private foundations" can be sued by the IRS for severe penalties. In other cases, the IRS can impose taxes and penalties on the charity itself. Not infrequently, if the IRS is successful in imposing the taxes and penalties against the charity, the officers and directors are sued by the attorney general of the state to force them to reimburse the institution. In some cases, taxes and penalties can be imposed against broad based public charities as well as private foundations.

The possibility of suit being brought by the attorney general can also involve investment losses as well as on the grounds that the charitable assets were improperly expended.

| Use a "Tax Poison" Partnership | Many families use partnerships to centralize the management of their assets and for other reasons, some of which are discussed in Chapter 14. In some cases, partnerships can, at least to a limited degree, be used to thwart claims of creditors against certain family members. Although owning an interest in a partnership, which in turn holds valuable assets, |

initially may be viewed as beneficial, in some cases it can be detrimental to creditors because income may be imputed to someone who holds an interest in the partnership.

TAXATION OF PARTNERS AND PARTNERSHIPS

Partnerships are not themselves taxed. Rather, all of the income, including capital gain, and other tax attributes, such as losses and deductions, are attributed directly to the partners of the partnership. That income is imputed to the partners whether or not any distributions are made from the partnership to the partners. In other words, a person who is a partner may be required to report income of the partnership and pay income tax on it even though the partnership makes no distributions to that or any other partner.

In some cases, partners are permitted to transfer their interests in the partnership to others. However, the persons receiving the partnership interests usually do not automatically become partners. Rather, they merely become "naked assignees." That means that they may be entitled to distributions made with respect to their assigned interests but they do not get to vote on any partnership matter (such as whether partnership distributions will be made or whether the partnership will be dissolved). On the other hand, as a general matter, such naked assignees do not become liable for debts and other liabilities of the partnership as a general partner of the partnership would.

ENTITLEMENT TO DISTRIBUTIONS AND PROCEEDS UPON LIQUIDATION

Under the partnership law of most states, any partner can withdraw and demand payment in liquidation of his or her partnership interest at any time unless the partnership agreement, in effect, provides otherwise by having the partnership last for a fixed number of years. Also, as a general rule, a partnership dissolves upon the death of a general partner, unless the partnership agreement provides otherwise. In fact, any written partnership agreement usually will specify the circumstances under which partners may be entitled to distributions of profits generated by the partnership or to receive proceeds in partial or total liquidation of the partnership. Whether or not there is a written partnership agreement, state partnership law may provide that a court having jurisdiction over the partnership may order its termination for any "equitable" reason.

Sometimes, the written partnership agreement will provide for different partners to receive different types of distributions and to receive distributions at different times. Some partners, for example, may be in the position of being the equivalent of "preferred shareholders." Those partners will be entitled to distributions of profits or payments in liquidation before the other ("common") partners are.

Sometimes, the partnership can provide for partnership interests to be converted from preferred to common or from common to preferred or into some other category when certain events occur. Generally, such rights and conversions set forth in the written partnership agreement are enforceable under the law.

WHAT HAPPENS WHEN A PARTNER IS SUED

Not infrequently, a partnership agreement will provide that a person will cease to be a partner upon certain events. Typically, those events include death, incompetency, bankruptcy, and, in some cases, any attempt to assign any partnership interest of the partner. Usually, those provisions are enforceable. Where the partnership agreement provides for a person's status as a partner to terminate, usually one of two results occurs.

In one case, the partnership, or the other partners, may be able to acquire the partner's interest in the partnership pursuant to a type of "buy-sell" provision. In many such circumstances, that partner is paid an amount equal to his or her capital account. Capital account normally consists of the contributions which the partner has made to the partnership plus his or her share of profits and gains but reduced by any losses allocable to that partner and distributions made to him or her. In other cases, some other buyout price is used, which may be very low.

In the other case, rather than having the partnership or the other partners buy out the partner's interest, the interest in the partnership continues to remain outstanding but only as a "naked" property interest rather than as a partnership interest. That means that the guardian of the incompetent (former) partner, the executor of the deceased (former) partner or the creditor of the (former) partner becomes an assignee of the interest in the partnership. However, as explained earlier, that assignee does not become entitled to participate in any management decisions of the partnership, including a decision to liquidate the partnership, which usually is reserved to the partners. Also, in some cases, where the interest of the incompetent, deceased or bankrupt partner is not purchased by the partnership or the other partners, the partnership agreement may authorize the partnership to convert the interest of such former partner into a different partnership interest. That might be, for example, an interest which is not entitled to distributions at the same time that the other partners are entitled to distributions.

How the Foregoing Might Be Used as a Shield Against Creditors

Almost everyone who held an interest in a tax shelter partnership eventually realized that it was detrimental to hold that interest after a few years. In most tax shelter partnerships, there came a point where income would be imputed to a partner even though the partner received no distributions. Lawyers and accountants often call that "phantom income." Under the law, the partner would be required to report a large amount of taxable income but there was no distribution from the partnership.

That bad situation can happen to partners in any kind of partnership. Lawyers, accountants, architects, engineers and other professionals who operate through partnerships often find that they are required to report a much larger amount as taxable income than the amount of distributions made during the year. For example, any amount of income retained by the partnership as a contribution to capital is nonetheless taxable to the partners even though the partners do not receive that amount. Usually, the partnership arranges so that all partners receive more than enough cash distributions to pay taxes on the amount imputed to the partners as taxable income. In some cases, however, partners may be liable for much more income tax on partnership income than the amount of distributions made from the partnership. As explained earlier, if there are different categories of partners (such as preferred, common and special partners), some may receive distributions (thereby providing them with the cash to pay taxes on imputed partnership income) and others may receive no distributions even though they are required to report taxable partnership income.

Where a family has banded together to make investments through a partnership, each will be taxed on a part of the partnership income and receive distributions from the partnership, all as provided in the partnership agreement. Those who are involved in the management of the family partnership may also receive other distributions, such as salaries or certain "guaranteed payments." Guaranteed payments are those which must be made regardless of whether the partnership has taxable income.

If one of the members of the family has a liability problem and his or her interest is attached by a creditor in a bankruptcy proceeding or otherwise, the creditor will succeed to the partnership interest but only, usually, as a naked assignee. As explained above, at that point, typically one of two things will occur. First, the partnership or the partners will exercise any right which it or they may have to acquire the interest at the price set forth in the partnership agreement. Alternatively, the creditor will remain an assignee of the partnership interest and will be taxed on partnership income and be entitled to distributions but only as provided in the partnership agreement. Neither of those may be beneficial for the creditor and the latter may be detrimental. For example, where the buyout option price, exercisable by the partnership or the partners, is significantly less than the proportionate value of the partnership assets, the creditor may find that the assigned interest does not have significant worth. Second, if the creditor remains an assignee of the partnership interest, the creditor will be taxed on income of the partnership but there may be no distribution.

Properly structured, the partnership agreement may provide for the remaining partners to receive distributions, either as salaries, guaranteed payments or other preferred partnership distributions, with no distributions being made to the creditor who holds the assigned partnership interest. As explained earlier, the creditor, even though holding an assigned partnership interest, will not be a partner for purposes of making decisions. Such a situation usually will be distasteful: The creditor is required to report partnership income but is entitled to no distribution. That situation may continue for several decades. In such a case, many creditors will agree to let their interest be acquired at a very small price. The reason, of course, is that the creditor winds up holding "tax poison" rather than a valuable property right.

DOES THE TAX POISON PARTNERSHIP REALLY WORK?

There does not appear to be any reported case in which the tax poison partnership as a method to deter creditors claims has been tested. It seems more likely that it will be effective if the operation of the partnership does not change dramatically after a creditor attaches the interest. For example, if the partnership has followed a practice of making regular distributions of all income and gain but ceases making those distributions once a creditor attaches the interest of one of the partners, the courts might be more prone to dissolve the partnership to allow the creditor access to the underlying assets in the partnership. On the other hand, a conversion of the interest automatically pursuant to the terms of the partnership when it is attached may well be respected by the courts. Moreover, the buyout provision may well be respected if it covers circumstances in addition to attachment by creditors (such as incompetency and death) and the buyout option has been consistently exercised every time an opportunity to exercise it has arisen.

However, as mentioned above, under the law of some states, the courts have the right to dissolve a partnership for any equitable reason. Obviously, there may be wide latitude in determining what is equitable and what is not. Where it is apparent that the only purpose for the provision in the partnership agreement is to hurt a naked assignee, there may be a greater chance that the court will order the dissolution of the partnership. On the other hand, where the provisions apply in several other cases (such as death), it seems that the probability of the provision being respected and the court refusing to terminate the partnership is much greater.

In any event, although the concept of using a tax poison partnership is new, there appears to be little downside. The creditor should not be entitled to attach any of the underlying assets of the partnership unless a court orders that. At a minimum, the creditor would be required to commence a suit and the probability of the suit being successful will not be assured. Not infrequently, lawsuits involving requests for dissolution of a partnership go on for many years even when the suit is commenced by a real partner and significant grounds for complaint are alleged. During that time, it is likely that the creditor-assignee will be taxed on income of the partnership. Especially where that amount is significant, the creditor may well settle for a rather nominal payment for its attached partnership interest.

Transfers to Others

Assets which you have transferred to others for full consideration in money or money's worth are not subject to claims from creditors unless you made the transfer with the actual intent to defraud creditors. For example, if you do not want your weekend home to be the subject of a claims proceeding, you could sell it to your children for full value, even after a judgment against you had been rendered (unless that judgment prohibits you from transferring any asset even for full value). Obviously, you face the risk of a contention by your creditors that you transferred the asset for less than full value or that the transfer was not in good faith. However, unless your creditors can prove that, they probably cannot attach it.

On the other hand, if you transfer an asset for less than its value in defraud of creditors, the transfer is voidable and the property (or its worth) is attachable in the hands of the person who received it from you. That applies whether the transfer is directly to individuals, to an entity they own (such as a corporation your children own) or a trust, and whether or not you were the original creator of the trust.

As a general matter, a transfer is considered in defraud of creditors if the creditor is known. Different states have different rules creating presumptions as to whether or not a transfer is in defraud of creditors. The usual time is one or two years but special rules apply sometimes extending that period. However, a transfer to immunize property from future creditors generally is not a transfer which is considered in defraud of creditors so as to make it void or voidable unless you are insolvent or are left with insufficient assets to pay foreseeable debts. You usually are permitted, for example, to transfer assets with an intention of preventing them from being subject to the claims of your future creditors. For instance, you engage in high risk activity where you may be personally liable. You transfer considerable assets to your spouse who will not engage in those activities and will not be liable on account of your activity. If liability should later arise, and theoretically just about regardless of how quickly, those assets should not be considered as having been transferred in defraud of creditors so as to make the transfers void or voidable and, therefore, attachable by your creditors.

How to Keep Your Spouse from Being Liable for Your Liability

Husbands and wives usually are not automatically liable for claims brought against the other. Often, however, one spouse will guarantee or co-sign on indebtedness where the other spouse guarantees or signs. To the extent possible, you should avoid having your spouse do that; otherwise, you expose your spouse's assets to claims of your creditors. In some cases, creditors may contend that both spouses are liable, even if only one spouse committed the act which gave rise to liability, because the spouses were operating in a general partnership. A few courts have found implied partnerships between husbands and wives in other contexts, such as where they become divorced and one seeks an interest in assets where the title is held by the other spouse. Those types of cases eventually may lead to circumstances where creditors are able to make both spouses liable even though the liability arose with respect to activities undertaken by only one of them.

Moreover, in some community property jurisdictions, the community property interest of each spouse may be liable where the liability arose on account of activity undertaken by one spouse on behalf of the community. If you live in a community property jurisdiction, and you wish to immunize your spouse's one-half community property interest from the claims of your creditors for certain high risk activities you undertake, you should discuss the matter with your lawyer. He or she can advise you whether having your spouse enter an agreement with you in which your spouse acknowledges that activity is a separate property activity of yours (and not a community property activity) will immunize your spouse's community property interest in other assets from those claims. It should be mentioned, however, that if you undertake a high risk activity, it may be that you can immunize yourself from claims by operating through another entity, such as a corporation. However, if you individually cause the damage, the corporate shell probably will not provide any real protection. That is the case, for example, for professionals who operate through professional corporations. Individuals who commit the act of malpractice are individually liable. However, in most cases, the other professionals in a limited liability entity, who were not involved in the activity, are not individually liable.

Moreover, for any asset you transfer to your spouse, you can immunize it, as a general rule, from claims of your spouse's creditor by transferring it in trust for your spouse. Transfers in trust for your spouse can be made in such a way so as not to be subject to gift tax while simultaneously preventing them from being subjected to the claims of your spouse's creditors. As a consequence, whenever you are considering making a significant transfer to your spouse, you should consider making it in trust. By the way, if the trustee eventually transfers the assets to your spouse, your spouse can retransfer the assets to you gift tax free.

How to Keep Other Family Members from Being Liable for Your Liability

Steps similar to those which attempt to avoid making your spouse's assets liable for claims of your creditors may be used for other family members as well. The good news is that creditors much more rarely attempt to attach assets of family members other than a spouse. On the other hand, when you transfer assets to the family members other than your spouse the transfers may be subject to gift tax, unless it falls under an exemption or exclusion. Those exemptions and exclusions are limited by law so that large transfers may well be subject to significant gift tax. If you are inclined to reduce estate taxes, making transfers subject to gift tax actually can be beneficial as is discussed in more detail in Chapter 14.

In any case, whenever you are contemplating a large transfer to other family members (such as children), consideration should be given to making the transfer in trust for them, even if they are adult and completely competent. Your children can have total investment authority over those assets and have certain other rights, as explained in Chapter 9, without exposing the assets to claims of the children's creditors which is likely to be the case if you make an outright transfer to them.

SUMMARY AND CONCLUSIONS

Many businesses and well-to-do individuals will face large claims from time to time. Insurance can provide some protection against the impact of those claims but that insurance often is expensive to acquire and, to some degree, makes the company or individual which is insured a more attractive target for a lawsuit. Both businesses and individuals can be liable for the acts of others. Businesses in almost all circumstances are liable for injuries caused by their employees, regardless of the safeguards which the company imposes. Individuals may be liable for the activities of others as well. Any individual who operates a proprietorship or is a general partner of a partnership usually is fully liable for all claims against that business. Claims can arise in other ways as well, such as those by certain family members for support, to the government for taxes or penalties, or to others for indebtedness and for guarantees. Businesses may be able to provide some protection for their assets by having certain activities held in different entities which immunize assets not directly involved in the activity or entity which gave rise to the claim. Individuals also can take action to protect themselves (and their family members) from claims. Exemptions provided under law (such as qualified retirement plan interests, and, in certain states, homes and cash value insurance) can help identify appropriate assets to acquire. Transferring assets to others may also protect the assets from the former owner's claims unless the transfers are in defraud of creditors. In addition to direct outright transfers to other family members, transfers to a foreign asset protection trust even for your own benefit may immunize assets. Transfers to trusts for family members can provide the double benefit of immunizing the property from claims of the former owner's creditors as well as the creditors of beneficiaries, so long as the transfer was not in defraud of creditors.

CHAPTER 17

HOW CAN I PROVIDE FOR A SPECIAL FRIEND OR A NON-MARITAL CHILD?

INTRODUCTION AND OVERVIEW OF CHAPTER

Not infrequently, an individual will want to provide discreetly for someone who is not an immediate family member. Unfortunately, the disposition of the estate of an individual, including one who is prominent within a community becomes a matter of public record. Even if the disposition initially is unknown, subsequent events, such as a challenge to the disposition by a family member, can cause it to become publicized. This Chapter discusses reasons why an individual may wish to provide for someone outside of the immediate family and some other ways to attempt to accomplish that.

MOTIVES FOR PROVIDING FOR A SPECIAL FRIEND OR NON-MARITAL CHILD

Some individuals sire or give birth to children outside of marriage. As a general matter, the illegitimate child of a female is regarded by the law as the woman's child even if the woman is not married. It is common today to refer to a child born out-of-wedlock as a "non-marital" child rather than "illegitimate" or "unlawful." The natural father of a non-marital child is not regarded as the child's parent for purposes of inheritance, in most states, unless there is some type of open acknowledgment of the parenthood or an order of paternity has been entered during the father's lifetime. Whether the child is born within or outside of wedlock, once a child is adopted by another family he or she is no longer considered a descendant of his or her natural family for most purposes under the law. Regardless of whether the law acknowledges the natural maternity or paternity, a natural parent may wish to provide for a child whom he or she does not openly acknowledge.

In addition, some individuals have a sexual relationship with someone outside of marriage and wish to provide for that person, in a discreet manner. Occasionally, one individual will want to help another even though there is no romantic or blood relationship. Sometimes, when that occurs, the individual wishing to bestow the benefit upon another will want to do so in a discreet rather than a public manner. For example, a college friend has a child who is extremely disabled. You would like to provide for that child but wish to do so in a confidential manner. For several other reasons, you may wish to provide for someone outside of your immediate family but will wish to do so only if the matter is kept as confidential as possible.

SPECIFIC METHODS

Legacy of Cash or Property

Obviously, making a legacy of cash or property to or in trust for the individual will benefit that person. As a general matter, your Will is a matter of public record. As a consequence, any bequest you make will be a matter of public record. Although, occasionally, individuals describe that special person as "my friend" or some other term, the community often infers such a description to mean "my lover" or another label which is inaccurate or which you do not wish to have placed on the relationship. Generally, it may be best not to provide a description at all if you decide to provide for another individual outside of your family.

An exception to that rule is where you are making bequests to many of your friends. If someone special is merely one of several individuals who receive bequests from you of approximately the same size or value, references to each of them as "my friend" is not likely in and of itself to cause the community to label one of them as other than a friend. Indeed, some individuals, in order to camouflage the most important object of their bounty, make gifts to many "friends" or relatives. Where the list includes relatives it may be best not to put any label on any of them at all. Your attorney (and your family) will know who is a relative and who is not. If the few non-relatives are "sprinkled" in among relatives, the pattern may appear to be very natural. Sometimes, godchildren or others with whom the property owner has had close long-term relationships are also made legatees.

Obviously, adding those persons in order to camouflage the real person intended to be benefitted is expensive in that money must actually be transferred to the others and taxes must be paid on their bequests as well as the bequests to the person whom you wish most to benefit.

Distribution Under a Living Trust

Another way to effect a transfer at death but reduce the amount of publicity within the community, in most cases, is to use a revocable living trust as a substitute, in whole or in part, for a Will. Revocable living trusts are discussed in more detail in Chapter 11. In most cases, your revocable living trust will not become a public document unless a legal proceeding with respect to it is commenced. That could happen, for example, if a member of family attempts to contest the distribution you have directed to be made to your special friend. However, such contests are much more rare when the "offensive" disposition is contained in a revocable living trust rather than in a Will. It is much more difficult to attack successfully transfers under a revocable living trust than under a Will. In part, that is because you will have registered title to property in the name of that trust and taken other actions with respect to it during your lifetime. That activity makes it extremely difficult for others to contend that you were unaware of its effect and purpose or were incompetent to execute it.

Moreover, the revocable living trust is less likely to receive close scrutiny by certain family members. You will still have a Will, naming an executor to carry out important decisions with respect to your estate. In addition, although a certified copy of your Will must be attached to your estate tax return, copies of such trusts are "buried", generally, as later exhibits to your estate tax return.

Nonetheless, members of your family will have many opportunities to "discover" the special disposition you have made. Where you want the matter kept more private than that, additional steps may have to be taken.

Lifetime Gifts

IN GENERAL

One of the most effective ways to provide for a special friend is to make lifetime transfers. Often, those transfers can be made to fall into the protection of exclusions from taxation and/or will be subjected to lower rates of taxation. In addition, they are very unlikely to become matters of public record after you die. During your lifetime, you may be able to control, to a greater degree than you could arrange for after your death, dissemination of information about transfers made during lifetime than transfers you make at your death. As a consequence, it is appropriate for you to consider making lifetime transfers if you wish to maximize the confidentiality of them.

Fortunately, now, most gifts made even within three years of death can be structured so as not to be includable, and as a general matter, not even fully reportable for estate tax purposes when you die. Nonetheless, at least in an indirect way, such gifts may have to be disclosed on your estate tax return. The reason for this is the manner in which the federal estate tax is computed. All **taxable** gifts (for example, those over $10,000 a year) made since 1976 have the effect of increasing the initial tax rates which your estate faces when you die. If you have made exceptionally large gifts during your lifetime, additional ones will have no further impact on your estate tax return and, accordingly, are less likely to draw close scrutiny.

If a member of your immediate family is the executor of your Will, that family member will have to sign the return, and in reviewing it, may ask questions about the gifts. As a practical matter, therefore, it may be best not to name an immediate family member as an executor as that may well reduce the probability of the lifetime gifts being discovered.

ANNUAL EXCLUSIONS

Gifts that fall under the protection of the $10,000 annual exclusion need not be reported on a gift tax return and, as a general matter, will not be includable in your estate when you die. However, to ensure that effect, it will be appropriate for you to discuss transfers, before they are made, with your tax advisor. For example, under current law, annual exclusion gifts made within three years of your death directly from your revocable living trust may be included in your estate.

Under a special provision of the tax law called "gift splitting", you and your spouse are permitted to agree, in effect, to treat gifts made by one of you as made by both, thereby doubling the annual exclusion gifts you can make each year from $10,000 to $20,000. To get the benefit of gift-splitting with your spouse, your spouse must sign your return and will see those transfers. Hence, if you want to give $20,000 away each year to a special friend free of gift tax, your spouse will have to agree to split those gifts. Certainly, there are some spouses who do not review tax returns they are asked to sign. However, you may be taking a risk and be unpleasantly surprised when your spouse does ask you about transfers to a particular recipient.

GENERATION-SKIPPING TRANSFER TAX CONSIDERATIONS

In addition to having to be concerned about gift tax, you must be concerned about generation-skipping transfer tax (discussed in more detail in Chapter 14) as well if the gift is to a person who is regarded as in the generation of your grandchildren or more remote descendants. Persons who are related to you by blood (going back to any grandparent of yours) are assigned to generations on the basis of their actual generation in your family. Non-relatives are assigned to generations based upon their relative age to you. Basically, if someone is more than 37$\frac{1}{2}$ years younger than you, that person is considered to be in your grandchildren's generation and, in addition to paying any gift tax, you may also have to pay generation-skipping tax or apply part of your GST exemption to avoid paying the tax on transfers to that person.

Generally, any transfer which falls under the protection of the $10,000 annual exclusion also qualifies for exemption from taxation for generation-skipping transfer tax purposes. In some cases, differences in the tax system occur and, again, if the person to whom you wish to make the gift would be assigned to your grandchildren's or a more remote generation, you should discuss the matter with your tax advisor before making the transfer.

Disclosure at Death of Large Gifts

Gifts in excess of the annual exclusion are subject to gift tax although the gift tax exemption equivalent (which can protect as much as $600,000 from federal gift tax) may apply to prevent the actual imposition of a tax. Nonetheless, if the transfer is in excess of the annual exclusion, a return is supposed to be filed even if no gift tax is due. Even if you fail to file the return, your executor will have to file one for you and disclose the gift on your estate tax return (because, as explained above, that gift will affect the amount of estate tax you pay at your death).

Do not make the mistake of believing that just because you made the transfer, your family did not catch you, and you did not file a return that the transfer will not be discovered after you die. The audits conducted by the IRS are extremely thorough and often uncover gifts, even though not reported, made long before death. In such a case, your estate faces not only the responsibility of filing a back gift tax return, but paying the tax, interest and probably penalties as well. In addition, in almost all cases, your estate taxes will increase. That kind of adverse consequence is more likely to draw your family's attention to the transfer than if you had made the gift, filed the return and paid any tax due.

In addition, if you live in one of the states which has a gift tax (or make a transfer of real or tangible property located in such a state even if you do not live there), you may have to pay a state gift tax even if you do not have to pay a federal one. The reason is that the gift tax exemption in some states is much smaller than the federal gift tax exemption. In a circumstance where writing a check to the IRS would draw attention from your family members, you had best make sure that you do not exceed the limit for gift tax free transfers. By the way, your check for gift taxes is made out to the IRS the same way that your income tax check is which, in some cases, may camouflage the reason for paying the tax.

The Friend's Trust

If you are making outright transfers to a special friend, it is possible that he or she may expend the gifts (even if you want them saved) or may build up a sufficient independent level of wealth so as to change the relationship that you have with that person. As a consequence, not infrequently, individuals who make transfers during lifetime wish for them to be in such a form that they can control their disposition. For example, you may wish to create a trust in which you control distributions to your friend so as not to change your relationship with that person but, nonetheless, have a fund available for him or her when you die.

If you retain such a power, the property will be includable in your estate when you die. As indicated above, it is difficult to forecast what kind of scrutiny such an inclusion will raise with your family or others. Generally, retaining such a power is not a wise thing to do. It may be better to have an independent entity (such as a bank, trust company, or one of your professional advisors) serve as the trustee in such a case.

Also, in some cases, individuals will wish to make their children or other descendants potential beneficiaries of the trust so that if the relationship with the friend changes the assets can be distributed to someone other than the friend. That may backfire. When the trustee gets ready to make distributions to your friend or the others, the trustee may feel compelled to tell the others of their rights in the trust. In fact, under the law of many states, if a proceeding with respect to the trust occurs (such as the trustee wants instructions as to the meaning of the trust agreement), all potential beneficiaries probably have to be made parties to the lawsuit. That will, so to speak, let the cat out of the bag.

If you wish there to be an "escape valve" so that distributions can be made to someone other than your friend, either during your lifetime or after your death, adding charities as potential recipients may be better. However, if you reside in a state where the attorney general, who is usually the statutory representative for unnamed charities in trusts and similar instruments, is active, you may find that even naming charities as discretionary distributees of trust assets may cause publicity with respect to it to occur.

Perhaps, the most confidential manner in which the trust can be structured to operate is to provide for distributions to be made to your friend after your death or, if your friend does not survive all distributions, to be distributed to your friend's family or in fixed shares to named charities.

The Importance of Using a Declaration of Trust

Trusts can be formed in a variety of different ways. The most common way is for the property owner to enter into a contract with a trustee for the benefit of a third person, the beneficiary or beneficiaries. Usually, the name of the property owner who creates the trust is recited in the agreement and that is a matter of public record.

The law, however, provides an alternative. The trustee may make a **Declaration of Trust** without disclosing who provided the assets of the trust. In effect, the trustee merely declares that the trust (pursuant to its terms) exists, and the identity of the person who provided the assets which comprise the trust is not disclosed in the document. By eliminating any reference to your family or institutions with whom you have a unique affiliation, the probability of discovery that you were the person who transferred the asset to the trust is greatly reduced. In fact, some individuals, to further heighten the confidentiality, have the Declaration of Trust made in another state (and, in some cases, a foreign country).

Although the Declaration of Trust is a good way to camouflage a transfer from you, it will not eliminate the need to disclose it on your estate tax return or to pay gift tax if the transfers to the trust exceed the annual exclusion (or do not fall under another exception). However, if someone other than you provides the initial funds placed in the Declaration of Trust and all transfers you ever make to the trust fall under the protection of the annual exclusion, your advisors may well conclude that no disclosure about the Declaration of Trust need be made on your estate tax return. How to make transfers to the trust so qualify is mentioned later in this Chapter. If the transfers are greater than that, they can affect the estate tax payable on your death and, therefore, must be disclosed on your estate tax return. Furthermore, if the trust owns insurance on your life, the policy must be disclosed on your estate tax return even if the proceeds are not subject to estate tax.

BUY-SELL OPTIONS IN ESTATE PLANNING

Introduction

As discussed in other Chapters, options are often an effective method to control the disposition of property both during lifetime and at death. In some cases, they can also be used to effect a transfer to a special friend in a way which camouflages the real intention of the transfer and, in certain cases, eliminates estate taxes with respect to it even if it occurs at death.

Business Circumstances

In General

Very often, businesses and their owners, or the owners alone, enter into an agreement relating to the transfer of business interests as the owners die. Typically, those are called "buy-sell" agreements. Usually, they provide for the sale of the deceased owner's interest in the business by his or her estate to the surviving co-owners (or to the business itself) at a preset price or pursuant to preset formulas. Except for certain buy-sell agreements among family members, those agreements may be structured in such a way so that the price set forth in the agreement or determined pursuant to the formula fixes the estate tax value of the interest. Where the price determined pursuant to the agreement is lower than actual fair market value, taxes may be reduced. The reason is that only the price paid pursuant to the agreement is includable in the estate.

Because such agreements are so common in business and investments, they usually do not draw close scrutiny by surviving family members (other than proof that the provision is enforceable). Sometimes, however, surviving family members will want to avoid enforcement of the buy-sell provision especially if it results in a purchase price significantly less than the asset's fair market value. Usually, however, the buy-sell agreements are accepted.

INVESTMENTS WITH YOUR FRIEND

As a consequence, entering into an investment or a business relationship with a special friend and providing for your interest to be transferred pursuant to a buy-sell agreement to that person at a favorable price and/or favorable terms may provide an excellent way to camouflage the real purpose for the transaction. However, the business arrangement must be bona fide. Moreover, under a new tax rule in most cases, the price established under a new buy-sell agreement does not fix estate tax value if the agreement is with a member of your family or a "natural object" of your bounty. The meaning of the "natural object" of one's bounty has never been defined in detail. It probably means those who inherit most of your wealth and would not necessarily include a special friend. In any case, it is unlikely that the IRS would inquire into the relationship you may have with the surviving investor or business owner if that individual is not otherwise a recipient of property upon your death. To further reduce the probability of any inquiry by your family or the tax authorities, you might have your special friend act through another entity, such as a corporation.

How to Enter Into a Buy-Sell Agreement with Your Special Friend

If your friend has money to invest, arranging for a joint investment or business venture with appropriate buyout provisions may not be difficult to set up. However, where your friend does not have significant wealth, making such a joint venture may be difficult. One way is to have your friend perform some management function for the venture or business and for that person to receive what is commonly called "carried interest." Usually, that means that the person earns a percentage of the growth as part of the payment for services. Although the income tax consequences of such a carried interest are not certain, in many situations, your tax advisor should be able to tell you what the likely ramifications will be. In any case, usually the ramifications are limited to the business and do not result in matters personal to you which are of the type which are likely to draw attention of your family members.

Stock Options Held by Your Friend

In some circumstances, such as where your special friend works in your business, he or she can be awarded stock options, the exercise of which can be tied into certain events, such as your death. Where your friend is a key employee (or can be made one), the fact that he or she is granted some options is not unusual. However, it may be difficult to expunge those options if your relationship with that person should change. Because the options presumably have been granted for employment reasons, a change in a personal relationship generally would not serve as the basis for terminating the options. Not infrequently, however, options are effective only if the employment of that person is not terminated prior to the exercise.

If you wish to consider using stock options (or comparable options in a partnership) for your friend, you should discuss the matter with your business and legal counsel.

Employment Contract Option for Your Friend

If your friend works or comes to work for your business, you can provide your friend with an option to continue working for your company. Not infrequently, such arrangements are set up as a consulting contract under which your friend is required only to provide services as demanded by the company and then only under appropriate circumstances and subject to certain maximum number of hours per month. Where your friend can provide valuable services to your company, providing for long-term employment or consulting services pursuant to a contract may provide a good base of continuing income for that person. Similarly, providing for non-qualified deferred compensation for such a person also can be an effective way of providing that person with an income stream. In many cases, you can hold the option to terminate the contract rights before they become effective. However, if you should attempt to do that, there may well be a claim made against you or your company contending that the termination of the right was improper and unlawful. In such a case, your special relationship with that person may well be disclosed. Hence, even if you hold the right to terminate the contract, it is doubtful that you will do so.

In any case, one of the benefits of providing for an income stream for a friend who also works for or with your business is that the payments probably are not subject to estate tax and probably are deductible to your business unless the payments are unreasonable under the circumstances. Your advisors can tell you whether the structure proposed is comparable to that provided for similarly situated employees and consultants. If it is, any challenge by the IRS to the tax treatment you propose becomes somewhat remote.

LIFE INSURANCE

Introduction

Life insurance often is an appropriate asset to effect a transfer of wealth at death. Generally, the value of the insurance does not fully "ripen" until you die. That means that funding insurance during your lifetime may not change your relationship with your friend in a way which you would regard as adverse.

Disclosure

As explained in more detail in Chapter 15, insurance which you own at or within three years of your death is includable in your estate when you die. Even if it is not includable in your estate for tax purposes, it nonetheless must be disclosed on your estate tax return. The fact that it has to be disclosed means that there may be an opportunity for your family members to discover its existence and to discover why insurance was owned by and/or made payable to someone who is not an immediate member of your family.

One of the ways in which that can be camouflaged is to have the insurance owned by and made payable to a business you have which passes, pursuant to a buy-sell agreement or otherwise, to your friend at your death. It might even be a business which your friend owns during your lifetime, and in which you have no ownership, but one in which you serve on the board of directors or perform some other role which would make it look more natural that the business would hold insurance on your life. Key person insurance is a common type of insurance to be owned by and paid to a business—its purpose is to provide that business with funds so that it can acquire an experienced replacement for you.

The Insurable Interest Rule

Under the law of all states, one person can acquire a policy of insurance from an insurance company on the life of another only if the acquiring person has an "insurable" interest in the person whose life is to be insured. Those who depend economically on the insured generally are regarded as having such an interest. Close family members almost always are deemed to have an insurable interest in the lives of each other. Where there is no family relationship between the insured and the person who wishes to acquire the policy, the insurable interest rule may prevent the acquisition. As explained above, a business for which you work, or of which you are a significant owner and/or director, probably would be regarded as having an insurable interest in you so that it could acquire a policy of insurance on your life. Moreover, co-owners of a business (or co-venturers in an investment) often are regarded as having an insurable interest in each others lives especially where there is a buy-sell agreement which will take effect when one of them dies.

Absent such an insurable interest, you will be (or someone on your behalf who has an insurable interest will be) required to acquire the insurance policy and to transfer it to or for the benefit of your friend. In virtually all states, you do not run afoul of the insurable interest rule if you acquire a policy of insurance on your own life even if you intend to assign it immediately to someone who does not have an insurable interest on your life.

One potential problem, however, of your acquiring the policy and transferring it to someone else is that, if you die within three years of the transfer, the proceeds will be includable in your estate and be subject to estate tax. That tax is more likely to draw the attention of your family to the recipient of the insurance.

JOINTLY-OWNED PROPERTY

Introduction

Property may be owned by two (or more) persons in a variety of different ways. Usually, the major distinction among the various types of common ownership is whether or not there are rights of survivorship when one of the owners dies. Some types of ownership provide that each owner may dispose of his or her undivided interest in the property upon death. Such property is said not to have "rights of survivorship." Where the interest of a deceased owner automatically passes to the survivor upon death, the property is said to contain "rights of survivorship." More detail about those types of property interest is contained in Chapter 10.

By owning property jointly with rights of survivorship with a friend, your interest in the property automatically will be transferred to your friend upon your death. However, the effects are likely to be so significant that close attention will be drawn to that transfer.

Tax Effects

Except when you have property placed in joint name with your spouse, you will be making a gift, in almost all cases, to the other co-owner when you place property in joint name with that person. The only exception is for transfers where you can revoke the other person's interest. Usually, that is the case only with bank accounts (although not in all states) where you retain control of the account, such as maintaining exclusive control of the passbook.

Whether or not a gift is made at the time you create the joint ownership arrangement, the asset will have to be disclosed on your estate tax return when you die. The tax law contains a presumption that all property jointly owned with rights of survivorship (with someone other than your spouse) is includable in your estate and it is up to the surviving co-owner to prove otherwise by establishing the part which he or she contributed towards the purchase price of the asset. That often is difficult to prove. The result usually is inclusion of the entire property in your taxable estate and the imposition of significant taxes. Moreover, if you fail to pay gift tax at the time you created the joint tenancy, the IRS may seek to impose back gift taxes, interest and penalties.

The conclusion is almost irresistible that attempting to transfer property to a special friend through a joint ownership arrangement is not a good plan.

Use of Trusts

As is discussed in more detail in Chapter 10, trusts are one of the most flexible arrangements under the law. Whenever you are attempting to take care of a person who is a minor or disabled, a trust is almost always the most effective method to achieve the desired results. The trust does not have to last, however, after your death if the person has reached majority and is not otherwise legally disabled (such as suffering from some mental impairment). Particularly where you want to assist with a non-marital child, who may be a minor, use of a trust, as a practical matter, is a necessity.

As explained above, confidentiality is more likely to be achieved if a Declaration of Trust is used in which your relationship as the grantor to the trust is not disclosed. Your attorney can advise you as to other matters with respect to the Declaration of Trust, including whether it is best to have it created in a state other than your home state.

Transfers in Trust

Outright transfers to another individual almost always qualify for the gift tax annual exclusion. As explained in more detail earlier in this Chapter, however, transfers in trust may be a better way to provide a fund for a special friend. Although transfers to a trust can be made to qualify for the annual exclusion (and in full, contrary to the belief of some advisors), you will need the assistance of tax specialist in order to ensure you achieve that result. Generally, once funds (or other assets) have been transferred to a trust, it may be invested in any way you wish, including, in some cases, acquiring insurance on your life. However, as is explained in more detail above, the trust may not be regarded as having an insurable interest on your life, thereby preventing it from acquiring insurance on your life. In such a case, you will have to acquire the insurance and transfer it to the trust yourself. That transfer also can be made to qualify for the annual exclusion (assuming its tax value is not in excess of the amount covered by the annual exclusion).

SUMMARY AND CONCLUSIONS

For a variety of reasons, a property owner may wish to provide for someone outside of the immediate family but wish to do so only in confidential manner. Making transfers at death usually is not the most effective way of achieving the goals of bestowing benefits and maintaining confidentiality. Lifetime gifts, especially those that fall under the protection of the annual exclusion, may be the best route to follow. Such gifts can be made either outright or in special forms of trust. Business arrangements, including use of a buy-sell agreement or insurance payable to a business, also can be effective means of bestowing benefits and maintaining confidentiality. Use of trusts may be especially appropriate. A Declaration of Trust may go far in camouflaging your identity as the person who provided the consideration for the creation of that arrangement. Nonetheless, the fact that you created the trust might have to be disclosed on your estate tax return even if the trust assets are not subject to estate tax in your estate. Nonetheless, if someone else makes the initial contribution to the Declaration of Trust and all transfers you make to it fall under the protection of the annual exclusion, your executor may well conclude that the Declaration of Trust does not have to be disclosed on your estate tax return unless it holds insurance on your life. In any case, where you wish to maintain confidentiality, consider appointing a third party as your executor rather than family members.

CHAPTER 18

HOW DO I SELECT THE APPROPRIATE LAWYER?

OVERVIEW AND INTRODUCTION

Even professional financial and estate planners go to other advisors with respect to their personal affairs. The economic, business tax and legal ramifications of action or inaction are so complicated that few, if any, can master all of the disciplines which relate to wealth protection planning and which should be considered in formulating and carrying out a plan. The planning for closely-held business owners adds an additional measure of complexity. Those who go forward without the advice of competent counsellors will fall short of achieving their goals. In some ways, the action they take without competent advice will result in worse consequences than if they did nothing. Selecting an appropriate advisor, therefore, is a critical step in the process of commencing and completing the planning process. This Chapter discusses the attributes which an appropriate advisor to you should have and how to find that advisor. Because of the critical role that the law plays in estate and financial planning, this Chapter emphasizes the selection of the appropriate legal team to assist you.

YOU CANNOT DO IT ALONE

Even excellent lawyers seek the advice of other lawyers when it comes to personal matters. The adage a "lawyer who represents himself or herself has a fool for a client" applies especially in the context of litigation but it also applies with respect to estate and financial planning. It is difficult for anyone to approach that planning objectively. It necessarily involves your money, your family, your loved ones, your friends and other matters which are close to your heart. To believe that you can objectively assess what is the best strategy may be foolhardy. You, as the busy owner of closely-held business, probably cannot master all the disciplines which are necessary to effect the appropriate plan, no matter what it is.

Therefore, one of the first and most important steps you can take is to find appropriate advisors. Your current attorney, accountant and other advisors may or may not be the best people to assist you in achieving your financial and estate planning goals. Most corporate lawyers, for example, do not have extensive experience with respect to estate or personal tax and creditor planning matters. Just because you may live in a modest-sized community does not mean that your planning, and its ramifications, is any less complex than someone in a larger community. In fact, in many ways, those in smaller communities and with a smaller base of wealth need more assistance: The loss of a few million dollars to a billionaire may not matter, but the loss of several hundred thousand dollars to you, your family and your business may mean the difference between successful completion of a plan and one which utterly fails.

WHERE YOU MAY NEED PROFESSIONAL ADVISORS

Motivation

Most successful business owners have spent their lives building their base of wealth. Many have not made detailed plans for the preservation and protection of that wealth, particularly as they approach retirement, the business matures and the reality of death and the passage of considerable property to others becomes a reality. For many owners, the development of their successful enterprises is their crowning achievement. It has made them important members of the community, provided an important base of wealth for their family, assured the education of their grandchildren and achieved important other goals. Unfortunately, however, it is sometimes difficult for those persons to face up to the need to do sophisticated and sometimes expensive financial and estate planning to prevent the erosion of those goals. As explained in detail in other Chapters, protection and preservation of your wealth, and achieving other important goals, almost always involves sharing responsibility of the management of your business and other assets and the sharing of the ownership of your enterprise and other property. That may run counter to your current wishes.

Reasoning such as "I need to be the complete owner of my business to effectively negotiate with customers" certainly is not a sound answer. Every hour of every day, chief operating officers of major (and minor) businesses, who have no ownership in the enterprise, negotiate just as effectively on behalf of their enterprises as you do on behalf of yours. To say "I don't really care what happens after I die and whatever my spouse and kids get from my estate is more than I started with" is to deny the importance of your business to you and is contrary to the care you have taken in the development of your business. Your business has value to your employees, your community and your family both during your lifetime and after your death. You have a responsibility to engage in responsible estate planning.

Sometimes, a primary reason for failure to act is related to fear of change. As said before, your position in your community and in your family may relate directly to your control of the business and the family's base of wealth. Sharing that control and that wealth may change your relationships and change usually is something human beings tend to avoid especially where the effect of the change is uncertain or could be adverse. Nonetheless, if you wish to achieve protection and preservation of your business and your base of wealth, it is necessary that you plan during your lifetime. If you are unwilling or unable to do so, perhaps, you would consider discussing the matter with a professional such as a psychologist.

Do not expect that all of your current advisors, such as your company's attorney and accountant, will give you straight advice. Most advisors, unfortunately, will do what is in their own best interests. It is in their best interests to keep their business relationship with you. Many advisors learn to read their clients and customers very well. Merely the way you phrase the questions will cause most advisors to answer in only one way. How do you think your advisors are going to react to a question like, "Don't you think that I need to keep complete control of the company and that I can do my estate planning next year?" Usually, the advisor will respond, "I couldn't agree with you more."

One of the most important things you can do, therefore, if you want the best advice, is to establish your goals with your advisors. If your primary goal is understood to be the preservation of your personal power base and wealth, that is what your advisors will seek to give you, regardless of any "lip service" you may give to other priorities. If you are committed to maximum wealth preservation and protection for your business and your family, subject to certain reasonable limitations, you have to make your advisors believe it. Otherwise, they are going to give you answers to your questions based on what they know are your real primary goals.

Establishing Goals, Priorities and Timetables

Before selecting your several advisors, it is appropriate for you to establish your goals, determine which have high priority and develop a timetable to implement and carry them through. Broad goals, such as providing the maximum base of wealth for your surviving spouse, minimizing the probability of your business being sold after you die, and similar ones are goals that some people can determine on their own without assistance. For many, however, even setting forth general goals is facilitated by using an advisor. Your company's lawyer or accountant, for example, may know you, your business and family situation adequately so that he or she can assist you in ascertaining those goals and generally how they can be attained.

Setting priorities is very important. Almost always, to some degree, they will conflict with each other. A common one, for a married property owner, is maximizing the base of wealth for a surviving spouse and minimizing overall taxation when property eventually passes to descendants. Leaving your estate to your spouse is likely to minimize tax at that time and, therefore, maximize your spouse's base of wealth, but that probably will mean more tax is due when your spouse dies. One of the reasons you need independent advisors who are experienced in such matters is that they can present evidence as to what the effects of the various, and to some degree competing, goals are so that you can make more informed decisions on priorities.

REVIEW

Often, property owners seek to have any plan involving significant ramifications reviewed by an outside expert. It is somewhat like getting a second opinion as to whether or not you need a serious operation. Keep in mind, however, that even an outside expert probably will be motivated to recommend what is in his or her best interests. Often, the outside advisor's motivation will be to try to become your primary advisor. Such an advisor may unnecessarily criticize the plan he or she is asked to review. Hence, you and your other advisors need to pick an expert who has a track record of giving independent objective advice to review the plan. Such an advisor will not attempt to aggrandize himself or herself or to "move in" on your other advisors.

Implementation

You also need experienced advisors for implementation. An expert may be able to tell you **how** to achieve goals, but you may also need another expert to carry them through. Some individual experts are excellent in making plans but are procrastinators in carrying them out. Among other things, you should obtain a definite timetable from your advisors as to when documents and other steps will be completed. Although there may be significant slippage, a commitment to a timetable will help make sure the plans are expediently carried out and probably will reduce the costs of doing so. When a matter has grown "cold" on an advisor's desk, interest in the matter wanes and the relearning process usually is an expensive one. A timetable also helps you move forward in the face of what you may perceive to be competing demands upon your time.

Follow Up and Monitoring

Asset protection and preservation, as with all financial and estate planning, is a lifetime process. Even after you have placed a plan into effect, following up and monitoring the steps and their ramifications will be important. You should seriously consider the continuing advice of an expert for such follow-up tasks.

PROFESSIONALS

Introduction

The list of professionals you need is a rather long one. It almost certainly will include an attorney, an accountant, a life insurance advisor, a member of the clergy, perhaps, and even others. To some degree, you can leave choices of collateral experts to some of you own advisors. However, it usually is appropriate for you to participate in the selection process or at least approve of one selected by others. You will have a better feel than your own advisors will as to whether or not one particular person is an appropriate advisor for you.

Your First Choice: Someone Whose Judgment You Trust

When you decide to make your list of advisors, an appropriate place to start may be with your current advisors, such as the attorney for your company or your personal accountant. Those individuals are likely to know the lay-of-the-land well and give you their views as to the type of experts you will need. However, it is natural for your current advisors to be fearful that they will lose your business if other experts are chosen. To some degree, you may be able to dissipate that fear if you decide to choose advisors from out-of-town and tell your local advisors that the outsider will work on a limited basis and work only in conjunction with your local and regular advisors.

In any case, one of the hallmarks of a real professional is his or her ability to give disinterested advice to you, whether you really want to hear it or not. You are most fortunate if you have even one advisor who will do that for you. However, if your reaction is negative each time you hear advice you do not like, your advisor will learn to give you answers which are not the ones which he or she believes are best but the ones he or she has learned are the ones you want.

You may have a friend, relative, associate or someone else, who is not a professional, but who is someone who will present you with an unbiased judgment as to which professionals you should select to advise you. Perhaps, if you know someone who has gone through the process of wealth preservation and protection and done so successfully, you might seek that person's recommendations as to the process by which you should choose advisors.

Attorneys

IN GENERAL

To paraphrase from the book *The Godfather*, a lawyer with his briefcase can steal more or do more damage than a hundred men with guns. On the other hand, your lawyer can be worth his or her weight in gold. Although lawyers are largely distrusted by Americans (and not very well liked) they are essential members of any team of advisors in any transaction involving the transfer or preservation of wealth.

In fact, your goal should not be to avoid lawyers, or minimize your contact with them, or even to have the fewest number to achieve the goals you want, but to choose the best ones and work with them. They are not perfect beings, but you have little choice but to accept the realty that they will play an important role throughout your life when it comes to your financial and related affairs. Your job is to select the best ones for you.

LAWYER SPECIALISTS

The practice of law is at least as specialized as the practice of medicine. The number of different types of medical experts have proliferated as their base of knowledge and experience has expanded. This has happened over a long span of time. For lawyers, however, expanding the number of areas of specializing merely takes the legislature passing new laws which require new expertise. Today, few can even claim to be tax experts in the law. Almost everyone who is a tax expert specializes in a certain subpart of the tax law. Some, for example, specialize only with respect to the taxation of life insurance companies (and, in fact, know very little about the taxation of the products themselves). Others specialize in the taxation of partnerships **or** corporations **or** S corporations **or** estate and related taxes **or** some other tax area.

Hence, you should be wary of any attorney who tells you that he or she is expert in all fields. That simply cannot be true today. It also means that you should appreciate that you may need several lawyers to accomplish your goals. An out-of-state expert, for example, probably will have to affiliate with a local lawyer to ensure to that the state ramifications of your plan do not run afoul of that state's rules. It also means that the attorneys who are probably closest to you may not be the ones who are experienced specialists in all the disciplines you will need to achieve financial and estate planning goals. Perhaps, other lawyers with the same law firm will be able to provide that expert advice. However, keep in mind that your law firm will have an interest in keeping all of your business. The concern is that once a crack in the relationship leaks, the whole wall of representation will come down and all of your business will go elsewhere. If you want disinterested and objective advice in the selection of other experts, make it clear (and really mean it) that your regular law firm will not lose the current work it does for you and your company.

OTHER ATTRIBUTES OF SPECIALISTS

Superior technical capacity is an essential ingredient of being an expert. However, other attributes are also critically important to be an effective one. The expert must have a track record of integrity and commitment to the best interests of the client to even be considered.

Other attributes you may want your expert advisors to have include a professional demeanor, an ability to produce significant quantities of work in a reasonable period of time, a proven track record that he or she is not a procrastinator, an ability to work with others and show respect for their judgments, a superior ability to lead other people, fairness in billing practices, a stable professional environment (for example, the lawyer does not constantly move from firm to firm and the lawyer's current firm is not in turmoil as many are) and sound common sense. Perhaps, it is not surprising that some individuals also seek lawyers with certain ethnic or religious backgrounds.

Of perhaps equal importance, however, is your personal reaction to the individual. Are you comfortable discussing private matters with that person? Does his or her approach to problems strike you as sensible? If you are not comfortable, consider going to someone else.

A few words about attorney ethics is appropriate. The Bar is largely a self-regulated body. The ethical rules which apply to lawyers are among the most strict, at least in theory, of any rules which regulate professionals or others. Most lawyers try to live up to the high ethical standards which are set for them. Sometimes, however, professionals will do anything to succeed for themselves or for their clients. Sometimes, they step over the line of ethics or morals so that the result sought will definitely be achieved. However, regardless of the apparent success of an attorney who has a track record of crossing over such lines, he or she probably is not an appropriate choice, especially in financial or estate planning areas.

Fees

The ethical rules relating to lawyers strongly suggest that a written fee agreement be entered into prior to any significant work being done for a client. Unfortunately, few lawyers even discuss fee arrangements with their client. That is unfortunate for many reasons. Clients tend to underestimate what the fees will be (and some mistakenly believe there will be no charge at all). The attorney, on the other hand, is confident that the client appreciates the extraordinary effort and work being produced and will be willing to pay almost any fee requested.

Although the burden should be on the lawyer, make sure you raise with each attorney (and other professionals you hire) exactly how fees will be charged. You should insist that the arrangement be agreed to in writing. You also may be interested in knowing that it is unethical for an attorney to charge an unreasonable fee. Obviously, different people can violently disagree as to what is reasonable and what is not. The way to avoid that disagreement, as a general rule, is by having a fee agreement in writing up front.

Common Methods of Setting Fees

Probably, the most common way for attorneys in the United States to charge for their work is by the hour (plus additional charges for disbursements and related services). Lawyers, like plumbers and other workers, have good days and bad days. You should expect to pay those standard time charges, if you agree to do so at the beginning of the representation, whether your lawyer has a great day or poor day for you. Often, the client and a lawyer will disagree vehemently as to whether or not the work done was productive. Obviously, you could reserve your right to object to paying a fee based upon the quality. However, you should anticipate that you will be forced to pay the attorney's fee unless you can establish that the work was not authorized or exceeded the limits of the authorization. Merely saying that you did not like the Will which you lawyer prepared usually would not be a ground to refuse to pay the lawyer's fee unless you could establish that the lawyer did not follow your instructions or the job is extremely unworkmanlike.

Lawyers (and other professionals, such as accountants) have now largely "unbundled" their charges. That means that you not only pay for the lawyer's time, but also for the time of assistants (including those who work in the attorney's library who are instructed to find materials for work done for you), secretaries, data processing experts, and others. Law firms also now use computers to produce work, including printing Wills and other documents. Many law firms charge for such services. Law firms also charge for photocopying, facsimile (FAX) transmission and messenger service. Usually, the charges for such additional services results in the law firm making a profit on them. For example, your law firm may charge 25 cents per page for photocopying. Obviously, you can go to a copy center and pay less. The law firm, however, usually will make a charge for such services similar to those of other law firms in its area. Whether or not you can negotiate a reduction for such charges depends upon the firm and the nature of the work it will do for you. If you do not want to pay for such matters (including secretarial overtime, cabs that attorneys will take home when they work late at night on your matter, etc.), it is appropriate to cover those matters when you discuss fees with your lawyer.

FIXED FEES

Not infrequently, an attorney will agree to complete a job for a fixed fee. Historically, attorneys charged a fixed fee based upon a percentage of the estate for work in administering one. Often, such fees are highly lucrative for law firms, exceeding (sometime by a significant multiple) what the hourly time charges would be at the firm's standard rates. In fact, some courts will no longer approve such fixed fees for such estate administration work and will award fees, where court approval is required (as it is in some states for estate administration work), only at a per hour charge.

Regardless of how your lawyer charges, you should insist that the attorney maintain contemporaneous records of all time spent and expenses incurred on your matters. That will be important proof if you and the attorney have a dispute as to fees. Most lawyers are not aware of it, but several courts have stated that the attorney's inability to prove what work was done is grounds for awarding no fee. An attorney who fails to maintain contemporaneous records of his or her work usually must engage in fiction writing when attempting to establish exactly what he or she did.

Fixed fees are sometimes used for financial and estate planning work, as opposed to after-death estate administration work. For example, your attorney may agree to prepare a Will or other document for you for a flat fee. Make no mistake about it, however: Once the attorney knows that the fee is fixed, he or she will be motivated to do the minimum work to complete the job. Few things will make lawyers more upset than another lawyer in the office who has taken on a matter for a fixed fee and then the cost of the services vastly exceeds that fee.

Sometimes, you can agree to get your attorney to put a cap on the fees. You will agree to pay by the hour but only up to a certain limit. Again, once the limit is reached it will be in the attorney's best interest to minimize the amount of additional work which is done.

Obviously, you will want your professionals to do the best job that they can. As you can see, using a fixed fee may not achieve that result.

CONTINGENT FEES

Occasionally, lawyers take cases on a contingent fee basis. Usually, that means that the attorney will be paid a percentage of the result the attorney achieves. Often that occurs where the attorney represents an individual or a company in a lawsuit in which a money judgment is sought. The attorney may receive a percentage (which sometimes is 50% or more) of the amount recovered. Contingent fees also can be used in tax refund cases. Sometimes attorneys are paid a percentage of the amount which they saved. For example, the IRS assesses an additional $3 million of taxes against your company. The Service appears to have a strong case. Your attorney agrees that he or she will be paid a percentage of the difference between the $3 million assessment and the amount the IRS ultimately receives (or settles for).

Contingent fees are sometimes difficult to use in the context of wealth preservation and protection. It is difficult for you to know how much your attorney will have saved your company or your family by certain planning steps. To some degree, you are at the mercy of your attorneys when they tell you that you have saved a tremendous amount of money by unique and innovative ideas which they have implemented. In a circumstance where you cannot readily perceive the results achieved, it may be inappropriate for you to agree to a contingent fee arrangement.

OTHER MATTERS ABOUT LAWYER FEES

The amount of cooperation the attorney receives (including cooperation of other professionals and you) may greatly affect the amount of time which the attorney has to expend. You, therefore, want to promote great cooperation among your professionals. It is likely to produce a better job at a lower cost. What has just been stated applies to you as well. Try to limit your use of your attorney's time to matters which should properly be referred to the attorney. Taking up his or her time with irrelevancies will increase the bill.

Moreover, you should have an agreement with your attorney as to the form of billing and information you will receive. Most law firms today keep computerized contemporaneously recorded entries of work done. You should have an agreement at the beginning of your representation that those records will be made available to you at your request. In fact, for many clients, the attorney may send only a one line bill ("for professional service rendered") and attach a copy of the contemporaneously recorded time charge entries. In some cases, however, you may want a narrative description. In any case, you should reserve the right to see the firm's records of time recorded regardless of the fee arrangement you use (and even if it is a fixed fee).

SUMMARY ABOUT FEES

In most circumstances, you will find that for planning, per hour charges are the best fee arrangement for you. If you become dissatisfied with that person's services, it may be easier to terminate the relationship and to settle outstanding fee matters if you have agreed to pay by the hour. That does not mean that you should not consider putting a limitation on the amount which an attorney can charge. In fact, at a minimum, for each project which is undertaken you should ask your attorney for a written estimate. Keep in mind, however, that estimates are only estimates.

ACCOUNTANTS

Your accountant, or one specifically hired for work in wealth preservation and protection, may be a very important advisor. Often, estate and financial planning will have an impact upon the official accounting records which your business maintains or which are maintained for you personally and used for other matters, such as securing loans from third parties. Moreover, many accountants have significant experience in tax and related matters. In some cases, they will have systems to do analysis which your lawyer will not have. Often, accountants are more cost efficient in preparation of certain tax returns than lawyers are.

Many of the attributes you seek for your lawyer may also be the ones you seek in an accountant. In any case, for an owner of a closely-held business, use of an accountant, or a number of accountants in the process of wealth preservation and protection can be efficient.

OTHER PROFESSIONALS

Depending upon your circumstances, you may seek the advice of other professionals. For example, if a member of your family is disabled or suffers from a unique problem, the advice from an expert who assists that person (such a medical specialist) may be important. For example, if special facilities will be needed for a family member, that should be reflected in your estate planning documents (such as an express authorization by a trustee to expend funds for psychiatric care, vocational training, physical therapy, institutionalization or whatever the need may be).

As explained in Chapter 4, you may need the advice of one or more investment advisors if you decide to sell your business. Seeking their advice long before the sales process begins probably is best. However, as mentioned in Chapter 4, many such advisors will be motivated to convince you to sell your business because their pay will be primarily or exclusively dependent upon arranging the sale. Again, having your other advisors, whose pay will not be affected whether a sale occurs or not, should be sought. Keep in mind, however, that your company's lawyers and accountants may wish you not to sell your business. One of the quickest ways to lose an important client is for the client to sell out to someone else. Again, try to pick out of your circle of advisors those who have the least personal motivation to give you anything but the most unbiased counsel.

HOW TO SELECT AN APPROPRIATE PROFESSIONAL FOR YOU

Start with a List of Attributes

As explained above, whether it is an attorney, accountant or other advisor, you may want to make a list of attributes which you want that professional to have. If you would be uncomfortable if the individual is not of a particular ethnic or religious background, you might as well put it on your list although you may be drastically reducing the pool of available talent.

As mentioned above, costs must be considered if your budget is limited. You should ensure that the professional you choose can work within your budgetary guidelines.

Consider a Peer Review

When I asked a family who had retained me how they had selected their prior attorney to represent them in the matter, I was told that they chose him because he had a large office, wore a large diamond ring and drove an expensive car. As ridiculous as that sounds, professionals are chosen often on such indirect manifestations of success. Making (or spending) more money than other professionals is not necessarily any indication of a professional's ability other than, perhaps, to maximize fees or borrow money. In virtually all areas of specialty (from auto mechanics to law to brain surgery), the best test of a person's ability usually is a peer review. If you want to find out who is the best landscaper in town ask the other landscapers for their advice, as to who, other than themselves, is the best. Obviously, professional jealousy sometimes will rear its head; however, over time, certain names will continue to appear and you will wind up with a short list of those who are best and have the attributes you want. Peer review probably is the most accurate system you can use to select a top notch person.

Interview At Least Two or Three People

Even if any one individual constantly rises to the top in recommendations, it will be appropriate for you to interview more than one or have your other advisors do so. You may discover in the interviewing process that the basic approach of one of them is more suitable for you than others. As mentioned earlier, if some of your advisors know you well, it may be appropriate for you to relegate a recommendation to them. In such a case, your job merely will be to conduct the final interview.

Look Ahead to When That Person Will No Longer Be in the Picture

However, people retire, go into other fields, get sick and die; because your wealth preservation and protection program will last through your lifetime and the lives of surviving family members, advisors will be needed for a very long time. Some experts tend to be in the mature stages of their career. Because of those factors, you should look at what successors to your advisor will be available either within that organization or at other organizations.

Choose the Best You Can Afford

Careful financial and estate planning may have a significant impact upon your, your business's and your family's economic strength. The variety in the quality of professionals you need to assist you in such planning is as great as in any other endeavor. Often, you will get what you pay for. Going for a low priced product often results in a low quality product. The same can be true for advisors. Obviously, price alone is not a complete indicator of quality. Nonetheless, in weighing the attributes of professionals, you should choose the best one for you to the extent you feel you reasonably can afford to engage their services.

HOW TO USE YOUR PROFESSIONALS EFFECTIVELY

Introduction

Setting your goals and selecting professionals is not enough. You have got to make them work together in a productive, cost efficient and timely way. You should take the time to become involved in the decision making process. No doubt, you will be paying your professionals well for their advice and, to a reasonable degree, you ought to learn as much from them as you can.

Chair an Initial Meeting

To see whether things get off to a proper start, it is appropriate for you to call a meeting of your professionals and for you not only to attend it but also to chair it. Your interest and command in doing that will help set an appropriate relationship between you and them. It may also prevent a professional from making decisions that you yourself should make. Your level of preparation for and participation in that initial meeting will go far in setting the attitude of your professionals in tackling your work. If you present your goals and your timetable for action in a thorough and thoughtful manner, your professionals are more likely to respond in kind than if you fail to attend the meeting, do not control it or do not have a well thought out agenda.

Set a Regular Meeting Schedule and Stick to It

How much time you spend with your professionals depends upon how important you regard the work they are doing, how much you want to control it and the speed with which you want it done. There is nothing like setting a deadline to have work done more quickly than when no deadline is set.

At a minimum of once a year, you should schedule a regular meeting with all of your professionals to cover the progress that has occurred since you last met and what new problems and new opportunities have arisen. Often, a client will attempt to reduce the number of professionals who attend such regular meetings because professionals usually charge for their time for being there. That is a little like owning a professional sports team and having a practice without all of the key positions being filled. The results are not as likely to be as good as if all the players can practice together. Probably, in the first stages of your planning, quarterly or more frequent meetings will be appropriate. After the initial stages of planning have been implemented, the frequency of meetings with all advisors present probably can decrease. In any event, you should have a regular meeting schedule and ensure that you carry it out.

Choose the Team Captain Before Any Major Family or Financial Decision Is Made

Even if you want to be the working captain of your estate and financial planning team, you need to have one of your advisors be your primary lieutenant. In fact, your interest in the process may be insufficient or your expertise not sufficiently developed so that one of your advisors really should be the captain. In any case, you should designate the point-person among your advisors who will be primarily responsible for ensuring that work for you is done in a timely and professional manner.

SUMMARY AND CONCLUSIONS

The advice of professionals is a necessary part of any wealth building, preservation or protection plan, whether it is for yourself during your lifetime or for your family after your death. For owners of closely-held businesses, the need for professional advice often is even greater because of the additional complications their financial picture represents and the special opportunities which the law provides them to use. The quality of professionals varies widely as does their approach to problem solving and completing other tasks. You may need the assistance of a professional to work with you in committing yourself to a program to carry out your plan. In any case, you will need professionals to continue to monitor and advise you about the results of the steps you have implemented to achieve your chosen goals. Understanding what professionals you will need and the attributes they should have is a major step in selecting appropriate ones for you. Getting independent advice is sometimes difficult to obtain from current professional advisors because of their concern of potential loss of business from you. One of the most effective ways you can select a professional is from a peer review. In any case, regardless of the professionals you choose, you should have a written understanding as to the scope of their engagement, how they will carry it out and how they will charge you for their work. Also, you should work as closely with your professionals as is reasonable and learn as much from them as possible so that you remain in control of your plans and how they are carried out.

INDEX